HOLY MEN
AND
HOLY WOMEN

SUNY Series in Medieval Studies
Paul E. Szarmach, Editor

HOLY MEN
AND
HOLY WOMEN

OLD ENGLISH PROSE SAINTS' LIVES
AND THEIR CONTEXTS

EDITED BY

PAUL E. SZARMACH

STATE UNIVERSITY OF NEW YORK PRESS

Published by
State University of New York Press, Albany

© 1996 State University of New York

For information, address State University of New York
Press, State University Plaza, Albany, N.Y. 12246

Production by Diane Ganeles
Marketing by Theresa Abad Swierzowski

Library of Congress Cataloging-in-Publication Data

Holy men and holy women : Old English prose saints' lives and their
    contexts / edited by Paul E. Szarmach.
        p.   cm. — (SUNY series in medieval studies)
    Includes index.
    ISBN 0-7914-2715-3. — ISBN 0-7914-2716-1 (pbk.)
    1. English prose literature—Old English, ca. 450–1100—History
and criticism.   2. Christian literature, English (Old)—History and
criticism.   3. Christian saints in literature.   4. Christian
hagiography.   I. Szarmach, Paul E.   II. Series.
PR226.H65   1996
274.2'03'0922—dc20   95-1192
                                                                  CIP

10   9   8   7   6   5   4   3   2   1

121096-3045 T1

Contents

Abbreviations and Short Titles

ASE *Anglo-Saxon England* (cited as a periodical by volume and year)

ASPR *Anglo-Saxon Poetic Records*, in 6 vols. ed. G. P. Krapp and E. V. K. Dobbie (New York, 1931–42; 2d printing 1958–65)

BHL *Bibliotheca Hagiographica Latina*, 2 vols. (Brussels, 1898–1901)

BL British Library, London (in citations of manuscripts)

BN Bibliothèque Nationale, Paris (in citations of manuscripts)

CCCC Cambridge, Corpus Christi College (in citations of manuscripts)

CCSL *Corpus Christianorum Series Latina,* cited by volume

CSEL *Corpus Scriptorum Ecclesiasticorum Latinorum,* cited by volume

CUL Cambridge, University Library (in citations of manuscripts)

EEMF *Early English Manuscripts in Facsimile*

EETS Early English Text Society (cited in the various series: OS, Original Series; ES, Extra Series; SS, Supplementary Series)

Ker, *Catalogue*
 N(eil) R. Ker, *Catalogue of Manuscripts Containing Anglo-Saxon* (Oxford, 1957)

MGH *Monumenta Germaniae Historica,* cited by subseries and volume

PG *Patrologia Graeca,* ed. J. P. Migne (Paris, 1857–67), cited by volume and column

PL *Patrologia Latina,* ed. J. P. Migne (Paris, 1844–91), cited by volume and column

Foreword

This collection of essays, conceived as the third in a series for the SUNY Press on Old English prose (OE), joining *The Old English Homily and Its Backgrounds* (1978) and *Studies in Earlier Old English Prose* (1986), focuses on the substantial body of saints' lives in Anglo-Saxon literature with special reference to Ælfric.[1] The aim of these three collections has been to stimulate scholarly and critical interest in OE prose, thus redirecting the energies of Anglo-Saxonists towards a large body of material that has had comparatively few interpreters.[2] This collection concerns itself with "holy narrative" or "holy biography" more than its two predecessors and pursues interdisciplinary connections in a more concerted way beyond the merely comparative-literary. As with the earlier collections, the writers here show a special concern for the contextualizing significance of the Latin tradition. For specialists in this area of study the expression *Anglo-Saxon* contains within it the happy ambiguity in covering both language forms, Old English and Latin, thus underlining the reality that high culture was bilingual in nature. Part One establishes some of the general contexts necessary for the study of OE lives, including history and art history, giving the broader view that work in other disciplines and collateral subjects proves necessary for a fuller understanding of the prose achievement or at least in some sense serves as a prolegomenon to it. Part Two focuses more closely on OE saints' lives as such, offering essays on manuscript contexts or interpretation of *vitae* from the varying perspectives of literary criticism. Though the whole collection gives explicit evidence of this plan, readers should readily discover that the contributors typically do not accept this scheme as a simple abstraction but rather see texts and contexts in a vital relation as they pursue their specific subjects.

The introduction to this collection is E. Gordon Whatley's "preface to study" on the sources and resources of the field. This essay is intended for individuals new to hagiography in Latin or Old English. Part bibliographical survey, part analysis of the state of the question, and part desiderata, it offers a well-marked and well-defined entry point into the subject of OE prose saints' lives. Arguing that OE saints' lives are best read in relation to Latin source texts and the larger tradition of Latin hagiography in England and on the continent, Whatley offers a list of extant OE saints' lives; discussions of resources for studying OE saints' lives, for nonnative saints' lives, for native saints' lives; and a list of Latin hagiographic manuscripts of Anglo-Saxon provenance. To assist the reader Whatley uses the Life of Julian and Basilissa as a representative object for research to show how the resources assist understanding. Whatley makes many observations along the way. Perhaps the most important of these is the disjunction between the insular and the continental: modern continental scholarship focuses on continental sources (and resources) such that the insular tradition may receive scant or misleading attention. Thus, the Anglo-Saxonist seeking to verify an OE translation of the life of a continental saint ought not to use a Latin edition based exclusively on continental manuscripts; conversely, continental scholarship often eschews vernacular evidence. The reader also derives the benefit of Whatley's experience when he points out problems for Anglo-Saxonists in the *Bibliotheca Hagiographica Latina* and reminds us that Anglo-Saxon writers may sometimes be the first witnesses to Latin translations from the Greek, that later vernacular writers seem to have focused on English saints grounded in historical reality, and that information about saints can come through sources other than strict *vitae*, such as Bede's *Historia Ecclesiastica.* As is appropriate for an essay in this genre of scholarly writing, Whatley presents a goldmine of footnotes and references.

Thomas D. Hill begins Part One by presenting an equivalent to Whatley's survey in the mode of literary history and generic analysis. Hill sketches various distinctions within the genre of saint's life. He describes "primary" hagiographic texts, essentially a historical witness to the life and works of a medieval saint, and "secondary" texts, which are either "legends" more or less connected with liturgical occasions and uses, or "art-*vitae*," which are sacred romances. After explaining these distinctions, Thomas Hill gives several broad comparisons to assist the literary understanding of the genre. These comparisons, sometimes drawn from beyond Anglo-Saxon England and its times, link hagiography with literary romance, religious art, typology, and "emblematic narrative." Like Hill's special formation art-*vita* this last phrase is an advance in generic analysis, describing more sharply what some scholars have seen in operation; viz., "a mode of narrative in which inner experience, either psychological or spiritual, is reflected by the external events of the narrative." Thomas Hill's essay suggests the complexities of the genre and the need for a continuing investigation that is both wide and deep in scope.

The next two essays develop Thomas Hill's contextual themes by considering these issues with respect to earlier Anglo-Saxon England, notably

Northumbria, which gave the period its first "Golden Age." Carol Neuman de
Vegvar examines the intellectual and material context for royal women
monastics as a group, including archaeological evidence, to provide a broader
cultural context to assist the interpretation of the written evidence; in other
words, she describes the "conditions of sanctity" for what Hill describes as
"primary" hagiographic texts. With rich and detailed documentation Neuman
de Vegvar connects royal sanctity and women's roles, explaining the institutional basis for what in current jargon we would call pro-active royal women.
Some of these women found themselves the head of that special early medieval institution, the double monastery, which had its greatest moment of
development in earlier Anglo-Saxon England and earlier Francia. As abbesses they often attained significant power and eternal sanctity, the latter
particularly remembered on earth in *vitae*. In these monasteries patterns of
life and learning were varied and complex; monastic rules and expectations
were not uniform and not necessarily very restrictive, while levels of literacy,
difficult to assess and elusive to describe, must have supported the contemplation of scripture and certainly allowed many women to pursue the life of
letters as well. The material evidence for intellectual activity helps support
the idea that royal women monastic saints well deserved the testimonials of
their hagiographers.

David Rollason continues the emphasis on deeper Latin contexts and
Northumbria in his treatment of the remarkable burst of hagiographical activity there in the late seventh and early eighth centuries. He explores the possibilities that these works, unusual in number for England, influence or attempt
to influence contemporary politics, both secular and ecclesiastical. Rollason
organizes his chapter around three major issues: Easter and the tonsure question, the figure of Wilfrid, and the unity of Northumbria. How to calculate the
date of Easter and the form of tonsure together made for one of the first
Anglo-Irish disputes, presumably settled at the Synod of Whitby in 664, but
Rollason sketches how this joint matter was a long process, rather than an
event, animating important saints' lives, which criticize or answer criticism
of the various contending parties. In this period Wilfrid of York was a domi-
nating and controversial figure, who controlled "a kingdom of churches" and
their riches, not to mention a following of armed men. The Life of Wilfrid
may therefore appear as an apologia, answering the lives of other great saints
on their terms, as well as seeking consolidation and continuation of Wilfrid's
power base by his successors. Finally, the political stability of Northumbria,
as the joining of its constituent states of Bernicia and Deira, is an expressed
or implied topic in the several saints' lives that describe the political tensions.
For scholars working on later treatments of the saints mentioned in this
Northumbrian canon Rollason's discussions are apposite; scholars are, for
example, well advised to note that Æthelthryth's friendship with Wilfrid has

a deep political resonance and that Martin of Tours is a hagiographical figure of political unity, having been appropriated in the story of Cuthbert for that purpose.

Michael Lapidge and Peter Jackson establish and clarify the basis for the vernacular tradition, especially the works of Ælfric, in their treatments of the liturgical calendar and the Cotton-Corpus legendary. Lapidge explains the distinction between *temporale* and *sanctorale* and then goes on to reconstruct Ælfric's *sanctorale* by reference to Anglo-Saxon and early medieval calendars. Granted that there is now no satisfactory manuscript for Ælfric's *Lives of Saints* (the famous Cotton Julius E.vii has its difficulties) and thus the mainline scholarly tradition in OE editing, where one corrects a "base text," must needs falter, reconstruction of Ælfric's likely idea of the calendar of saints is the only reasonable recourse. When Ælfric follows the tradition, he is no more interesting than when he differs from it. It is particularly interesting, say, to note that this Winchester-trained Benedictine monk omits lives of key saints and their observances such as Æthelwold, his mentor, and the Translation of St. Benedict, among others. As Lapidge argues, liturgical design is logically prior to questions of source, style, and lexis. Lapidge and Jackson further clarify the contents and nature of the Cotton-Corpus legendary, a collection now extant in a form dateable to the third quarter of the eleventh century and to Worcester but probably originating in northern France or Flanders in the late ninth or early tenth century. By the later tenth century a version of the legendary was available in Anglo-Saxon England, and Ælfric clearly used it extensively. The Jackson and Lapidge list can thus provide the first step for understanding what Latin hagiographic texts were known in later Anglo-Saxon England.

In her study of the idea of the "active and contemplative" lives and its relation to the image of sanctity in OE saints' lives and particularly Ælfric, Mary Clayton demonstrates how a key set of concepts from the history of the early medieval church can provide a fuller understanding for developments in later Anglo-Saxon England. Clayton traces the various forms of the solitary life and the communal life as they interact with *saeculum* from the patristic period through the Golden Age of Northumbria through the time of Ælfric. As she has done in her other work, Clayton shows how Ælfric has a distinctive interpretation of an issue in early Christian thought. The exemplary text is the homily for the Assumption, where Ælfric makes choices among patristic sources to illustrate the story of Martha and Mary in the Gospel of Luke, who are traditionally types of the active and the contemplative. Ælfric avoids choices that promote the contemplative life and seeks to promulgate the active life of teaching. Thus, what critics of style might see as another example of Ælfric's tendency to abbreviate sources is, as Clayton demonstrates, a considered choice within the options available to an early medieval religious thinker. One can easily understand why Ælfric avoids writing about hermit saints and why martyrs and confessors, who gave up their lives or alternatively bore witness through their works, are so prominent. Accordingly, Æflric offers no account of the great solitary Guthlac and shapes the Life of Cuthbert so that Cuthbert's biography is more that of a preacher and teacher than that of an ascetic. Ælfric offers models of sanctity that propagate the special ideal of active, pastoral Benedictinism, which was current in his time.

Barbara Abou-El-Haj concludes Part One of this collection with a wide-ranging contextual study of the cult of St. Cuthbert, who, as Reginald of Durham tells us, ranked with Eadmund and Ætheldreda as one of the most revered saints of the twelfth century. Abou-El-Haj describes how the cult developed over time and major discontinuities; for example, more than 200 years intervened between Bede's prose life and the record, mostly of royal donations, drawn up, amplified, and rewritten in a series of chronicles beginning in the mid-tenth century. She brings together hagiography, historical documents, and manuscript illuminations to mark the shifts in emphasis arising from the post-Conquest consolidation, particularly violent in Northumbria and at Durham, where it was marked by assassinations of William the Conqueror's early appointees. In these years, Durham was incorporated in the Norman ecclesiastical hierarchy, and Cuthbert's community of clerks lost its shrine to a new community of Benedictine monks installed by Durham's first Norman bishop, William of St. Calais, and the cult was activated as a part of a sweeping campaign of economic and spiritual reform. The monks advanced the cult independent of the vicissitudes of Anglo-Norman political and ecclesiastical politics and also in response to it. Between 1100 and 1104 the monks completed their most elaborate additions to the cult and confirmed its possession by acquiring the last segments of Cuthbert's ancient patrimony, illustrating a new copy of Bede's life and recent miracles strategically related to these activities, and by orchestrating the discovery of Cuthbert's incorrupt body, which was disputed and publicized before a suitable audience. Thus, Abou-El-Haj continues a major theme in the study of Anglo-Saxon saints: their reception and appropriation in post-Conquest England.

Part Two of the collection shifts to a primary engagement with Old English prose saints' lives. D. G. Scragg and Joyce Hill present basic information on the body of OE prose saints' lives with their consideration of the corpus of lives and their dissemination. Scragg offers a piece on the anonymous lives, which is effectively a companion to his fundamental essay on anonymous homilies.[3] He surveys the manuscript context of this corpus to try to determine more about the tradition before Ælfric. After an analysis of the manuscript collections and their contents in the light of the most recent scholarship, Scragg concludes that many of the extant pieces existed before the year 1000 and that when Ælfric's Lives became available, the Anglo-Saxon audience had a wide choice of hagiographical material. Ælfric thus did for the saint's life what he did for the sermon, that is, provide a more comprehensive set of lives for a genre already well established. Joyce Hill amplifies further the Ælfric connection in her preliminary survey of the dissemination and use of Ælfric's *Lives of Saints*. She notes where individual items occur other than in the best manuscript (though not authorial) BL Cotton Julius E.vii, their relative apparent popularity, and the extent to which they are drawn by association and adaptation into homiletic contexts that are non-Ælfrician. Since the evidence is incomplete, there is every reason to be very cautious in the extrapolation of grand conclusions. Nevertheless, Joyce Hill is able to suggest a broad contrast between the use of hagiographical and non-hagiographical, which often attaches itself to the *Lives,* and to show, as is to be expected (despite Ælfric's concerns for the integrity of his own work), no distinction operating between Ælfric's lives and those written by others, now anonymous.

M. R. Godden explains how Ælfric's literary achievement in the genre of a saint's life developed from a series of experiments in the precursors to the *Lives of Saints*, the First and Second Series of the *Catholic Homilies.* Godden isolates three major issues that Ælfric had to face in adapting hagiographic material for a preaching collection: (1) the truth content and authority of hagiography and its relation to history; (2) the conception or characterization of the holy person, particularly the issue of whether a given saint was an individual or a type; (3) the *sententia* or 'meaning' of a life, especially as a pattern of life reflecting on the lives of others. Godden clarifies these issues through an analysis of six items from the *Catholic Homilies.* His method lies in a wide-ranging and analytic use of source criticism in a context of nuanced reading sensitive to doctrinal issues. Godden shows how Ælfric's consideration of the issues varies in emphasis and nature, depending on the particular *donnée* of a saint's biography. Ælfric's treatment of Gregory the Great, for example, combines hagiography, history, and preaching. Godden argues that the later lives in the *Catholic Homilies* concentrate on narrative rather than preaching and debate, employing hagiographic diction and rhythmical prose style, which set the pattern for the *Lives of Saints.* The overall analysis is a convincing demonstration of how Ælfric changes as a writer, responding in a considered way to the implications of the material he receives.

In his essay on Ælfric, Frederick M. Biggs shows how much scope remains for source criticism heightened by precise analysis when he examines the relations between extant *Martiniana* and Ælfric's two treatments of the Life of Martin. Previous work long ago demonstrated Ælfric's indebtedness to Sulpicius Severus and Gregory of Tours, and Patrick Zettel improved our understanding of the issue by indicating the importance of the Cotton-

Corpus legendary, which included Alcuin's treatment of Martin in *Laudationes*. But Biggs goes one step further by tracing Ælfric's selection and ordering of details with the Latin as a total framework for understanding. He is able to substantiate the view that Ælfric has an interest in "chronologically accurate narrative," which in turn implies Ælfric's active discrimination of the value of historical sources. Like Bede Ælfric thus has an interest in the "truth value" of holy biography. For Biggs source criticism becomes open ended, not close ended: the critic does not establish documentary evidence only and merely but rather uses it to discover what Ælfric thought of his sources and to uncover his active process of engagement with the Latin tradition. Ultimately the critic can construct a biography of the literary imagination. Biggs, in fact, offers source criticism in a newer key.

Hugh Magennis takes source study of Ælfric in a different direction in his consideration of Ælfric and the Seven Sleepers and highlights another aspect of Ælfric's adaptation of the Latin tradition. Like Biggs, Magennis sees in Ælfric a mind active in selection and discrimination and, while granting the importance of the Cotton-Corpus legendary, shows that surviving copies of this legendary do not account for all that Ælfric does. Magennis is further aided in his analysis by a near-contemporary anonymous OE version that offers comparative, if not "intertextual," material. Ælfric's treatment of the Seven Sleepers shows how a *vita* can serve the ends of doctrine. Ælfric, reflecting major tendencies in early hagiography, produces a severe or austere life, in some respects dehumanized and deprived of detail, to explain the doctrine of the resurrection of the body. So "pure" an approach to antecedent holy narrative marks Ælfric as a sharply different writer from his contemporaries.

The final two essays depart from established methods and established concerns in the study of OE saints' lives. Ruth Waterhouse presents interpretations of Ælfric's Life of Oswald and Life of Æthelthryth based on a new model of understanding that relates writer, text, and reader. This new model, a form of discourse analysis, outlines the three-way transaction among these elements in their complexity and detail, making more explicit matters of influences and intertextuality, but above all bringing the audience-reader back into the creation of meaning. The Life of Æthelthryth, Waterhouse argues, is an example of a text that for a twentieth-century reader seems to combine comic elements and elements offensive to a feminist reader. Æthelthryth's reluctance to bathe, bizarre as it might seem now, takes on another meaning altogether when a study of the semantic field of "baþian" discloses a higher level of symbolic signification. Æthelthryth's virginity despite her marriages, which a twentieth-century feminist reader might link to concerns of patriarchal hegemony, is a theme that on closer examination shows Ælfric's recognition of a potential audience's understandable incredulity, which he counters in such a way as to bring out the distance between the saint's exemplary behavior and the more pragmatic behavior that can be expected from a lay audience. Waterhouse's application of discourse analysis to the Life of Oswald similarly seeks to describe the transaction of meaning among writer, text, and audience.

The concluding essay likewise contains some new themes for study in its analysis of the Life of Euphrosyne. Once considered to have been written by Ælfric and then relegated to the anonymous tradition, this Life would appear to be a likely candidate for literary obscurity. Yet most recent interest in women in Anglo-Saxon culture (and literature), as well as the growing study of Old English prose for its own sake, may make it possible to retrieve this work for the future canon of prose works to be actively read both for cultural meaning and literary style. Within this dual movement towards new topics and new works my concluding paper offers a reading of the Life with some treatment of source relationships with the Latin and a brief review of scholarship, particularly of this subgenre of *vita*. The focus must nevertheless be on sexuality, both explicit and implicit, and Euphrosyne's holy transvestitism that enables her to live as a man in a monastery for some thirty-eight years and to convert her father to the good life. Since Ælfric is the measure for achievement in prose, how the anonymous writer treats themes similarly found in Ælfric is a necessary theme. All such saints' lives have been called *sensational novelettes,* containing episodes "unelevated even when the underlying doctrine is remembered," but the final point here will be that the renewed interest in human sexuality, fostered in part by issues highlighted by women's studies, has a liberating effect in the study of Old English prose.

These essays seek to continue the further development of the study of OE prose by opening up the interdisciplinary, literary, and cultural potential inherent in the study of early English saints' lives. The methodologies employed here are various: traditional in the emphasis on manuscript, original evidence, and Latin sources, "newer" in their emphasis on new topics and new perspectives. Even the first two SUNY collections, which came forward before the *adventus theoriae* dominated discussion, were concerned with canon formation, though the phrase was scarcely known then in Anglo-Saxon studies; so too does this collection aim to continue the redirection of field interest toward the largest body of vernacular prose in early medieval Europe. It is an irony and a paradox of Old English studies that, when scholars offer new work in OE prose, however grounded in methodology old or new, they are advancing the newer intellectual strategy of expanding the canon, and when scholars offer newer theoretical insights for OE poetry, they are, in a basic sense, treading rather well-worn paths. It seems inconceivable that anyone interested in a cultural study of Anglo-Saxon England would want to do so without incorporating the body of OE prose and the broad perspectives implied in the study of that corpus. One can only stress, for example, that the women of *Beowulf* are, after all, only some of the women, and a theory of the representation and reality of women in Anglo-Saxon England must needs take into account the real and imagined women who were their holy exemplars. As it turns out, several of the contributors to this collection are very much interested in reediting Ælfric's *Lives of Saints,* which would suggest the recursiveness of the various modes of scholarship: editions stimulate studies, but studies can equally inspire new and improved editions.

It is more than required at this point to thank the many contributors to this enterprise. As happens in an activity that requires the synchrony of more than fifteen personal and professional lives, the essayists were called upon to exercise patience with each other and with the editor. No contributor to this collection has been unbusy, with many, other pursuits. A new factor that confronted us all was the spectre of the computer. Offering the three temptations of multiple and easy revisions, ultimate economy in typesetting, and easy, combinative editing, the machine turned out to be a near demon. Incompatible systems, for example, lead scholars off to strange places in manuscript preparation and scanners could not cope with the special OE characters. My collaborators remained cheerful as we all suffered the joys of progress.

This collection has been a project of the Center for Medieval and Early Renaissance Studies at the State University of New York at Binghamton, enjoying mainly indirect support from staff and facilities. I would like to thank my colleague Robin S. Oggins, under whose directorship this project came to completion, and Ann DiStefano, who with several student assistants, helped lead us all out of the computer maze. These student assistants include Sandra Sammartano, Helene Scheck, and Holly Holbrook. At Western Michigan University, where this project was completed, Gregory Beckelhymer gave invaluable help to the editor, who is accordingly most grateful.

As a final bibliographical note, the contributors have made a reasonable effort to incorporate scholarship through the end of 1992 in their essays.

Notes

1. The complete references are Paul E. Szarmach and Bernard F. Huppé, eds., *The Old English Homily and Its Backgrounds* (Albany, N.Y., 1978); Paul E. Szarmach, ed., *Studies in Earlier Old English Prose* (Albany, N.Y., 1986).

2. See my "Old English Prose," which is part of the special issue *Old English Studies: Current State and Future Prospects, ANQ,* n.s. 3, no. 2 (1990): 56–59.

3. D. G. Scragg, "The Corpus of Vernacular Homilies and Prose Saints' Lives Before Ælfric," *ASE* 8 (1980): 223–77.

Introduction

An Introduction to the Study of
Old English Prose Hagiography: Sources and Resources

E. Gordon Whatley

Many of the essays in this volume are by scholars who have been active in the area of Old English prose homilies and saints' lives for some time. Their contributions illustrate not only a variety of seasoned critical approaches but also considerable methodological expertise. This introductory chapter (more a collection of notes than an essay) is addressed to those students and scholars, from whatever discipline, who are attracted to, but not yet very familiar with, the field of Anglo-Saxon hagiography or Western hagiography at large. The aim of the chapter is to survey some of the principal research tools necessary for original work in the corpus of Old English lives (those by Ælfric and the anonymous individual lives) and the Latin texts that lie behind them. I have purposefully avoided certain topics that might otherwise require treatment here but are dealt with in detail elsewhere in this volume; for example, the manuscripts containing the Old English texts themselves are discussed in the chapters by Joyce Hill and Donald Scragg, and what is probably the most important of the Anglo-Saxon manuscripts containing Latin hagiographic texts, the "Cotton-Corpus" legendary, figures largely in the chapter by Michael Lapidge and Peter Jackson. Purely for practical reasons, I have also excluded from consideration major Old English prose works that are hagiographic in content but collective in form: the Old English Bede, Gregory's *Dialogues*, and the Old English *Martyrology*.

Hagiography is narrative, but it is framed by lists, including calendars of saints' feast days, martyrologies, litanies, lists of relics and miracles, and even lists of manors and fields "owned" by the saints for the ecclesiasts under their patronage. This chapter has five sections of which the first and last are lists (more lists are in the notes). The first section lists the saints whose acts are narrated in one form or another in Old English prose. The last section lists the surviving manuscripts from the Anglo-Saxons' own collections of Latin

3

hagiography and itemizes the Latin saints' lives in each one. In between, the sections focus by turns on the scholarly resources for studying the Old English texts, Latin hagiography of continental origin, and Anglo-Latin hagiography. The chapter's progression from published Old English texts to largely unpublished Latin manuscripts betrays its underlying theoretical bias: that the Old English saints' legends are best read in relation to their individual Latin source texts and in the larger context of Latin hagiography in England and Europe in the early medieval period. The more we can learn about the Latin tradition, the better we will understand the 100 or so vernacular texts that for many English men and women, clerical as well as lay, replaced the Latin tradition in the tenth and eleventh centuries.

List of Old English Prose Saints' Lives

Following is a list of all the texts of individual saints' lives in Old English prose, the majority by Ælfric, the rest anonymous, that I have located through printed sources. The texts are listed alphabetically by saint's name. Where there is more than one version of a saint's life, Ælfric's is listed first. Each text is identified by the conventional short title, as used by the *Dictionary of Old English*[1]: *ÆCHom* = Ælfric's *Catholic Homilies*, Series I and II; *ÆLS* = Ælfric's *Lives of Saints*; *ÆHomM* = Ælfric's *Homilies* (ed. Pope); *LS* = the anonymous saints' lives, or *Sanctorale*. In the case of Ælfric's *Catholic Homilies*, my numbering of the First Series is that of Thorpe's edition only; for the Second Series homilies I have given two numbers, the first from Thorpe, the second from Godden's recent EETS edition: thus *ÆCHom* II, 20/18 is number XX in Thorpe's, XVIII in Godden's edition of the second series.[2]

The short title is followed by the text's identification number from the authoritative "List of Texts" by Frank and Cameron in their plan.[3] For example, the first text in my list, Abdon and Sennes, has the short title *ÆLS* 24, and the identification number B1.3.24. I have given page (and sometimes line) numbers only where the piece in question is part of a larger text.

For reasons of space and to avoid redundancy, I have not given manuscript information or, in most cases, citations of printed editions; both are supplied at the appropriate place in the *Plan* (which does not, however, include references to Godden's later edition of *ÆCHom* II). Editions printed since the publication of the *Plan* may be located in the bibliography of Luke Reinsma for Ælfrician texts and that of Karen Quinn and Kenneth Quinn for non-Ælfrician texts[4] (see second section), but I have included references (in the Notes) to important editions not mentioned in the *Plan*, Reinsma, or Quinn and Quinn. Readers should note that not all the texts that follow are "hagiographical" in the strict sense; most of Ælfric's homilies on the various feasts of the Virgin, for example, take their narratives from scripture, not from the apocrypha.

Abdon and Sennes, *ÆLS* 24, B1.3.24.[5]
Æthelthryth, *ÆLS* 21, B1.3.21.
Agatha, *ÆLS* 9, B1.3.9.
Agnes, *ÆLS* 8 (part 1), B1.3.8 (with Gallicanus, John and Paul).
Alban, *ÆLS* 20, B1.3.20.
Alexander, Eventus, and Theodolus, *ÆCHom* II 20/18, B1.2.23, B1.4.24.
Andrew i, *ÆCHom* I 38, B1.1.40.
Andrew ii, *LS* 1, B3.3.1.[6]
Apollinaris, *ÆLS* 23, B1.3.23.[7]
Apollonius (Apollo) of Egypt (part 2 of Maccabees).
Augustine of Canterbury, *LS* 2, B3.3.2 (fragment).
Bartholomew, *ÆCHom* I 31, B1.1.33.
Basil, *ÆLS* 4, B1.3.4.
Benedict, *ÆCHom* II 11, B1.1.12 (see also Gregory the Great's *Dialogues* 2).
Cecilia, *ÆLS* 32, B1.3.32.
Chad, *LS* 3, B3.3.3.
Christopher, *LS* 4, B3.3.4.[8]
Chrysanthus and Daria, *ÆLS* 33, B1.3.33.
Clement, *ÆCHom* I 37, B1.1.39.[9]
Cross (Exaltation), *ÆLS* 27, B1.3.27.
Cross (History), *LS* 5, B3.3.5.
Cross (Invention i), *ÆCHom* II 19/18. B1.2.22.
Cross (Invention ii), *LS* 6, B3.3.6.[10]
Cuthbert, *ÆCHom* II 10/10, B1.2.11.
Denis and companions, *ÆLS* 29, B1.3.29; also in Clement, pp. 558–60.
Edmund (king and martyr), *ÆLS* 31, B1.3.31.
Eugenia, *ÆLS* 2, B1.3.3.[11]
Euphrosyne, *LS* 7, B3.3.7.[12]
Eustace and Companions, *LS* 8, B3.3.8.
Forty Soldiers, *ÆLS* 12, B1.3.12.
Four Evangelists (Mark, part 2), *ÆLS* 16, B1.3.16, pp. 326–36.
Fursey (*visio* only), *ÆCHom* II 22/20, B1.2.25.
Gallicanus (see John and Paul).
George, *ÆLS* 15, B1.3.15.[13]
Giles, *LS* 9, B3.3.9.[14]
Gregory, *ÆCHom* II 9, B1.2.10.
Guthlac, *LS* 10, B3.3.10.[15]
James the Greater (i), *ÆCHom* II 31/27, B1.2.34.

James the Greater (ii), *LS* 11, B3.3.11.[16]

James the Less (see Philip and James the Less).

John and Paul with Gallicanus (Agnes, part 2), *ÆLS* 8, B1.3.8, pp. 186–94.

John the Baptist (Decollation), *ÆCHom* I 32, B1.1.34.

John the Baptist (Nativity i), *ÆCHom* I 25, B1.1.27.

John the Baptist (Nativity ii), *LS* 12, B3.3.12.

John the Evangelist (Assumption), *ÆCHom* I 4, B1.1.5.[17] Extract also in Ælfric's "Letter to Sigeweard," B1.8.4 (Crawford's ed., ll. 1017–1153).[18]

Julian and Basilissa, *ÆLS* 5, B1.3.5.

Laurence, *ÆCHom* I 29, B1.1.31.

Lucy, *ÆLS* 10, B1.3.10.

Macarius of Egypt (part two of Swithun).

Maccabees, *ÆLS* 25, B1.3.25;[19] appends Apollonius episode, pp. 122–24, ll. 833–62 (from Rufinus, *Historia monachorum*, *PL* 21.411–12).

Machutus, *LS* 13, B3.3.13.

Malchus (*Vitas Patrum*, part 2), *LS* 35, B3.3.35, pp. 199–207.[20]

Margaret (i), *LS* 14, B3.3.13.

Margaret (ii), *LS* 15 (burnt), B3.3.15.

Margaret (iii), *LS* 16, B3.3.16.

Mark, *ÆLS* 16, B1.3.16.

Martin (i), *ÆCHom* II 39/34, B1.2.42.

Martin (ii), *ÆLS* 30, B1.3.30.

Martin (iii), *LS* 17, B3.3.17.[21]

Mary of Egypt, *LS* 23, B3.3.23.

Mary Virgin (Annunciation), *ÆCHom* I 13, B1.1.14

Mary Virgin (Assumption i), *ÆCHom* I 30, B1.1.32 (plus two Marian miracles: Theophilus, p. 448; slaying of Julian Apostate by Mercurius, pp. 448–54).

Mary Virgin (Assumption ii), *ÆCHom* II 34/29, B1.2.36.

Mary Virgin (Assumption iii), *LS* 20, B3.3.20.

Mary Virgin (Assumption iv), *LS* 21, B3.3.21.[22]

Mary Virgin (Nativity i), *ÆCHom* II 36/31, B1.2.39; see also *ÆHomM* 8, B1.5.8.[23]

Mary Virgin (Nativity ii), *LS* 18, B3.3.18.[24]

Mary Virgin (Nativity iii), *HomU* 10 (*VercHom* 6, B3.4.10).[25]

Mary Virgin (Purification i), *ÆCHom* I 9, B1.1.10

Mary Virgin (Purification ii), *LS* 19, B3.3.19.[26]

Mary Virgin (Sermon of Ralph D'Escures), *LS* 22, B3.3.22.

Matthew (see also Andrew ii), *ÆCHom* II 37/32, B1.2.40.

Maur, *ÆLS* 7, B1.3.7.

Maurice and companions, *ÆLS* 28, B1.3.28.

Mercurius (slaying of Julian Apostate: see Basil; see also Mary Virgin, Assumption i).

Michael (i), *ÆCHom* I 34, B1.1.36.

Michael (ii), *LS* 24, B3.3.24.[27]

Michael (iii), *LS* 25, B3.3.25.

Mildred (i), *LS* 26, B3.3.26.

Mildred (ii? see Sexburga), *LS* 27, B3.3.27.

Neot, *LS* 28, B3.3.28.

Nicholas, *LS* 29, B3.3.29.

Oswald (king and martyr), *ÆLS* 26, B1.3.26.[28]

Pantaleon, *LS* 30, B3.3.30.

Paul (apostle), *ÆCHom* I 27, B1.1.29.

Paulinus, *LS* 32, B3.3.32.

Peter, *ÆCHom* II 28/24, B1.2.31 (exegetical, not hagiographical).

Peter (Chair of), *ÆLS* 11, B1.3.11 (includes Petronilla and Felicula, ll. 232–93).

Peter and Paul (i), *ÆCHom* I 26, B1.1.28.[29]

Peter and Paul (ii), *LS* 32, B3.3.32.

Petronilla and Felicula (see Peter, Chair of).

Philip and James the Less, *ÆCHom* II 18/17, B1.2.21.

Quintin, *LS* 33, B3.3.33.

Sebastian, *ÆLS* 6, B1.3.6.[30]

Seven Sleepers (i), *ÆCHom* II 32/27, B1.2.34.

Seven Sleepers (ii), *LS* 34, B3.3.34.

Sexburga (see also Mildred ii?), B3.3.27 (one portion of the fragmentary text in MS London, Lambeth Palace 427, ff. 210–11, may be from a life of Sexburga).[31]

Simon and Jude, *ÆCHom* II 38/33, B1.2.41.

Stephen Protomartyr (i), *ÆCHom* I 3, B1.1.4.

Stephen Protomartyr (ii), *ÆCHom* II 2, B1.2.3.

Swithun, *ÆLS* 22, B1.3.22; part two is Macarius, pp. 470–72, ll. 471–93 (cf. Rufinus's *Historia Monachorum*, *PL* 21.451); same story in AEHom 29, B1.4.30 (Pope's ed., pp. 790–96).

Theophilus (see Mary, Virgin, Assumption i).

Thomas, *ÆLS* 34, B1.3.34.

Veronica, *VSal*, B8.5.4.

Vincent, *ÆLS* 35. B1.3.35 (see also *ÆHomM*, B1.5.9, "On a Martyr's Day").[32]

Vitas Patrum (see also Apollonius, Macarius, Malchus), *LS* 35, B3.3.35.[33]

Resources for Studying Old English Prose Saints' Lives

The splendid *Bibliography of Publications on Old English Literature* by Stanley Greenfield and Fred Robinson (Greenfield/Robinson) is the standard bibliography for the field.[34] But with its formal orientation toward the history of scholarship, it does not attempt to serve as a guide to Old English prose hagiography as such. Nowhere in the text or index is there anything resembling a comprehensive list of the Old English prose saints' lives, nor can such a list be drawn up piecemeal using Greenfield/Robinson only. A necessary complement to Greenfield/Robinson is the redoubtable *Plan for the Dictionary of Old English*, mentioned earlier. The third and longest section, by Angus Cameron, comprises an elaborately classified and numbered list of all the extant texts of Old English, verse and prose, with all known manuscript copies of each text (keyed to entries in Ker's *Catalogue*) and its most recent or standard printed edition. The numbering works according to a classification system likely to become very familiar to Anglo-Saxonists as the *Dictionary of Old English*, with its ancillary publications, becomes more widely known and used.[35] Thus section A in the *Plan* comprises all the poetic texts; section B consists of twenty-eight categories of prose texts; section C comprises glosses, and so on. Most relevant to hagiography are B1, the works of Ælfric (the two series of *Catholic Homilies*, B1.1–B1.2, and the *Lives of Saints*, B1.3); B3.3, the "Sanctorale" or anonymous prose saints' lives; and B19 (the Old English *Martyrology*).[36] The Ælfrician texts in the *Plan* B1. 1–3 are listed more or less according to their order in the standard printed editions (which is the calendar order of the saints' feast days in the chief manuscripts), but those in B3.3, "Sanctorale," are listed alphabetically by saints' names.

Cameron's lists of prose lives, despite their mixture of calendar and alphabetical formats, are the most convenient and complete, and they are an essential starting point for the study of the corpus of Old English prose hagiography.[37] They can be improved slightly, as I have tried to do in the preceding list by adding separate entries for Apollonius, the Four Evangelists, John and Paul, Macarius, the Maccabees, Malchus, Sexburga, and Veronica, all of whom are the subjects of separate Old English texts, or distinct parts of texts, but are not identified in the *Plan*.

The *Plan* offers a listing of texts, manuscript copies, and standard editions up to 1972. It is not a bibliography as such. Two newer works cited earlier, by Reinsma and the Quinns,[38] provide more specialized bibliographical support and guidance to students of Old English prose hagiography. Reinsma's bibliography of editions and scholarship on Ælfric's works includes sections specifically on the homilies and saints' lives, arranged chronologically by date of publication, and provides a helpful abstract of each item listed. Manuscripts, subjects, and modern authors each have separate indices, allowing one to locate studies and editions of individual saints' lives. The Quinns' *Manual* deals with the non-Ælfrician corpus of Old English prose. Unlike Greenfield/Robinson's and Reinsma's bibliographies, which plot the development of modern scholarship chronologically, the Quinns have provided a guide to the texts themselves, organized on the model of the Toronto *Plan*, including the *Plan* reference numbers. Thus the "Sanctorale" section of the *Manual* essentially duplicates that of *Plan*, but with more information about each separate text, including incipits, manuscripts, brief descriptions of each text, all known editions, and pertinent studies. The *Manual* also, however, repeats some of the *Plan*'s problems and omissions, for example, of Malchus, Sexburga, and Veronica, although Malchus at least is visible through the General Index.

Both Reinsma's and the Quinns' valuable works incorporate bibliograpical items appearing as late as 1982 (and occasionally later). For more recent material, the best resource, in addition to the standard literature bibliographies, is the bibliography of Anglo-Saxon studies compiled annually by Carl Berkhout, published in the spring issue of the *Old English Newsletter*, especially section 3c, dealing with prose literature.[39] Reinsma and the Quinns include unpublished doctoral dissertations among their citations, as does Berkhout. A recent convenient bibliography of dissertations on Old English is that of Pulsiano;[40] for current information about dissertations, the standard source is, of course, *Dissertation Abstracts International*, especially the A volume, covering the humanities and social sciences in North America, and the C volume, covering Europe and elsewhere (all fields, but selectively).[41] More specialized annual reports and summary catalogues are usually available in major research libraries for locating dissertations abroad and in specialized subjects.

Resources for Studying the Latin Sources of Old English Prose Saints' Lives: Non-native Saints

The great majority of the printed texts of Old English prose saints' lives are accessible only in older, collective editions, where one is faced with the Old English text, information about its manuscript sources and language, and little else. A few lives are available in individual editions, and a handful of these print and discuss the Latin source of the Old English text.[42] In most cases, therefore, one must make use of the standard resources of hagiographic scholarship at large, and do for oneself the "Quellenforschung" usually provided in a good critical edition, to gain some understanding of the Latin tradition in which the Old English hagiographer worked and to which that text, in one way or another, responds.

To illustrate the use of these hagiographic sources and resources and some of their attendant problems, I selected more or less at random, as a representative text for source study, one of the pieces in Ælfric's *Lives of*

Saints: the story of SS. Julian and Basilissa, who represent, as "virgin spouses," an interesting subcategory of Ælfric's martyred saints (cf. also Cecilia and Valerianus, Chrysanthus and Daria). Ælfric's source in this case was a Latin legend, the *Passio SS. Juliani et Basilissae*, of which more shortly.

At the outset in a study of this kind, it is advisable to consult an encyclopedia for general information about the saint's origins, legend, cult, and iconography. The best of those devoted to hagiography is the Italian *Bibliotheca Sanctorum*.[43] I should mention at this point also that the only general guide to the Anglo-Saxons' use of Latin texts, including saints' lives, has been Ogilvy's *Books Known to the English*. Although less than thorough in its coverage and prone to various kinds of errors, Ogilvy's book is nonetheless valuable in the early stages of source study of Old English literature, and his list of texts and references forms the original basis of the forthcoming *Sources of Anglo-Saxon Literary Culture*, designed to replace *Books Known*.[44]

Two German dissertations, both published in 1892, laid the foundations for subsequent study of Ælfric's Latin hagiographic sources: those of Förster, on the "legends" in *Catholic Homilies*, and Ott, on those in volume 1 of Skeat's edition of *Lives of Saints*.[45] The lives in volume 2 were first sourced by Loomis and others, and source studies of specific hagiographic texts by Ælfric continue to appear.[46] The important work of Patrick Zettel on the Latin hagiographic sources of both the *Homilies* and *Lives* is discussed later in this chapter as well as in that of Lapidge and Jackson in this volume. Less work has been done on the sources of the anonymous lives.[47]

According to Ott, Ælfric's Latin source for our sample text, his life of SS. Julian and Basilissa (hereafter *ÆLS* 4), was a seventh-century Latin prose *passio* (hereafter *Pas.Jul.Bas.*) very similar to that printed in the *Acta Sanctorum, Ianuarius*, volume 1,[48] but having more details in common with some of the manuscripts cited there for variant readings. *Acta Sanctorum*, the work of a dedicated group of Jesuit scholars, Société des Bollandistes, is perhaps the best known (and certainly the bulkiest) of the resources of modern hagiographic scholarship. Its hefty folio tomes contain *vitae* or *passiones* of nearly all the known saints of the Christian Middle Ages whose feast days occur from January through November.[49] The texts are printed in the order of the saints' feast days. Thus the first three volumes of *Acta Sanctorum* are devoted to the saints with feast days in January, including Julian and Basilissa on January 9, although in the early Middle Ages the pair were associated in some calendars and martyrologies with January 6 or 8. This sort of variation in feast days is typical.[50]

Having reached the *Acta Sanctorum* edition of *Pas.Jul.Bas.* we confront a major difficulty. Although *Acta Sanctorum* remains the greatest single collection of hagiographic texts, it is also, like J.-P. Migne's more familiar library of patristic texts, *Patrologia Latina*, out of date and deficient by modern scholarly standards. Moreover, it is incomplete: the lives of the saints of December have not been edited for *Acta Sanctorum*.[51] The great majority of the volumes were published in the seventeenth and eighteenth centuries, and although they contain editions that are in some cases still valuable today,[52] only the November volumes (1887–1925) reflect truly modern standards of textual scholarship. The *Acta Sanctorum* edition of *Pas.Jul.Bas.*, for example, is based on an unnamed, undated "very old manuscript" collated with several others that have taken a good deal of modern scholarship just to identify.[53] The early Bollandists frequently, though not always, made use of relatively late manuscripts, preferring usually more polished (but often much revised and interpolated) redactions, in legendaries of the twelfth or thirteenth centuries, to the cruder but more "authoritative" recensions of the early medieval period. The *Acta Sanctorum* editions of late classical and early medieval texts such as *Pas.Jul.Bas.*, therefore, are not usually representative of the sort of texts that Anglo-Saxons such as Aldhelm or Ælfric used in their own hagiography, and detailed critical comparisons between an Old English text and a Latin text from *Acta Sanctorum* alone should be avoided if possible.[54]

The modern Bollandists, on the other hand, have provided us with several tools for either tracking down more recent and rigorous printed editions, or, failing that, for finding more authoritative, earlier manuscripts. Their journal *Analecta Bollandiana*, founded in 1882, publishes articles in the whole field of hagiography, Eastern as well as Western, including editions of shorter hagiographic texts, critical studies, manuscript information, hagiographic catalogues of smaller manuscript collections, and review notices of new books and articles in the field. It is well indexed (every twenty volumes), viz., by saints, manuscripts, and modern authors, as is each fascicle of the journal. Needless to say, working through the copious indices for notices of one's chosen saint, text, or manuscript, can be tedious, but it is a necessary and invariably rewarding task for anyone in the early stages of a hagiographic project.

The accompanying monograph series, *Subsidia Hagiographica*, includes editions of longer texts, special studies, and catalogues of hagiographic texts in medieval manuscripts in the larger and smaller libraries of Europe. Among the most important volumes in the *Subsidia* series are the great hagiographic catalogues of the libraries of Paris, Brussels, and Rome,[55] which include manuscripts of insular origin, some of the most significant of which, for hagiography in Anglo-Saxon England, have only recently begun to be recognized as insular.[56] More recently, the Bollandists have concentrated their cataloguing efforts on the provincial libraries of France.[57]

Perhaps the most widely used volume in the *Subsidia* series, in addition to Delehaye's classic popular introduction to hagiographic literature,[58] is the Bollandists' handlist of medieval Latin hagiographic texts, *Bibliotheca*

Hagiographica Latina (*BHL*),[59] an alphabetical listing of all the Christian saints, Eastern as well as Western, whose lives are preserved in Latin.[60] The different *vitae* or *passiones* of each saint are arranged in ostensibly chronological order, with a separate identification number, incipit, and desinit (*BHL* does not use explicit), and where possible, citations of printed editions of (and printed excerpts from) each variant version of the life. Where there is no printed edition of a particular recension or redaction, *BHL* cites published notices of manuscript copies.

Thus in the first edition of *BHL*, the entry for SS. Julianus and Basilissa lists six different literary memorials, the earliest of which is the anonymous *passio* (our *Pas.Jul.Bas.*) as printed in *Acta Sanctorum*, here numbered *BHL* 4529, along with three variant versions, *BHL* 4530–32, encountered by the Bollandists in their manuscript researches. *BHL* 4532, for example, differs from 4529 in omitting the prologue and most of the last chapter. On the other hand, the next three items under Julianus and Basilissa, *BHL* 4533–35, comprising poems by various authors in praise of the two saints, are not simply variant versions of the *passio prima* (*BHL* 4529), but distinct works, although based ultimately on some version or other of the basic *passio*. The earliest of these, *BHL* 4533, a lengthy section of Aldhelm of Malmesbury's major work *De Virginitate*, is obviously relevant to the Anglo-Saxon context, because, as a work well known to the later Anglo-Saxon literati, it may turn out to have influenced Ælfric's treatment or selection of the legend of Julian and Basilissa.[61]

There are two supplements to *BHL*, published in 1911 and 1986,[62] the second of which, the *Novum Supplementum*, supersedes the former. In the case of *Pas.Jul.Bas.*, it incorporates the references made in the 1911 *Supplément* to additional variant recensions (*BHL* 4532b–d), and cites two new printed editions of *BHL* 4529, both based on important early manuscripts, and a study, by Delehaye, of the cults of the martyrs of Egypt, including Julian and Basilissa.[63] The two supplements also reveal, however, that the numerical classification system of *BHL*, as set up in the first edition, does not always reflect the textual facts as revealed by more exhaustive research and more recent manuscript discoveries. The system has come to appear somewhat cumbersome (e.g., the proliferation of alphabetical modifiers, such as *BHL* 4532b–d, mentioned previously), and even misleading. A famous example concerns the *passio* of St. Alban, Britain's "protomartyr," where the original *BHL* numbering system conveys a topsy-turvy picture of the history of the text as it has been reconstructed since the turn of the century.[64]

Despite these drawbacks, *BHL* remains the essential guide (Ker's *Catalogue*, for example, usually indicates hagiographic Latin sources solely by *BHL* number). It offers at a glance a sketch of the literature inspired by a saint's cult, with the main bibliographical information. Especially now with its updated supplement, it provides a vivid if schematic picture of the rich instability of hagiographic texts in the Middle Ages. Each recension represents a different interpretation of the inherited legend, and to speak of *the* life or passion of a particular saint becomes meaningless in the light of the textual variety revealed in *BHL* and its supplements.[65]

A substantial number of the Latin hagiographic texts current in Anglo-Saxon England, including *Pas.Jul.Bas.* and the ultimate sources of many of the prose lives and the poems *Elene* and *Andreas*, were originally composed in Greek. Many cults of originally Greek or otherwise "Oriental" saints had migrated to Italy, Gaul, and Spain by the sixth and seventh centuries and thence to England and Ireland. For our purposes, the best scholarly treatment of the hagiographic repercussions of this migration is that of Siegmund, whose book on Greek Christian literature in the West is particularly detailed in its attention to hagiography and hagiographic manuscripts and has not in this respect been replaced by Berschin's otherwise superior study.[66]

Siegmund lists and discusses the earliest surviving manuscript copies of the principal Latin versions of Greek saints' legends popular in the West, invariably identifying them by their *BHL* numbers.[67] He dates *Pas.Jul.Bas.* among the texts translated into Latin in the seventh century or earlier, citing as evidence Aldhelm's knowledge of it, and early manuscript copies such as the late seventh century "Luxeuil Lectionary" and some early legendaries (anthologies of hagiographic texts for liturgical or devotional reading) such as Munich, Bayerisches Staatsbibliothek 3514 and 4554 (early and late eighth century, respectively).[68] Today, in certain instances, Siegmund's references to legendaries can be supplemented from Cross's work on the hagiographic sources of the ninth-century Old English *Martyrology*.[69] For example, Cross mentions unpublished early recensions of *Pas.Jul.Bas.* in legendaries of the ninth and tenth centuries in the Vatican and in Montpellier.[70] The legendaries in general are discussed by Philippart in a volume of the *Typologie* series, with a table of the oldest (seventh- and eighth-century) legendaries and much valuable information about hagiographic texts of various kinds.[71]

Manuscripts such as those cited by Siegmund and Cross, and the modern editions based on them, are, compared to the early printed editions, potentially more valuable witnesses to the recensions of *Pas.Jul.Bas.* current during the Anglo-Saxon period. But the earliest manuscripts are rarely of English provenance. It is possible that an early manuscript from outside England could be very similar to the recension used by Ælfric himself, because, as is well known, the tenth-century revival of monastic culture and Latinity in England was strongly influenced from abroad and manuscript books were brought from the continent in significant numbers.[72] But it seems only logical that manuscripts of demonstrably English provenance, if they exist, are likely to take us closest to the sources of the Anglo-Saxon hagiographers. Unfortunately, the Bollandists did not prepare a Latin hagiographic catalogue to the

English libraries,[73] and the only major survey of hagiographic manuscripts in British libraries, that of Sir Thomas Duffus Hardy, covers texts about British saints and British history only (see later). The new reference work in progress, *Sources of Anglo-Saxon Literary Culture*, will go some of the way to compensating for the lack of a Bollandist-type catalogue.[74] Helmut Gneuss's published list of manuscripts extant from Anglo-Saxon England is one of the project's more important bases and a necessary reference point for any research involving Anglo-Saxon manuscript sources.[75]

With regard to Ælfric's hagiographic sources, however, an unpublished Oxford dissertation by Patrick Zettel has drawn attention to a mid-eleventh century English legendary, the so-called Cotton-Corpus legendary, which seems very similar, if not identical, to the collection of hagiographic texts that Ælfric drew on for the non-English saints' legends included in *Catholic Homilies* and *Lives of Saints*.[76] In the case of Julian and Basilissa, for example, Zettel's textual analysis of parallels between *ÆLS* 4 and several Latin recensions strongly suggests that the text of *Pas.Jul.Bas.* in BL Cotton Nero E. i is closely related to Ælfric's source.[77] The Cotton text, which according to Zettel is of the same type as *BHL* 4532, shares with the Old English several detailed divergences from the printed versions of *BHL* 4529, including occasional errors. Especially significant, however, is the fact that the Cotton text of *Pas.Jul.Bas.*, like *ÆLS* 4, is considerably abbreviated in comparison with *BHL* 4529. Whereas Anglo-Saxonists have normally credited Ælfric himself with reducing and simplifying the legend (*ÆLS* 4 is half as long as *BHL* 4529), some of the detailed work of editing and abbreviation (including the omission of some potentially sensitive material on the asexuality of monks and nuns) had already been done for him by the nameless scribes responsible for the transmission of Ælfric's source text. Even though the Cotton manuscript is a half-century or more later than Ælfric's time, it appears to derive from a collection of saints' lives, a legendary in effect, in use in late tenth-century England, which in turn derived from a late ninth-century continental collection.

Zettel's work implies that Ælfric's "interpretation" of a text such as *Pas.Jul.Bas.* is not as easily isolated as previous critics have assumed. To place his hagiographic achievement in perspective, it must be viewed as part of a larger process of textual transcription, redaction, and transmission. We need to find out as much as possible about the Anglo-Saxons' own Latin recensions of the legends before we can approach the vernacular versions with critical confidence. The manuscript sources for this are few enough, but until Zettel's work began to attract attention they had been all but ignored. In addition to the major collection known as the Cotton-Corpus legendary, with its later affiliates,[78] three manuscripts in particular are worthy of note and, to the best of my knowledge, have been little studied for their possible relevance to the extant Old English prose saints' lives, except by Cross in his work on the Old English *Martyrology*[79]: London, BL Harley 3020 (late tenth century, Christ Church, Canterbury?[80]), Paris BN Lat. 5574, ff. 1–39 (possibly Mercian, early tenth century[81]), BN Lat. 10861 (early ninth century, Christ Church, Canterbury[82]). The hagiographic texts in these manuscripts are identified by saints' names in the final section of this chapter.

Resources for Studying the Sources of Old English Prose Saints' Lives: Native English Saints

Although foreign saints, from continental Europe and Eastern Christendom, make up the majority of those whose legends were rendered into Old English prose, several vernacular lives of native or insular saints have been preserved. As our initial list of texts indicates, Ælfric composed narrative accounts of six native saints: Alban, Æthelthryth, Cuthbert, Edmund, Oswald, and Swithun, along with Gregory the Great, a sort of honorary Englishman by virtue of his having directed the mission of St. Augustine of Canterbury.[83] Ælfric also recounted substantial portions of the visions experienced by the Irish *peregrinus* St. Fursey in East Anglia. Anonymous accounts, or fragments of them, are extant for Augustine, Chad, Guthlac, Mildred, Neot, Paulinus, and possibly Sexburga. Short accounts of some of these and of other native saints (mainly Northumbrian) are included in the Old English *Martyrology*.[84]

This is all that has survived from what was probably a larger corpus of vernacular prose lives of English saints. We know, for example, that underlying a twelfth-century Latin account of Æthelthryth of Ely there was an Old English life, longer and more detailed than Ælfric's version in *Lives of Saints*, which was probably composed at Ely in the eleventh century. A life of St. Wulfstan, bishop of Worcester (1062–95), composed in Old English by Coleman of Worcester soon after Wulfstan's death, is lost, but a Latin translation by William of Malmesbury, *BHL* 8756, survives. The recent work of David Rollason on Mildred of Thanet and that of Susan Ridyard on several other Anglo-Saxon royal saints point to the existence of other lost vernacular and/or Latin lives of native saints, demonstrating the value of studying the post-Conquest manuscripts for literary evidence of the pre-Conquest saints' cults and the interesting connections and contrasts between the two periods.[85]

The Anglo-Saxons of the tenth and eleventh centuries do not appear to have composed new Latin lives of non-English saints (such as the twelfth century Anglo-Latin poems on the desert saints Malchus and Paul or the martyrs Laurence and Catherine). Their efforts, and those of the foreign hagiographers who wrote in England, were concentrated rather on the native saints of their own and earlier ages. Of these lives there is a substantial number. Unlike many of the saints whose cults reached England from the continent and the Mediterranean, and whose *"legenda"* are usually dismissed mainly as pious fictions, many of these *vitae* of native Anglo-Saxon saints are believed to be at least rooted in genuine history and local tradition, even if they are not reliable in every detail, and they have always received a good deal of attention from historians. As a result, historical scholarship on the Latin sources of native Anglo-Saxon hagiography, and on the larger corpus of Anglo-Latin lives in general, is more current and more accessible than the scholarship on many of the continental saints who chiefly occupied Ælfric and the other vernacular hagiographers. This is true both for the early Anglo-Saxon period, up to the early ninth century, and the later period, when the vernacular prose lives appear to have been composed.

For example, Bertram Colgrave's critical editions of the Latin lives from the early period (Cuthbert, *BHL* 2019, 2021; Guthlac, *BHL* 2723; Wilfred, *BHL* 8889; and Gregory the Great, *BHL* 3637) were recently reprinted in paperback.[86] Wallace-Hadrill's 1988 commentary on Bede's *Ecclesiastical History* (*inter alia* a compendium of early Anglo-Saxon saints' lives) complements the 1969 edition and translation by Colgrave and Mynors.[87] The two surviving hagiographic poems of the late eighth–early ninth century by Alcuin (whose *Versus de Patribus Regibus et Sanctis Euboricensis Ecclesiae* includes a virtual life of King Oswald martyr) and Æthelwulf (*De Abbatibus*) are now accessible in modern critical editions.[88] The anonymous life of Ceolfrid, *BHL* 1726, and Bede's metrical life of Cuthbert, *BHL* 2020, are the subjects of important new essays, the latter in a major commemorative collection on Cuthbert's history, cult, and memorials.[89] Bede's apparently lost recension of the *passio* of St. Anastasius, a Persian martyr venerated in Rome from the seventh century, has now been identified as one of the extant versions, *BHL* 408.[90]

New editions and translations of the Latin lives of the later Anglo-Saxon saints have either appeared within the recent past or are forthcoming (as cited and noted by Keynes in his 1987 bibliography discussed later[91]): Æthelwold, *BHL* 2646–47 (by Ælfric and Wulfstan of Winchester); Dunstan, *BHL* 2342–43 (by *B* and Adelard); Edward martyr, *BHL* 2418 (anonymous *passio*); Edmund martyr, *BHL* 2392 (the *passio* by Abbo of Fleury); Oswald of York, *BHL* 6374 (the life now credited to Byrhtferth of Ramsey); Swithun, *BHL* 7944–45 (by Lantfred).[92] Æthelwold and Dunstan are the subjects of recent major collections of essays.[93]

Studies and editions of texts from this later period that are not listed by Keynes concern the memorials of more shadowy saints from earlier periods or learnedly poetic versions of existing prose texts: Æthelred and Æthelbert, *BHL* 2643 (late tenth century *passio* preserved in the "Simeon of Durham"

Historia Regum and attributed by Michael Lapidge to Byrhtferth of Ramsey); Ecgwine, *BHL* 2432 (*vita* by Byrhtferth); Grimbald (*BHL Nov. Suppl.*, p. 407: *vita* preserved in a thirteenth-century breviary); Indract, *BHL* 4271 (not William of Malmesbury's but more probably tenth–eleventh century); Kenelm, *BHL* 4641m (*passio*); Neot, *BHL* 6052 (*vita prima*); Rumwold, *BHL* 7285 (*vita*); Swithun, *BHL* 7947 (*miracula* in verse, by Wulfstan of Winchester); Wilfred, *BHL* 8891 (*vita* in verse, by Frithegod).[94]

Although there is no standard study of or detailed guide to Anglo-Saxon hagiography as such, several books, complementary in approach, offer help. Wolpers's *Die Englische Heiligenlegende*, purely literary in approach (and now somewhat old fashioned in its *formgeschichtlich* focus), deals selectively with both Latin and vernacular texts and their relationships. The pertinent chapters of Gransden's *Historical Writing* provide a detailed survey of major and minor Latin texts and contexts, but from a purely historical perspective. Also valuable for its succinct but thorough coverage of the chief hagiographies is Lapidge's broad survey of Anglo-Latin literature as a whole in the new edition of Stanley Greenfield's history of Old English literature.[95]

Thanks to the work of these scholars, and to the appearance of excellent special bibliographies on Anglo-Saxon historical materials, there is no need here for a detailed consideration of the native English saints and their sources. The bibliographies of Anglo-Saxon history by Rosenthal and Keynes are valuable updates of (and introductory alternatives to) the relevant portions of the more comprehensive older bibliographies of Graves on English history and Bonser on Celtic and Anglo-Saxon. Celtic-Latin sources are the subject of a recent bibliography by Lapidge and Richard Sharpe.[96] The Keynes bibliography, which costs a pittance, is explicitly intended as an introductory bibliography, and as such constitutes a detailed guide to the themes and periods of Anglo-Saxon history, culture, and their written sources. Particularly relevant to hagiographic study are the general sections "Royal Biography," "Hagiography," "Local Histories," and "Manuscripts," but there is little that one can afford to ignore in the sections devoted to the chronologically arranged topics in the rest of the book. In Rosenthal's bibliography the section "Ecclesiastical History," including "Ecclesiastical Biography," complements the hagiographic and ecclesiastical sections of Keynes but reaches further into the secondary scholarship.

A recent book by Rollason,[97] surveying the cults of Anglo-Saxon saints as a whole, provides the essential historical background to any future study of individual texts, Latin or vernacular. This is both a highly informative and judicious historical survey of the saints' cults, and a rich and thoughtful study of their liturgical, social, and political contexts, against the background of continental saints' cults and hagiography. Ridyard's detailed monograph,[98] on West Saxon and East Anglian royal saints, is a more focused, more textually oriented study of a small group of saints and their literary memorials (including King Edmund, Æthelthryth, and Sexburga), which emphasizes, like Rollason, the role of the saints' cults as instruments of policy, deeply involved with the activities of elite groups in English society.[99]

Despite this copious and growing body of historical and textual scholarship on native Anglo-Saxon hagiography, there is still no comprehensive listing of the texts and manuscripts to compare with the *Plan*'s list of vernacular works (see the first section of this chapter) or the list of Celtic saints' lives in Lapidge and Sharpe. Something like such a list will emerge from the complete version of *Sources of Anglo-Saxon Literary Culture*. As mentioned earlier, the Bollandists did not catalogue the Latin hagiographic manuscripts of English libraries. The only major work of reference that remotely resembles a *Wegweiser* to English hagiography is Hardy's sprawling and outdated *Descriptive Catalogue* in the Rolls Series.[100] Its notices of unpublished manuscripts are cited frequently in *BHL* and it is still useful in the early stages of a project in English hagiography, particularly for lists of manuscripts of a specific work that are in major British libraries and for early editions, but its coverage of continental libraries is erratic, and Hardy, working in the mid-nineteenth century, naturally missed many manuscripts in British libraries that were not yet properly catalogued. Occasionally, he missed a work or saint altogether; for example, King Oswald of Northumberland, one of the heroes of Bede's *Ecclesiastical History*, subject of a separate prose life by Ælfric (see the first section) and of several Latin lives by hagiographers on the continent, where Oswald's cult flourished throughout the Middle Ages.[101]

List of Latin Manuscripts of English Provenance, up to 1100, Containing Hagiographic Texts

Omitted here are manuscripts containing only collective hagiographies such as Bede's *Ecclesiastical History*, Aldhelm's *De Virginitate* (prose or verse), Gregory the Great's *Dialogues* or Prudentius's *Peristephanon*. Marian texts are also excluded. Manuscripts marked with ? in parentheses are either rather late to be considered Anglo-Saxon (although of possible importance for Anglo-Saxon studies) or are not definitely of Anglo-Saxon provenance or quondam ownership. After each manuscript's catalogue number (italicized), the lives it contains are listed by saints' names in the square brackets, with any known authors in parentheses. For reasons of space and eyestrain, contents of some of the larger MSS (e.g. Cotton-Corpus legendary) are not detailed here, but the reader is referred to appropriate printed catalogues.

Arras. Bibliothèque Municipale *1029* [Cuthbert (Anon.), Dunstan ("B"), Filibert, Guthlac (Felix)].

Avranches. Bibliothèque Municipale *29* [Martin (Sulpicius, et al.)].

Boulogne. Bibliothèque Municipale *106* [Aichard, Bavo, Filibert, Guthlac (Felix), Walaric].

Brussels. Bibliothèque Royale *9850–52* [Vitae Patrum].

Cambridge. Corpus Christi College *9* [second part of Cotton-Corpus legendary, with BL *Cotton Nero E. i*, from Worcester, mid-eleventh century; another copy in Salisbury Cathedral Library *221 + 222*; contents of *CCCC 9* listed by M. R. James, *A Descriptive Catalogue of the Manuscripts in the Library of Corpus Christi College, Cambridge*, vol. 1 (Cambridge, 1912), pp. 21–30], *183* [Cuthbert (Bede, pr. and metr.)], *307* [Guthlac (Felix)], *312* [Augustine Cant. (Goscelin)], *367* [Kenelm], *389* [Guthlac (Felix), Paul Hermit (Jerome)]; Pembroke College *24* [Denis (Haymo), Finding of the Cross, James the Greater, John Evang., Mark, Philip], *25* [Andrew, John Evang., Martin (Alcuin)], *91* [Bartholomew]; St. John's College *164* [Benedict (Adrevald, Odo)]; Trinity College *O.10.31* (?) [Finding of the Cross]; Trinity Hall *21* [Martin (Sulpicius et al.)].

Copenhagen. Kongelige Bibliotek *G.K.S. 1588* [Edmund (Abbo)], *2034* [Cuthbert (Bede, metr.)].

Dublin. Trinity College *174* (?) [Achatius (Anastasius), Afra, Amalberga, Andrew (Gregory of Tours et al.), Balthildis, Barnabas, Crispina, Cyprian, Didimus and Theodora, Euphemia and soc., Euphrasia, Giles (Fulbert), Guthlac (Felix), Julian of Le Mans, Julian and Basilissa, Leonard, Lucy of Rome, Luke (Paul the Deacon), Maccabees (Gaudentius), Nicholas (John of Bari), Paternus (Fortunatus), Rufinus and Valerus (Paschasius R.), Servatius (Radbod), Spes and sor., Stephen (Augustine, et al.), Thecla, Theodota and fil., Victor and Corona, Vincent (Augustine, anon.)].

Durham. Cathedral Library *A.III 29* [Benedict (Odo)].

Edinburgh. Advocates Library *18.7.8* [Lawrence].

Exeter. Cathedral Library *FMS/3* [Basil].

Hereford. Cathedral Library *O.6.xi* [Martin (Sulpicius), Maur], *P.2.v.* [John Almoner, Margaret, Mary Magd., Nicholas (John the Deacon), Vit. patr.].

Leningrad. Public Library *O. v. XIV.1* [Wilfred (Frithegod, metr.)], *Q. v. XIV.1* [Felix of Nola (Paulinus)].

London. British Library: *Additional 40074* [Martin (Sulpicius et al.)]; *Arundel 91* (?) [legendary, 63 items: see *Catalogue of MSS in the British Museum*, new ser., Vol 1, Part 1, *The Arundel Manuscripts* (London, 1834), pp. 24–26]; *Cotton Caligula A. xv* [Paul Hermit (Jerome)], *Claudius A. i* [Wilfred (Frithegod, metr.)], *Cleopatra B. xiii* [Dunstan ("B")], *Nero E. i* [part of Cotton-Corpus legendary (see also *CCCC 9*): contents listed in J. Planta,

A Catalogue of Manuscripts in the Cottonian Library Deposited in the British Museum (London, 1802), pp. 239–41; see also Zettel, "Ælfric's Hagiographical Sources," pp. 15–34 and Lapidge and Jackson in this volume], *Otho A. viii* (?) [Mildred (Goscelin)], *A. xii* (?) [Ælfheah (Osbern)], *A. xiii* [visio Baronti], *Tiberius B. ii* [Edmund (Abbo, Hermann)], *Vespasian B. xx* (?) [lives of Augustine and other Canterbury SS. (Goscelin)], *D. vi* [Wilfred (Eddius Stephanus)], *A. xix* [Cuthbert (Bede, pr. and metr.)]; *Harley 526* [Cuthbert (Bede, metr.), Edward Conf.], *652* [lections for Canterbury SS.], *1117* [Cuthbert (Bede, pr. and metr.)], *3020* [Historia abbatum. . . . Benedict Biscop et al. (Bede), Ceolfred (anon. "Historia abbatum"), Pope Caelestus, Pope Cornelius, Pope Felix II, Abdon and Sennes, Agapitus, Faustinus and Beatrix, Felicitas, Juliana, Theophilus], *3097* (?) [Botulf, Guthlac (Felix), Nicholas (Otloh), Thorney SS.]; *Royal 4. A. xiv* [Guthlac (Felix)], *5. B. xv* [Lethardus], *6. A. vii* [Gregory (John the Deacon)], *13. A. x* [Machutus (Bili)], *13. A. xv* [Guthlac (Felix)], *15. C. vii* [Swithun (Lantfred, Wulfstan metr.)]. Lambeth Palace *173* [Abraham Hermit, Euphrasia, Fursey, Pelagia (Eustochius), Visions of Barontus, Dryhthelm, Fulrad, and Wettin], *362* [Edmund (Abbo)].

Munich. Bayerische Staatsbibliothek *22053* (?) [Finding of the Cross].

New York. Pierpont Morgan Library, *926* (?) [Alban (lections, from Bede), Alexius, Dunstan (Adelard), John Almoner].

Orléans, Bibliothèque Muncipale *342/290* [Alexis, Anastasius, Athanasius, Exaltation of the Cross, Judas Quiriacus, Nicholas (John the Deacon), Thecla].

Oxford. Bodleian Library: *Auctarium F.2.14* [Swithun (Wulfstan, metr.)]; *Bodley 109* [Cuthbert (Bede. pr. and metr.)], *163* [De abbatibus (Æthelwulf), Oswald (lections)], *381* [Gregory (John the D.)], *535* [Denis, Machutus (Bili), Mary Magd., Neot], *596* (?) [Cuthbert (Bede, pr. and metr.), Julian of Le Mans]; *Digby 175* (?) [Cuthbert (Bede, pr. and metr.), Oswald, Aidan]; *e Museo 6* [Augustine of Hippo (Possidius)]; *Jesus College 37* [Gregory (John the D.)]; *Trinity College 4* [Maurice and soc.].

Paris. Bibliothèque Nationale, *Lat. 1771* (?) [Ambrose (Paulinus)], *2769* (?) [Finding of the Cross], *2825* [Cuthbert (Bede, metr.)], *5774* [Christopher, Finding of the Cross, Exaltation, Juliana, Margaret], *8431* (ff. 21–48) [Wilfred (Frithegod, metr.)], *10861* [Afra, Agatha, Agnes, Cecilia, Cyprian, Cosmas and Damian, Erasmus, Eulalia, Euphemia, Felix of Thibiuca, Gallicanus and John and Paul, Gervase and Protasius, James the Great, Juliana, Philip, Sebasteni (= Forty Martyrs), Sebastian, Sympronianus and companions (= Four Crowned Ones), Vincent].

Rome. Vatican City, Bibliotheca Apost. Vaticana: *Pal. Lat. 235* [Felix of Nola (Paulinus)], *Reg. Lat. 204* [Cuthbert (Bede, metr.)], *489* [Brice, Martin (Sulpicius)], *566* [Swithun (Lantfred)].

Rouen. *1385* [Swithun (Lantfred)].

Salisbury. Cathedral Library *11* [Peter (Ps.Clement, *Recognitiones*)], *221,
222,* [= former Oxford Bodl., Fell 4 and 1, a late eleventh century Salisbury
legendary, copied from same exemplar as BL *Cotton Nero E. i + CCCC
9*; contents listed in Zettel, "Ælfric's Hagiographical Sources," pp. 15–34
and Teresa Webber, *Scribes and Scholars at Salisbury Cathedral c. 1075–
c. 1125* (Oxford, 1992), pp. 154–57], *223* [= former Oxford Bodl. Fell 3,
a late eleventh century legendary, St. Augustine's Canterbury; partial list
of contents in Levison, "Conspectus Codicum," *MGH SRM* 7, no. 632, full
list in Webber, pp. 169–70].

St. Gall. Stadtsbibliothek *337* [Dunstan ("B")].

Worcester. Cathedral Library *F. 48* [Hilarion (Jerome), Paul Hermit (Jerome),
Vitae Patrum (Rufinus et al.)], *F. 94* [Benedict (Odo)].

Note that this is not a complete list; some catalogues remain to be
checked.

Notes

1. Angus Cameron, Ashley Crandell Amos, Antonette diPaolo Healey, et al.,
Dictionary of Old English (Toronto, 1986–).

2. The principal editions of Ælfric's hagiographic works are Benjamin Thorpe,
ed., *The Homilies of the Anglo-Saxon Church. The First Part, Containing the Sermones
Catholici, or Homilies of Ælfric*, 2 vols. (London, 1843–46) [= *ÆCHom*]; Malcolm
Godden, ed., *Ælfric's Catholic Homilies. The Second Series: Text*, EETS SS 5 (London, 1979) [= *ÆCHom* II]; W. W. Skeat, ed., *Ælfric's Lives of Saints*, EETS OS 76,
82, 94, 114 (Oxford, 1881–1900; reprinted in 2 vols., 1966]; J. C. Pope, ed., *Homilies
of Ælfric: A Supplementary Collection*, EETS SS 259–60 (Oxford, 1967–68) [=
ÆHom]. For other editions of Ælfric's and the anonymous homilies, see Frank and
Cameron, *Plan*, cited in the next note, the bibliographies of Reinsma and the Quinns
(see note 4), and the notes that follow.

3. Roberta Frank and Angus Cameron, *A Plan for the Dictionary of Old English*,
Toronto Old English Series, 2 (Toronto and Buffalo, 1973), pp. 25–306. For an
explanation of *Plan*'s numbering system, see the second section of text.

4. Luke M. Reinsma, *Ælfric: An Annotated Bibliography* (New York, 1987);
Karen J. Quinn and Kenneth P. Quinn, *A Manual of Old English Prose* (New York
and London, 1990).

5. Rowland L. Collins and Peter Clemoes, "The Common Origin of Ælfric Fragments at New Haven, Oxford, Cambridge, and Bloomington," in Robert B. Burlin and
Edward B. Irving, Jr., eds., *Old English Studies in Honour of John C. Pope* (Toronto
and Buffalo, N.Y., 1974), pp. 285–326, especially pp. 313, ll. 23–32, p. 314, ll. 1–31.

6. Frederick G. Cassidy and Richard N. Ringler, eds., *Bright's Old English Grammar and Reader*, 3d. ed. (New York, 1971), pp. 203–19.

7. Collins and Clemoes, "Common Origin," pp. 309–10, p. 313, ll. 1–22.

8. J. McGowan, "Notes on the Old English Version of the *Vita Sancti Christophori*," *Neophilologus* 75 (1991): 451–55.

9. Else Fausbøll, ed., *Fifty-Six Ælfric Fragments* [with facsimiles] (Copenhagen, 1986), pp. 71–89.

10. Mary-Catherine Bodden, ed., *The Old English Finding of the True Cross* (Cambridge, 1987).

11. S. D. Lee, "Two Fragments from Cotton Ms. Otho B.x," *British Library Journal* 17 (1991): 83–87, especially p. 85.

12. Ibid., p. 85.

13. Klaus Sperk, *Medieval English Saints' Legends*, English Texts 6 (Tübingen, 1970), pp. 102–6.

14. Anna Maria Luiselli Fadda, "La Versione Anglo-sassone della Vita Sancti Aegidii Abbatis," *Romanobarbarica* 7 (1982–83): 273–352.

15. D. G. Scragg, ed., *The Vercelli Book and Related Texts*, EETS OS 300 (Oxford, 1992), pp. 383–92.

16. Viktor Schmetterer, ed., "Drei altenglische religiöse Texte aus der Handschrift Cotton Vespasianus D XIV," dissertation, University of Vienna 150 (1981), pp. 54–93

17. Cassidy and Ringler, *Bright's Grammar and Reader*, pp. 222–38.

18. Cf. Peter Clemoes, "The Chronology of Ælfric's works," in Clemoes, ed., *The Anglo-Saxons: Studies in Some Aspects of Their History and Culture Presented to Bruce Dickins* (London, 1959), pp. 238, n. 3; reprinted *Old English Newsletter, Subsidia* 5 (1980): 28.

19. Collins and Clemoes, "Common Origin," p. 318, ll. 27–32.

20. See Peter Clemoes in Bruno Assmann, *Angelsächsische Homilien und Heiligenleben*, Bibliothek der Angelsächsischen Prosa 3 (Kassel, Germany, 1889; reprinted Darmstadt, 1964), pp. xxxiv–xxxv. Ælfric provides a brief summary (only partially preserved) of the legend of Malchus at the close of his rendering of the book of Judith: Assmann, ibid., pp. 115–16, ll. 445–end.

21. Scragg, *Vercelli Book*, pp. 290–308.

22. Raymond J. S. Grant, ed., *Three Homilies from Cambridge, Corpus Christi College 41* (Ottawa, 1982), pp. 18–41.

23. Cf. Julius Zupitza, "Die Legende vom Trinubium der heiligen Anna," in Wolfgang Keller, ed., *Probleme der englischen Sprache und Kultur. Festschrift Johannes Hoops zum 60. Geburtstag . . .* , Germanische Bibliothek, II. Abt., Untersuchungen

und Texte 20 (Heidelberg, 1925), pp. 105–30.

24. See Clemoes in Assmann, *Angelsächsische Homilien*, (1964 ed.), pp. xxix–xxx.

25. Scragg, *Vercelli Book*, pp. 128–31.

26. Ibid., pp. 281–86.

27. Grant, *Three Homilies*, pp. 56–77.

28. Cassidy and Ringler, *Bright's Grammar and Reader*, pp. 239–54.

29. Fausbøll, *Fifty-Six Fragments*, pp. 43, 45.

30. Lee, "Two Fragments," pp. 85–86.

31. David W. Rollason, *The Mildrith Legend: A Study in Early Medieval Hagiography in England* (Leicester, England, 1982), p. 30, and Richard M. Wilson, *The Lost Literature of Medieval England*, 2d ed. (London, 1970; reprinted 1972), p. 89.

32. See Clemoes, "Chronology," p. 236 (reprint, p. 26), and n. 1. Cf. A. Nicholls, "Ælfric's 'Life of Vincent': The Question of Form and Function," *Notes and Queries*, n.s. 38 (1991): 445–50.

33. Several extracts from different parts of *Verba Seniorum* and *Historia Monachorum* are among the writings of Ælfric. Further, an anonymous brief extract (two anecdotes) from *Verba Seniorum* is printed by Assmann, *Angelsächsische Homilien*, (1964 ed.), pp. 195–97, along with Malchus, pp. 197–207, as portions of the same work, but Malchus is a separate text. For a survey of the Anglo-Saxons' knowledge and use of the various texts making up the *Vitas Patrum*, see Peter Jackson's entry in the projected *Sources of Anglo-Saxon Literary Culture*. See his sample entry in Frederick M. Biggs, Thomas D. Hill, and Paul E. Szarmach, eds., *Sources of Anglo-Saxon Literary Culture: A Trial Version*, Medieval and Renaissance Texts and Studies 74 (Binghamton, N.Y., 1990), pp. 162–65; also "The *Vitas Patrum* in Eleventh Century Worcester," in C. Hicks, ed., *England in the Eleventh Century*, Proceedings of the 1990 Harlaxton Symposium (Stamford, 1992), pp. 119–34.

34. Stanley B. Greenfield and Fred C. Robinson, *A Bibliography of Publications on Old English Literature to the End of 1972* (Toronto, 1980).

35. See also Antonette diPaolo Healey and Richard Venezky, *A Microfiche Concordance to Old English: The List of Texts and Index of Editions* (Toronto, 1980).

36. Frank and Cameron, *Plan*, pp. 44–76 (B1.1–3). Section B1.4 includes some additions to the hagiographical items in B1.1–3. The *Plan*'s number for the *Old English Martyrology*, B19.1–6, has been adapted by Donald Scragg and Paul Szarmach to provide separate numbers for individual entries in the martyrology. See Biggs, Hill, and Szarmach., eds. *Sources of Anglo-Saxon Literary Culture*, Appendix A, Martyrology, pp. 208–20.

37. There is an alphabetical list of the saints' texts, both Ælfric's and anonymous, in Ker's *Catalogue*, Index I, pp. 530–32, under Homilies I (b) Sanctorale. Most of the

anonymous lives are also listed alphabetically in the Quinns' *Manual of Old English Prose*, pp. 44–53.

38. See note 4.

39. See also the annual bibliography by Berkhout in *ASE*. In the future (starting with vol. 24) the bibliography issue of *Old English Newsletter* will appear in the summer, replacing the spring issue.

40. Phillip Pulsiano, *An Annotated Bibliography of North American Doctoral Dissertations on Old English Language and Literature* (Lansing, Mich., and Woodbridge, Suffolk, 1988).

41. Published by University Microfilms Inc., Ann Arbor, Mich., 1952–.

42. By my count, of the editions cited in the *Plan*, only those of Chad (B3.3.3, ed. Vleeskruyer) and Christopher (B3.3.4, ed. Rypins) print a Latin source text. Add to these Hervey's edition of Ælfric's *Edmund* (see Greenfield/Robinson, no. 5343A), along with that of Giles by Fadda (note 14), Machutus by Yerkes (Quinn and Quinn, *Manual*, p. 265, no. 518), James the Greater by Schmetterer (note 16), and Margaret by Assmann, *Angelsächsische Homilien*, pp. 208–20.

43. *Bibliotheca Sanctorum*, 12 vols + index (Roma, 1961–70). For Julian and Basilissa, see vol. 6 (1965), 1120–23. In English, see Herbert Thurston and Donald Attwater, eds., *Butler's Lives of the Saints*, 2d ed., 4 vols. (London, 1956): this varies in quality (e.g., entry for Julian and Basilissa is perfunctory) but is good for narrative summaries and occasionally for older bibliography, not always accurately cited. In French, see *Vies des Saints et des Bienheureux selon l'Ordre du Calendrier avec l'Histoire des Fêtes*, 13 vols. (Paris, 1935–59). On iconography, see *Lexikon der Christlichen Ikonographie*, 8 vols. (Rome, Basel, Freiburg, and Vienna, 1968–76), especially vols. 5–8 on the iconography of the saints. The standard modern ecclesiastical encyclopedias, e.g., *Dictionnaire d'Histoire et de Géographie Ecclésiastique* (Paris, 1912–), and *Dictionnaire d'Archéologie Chrétienne et de Liturgie* (Paris, 1907–53) are also worth consulting.

44. J. D. A. Ogilvy, *Books Known to the English 597–1066* (Cambridge, Mass., 1967); "Addenda et Corrigenda," in *Mediaevalia* 7 (1984 for 1981): 282–325, reprinted *Old English Newsletter, Subsidia*, 11 (1985). An important alternative to Ogilvy's notes on manuscript sources is Helmut Gneuss, "A Preliminary List of Manuscripts Written or Owned in England up to 1100," *ASE* 9 (1981): 1–60. On *Sources of Anglo-Saxon Literary Culture*, see note 74. See also, on the native Anglo-Saxon sources of the later Old English prose writers, Adam D. McCoy, "The Use of the Writings of English Authors in Old English Homiletic Literature," dissertation, Cornell University, 1973. I owe this reference to Thomas D. Hill (and see Reinsma, *Ælfric*, no. 745).

45. Max Förster, *Über die Quellen von Ælfrics Homiliae Catholicae. I. Legenden* (Berlin, 1892), Greenfield/Robinson no. 5300; J. Heinrich Ott, *Über die Quellen der Heiligenleben in Ælfrics Lives of Saints I* (Halle, Germany, 1892), Greenfield/Robinson no. 5351. See also, *inter alia*, nos. 5303, 5305, 5317, 5331, 5333, 5338.

46. C. Grant Loomis, "Further Sources of Ælfric's Saints' Lives," *Harvard Studies and Notes in Philology and Literature* 13 (1931): 1–8, Greenfield/Robinson no. 5358. See also nos. 5153, 5317, 5352, 5356–57, 5360, 5365, 5366. See also Reinsma, *Ælfric*, nos. 808, 834, 841, 842, 845, 847, 851, 852, 855, none of which is in Greenfield/Robinson. Most recently, see Joyce Hill, "Ælfric, Gelasius and St. George," *Mediaevalia* 11 (1989 for 1985): 1–17, and essays by Biggs, Magennis, and Szarmach in this volume.

47. Notable exceptions are Cassidy and Ringler, *Bright's Grammar and Reader*, pp. 203–5 (Andrew); Hugh Magennis, "On the Sources of the Non-Ælfrician Lives in the Old English Lives of the Saints, with Reference to the Cotton-Corpus Legendary," *Notes and Queries*, n.s. 230 (1985): 292–99 (Euphrosyne, Eustace, Mary of Egypt, Seven Sleepers); Mary Clayton, *The Cult of the Virgin Mary in Anglo-Saxon England*, Cambridge Studies in Anglo-Saxon England 2 (Cambridge, 1990); Jane Roberts, "The Old English Prose Translation of Felix's *Vita sancti Guthlaci*," in Paul E. Szarmach, ed., *Studies in Earlier Old English Prose* (Albany, N.Y. 1986), pp. 363–79 (includes refeferences to earlier work by Roberts and others). See Fadda's ed. of *LS* 9, Giles (note 14).

48. *Ioannes Bollandus et al., Acta Sanctorum quotquot orbe coluntur . . . Ianuarii t. I* (Antwerp, 1643), pp. 575–87.

49. Because of its long and complicated publishing history, bibliographical citations of *Acta Sanctorum* are fraught with peril. The first edition (71 volumes, Antwerp and Brussels, 1643–1931; reprinted, 65 vols., Brussels, 1965–70) covers the saints of January–November, including (*Novembris*, vol. 2, pt. 2), the valuable edition and commentary on the so-called Jerome martyrology, Hippolyte Delehaye and Henri Quentin, *Commentarius Perpetuus in Martyrologium Hieronymianum* (Brussels, 1931). The third edition (Paris, 1863–69) was a reprint of the original January–September volumes, plus the then newly published but incomplete October (ten out of the eventual total of thirteen volumes). The first and third editions have different paginations. Most libraries have either the first or third edition or the new reprint of the former. The second edition (Venice, 1734–70) is rare. For a brief history of the Bollandists' work, see David Knowles, *Great Historical Enterprises and Problems in Early Monastic History* (Edinburgh, 1963).

50. On calendars and martyrologies, see the citations in Richard W. Pfaff, *Medieval Latin Liturgy: A Select Bibliography*, Toronto Medieval Bibliographies, 9 (Toronto, Buffalo, N.Y. and London, 1982), pp. 45–46, 55–56.

51. The last volume published in the series was an edition of the Roman Martyrology: Delehaye et al., eds., *Propylaeum ad Acta Sanctorum Decembris. Martyrologium Romanum* (Brussels, 1940). There appear to be no plans for further volumes. For another valuable piece of prolegomena, however, see Delehaye, *Étude sur le Légendier Romain: les Saints de Novembre et de Décembre*, Subsidia Hagiographica, 23 (Brussels, 1936; reprinted 1968).

52. For example, the *Vita sancti Aichardi* in *Acta Sanctorum Sept.*, t. 5 (Antwerp, 1755), pp. 85–99, edited from an important tenth century Anglo-Flemish manuscript

(Arras, BM 1029/812), preserves a text that has since been lost from the manuscript. Philip Grierson, "Les Livres de l'Abbé Seiwold de Bath," *Revue Bénédictine* 52 (1940): 96–116.

53. The manuscript referred to in Bolland's preface, *Acta Sanctorum. Ian.*, vol. 1, p. 570, as S.Maximini is almost certainly the great thirteenth century legendary from the church of St. Maximinus, Trier. The January portion is now Paris, BN lat. 9741. See *Catalogus Codicum Hagiographicorum Latinorum ... in Bibliotheca Nationali Parisiensi*, Subsidia Hagiographia 2, 4 vols. (Brussels 1889–93), vol. 2, pp. 584–88. *Pas.Jul.Bas.* is item no. 15.

54. In addition to *Acta Sanctorum* and *PL*, e.g., vols. 73–74, *Vitae Patrum*, the most important older hagiographic collections are those of B. Mombritius (= Bonino Mombrizio), *Sanctuarium seu vitae sanctorum*, 2 vols. (Milan, 1480), 2d ed., 2 vols. (Paris, 1910), and Luc D'Achery and Jean Mabillon, *Acta Sanctorum Ordinis S. Benedicti (A.D. 500–1100)*, 9 vols. (Paris, 1688–1701; reprinted, Venice, 1733–40).

55. I cite only the Latin MS catalogues: *Catalogus Codicum Hagiographicorum Bibliothecae Reginae Bruxellensis, Pars I. Codices Latini Membranei*, Subsidia Hagiographica 1, 2 vols. (Brussels, 1886–89); Albert Poncelet, *Catalogus Codicum Hagiographicorum Latinorum Bibliothecarum Romanarum praeter quam Vaticanae*, Subsidia Hagiographica 9 (Brussels, 1909; reprinted 1979); Poncelet, *Catalogus Codicum Hagiographicorum Latinorum Bibliothecae Vaticanae*, Subsidia Hagiographica 11 (Brussels, 1910; reprinted 1961). For the Paris catalogue, see note 53.

56. For example, Paris, BN lat. 5774, 10861 (see the last section).

57. Joseph van der Straeten, *Manuscrits Hagiographiques d'Arras et de Boulogne-sur-Mer*, Subsidia Hagiographica 50 (Brussels, 1971); *Les Manuscrits Hagiographiques de Charleville, Verdun et Saint-Mihiel*, Subsidia Hagiographica 56 (Brussels, 1974); *Les Manuscrits Hagiographiques d'Orléans, Tours et Angers*, Subsidia Hagiographica 64 (Brussels, 1982). See *Analecta Bollandiana* 85, 86, 87 (1967–69), for his catalogues of Bourges, Avranches, and Boulogne-sur-Mer, respectively. See also Guy Phillipart, "Manuscrits Hagiographiques de Châlons-sur-Marne," *Analecta Bollandiana* 89 (1971): 67–102. A list of the Bollandists' earlier hagiographic catalogues, including the many published as articles in *Analecta Bollandiana*, up to 1937, is provided by Siegmund (cited in note 66), p. 211, n. 1, and by Dubois, *Sources et Méthodes*, pp. 27–30 (see next note).

58. Delehaye, *Les Légendes Hagiographiqes*, Subsidia Hagiographica 18A, 4th ed. (Brussels, 1955; reprinted 1973), trans. Donald Attwater, *The Legends of the Saints* (Notre Dame, Ind., 1962). The translation by Virginia M. Crawford (London, 1907; reprinted Norwood, Pa., 1974) is from the second edition. Among more recent general guides to hagiography are those of René Aigrain, *L'Hagiographie: ses Sources, ses Méthodes, son Histoire* (Paris, 1953), R. Grégoire, *Manuale di Agiologia: Introduzione alla Letteratura Agiografica*, Bibliotheca Montisfani 12 (Fabriano, Italy 1987), Jacques Dubois and J.-L. Lemaitre, *Sources et Méthodes de l'Hagiographie Médiévale* (Paris, 1993), and the new literary-historical survey by Walter Berschin, *Biographie und Epochenstil im lateinischen Mittelalter: Vol. 1, Von der Passio Perpetuae*

zu den Dialogi Gregors des Grossen; Vol. 2, Merowingische Biographie. Italien, Spanien und die Inseln im Frühen Mittelalter; Vol. 3, Karolingische Biographie 750– 920 n., Chr., Quellen und Untersuchungen zur lateinischen Philologie des Mittelalters 8–10 (Stuttgart, 1986, 1988, 1991). A new collaborative history of hagiography (Latin and vernacular) is forthcoming, under the direction of Guy Philippart. Delehaye's other monographs in the *Subsidia* series, now of greater value than *Les Légendes Hagiographiques*, deserve a wider audience: e.g., *Les Origines du Culte des Martyrs*, no. 20 (2d ed., 1933; reprinted 1976); *Les Passions des Martyrs et les Genres Littéraires*, no. 13B (2d ed., 1961); *Les Saints Stylites*, no. 14 (1923; reprinted 1962). See also *Subsidia* 17, 21, 42, and, for 23, see note 51.

59. *Bibliotheca Hagiographica Latina Antiquae et Mediae Aetatis*, Subsidia hagiographica 6, 2 vols. (Brussels, 1898–1901); *Supplément*, Subsidia Hagiographica 12 (Brussels, 1911); *Novum Supplementum* (H. Fros), Subsidia Hagiographica 70 (Brussels, 1986).

60. The equivalent guide to Greek hagiographic texts is that of François Halkin, *Bibliotheca Hagiographica Graeca*, 3d ed., Subsidia Hagiographica 8A, 3 vols. (Brussels, 1957), with Halkin's *Auctarium Bibliotheca Hagiographicae Graecae*, Subsidia Hagiographica 47 (Brussels, 1969).

61. *PL* 89, 260–63; Rudolf Ehwald, *Aldhelmi Opera Omnia, MGH Auctores Antiquissimi* 15 (Berlin, 1919), pp. 405–13 (ll.1251–1449); prose *De Virginitate*, ibid., pp. 280–84. For English translations of both prose and verse, see Michael Lapidge and Michael Herren, *Aldhelm the Prose Works* (Ipswich, Cambridge, and Totowa, N.J., 1979), pp. 99–102, and Lapidge and James Rosier, *Aldhelm the Poetic Works* (Cambridge and Dover, N.H., 1985), pp. 130–35. For Aldhelm's influence in later Anglo-Saxon England, see the various studies by Lapidge cited in his valuable survey, "The Anglo-Latin Background," in Stanley B. Greenfield and Daniel C. Calder, *A New Critical History of Old English Literature* (New York, 1986), pp. 5–37.

62. For *BHL* and supplements, see note 59.

63. "Les Martyrs d'Égypte," *Analecta Bollandiana* 40 (1922): 5–154, especially 66, 86, 118, 120–21, 123–24.

64. See Wilhelm Levison, "St. Alban and St. Albans," *Antiquity* 15 (1941): 337–59. In addition to *BHL*, it is advisable to consult Eligius Dekkers, *Clavis Patrum Latinorum*, 2d ed., *Sacris Erudiri* 3 (Bruges and The Hague, 1961), a *vade mecum* to pre-800 authors, including anonymous saints' lives, pp. 468–501, indexed by saints' names, pp. 550–54. For the saints' lives cited in the ongoing edition of the *Vetus Latina* version of the bible, see H. J. Frede, ed., *Vetus Latina. Die Reste der Altlateinischen Bibel*, 1, 1, *Kirchensschriftsteller, Verzeichnis und Sigel* (Freiburg, Germany, 1981), pp. 25–58, with supplements, *Aktualisierungsheft* 1984, 1988. For most recent bibliographical information, see the sections devoted explicitly to "Vitae Sanctorum" and "Agiografia" in the annual *Medioevo Latino, Bolletino Bibliografico della Cultura Europea dal Secolo VI al XIII*, ed. Claudio Leonardi (Spoleto, 1980–).

65. See Colin Chase, "Source Study as a Trick with Mirrors: Annihilation of Meaning in the Old English 'Mary of Egypt'," in Paul E. Szarmach, ed., with Virginia

Darrow Oggins, *Sources of Anglo-Saxon Culture*, Studies in Medieval Culture, 20 (Kalamazoo, Mich., 1986), pp. 23–33.

66. Albert Siegmund, *Die Überlieferung der Griechische Christlichen Literatur in der Lateinischen Kirche bis zum Zwölften Jahrhundert*, Abhandlungen der Bayerischen Benediktiner-Akademie 5 (Munich 1949), especially pp. 195–277. Walter Berschin, *Griechisch-lateinisches Mittelalter* (Munich, 1980), now in English, trans. Jerold C. Frakes, *Greek Letters and the Latin Middle Ages from Jerome to Nicholas of Cusa*, rev. and expanded ed. (Washington, D.C., 1988). See also Eugen Ewig, "Die Verehrung Orientalischer Heiliger im Spätrömischen Gallien und im Merowingerreich," in his *Spätantikes und Fränkisches Gallien. Gesammelte Schriften (1952–73)*, vol. 2 (Munich, 1979), pp. 393–410.

67. The 1986 *Novum Supplementum* of *BHL*, pp. 922–23, has a concordance of *BHL* numbers and the relevant pages in Siegmund.

68. Siegmund, *Die Überlieferung*, p. 238. He identifies its Greek source text as *BHG* 970, which has recently been edited by François Halkin, "La Passion Ancienne des Saints Julien et Basilisse (*BHG* 970–971)," *Analecta Bollandiana* 98 (1980): 241–96. For the Luxeuil recension, see Paris, BN lat. 9427, ed. Pierre Salmon, *Le Lectionnaire de Luxeuil, vol. 1: Édition et Étude Comparative*, Collectanea Biblica Latina 7 (Rome, 1944), pp. 24–57.

69. James E. Cross, "Identification: Towards Criticism," in Phyllis Rugg Brown, Georgia Ronan Crampton, and Fred C. Robinson, eds., *Modes of Interpretation in Old English Literature. Essays in Honor of Stanley B. Greenfield* (Toronto, Buffalo, N.Y. and London, 1986), pp. 229–46, especially 232–34.

70. Vat. Reg. Lat. 516, and Montpellier, Bibliothèque Interuniversitaire, Section Médicine H 156 (Cross, p. 233). Another early copy is Vat. Reg. Lat. 577 (s. ix/x), cited by Delehaye (note 51), p. 124.

71. Guy Philippart, *Les Légendiers et Autres Manuscrits Hagiographiques*, Typologie des Sources du Moyen Age Occidental, fasc. 24–25 (Turnhout, Belgium, 1977). See also Siegmund, *Die Überlieferung*, pp. 200–8. On Philippart's book and on the use of legendaries, see Baudoin de Gaiffier, "A Propos des Légendiers Latins," *Analecta Bollandiana* 97 (1979): 57–68. On early medieval manuscripts in general, see the catalogue series by Elias A. Lowe, *Codices Latini Antiquiores: A Palaeographical Guide to Latin Manuscripts Prior to the Ninth Century*, 12 vols. (Oxford, 1934–72), and on Carolingian manuscripts in particular, see the various studies by Bernard Bischoff, including *Die Südostdeutschen Schreibschulen und Bibliotheken in der Karolingerzeit*, Vol. 1. *Die Bayrischen Diözesen* (Leipzig, 1940; 3d ed., Wiesbaden, 1974); Vol. 2. *Die Vorwiegend Österreichischen Diözesen* (Wiesbaden, 1980); *Mittelalterliche Studien: Ausgewählte Aufsätze zur Schriftkunde und Literaturgeschichte*, 3 vols. (Stuttgart, 1966–81).

72. Frank Rella, "Continental Manuscripts Acquired for English Centers in the Tenth and Early Eleventh Centuries," *Anglia* 98 (1980): 107–16.

73. They did survey the English holdings of Greek hagiography: Charles Van de Vorst and Delehaye, *Catalogus Codicum Hagiographicorum Graecorum Germaniae Belgii Angliae*, Subsidia Hagiographica 13 (Brussels, 1913; reprinted 1968). Subject indices to manuscript catalogues of individual libraries are rarely exhaustive. One of the best is the British Library's *Subject Index*. The best guide to catalogues of manuscript collections is that of Paul O. Kristeller, *Latin Manuscript Books Before 1600: A List of the Printed Catalogues and Unpublished Inventories of Extant Collections*, 3d ed. (New York, 1965). See also (on England) Leonard E. Boyle, *Medieval Latin Paleography*, Toronto Medieval Bibliographies, 8 (Toronto and Buffalo, N.Y., 1984), pp. 225–28.

74. The projected completion date for the first of likely three volumes is 1996. In the meantime, see the introduction and sample entries in *Sources of Anglo-Saxon Literary Culture* (note 33). A corollary but much larger project, *Fontes Anglo-Saxonici*, is underway in England. See the first report in *Old English Newsletter* 19, no. 2 (Spring 1986): 17–19, updated annually thereafter.

75. See note 44.

76. Patrick H. Zettel, "Ælfric's Hagiographic Sources and the Legendary Preserved in B.L. MS Cotton Nero E. i + CCCC MS 9 and Other Manuscripts," dissertation, Oxford University (1979); see also Zettel, "Saints' Lives in Old English: Latin Manuscripts and Vernacular Accounts: Ælfric," *Peritia* 1 (1982): 17–37. For an analysis of the contents of the Cotton-Corpus legendary see the study by Jackson and Lapidge in this volume. Despite the general importance of Zettel's findings, detailed studies of individual Ælfrician texts are necessary to develop and refine his thesis, which will doubtless undergo considerable modification. See, e.g., the recent work of C. Morini, "Le fonti della *Passio S. Agathae* di Ælfric," *AION-Filologica Germanica* 30–31 (1991 for 1987–88): 83–94.

77. Zettel, "Ælfric's Hagiographic Sources," pp. 143, 201–8.

78. Described in Zettel's article, "Saints' Lives in Old English," pp. 18–20. In addition to the mid-eleventh century collection in BL Cotton Nero E. i and Cambridge, Corpus Christi College 9, the other major representative of the legendary is Salisbury Cathedral 221–222 (formerly, Oxford, Bodleian Library, Fell 4 and 1).

79. Cross refers to Paris, BN lat. 10861 in connection with several of the *Martyrology* entries; e.g., "Eulalia of Barcelona," *Notes and Queries*, n.s. 28 (1981):482–84.

80. Nicholas Brooks, *The Early History of the Church of Canterbury* (Leicester, England, 1984), p. 268; David N. Dumville, *Liturgy and the Ecclesiastical History of Late Anglo-Saxon England: Four Studies* (Woodbridge, England 1992), pp. 110–11 (n. 92), 140.

81. François Avril and Patricia Danz Stirnemann, *Manuscrits Enluminés d'Origine Insulaire viie–xxe Siècle* (Paris, Bibliothèque Nationale, 1987), p. 11. I am grateful to Frederick Biggs for drawing the manuscript and this catalogue to my attention.

82. Michelle P. Brown, "Paris, Bibliothèque Nationale, lat. 10861 and the Scriptorium of Christ Church, Canterbury," *ASE* 15 (1986): 119–37.

83. The omission of Augustine of Canterbury from *Catholic Homilies* and *Lives of Saints* is surprising because his feast day in England appears to have been among the most important after the apostles. In addition to the calendars edited by Francis Wormald, *English Kalendars Before* A.D. *1100*, Henry Bradshaw Society 72 (London, 1934), see the Old English verse *Menologium*, lines 95–106, ed. Elliott V. K. Dobbie, *The Anglo-Saxon Minor Poems*, *ASPR* 6 (New York and London, 1942), pp. 51–52. On the hagiological background to Ælfric's saints' legends, see Bernadette Moloney, "*Be Godes Halgum*: Ælfric's Hagiography and the Cult of the Saints in England in the Tenth Century," in V. John Scattergood, ed., *Literature and Learning in Medieval and Renaissance England: Essays Presented to Fitzroy Pyle* (Dublin, 1984), pp. 25–40, and, more recently, Lapidge (see note 97).

84. Æthelwald (hermit of Farne), Aidan, Alban, Augustine, Benedict Biscop, Ceadwalla, Ceolfred, Chad, Eadberht, Eosterwine, Æthelburga, Æthelthryth, Fursey, Gregory, Guthlac (and Pega), the two Heawalds, Hilda, Hygebald of Lindsey, John of Beverley, Oswald, and Wilfred: the main source for these *Old English Martyrology* entries is Bede's *Ecclesiastical History*. See Cross, "A Lost Life of Hilda of Whitby: The Evidence of the *Old English Martyrology*," in William P. Snyder, ed., *The Early Middle Ages*, Acta 6 (Binghamton, N.Y., 1982), pp. 21–43. On the use, in later Old English prose homilies and saints' lives, of English authors such as Bede, see McCoy's dissertation, note 44.

85. *The Vita Wulfstani of William of Malmesbury*, ed. Reginald R. Darlington, Camden Society, 3rd Ser., 40 (London, 1928), trans. Michael Swanton, *Three Lives of the Last Englishmen* (New York, 1984). For Rollason on Mildred, see note 31. Susan Ridyard, *The Royal Saints of Anglo-Saxon England: A Study of West Saxon and East Anglian Cults*, Cambridge Studies in Medieval Life and Thought, 4th ser., 9 (Cambridge, 1988), p. 29, on Edburga (lost Latin life); for lost OE lives of Sexburga and Æthelthryth, pp. 54–58. Simon Keynes and A. Kennedy will present an edition of the twelfth century Latin version of the lost tenth century Old English "Book of St. Æthelwold," which relates mainly to Ely Abbey.

86. For Colgrave's editions, see Simon Keynes, *Anglo-Saxon History: A Select Bibliography*, Old English Newsletter Subsidia 13 (1987): 5, nos. B33–35, B38; in the second, revised version (1993), p. 7, nos. 130, 135, 140, 155.

87. John M. Wallace-Hadrill, *Bede's Ecclesiastical History of the English People: A Historical Commentary* (Oxford, 1988); Bertram Colgrave and Roger A. B. Mynors, eds., *Bede's Ecclesiastical History of the English People* (Oxford, 1969). See the list of studies of Bede and his *Ecclesiastical History* in Keynes's bibliography, 1st ed., pp. 20–21, 2d, rev., ed., pp. 28–29; see also the introductory study by George H. Brown, *Bede the Venerable* (Boston, 1987).

88. Peter Godman, ed., *Alcuin, the Bishops, Kings, and Saints of York* (Oxford, 1982); Alisair Campbell, ed., *De Abbatibus* (Oxford, 1967).

89. Judith McClure, "Bede and the Life of Ceolfrid," *Peritia* 3 (1984): 71–84. Lapidge, "Bede's Metrical Life of Cuthbert," in Gerald Bonner, David Rollason, and Clare Stancliffe, eds., *St. Cuthbert, His Cult and Community to* A.D. *1200* (Woodbridge, England; Suffolk, and Wolfboro, N.H., 1989), pp. 77–93 (among the many important contributions to this volume those by James Campbell, Rollason, Luisella Simpson, Stancliffe, Alan Thacker, and Benedicta Ward are particularly relevant here).

90. Carmela Franklin and Paul Meyvaert, "Has Bede's Version of the 'Passio S. Anastasii' Come down to Us in 'BHL' 408?" *Analecta Bollandiana* 100 (1982): 373–400.

91. *Anglo-Saxon History* , 1st ed., pp. 4–5, 2d ed., p. 6.

92. Recently published is Michael Lapidge and Michael Winterbottom, eds., *Wulfstan of Winchester: The Life of St Æthelwold* (Oxford, 1991). Lapidge's forthcoming edition of the Swithun texts will include new editions of the texts numbered by the Bollandists *BHL* 7944–49. For his convincing evidence regarding Byrhtferth's authorship of the *Vita S. Oswaldi*, and for valuable discussion of the style of several of the lives listed here and later, see his article, "The Hermeneutic Style in Tenth-Century Anglo-Latin Literature," *ASE* 4 (1975): 67–111, especially 90–95. See also note 94, regarding other hagiographic works by Byrhtferth.

93. Barbara Yorke, ed., *Bishop Æthelwold: His Career and Influence* (Woodbridge, England; Suffolk, and Wolfboro, N.H., 1988); N. L. Ramsay, M. Sparks, and T. Tatton-brown, eds., *St. Dunstan and His Times* (Woodbridge, 1992). For a comparative analysis of the lives of Dunstan by "B" and Osbern of Canterbury, see David Townsend, "Anglo-Latin Hagiography and the Norman Transition," *Exemplaria* 3 (1991): 385–433, especially 393–403.

94. Lapidge, "The Medieval Hagiography of St. Ecgwine," *Vale of Evesham Historical Society Research Papers* 6 (1977): 77–93; "The Digby-Gotha Recension of the Life of St. Ecgwine," ibid. 7 (1979): 39–55; "Byrhtferth and the Vita S. Ecgwini," *Medieval Studies* 41 (1979): 331–53; Janet M. Bately, "Grimbald of St. Bertin's," *Medium Ævum* 35 (1966): 1–10; Lapidge, "The Cult of St Indract at Glastonbury," Dorothy Whitelock et al., eds., *Ireland in Early Medieval Europe* (Cambridge, 1982), pp. 179–212; Ruri von Antropoff, *Die Entwicklung der Kenelm-Legende*, (dissertation, University of Bonn (1965); Lapidge and David Dumville, eds., *Annals of St Neots with Vita Primi Sancti Neoti, The Anglo-Saxon Chronicle: A Collaborative Edition*, 17 (Cambridge and Wolfboro, N.H., 1985); Mary Richards, "The Medieval Hagiography of St. Neot," *Analecta Bollandiana* 99 (1981): 259–78; Vita S. Rumwoldi, *Acta Sanctorum, Nov.*, vol. 1, pp. 685–90; Alistair Campbell, ed., *Frithegodi Monachi Breuiloquium Uitae Beati Wilfredi et Wulfstani Cantoris Narratio metrica de Sancto Swithuno* (Zurich, 1950); Lapidge, "A Frankish Scholar in Tenth-Century England: Frithegod of Canterbury/Fredegaud of Brioude," *ASE* 17 (1988): 45–65. A new edition and translation by R. C. Love of the eleventh-century lives of Kenelm, Romwald, and Birinus of Wessex is forthcoming in Oxford Medieval Texts. See also David Townsend, "An Eleventh-Century Life of Birinus of Wessex," *Analecta Bollandiana*

107 (1989): 129–59. The substantial number of *vitae* composed in the later eleventh century and early twelfth century by such authors as Folcard, Goscelin, Osbern, and Eadmer fall outside the strict purview of this article. See Antonia Gransden, *Historical Writing in England c.550 to c.1307* (Ithaca, N.Y., 1974), pp. 105–35, for a preliminary survey.

95. Theodor Wolpers, *Die Englische Heiligenlegende des Mittelalters* (Tübingen, 1964), Greenfield/Robinson no. 678; Gransden, especially Chapters 2, 4, and 5; Lapidge, in Greenfield and Calder, Chapter 1. Lapidge's numerous important papers are collected in his *Anglo-Latin Literature, 900–1066* (London, 1993). See also Ridyard, *The Royal Saints*, and Rollason, *Saints and Relics* (see note 97).

96. Wilfrid Bonser, *An Anglo-Saxon and Celtic Bibliography (450–1087)*, 2 vols. (Oxford, 1957); Edgar B. Graves, *A Bibliography of English History to 1485* (Oxford, 1975), especially pp. 319–83; Simon Keynes, *Anglo-Saxon History, a Select Bibliography*, Old English Newsletter *Subsidia*, 13 (1987): 2d rev. edition (1993); Michael Lapidge and Richard Sharpe, *A Bibliography of Celtic-Latin Literature 400–1200*, Royal Irish Academy Dictionary of Medieval Latin from Celtic Sources, Ancillary Publication 1 (Dublin, 1985); Joel T. Rosenthal, *Anglo-Saxon History: An Annotated Bibliography* (New York, 1985). On women in Anglo-Saxon historical and hagiographic sources, see most recently Rosenthal's essay and bibliography, "Anglo-Saxon Attitudes: Men's Sources, Women's History," in Rosenthal, ed., *Medieval Women and the Sources of Medieval History* (Athens, Ga., and London, 1990), pp. 259–84; Stephanie Hollis, *Anglo-Saxon Women and the Church* (Woodbridge, England, 1992); Gopa Roy, "Women and Sanctity: Lives of the Female Saints Written in English from Cynewulf to the Katherine Group," dissertation, University of London (1991). Of pertinent annual bibliographies, in addition to those in *Anglo-Saxon England* and the *Old English Newsletter*, *Medioevo latino*, and the "Bulletin" pages of each fascicle of *Analecta Bollandiana*, the following are particularly valuable: *Writings on British History* (London, Institute for Historical Research, 1971–); *International Medieval Bibliography*, quarterly installments (Minneapolis and Leeds, 1967–).

97. David Rollason, *Saints and Relics in Anglo-Saxon England* (Oxford, 1989). See also Lapidge, "The Saintly Life in Anglo-Saxon England" in Malcolm Godden and Michael Lapidge, eds., *The Cambridge Companion to Old English Literature* (Cambridge, 1991), pp. 243–63; and V. Ortenberg, *The English Church and the Continent in the Tenth and Eleventh Centuries* (Oxford, 1992).

98. See note 85.

99. Rollason, *Saints and Relics*, however, pp. 186–87, sees the saints' cults of later Anglo-Saxon England, unlike those of the seventh and eighth centuries, as deliberately reaching outside the elite groups to embrace the population as a whole.

100. Thomas Duffus Hardy, *A Descriptive Catalogue of Materials Relating to the History of Great Britain and Ireland to the End of the Reign of Henry VII*, 3 vols. in 4, Rolls Series 26 (London, 1862–71; reprinted Millwood, N.Y., 1966).

101. Peter Clemoes, *The Cult of St Oswald on the Continent*, Jarrow Lecture 1983 (Jarrow, England, 1984).

Part One

The Contexts

Imago Dei:
Genre, Symbolism,
and Anglo-Saxon Hagiography

Thomas D. Hill

The Oxford Dictionary of the Christian Church defines *hagiography* as "the writing of the lives of the saints,"[1] and this definition has the advantages of being succinct, broad in scope, and uncontroversial. But it has the disadvantage of subsuming all of the enormous and very diverse corpus of medieval hagiography under one heading,[2] and to discuss these texts as literature it is necessary to make some generic distinctions and sketch out some of the less familiar literary and aesthetic conventions of these texts. The term *sketch* is deliberately chosen because the topic is a vast one and relatively little explored and this chapter is intended to be open ended and suggestive rather than even an attempt at a definitive statement. At any rate, to begin with some terminology, *genre* is, of course, a much debated term in contemporary literary studies. The "genres" with which I am concerned in this chapter are "poetic" rather than "ethnic" genres; that is, with generic distinctions as defined by literary historians and critics rather than generic distinctions that medieval hagiographers would themselves have recognized and named.[3] Again, this discussion is written necessarily from the particular perspective of a literary critic interested in Old English, Anglo-Latin, and Middle English literature. A broad comparative perspective is desirable, and all of the medieval vernacular hagiographic traditions are dependent to one degree or another on Medieval Christian Latin prototypes and exemplars, but it is necessary to view the European hagiographic tradition from some perspective, and the English hagiographic tradition is both varied and extensive.

In addition to discussing the various generic forms of medieval hagiography, I would also like to discuss some aspects of the problem of hagiographic symbolism. Medieval literary hagiography has been relatively little studied from a literary viewpoint, and its aesthetic dimension is closely related to its symbolic context. Not all medieval hagiographic texts bear symbolic significance, but some do, and those that do are among the most interesting and significant texts that are preserved. But before one can begin to argue about the literary or symbolic significance of one or another saint's life, it is necessary to make certain specific generic distinctions.

The first such distinction, which is less a literary than a historiographic one, is between "primary" medieval hagiographic texts and all others. What I mean by a *primary* hagiographic text is a text that is itself a primary written witness to the life and deeds of a medieval saint. (For a variety of reasons the "classic" saint's lives of the late patristic period fall outside the scope of this discussion.) Typically, a member of a given Christian community would acquire a reputation for sanctity during his or her life, and after his or her death the local people would begin to pray at the tomb. Then, if local enthusiasm continued and it did indeed seem that the cult of this individual had some basis—that "miraculous" cures and benefits were being obtained—some figure in authority would turn to an appropriately literate member of the community and ask him or her to write a *vita* of this newly discovered saint. At this point the hagiographer, on the basis of personal knowledge, oral tradition, and possibly even of written records, would construct a *vita*. Our sense of the highly conventional nature of medieval hagiography and our awareness of the enormous hagiographic corpus that is preserved should not blind us to the fact that the hagiographer who wrote the primary *vita* was making a very radical claim. Not only is the subject a monk, priest, or lay person who led an exemplary life, he or she is to be accepted as a saint whose life found such favor with God that He has made that sanctity manifest in miracles. It now is appropriate to revere the departed individual and to ask the saint to intercede for the members of the community in which he or she once lived. The constraints of hagiographic convention are quite rigid, but even so, the author of the primary text has very considerable latitude in the claims one can make, the incidents one can include, and the ordering of the narrative as a whole. For this reason, primary saints' lives are among other things important historical sources, both for what they reveal about the life and the historical world of the saint and perhaps more important for what they reveal about the *mentalité* of the author and his or her audience. This aspect of hagiography has attracted considerable attention recently,[4] but there is still relatively little interest even in primary hagiographic texts as literary texts.

"Primary" saints' lives, however, often present a variety of particular and specific historical problems; and both because of these problems and because such primary texts are relatively rare, "secondary" saints' lives, lives of men and women whose sanctity could simply be taken for granted by the author, are more characteristic of the genre of hagiography as a whole and are generally more appropriate texts for literary analysis. But given this still enormous corpus of "secondary" hagiographic texts, further discriminations seem appropriate, and an immediate one concerns the way in which a given text was intended to be used. Hagiographic texts served two main functions—functions that were not mutually exclusive, but that in practice led to the development of two quite distinct modes of hagiographic literature. On the one hand, such texts could be read as Christian literature—texts to be read in public or in private for pleasure and for instruction—and on the other, certain hagiographic texts served a specific quasi-liturgical function. Both "secular" and "regular" religious services commemorated the saints, and there were various occasions, both in the liturgy of the Mass and the daily order of religious observances of monastic and other comparable groups in which hagiographic texts could appropriately serve as readings, "legends" in the service. Obviously, for example, the life of a given saint would make a suitable text to read on the festival of that saint in the regular order of "secular" worship. And among the religious, the Rule of Benedict provides a variety of contexts in which saints' lives might appropriately be read. A given saint's life could obviously be read both in church as a *legendum* (as it came to be called in the later Middle Ages), and in private as a literary work, but equally obviously these different contexts had a direct influence on the development of the *vita*. A *vita* (or *passio*, because the distinction is not really relevant to the present argument) intended for "legendary" use will tend to be relatively brief and straightforward. The constraints of time—the reading is only one portion of the service as a whole—mean that there will be an ongoing tendency to abbreviate the text. And the fact that the reading is a part of a religious service will similarly mean that there will be a tendency to make the *vita* as readily comprehensible as possible. The author has, in a sense, a responsibility to the community as a whole. By contrast the author of a literary *vita* faces no such constraints. One can elaborate the *vita* to one's heart's content; it can be as long and as difficult as one wishes. I would call such a *vita* an art *vita*, a term patterned after the model of "art song." Examples of art *vitae* would be the extended Old English saints' lives—*Elene, Juliana,* and the Guthlac poems of the *Exeter Book*—the Middle English *St. Erkenwald,* or the Old French *St. Alexis.* Whatever the merits or demerits of these poems, they are clearly ambitious literary works, which treat the live of a given saint with some fullness, and are too long to be read (as a whole at least) in a single church service or for public monastic reading. By contrast the saints' lives found in such collections as the OE *Martyrology* or such later collections as the *Legenda Aurea* of Jacobus de Voragine and the *South English Legendary* are eminently suitable for public reading in the context of a religious service.[5]

If these distinctions seem cogent, it follows that a scholar interested in literature is more likely to be concerned with the art *vitae* than with either *legenda* or "primary" saints' lives. And one immediate feature of the art *vita* that sets it apart from other hagiographic texts—particularly from legenda— is that characteristically the art *vita* is a hagiographic text that imitates some secular literary form. Such a text as the *Vita Sancti Martini* of Sulpicius Severus is, of course, an account of the life of a great Christian saint of the late ancient world. But at the same time, this text reflects the conventions, traditions, and assumptions of late antique prose biography.[6] Similarly, it is conventional to speak of the extended Old English poetic saints' lives as hagiographic texts, a convention that is surely correct. But at the same time these texts are patterned after Old English secular heroic poetry, and one of the major aesthetic problems for literary scholars who discuss these texts is whether this fusion of diverse elements is aesthetically successful. Similarly Old French verse art *vitae* can be seen as sacred romances, in that many of these texts reflect both the form—that is, the octosyllabic couplet—and many of the conventions of Old French romance. Again, much of the oddity of medieval Irish hagiographic narrative reflects the influence of secular Irish heroic prose narrative. None of these suggestions is particularly novel, but if one accepts the assumption that art *vitae* are a particular and to some extent discrete hagiographic form, then the pervasive fusing of religious content and secular form so characteristic of these various texts is more readily comprehensible.

Even art *vitae*, though, have often been treated with reserve in the relevant literary histories, and the rationale for this attitude stems from several related sources. On the one hand, traditional historians have turned to these texts as historical sources and have, perhaps inevitably, been frustrated by the extremely conventional quality of hagiographic language and narrative. Similarly literary historians, at least until quite recently, have neglected hagiographic texts, because these texts seemed unpromising, and because there is, after all, so much else to do.

A larger reason, however, for the comparative neglect of even the art *vitae* by literary historians and others is that the conventions of this genre are only beginning to be understood. These problems can most simply be approached by analogy, the time-honored procedure of comparison and contrast. Once the generic expectations of hagiography have been clarified to some degree by analogy, it will be appropriate to turn to the more specific and localized issues of latent symbolic context in these texts, the problem of typology and the characteristic development of metaphor in hagiographic narrative.

The first and broadest literary comparison I wish to propose is between hagiography and the contemporaneous genre of medieval romance. There exist obvious general similarities between *vitae* and medieval romance.[7] Neither hagiographers nor the authors of romances are concerned with verisimilitude as such. As the etymological development of the word *legend* suggests, hagiographers were not concerned with the plausibility of their narratives, and one way of defining *romance* is to point out that most romances are specifically set apart from the ordinary contingencies of history and experience. It is no accident that the great *locus* of medieval romance is the court of King Arthur, a court that can never have existed in anything like the form assigned to it by medieval romancers.

The *vitae* are similarly autonomous and divorced from the sequence of history. It might of course be objected that the saints were (or at least often were) real people who lived at a given moment of historical time and whose bodies are preserved for the edification and comfort of the faithful. But for a variety of reasons the saints' lives are characteristically unhistorical as a genre. The mode of the saints' existence within time, as viewed by their successors, differs from that of ordinary Christians. Ordinary lives are defined by history, whereas the saints transcend it. Christians can only speculate about the final significance of the lives of most of the faithful, but medieval Christians knew that God had already made manifest his judgment that the saints' lives were holy. And this fact is more important from the hagiographer's perspective than the specific historical context in which the saint lived and worked.

Another obvious feature that saints' lives and romances share, distinguishing them from more realistic modes of literature, is the constant presence of the supernatural, the miracles of hagiography and the marvels of romance. Although these marvels are seemingly unmotivated and unpredictable, the general structure and ultimate outcome of the story are very predictable in both genres. The supernatural elements are thus marvelous and surprising, but they occur within a narrative framework whose form is predetermined.

Both hagiography and romance are concerned with ideal types. In hagiography consistently the saint does not hesitate—he or she lives in a world where good and evil are clearly defined and where ambiguities are explicitly excluded. To cite one example (drawn form the corpus of Old English poetry since the rhetorical elaboration of West Germanic poetry illustrates the point with especial clarity) in the Old English *Juliana*, the heroine is the secretly Christian daughter of a pagan father. When the moment of choice approaches, the father first speaks to his daughter in terms of their relationship: "Đu eart dohter min   seo dyreste / ond seo sweteste   in sefan minum, / ange for eorþan, minra eagena leoht, / Iuliana!" (93–96).[8] A few lines later, however, after Juliana has affirmed her Christian faith, her father turns upon her: "Đa waes ellenwod,   yrre and reþe, / frecne and ferðgrim,   fæder wið dehter. / Het hi

þa swingan,   susle þreagan, / witum wægan,   ond þaet word acwaeð: /
'Onwend þec in gewitte, ond þa word oncyr / þe þu unsnyttrum   ær
gespræce, . . .' " (140–45). A little later, he sends her Heliseus (Juliana's
pagan would-be husband) and a martyr's death without hesitation.

What is striking about this episode is not so much the conflict between
father and daughter, which has scriptural precedent and anticipates the frustrated, violent, and yet curiously sexual relationship between Heliseus and
Juliana,[9] as the absence of any (even momentary) ambiguity. Once it is clear
that Juliana is Christian, her father responds like any other persecutor, mer-
cilessly torturing the "light of his eyes" without any apparent regret. It is
customary to explain (insofar as any explanation is offered) episodes of this
sort by reference to the naiveté of the hagiographers or their audiences. But
although such explanations are no doubt true in part, the naiveté is curiously
stylized. Where one might expect the poet to focus upon the tragic conflict
between Juliana's father's private feeling and public conviction, where the
narrative virtually demands such a response, the poet rigorously excludes any
depiction of doubt or hesitation, not only on the part of the saint but on the
part of her pagan and (presumably) damned father as well. The Old English
Juliana is a text that is a considerably elaborated version of a Latin *vita*, so
there is no question that the poet could have expanded upon his source here
if he (or she) wished. Similarly in romance, the line between good and evil
is ordinarily very clearly drawn; there is no hesitation or ambiguity. The
hero's strength, virtue, and courage and his mistress's beauty are beyond
question.

As a result, realistic characterization is not a normal feature of either
hagiography or romance; the hero or heroine in either genre is beyond
reproach and serves as a model, an exemplar, who perfectly fulfills the
values of Christian culture or those of the court. It follows from these
remarks, and is indeed very clear, that most saints' lives, like most romances, are "escapist" literature, many of them in the most pejorative sense
of that rather ambiguous term. The *vitae*, even art *vitae*, reflect a world
where God's presence and judgment, rather than being as agonizingly re-
mote as they often seem to be in the world of experience, are immediate
and omnipresent and where Christian ideals and values have decisive finality
unhindered by any "realistic" considerations. Similarly romances reflect a
world where aristocratic values are exemplified without any of the distractions the real world imposes.

Yet both saints' lives and romances are more than their weakest exemplars and can transcend the kind of weakness that my characterization of
them might imply, in that there is a tendency in both genres toward symbolism. This aspect of hagiography is (at least theoretically) quite widely granted,
and the importance of symbolism in some of the most famous romances such

as Wolfram's *Parzival* or *Gawain and the Green Knight* is similarly accepted, although the terms and the significance of the symbolic aspect of these works are still a matter of scholarly argument.[10] I do not mean by these suggestions to gloss over the very real differences between hagiography and romance as literary genres; the values the genres reflect are clearly very different, but a preliminary definition of hagiography as sacral romance may help us in accustoming ourselves to discussing hagiography as literature.

Another useful analogy is between hagiography and iconography—or perhaps to make the comparison somewhat less specific, between hagiography and the religious art of early medieval Europe. The initial point to emphasize is the essential similarity of the assumptions of both hagiographers and iconographers (if I may use this term loosely to include both sculptors and illuminators) concerning the relationship of external reality and its representation in art or literature.

It is commonplace in art history to point out that the visual artists of medieval Europe were less concerned with *mimesis*, with the imitation of external reality, than with portraying the earthly reflection, the *image* of a noumenal reality whose essential contours had been revealed in the Bible and defined and elaborated in the first four or five centuries of Christian tradition. The philosophical presumptions which underlie this aesthetic tradition are suggested by a comment of Peter Brown's concerning Augustine's intellectual stance:

> Augustine, however, was a man steeped in Neo-Platonic ways of thought. The whole world appeared to him as a world of "becoming," as a hierarchy of imperfectly realized forms, which depend for their quality, on "participating" in an Intelligible World of Ideal Forms. This universe was in a state of constant, dynamic tension, in which the imperfect forms of matter strove to "realize" their fixed, idealstructures, grasped by the mind alone.[11]

The intellectual imagination of patristic and early medieval Christianity was dominated by this kind of Neo-Platonic thought, and one consequence was the emphasis in both art and literature upon the reality that, from this perspective, underlies the ephemeral detail of ordinary experience and perception. Even Augustine's *Confessions*, a work that seems intensely concrete and historical, is, if Courcelle and those Augustinian scholars who accept his views are right, structured in terms of biblical type and allusions;[12] and the turning away from concrete specific history is much more sharply marked in the visual arts and hagiography.

Perhaps an analysis of a single specific example of an iconographic form will help to clarify the analogy between iconography and hagiography. One of the standard depictions of Mary with the Christ child shows the latter seated rigidly, as if on a chair, on the knees of the former. This unnatural posture can hardly be attributed to the technical unsophistication of medieval artists, who, whether they were capable of depicting the human form accurately or not, could obviously have chosen to represent the two figures in any posture they wished; and art historians are generally agreed that this pose represents Christ as Wisdom seated upon the throne of Solomon.[13] Because its iconographic meaning is so well understood, this image can serve as a specific example of the iconographic mode.

The image in question is neither wholly representational nor wholly abstract. Christ and the Virgin Mary are emphatically real historical persons, who lived at a specific moment in historical time. Yet their relationship, and the significance of their relationship, is not fully defined by historical circumstances. Christ was once a baby, wholly and utterly human in his weakness, and yet at the same time He was also the *Logos*, united and coequal with God the Father. And it is precisely the distortion, the unrealistic aspect of the iconographic form (in this case the stiff hieratic posture of the Christ child) that serves to convey both dimensions of Christ's being. If the image were wholly representational, the viewer might ignore or forget the mystery that the very existence of Christ presents. On the other hand, if the image were wholly abstract—if the figures of Mary and the Christ child were not immediately recognizable as mother and child—the viewer might forget that Christ was man as well as God. Thus the distortion of form so characteristic of early medieval Christian art serves to convey spiritual, noumenal truths concerning the figures the artist depicts. Paradoxically, the technical limitations of this mode of art are appropriate to the mode of Christian truth with which it is concerned.

Another aspect of the image of the Christ child enthroned upon the Virgin Mary is, I believe, significant, though difficult to define with any assurance. The depiction of Christ as an infant, seated upon the knees of his mother, can be seen as an image that contrasts very strikingly with the usual representation of a king or even God enthroned in majesty, precisely because it suggests these images. Christ rules not only as a king on a throne, but also as a baby upon his mother's knee, and this iconographic image evokes the biblical theme of "the power of the weak," a theme prominent in the Pauline epistles and in Christian thought from that point on.[14]

Part of the resonance of the image of Christ enthroned upon his mother's knees lies in the fact that early medieval society (which consisted essentially of an agrarian social structure ruled by a military caste) was dominated by masculine authority based ultimately upon violence. And yet at the same time the continuity of society, and whatever hope people might have for peace and justice, depended, on the one hand, upon the fertility of women and, on the other, upon a general recognition of the essential dignity of those who could not defend their rights by force. And it would not, I believe, be overinterpreting this image to suggest that this representation of the infant Christ with his mother at least suggests these concerns. I am not, of course, arguing that the image is somehow unorthodox, but simply that the efficacy of Christian "myth" depends in part upon the fact that aspects of these myths express universal concerns.

Another important dimension of hagiography is *figuration* or *typology*—two terms that are in effect synonymous. Erich Auerbach was the first scholar to call attention to the implications of this mode of understanding the significance of biblical history for the study of medieval literature, and in his essays *"Figura"* and "St. Francis of Assisi in Dante's *'Commedia,'*" he both defines this concept and illustrates how Dante, in his depiction of the life of Francis, is influenced not so much by the specific historical facts of Francis's life, but what he perceives as the essential figural patterns underlying it.[15] Figuration is, of course, only one of the various levels on which the medieval Church perceived the larger meaning of the biblical text, but it is of particular importance in hagiography because a saint's life deals with history. Other aspects of biblical symbolism, such as numerical symbolism or the specific iconographic meaning of given animals or objects, are sporadically relevant; but figuration is relevant in a more general way because it concerns history and its meaning, and hagiography is, among other things, one mode of understanding Christian history.

One immediate problem with the typology of saints' lives is that this entire subject is only beginning to be explored; yet even so, there are learned and in my judgment convincing analyses of typological patterning and allusion in Augustine's *Confessions*,[16] Gregory's "Life of Benedict,"[17] which consists of one book of the *Dialogues*, and the *Vita S. Martini* of Sulpicius Severus.[18] These texts were central in the tradition of medieval religious literature; and if we are prepared to grant that they exhibit figural patterning, then it follows that we must be prepared to take the possibility of figuration in any given saint's life very seriously indeed.

I would not, of course, argue that every saint's life that seems in some way incoherent exhibits complex figural patterns; many saints' lives are indeed badly composed series of stereotypes. But I would insist that we must be hesitant before we dismiss a text as incoherent. Thus the Old English *Juliana* was for long considered the weakest and least interesting Old English poetic saint's life, yet Joseph S. Wittig has convincingly demonstrated figural patterning in the poem.[19] There is a tendency among scholars concerned with medieval literature to move very quickly—particularly in the case of lesser known works—from a reasonable doubt concerning the merits or coherence of a given work to outright condemnation. It seems to me, however, that we should be more ready to live with open questions. It may be quite a long time before we have explored medieval Christian symbolism very carefully, and in the meantime many of our judgments concerning saints' lives, and indeed much medieval religious literature, will necessarily have to be tentative.

As I have suggested, figuration is a mode of viewing history, and as Auerbach and others have perceived, it is an integral aspect of biblical thought. What set Israel apart, conceptually at least, from the great imperial states of the ancient world such as Egypt, was that Israel's God, Yahweh, acted within time and history, whereas the gods of the neighboring states were worshipped in rituals that implied a cyclical and hence ahistorical perception of time. The history of Israel is thus the history of Israel's relationship with Yahweh. From the perspective of ancient Israel, one perceives the meaning and order of history by examining the record of God's actions toward Israel, and one can extrapolate the future on the basis of Yahweh's actions in the past. This future, however, is wholly distinct and set apart from the historical events that preceded it. Therefore when Paul defined Christian experience in terms of the story of Exodus—time and familiarity have, I believe, dulled the bold-ness of this imaginative leap for us—he was, at the very least, extrapolating on the basis of a traditional and indeed ancient mode of understanding the meaning of the history of Israel.[20] For us, however, to speak of a given saint's life as figural narrative might seem to suggest an implicit contradiction in terms. One can of course speak of the figural understanding of a narrative such as the sacrifice of Isaac, which prefigures the crucifixion; but since the life of Benedict in Gregory's *Dialogues* simply reiterates figures and episodes that have already been fulfilled in Christ, in what sense can it be defined as "figural"?[21] There are, I believe, two separate answers. On the one hand, one can insist upon the fact that terms such as *figuration* and *typology* are defined by critical usage—Auerbach, who after all was one of the first modern schol-ars to explore this aspect of medieval thought, speaks of such texts as Dante's "Life of St. Francis" in the *Paradiso* or the Life of St. Mary of Egypt as figural narratives,[22] by which he presumably means that these narratives stand in the same relation to the "figural" mode of understanding history as "real-istic" narrative does to "realism."

But apart from this appeal to Humpty-Dumpty's axiom in *Alice in Won-derland* that we can make words mean what we want them to, there is another larger sense in which texts such as the Life of Benedict or the Life of St. Martin are typological in much the same sense that biblical texts are. For, if Christ's life fulfills the types of the Old Testament, it does not exhaust them. Daniélou has spoken of how the events of Christ's life not only fulfill Old Testament types but also prefigure the events of the final times.[23] Christian history contin-ues beyond the events of the New Testament. It is possible for medieval historians and hagiographers to perceive such events as the conversion of England, or the Crusades, or the life of a specific local saint in terms of figural patterns. This perception is not merely arbitrary or absurd; it is simply one way, and I would submit a legitimate way, of understanding the sequence of history. At any rate, a given *vita* may thus be "figural" in that its narrative echoes certain specific biblical types and itself prefigures their fulfillment in the lives of the reader and (perhaps) in the drama of the last times.

Another dimension of the art of hagiography that I would like to explore has received even less attention than figuration and yet is, I believe, virtually as important for our understanding of the genre. Although this aspect of hagiography has been recognized in specific instances, I have never seen a specific term for it, and I would suggest here the phrase *emblematic narrative* as a mode of narrative in which inner experience, either psychological or spiritual, is reflected by the external events of the narrative. (T. S. Eliot's phrase *objective correlative* might seem apposite, but the meaning of Eliot's phrasing is disputed and I am concerned with a relatively simple literary phenomenon). Characteristically in emblematic narrative, metaphors concerning religious truths or aspects of the psychology of a saint are expressed in narrative form. This is a characteristic technique of New Testament narrative; to quote Daniélou, "thus as often in the Gospel of John, the visible reality appears as a sign of an invisible reality. The loaves of the multiplication are figures of the word of God and the Eucharist."[24] The kind of metaphoric usage that Daniélou is discussing here is significantly different from typology as this is usually understood, since there is no question of a relationship between two historical events, but rather between a biblical object—bread that is mysteriously increased—and a general concept—"the Word of God."

At any rate, let me attempt to illustrate the conception of "emblematic narrative" from a well-known hagiographic text. In Gregory's "Life of Benedict" in the *Dialogues*, Benedict at one point goes to visit his sister Scholastica. They spend the day together talking and at the end of the day Scholastica implores Benedict and his companion to spend the night with her "talking about the joys of heaven until the morning." Benedict refuses since he feels that he must return to the monastery.

> Tanta uero erat caeli serenitas, ut nulla in aere nubes appareret. Sanctimonialis autem femina, cum verba fratris negantis audisset, insertas digitis manus super mensam posuit, et caput in manibus omnipotentem Dominum rogatura declinauit. Cumque leuaret de mensa caput, tanta coruscationis et tonitrui uirtus, tantaque inundatio pluuiae erupit, ut neque uenerabilis Benedictus neque fratres, qui cum eo aderant, extra loci limen quo consederant, pedem mouere potuisissent. Sanctimonialis quippe femina,

caput in manibus declinas, lacrimarum fluuios in mensam fuderat, per quas serenitatem aeris ad pluuiam traxit. Nec paulo tardius post orationem inundatio illa secuta est, sed tanta fuit conuenientia orationis et inundationis, ut de mensa caput iam cum tonitruo leuaret, quatenus unum idemque esset momentum, et leuare caput et pluuiam deponere. Tunc uir Dei inter coruscos et tonitruos atque ingentis pluuiae inundationem uidens se ad monestarium non posse remeare, coepit conqueri contristatus, dicens: "Parcat tibi omnipotens Deus, soror, quid est quod fecisti?" Cui illa respondit "Ecce te rogaui et audire me noluisti. Rogaui Dominum meum, et audiuit me."[25]

This episode has been discussed from the perspective of folklore—in terms of the motif of tears bringing rain[26]—and A. de Vogüé has written convincingly on the typological implication of the narrative,[27] but the problem that interests me here is the link between the emotional prayer of Scholastica and the storm that prevents Benedict from returning home. The two are explicitly linked in the *Dialogues*; it is not merely that Scholastica has prayed for rain, but to paraphrase Gregory, "she poured rivers of tears upon the table *by which* she drew rain from the clear sky." Her tears and the rain are somehow inextricably associated. The point of the miracle would seem to be that God, in effect, externalized the "storm" of Scholastica's grief in the rainstorm that prevented Benedict from returning to his monastery. This physical storm is thus a concrete external "emblem" of an internal phenomenon—that is, Scholastica's grief. It is very easy for a modern reader to see this entire brief narrative as the symbolic expression of a quite simple and normal experience. Benedict had initially intended to return to his monastery, but the violent "storm" of his sister's grief convinced him that it was God's will to respect the law of charity more than the monastic rule, which forbids unnecessary lingering outside the monastery. But such a realistic interpretation of the narrative would deny its most striking characteristic—the miracle that is the occasion for Gregory's inclusion of this episode in his Life of Benedict. This problem frequently occurs in hagiography; are, for example, the demons who appear to St. Anthony "emblems" of temptation, a reflection of aspects of the consciousness of the saint, or representations of external demonic forces? The answer would seem to be all of the above; other monks in the tradition of the desert fathers recognized that "we are our own demons,"[28] but they did not therefore deny that real demons tempted the ascetic heroes of old. The point is that hagiographers and their audience believed simultaneously in the reality of the miraculous and yet were aware that a given miracle in a specific saint's life might bear symbolic meaning as well. And if it was only a symbol, if the miracle never existed as an event within history, this did not affect the lager truth of the narrative as a whole. Jacobus de Voragine makes this point explicitly in remarking about his narrative of the assumption of the Virgin Mary, "porro alia multa sunt ibi posita *potius ad simulationem, quam ad veritatem.* . . ."[29]

Emblematic narrative is really quite common in hagiographic narrative, and its general purport has been widely apprehended in specific instances. Once the question was posed, few critics would deny that the heretic Simon's fall from the air in the *Acts of Peter and Paul* is at least generally related to his overweening spiritual aspirations or that St. Christopher's quest for the most powerful man on earth is not merely a historical account of his adventures. But often there are instances in which our own lack of knowledge is sufficient to obscure for us the full meaning of an episode in a hagiographic text. Some years ago in the course of his work on the directional symbolism of Dante's *Commedia*, John Freccero pointed out that the scene in the "Life of St. Peter" in which Peter requests to be crucified head downward depends upon a complex sequence of cosmological speculation that is originally based on Aristotelian cosmology.[30] And there are no doubt many episodes in hagiographic texts that at present seem to us either grotesque or gratuitous, which will eventually be interpreted much more adequately than they are now. But for the moment all I am concerned with is to establish that in some instances we should consider the possibility of "emblematic" as well as figural meaning in interpreting texts of this sort.

Hagiography, as I have been discussing it, is a curious literary form indeed. On the one hand, every *vita*, no matter how simple or complex, is based upon a radically historical claim. If the given saint did not live, die, and make his or her powers manifest as the *vita* claims, then the *vita* is not merely in error, it is potentially at least destructive. It is hardly worthwhile invoking a saint who is not there. Yet the *vitae* are profoundly unhistorical as a genre. Still another of their functions is to provide moral *exempla*; and yet it could easily be argued that typically the *vitae* are so utterly unrealistic that they hardly provide appropriate *exempla* for real Christians living in the world of history. It could even be argued that the world of absolutely clearest moral choice depicted by the *vitae* conflicts with that fundamental aspect of Christian ethics which forbids one Christian to offer final judgment upon another. The absolute certitude with which Juliana can repudiate her father and potential husband is rarely appropriate for Christians in the real world of mixed motives and confused intentions. But these criticisms are historically inappropriate. The *vitae* were repudiated by the reformers in the sixteenth century and have gradually been discarded in the tradition of Roman Catholic spirituality in the centuries since. But if the tradition of the *vitae* is problematic historically and to some degree morally, this does not mean that we cannot still appreciate the very real aesthetic merit of the best of the art *vitae*. They offer a vision of sanctity, and if it is an abstract, stylized, and in some ways partial one, it still demands our respect if not our assent.

Notes

1. *The Oxford Dictionary of the Christian Church*, ed. F. L. Cross, 2d ed. (London, New York, and Toronto, 1983), ad loc.

2. For a recent discussion of hagiography that, however, treats hagiography as a whole as one undifferentiated genre, see Thomas J. Heffernan, *Sacred Biography: Saints and Their Biographies in the Middle Ages* (New York, 1988). For an earlier and very suggestive study see James W. Earl, "Typology and Iconographic Style in Early Medieval Hagiography," *Studies in the Literary Imagination* 8 (1975): 15–46; a revised version of Earl's essay with the same title is reprinted in *Typology and English Medieval Literature*, ed. Hugh T. Keenan (New York, 1992), pp. 89–120.

3. For this distinction, see Dan Ben-Amos, "Analytical Categories and Ethnic Genres," in *Folklore Genres*, ed. Dan Ben-Amos, Publications of the American Folklore Society 26 (Austin, Texas, 1976), pp. 215–42.

4. For a convenient introduction to this literature, see Stephan Wilson, "Annotated Bibliography," in *Saints and Their Cults*, ed. Stephan Wilson (Cambridge, 1983), which includes over 1,300 entries. Another recent survey with some bibliography is that of Pamela Sheingorn, "The Saints in Medieval Culture; Recent Scholarship," *Envoi* 2 (1990): 1–30.

5. The problem of reconstructing actual liturgical usage for the early medieval period is a very difficult one, and for this reason I have limited myself to what I hope are plausible generalities. For one preliminary discussion of the problem of the early English liturgy, see Milton M. Gatch, "Old English Literature and the Liturgy," *ASE* 6 (1977): 237–47.

6. See the comments of Jacques Fontaine in his edition of the *Vita Sancti Martini* of Sulpicius Severus; Sulpice Sévère, *Vie de St. Martin*, Sources Chrétiennes 133 (Paris, 1967), vol. 1, pp. 97–123.

7. The comparison is, of course, commonplace; for a gathering of papers concerned with this problem, see the journal *Medievalia et Humanistica*, n.s. 6 (1975). See also Northrup Frye, *The Secular Scripture: A Study of the Structure of Romance* (Cambridge, Mass., 1976), p. 3 and passim.

8. All quotations of Old English poetry are from the *ASPR* by line numbers. The two passages of *Juliana* that I quote may be translated as follows. "You are my daughter, dearest and sweetest to my mind before any upon this earth, the light of my eyes, Juliana. . . . " "Then he was furiously angry, fierce and wrathful, terrible and grim in mind, the father against the daughter. He commanded her to be beaten, to endure torture, to bear torments and uttered this saying: 'Turn in mind and reverse those words which you unwisely spoke before'."

9. Heliseus has her stripped naked and flogged (185–88), and then hung by her hair (presumably still nude) on a high tree (225–32). During these tortures—which in part are predicated upon Juliana's refusal to engage in the sexual relationship of marriage with Heliseus—he watches and exults in her sufferings.

10. For discussion of this aspect of *Gawain*, see Larry D. Benson, *Art and Tradition in Gawain and the Green Knight* (New Brunswick, N. J., 1965), pp. 207–48. For discussion of one startlingly exact pattern of chronological symbolism in *Parzival*, see Arthur Groos, "Time Reference and the Liturgical Calendar in Wolfram von Eschenbach's *Parzival*," *Deutsche Viertjahrsschrift für Literaturwissenschaft und Geistesgeschichte* 49 (1975): 44–65.

11. Peter Brown, *Augustine of Hippo* (Berkeley and Los Angeles, 1969), pp. 221–22. See also, Peter Brown, *The Cult of the Saints* (Chicago, 1981), which focuses on Latin patristic texts.

12. Pierre Courcelle, *Les "Confessions" de Saint Augustin dans la tradition littéraire, antécédents et postérité* (Paris, 1963) and *Recherches sur les Confessions de Saint Augustin* (Paris, 1968).

13. The figure is referred to by art historians as the *Majestas Mariae*. For discussion and examples, see Gertrud Schiller, *Iconography of Christian Art*, trans. Janet Seligman (Greenwich, Conn., 1971), vol. 1, 23–25, plate references ad loc.

14. Thus, such texts as 2 Corinthians 12:9, Romans 5:3 and Phil. 4:12 explicitly articulate this theme, and it is implicit in a number of famous biblical narratives. Jacob, Joseph, and David are all younger brothers, who in the normal course of events would be subservient to their elders.

15. Erich Auerbach, "*Figura*," and "Saint Francis of Assisi in Dante's *Commedia*," in *Scenes from the Drama of European Literature* (New York, 1959), pp. 11–98; for publication data on the German texts of these articles, see p. 5.

16. See Courcelle, *Les "Confessions."*

17. M. Mähler, "Evocations bibliques et hagiographiques dans la Vie de Saint Benoit par Saint Grégoire," *Revue Benedictine* 83 (1973): 398–429.

18. On typology in the *Vita Sancti Martini*, see Fontaine, *Vita Sancti Martini*, pp. 127–34, and passim.

19. Joseph S. Wittig, "Figural Narrative in Cynewulf's *Juliana*" *ASE* 4 (1975): 37–55.

20. Thus in biblical thought God is revealed in history: God is "the God of Abraham, Isaac and Jacob" (Exodus 3:6). Each new aspect of Israel's history thus reveals something further about Him. Paul therefore saw the crucified Christ as, at the same time, the fulfillment and the end of the history of Israel.

21. See Friedrich Ohly, "Halbbiblische und Ausserbiblische Typologie," reprinted in *Schriften zur Mittelalterlichen Bedeutungsforschung* (Darmstadt, Germany, 1977) pp. 361–400.

22. Auerbach, *Scenes*, pp. 78–98.

23. Jean Daniélou S. J., *The Bible and Liturgy*, trans. anon. (Notre Dame, Ind., 1956), pp. 156–61 and passim.

24. Ibid., pp. 209–10.

25. *Dialogi*, II, 33; Grégoire le Grand, *Dialogues*, ed. Adelbert de Vogüé and Paul Antin, Sources Chrétiennes, nos. 251, 260, 265 (Paris, 1978–80), vol. 2, p. 232. "The sky was so clear at the time that there was not a cloud in sight. At her brother's refusal Scholastica folded her hands on the table and rested her head upon them in earnest prayer. When she looked up again, there was a sudden burst of lightening and thunder, accompanied by such a downpour that Benedict and his companions were unable to set a foot outside the door. By shedding a flood of tears while she prayed, this holy nun had darkened the cloudless sky with a heavy rain. The storm began as soon as her prayer was over. In fact, the two coincided so closely that the thunder was already resounding as she raised her head from the table. The very instant she ended her prayer, the rain poured down. Realizing that he could not return to the monastery in this terrible storm, Benedict complained bitterly. 'God forgive you, sister!' he said 'What have you done?' Scholastica simply answered, 'When I appealed to you, you would not listen to me. So I turned to my God and He heard my prayer.' " The translation is that of O. J. Zimmerman O.S.B. from, Saint Gregory the Great, *Dialogues*, Fathers of the Church 39 (New York, 1959), pp. 102–4.

26. A. J. Festugière, "Lieux commun littéraires et thèmes de folklore dan l'hagiographie primitive," *Wiener Studien: Zeitschrift für Klassische Philologie* 73 (1960): 123–52.

27. A. de Vogüé, "La rencontre de Benoît et de Scholastique," *Revue d'Histoire de la Spiritualité* 48 (1972): 262–73.

28. Thus Ambrose *Exameron* I. viii. 31; *CSEL* 32.1, p. 31; *PL* 14, 140. For a gathering of instances of this motif, see the *Review of English Studies* 30 (1979): 182–83.

29. Jacobus a Voragine, *Legenda aurea*, ed. T. Graesse, 2d ed. (Leipzig, 1850), pp. 509–10.

30. John Freccero, "Infernal Inversion and Christian Conversion (*Inferno* XXXIV)," *Italica* 42 (1965): 35–41.

Saints and Companions to Saints:
Anglo-Saxon Royal Women Monastics in Context

Carol Neuman de Vegvar

One of the more prominent and unusual factors in the conversion of the Anglo-Saxons is the role played by royal women monastics in the development of the Church.[1] Many of these women eventually came to be recognized as saints; yet for them, unlike their male counterparts, there are no surviving independent early *vitae*. Documentary sources on these women and their lives, however, are remarkably plentiful for so early a period. References to these women abound in Bede's *Historia Ecclesiastica*, sometimes implying lost *vitae*, and in the surviving *vitae* and correspondence of the male saints with whom they are associated, as well as in documents associated with women monastics and their foundations.[2] Further, as the archaeological exploration of these foundations progresses, we have become increasingly aware of the material setting in which these women lived and participated in the events of their age.

The royal women monastics, saints and otherwise, have not been neglected in the scholarship on early Anglo-Saxon England. Since the nineteenth century, writers have focused on the individual accomplishments of these women, the biographical and geographical details of their lives as they can be gleaned from documents, their respective places and relationships within the royal genealogies, and the roles of their individual foundations. It is not my purpose to reiterate here what has already been examined in detail elsewhere. Nor will I present new information here; the documents are well known, and the cited archaeological evidence has been published in the context of find sites. Rather, I propose to examine the intellectual and material context of the early conversion-period royal women monastics as a group, on the basis of documents and site evidence, and to attempt to determine to what extent they were extraordinary or typical within the broader range of attitudes and activities of their class and sex in their time. The understanding of a

broader cultural context may perhaps assist in the interpretation of the surviving documentation, including the synopsized *vitae* in Bede.

I. Royalty and Women's Roles

A brief overview of the female Anglo-Saxon saints of the pre-Viking
period reveals that over half of them are royal, the widows or daughters of
kings, or otherwise closely related to the royal houses of the various Anglo-
Saxon kingdoms. Of the rest, some are prominent nonroyal abbesses, a few
derive their sainthood from association with or miracles involving another,
often royal, female saint; for the remainder, the majority are little-known
figures, appearing exclusively as the otherwise undocumented foci of localized cults or of much later (post-Conquest) and often historically questionable hagiographic literature. The preponderance of royalty among the
well-documented female saints in pre-Viking sources is overwhelming,
parallelling the association with royalty by early participation in the royal
entourage among male saints and monastic founders.[3] This relationship is
evident from an overview of the documents, as they concern themselves
almost exclusively with the doings of the royal and the holy. Commoners
occur in Bede's *Historia Ecclesiastica* and in early Anglo-Saxon hagiographical
sources usually in crowds, as a sort of Greek chorus to the deeds of saints,
or individually as the objects or observers of miracles or bit players at important events.

There are however also institutional reasons for the preponderance of
royalty among Anglo-Saxon female saints of the early period. In the early
Anglo-Saxon context, sainthood was often conferred on founders of monastic
communities and important abbots and abbesses. The cults of these saints
arose in the context of the monastic communities with which the saints were
most closely associated and were often later confirmed by the translation of
the saint from the monastic cemetery to the interior of a monastic church. The
frequency of royalty among Anglo-Saxon women saints parallels the frequency with which monastic communities were founded by royal women.[4] It
was not uncommon in this period for royal widows to found and retire to
monastic communities. Michael Enright's recent discussion of the role of
queens in the political structure of the early Germanic kingdoms demonstrated that the confinement, voluntary or otherwise, of royal widows to
monastic communities was sometimes a necessary side effect of the smooth
transition of power and material wealth from a deceased king to his successor; parallel circumstances were found in contemporary Spain, where the
third Synod of Saragossa mandated that royal widows always enter convents.[5]
Other royal women also entered religion for a variety of reasons; Ælfflæd,

eventual abbess of Whitby, was vowed in infancy to a life in religion by her father, Oswy of Northumbria.[6] Others founded or joined religious communities in response to a spiritual calling, some abandoning marriages to do so; including Æthelthrith, wife of Ecgfrith of Northumbria, and possibly also Cyneburg, wife of Alchfrith, under-king of Deira, and Cuthberg, wife of Aldfrith.[7]

In rejecting William Chaney's assertion that the sanctification of royalty in early Anglo-Saxon England was a natural continuation of preconversion Germanic sacral kingship, Susan Ridyard has recently pointed out the distinction between earthly and spiritual glory drawn by Bede and the other hagiographers of the age and demonstrated that the sanctity of the royal women saints was signaled in life by their rejection of earthly pleasures associated with their former rank in secular society.[8] To a certain extent, however, the descriptions of the personal austerities of the royal women monastics, whether based on biographical fact or textual hyperbole, need not blind us to the continuing functioning of cloistered royal women, especially monastic founders and including several saints, in the broader field of the relationship between kings and the Church. As Margaret Deanesly pointed out, monastic foundations established or maintained by royal women had advantages for the kings to whom their founders were related.[9] Kings and their households were converted to Christianity well before the general population of their kingdoms, and kings were expected by their bishops to fund and otherwise support the continuing missionary effort in the neighboring countryside. The foundation of monastic communities had the double advantage of providing centers for a monastic life within the region and of establishing training centers for the necessary clergy of the new faith. The six bishops trained at Whitby in the time of Abbess Hilda, niece of Edwin of Northumbria, probably constitute only the most prominent example, by both quality and quantity, of the training of clergy under royal abbesses.[10] Further, in the newly converted regions of northern Europe, landed endowment for the clergy was provided by kings. Although providing an income for the bishop and his household was a primary concern, additional clergy could be supported on wealth or land that might have been otherwise given to a daughter as a dowry or taken by a widowed queen into a second marriage, by allowing her to found a monastic community.[11] Widows who would otherwise continue to reside within a royal household would also be encouraged to found monastic communities with lands received as dowries, as marriage portions from their husbands, or as inheritances from parents.[12] Toponymic evidence indicates ownership of land by women in the Anglo-Saxon period, and enough of this evidence is early in date to indicate that the inheritance practices that supported such ownership were not the invention of the Alfredian age but a continuation of preconversion Germanic custom.[13]

Anglo-Saxon kings who not only allowed but encouraged their female relatives to set up monastic communities were taking best advantage of available talent. The installation of royal women as monastic founders avoided the necessity of the use in the same role of male relatives, who were needed at the king's side, as part of the complex social structure of kinship and loyalties that held together the warband, the foundation of secular power. On the other hand, the role of royal abbesses as advisors, hostesses, and diplomats in many ways echoed that of their sisters in the secular world. The role of secular royal women was largely acted out in diplomatically advantageous marriages, which were intended to construct and maintain links of mutual support and trust between royal houses. This role was often not merely a passive presence at a foreign court and the provision of male heirs to a politically important spouse. Recent analysis of the roles of the female characters in *Beowulf* indicates that, although the role of women was subordinate to that of men at court, their part was not passive.[14] Setsuko Haruta has suggested that the failure of passive female characters, Hildeburh and Freawaru, is deliberately contrasted in the poem to the at least temporary success of Wealhtheow and Hygd as diplomats between nations, hostesses and keepers of the peace at court, and protectors of national continuity.[15] These tasks cannot be accomplished by passivity, and indeed these women use wisdom and eloquence with the directness and dexterity with which their male counterparts use physical violence. The poet praises them directly for their wisdom: Wealhtheow is *mode geðungen* ("mature of mind"), and Hygd is *wis welðungen* ("wise and well taught"), which implies a trained rather than an entirely inborn talent for diplomacy.[16]

Given the controversy over the date of *Beowulf*, readers may be inclined to suggest that the poem may well not be an accurate representation of early Anglo-Saxon social practices.[17] However, the role of queens as diplomats and councilors to their husbands is clearly demonstrated by a close reading of Bede and of early Anglo-Saxon *vitae*. Christian princesses married to pagan kings were important points of access for the church in the conversion of Kent, Northumbria, and the East Saxons; indeed Pope Boniface wrote not only to Edwin of Northumbria but also to his Christian queen, Ethelburga, in an attempt to convince the king to convert.[18] Rædwald's pagan queen prevented the murder of Edwin, in exile at the East Anglian court, and later persuaded Rædwald to renounce exclusive faith in Christianity.[19] Queen Eanfled's persistence in celebrating Easter according to the Roman calendar, despite her husband Oswy's adherence to the calendar in use in the Columban foundations, was one of the major factors precipitating the Synod of Whitby.[20] Sebbi of the East Saxons was prevented from becoming a monk by his wife's insistence; only in his final illness did she relent.[21] According to "Eddius,"

Ecgfrith's queen, Iurminburgh, was instrumental in turning her husband against Wilfrid, as was her sister, queen to Centwini of the West Saxons.[22]

Given the extent of activity of secular royal women, it is not surprising to find royal abbesses not only playing a large part in the formation of the church through the training of clergy, but also taking an active role in contemporary events, often by their presence at court and at synods. Hilda of Whitby played an allegedly silent, albeit partisan, role as hostess at the Synod of Whitby, and was called *advisor to kings and princes* by Bede.[23] Æbbe, sister to Oswy of Northumbria and abbess of Coldingham, and a "very wise and holy woman," was present at court at the time of the humiliation and imprisonment of Wilfrid and threatened Oswy's son and successor Ecgfrith with the wrath of God if he would not allow Wilfrid to leave the realm unmolested.[24] Hilda's protegé and successor Ælfflæd not only served, along with another abbess, Æthilberg, as witness to her half brother Aldfrith of Northumbria's deathbed wish for reconciliation with Wilfrid, but attended the synod on the east bank of the Nidd to relay this message and advise the assembled clergy; "Eddius" described her as "the best of advisors and a constant source of strength to the whole realm."[25] By supporting the establishment of monastic foundations, Anglo-Saxon kings were able to provide a niche and position of rank for some of their female relatives, from which they might draw upon their diplomatic talents, in an intermediate position between church and state, just as their secular sisters provided the same kind of social and diplomatic bonding within and between kingdoms.

The Double Monastery as Institution

The monastic communities of the early Anglo-Saxon period varied considerably in size, from grand establishments with large numbers of residents, stone structures, and substantial legacies of intellectual endeavor and artistic production to small communities occupied by the founder and a few followers. Several of the more prominent of the monastic communities founded by royal women were double monasteries, with both male and female monastic communities in residence. Given the need for clergy in the period, it is not surprising that this somewhat unusual arrangement had the blessings of both the clergy and the secular authorities.[26] The probable source of the double monastery as institution in the Anglo-Saxon kingdoms was Merovingian Francia, where the double monastery had developed similarly, under royal patronage and usually under the direction of abbesses rather than abbots.[27]

The rule of the Frankish double monasteries was not uniform. Jouarre, founded by Columbanus, and Remiremont, founded as a daughter house of

Luxeuil, initially followed Columbanus' *regula*, as may have Nivelles, Stablo-
Malmedy, and Montierender.[28] Waldebert, assistant at the foundation of
Faremoutiers and St. John the Baptist at Laon and later third abbot of Luxeuil,
composed a rule for nuns, the *Regula cuiusdem patris ad virgines*, a combination of Columban and Benedictine ideas, which was instituted first at
Faremoutiers and later at Remiremont.[29] Sadalberga's foundation of St. John
the Baptist at Laon followed the *regula* of Bishop Donatus of Besançon,
which included elements of the rules of Columbanus and Benedict and the
Regula ad virgines of Caesarius of Arles.[30] Chelles, Bèze, and later Jouarre
followed a combination of the Benedictine and Columban rules.[31] Thus practices must have varied from house to house.

    One factor held in common by many of the Frankish double monasteries
was their affiliation with Frankish royalty and nobility, and often with women
of this class. Stablo-Malmedy was founded in 648 under Sigibert III of
Austrasia, along with his major domo Grimoald and Bishop Kunibert of
Cologne; and the initial endowment for Montierender came from Chilperich
II of Austrasia.[32] Chelles was initially founded in the sixth century by
Chrodechilde, wife of Clovis I, on an old royal property dating from the reign
of Chilperich I, and was enlarged and regularized under Queen Balthildis.[33]
Balthildis also provided a rich endowment for Faremoutiers; but it was to
Chelles that she retired, more or less voluntarily.[34] Nivelles became a double
abbey under Abbess Gertrude, daughter of Pepin the Elder.[35] Faremoutiers
was founded in 613–614 by Burgundofara, daughter of Chagnerich of Meaux.[36]

    According to Bede, Faremoutiers, Chelles, and Andelys outside Paris
were the primary centers to which girls of royal and noble Anglo-Saxon
families were sent to be educated or to join convents in the mid-seventh
century, as there were at that time only a few monastic communities in
England.[37] Monastic establishments for women were rare in England in this
period. All the documented examples were very recent foundations: Eanswith's
convent at Folkestone, founded around 630 but known only through later
documents; Æthelburga's double monastery at Lyminge, founded sometime
after 633; and the possibly double foundation at Hartlepool, probably established in the 640s by Heiu, according to Bede the first woman in Northumbria
"to take vows and be clothed as a nun."[38] Royal and noble parents no doubt
felt more comfortable sending their daughters to places with better established reputations. Francia was familiar through links of royal marriage and
trade, and the houses to which Anglo-Saxon women of high status were sent
had in many cases the amenities afforded by royal endowments.[39] Anna of
East Anglia's daughter Ethelberga and his stepdaughter Sæthryd both became
abbesses at Faremoutiers, where Earcongota, daughter of Earconbert of Kent,
lived and died as a young nun; and Hereswith, niece of Edwin of Northumbria
and sister to Hilda of Whitby, became a nun at Chelles.

It must have been apparent to the sisters and female cousins of these emigré royal monastic women that, in founding monastic communities at home, the royally endowed Frankish double monasteries were a model well worth considering. According to Bede, when Hilda of Whitby turned to religion in 647, she had every intention of following Hereswith from East Anglia to Chelles.[40] Bishop Aidan, however, prevailed upon her to return to Northumbria and govern a small community endowed with a single hide of land on the river Wear, perhaps as a test of her vocation and abilities. Her next charge was Heiu's foundation of Hartlepool, where she imposed a regular rule, possibly in emulation of what she knew of Frankish practice. Her first opportunity to found a monastic community of any size came in 657, when she established the double monastery at Whitby. Many subsequent communities founded, ruled, or endowed by royal women were double houses: Coldingham, Ely, Wimbourne, Wenlock, Thanet, and Queen Osthryth of Mercia's endowment at Bardney, and possibly also Lyminge, Thanet, and Hackness.[41] In the same period there were, however, also royal foundations that were not double but exclusively for women, including Minster in Sheppey; double foundations that were not royal, such as Barking, Hartlepool, and possibly Repton; and convents for women that were neither royal nor double, such as Watton.[42]

The Anglo-Saxon double monastery as institution was tolerated by church authorities, although not without a degree of ambivalence among those who knew that the institution had been condemned elsewhere. In the *Penitential* of Theodore of Tarsus it is noted: "Non licet viris feminas habere monachas neque feminis viros; tamen consuetudinem istius provinciae non destruamus."[43] Such tolerance was extended because the double monastery was an efficient use of revenue, in a frontier situation of scarce resources, in providing a center of both monastic life and clerical training and because it had the support of the royal houses of many of the Anglo-Saxon kingdoms.

As at the Frankish double monasteries, the rule and consequently the custom of abbess and community varied substantially among the Anglo-Saxon double houses. Each founder was essentially free to assemble his or her own rule, establishing the priorities of life within the community, providing that the rule was consistent with the tenets of monastic life as based on preexisting models and was applied with a degree of consistency. Bede notes that Earconwald, bishop of London, devised and established "an excellent form of monastic rule" in both his own monastery at Chertsey and in the community he founded for his sister Æthilburh at Barking.[44] Hilda's rule at Hartlepool and Whitby was premised on "righteousness, mercy, purity, and other virtues, but especially of peace and charity," and was devised in consultation with Bishop Aidan "and other devout men," who visited her to offer guidance.[45]

Custom and Practice Among Women Monastics

Variations in the rule, the endowment and the makeup of the community could directly effect the degree of enclosure or access to the world, the relative degree of poverty or luxury of the community's customs, the level of literacy, the uses and arrangement of the monastic site and buildings, and the kind and quality of art produced by or for the community.

The degree of enclosure varied radically among Anglo-Saxon convents and royal houses.[46] At one extreme was Wimbourne, as described in the *Life of Saint Leoba*, written by Rudolf of Fulda between 800 and 850.[47] Under Abbess Tetta, Leoba's teacher, the residences of men and women were so segregated that neither sex was permitted to enter the residence of the other, except priests who came into the women's quarters to celebrate mass and then left immediately. Even the abbess confined herself to the women's residence and gave her orders and advice through a window. Such strict enclosure is reminiscent of the rule of Caesarius of Arles, which was very influential in Francia.[48] However, such rigid enclosure was not the norm in England, and Rudolf's description may be biased by his knowledge of the more strictly regulated communities of the ninth century.[49] Although residential buildings were consistently separated, there are many incidents in Bede where contact between men and women occur within monastic communities as a natural part of daily events. At Barking, the church was apparently in use simultaneously by nuns and monks for predawn offices, as Bede tells us that at the time of the miracle revealing the site for the nuns' cemetery, the nuns had just left the church, while two monks remained there.[50] Also at Barking, a boy oblate named Æsica was a student among the nuns; in his dying breath he called for one of them by name.[51] Hilda attended the synod at Whitby; the reeve at Whitby brought Cædmon directly to Hilda to reveal his miraculous gift of poetry; and the monks from Whitby who told the nuns at Hackness of Hilda's death spoke directly to them.[52] While visiting Queen Osthryth at the men's community at Bardney, Abbess Æthilhild mentioned that at her own neighboring house, she and one of the nuns had gone at night to the abbey guesthouse quarters to comfort a male guest tormented by an evil spirit.[53]

Abbesses sometimes traveled further afield outside their monastic communities, both to court and to synods, as previously discussed. Quite a few abbesses and their nuns went the far greater distance to Rome. The correspondences of Boniface reveal that the church was ambivalent about such journeys, both because it allowed monastics to wander abroad from their communities and because, in the case of women monastics, the dangers of travel in the seventh and eighth century were not to be underestimated. Boniface's early letter from Eangyth and Heaburg, around 720, reveals that the women were aware of both issues and sought Boniface's advice.[54] In a letter of about 725 to Bucge, possibly identical with Heaburg, he somewhat reluctantly conceded that if she could not find peace in her home community, she might seek it in Rome, but that she should at least wait until the wars of the "Saracens" had ceased.[55] Boniface later met Bucge in Rome; her kinsman Æthelbert II of Kent, citing her as an intermediary in his correspondence with Boniface, mentioned that meeting.[56] Not all women who set out from England for Rome, however, ever set eyes on their goal. In his famous letter of 747 to Cuthbert, Archbishop of Canterbury, Boniface deplored the number of "veiled women and matrons" who had run out of funds in foreign towns and had turned to prostitution, and he asked Cuthbert to have a synod forbid pilgrimage by women. One may speculate whether this reflected a change in circumstances between 725 and 747, such as an increasing number of women undertaking the dangerous journey without adequate funds or contacts, or whether Boniface was inclined to forbid in general what he might allow in individual cases, or whether the shift reflects a change of attitude, personal or widespread, toward the mobility of women.[57] However, there is evidence that the abbesses did do whatever was possible to smooth the road for one another: a letter from Ælfflæd to Abbess Adolana of Pfälzel (Palatiolum) near Trier survives, asking Adolana's assistance for an unnamed abbess enroute to Rome.[58] It has been suggested that the unnamed traveler was abbess of one of the daughter houses of Whitby and that Ælfflæd was writing a superior's letter of introduction for her; but it could as easily reflect a supportive personal friendship between Ælfflæd and a younger colleague.

Abbesses also cultivated friendships with male colleagues, received them as guests, and arranged to meet them both within and outside their respective communities. Aidan and others visited Hilda at Hartlepool to assist her in instituting a regular life there.[59] Cuthbert visited both Æbbe at Coldingham and Verca at South Shields.[60] Ælfflæd met Cuthbert of Lindisfarne twice, once at the monastery on Coquet Island, and once at the consecration of a church on her estates; both meetings were arranged at her request.[61] Bede notes these incidents because of the miracles of prophecy performed by Cuthbert on these occasions and apparently not because there was anything unusual about such meetings. The deep affection between abbots and abbesses, often future saints, is also apparent in the descriptions of personal gifts they sent one another: Cuthbert sent Ælfflæd a linen cincture, which cured her of a crippling ailment.[62] Verca of South Shields gave Cuthbert a linen cloth, which he chose to set aside for use as a shroud.[63] Similarly, Abbess Ecgburh sent Guthlac a lead coffin and a linen burial cloth.[64] Gifts are also often mentioned in the correspondences of Boniface and his colleagues with women monastics in England and in the new German communities; these include clothing, altar cloths, books, verses, and scriptural passages sent in both directions.[65] Further, these letters often use empassioned terms of endearment, for all that the terms are often quotations from Scripture and the endearment spiritual. The depth of this affection extended to Boniface's wish to have Leoba, abbess of Bischofsheim, buried beside him, a wish that the monks at Fulda declined to fulfill.[66]

Despite the relative openness of many Anglo-Saxon women's and double communities, only one scandal is prominent in the pages of Bede's *Historia*, the behavior of the residents of the double monastery at Coldingham.[67] Bede significantly does not mention specific sexual misconduct but rather emphasizes sloth, gluttony, drunkenness, idle conversation, and especially a tendency among the nuns to fine clothes, with which they intended to "attract the attention of strange men," presumably lay visitors to the community. Aldhelm's prose treatise *De Virginitate*, addressed to the nuns at Barking, also stresses the spiritual danger of fashionable dress, curled hair, and manicured nails, and the nineteenth, twentieth and twenty-eighth canons of the 747 Synod of Clovesho similarly decry colorful dress in monastic communities, as does Boniface's letter to Cuthbert of Canterbury.[68] Alcuin later repeats this warning in his letters to Ethelred of Northumbria and to the monks of Lindisfarne.[69] Given that many of the superiors in the leading communities came to monastic life after active lives in the secular world and that we may assume a similar lay background for most monks and nuns, such a delight in color and ornamentation, as is paralleled in surviving jewelry in secular graves, should come as no surprise. In the eighth century, there are graver lapses of monastic discipline, specifically of chastity, but by that date the original inspiration of the communities had lapsed with the deaths of the founding abbesses. Further, the ties of the monastic communities with royal houses and the secular world as a whole seems to have had a part in the development of this problem. Boniface's letter to Æthelbald of Mercia rebukes the king for immorality with nuns and novices, whom Boniface calls *loose women*; the letter mentions that the sanctity of monastic communities were respected until the reign of Osred of Northumbria (706–717) and Ceolred of Mercia (709–716), who also indulged in "the seduction of nuns and the contemptuous treatment of monastic rights."[70]

The wealth of communities and the material luxuries of the lives of the residents also seems to have varied, both on the basis of the former secular status of the abbess and on the importance affixed to religious poverty in the community's rule. Communal living was part of the rule at Whitby; according to Bede, all property there was owned in common, "after the example of the primitive church," and there were consequently no distinctions of wealth and poverty in the community.[71] However, the 1867 discovery in the so-called kitchen midden at Whitby of an early Anglo-Saxon bone comb with personalized runic inscription, "My God, may God Almighty help Cy . . ." (Figure 1), suggests that Bede's vision of a communal utopia at Whitby may

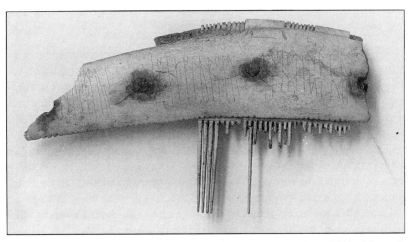

Figure 1. Bone comb with runic inscription from Whitby Abbey (Whitby, Whitby Museum). Photo: Whitby Literary and Philosophical Society (W. Leng). By permission.

not have been accurate, or may have included an element of optimistic hyperbole.[72] Other finds from the site indicate a comparatively luxurious pattern of life. Among early finds, the bone comb with runic inscription, an openwork cast comb (possibly a Frankish import), and an additional fragmentary two-edged bone comb, may well have had liturgical functions.[73] Additional possibly liturgical combs were found in the Office of Works excavation between 1920 and 1928.[74] The hanging bowls probably indicated by fragments found in the same excavation may also have been liturgical rather than secular in function.[75] However, a jet bead and possible fragments of jewelry among the early finds, and the rings, brooches, "chatelaines," pins with ornamented heads, glass beads, and a segment of a glass bracelet found in the Office of Works excavation are certainly personal ornaments.[76] The Office of Works excavation also uncovered toilet articles, including not only tweezers but also ear and nail cleaners common in pagan Anglo-Saxon sites and also with clear Frankish precedents, evidence of a standard of personal hygiene based on both Anglo-Saxon secular and continental practice.[77] Rim fragments of possibly imported glass cups, and six examples of imported Frankish pottery, probably from the Rhineland, suggest both the extent of links to the continent and the comparative standard of living at Whitby.[78] Moreover, not all members of such communities were on an equal footing: in addition to the internal hierarchy of the religious community, there were also servants in the more preeminent Anglo-Saxon monastic houses. At Whitby, Hilda had a reeve and a stable keeper and Ælfflæd had shepherds; and Abbess Æthilhild had servants of both sexes in her community in Mercia.[79]

Learning among women monastics

The level of learning in the convents and double monasteries of early Anglo-Saxon period is difficult to assess with precision and varied considerably within and between communities. Basic literacy was probably imperative for the contemplation of scripture, which was an essential part of the rule at most houses of the period and strongly endorsed by both synods and writers on monastic life, although standards seem to have varied over time and oral repetition and memorization played a significant role as well. The seventh canon of the Synod of Clovesho (747) expressed concern about the level of learning in monasteries, endorsed study of scripture at monastic houses, and exhorted bishops, abbots, and abbesses to work toward its revival and strengthening.[80] The same canon also decreed that *pueri* should be educated in monastic schools so that they might gain a love for sacred knowledge and be useful members of the church; but it neither specifies the extent of this education nor does it indicate whether these young people are novices or members of the laity with no plans for careers in the church. Further, the use of the word *pueri* does not exclude the possibility of women's education in similar "schools."[81] Bede does say that in the seventh century Anglo-Saxon women of rank went to the French monastic communities at Andelys, Chelles, and Faremoutiers "for their education, or to be betrothed to their heavenly bridegroom," which implies that not all went to Francia also took the veil there. The documents, however, do not provide evidence that the Frankish convents contained organized schools nor does Bede mention any of their students who returned to secular life in England. The level of literacy of secular women in early England remains unknown: one wonders if Ethelberga of Northumbria could read the letter sent to her by Pope Boniface.[82]

In England, the double monasteries at Whitby and Barking were important centers of learning in the second half of the seventh century. Whitby is famous for having provided the education of six bishops.[83] Yet the education received by these men at Whitby was not as complete as at least two of them wished; Oftfor and John went on to study at Canterbury, and as Bertram Colgrave suggested, this may have been the norm.[84] Oftfor is said by Bede to have studied primarily reading and the application of scripture at Whitby, and this may have been the whole of the curriculum there; of Hilda's rule, Bede says, "Those under her direction were required to make a thorough study of the Scriptures and occupy themselves in good works."[85] This dictum seems to have applied without consideration of sex. The bookcover mounts and hinge plates found in the Office of Works excavation at Whitby and perhaps also the metal tags tentatively identified by Peers and Radford as bookmarkers also indicate the presence of books, but not their content.[86] The *Life of Gregory the Great*, the only surviving text written at Whitby, by an anonymous writer of the early eighth century, demonstrates a thorough knowledge of scripture.[87] The writer also knew most of the major works of Gregory, albeit such references need not have been a permanent part of the Whitby library; for such special projects it was common to borrow sources from other centers, as was the case for Bede's compilation of the *Historia Ecclesastica*.[88] The Whitby monk's references to Augustine and Jerome suggest some element of patristic literature at Whitby, but whether in the original sources or in anthologies is difficult to determine; his one quotation from Horace is probably from a grammar text.[89] On the other hand, Aldhelm's prose *De Virginitate*, dedicated to Abbess Hildilith and several of the nuns of Barking, indicates that their level of learning was possibly more sophisticated than that of their contemporaries at Whitby: they studied not only scripture but also patristic writings, exegetical literature, history and chronology, grammar, and the rules of Latin poetry.[90] Aldhelm also recommended readings to them including the *Collationes Patrum* of Cassian and the *Moralia in Job* of Gregory the Great.[91] It would be unrealistic and possibly insulting for him to suggest such readings if the nuns at Barking had no access to such works, which suggests the presence of an extensive library, as does their curriculum. Although possibly not on a par with the libraries available to Bede at Jarrow and Wearmouth, the library at Barking was exceptional enough in scale and scope to commend it to Aldhelm.[92] Others did not have access to such resources: Bucge wrote to Boniface that she would send him the martyrology he had requested as soon as possible, but that so far she had not been able to obtain it.[93] Elsewhere a solitary *ex libris* hints at a lost library of unknown scale; an Italian manuscript of Jerome's commentary on Ecclesiastes is inscribed, "Cuthsuuithae. boec. thaerae abbatissan," as owned by Cuthswith, a seventh-century abbess, possibly of Inkberrow.[94]

It is more difficult to ascertain the level of writing ability among religious women in the early Anglo-Saxon period, but again variability is probable. The women whose writings are included in the Bonifacian correspondences certainly demonstrate that they could write as well as read, but they make up in enthusiasm what they lack in grace of style.[95] The imitation by at least two of these writers, Leoba and Berhtgyth, of the style of Aldhelm, however, indicates that they recognized and acknowledged his standards of quality and complexity in prose.[96] The use of quotations to enrich the text and its meaning is as common among women writers as among the men of their age; biblical quotations are naturally the most prominent. Egberga quotes from the *Aeneid* and Jerome's letter to Ruffina; the quotations in a grammar text could have provided her with these fragments.[97] The skill of writing verse was not limited to the studious nuns of Barking; Leoba sent verses to Boniface, claiming to have learned the craft of metrical poetry from Eadberga, and Lul submitted his verses to an unnamed abbess and a nun for their criticism.[98]

Were there organized scriptoria at the double monasteries and convents of England in this period? Again the evidence is uncertain.[99] Boniface writes to Eadberga, abbess of Thanet, to copy out the *Epistles of Peter* for him in letters of gold.[100] Was this volume also to have been illuminated? The book itself does not survive, but we have Boniface's request that it be in gold so "that the Holy Scriptures may be honored and reverenced when the preacher holds them before the eyes of the heathen," and rich ornament would certainly be more convincing for the illiterate than golden words alone.[101] This passage, however, may refer to a single scribe or illuminator working in comparative isolation, as might early documentary evidence elsewhere.[102] The earliest scriptorium demonstrably including women as scribes was at Chelles under the abbacy of Gisla, where a consortium of at least nine nuns worked as scribes, probably in a mixed scriptorium; their surviving manuscripts are not illuminated.[103] For manuscripts illuminated by nuns, our earliest certain example is the Spanish *Gerona Apocalypse* (Gerona Cathedral), dated 975 and illuminated at least in part by the nun En or Ende, who appears as "En depintrix et Dei aiutrix," in the colophon at the end of the codex.[104]

The archaeological evidence of writing at women's convents and double houses in England in the early Anglo-Saxon period comes exclusively from excavated sites and therefore probably does not afford a complete picture of the historical situation. Whitby is the richest source of evidence. Among recorded early finds that do not survive, Andrew White lists a curved horn nine inches in length and divided into two compartments, which would have been inconvenient as a drinking vessel but useful as a well for ink of differing colors.[105] The 1920–25 Office of Works excavation turned up five bronze styli and the head of a sixth.[106] Sir Charles Peers and C. A. R. Radford, in their much delayed 1943 report of that excavation, noted that styli are not common on Saxon sites; only two were found at the pre-Conquest levels of St. Augustine's, Canterbury, and one at Blythburgh.[107] However, this evidence may be skewed by factors of survival and selective excavation; it does not necessarily indicate that more people were writing at Whitby than elsewhere. Styli were used not so much in the production of manuscripts as in the use of waxed tablets for learning letter forms and taking notes for various purposes; they do not constitute evidence of the presence of a scriptorium. Rosemary Cramp's very welcome attempt to reconstruct the sites of the small finds at Whitby based on the finds register of the 1920–25 excavation has placed some of the styli in the same spaces, sections 5, 6, 7, 9, and 11, and Building G, with loom weights, needles, and other evidence of primarily feminine domestic activities.[108] However, in both sections 5 and 7, the styli and the decidedly feminine domestic implements are on different levels. In sections 6 and 11, spindle whorls and styli occur in the same level, and in Building G two styli share the lower level with dress fastenings and eighteen loom weights, but even here the evidence cannot determine if the same gender component of the monastic population necessarily used both the styli and the domestic implements, as a level may represent several years if not decades of use of the structures, possibly for a series of functions. Thus even the rich evidence from Whitby cannot lead to unambivalent conclusions of book production by the female residents.[109]

The Monastic Community as Physical Setting

What of the architectural settings in which these activities were pursued? The documents give some sense of the buildings and other elements of the monastic environment. The monastic communities of the period, regardless of their scale or the gender of their occupants, seem to have been consistently surrounded by a barrier, a *vallum monasterii*, which was more a symbol of the enclosure of the inhabitants and their separation from the secular world than a defensive outworks.[110] The material seems to have varied: according to Rudolf's *Life of Leoba*, Wimbourne, with its strict laws of enclosure, had a high stone wall.[111] Internal subdivisions sometimes took the form of a physical partition: at Æthelhild's monastery, the women's house was enclosed and separated from the men's residence by a gate, presumably set in a wall or fence.[112] Strict separation of residences by sex was also in effect at Barking under Æthelburh, and presumably also at the other double houses. Within the communities, a monastic church would normally provide a spiritual if not a spatial focal point.[113] In the communities described in the documents, there were both communal buildings and more private ones. In the women's part of the community at Barking, there were both a communal dormitory for the sisters and individual *cubiculi* or residential cells for the aged and infirm nuns; an arrangement paralleled at Brie, where Earcongota visited each of the cells on the day of her death.[114] At Coldingham, according to Rosemary Cramp's insightful interpretation of Bede's description, there were probably both communal dormitories and private cells used for reading and meditation, called *domunculae*, or "little houses."[115] Hackness too had a communal dormitory.[116] Whitby had a house for postulants in the "remotest corner of the monastery" and an infirmary.[117] Refectories were presumably communal, as were buildings used for crafts requiring considerable space, such as weaving. A guesthouse is mentioned at Barking, outside both the women's and the men's residential precincts. Cemeteries were also provided: at Barking, where the church was apparently shared by the monks and nuns, the use of the two early cemeteries was segregated by sex until overcrowding forced translation from both into a communal ossuary in the church.[118]

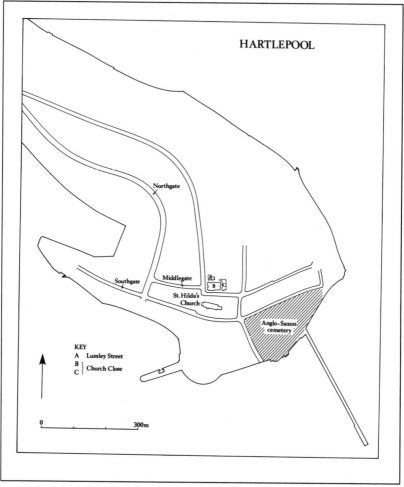

Figure 2. Hartlepool: "Map showing the location of the Lumley Street excavation (A) and the Church Close excavations (B, C);" from Rosemary Cramp and Robin Daniels, "New Finds from the Anglo-Saxon Monastery at Hartlepool, Cleveland," *Antiquity* 61 (1987): 425, Fig. 1. Used by permission of Robin Daniels and Oxford University Press.

Excavations have revealed the layout of several early monastic sites, including Hartlepool and Whitby. Hartlepool occupies a headland which was severed from the rest of the mainland in the medieval period by a wall and a ditch (Figure 2). Excavations by the Department of Archaeology of Durham University near Lumley Street in 1968 and by the Cleveland County Archaeology Section in 1984–85 revealed the remains of twenty-three or twenty-four timber buildings constructed in two methods, trench or slot

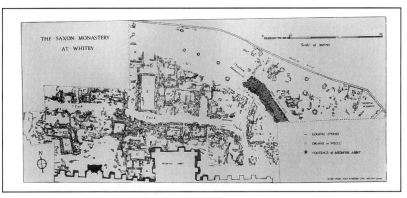

Figure 3. Redrawn plan of Whitby Abbey. From Rosemary Cramp and Philip Rahtz *The Archaeology of Anglo-Saxon England*, ed. David Wilson (London, 1976), Figure 5.7. Used by permission of Methuen and Co., London.

construction and individual-post construction; gabled roofs are inferred. The 1984–85 finds included ten complete structures, with three plan types: simple rectangular buildings, buildings with internal partitions creating a larger room and a smaller room, and a single longer building consisting of two distinct units. There were no indications of hearths. The settlement was largely enclosed by a boundary of posts, superseded by a palisade trench, but buildings occur outside this perimeter. The relative date, and consequently the possible interpretation of these buildings, awaits radiocarbon analysis.[119]

At Whitby, the 1920–25 Office of Works excavation has been reexamined by Rosemary Cramp and Philip Rahtz (Figure 3).[120] The Anglian monastery is overlain by the remains of the medieval church. Here, as at Hartlepool, the *vallum monasterii* has been tentatively identified, but if this is an accurate determination, there are many extramural structures that may predate or postdate the use of the site by the monastic community. The remains of buildings here were of stone, with walls ordinarily two feet thick, set on packed clay foundations. Some of the buildings had internal partitions; the roofs were most probably thatched. There were also remains of wattle and daub, which were believed by Peers and Radford to have been part of the internal partitions of buildings; Rahtz has made the interesting suggestion that these may represent an earlier phase of construction on the site.[121] Bede does not specify whether Hilda founded the monastery at Whitby or whether she took over a preexisting community; if the latter is the case, then Rahtz's theory may support the chronology of successive settlements on the site. The use of stone at Whitby, as opposed to the timber construction observed at Hartlepool, suggests the impact of Hilda's, and her successors Eanflæd's and

Figure 4. Hackness, St. Peter's Church, chancel arch impost: relief of zoomorphic interlace. Photo: Department of Archaeology, University of Durham. Used by permission.

Ælfflæd's, royal connections, in terms both of comparative wealth and the continental taste for stone construction manifested here.

Two structures at Whitby were subdivided with a living space and hearth in one half and a bedroom and lavatory in the other half, suggesting a private bed-sitter arrangement for the abbess and possibly for the prioress or for a royal ward or retiree at the monastic community. Similar partitioning is found in presumably residential buildings at Jarrow and is echoed in the partitioned wooden structures at Hartlepool, suggesting a similar standard of living and possibly the use of a common model or the copying of the forms of one of these monastic centers by the others.[122] As the internal chronology of all three sites is as yet indeterminate, relative chronology among the sites remains obscure. However, the evidence seems to indicate a fairly elegant living arrangement by early medieval standards for the superiors in monastic communities, and the use of mainstream building types regardless of the gender of superior or community; as far as building types are concerned, Anglo-Saxon women monastics were clearly not excluded from currents of architectural development, neither in terms of access to design or media of construction nor in terms of financial means.

The buildings excavated at Whitby to the north of the medieval church are small; Cramp has suggested that these may be *domunculae* as at

Coldingham and that the larger communal buildings may have been located to the south of the medieval church, where foundations were noted by Peers and Radford.[123] One might also suggest that the foundations of the monastic church are probably under those of the medieval church, according to the medieval tradition of rebuilding churches on the sites of their predecessors.

Fragments of architectural remains of early churches survive at Hackness and at Hart, associated by H. M. Taylor and Joan Taylor with the early monastery at Hartlepool. St. Peter at Hackness preserves an early chancel arch with an impost carved with zoomorphic interlace (Figure 4) in a style typical of the second half of the eighth century and three of the side-alternate quoins of the nave.[124] These are all that remains of the two pre-Conquest churches associated with the site of the monastery at Hackness, founded by Hilda in 680 as a cell of Whitby. St. Mary Magdalene at Hart retains similar vestiges of Anglian construction: four original nave quoins; the head of the early chancel arch above the wider Norman arch, with a triangular-headed doorway above it; and fragments of carved stones, including two probably lathe-turned baluster shafts and a sundial (Figures 5–8). The presence of baluster shafts links this church to those at Jarrow and Monkwearmouth, albeit the technology of baluster turning differs between Hart and Jarrow-Monkwearmouth, suggesting different workshops but similar, probably continental models.[125]

The connections demonstrated by the architectural ornament at Hackness and Hart indicate, as might be expected, that the royal double monasteries and their dependencies had a broad range of connections within the art-producing world of the early Northumbrian monastic establishments and were able to command the highest available level of craftsmanship of their day. These standards are borne out by an examination of sculptural remains from Whitby, Hartlepool, and Hackness and by evidence of metalworking from Hartlepool. From Whitby, the Peers and Radford site report includes a reused stone slab (slab no. 1) with an early incised cross on one side and an elegant quadruped and vegetal motif framed by a double pearl border on the other (Figure 9).[126] The slab may have been used as part of a tomb shrine, as Peers and Radford suggest, or equally possibly as part of a screen or some other aspect of the architectural ornament of a church. The numerous plain and inscribed funerary cross slabs from Whitby and the grave slabs from Hartlepool (Figure 10) generically resemble stones found at Monkwearmouth (Figure 11), Lindisfarne, and elsewhere.[127] Local idiom prevails in the configuration and ornamentation of these slabs and in variations in their usage, notably at Hartlepool where it is possible that the stones were found in rather than above the graves.[128] The usage of incised cross slabs in funerary contexts is a common practice in Northumbrian monasteries, not excluding double houses.[129] Again, given the range of contacts among major monastic

Figure 5. Hart, part of a cross shaft (Hart, St. Mary Magdalene; west end of nave). Photo: Department of Archaeology, University of Durham. Used by permission.

communities in the region and period, this similarity of basic forms is not surprising.

Similarly the Hackness Cross, associated with the cell of Whitby at Hackness, shows many parallels with regionally well-established forms.[130] Two fragments of the shaft of this cross are preserved in the church of St. Peter at Hackness. The upper fragment is in better condition: its upper west

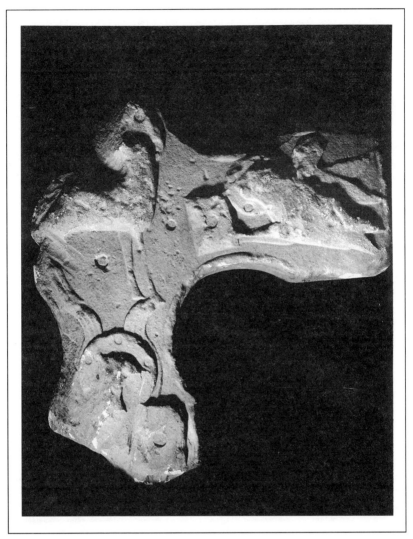

Figure 6. Hart, incomplete cross head (Hart, St. Mary Magdalene; near pulpit). Photo: Department of Archaeology, University of Durham. Used by permission.

face (Figure 12) displays a well-preserved two-volute simple scroll with ridged nodes, long triangular berry bunches, and double scooped drop leaves. These fill a square-molded panel, above a fragmentary panel containing a badly abraded head. The east face of the upper block preserves a three-knot example of type-B simple-pattern interlace.[131] The west face of the lower slab (Figure 13) includes the lower part of a panel containing two confronted

Figure 7. Hart, fragment of baluster shaft (Hart, St. Mary Magdalene; west end of nave).
Photo: Department of Archaeology, University of Durham. Used by permission.

quadrupeds. The division of the cross into square-molded panels is not uncommon, and the figural and ornamental motifs that fill them are neither
unusual nor significantly higher or lower in quality of execution than other
Northumbrian crosses of the second half of the eighth and first half of the
ninth century.[132]

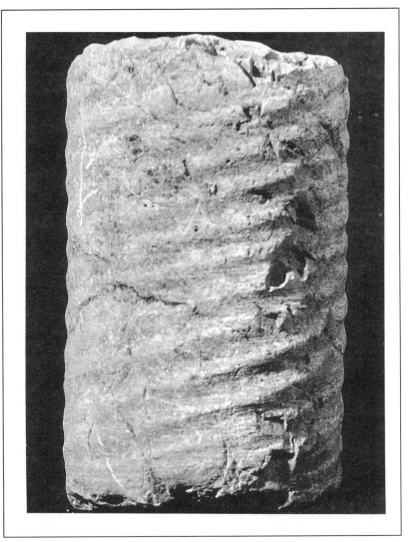

Figure 8. Hart, fragment of column or baluster shaft (Hart, St. Mary Magdalene; west end of nave). Photo: Department of Archaeology, University of Durham. Used by permission.

No aspect of the art produced for double houses and women's religious communities in the early Anglo-Saxon setting truly distinguishes it from the art produced for other monastic centers of the same cultural milieu. Indeed, the recent discovery of metalworking equipment in the debris fill in the boundary trench at Hartlepool confirms the links between Hilda's foundations and communities elsewhere. Molds found at the site

Figure 9. Whitby, slab no. 1. Photo: From Sir Charles Peers and C. A. Ralegh Radford, "The Saxon Monastery of Whitby," *Archaeologia* 89 (1943), pl. 20b. Used by permission of the Society of Antiquaries, London.

included three with decoration, of which one showed a calf with a trumpet in its mouth (Figure 14). The trumpetting calf may well be linked to the apocalyptic series of evangelist symbols with trumpets reflected in the evangelist portrait sequence in the Lindisfarne Gospels (Figure 15).[133]

In considering the evidence of work in stone and metal at the double monasteries, we are most probably looking at the work of male monastics and lay craftsmen affiliated with the monasteries, whether for the duration of a particular project or for a lifetime, rather than at the handiwork of royal monastic women themselves. On the other hand, references to textile work, especially embroidery, in the *vitae* of the early-eighth-century saints Harlindis and Relindis, as well as the repeated references to the weaving and ornamentation of textiles in the correspondence of Boniface with and about his female contemporaries, suggests a tradition of such handcraft among the leading women monastics of the period.[134] The two surviving pieces of late eighth- or early-ninth-century embroidery at Maaseik are our only richly ornamented fragments that may arguably be linked to the early Anglo-Saxon period; all other examples are substantially later.[135] Nor do we have substantial evidence for production of liturgical cloths by lay women of the period, although there is no evidence to suggest that they did not also embroider cloths for the church as well as for secular use.[136]

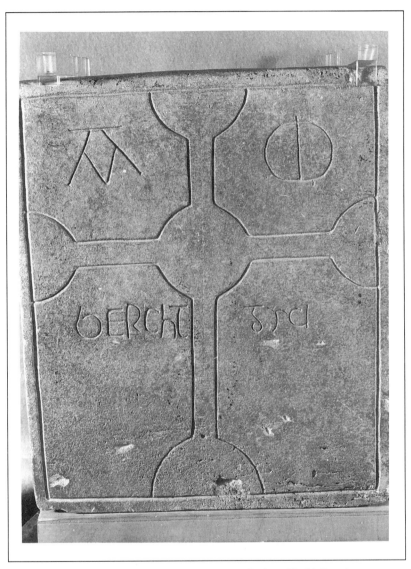

Figure 10. Hartlepool, recumbent grave marker or cover, (Durham, Monk's Dormitory, no. XXVIII). Photo: Dean and Chapter of Durham. Used by permission.

The lives and contributions of the Anglo-Saxon royal women monastics may in all be said to be part of the broader context of Anglo-Saxon religious life. Because of their original context and continuing contacts, the royal women monastics lived in a liminal context, between court and church. Because of these unusual circumstances, their lives and customs, as demonstrated by the

Figure 11. Monkwearmouth, grave marker or cover, (Monkwearmouth, St. Peter; showcase, north aisle). Photo: Department of Archaeology, University of Durham. Used by permission.

documentary and archaeological evidence, find close parallels both in the monastic communities of their male contemporaries and in the lives of their female relatives at court. Because the particular dynamics of the relationship of court and convent, the Anglo-Saxon royal women monastics found themselves in a position, like that of their secular female relatives, in which they could be profoundly involved and influential in the events and developments

Figure 12. Hackness, upper cross shaft fragment, upper west face: two-volute scroll and head of a figure. Photo: Department of Archaeology, University of Durham. Used by permission.

of their day. Far from being isolated by their spirituality, it became their passport to a level of power parallel to if not higher than that of their queenly cousins. In this equation their membership by birth in the aristocracy of the period played a critical role.[137]

The heyday of Anglo-Saxon royal abbesses was shortlived. The usefulness of double houses was closely tied to the needs of the conversion period;

Figure 13. Hackness, lower cross shaft fragment, west face: confronted quadrupeds. Photo: Department of Archaeology, University of Durham. Used by permission.

once that period was over, these foundations went into gradual decline. Some double houses may have gradually become women's communities; in Bede's *Life of Cuthbert* (Chapter 23) Ælffæd is seens as ruling a women's community at Whitby.[138] Other originally double communities were destroyed in the Viking invasions; those that were later refounded took the form of single-sex communities. Very few double houses persisted into the tenth century.[139]

The institutional church was not opposed to this decline; the double monastery was a heterodox regional institution within which royal abbesses were privileged to operate with minimum episcopal direction. By the middle of the eighth century two major trends made churchmen less disposed to accept these abbesses' self-direction, mobility, and involvement in regional politics: the increasing centralization of spiritual and institutional authority in the hands of bishops and the movement toward strict active enclosure of female monastics, concurrently gaining momentum on the continent.[140] Further, clerics began to look with increasing disfavor on the pastoral role of abbesses in regard to neighboring lay communities. By mid-century there was a sufficient number of trained and ordained clergy in England that sacerdotal alterization and elitism could be logistically supported.[141] Stephanie Hollis

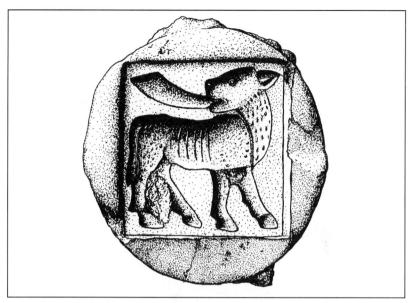

Figure 14. Hartlepool, "Mould 2: the Apocalyptic animal"; from Rosemary Cramp and Robin Daniels, "New Finds from the Anglo-Saxon Monastery at Hartlepool, Cleveland," *Antiquity* 61 (1987): 430, 7b. Used by permission of Robin Daniels and Oxford University Press.

has suggested an active campaign of suppression of the history of the accomplishments of the royal abbesses in Bede's *Historia Ecclesiastica* and in his prose revision of the *Life of Cuthbert.* In other cases, *vitae* of the abbesses composed within their communities may have been allowed to slip into oblivion with their communities.[142]

Toward a Contextual Methodology

A discussion of the documentary and archaeological evidence concerning the physical and cultural setting of early royal women monastics may seem out of place in a volume on Old English prose saints' lives, particularly for scholars for whom the lives themselves have been a primary focus of investigation. Further, the documentary sources adduced here have been the early Latin sources rather than the later Old English ones, where contextual evidence may well have been adjusted to fit an updated view of monastic life. In the exploration of the cult of saints in early medieval England, the broader area of inquiry in which this volume of studies belongs, there is nonetheless a need for the consideration of both texts and contexts. At the same time

Figure 15. London, British Library Cotton MS Nero D IV, f. 93v; *The Lindisfarne Gospels; Evangelist Portrait of Mark.* Photo: By permission of the British Library.

these approaches can be mutually supportive. The surviving evidence from pre-Viking England is so fragmentary that data from different lines of inquiry should optimally be coordinated and cross-checked to provide a relatively consistent view of the period. I do not propose a monolithic view of history, but suggest that the scarce, scattered, and often hotly debated remains of the past may make better sense if they are periodically considered across modern disciplinary fences.

Contextual methodology has recently come under fire in Anglo-Saxon studies with regard to the study of archaeology in conjunction with the Old

English poetic record. In her recent article, *"Beowulf* and Sutton Hoo: The Odd Couple,"* Roberta Frank documents the cumulative comedy (or tragedy) of errors that has resulted from successive attempts to read the poem and the ship burial in a one-to-one source-site equation as reflective of the cultural experience.[143] Frank suggests that *Beowulf* and Sutton Hoo be allowed a "creative divorce." Nonetheless, studying texts and sites in complete mutual isolation would be an excessive response to such criticism; after all, in "creative divorce," communication can and often does continue. However, instead of building one-to-one correspondences between texts and sites of objects, as such hypotheses are all too subject to the changing interpretation of their individual components, a less specific approach may be more consistently useful, seeking repeated patterns of evidence in the textual and archaeological source material.[144] A case in point is the relevancy of archaeological finds possibly reflecting writing by women in Anglo-Saxon England, presented in part in the present chapter, to current studies of women's production of texts in the same cultural environment.[145] The potential of archaeology and text study to broaden each other's range of understanding deserves reconsideration. This chapter is an attempt to leave the lines of communication open as regards the cult of saints in early Anglo-Saxon England.

Notes

1. My thanks are due to Hilda Wick, Rare Books Consultant, Beeghly Library, Ohio Wesleyan University, for the opportunity to read her unpublished article on Hilda of Whitby, which immensely facilitiated my own survey of the literature. I also thank Laurie Churchill, Ohio Wesleyan University, and Thomas Ohlgren, Purdue University, for the opportunity to present segments of this chapter, respectively, in the New Women Faculty lecture series at Ohio Wesleyan University and in the eighth symposium on the Sources of Anglo-Saxon Culture at the 25th International Congress on Medieval Studies at Western Michigan University, Kalamazoo.

2. Bede on Æthelburh of Barking, *HE* IV.7–10, pp. 356–65; on Ætheldreda, *HE* IV.19, pp. 390–97; on Hilda, *HE* IV.23–24, pp. 404–21. See also Bertram Colgrave, *The Life of Bishop Wilfrid by Eddius Stephanus* (1927; reprinted Cambridge, 1985), hereafter cited as Eddius, *Life of Bishop Wilfrid*; Bede, *Prose Life of Saint Cuthbert*, in Bertram Colgrave, *Two Lives of St. Cuthbert* (1940, reprinted Cambridge, 1985), hereafter cited as Bede, *Prose Life of St. Cuthbert*; Edward Kylie, *The English Correspondence of Saint Boniface* (London, 1924); P. H. Külb, *Sämmtliche Schriften des heiligen Bonifacius, des Apostels der Deutschen* (Regensburg, 1859); and "The Correspondences of Saint Boniface," in C. H. Talbot, ed. and trans., *The Anglo-Saxon Missionaries in Germany* (London, 1954), hereafter cited as Talbot, "Correspondences of St. Boniface." See also J. E. Cross, "A Lost Life of Hilda of Whitby: The Evidence of the *Old English Martyrology*," in William H. Snyder, ed., *The Early Middle Ages*, *Acta* 6 (1982 for 1979): 21–43.

3. Wilfrid was of noble family; his parents hosted the royal entourage (Eddius, *Life of Bishop Wilfrid,* ch. 2, pp. 4–7). Guthlac was of a collateral line of the royal house of Mercia and leader of a warband (Bertram Colgrave, *Felix's Life of Saint Guthlac* [1956, reprinted Cambridge, 1985], hereafter cited as Felix, *Life of St. Guthlac,* ch. 2, pp. 74–75; ch. 17, pp. 80–81. Benedict Biscop and Ceolfrith were both members of noble families, and Benedict served in the warband of King Oswy of Northumbria; see Bede, *Lives of the Abbots,* ch. 1, and *The Anonymous Life of Ceolfrith, Abbot of Jarrow,* ch. 2, in Clinton Albertson, *Anglo-Saxon Saints and Heroes* (New York, 1967), pp. 225–26, 247.

4. Lina Eckenstein, *Women Under Monasticism* (New York, 1963), pp. 79–80. A survey of the 48 Anglo-Saxon female saints in David H. Farmer, *The Oxford Dictionary of Saints,* 2d. ed. (Oxford and New York, 1987), reveals that twenty-nine are known to be royal, six are possibly royal, two are noble or wealthy, two are nonroyal but associated with royal foundations, one is nonroyal with no royal associations, and eight are nonroyal but obscure and in some cases historically questionable.

5. Michael Enright, "Lady with a Mead Cup: Ritual Group Cohesion and Hierarchy in the Germanic Warband," *Frühmittelalterliche Studien* 22 (1988):195.

6. Bede, *HE* III.24, pp. 290–93.

7. Eckenstein, *Women Under Monasticism,* p. 106.

8. Susan Ridyard, *The Royal Saints of Anglo-Saxon England: A Study of West Saxon and East Anglian Cults* (Cambridge, 1988), pp. 74–79, 82–92; cf. William Chaney, *The Cult of Kingship in Anglo-Saxon England: The Transition from Paganism to Christianity* (Manchester, 1970), p. 81.

9. Margaret Deanesly, *The Pre-Conquest Church in England* (London, 1961) pp. 199–207.

10. Bede, *HE* IV.23, pp. 408–11.

11. Deanesly, *The Pre-Conquest Church,* p. 200; Enright, "Lady with a Mead Cup," pp. 192–98.

12. Eckenstein, *Women Under Monasticism,* p. 81. Stephanie Hollis, *Anglo-Saxon Women and the Church: Sharing a Common Fate* (Woodbridge, England and Rochester, N.Y., 1992), p. 80, suggests that going into monastic orders was often a widow's means to protect her inheritance; she cites evidence from Anglo-Saxon law codes indicating that a widow often enountered hostility from her husband's relatives over inherited property.

13. Frank M. Stenton, "The Historic Bearing of Place-Name Studies: The Place of Women in Anglo-Saxon Society," *Transactions of the Royal Historical Society* 4th ser., 25 (1943): 1–13; Christine Fell et al., *Women in Anglo-Saxon England and the Impact of 1066* (Bloomington, Ind. 1984), pp. 95–100. The evidence of wills is mostly tenth century or later.

14. Enright, "Lady with a Mead Cup," pp. 170–203; Larry H. Sklute, "*Freoðuwebbe* in Old English Poetry," *Neuphilologische Mitteilungen* 71 (1970): 534–41. I have avoided the use of the term *freoðuwebbe* for the diplomatic role of women in the Anglo-Saxon secular world because, as Kelley Wickham-Crowley has recently pointed out, the use of the term is rare and exclusively literary: "Archaeology, Weaving and Women in the Anglo-Saxon World," Session 38, Twenty-fifth International Congress on Medieval Studies, Western Michigan University, Kalamazoo, 1990.

15. Setsuko Haruta, "The Women in *Beowulf*," *Poetica* 23 (1986): 1–15.

16. *Beowulf* 624a, 1927a (Haruta, ibid., p. 5).

17. The controversy concerning the date of *Beowulf* has expanded radically in the last decade; for an introduction to major issues, see Colin Chase, ed., *The Dating of Beowulf*, Toronto Old English Series, 6 (Toronto, 1981).

18. Bede, *HE* I.25–26, pp. 72–79; II.9, pp. 162–67; II.11, pp. 172–75; IV.13, pp. 370–73. On the commercial inducements to such marriages, see A. Lohaus, *Die Merovinger und England*, Münchener Beiträge zur Mediävistik und Renaissance-Forschung 19 (Munich, 1974), pp. 26–27.

19. Bede, *HE* II.11, pp. 180–81; II.12, pp. 190–91.

20. Bede, *HE* III.25, pp. 296–97.

21. Bede, *HE* IV.11, pp. 364–67.

22. Eddius, *Life of Bishop Wilfrid*, ch. 24, pp. 48–49; ch. 40, pp. 80–81; and Hollis, *Anglo-Saxon Women*, pp. 208–42.

23. Bede, *HE* III.25, pp. 298–99; IV.23, pp. 408–9, and see also Hollis, ibid., p. 181, who implies that Hilda's silence at Whitby in *HE* III.25 is a reflection of Bede's opinion of the proper role of monastic women rather than a historical fact.

24. Eddius, *Life of Bishop Wilfrid*, ch. 39, pp. 78–79.

25. Ibid., chs. 59–60, pp. 126–33. See also Janet L. Nelson, "Women and the Word in the Earlier Middle Ages," in W. J. Shiels and Diana Wood, eds., *Women in the Church* (Oxford and Cambridge, Mass., 1990), p. 65. Nelson makes the important point that the role of abbesses at court and synod was not ex officio but rather the result of their personal royal connections.

26. Theodore, *Poenitentiale*, VI.8, in A. W. Haddan and W. Stubbs, *Councils and Ecclesiastical Documents Relating to Great Britain and Ireland* (1871, reprinted Oxford, 1964), vol. 3, p. 195.

27. P. Stephanus Hilpisch, *Die Doppelklöster; Entstehung und Organisation* (Münster in Westphalia, 1928), pp. 44–46. For an overview of the history of the double monastery, see Hilpisch, ibid., pp. 1–87; and Friedrich Prinz, *Frühes Mönchtum im Frankenreich* (Munich and Vienna, 1965), passim.

28. Prinz, ibid., pp. 142, 170, 182, 186. See also Michel Parisse, *Les nonnes au Moyen Age*, ed. Christine Bonneton (Le Puy, France, 1983); Suzanne F. Wemple, *Women in Frankish Society: Marriage and the Cloister* (Philadelphia, 1985), pp. 158–65.

29. Prinz, ibid., pp. 81, 142–43.

30. Ibid., p. 145.

31. Ibid., pp. 175, 179. Although Chelles may not have been a double house from the moment of its foundation by Queen Balthildis in the seventh century, as revealed by careful analysis of the early anonymous *vita* of Balthildis, it was certainly double by the second half of the eighth century, at the time of the composition of the *Vita s. Bertilae*. See Suzanne F. Wemple, "Female Spirituality and Mysticism in Frankish Monasteries: Radegund, Balthild and Aldegund," *Medieval Religious Women*, vol. 2, *Peaceweavers*, ed. John A. Nichols and Lillian Thomas Shank (Kalamazoo, Mich., 1987), pp. 42–43. At what point Chelles became double certainly has a bearing on the extent of its influence on the development of the double monasteries of England, but the not uncommon institution of double houses on the continent is fairly certain, and thus an available model for Anglo-Saxon foundations.

32. Prinz, ibid., pp. 169, 182.

33. Ibid., pp. 174–75.

34. Ibid., pp. 143, 174.

35. Ibid., p. 186.

36. Ibid., p. 142.

37. Bede, *HE* III.8, pp. 236–39.

38. Eckenstein, *Women Under Monasticism*, pp. 199–200; Bede, *HE* IV.23, pp. 406–7; Christine E. Fell, "Hild, Abbess of Streonaeshalch, in Hagiography and Medieval Literature," *Proceedings of the Fifth International Symposium of the Center for the Study of Vernacular Literature in the Middle Ages*, ed. P. Foote, J. H. Jorgensen, and T. Nyberg (Odense, Denmark, 1981), p. 82; S. E. Rigold, "The 'Double Minsters' of Kent and Their Analogies," *Journal of the British Archaeological Association*, 3rd ser., 31 (1968): 31.

39. Lohaus, *Die Merovinger*, pp. 26–27. See W. Levison, *England and the Continent in the Eighth Century* (Oxford, 1943) for an overview of channel trade in the Middle Ages.

40. Bede, *HE* IV.23, 406–7; and see note 31.

41. Rigold, "The 'Double Ministers'," p. 31; Bede, *HE* III.11, 246–47; Fell, "Hild, Abbess of Streonaeshalch," p. 83, on the identity of "Hacanos" and Hackness; A. Hamilton Thompson, "The Monastic Settlement at Hackness and Its Relation to the Abbey of Whitby," *Yorkshire Archaeological Journal* 27 (1924): 389.

42. Eckenstein, *Women Under Monasticism*, p. 108 on Repton; Bede, *HE* V.3, pp. 460–61 on Watton.

43. Haddan and Stubbs, *Councils*, vol. 3, p. 195. "It is not permitted for women religious to have men [among them], nor for the men [to have among them] women; nonetheless we will not dismantle what is customary in this province."

44. Bede, *HE* IV.6, pp. 354–57.

45. Bede, *HE* IV.23, pp. 406–07.

46. Eckenstein, *Women Under Monasticism*, p. 117.

47. "*The Life of Saint Leoba* by Rudolf, Monk of Fulda," in C. H. Talbot, *The Anglo-Saxon Missionaries to Germany* (London, 1954), p. 20; hereafter cited as Rudolf, *Life of St. Leoba.*

48. Jane T. Schulenberg, "Strict Active Enclosure and Its Effects on the Female Monastic Experience (ca. 500–1000)," *Medieval Religious Women*, vol. 1, *Distant Echoes*, ed. J. A. Nichols and L. T. Shank, Cistercian Religious Studies Series 71 (Kalamazoo, Mich., 1984), pp. 54–55, 59–60.

49. Joan Nicholson, "*Feminae gloriosae*: Women in the age of Bede," *Medieval Women*, ed. D. Baker (Oxford, 1978), p. 19, and see also Hollis, *Anglo-Saxon Women*, p. 272.

50. Bede, *HE* IV.7, pp. 356–59.

51. Bede, *HE* IV.8, pp. 358–59.

52. Bede, *HE* III.25, pp. 298–99; IV.24, pp. 416–19; IV.23–24, pp. 412–19.

53. Bede, *HE* III.11, pp. 248–49.

54. Kylie, *The English Correspondence*, no. 8, pp. 61–67.

55. Ibid., no. 9, p. 69.

56. Ibid., no. 38, pp. 154–55.

57. Ibid., no. 42, p. 188; Haddan and Stubbs, *Councils*, vol. 3, p. 381. Hollis, *Anglo-Saxon Women*, pp. 71, 115, 149–50, has pointed out that Boniface's letter to the Archbishop of Canterbury comes at the end of his career, when he had become a spokeman for the continental reform movement with its "elitist conception of ecclesiastical office and a hostile and derogatory attitude towards women" (p. 115), but that like Bede (p. 269), Boniface was inclined to be more conciliatory with regard to women whom he knew personally and particularly toward upper-class women (p. 71).

58. Külb, *Sämmtliche Schriften*, no. 166, pp. 410–12.

59. Bede, *HE*, IV.23, pp. 408–9.

60. Bede, *Prose Life of St. Cuthbert*, ch. 10, pp. 188–89; ch. 15, pp. 264–65.

61. Ibid., ch. 24, pp. 234–39; ch. 34, pp. 260–65, and see also Hollis, *Anglo-Saxon Women*, pp. 121–23, 185–207.

62. Bede, ibid., ch. 23, pp. 230–35. Hollis has suggested that gifts involving personal objects conveyed from a sainted bishop to an abbess are a hagiographic *topos* symbolically identifying the bishop with Christ and the abbess with Mary/Ecclesia as recipient and guardian of relics.

63. Bede, ibid., ch. 37, pp. 272–73. Reginald of Durham describes a sheet of linen enshrouding the body of St. Cuthbert at the 1104 translation, but he may have been mistaken in identifying it as the original textile presented by Verca; see C.F. Battiscombe, "Historical Introduction," in *The Relics of St. Cuthbert*, ed. C. F. Battiscombe (Oxford, 1956), pp. 23–24.

64. Felix, *Life of St. Guthlac*, ch. 48, pp. 146–49.

65. Kylie, *The English Correspondence*, no. 4, p. 50; no. 9, p. 69; no. 14, pp. 90–91; no. 15, p. 92; no. 18, pp. 110–11; Thomas Allison, *English Religious Life in the Eighth Century* (London, 1971), pp. 108–9.

66. Rudolf, *Life of St. Leoba*, p. 224. Hollis, *Anglo-Saxon Women*, pp. 71, 113, 130–43, 283–97, sees the spiritual love or *caritas* of early Anglo-Saxon monasticism in general and the Bonifatian circle in particular as analogous to and in some respects a replacement for the kinship groups of secular society.

67. Bede, *HE* IV.25, pp. 420–27. Hollis, ibid., pp. 101–2, reads Bede's report of the Coldingham scandal as a warning against the double monastery as institution and as a promotion of strict, active enclosure of women monastics.

68. Aldhelm, *De Virginitate*, ch. 58, in Michael Lapidge and Michael Herren, *Aldhelm; The Prose Works* (Cambridge and Totowa, N.J., 1979), hereafter cited as Aldhelm, *De Virginitate*, pp. 127–28; Haddan and Stubbs, *Councils*, vol. 3, pp. 368–69, 376–83. Note also the gold thread fragments found at Barking Abbey, which, as Leslie Webster has observed, may have come from a personal garment or from an eccclesiastical vestment; see Leslie Webster and Janet Backhouse, eds., *The Making of England: Anglo-Saxon Art and Culture A.D. 600–900* (London, 1991), pl. 67a, 88–89. Hollis, ibid., pp. 98–107, points out that the warning in Aldhelm's *De Virginitate* against self-adornment is a much-repeated *topos* originating with St. Paul that alludes to woman as temptress. Hollis, ibid., pp. 99–100, also suggests that Aldhelm realized that the nuns of Barking, to whom he directed his treatise, were not guilty of self-adornment, but that he felt obliged to preach on a topic appropriate to an upper-class female audience; but the archaeological evidence is ambiguous on this point.

69. Colin Chase, ed., *Two Alcuin Letter-Books from British Museum Ms. Cotton Vespasian A XIV* (Toronto, 1975), pp. 51, 55.

70. Talbot, "Correspondences of St. Boniface," no. 32, pp. 120–26; Enright, "Lady with a Mead Cup," p. 197, on claiming territory through the possession of women, including nuns. See also Hollis, *Anglo-Saxon Women*, p. 97.

71. Bede, *HE* IV.23, pp. 408–9.

72. Andrew White, "Finds from the Anglian Monastery at Whitby," *The Yorkshire Archaeological Journal* 56 (1984): 33–40.

73. Ibid., p. 38.

74. C. Peers and C. A. R. Radford, "The Saxon Monastery at Whitby," *Archaeologia* 89 (1943): 70–71; nos. 105–6.

75. Ibid., pp. 47–50; nos. 1–11.

76. Ibid., pp. 58–61, 63–64, 73; nos. 49–65, 76–79, 102–24; White, "Finds," pp. 37, 39; nos. 2, 4, 13.

77. Peers and Radford, ibid., pp. 61–63; nos. 66–75.

78. Ibid., pp. 72–73; nos. 125–26; G. C. Dunning, "The Pottery," in ibid., pp. 80–82; nos. 27–32. Of the Whitby pottery designated "continental" by Dunning, some has been more recently reconsidered as insular in production. See J. Hurst, "The Pottery," in D. M. Wilson, *The Archaeology of Anglo-Saxon England* (London, 1976), pp. 283–348. A significant portion of the Whitby pottery, however, remains continental in accepted provenance; Rosemary J. Cramp, "A Reconsideration of the Monastic Site of Whitby," in R. Michael Spearman and John Higgitt, eds., *The Art of Migrating Ideas* (Edinburgh, 1993), p. 71. Glass fragments have also been found at Brandon and at Barking; Webster and Backhouse, *The Making of England*, pl. 66w–x, 67m–t, pp. 87–88, 90–93.

79. Bede, *HE* III.11, pp. 248–49; IV.24, pp. 416–17; Bede, *Prose Life of St. Cuthbert*, ch. 34, pp. 264–65.

80. Haddan and Stubbs, *Councils*, vol. 3, p. 365.

81. My thanks are owed to Donald Lateiner, Department of Humanities/Classics, Ohio Wesleyan University, for pointing out the possible gender-ambiguous use of the word *puer* in antiquity: see *The Oxford Latin Dictionary* (Oxford, 1968), pp. 1614–15. This ambiguity continues in the Vulgate (John 21:5), where *puer* is given for "child"; see A. Blaise, "Le Latin Chrétien," *Dictionnaire Latin-Francais des auteurs chrétiens* (Strassbourg, 1954), p. 683; but exclusively medieval Latin usages are limited to predominantly male roles: (implied male) servant or slave, armed retainer, vassal, champion, son, young prince, squire, or clerk in minor orders; so the meaning of the term in the proceedings of the Synod of Clovesho remains unclear. See J. F. Niermeyer, *Mediae Latinitatis Lexicon Minus* (Leiden, 1984), p. 870; *Lexicon Latinitatis Medii Aevi* (Turnhout, 1975), p. 751.

82. Bede, *HE* III.8, pp. 236–39. Hollis, *Anglo-Saxon Women*, p. 258, outlines the documentary evidence concerning the extent of literacy at Chelles under Abbess Bertila. See also Janet L. Nelson, "Les Femmes et l'Evangelization au IXème siècle," *Revue du Nord* 68 (1986): 471–85; C. P. Wormald, "The Uses of Literacy in Anglo-Saxon England and Its Neighbors," *Transactions of the Royal Historical Society*, 5th ser., 27 (1977): 95–114; and Shari Lynn Horner, "Women's Literacy and Female Textuality in Old English Poetry," dissertation, University of Minnesota (1992), pp. 18–21, which stresses the role of secular women in the ninth century. It remains

unclear, however, how widespread literacy may have been among upper-class secular Anglo-Saxon women in the second half of the seventh and first half of the eighth century.

83. Bede, *HE* IV.23, pp. 408–11.

84. Bede, *HE* V.3. pp. 460–61; Bertram Colgrave, *The Earliest Life of Gregory the Great* (1968; reprinted Cambridge, 1985), p. 37. John referred to Theodore's medical knowledge from personal memory.

85. Bede, *HE* IV.23, pp. 408–9. Hollis, *Anglo-Saxon Women*, p. 78, suggests that Hilda was educated by Aidan and (p. 125) was herself the teacher of the clergy trained at Whitby in her day. She notes, p. 257 n. 70, that modern scholars have taken their cue from Bede as to the state of the curriculum at Whitby and have read his silence on Hilda's role to imply that she was a visionary administrator but no teacher. Hollis, ibid., p. 270, however, presents a case that Bede systematically underplays the role of the royal abbesses and that his statements ought not to be read as a complete and unbiased historical record. In *HE* III.24, pp. 292–93, Hilda's successor Ælfflæd is named both *discipula* and later *magistra* of life under the monastic rule.

86. Peers and Radford, "The Saxon Monastery," pp. 50–58; nos. 12–30, 35–48.

87. Colgrave, *Earliest Life of Gregory*, pp. 45–49, 53–54. Peter Hunter Blair, "Whitby as a Centre of Learning in the Seventh Century," in *Learning and Literacy in Anglo-Saxon England: Studies Presented to Peter Clemoes*, ed. Michael Lapidge and Helmut Gneuss (Cambridge, 1985), p. 30, n. 150, and Hollis, *Anglo-Saxon Women*, pp. 126, 270, note that nothing precludes the possibility that the Whitby *Life of St. Gregory* may have been written by a Whitby nun. It is fairer to say that the sex of the author, who was certainly a member of the Whitby community, remains unknown.

88. Colgrave, *Earliest Life of Gregory*, p. 53; Bede, *HE*, Praefatio, pp. 2–7.

89. Colgrave, ibid., pp. 37, 53–54.

90. Aldhelm, *De Virginitate*, ch. 4, pp. 61–62.

91. Ibid., ch. 14, p. 70. Hollis, p. 79, suggests that, although the curriculum of Barking may have been enriched by contact with Archbishop Theodore's school at Canterbury through Aldhelm, the nuns seem to have had limited access to the new learning; they do not seem to have studied *computus* and astronomy, which were offered at Canterbury.

92. Given that Barking was a double monastery, one is left to wonder about the role of the brothers in the intellectual life of the community because Aldhelm's treatise is addressed only to the abbess and several female members of the community. As Aldhelm includes more examples of male than of female virginity, his treatise may be directed to both male and female components of the community and the addressing of his treatise to the women of Barking may in this case be more or less a pro forma honorary dedication (see Janemarie Luecke, "The Unique Experience of Anglo-Saxon Nuns," in *Medieval Religious Women*, vol. 2, *Peaceweavers* (Kalamazoo, Mich., 1987), pp. 61–63). Alternatively the monks of Barking may have been a minority in

the community, serving as manual-labor support staff to the female residents (see Rigold, "The 'Double Minsters,' " p. 27) and were not considered by Aldhelm among the intellectual elite of the community.

93. Kylie, *The English Correspondence*, no. 4, p. 50.

94. Fell, *Women in Anglo-Saxon England*, p. 113; Patrick Sims Williams, "Cuthswith, Seventh-Century Abbess of Inkberrow, near Worcester, and the Würzburg Ms. of Jerome on Ecclesiastes," *ASE* 5 (1976): 1–21.

95. Eckenstein, *Women Under Monasticism*, p. 126.

96. Fell, *Women in Anglo-Saxon England*, pp. 114–15.

97. Kylie, *The English Correspondence*, no. 7, pp. 57–66.

98. Ibid., no. 18, pp. 98–101; no. 23, pp. 110–11; E. S. Duckett, *Anglo-Saxon Saints and Scholars* (New York, 1948), p. 385.

99. Fell, *Women in Anglo-Saxon England*, pp. 112–14.

100. Kylie, *The English Correspondence*, no. 14, pp. 90–91. Allison suggested some time ago that the letter implies that Eadberga was to have the text copied out by a scribe, not necessarily even in her own community (Allison, *English Religious Life*, p. 61), but if the Eadberga of this letter is the same as the Eadberga to whom Lul sent a silver stylus, then we must assume that the gift was appropriate to the recipient (Kylie, ibid., no. 22, pp. 108–9).

101. Kylie, ibid., no. 14, p. 90.

102. Annemarie W. Carr, "Women Artists in the Middle Ages," *Feminist Art Journal* 5 (1976): 5, 9, n. 3.

103. Bernhard Bischoff, "Die Kölner Nonnenhandschriften und das Skriptorium von Chelles," *Karolingische und Ottonische Kunst: Werden, Wesen, Wirkung* (Wiesbaden, 1957), pp. 395–411. As Chelles was a double house by Gisla's day, it may be assumed that the population of its scriptorium was mixed (Carr, ibid., p. 6.).

104. Carr, ibid., p. 6; D. Miner, *Anastasie and Her Sisters; Women Artists of the Middle Ages* (Baltimore, 1974). The majority of later examples of illumination by women in the West come from Germany, where aristocratic canonical convents persisted into the twelfth century as centers of women's intellectual endeavor. See Carr, ibid., pp. 6–8. Elsewhere, notably in Byzantium, the evidence is more scarce and predominantly later in date. See Annemarie W. Carr, "Women and Monasticism in Byzantium: An Introduction from an Art Historian," *Byzantinische Forschungen* 9 (1985): 1–15.

105. White, "Finds," p. 40.

106. Peers and Radford, "The Saxon Monastery," pp. 64–65, nos. 80–85.

107. Ibid., p. 64. Since Peers and Radford were published in 1943, additional (although still not numerous) styli have come to light elsewhere, both at Brandon and

Barking, and at Flixborough (S. Humberside); see Webster and Backhouse, *The Making of England*, pl. 66r–t, 67i–k, 69w, pp. 86–87, 90 100–1. Flixborough was an eighth-and ninth-century (very probably) monastic community, the site of which produced loom weights, two styli (one of silver, paralleling Lul's gift to Eadberga), and an inscribed lead plaque, bearing both male and female names ending with EDEL NUN, the last word possibly an abbreviation of *nunna* or "nun." Michelle P. Brown, in Webster and Backhouse, ibid., p. 95, believes the palaeography of this inscription to indicate that the scribe was familiar with a Mercian hybrid minuscule used in charters of the eighth and ninth centuries and in two Mercian prayerbooks of the later Tiberius group; this inscription overlies an older one in Lindisfarne display script. It must remain in the realm of speculation, however, whether these ingredients reflect the historical reality of a double monastery with a scriptorium, possibly with female scribes or illuminators.

108. Rosemary Cramp, "Appendix B: Analysis of the Finds Register and Location Plan of Whitby Abbey," in *The Archaeology of Anglo-Saxon England*, ed. D. M. Wilson (Cambridge, 1976), pp. 453–57.

109. Rosemary Cramp, "Monastic Sites," in *The Archaeology of Anglo-Saxon England*, ibid., p. 229. More recently, Rosemary Cramp has emphasized that it is impossible to stratify the Whitby objects reported by Peers and Radford, but suggests that there is no evidence in the artifactual record for changes in the specific uses of area of the site; see Cramp, "A Reconsideration," pp. 64, 68. In the absence of stratigraphy, however, it is also impossible to rule out such changes, especially for such "light industries" as weaving and writing, which may be present either sequentially or simultaneously.

110. Rosemary Cramp, "Monastic Sites," p. 204; Edward James, "Archaeology and the Merovingian Monastery," in *Columbanus and Merovingian Monasticism*, ed. A. B. Clarke and M. Brennan, BAR International Series 113 (Oxford, 1981), pp. 40–41.

111. Rudolf, *Life of St. Leoba*, p. 207.

112. Bede, *HE* III.11, pp. 248–49.

113. Bede, *HE* IV.7, 356–57. See also Hollis, *Anglo-Saxon Women*, p. 259, on the construction of churches under Seaxburg at Minster-in-Sheppey (*Fragmentary Life of S. Mildryth*) and Eadburg at Thanet (*Lambeth Fragment*).

114. Bede, *HE* III.8, pp. 238–39; IV.8–9, pp. 358–61.

115. Cramp, "Monastic Sites," 206–7; Bede, *HE* IV.25, pp. 424–25. The same term is used by the writer of the *Anonymous Life of St. Cuthbert* to describe the various structures of the saint's hermitage on Inner Farne. See Bertram Colgrave, *Two Lives of St. Cuthbert* (1940; reprinted Cambridge, 1985), ch. 1, pp. 96–97. Bede describes the hermitage more completely as consisting of an oratory and a "habitation"; see Bede, *Prose Life of St. Cuthbert*, ch. 17, pp. 216–17.

116. Bede, *HE* IV.23, pp. 412–15.

117. Bede, *HE*, IV.23, pp. 414–15; IV.24, pp. 418–19.

118. Bede, *HE* IV.10, pp. 362–65. Mixed cemeteries were the norm at double houses; Hollis, *Anglo-Saxon Women* pp. 103, n. 144, 111, ascribes the segregated cemeteries at Barking to the influence of Theodore, as *Theodore's Penitential* II.vi.8 specifies segregated burial of monks and nuns.

119. Rosemary Cramp and Robin Daniels, "New Finds from the Anglo-Saxon Monastery at Hartlepool, Cleveland," *Antiquity* 61 (1987): 424–32. Recently Cramp has pointed out additional links between metalwork from Whitby and examples from elsewhere in the British Isles; see Cramp, "A Reconsideration," pp. 66–68.

120. Cramp, "Monastic Sites," pp. 223–29; P. Rahtz, "The Building Plan of the Anglo-Saxon Monastery of Whitby Abbey," in *The Archaeology of Anglo-Saxon England*, ed. D. M. Wilson (London, 1976), pp. 459–62.

121. Rahtz, ibid., p. 461.

122. Cramp, "Monastic Sites," pp. 236–39.

123. Ibid., p. 229.

124. Harold M. Taylor and Joan Taylor, *Anglo-Saxon Architecture*, vol. 1 (Cambridge, 1965), pp. 268–70.

125. Ibid., vol. 1, pp. 287–89; Rosemary Cramp, *Corpus of Anglo-Saxon Stone Sculpture*, vol. 1, pt. 1 (Oxford, 1984), pp. 96–97, notes that, whereas the stone is the same material as the Monkwearmouth examples and is like them turned on a lathe, the technique is different, producing pointed grooved moldings seen only here and at Greatham. This may suggest evolution or variation within a workshop, possibly over generations, or different shops referring to similar models.

126. Peers and Radford, "The Saxon Monastery," pp. 33–35, pl. 20. Peers and Radford date this slab to the seventh century.

127. Cramp, *Corpus*, vol. 1, pt. 1, pp. 97–101; vol. 1, pt. 2, pls. 84–85; G. Baldwin Brown, "The Hartlepool Tombstones and the Relations Between Celtic and Teutonic Art in the Early Christian Period," *Proceedings of the Society of Antiquaries of Scotland* 53 (1918–19): 195–228; Forrest S. Scott, "The Hildithryth Stone and the Other Hartlepool Namestones," *Archaeologia Aeliana* 43 (1956): 191–212; Peers and Radford, ibid., pp. 35–47; Catherine Karkov, "The Insular Chalice-Cross," dissertation, Cornell University (1990), pp. 72–76. Recently, Cramp, "A Reconsideration," pp. 68–70, has discussed connections of surviving examples of sculpture at Whitby, particularly the unornamented crosses, with the "stelae" at York and with continental examples concentrated in the Vexin. She sees the introduction of stonecarving at Whitby in conjunction with the construction of a second generation mortared-stone church, possibly by masons from York. For the relief animal in a vinescroll on slab no. 1, Cramp, ibid., p. 71, identifies the closest parallel in a fragmentary cross-shaft at Dacre, Cumbria; see Cramp, "Dacre, CU. (St. Andrew): 1. Part of cross-shaft," in Richard N. Bailey and Rosemary Cramp, *Corpus of Anglo-Saxon Stone Sculpture*,

vol. 2, *Cumberland, Westmoreland, and Lancaster North-of-the-Sands* (Oxford, 1988), pp. 90–91, ills. 235–39.

128. Cramp, *Corpus*, vol. 1, pt. 1, p. 97; Scott, "The Hildithryth Stone," 197; Daniel H. Haigh, "Notes on the Monumental Stones Discovered at Hartlepool in the Years 1833, 1838, 1843," *Journal of the British Archaeological Association* 1 (1846): 185–96.

129. Karkov, "The Insular Chalice-Cross," pp. 29–48.

130. G. Baldwin Brown, "The Hackness Cross," in *The Arts in Early England,* vol. 6, pt. 1 (London, 1930), pp. 52–75; A. W. Clapham, "Hackness, the Church and Pre-Conquest Crosses," *Archaeological Journal* 105 (1948): 82; John Higgitt and Raymond I. Page, "Hackness, NR (St. Peter) 1a–b. Part of Cross-Shaft, in Two Pieces," in James Lang, *Corpus of Anglo-Saxon Stone Sculpture*, vol. 3, *York and East Yorkshire* (Oxford, 1991), pp. 135–41.

131. Cramp, *Corpus*, vol. 1, pt. 2, xli, Fig. 23b.

132. See Higgitt and Page, "Hackness," pp. 138–40. Both the north and south faces of the upper fragment and the north face of the lower fragment include Latin commemorative inscriptions. On the east side of the upper fragment is a partially preserved inscriptive panel that begins in runelike letters, continues in *halal*-runes, and ends in three Latin letters. On the south side of the lower slab is an inscription in an oghamlike cipher. The latter two inscriptions led R. A. S. MacAlister (in Baldwin Brown, "The Hackness Cross," p. 64.) to consider the possibility of the use of ciphers for private documents in the typical convent of the period, which he described as "virtually a religious secret society." Given the general openness to ecclesiastical and secular contacts of early Anglo-Saxon convents, such secretive practices would seem atypical, but the use of runes and ciphers is not uncommon in the Anglo-Saxon monastic context; see R[aymond] I. Page, *An Introduction to English Runes* (London, 1973), p. 67.

133. Cramp and Daniels, "New Finds," pp. 429–31.

134. Mildred Budny, "The Anglo-Saxon Embroideries at Maaseik: Their Historical and Art Historical Context," *Mededelingen van de Koninglijke Academie vor Wettenschappen, Letteren en Schone Kunsten van Belgie; Klasse der Schone Kunsten* 45, pt. 2 (1984): 50–133; Mildred Budny and Dominic Tweddle, "The Maaseik embroideries," *ASE* 13 (1984): 65–96.

135. Fell, *Women in Anglo-Saxon England*, p. 116; and see Budny and Tweddle, ibid., pp. 78–84, dating these embroideries in the late eighth or early ninth century.

136. Budny and Tweddle, ibid., pp. 84–85, n. 59; gives reference to embroidered fragments of wool twill in amuletic boxes from seventh-century graves. See also Audrey Meaney, *Anglo-Saxon Amulets and Curing Stones*, BAR British Series 96 (Oxford, 1981), pp. 184, 186–87.

137. Hollis, *Anglo-Saxon Women*, pp. 106, 182.

138. Bede, *Prose Life of St. Cuthbert*, pp. 230–31; Hollis, ibid., p. 268.

139. Hollis, ibid., p. 300.

140. Ibid., passim.

141. Ibid., pp. 130–37, 163–64. Late, mid-eighth century, interpolations in *Theodore's Penitential* rule against the administration of penance by women (II.vii.2) and against their active participation in the liturgy (II.vii.1).

142. Ibid., pp. 179–207, 234–70.

143. Roberta Frank, "*Beowulf* and Sutton Hoo: The Odd Couple," in *Voyage to the Other World: The Legacy of Sutton Hoo*, ed. C. B. Kendall and P. S. Wells (Minneapolis, 1992), pp. 47–64.

144. Such an approach to the combined study of documentary and archaeological materials was also suggested by Rosemary Cramp in her concluding remarks to the Insular Traditions conference, held at the twenty-sixth International Congress on Medieval Studies at Western Michigan University (Kalamazoo), May 9–11, 1991. This method is significantly more useful for the postconversion period, for which we have contemporary written records, than for the preconversion period, for which all written sources except Gildas postdate the period itself; see Barbara Yorke, "Fact or Fiction? The Written Evidence for the Fifth and Sixth Centuries A.D.," *Anglo-Saxon Studies in Archaeology and History* 6 (1993): 45–50.

145. See Horner, "Women's Literacy and Female Textuality," and also Patricia A. Belanoff, "Women's Songs, Women's Language: *Wulf and Eadwacer* and *The Wife's Lament*," in *New Readings on Women in Old English Literature*, ed. Helen Damico and Alexandra Hennessey Olsen (Bloomington and Indianapolis, Ind., 1990), pp. 193–203, and especially n. 2.

Hagiography and Politics in Early Northumbria

David Rollason

The study of saints' lives can have a number of quite different goals, including evaluating their literary value and style, discerning their significance for the liturgy of the Church, isolating the reflections in them of contemporary attitudes, or garnering the incidental information they contain about social organization and manners. In recent years, historians concerned with early Northumbria have subjected the saints' lives written there in the eighth century, all of which are in Latin, to searching analyses with a view to discovering how their composition was related to the political situation of the Church, the kings, and the aristocracy. The results of this work have been exciting, even if many aspects of them remain controversial. The aim of this chapter is to summarize the research of the scholars involved and present their findings as briefly and succinctly as possible, partly for the benefit of students of Northumbria, partly in the hope that those working on other saints' lives including, of course, the Old English lives with which this volume is chiefly concerned, may wish to consider the possible relevance of the approaches outlined here to their own studies. The basis of the problem that scholars working on Northumbria have been confronting is best presented by surveying the nature and chronological distribution of the lives in question.

In the late seventh and early eighth centuries Northumbrian writers produced a remarkably large number of Latin saints' lives.[1] These included a *Life of Pope Gregory the Great*, written by an anonymous monk of the abbey of Whitby, probably between 704 and 714;[2] a *Life of St. Cuthbert*, bishop of Lindisfarne (d. 687), by an anonymous monk of that church between 699 and 705;[3] two further lives of the same saint by Bede, one in verse written soon after 705 but seemingly revised sometime in the second decade of the eighth century;[4] and another in prose composed before (possibly some years before) 721;[5] and a *Life of St. Wilfrid*, bishop of York (d. 710), written by Stephen, a monk of Ripon, before 715 but apparently afterward revised, perhaps

c. 731–734 or even later.[6] Although these are the only works from seventh- and eighth-century Northumbria devoted to individual saints, we should consider in addition to them a *Life of Ceolfrith*, abbot of Wearmouth-Jarrow, written probably in 716, possibly by Bede himself, and concerned with the founder of Wearmouth-Jarrow, Benedict Biscop, and other abbots as well as with Ceolfrith himself;[7] and the *History of the Abbots of Wearmouth-Jarrow*, certainly composed by Bede after 716, possibly around 730, and dealing with similar matter.[8]

This burst of hagiographical activity occurred in a restricted area and a restricted time span. The number of these works is unusual for England, although it would not be remarkable by continental standards.[9] From south of the Humber in approximately the same period we have only a *Life of St. Guthlac*, composed by a certain Felix in East Anglia, probably between 730 and 740 or thereabouts,[10] together with vernacular lives of this same Guthlac and also St. Chad of Lichfield, which are hard to date and may be substantially later.[11] Some hagiographical writings have evidently been lost, for Bede refers in his *Ecclesiastical History of the English People* to an otherwise unknown account of the saints of Barking,[12] and the earliest version of the cycle of stories concerning St. Mildrith of Thanet, the work of Byrhtferth of Ramsey in the tenth century, has traces of a text originally composed in the eighth century.[13] Nevertheless, the Northumbrian group is remarkable, especially as there is no sign of the composition of such free-standing saints' lives in Northumbria earlier in the seventh century or after the middle of the eighth.

How can this burst of hagiographical activity be accounted for? There was no dearth of subjects for hagiographical composition outside Northumbria, but aside from Bede's notices in his *Ecclesiastical History* even such a promising potential saint as Æthelthryth of Ely was not honored with a free-standing life.[14] and Botulf of East Anglia, an important monastic figure who contributed to the education of Ceolfrith of Monkwearmouth-Jarrow, received only a passing reference in the *Life of Ceolfrith*.[15] Of course, the composition of a life was not an absolute necessity for the promotion of a saint's cult, although it may have been helpful to it.[16] The cult of Chad at Lichfield clearly flourished and so did that of Eorcenwald at London, although in neither case (with the possible exception of the vernacular *Life of St. Chad* noted previously) is there any evidence of hagiographical writing devoted to them in the seventh and eighth centuries.[17] Moreover, to judge by their language and complex scriptural and literary allusions, the Northumbrian lives must have had a predominantly ecclesiastical readership and can hardly have been intended to gain large numbers of devotees for the cults in question.[18]

These features of the Northumbrian lives might lead us to explain them as an aspect of the scholarly and literary development of the early eighth-century "Golden Age of Northumbria," for they are clearly to be associated with Bede's *Ecclesiastical History*, completed c. 731 and containing much material of a hagiographical character.[19] The lives would certainly not have been written but for the tide of scholarship and literature at that time in Northumbria, but this cannot be accepted as the sole reason for the unusually prolific output. Why were these saints and not others chosen as subjects of hagiographical writing? If such works were simply an expression of scholarly and literary culture we should expect to have early lives of the Northumbrian royal saints Oswald and Oswine, Hilda of Whitby, and other saintly figures of whom the only literary memorial we have is in the *Ecclesiastical History*.[20] We should also expect to have lives from the later eighth century in Northumbria, which, despite political turbulence, was evidently the scene of considerable scholarly and literary activity, as witnessed in Alcuin's poem *The Bishops, Kings and Saints of York*,[21] and the early ninth-century *De Abbatibus*, a poem on the abbots and saints of an unidentified Northumbrian monastery by an otherwise unknown member of that community called Æthelwulf.[22] Yet we have no lives as such from that period, despite the existence of obvious candidates such as the two hermits Echa of Crayke and Balthere of Tyningham whose miraculous activities are briefly described in Alcuin's poem.[23]

In the light of all this, we need to explore the possibility that the late seventh- and early eighth-century Northumbrian lives were composed as a response to the particular circumstances of that period and that their composition is at least in some measure explicable in terms of ecclesiastical and secular politics.[24] Although this may seem at first sight an unpromising line of thought given that the audience for the lives probably consisted mainly of churchmen, it should be emphasized that the religious communities in which or for which they were written had deep political involvement. Lindisfarne, for example, had been founded in close association with King Oswald of the Northumbrians. It lay a short boat journey from the royal stronghold of Bamburgh, and its relationship with the Northumbrian kings evidently remained close. It was the place to which King Ceolwulf retired after his final abdication in 737;[25] and in 750 the church of Lindisfarne seems to have been supporting Offa, son of the former King Aldfrith, in a bid for power, because we read that King Eadberht took Bishop Cynewulf prisoner, had the church of St. Peter on Lindisfarne besieged, and dragged away Offa from the relics of its principal saint Cuthbert, where he had taken sanctuary.[26] Later, Lindisfarne may have supported nonroyal potentates and claimants to the throne, for it was there in 793 that Sicga the patrician, who was responsible for the murder of the previous king, Ælfwold, was buried; and in 796 another patrician called Osbald, having been raised briefly to the throne and then deposed, came first to Lindisfarne and then, with some of the monks, he sailed away to take refuge with the king of the Picts.[27]

Nor was Lindisfarne unique in this respect. In the case of Hexham and Ripon, the high political profile of their founder Wilfrid is well documented in the life by Stephen, and it seems certain that their political involvement did not cease with his death.[28] In his will he left a third of his treasure to the abbots of these two monasteries to enable them to purchase the friendship of kings and bishops.[29] Later in the eighth century, Hexham appears as the burial place in 788 of the murdered King Ælfwold of the Northumbrians, whose cult (which can hardly have lacked political resonance) appears to have been fostered by the abbey.[30] Ripon seems to have been involved in the career of the future king of the Northumbrians, Eardwulf, who was in 790 captured and taken to the abbey where King Osred II ordered his execution. According to legend, he was killed outside the gates of the monastery and the monks placed his body outside the church in a tent, but after midnight he was found alive in the church. This story (to which Alcuin alludes in a later letter to Eardwulf) implied that the monks of Ripon were somehow instrumental in his survival.[31]

Less is known of the political associations of Whitby, although its royal foundation and its royal abbesses Eanfled and her daughter Ælfflæd would suggest that it too had a definite political role. Indeed it is clear that Ælfflæd played an important part in the resolution of the political difficulties that beset Wilfrid.[32] Nor should Bede's emphasis on the saintliness of the abbots of Monkwearmouth-Jarrow obscure the political importance of these two linked monasteries. Jarrow was founded in association with King Ecgfrith; and the reason given in the anonymous *Life of Ceolfrith* for the first abbot, Benedict Biscop, appointing an assistant is that he was often summoned to give advice to the king.[33] Moreover, Bede evidently saw himself as an actor on the political stage, despite his long residence in the monastery. The association between Bede and King Ceolwulf, manifest in the Preface to the *Ecclesiastical History*, may have been closer than is normally supposed, for it appears to have had a major impact on the content of that history, especially the inclusion in it of material relating to the Irish mission of St. Aidan. It is likely that Ceolwulf was particularly interested in this as a result of his connection with Lindisfarne.[34] Bede's letter to Bishop Egbert, written at the end of his life, also reveals a keen interest in the ecclesiastical and political development of Northumbria, which Bede clearly believed himself able to influence.[35] Indeed, it is now apparent that the *Ecclesiastical History* is in part at least to be understood as a work aimed at reform in Bede's own day.[36]

We should not find it surprising that monasteries were concerned in political developments, given that their members seem to have been drawn from the aristocracy: men like the nobles at Jarrow who objected to the monastic rule imposed on them by Ceolfrith or the retired warrior in the company of whom Wilfrid entered Lindisfarne.[37] After becoming monks, such aristocrats may well have continued to enjoy a way of life that had much in common with that of their lay contemporaries, for we have evidence of their concern with wealth, with feasting, with fine clothes, and with listening to recitations of heroic Germanic legends.[38] Against this background the possibility exists that political concerns lay behind the genesis of the Northumbrian saints' lives and that these texts were conceived of in some measure to express those concerns. The discussion that follows focuses on what may be regarded as three of the major issues of Northumbrian history in the seventh and eighth centuries: (1) the Easter and tonsure questions and the related problem of Northumbrian relations with the Picts and Scots; (2) the disputes involving Wilfrid and the general issue of ecclesiastical organization; and (3) the territorial and dynastic unity of Northumbria itself.

The Easter and Tonsure Questions

The method of calculating the date of Easter embodied a group of subsidiary problems about the correct Easter cycles to use, the date of the vernal equinox, and the appropriate days in the first week of the Hebrew month Nisan (as laid down in the Old Testament prescriptions concerning the keeping of the Passover). Its relevance to the Northumbrian church arose from the fact that the Irish monks such as Aidan who evangelized Northumbria used an Easter calculation that differed from that used elsewhere in Christendom, notably in the church of Rome. In fact the Irish church was in the process of adopting the calculation used in Rome, the southern Irish churches having agreed to use it in the 630s and the northern Irish churches under the leadership of Armagh sometime in the third quarter of the seventh century. But the church that had the greatest importance for Northumbria was Iona, which had dependent monasteries in Ireland and elsewhere in Scotland and which refused to accept the Roman Easter calculation until 716. As regards the tonsure question, Irish churchmen shaved only the front of their heads and those who claimed to be the following Roman traditions shaved the middle of the pate to produce a tonsure in the shape of a crown. Both these issues culminated at the Synod of Whitby in 664, when King Oswiu of the Northumbrians declared himself in favor of the Roman Easter and by implication of the Roman tonsure also.[39]

The degree of bitterness of this dispute in Northumbria is not easily assessed from our principal sources. Bede, as the greatest master of his day in the science of computing the church's calendar, may have adopted an exaggerated view of the importance of the Easter problem, and Stephen as biographer no doubt wished to emphasize the role of his hero Wilfrid, who had represented the Roman view in his successful participation in the Synod of Whitby. Nevertheless, there is no doubt that the bishop of Lindisfarne, Colman, left his see and went to Ireland with some of the community of his church as a result of the decision at Whitby, and it is clear too that at least some English churchmen regarded those who still adhered to the Irish methods of Easter calculation as schismatics or even heretics.[40] Moreover, in the eighth century, the whole question became bound up with Northumbrian relations with the Picts and Scots. In particular, King Nechtan of the Picts wrote to Abbot Ceolfrith of Monkwearmouth-Jarrow to ask advice on these very points.[41] It is likely that his adoption of Roman practices as a result of the reply he received from Ceolfrith had political ramifications and was connected with the explusion of (presumably recalcitrant) churchmen connected with Iona from Pictland in 717.[42] Although the Easter question was the more important problem, we should not underestimate the significance of the tonsure, which was clearly taken seriously in the early medieval church.[43]

How far did the saints' lives reflect and seek to influence these disputes? At one level, we may note Stephen's presentation of Wilfrid's role and speech at the Synod of Whitby, and in particular his claim that Wilfrid was expelled from the see of York, which he received after the synod, by "Quartodecimans"; that is, those who celebrated Easter on the fourteenth day of the month Nisan regardless of whether it was a Sunday.[44] In the first place, the Irish churchmen were not Quartodecimans because they always celebrated Easter on a Sunday,[45] and the life seems thus to embody a deliberate and propagandist slur on their position. In this connection we should not forget the possibility that Wilfrid's expulsion was connected with a political dispute between the reigning king of the Northumbrians, Oswiu, and his son Alhfrith, who appears to have been king of Deira and subordinate to his father. Alhfrith supported and patronized Wilfrid (it was he who granted him the monastery of Ripon), but he disappears from the historical record after the Synod of Whitby, and it is very likely that he rebelled against Oswiu and was killed.[46]

The prose lives of Cuthbert show a similar preoccupation with the question. Cuthbert must have followed Irish practices in his early years since he was trained at the Irish-influenced monastery of Melrose, and he was one of the monks of Ripon expelled by Alhfrith for refusing to adopt Roman practices. Nevertheless the *Life of Cuthbert* by an anonymous monk falsifies the historical record by claiming that Cuthbert received at Ripon the tonsure attributed to St. Peter and regarded as Roman, whereas we know from Bede that he was in fact tonsured at the Irish-influenced monastery of Melrose. The anonymous monk's aim was clearly to associate Cuthbert with Roman practices even when this was not justified by the facts of history.[47] The same is true of Bede's prose *Life of Cuthbert*, which, although it does not repeat the falsehood about Cuthbert's tonsure, does put words into the saint's mouth to the effect that the monks should have no communion with those who did not accept the Roman calculation of Easter any more than with those who persisted in evil living.[48] In view of Cuthbert's connections with Melrose and his contacts with the Picts (see later), the vehemence of this speech is unlikely to reflect his real views, and Bede was clearly making a propagandist point similar to that made by the anonymous monk with regard to the tonsure.

The dispute may also explain the choice of subject matter in the *Life of Gregory* by an anonymous monk of Whitby, for the composition of this text devoted to a Roman pope may have "enabled a Romanized church to discover its true beginnings in the missionary aspirations of a Roman pope— half a century before Aidan—who personified an orthodoxy which had now been officially proclaimed."[49] The inclusion in this life of a long section devoted to King Edwin of the Northumbrians and his conversion to Christianity by the Roman missionary Paulinus can only partly be attributed to Whitby being the burial place of Edwin.[50] It must also have been intended to emphasize the links of the Northumbrian with the Roman church. In reality, the conversion of Northumbria initiated under Edwin was transitory and more or less ended with his death.[51] But the life makes no allusion to Aidan and the Irish monks under whose guidance a definitive conversion was achieved. Rather, it merely gives the impression that Edwin was the key figure and that Pope Gregory's missionary Paulinus was the real agent of conversion. Here then was further propaganda for the Roman church and against the Irish.

So far we have been concerned only with the content of the lives. Their overall form and the circumstances of their composition may also have lent them significance in relation to the Easter question. This possibility is of importance with regard to the *Life of Cuthbert* by the anonymous monk and the *Life of Columba* written between 689 and 704 (probably after 697) by Adomnan, abbot of the abbey of Iona, which, although in the kingdom of Dalriada in western Scotland, had close links with Northumbria, arising from its having sent missionaries to that kingdom in the 630s and having at various times in the seventh century given refuge and possibly also assistance to Northumbrian royal exiles.[52] The latter is self-evidently aimed at enhancing the reputation of Columba as a saint, and given that it makes no explicit reference to the Easter question, it may well be that its underlying purpose was to defend Columba's sainthood in the face of criticisms of his adherence to Irish practices with regard to Easter and the tonsure. Such criticisms came in part from Ireland, for the southern Irish churches had adopted the Roman Easter in 633, with Armagh and churches dependent on it following suit in the late seventh century. We possess a letter from the Irish abbot Cummian to Abbot Segene of Iona urging him in vain to do the same.[53]

Equally the Northumbrian party in favor of the Roman Easter was skeptical of Columba's claim to sainthood. According to Stephen in his *Life of Wilfrid*, the Irish bishop of Lindisfarne, Colman is said at the Synod of Whitby to have defended his practice on the grounds that it had been that of Columba who was inspired by the Holy Spirit, but the synod was guided by Oswiu in rejecting this on the grounds that Columba was inferior to Peter.[54] Bede echoes this and puts into Wilfrid's mouth remarks skeptical of Columba's claim to divine inspiration, even implying that Columba is not a saint at all.[55]

In view of all this is not unreasonable to see the composition of the *Life of Columba* as a response to this criticism. Its underlying message was not only that Columba was indeed a holy man who worked miracles and saw visions, but also that the Easter question was not of such importance that it should divide Christians.[56] It is striking in this context that the first chapter of the *Life of Columba* deals with the Battle of Heavenfield, in which King Oswald won his throne by overcoming the British king Cadwalla. According to the life, Columba appeared to Oswald in a vision on the night before the battle and promised him victory, which he duly gained. Adomnan gives this further significance by saying that Oswald's followers agreed provisionally to become Christians dependent on the upshot of the battle.[57] No mention of Columba's supposed intervention is to be found in any other source, and it seems likely that we are reading in this a claim by Adomnan not only that Cuthbert was a great saint, but also that, quite contrary to the gibes of Wilfrid and his like, it was under him that the kingdom of the Northumbrians prospered in war and religion.[58]

The *Life of Columba* now seems to be more or less contemporaneous with the *Life of Cuthbert* by an anonymous monk and, although the two lives differ in structure and subject matter, they do share striking features, notably a passage in their respective prologues and a miracle story about a monk who was punished for eavesdropping on the respective saint's pious practices.[59] This suggests a relationship between them, and it is at least a possibility that the *Life of Cuthbert* is a response by the Romanized Northumbrian church to the composition of the *Life of Columba*.[60] As Adomnan laid stress on Columba's sainthood and played down the significance of the Easter controversy, so the Lindisfarne monk glorified a saint who could be represented (albeit inaccurately) as a product of the Roman traditions of the church in Northumbria.

Given that these lives belong to the last years of the seventh century and the early years of the eighth century, when the Synod of Whitby was already some decades in the past, it might be objected that the Easter question was too far in the past for it to have been a living issue meriting propaganda in hagiographical form, at any rate for the Northumbrian church. This objection, however, is unlikely to be valid. Bede gave the question much prominence in his *Ecclesiastical History*, in which the Synod of Whitby is represented as a major turning point and the conversion of Iona to the Roman Easter in 716 appears as (to use Professor Duncan's words) the *consummatum est* of the *History*. The prominence given to this latter event may in part have derived from the fact that Bede's informant on affairs in Scottish Dalriada and Pictland was the English monk Egbert, who was personally responsible for the change in the timing of Easter in Iona.[61] But it seems likely that, even allowing for Bede's personal interest in the subject, the Easter question was of continuing importance precisely because in the early eighth century it was unresolved in those areas in which the Northumbrian kings had interests of their own. Aldfrith in particular may have owed his throne to Scottish and Pictish support, and although there was peace with the Picts when Bede was writing the *Ecclesiastical History*, it appears from his chronological summary that there have been wars with the Picts as recently as 698 and 711.[62] Certainly there are signs that Cuthbert's dealings with the Picts are handled differently in the life by the anonymous monk and in the life by Bede. In the former, the saint's visit to the *Niduarii* Picts is treated as a deliberate act; in the latter it appears as the fortuitous result of a storm. This discrepancy may be the result of Bede's attribution to Cuthbert of a wish to have nothing to do with Easter schismatics, but it is also possible that it is a reflection of Bede's judgment of the political situation with regard to the Picts in the time of writing of his prose life.[63]

Wilfrid and Ecclesiastical Organization

It is not easy to discern the real reasons for the long series of disputes that involved the Northumbrian kings and led to Wilfrid's removal from his see in 664–666, his explusion in 678 and 691 and his imprisonment in 680–681.[64] The diocesan organization of Northumbria was evidently a factor, with Archbishop Theodore of Canterbury wishing to subdivide it as he had done with large southern sees such as that of the Mercians and Wilfrid seemingly wishing to keep it intact. This cannot, however, be the whole reason for the dispute, because it is apparent that Wilfrid was willing at an early stage to accept such a subdivision provided he had some influence over the choice of the other bishops.[65] The sheer scale of Wilfrid's wealth may also have made problems for him. In connection with the explusion of 679, Stephen represents Ecgfrith's queen Iurminburg complaining to the king of Wilfrid's riches, his numerous monasteries, the scale of his buildings, and his large following of armed men, royally dressed.[66] Wilfrid certainly controlled many monasteries in Northumbria, Mercia, and elsewhere in the south, some of which he had founded, some of which had been made over to him by will. Stephen calls them a "kingdom of churches" (*regnum ecclesiarum*).[67] It has been suggested that the real object of Northumbrian royal policy toward Wilfrid was to break up his "supratribal monastic connection."[68] If so, Wilfrid would be defending the unity of his see against Theodore and the integrity of his ecclesiastical "empire" against the Northumbrian kings.

No doubt there were other political ramifications. Wilfrid's connection with King Alhfrith may, as mentioned previously, have been the reason for the loss of his see in 664, and there is in general terms no doubt that Wilfrid was intimately involved in royal politics in Northumbria and elsewhere. In the case of the Frankish kingdom, Stephen says that he secured the return of King Dagobert II from exile in Ireland and that after that king's decease he was threatened with death in Frankia because of his former association with him.[69] Stephen makes similar claims for Wilfrid's role in the Northumbrian royal succession. On Aldfrith's death in 705, it appears that his successor was an otherwise unknown Eadwulf, whose son was in Wilfrid's company. The new king rashly (in Stephen's view) rebuffed Wilfrid's overtures of friendship and condemned him to exile, as a result of which the king was expelled by a conspiracy after a reign of only two months. No doubt Wilfrid's role in this coup was not as great as Stephen wished his readers to infer, but it seems clear that Wilfrid was a sufficiently important figure to emerge as the godfather of the new king Osred, son of Aldfrith, and to be in a position under him not only to remain in Northumbria but also to recover his two prime monasteries of Hexham and Ripon.[70]

In all this, Stephen's primary aim was to support Wilfrid's case and that of his "kingdom of churches," and he achieved this by a polemical treatment of events such as the synod of 703, at which Wilfrid's opponents were said to have been aiming to deceive him by recourse to treachery and by the inclusion verbatim of documents relating to Wilfrid's appeals to Rome. In the Preface, Stephen strikes a combative note that is maintained throughout: "Obsecro itaque eos qui lecturi sunt, ut fidem dictis adhibeant, relinquentes antiqui hostis millenos invidiae stimulos et recolentes, quod eloquentia pertonabat. Semper enim in propatulo fortitudo emulos habet: feriuntque summos fulgora montes."[71]

It might be objected that the *Life of Wilfrid* dealt with matters that cannot have continued to be burning issues much after Wilfrid's death in 710, but this judgment seems unlikely to be correct. The saint's demise must have left his religious communties, especially Hexham and Ripon, very vulnerable, as Stephen seems to hint; and the need to justify Wilfrid's claims and the legality of his actions must have been all the greater. That political problems continued to beset Wilfrid's churches is suggested by the fact that Acca, his successor at Hexham, was expelled in 731, the year in which King Ceolwulf was deposed and forcibly tonsured. The two events may well have been connected, a circumstance that would point clearly to the continuing political involvement of Hexham.[72] Now the *Life of Wilfrid* appears to have been written originally between Wilfrid's death in 710 and the death of Abbess Ælfflæd in 715, so its original composition fell in the situation of potential danger for Wilfrid's heirs shortly after his death. There are clear signs, however, that the surviving version of the life was subsequently modified, notably in that it gives two different accounts of Wilfrid's designation of his heir, the second of which names Tatberht, who actually did succeed him at Ripon and may therefore be a later tradition emanating from Tatberht himself or from his supporters. Certainly it would appear to have been written after Acca's expulsion for it refers to him as "of blessed memory," although it is clear that he was still alive at the time of writing.[73]

As with the *Life of Columba* and the *Life of Cuthbert* by the anonymous monk, the composition of the *Life of Wilfrid* may have been politically significant.[74] According to Bede's *Life of Cuthbert*, after that saint's death the church of Lindisfarne was afflicted with such trials and dangers that many of the monks left. It is clear from the *Ecclesiastical History* that these trials were coincident with the period in 687–688 when Wilfrid administered the see of Lindisfarne.[75] It seems then that there was bitterness at Lindisfarne toward Wilfrid and his churches, and it may be that this is reflected in the hagiography of Cuthbert and Wilfrid, respectively. It is striking in this connection that the *Life of Wilfrid* (written originally between 710 and 715) seems deliberately to draw many elements of its Preface from the *Life of Cuthbert* by the anonymous monk (between 698 and 705).[76] Alan Thacker has suggested that the *Life of Wilfrid* may have been written as a counterblast to the *Life of Cuthbert*, just as the *Life of Cuthbert* may have been composed as a counterblast to the *Life of Columba*. In other words, one of the purposes of writing the *Life of Wilfrid* was to show to Lindisfarne that Wilfrid was every bit as good a saint as Cuthbert (and Columba for that matter). Thacker has further suggested that Bede may have written his prose *Life of Cuthbert* so soon after the anonymous monk's life with the object of countering the *Life of Wilfrid* and of drawing attention to the trials that befell Lindisfarne.[77]

The Unity of Northumbria

From the accession of King Oswald in 634 until the early eighth century, Northumbrian kingship enjoyed an extraordinarily stable succession, being exclusively in the hands of the line to which Oswald belonged, all direct descendants of King Æthelfrith (d. ?616). Bede is at pains to lay emphasis on this stability and to paint a picture of peace and tranquillity. But, as David Kirby has observed, such stability can have been achieved, given the customs of royal succession in the period, only by the ruthless exclusion or liquidation of representatives of collateral lines who also had a legitimate claim to the throne. The existence of such collateral lines is demonstrated by the reemergence in the eighth century of surviving members of them, such as Bede's own king Ceolwulf, claiming descent from the very first king of Bernicia, Ida.[78]

Another source of unrest arose from Northumbria's original division into two kingdoms, Bernicia in the north and Deira in the south, the frontier being more or less on the River Tees.[79] Æthelfrith of the Bernician royal house ruled both kingdoms until he was killed in battle and displaced by the Deiran king Edwin, who in his turn died in battle in 633, after which Bernicia and Deira took separate kings of their royal families. When these were also killed, both kingdoms came into the power of the Bernician Oswald, who had been in exile during Edwin's reign. On his death, his brother Oswiu ruled all Northumbria, but he had to accept as king of Deira a member of the Deiran royal house called Oswine. Oswiu had Oswine murdered in 651 and then ruled both kingdoms and no more was heard of Oswine's line.[80] Bede was anxious to present the fusion of Deira and Bernicia as a successful process, with Oswiu making amends for the killing of Oswine by founding the monastery of Gilling in Deira, and subsequently founding six more monasteries in Deira and six in Bernicia, presumably as an indication of his evenhanded commitment to both kingdoms.[81] The unity was nevertheless fragile. Although no member of the Deiran royal family subsequently reigned, the Bernician kings clearly felt impelled to install kings of their own line in Deira. These included Oethelwald, son of King Oswald, and probably Alhfrith, son of King Oswiu. It is significant that Oethelwald certainly revolted against his uncle Oswiu at the Battle of the Winwaed in 654,[82] and as we have seen it is likely that Alhfrith did the same a decade later. The rift in the interests of Bernicia and Deira was therefore not exclusively dynastic and outlived the extinction of the Deiran royal house.

How far were these problems and tensions reflected in the lives we have been discussing? The *Life of Gregory* may be influenced by Bernician-Deiran tensions in the early eighth century, for it was composed at Whitby and in part devoted to Edwin of Deira, whose body was buried at Whitby and his cult fostered there. In that connection, it is striking that the author of the life links the cult with Mercia, where Edwin's body originally lay, and refers to his people as the *Humbrenses* (? dwellers around the Humber). The use of this term may imply that he envisaged links across the Humber between Deirans and the inhabitants of Lindsey to resist the dominance of the Bernicians. Certainly it is notable that Bede, who probably did know the life, made no mention of the resting-place or cult of Edwin, and he was always scrupulous in referring to the "Northumbrians" as a whole.[83]

Bede's sympathies clearly lay with the Bernicians and the unification of Northumbria, and Alan Thacker has argued that the lives of Cuthbert were seeking to present him as the patron saint of a united Northumbria and that this was in part why they included reflections of the hagiography of St. Martin, who played a similar role as patron saint of the Frankish kingdom. Cuthbert was to be the Northumbrian Martin.[84] Bede is explicit about Cuthbert's importance to the English at large in his metrical life of the saint. Just as Peter and Paul were the lamps of Rome, John of Asia, Bartholomew of the Indies, Mark of the Nile, Cyprian of Africa, Hilary of Poitiers and John Chrysostom of Constantiople, so it was Cuthbert who "leading his life among the stars, now taught the English to climb the heavens in his footsteps" ("Cuthbertus agens per sidera uitam / Scandere celsa suis docuit iam passibus Anglos").[85] More specifically to Northumbria, the lives show him as closely associated with King Ecgfrith and other members of the Bernician royal house such as Abbess Ælfflæd of Whitby, daughter of King Oswiu, the latter especially significant because, as suggested earlier, Whitby may well have been a focus of Deiran loyalties.[86]

There may be more specific propagandist elements in the lives' accounts of the dealings of saints and kings. We have already noted the associations made in the lives between Cuthbert and members of the Bernician royal house and this may be taken to imply not only that Cuthbert was being presented as a patron saint, but also that Lindisfarne had a particular interest in supporting that family. This is suggested particularly in the lives by a story of a meeting on Coquet Island off the Northumbrian coast between Cuthbert and the Abbess Ælfflæd of Whitby, whose brother Ecgfrith was then the reigning king. Cuthbert is supposed to have prophesied to Ælfflæd the imminent demise of her brother Ecgfrith and she to have asked him who should succeed seeing that the king had no brothers. The saint is then said to have reminded her that Ecgfrith did indeed have a brother, namely Aldfrith who (we learn elsewhere) was illegitimate and was then in exile in Iona ostensibly for the "study of letters" but no doubt in reality because his claim to the throne made him a danger to Ecgfrith.[87] As Hermann Moisl was emphasized, Aldfrith was clearly being prepared for the church and not for the throne, and we may infer that his eventual succession was achieved only with Pictish and Scottish assistance.[88] Cuthbert's prophecy, which appears in the life by the anonymous monk written in or immediately after Aldfrith's region, looks very like a statement of support by the Lindisfarne community for Aldfrith and his family. This support is notable in view of the incident referred to earlier in which we find Aldfrith's son Offa being granted sanctuary at Lindisfarne and its bishop being imprisoned by Offa's enemy, presumably for granting it to him.

Stephen's *Life of Wilfrid* is equally preoccupied with the relationship between the saint and the Northumbrian kings, especially in the latter
part of Wilfrid's life, but the emphasis is more parochial. As Gabriele
Isenberg has pointed out, a major theme of the work is the duty incum-
bent on the Northumbrian kings to do well by Wilfrid and his churches.[89]
While King Ecgfrith and Queen Æthelthryth were obedient to Bishop
Wilfrid, they enjoyed peace, joy and victory,[90] and Ecgfrith's kingdom
increased alongside Wilfrid's "kingdom of churches."[91] But when, on his
new queen Iurminburg's advice, Ecgfrith had Wilfrid condemned and
expelled, the saint prophesied that there would be weeping and confusion.
Things did indeed so turn out, for on the date Wilfrid had predicted
Ælfwine, Ecgfrith's colleague in the royal office, was killed in battle and
Ecgfrith gained no victories thenceforward.[92] Isenberg has drawn particular attention to the oath King Aldfrith swore after he had been stricken
with illness for refusing to receive Wilfrid on the latter's return in 705
from his final appeal to Rome.[93] According to Stephen, he made a vow to
God and St. Peter that, if he recovered, he would reinstate Wilfrid according to the latter's wishes and those of the pope, but if he died, he would
bind his successor to make such reinstatement.[94] In fact, Aldfrith did
expire and the oath by which he had bound his successors is represented
by Stephen as a major factor in their behavior toward Wilfrid. At the 706
synod that restored Hexham and Ripon to the saint, Stephen makes Abbess Ælfflæd repeat the oath verbatim to support the case for making
concessions to Wilfrid. She was seconded by Berhtfrith, "chief man of the
king" *(regis princeps)*, who is supposed to have attributed the succession
of the reigning king Osred to a vow that he and his comrades had made
concerning Wilfrid.[95] Considering the continuing importance and political
connections of Ripon, such claims as these cannot have been without
some impact on the political scene, not only at the time of the life's composition but also, we may conjecture, at the time of its revision in the 730s
if only as a threat of retribution against kings who did not respect the
interest of Wilfrid's churches. Stephen was emphasizing, as Isenberg has
formulated it "dass das Königtum nur dann sein Gehorsamsgelübde an Petrus
erfüllen konnte, wenn es zur Zusammenarbeit mit Wilfried berit war."[96]

   In short, the research reviewed in this chapter illustrates both the potential and the complexities of attempting to set saints' lives in a political context and to assess their possible influence on that context. It may be that the
early Northumbrian lives are to some extent exceptional, but the approaches
embodied in this research and the sophistication with which they have been
pursued must nevertheless have a wider relevance to the study of saints' lives
in the vernacular as well as in Latin.

Notes

1. For a general discussion, see Bertram Colgrave, "The Earliest English Saints' *Lives* Written in England," *Proceedings of the British Academy* 44 (1958): 35–60. See also Walter Goffart, *The Narrators of Barbarian History (A.D. 550–800); Jordanes, Gregory of Tours, Bede, and Paul the Deacon* (Princeton, N.J., 1988), Chapter 4, especially pp. 256–58. Goffart's discussion in that chapter runs parallel in certain respects to that in the present chapter and should be compared with it.

2. Bertram Colgrave, ed. and trans., *The Earliest Life of Gregory the Great by an Anonymous Monk of Whitby* (Lawrence, Kans., 1968; reprinted Cambridge, 1985). On the dating, see pp. 45–49.

3. Bertram Colgrave, ed. and trans., *Two Lives of St. Cuthbert* (Cambridge, 1940; reprinted 1985), pp. 60–139. On the date, see p. 13.

4. Werner Jaager, ed., *Bedas metrische Vita sancti Cuthberti*, Palaestra 198 (Leipzig, 1935). For the date of the original composition and its postulated revision, see Michael Lapidge, "Bede's Metrical *Vita S. Cuthberti*," in *St. Cuthbert, His Cult and His Community to A.D. 1200*, ed. Gerald Bonner, David Rollason, and Clare Stancliffe (Woodbridge, England, 1989), pp. 77–93, especially p. 85 and nn. 29 and 30.

5. Colgrave, *Two Lives*, pp. 142–307. Modification to the dating given on p. 16 is suggested by Clare Stancliffe, "Cuthbert and the Polarity Between Pastor and Solitary," in *St. Cuthbert*, ed. Bonner et al., pp. 21–44, at p. 24.

6. Bertram Colgrave, ed. and trans., *The Life of Bishop Wilfrid by Eddius Stephanus* (Cambridge, 1927; reprinted 1985). On the date and authorship, see D[avid] P. Kirby, "Bede, Eddius Stephanus and the 'Life of Wilfrid,'" *English Historical Review* 98 (1983): 101–10, and Goffart, *Narrators*, pp. 281–83.

7. Charles Plummer, ed., *Venerabilis Baedae Opera Historica*, vol. 2 (Oxford, 1896), pp. 388–404; and Dorothy Whitelock, trans., *English Historical Documents*, 2d. ed., vol. 1 (London, 1979), pp. 758–70. On the date and authorship, see Judith McClure, "Bede and the Life of Ceolfrid," *Peritia* 3 (1984): 71–84.

8. Plummer, *Opera Historica*, vol. 2, pp. 364–87; and D. H[ugh] Farmer, trans., *The Age of Bede* (Harmondsworth, England, 1983), pp. 183–208. For the date, see McClure, pp. 83–84.

9. A[lan] T. Thacker, "Origins of the Cult," in *St. Cuthbert*, ed. Bonner et al., pp. 109–10.

10. Bertram Colgrave, ed. and trans., *Felix's Life of Saint Guthlac* (Cambridge, 1956; reprinted 1985). For date and author, see pp. 15–19.

11. Jane Roberts, ed., *The Guthlac Poems of the Exeter Book* (Oxford, 1979), and "An Inventory of Early Guthlac Materials," *Mediaeval Studies* 32 (1970):

193–233; and R. Vleeskruyer, ed., *The Life of St. Chad: An Old English Homily* (Amsterdam, 1953).

12. Bertram Colgrave and R[oger] A. B. Mynors, eds. and trans., *Bede's Ecclesiastical History of the English People* (Oxford, 1969), vol. 4, 7–10, pp. 356–65, especially pp. 356 and 364.

13. D[avid] W. Rollason, *The Mildrith Legend: A Study in Early Medieval Hagiography in England* (Leicester, England, 1982), pp. 15–18 and 33–40.

14. Colgrave and Mynors, *Bede's Ecclesiastical History*, vol. 4, 19(17), pp. 390–97.

15. *Life of Ceolfrith*, Ch. 4 (Plummer, *Opera Historica*, vol. 1, p. 389; Whitelock, *English Historical Documents*, p. 759); and Charles Plummer and John Earle, eds., *Two of the Saxon Chronicles Parallel* (Oxford, 1892), vol. 1, p. 28 (s.a. 654 (A)).

16. Thacker, "Origins of the Cult," pp. 109–10.

17. Colgrave and Mynors, *Bede's Ecclesiastical History*, vol. 4, 3 and 6, pp. 344–47 and 354–55.

18. A[lan] T. Thacker, "The Social and Continental Background to Early Anglo-Saxon Hagiography," D. Ph. thesis, University of Oxford (1976); and in particular Gabriele Isenberg, *Die Würdigung Wilfrieds von York in der Historia Ecclesiastica gentis Anglorum Bedas und der Vita Wilfridi des Eddius* (Münster, Germany, 1978), especially p. 88. See also William Trent Foley, *Images of Sanctity in Eddius Stephanus' Life of Bishop Wilfrid, an Early English Saint's Life* (Lampeter, Wales, 1992).

19. See, for example, Peter Hunter Blair, *The World of Bede* (London, 1970).

20. Colgrave and Mynors, *Bede's Ecclesiastical History*, vol. 3, 2 and 9–14, vol. 4, 14 and 23(21), pp. 214–19, 240–61, 378–81, and 404–15, respectively.

21. Peter Godman, ed. and trans., *Alcuin: The Bishops, Kings, and Saints of York* (Oxford, 1982).

22. Alistair Campbell, ed. and trans., *Æthelwulf: De Abbatibus* (Oxford, 1967). See David Howlett, "The Provenance, Date and Structure of *De Abbatibus*," *Archaeologia Aeliana*, 5th ser., 3 (1975): 121–30; and Katherine Ward, "The Monastery of the *De Abbatibus:* A Reconsideration of its Location," *Durham Archaeological Journal* 7 (1992): pp. 123–27.

23. Godman, *Alcuin*, lines 1319–95, pp. 104–9.

24. On the political connotations of saints' cults in this period, see David Rollason, *Saints and Relics in Anglo-Saxon England* (Oxford, 1989), pp. 105–29.

25. Thomas Arnold, ed., *Symeonis Monachi Opera Omnia*, Rolls Series 75 (London, 1882–85), vol. 1, p. 47, vol. 2, p. 32; cf. Colgrave and Mynors, *Bede's Ecclesiastical History*, pp. 572–73.

26. Arnold, ibid., vol. 2, pp. 39–40; cf. vol. 1, p. 48.

27. Ibid., vol. 2, pp. 54 and 57.

28. Colgrave, *Life of Wilfrid*, passim; and Isenberg, *Die Würdigung Wilfreds*, pp. 89–94.

29. Colgrave, ibid., Ch. 63, pp. 136–37; on this, however, see also Isenberg, ibid. pp. 78–79 with regard to canon law.

30. Arnold, *Symeonis Monarchi Opera Omnia*, vol. 2, p. 52.

31. Ibid., vol. 2, p. 52; and D[avid] W. Rollason, "The Cults of Murdered Royal Saints in Anglo-Saxon England," *ASE* 11 (1983): 1–22, especially pp. 3–4, where Ælfwold is also discussed.

32. Colgrave and Mynors, *Bede's Ecclesiastical History*, bk. 3, 24 and bk. 4, 26, pp. 292–93 and 428–31; and Colgave, *Life of Wilfrid*, Ch. 60, pp. 130–33.

33. Plummer, *Opera Historica*, Ch. 12, vol. 1, p. 392.

34. D[avid] P. Kirby, "King Ceolwulf of Northumbria and the *Historical Ecclesiastica*," *Studia Celtica* 14–15 (1979–80): 168–73.

35. Plummer, *Opera Historica*, vol. 1, pp. 405–23; and Whitelock, *English Historical Documents*, vol. 1, pp. 799–810. See Goffart, *Narrators*, pp. 235–57.

36. James Campbell, *Essays in Anglo-Saxon History* (London and Ronceverte, W. Va., 1986), pp. 37–40; Alan Thacker, "Bede's Ideal of Reform," in *Ideal and Reality in Frankish and Anglo-Saxon Society*, ed. Patrick Wormald, Donald Bullough, and Roger Collins (Oxford, 1983), pp. 130–53, especially pp. 142–53; and D. P. Kirby, *Bede's Historia Ecclesiastica Gentis Anglorum: Its Contemporary Setting*, Jarrow Lecture 1992 (Jarrow, England, 1993).

37. *Life of Ceolfrith*, Ch. 8, Plummer, *Opera Historica*, vol. 1, pp. 390–92; Whitelock, *English Historical Documents*, vol. 1, pp. 760–61.

38. J[ames] Campbell, "Elements in the Background to the *Life of St. Cuthbert* and his Early Cult," in *St. Cuthbert*, ed. Bonner et al., pp. 3–19.

39. Henry Mayr-Harting, *The Coming of Christianity to Anglo-Saxon England*, 3d ed. (London, 1991), pp. 7–9 and 103–13; and Plummer, *Opera Historica*, vol. 2, pp. 348–54.

40. Colgrave and Mynors, *Bede's Ecclesiastical History*, vol. 3, 25, pp. 308–9; and Clare Stancliffe, "Cuthbert and the Polarity Between Pastor and Solitary," in *St. Cuthbert*, ed. Bonner et al., pp. 21–22. Cf. Goffart's subtle argument (*Narrators*, pp. 326–27) that Bede was forced to emphasize the Easter question because, in refuting the importance of Wilfrid, he had to give prominence to the Irish.

41. Colgrave and Mynors, ibid., bk. 5, 21, pp. 532–53.

42. Archibald A. M. Duncan, "Bede, Iona, and the Picts," *The Writing of History in the Middle Ages*, ed. R[alph] H. C. Davis and J. M[ichael] Wallace-Hadrill (Oxford, 1982), pp. 1–42, especially p. 27; and Plummer, *Opera Historica*,

vol. 2, p. 331. It is less clear, however, how topical the problem was in the 730s when it affected chiefly the Britons. Compare James Campbell, *Essays in Anglo-Saxon History* (London and Ronceverte, W. Va., 1986), pp. 23–24, with Goffart, *Narrators*, p. 253 and n. 94.

43. Edward James, "Bede and the Tonsure Question," *Peritia* 3 (1984): 85–98.

44. Colgrave, *Life of Wilfrid*, Chs. 12, 14, and 15, pp. 24–25 and 30–33.

45. Mayr-Harting, *The Coming of Christianity*, pp. 103–4.

46. Eric John, "The Social and Political Problems of the Early English Church" in *Land, Church and People: Essays Presented to H. P. R. Finberg*, ed. Joan Thirsk (Reading, England, 1970), pp. 39–63, especially p. 52; and Mayr-Harting, ibid., p. 108 (but cf. pp. 7–9).

47. Colgrave, *Two Lives*, anonymous vol. II, 2, pp. 76–77; Colgrave and Mynors, *Bede's Ecclesiastical History*, vol. 4, 27(25), pp. 430–31; and Stancliffe, "Cuthbert and the Polarity," pp. 23–24.

48. Colgrave, *Two Lives*, Bede Ch. 39, pp. 384–85.

49. Donald Bullough, "Hagiography as Patriotism: Alcuin's 'York Poem' and the Early Northumbrian 'Vitae Sanctorum,' " in *Hagiographie, cultures et sociétés, IVè–XIIècles* (Paris, 1981), p. 342.

50. Colgrave, *Life of Gregory*, Chs. 14–19, pp. 96–105.

51. Mayr-Harting, *The Coming of Christianity*, p. 69.

52. A. O. Anderson and M. O. Anderson, ed. and trans., *Adomnan's Life of Columba*, 2d ed. (Oxford, 1991).

53. *Cummian's Letter De controversia paschali*, ed. and trans. Mary Walsh and Dáibhí O Cróinín (Toronto, 1988). See also J. M. Picard, "The Purpose of Adomnan's *Vita Columbae*," *Peritia* 1 (1982): 160–77, especially pp. 171–72, and Mayr-Harting, *The Coming of Christianity*, p. 110.

54. Colgrave, *Life of Wilfrid*, Ch. 20, pp. 22–23.

55. Colgrave, and Mynors, *Bede's Ecclesiastical History*, vol. 3, 25, pp. 306–7. Cf. Goffart, *Narrators*, pp. 312–13.

56. Picard, "The Purpose," pp. 165 and 172–75.

57. Anderson and Anderson, *Adomnan's Life of Columba*, I.1.

58. Picard, "The Purpose," p. 175.

59. Donald Bullough, "Columba, Adomnan and the Achievement of Iona," *Scottish Historical Review* 43 (1964): 125–30; and 44 (1965): 17–21 and 26–28.

60. Stancliffe, "Cuthbert and the Polarity," pp. 22–23 and 43–44.

61. Duncan, "Bede," pp. 1–42.

62. Hermann Moisl, "The Bernician Royal Dynasty and the Irish in the Seventh Century," *Peritia* 2 (1983): 120–24; and Colgrave and Mynors, *Bede's Ecclesiastical History*, vol. 5, 23, pp. 560–61 and vol. 5, 24, pp. 564–67. Cf. note 42.

63. Colgrave, *Two Lives*, anonymous II.4, pp. 82–83, and Bede, Ch. 11, pp. 192–93; cf. D[avid] P. Kirby, "Bede and the Pictish Church," *Innes Review* 24 (1973): 6–25.

64. For this and what follows, see Mayr-Harting, *The Coming of Chrisianity*, pp. 129–47, and references there.

65. Colgrave, *Life of Wilfrid*, Ch. 32, pp. 64–65.

66. Ibid., Ch. 24, p. 49

67. Ibid., Ch. 21, pp. 42–43.

68. John, "Social and Political Problems," p. 51.

69. Colgrave, *Life of Wilfrid*, Ch. 28, pp. 54–55, and Ch. 33, pp. 66–69.

70. Ibid., Ch. 59, pp. 126–29.

71. Ibid., Preface. p. 2; trans. p. 3: "So I beseech my readers to believe my report, neglecting the thousand envious pricks of the ancient foe and reflecting on what has been eloquently proclaimed. For boldness ever has its rivals in public places—the lightnings strike the tops of the mountains."

72. "Continuations from the Moore Manuscript," in Colgrave and Mynors, *Bede's Ecclesiastical History*, pp. 572–73; and D[avid] P. Kirby, "Northumbria in the Time of Wilfrid," in *St. Wilfrid at Hexham*, ed. D[avid] P. Kirby (Newcastle upon Tyne, England, 1974), pp. 1–34, especially p. 24.

73. Kirby, "Bede, Eddius Stephanus," pp. 106–8.

74. Colgrave, *Two Lives*, Bede, Ch. 40, pp. 286–87.

75. Colgrave and Mynors, *Bede's Ecclesiastical History*, vol. 4, 29, pp. 442–43.

76. Colgrave, *Life of Wilfrid*, Preface, p. 2.

77. Thacker, "Origins of the Cult," pp. 115–22. Similar conclusions, relating also to the *Ecclesiastical History*, had been reached independently by Goffart, *Narrators*, pp. 307–24. See also W. Goffart, "*The Historia Ecclesiastica*: Bede's Agenda and Ours," *Haskins Society Journal* 2 (1990): 28–45. Reference should be made to the critique by Kirby, *Bede's Historia Ecclesiastica*, pp. 18–19.

78. Kirby, "Northumbria," pp. 20–21.

79. Peter Hunter Blair, "The Boundary Between Bernicia and Deira," *Archeaologia Aeliana*, 4th ser., 27 (1949): 46–59, reprinted *Anglo-Saxon Northumbria*, ed. M[ichael] Lapidge and P[auline] Hunter Blair (London, 1984), item 5.

80. F[rank] M. Stenton, *Anglo-Saxon England*, 3d ed. (Oxford, 1971), pp. 75–85.

81. Colgrave and Mynors, *Bede's Ecclesiastical History*, vol. 3, 14, pp. 256–57 and vol. 3, 24, pp. 292–93; see Thacker, "Bede's Ideal of Reform," pp. 146–47.

82. Colgrave and Mynors, ibid., vol. 3, 23, and 24, pp. 254, 286, and 290, respectively.

83. Colgrave, *Life of Gregory*, Chs. 18–19, pp. 100–5; Thacker, "Bede's Ideal of Reform," p. 147; and Alan [T.] Thacker, "Kings, Saints, and Monasteries in Pre-Viking Mercia," *Midland History* 10 (1985): 2–4.

84. Thacker, "Bede's Ideal of Reform," pp. 147–50, and J. M[ichael] Wallace-Hadrill, "Bede and Plummer," in his *Early Medieval History* (Oxford, 1975), pp. 90–91.

85. Jaager, *Bedas Metrische Vita*, Prologue, p. 60.

86. Thacker, "Bede's Ideal of Reform," p. 148, and "Origins of the Cult," p. 117.

87. Colgrave, *Two Lives*, anonymous, III.6 and Bede, Ch. 24, pp. 102–3 and 234–39. The place of Aldfrith's exile is given as Ireland in an erroneous citation in Rollason, *Saints and Relics*, p. 99.

88. Hermann Moisl, "The Bernician Royal Dynasty and the Irish in the Seventh Century," *Peritia* 2 (1983): 120–24.

89. Isenberg, *Die Würdigung*, p. 73.

90. Colgrave, *Life of Wilfrid*, Ch. 19, pp. 40–41. Cf. Ch. 20, pp. 42–43.

91. Ibid., Ch. 21, pp. 42–43.

92. Ibid., Ch. 24, pp. 50–51.

93. Isenberg, *Die Würdigung*, p. 73.

94. Colgrave, *Life of Wilfrid*, Ch. 59, pp. 126–27.

95. Ibid., Ch. 60, pp. 130–33.

96. Isenberg, *Die Würdigung*, p. 73: "that kingship could only then fulfill its proper vow to Peter, if it was ready for cooperation with Wilfrid."

Ælfric's *Sanctorale*

Michael Lapidge

Modern study of Ælfric's saints' lives and homilies, with its emphasis on source analysis, prose style, Winchester-school lexis, and similar topics, often runs the risk of overlooking a simple but fundamental aspect of this literary production; namely, that Ælfric was attempting above all to make the Christian devotions of the liturgical year comprehensible to a lay audience. In compiling his three great collections of reading (and preaching) material, Ælfric was motivated by a basic, but individual, awareness of what constituted the liturgical year, or *circulum anni* as he calls it: which feasts had the greatest significance and required the most careful explication and which had a lesser importance and could accordingly be omitted.[1] Ælfric's work of compilation was a process of judgment and selection, therefore, and we approach closest to his own concerns if we too maintain a continual awareness of the structure and outline of the liturgical year, which his saints' lives and homilies represent.

The liturgical year consists of two great, overlapping cycles of feasts: the *temporale* and the *sanctorale*. The *temporale* consists of those Sundays (and associated days) linked to Easter; and because Easter originated as a feast (Passover or *pasch*) in the Hebrew lunar calendar, it falls on a different Sunday—and hence different calendar day—each year. The *sanctorale*, on the other hand, consists of those feasts that are celebrated each year on the same day of the Roman or solar calendar. The different origins of these feasts— in the Hebrews' lunar calendar or in the Roman solar calendar—explain why, for example, Christ's birth is celebrated on a fixed day, December 25, every year, whereas His resurrection at Easter is celebrated on different Sundays each year.[2] The feasts of the *temporale* were celebrated universally throughout Christendom: Shrove Sunday (*Quinquagesima*), the first Sunday in Lent (*Quadragesima*), Palm Sunday, Easter with "Holy Week," Ascension, Pentecost or Whitsun, and so on. With the *sanctorale*, however, matters were somewhat different. Some feasts were apparently universal from the earliest days of Christianity (Christmas itself, and Epiphany, for example), and others, such as the Purification of the Virgin on February 2, were in due course to become universal. But many, perhaps the majority, of feasts in the *sanctorale* varied from church to church, depending (say) on whether a church possessed a particular saint's relics or whether a local bishop felt an especial veneration for a particular saint. It is usually the individual, localizable features in any *sanctorale*—whether in a liturgical calendar, sacramentary, breviary, homiliary, or whatever—that enable modern liturgists to infer the origin of a liturgical book and the structure of the particular liturgy it represents.

Ælfric composed his collections of homilies and saints' lives with a sharp awareness of how the individual items would fit into the overall pattern of the liturgical year and whether they pertained to the *temporale* or *sanctorale*. Such awareness implies in turn that Ælfric was working with a liturgical calendar. With each item, regardless of its literary form,[3] Ælfric specified the liturgical destination by means of a rubric, which made clear whether the text was intended for the *temporale* or the *sanctorale*. In this chapter I shall be concerned solely with those texts which Ælfric specifically designated for the *sanctorale*.[4] Considered as a group these texts throw an interesting light on how Ælfric conceived the structure of the liturgical year and what feasts he regarded as most important.[5] By isolating the texts intended by Ælfric for the *sanctorale*, it is possible to reconstruct the general outlines of the liturgical calendar that Ælfric had in mind as he assembled his collections of reading (and preaching) material.[6] It is then possible to compare this reconstructed calendar with those that have survived from late Anglo-Saxon England (including those from Winchester, where Ælfric was trained), and such comparison serves to highlight many unexpected and eccentric features of Ælfric's liturgical practice.[7] In what follows, I shall first list all those Ælfrician texts that are specified for a particular feast in the *sanctorale*, then compare this reconstructed *sanctorale* with those known from Anglo-Saxon liturgical calendars, and finally attempt some explanation of the individual features of Ælfric's *sanctorale*.

Let us proceed in chronological order through Ælfric's collections of homilies and reading pieces, beginning with the First Series of *Catholic Homilies*,[8] issued possibly as early as (but no earlier than) 990 and no later than 994.[9] This First Series consists of forty homilies and combines those for the *temporale* and *sanctorale* in a single sequence, beginning with Christmas. Nineteen of the forty items are specified for a particular feast in the *sanctorale*,[10] as follows (note that I give first the number of the homily within the collection, then the feast in question, then the specification as given in the rubric, in Roman reckoning,[11] and finally, in square brackets, the corresponding date in modern reckoning):

ii.	Christmas (*Natiuitas Domini*): *.viii. kl. Ian.* [December 25]
iii.	St. Stephen: *.vii. kl. Ian.* [December 26]
iv.	Assumption of St. John the Apostle: *.vi. kl. Ian.* [December 27]
v.	Holy Innocents: *.v. kl. Ian.* [December 28]
vi.	Circumcision (Octave of the Nativity): *Kl. Ian.* [January 1]
vii.	Epiphany: *.viii. id. Ian.* [January 6]
ix.	Purification of the Virgin: *.iiii. non. Febr.* [February 2]
xiii.	Annunciation of the Virgin: *.viii. kl. Apr.* [March 25]
xxv.	Nativity of John the Baptist: *.viii. kl. Iul.* [June 24]
xxvi.	SS Peter and Paul: *.iii. kl. Iul.* [June 29]
xxvii.	St. Paul: *.ii. kl. Iul.* [June 30]
xxix.	St. Laurence: *.iiii. id. Aug.* [August 10]
xxx.	Assumption of the Virgin: *.xviiii. kl. Sept.* [August 15]
xxxi.	St. Bartholomew: *.viii. kl. Sept.* [August 25]
xxxii.	Decollation of John the Baptist: *.iiii. kl. Sept.* [August 29]
xxxiv.	St. Michael (*Dedicatio ecclesiae*): *.iii. kl. Oct.* [September 29]
xxxvi.	All Saints: *Kl. Nou.* [December 1]
xxxvii.	St. Clement: *.ix. kl. Dec.* [November 23]
xxxviii.	St. Andrew: *.ii. kl. Dec.* [November 30]

Ælfric's Second Series of *Catholic Homilies*,[12] issued later than the First Series, but not later than 994 (inasmuch as it too was dedicated to Archbishop Sigeric)[13] similarly consists of forty items, of which fifteen (or sixteen)[14] are specified for the *sanctorale*:

i.	Christmas (*Natiuitas Domini*): *.viii. kl. Ian.* [December 25]
ii.	St. Stephen: *.vii. kl. Ian.* [December 26]
iii.	Epiphany: *.viii. id. Ian.* [December 6]
ix.	St. Gregory: *.iiii. id. Mart.* [March 12]
x.	St. Cuthbert: *.xiii. kl. Apr.* [March 20]
xi.	St. Benedict: *.xii. kl. Apr.* [March 21]
xvii.	SS Philip and James: *Kl. Mai.* [May 1]
xviii.	Invention of the Holy Cross; SS Alexander, Eventius and Theodulus:[15] *.v. non. Mai.* [May 3]
xxiv.	St. Peter: *.iii. kl. Iul.* [June 29]
xxvii(a).	St. James: *.viii. kl. Aug.* [July 25]
xxvii(b).	SS Septem Dormientes: *.vi. kl. Aug.* [July 27]
xxix.	Assumption of the Virgin: *.xviii. kl. Sept.* [August 15]
xxxii.	St. Matthew: *.xi. kl. Oct.* [September 21]
xxxiii.	SS Simon and Jude: *.v. kl. Nou.* [October 28]
xxxiv.	St. Martin: *.iii. id. Nou.* [November 11]

It will be noted that this list of feasts overlaps in several respects with that in the First Series of Catholic Homilies.

Ælfric's other major collection of liturgical reading pieces is his so-called *Lives of Saints*,[16] compiled after the two series of Catholic Homilies but no later than 998.[17] Unlike the two series of Catholic Homilies, we do not have the collection of *Lives of Saints* in precisely the form in which Ælfric issued it. The earliest and most complete manuscript (London, BL, Cotton Julius E. vii) contains various non-Ælfrician interpolations, and it is not always possible to be certain that the order of items in Julius E. vii is Ælfric's own. As represented in Julius E. vii, Ælfric's collection of *Lives of Saints* contains twenty-nine items intended for the *sanctorale*. In default of another, more reliable, manuscript, I give the contents of Julius E. vii (omitting those items that, on stylistic and other grounds, are deemed to be non-Ælfrician); note that the numbers given in the left-hand margin are those of Skeat's edition, not of the manuscript itself.[18]

i.	Christmas (*Natiuitas Domini*): *.viii. kl. Ian.* [December 25]
ii.	St. Eugenia: *eodem die* [December 25]
iii.	St. Basil: *Kl. Ian.* [January 1]
iv.	SS Julian and Basilissa: *Id. Ian.* [January 13]
v.	St. Sebastian: *.xiii. kl. Febr.* [January 20][19]
vi.	St. Maur: *.xviii. kl. Febr.* [January 15]
vii.	St. Agnes: *.xii. kl. Febr.*[20] [January 21]
viii.	St. Agatha: *Non. Febr.* [February 5]
ix.	St. Lucy: no date specified[21]
x.	*Cathedra S. Petri*: *.viii. kl. Mart.* [February 22]
xi.	*Quadraginta milites*: *.vii. id. Mart.* [March 9]
xiv.	St. George: *.viiii. kl. Mai.* [April 23]
xv.	St. Mark: *.vii. kl. Mai.* [April 25]
xix.	St. Alban: no date specified[22]
xx.	St. Æthelthryth: *.viiii. kl. Iul.* [June 23]
xxi.	St. Swithun: *.vi. non. Iul.* [July 2]
xxi(a).	St. Macarius: no date specified[23]
xxii.	St. Apollinaris: *.x. kl. Aug.* [July 23]
xxiv.	SS Abdon and Sennes: *.iii. kl. Aug.* [July 30]
xxv.	Holy Maccabees: *Kl. Aug.* [August 1]
xxvi.	St. Oswald, king and martyr: *Non. Aug.* [August 5]
xxvii.	Exaltation of the Holy Cross: *.xviii. kl. Oct.* [September 14]
xxviii.	St. Maurice and companions: *.x. kl. Oct.* [September 22]
xxix.	St. Dionysius and companions: *.vii. id. Oct.*[24] [October 9]
xxxi.	St. Martin: no date specified[25]

xxxii.	St. Edmund, king and martyr: *.xii. kl. Dec.* [November 20]
xxxiv.	St. Cecilia: *.x. kl. Dec.* [November 22]
xxxv.	SS Chrysanthus and Daria: *.iii. kl. Dec.* [November 29]
xxxvi.	St. Thomas: *.xii. kl. Ian.* [December 21]

In addition to the items intended for the *sanctorale* in Ælfric's major collections are two additional items, which circulated separately: a life of St. Vincent,[26] specified for *.xi. kl. Febr.* [= January 22], and a homily for the Nativity of the Virgin Mary, intended for *.vi. id. Sept.* [= September 8].[27] Taking these two separate items together with those in the three larger collections and ignoring the duplications of feasts such as Christmas, we are left with a total of fifty-four feasts specified by Ælfric for the *sanctorale*.

From these fifty-four feasts it is possible to reconstruct the liturgical calendar, which is implied by the specification of dates that the texts contain and that represents Ælfric's liturgical use. A reconstructed calendar is given in the Appendix to this chapter. The calendar highlights various features of Ælfric's use. On the whole, Ælfric has distributed his feasts evenly over the liturgical year. Some months, such as February and October, are thinly represented. In other months there are apparently striking gaps: in April there is no feast earlier than that of St. George on the 23; there is no feast in late May or early June (in fact none between May 3 and June 22); and no feast in early December, the earliest being that of St. Thomas on the 21. These gaps are readily explicable in liturgical terms. The gap in April is explained by the fact that Easter with all its attendant feasts normally falls at that time (the outer dating termini being March 22 × April 18); that in late May and early June by the fact that Ascension and Pentecost normally fall then, with the latest possible limit being June 13; and the feasts of Advent fall in early December. In other words, these apparent gaps in Ælfric's *sanctorale* are explicable in terms of feasts of the interconnected *temporale*.

Nevertheless, various omissions from Ælfric's *sanctorale* require comment and cannot be accounted for by reference to the *temporale*. Let us consider these omissions in four separate categories.

Feasts of Universal Observance Omitted by Ælfric

January:	S. Simeon (5), S. Felicis in Pincis (14), Conuersio S. Pauli (25)
February:	S. Brigide (1), S. Iuliane (16), S. Mathiae apostoli (24)
March:	Perpetuae et Felicitatis (7)
April:	S. Ambrosii (4)

May:	SS Gordiani et Epimachi (10), Nerei, Achillei, Pancratii (12)
June:	Barnabe (11), Geruasii et Protasii (19)
July:	Ordinatio S. Martini (4), Translatio S. Benedicti (11), Pantaleonis (28)
August:	Inuentio S. Stephani (3), S. Augustini (28)
September:	Proti et Iacincti (11), Cosme et Damiani (27), S. Hieronymi (30)
October:	S. Lucae (18)
November:	Eustachii (2), Quattuor coronatorum (8)
December:	S. Siluestri (31)

There are some curious omissions here. Among evangelists, Ælfric includes Mark (April 25), Matthew (September 21) and John (December 27), but oddly omits Luke. Among apostles, the omission of Matthias and Barnabas is striking. Among martyrs, the feasts of Gervasius and Protasius, Cosmas and Damianus, and the Four Crowned Martyrs were universally celebrated in Anglo-Saxon England, to judge from surviving liturgical calendars. Among Doctors of the Church, Ælfric includes St. Gregory (March 12), but omits Ambrose,[28] Augustine, and Jerome. Among virgin martyrs, one might have expected Ælfric to include Perpetua and Felicitas, who were commemorated in the *Nobis quoque peccatoribus* of the mass and whose names headed the list of virgin martyrs in most Anglo-Saxon litanies of the saints. Finally, note the omission of the Translation of St Benedict, an important feast that was celebrated, especially in Benedictine houses, on July 11. It is a curious omission for a Benedictine monk.

Frankish and Flemish Saints Widely Venerated in Late Anglo-Saxon England but Omitted by Ælfric

February:	SS Vedasti et Amandi (6)
August:	S. Audoeni (24)
September:	S. Bertini (5), S. Audomari (9), S. Landberti (17)
October:	S. Quintini (31)

Ælfric does include three saints of Frankish origin who had cults, especially in France: St. Maur (January 15), whose cult originated at Glanfeuil and who had a cult at Saint-Germain-des-Prés. St. Maurice and the Theban Legion (September 22), with a cult at Agaune in Burgundy, and St. Dionysius and companions (October 9), with cults principally in Paris. But his omissions are equally striking, in view of developments in the tenth-century Anglo-Saxon church. From the middle of the tenth century onward, the close links between the Benedictine reformers in England and the monasteries of northern France and Flanders resulted in the growth of the cults of certain Frankish saints in England. This growth is reflected in liturgical books. To choose one example, St. Vedastus is especially commemorated in the "Leofric Missal" (a sacramentary written in NE France or Flanders c. 900 that was in England, perhaps at Winchester, by the later tenth century) and in the famous "Benedictional of St Æthelwold."[29] By the same token, the Cotton-Corpus Legendary, which was certainly used by Ælfric, reflects an especial reverence for St. Vedastus,[30] but also includes SS Amandus, Bertinus, Audomarus, and Quintinus. It is surely odd that Ælfric should have omitted saints such as these.

English Saints (Excluding Those Venerated at Winchester) Omitted by Ælfric

March:	S. Ceadde (2), S. Eadwardi regis et mart. (18)
April:	S. Guthlaci (11)
May:	S. Dunstani (19), S. Augustini archiep. (26)
June:	S. Bonifacii mart. (5), S. Eadburge (15)
July:	S. Mildrede (13), S. Kenelme (17)

Ælfric's *sanctorale* includes a substantial number of (pan-)English saints: St. Cuthbert (March 20), St. Alban (June 22), St. Æthelthryth (June 23), St. Oswald king and martyr (August 5) and St. Edmund king and martyr (November 20). Given Ælfric's inclusion of these English saints, it is worth inquiring about his (equally striking) omissions. Possibly St. Dunstan (who died in 988) and King Edward (who was killed in 978) were omitted because their status as saints was too recent a phenomenon, and their cults were not yet established nationally at the time Ælfric was writing.[31] The cults of SS Eadburg,[32] Mildreth,[33] and Kenelm were probably too local in nature to command the attention of Ælfric. But his omissions of Augustine, the first archbishop of the English (whose role as leader of the successful Gregorian mission to convert the English will have been well known to Ælfric from the pages of Bede's *Historia Ecclesiastica*) and Guthlac (whose saintly life was well known from Felix's *Vita S. Guthlaci*)[34] are less easily explicable.

Saints with Cults Specifically at Winchester but Omitted by Ælfric

January:	Translatio S. Iudoci (9)
July:	S. Grimbaldi (8), Translatio S. Swithuni (15)

August: S. Æthelwoldi (1)
September: Translatio S. Birini (4), Translatio S. Æthelwoldi (10)
October: S. Iusti mart. (18)
November: S. Byrnstani (4)
December: S. Birini (3), S. Iudoci (13)

Ælfric was trained at Winchester and continued in later life to regard himself as an alumnus of Bishop Æthelwold.[35] It is not surprising, therefore, that he should have included in his *sanctorale* a commemoration of St. Swithun, the patron saint of Winchester. What is curious, however, is that his life of St. Swithun is specified for that saint's *depositio* on July 2 rather than for the *translatio* on July 15, which was by far the more widely celebrated feast. There are other curiosities. Ælfric omits all the continental saints whose relics were at Winchester and who were specifically revered there: Grimbald of Saint-Bertin, first abbot of the New Minster; St. Iudoc, whose relics the New Minster possessed; and St. Iustus, the boy martyr of Beauvais, whose relics were at the Old Minster. It is possible that Ælfric omitted Byrnstan, a relatively obscure bishop of Winchester in the earlier tenth century (931–934) because too little was known of him, but the omissions of Birinus and Æthelwold are less easy to explain. In 1006 Ælfric produced an abbreviated version of Wulfstan of Winchester's *Vita S. Æthelwoldi*, and it is possible that this Latin abbreviation marked Ælfric's first step toward an eventual English life of St. Æthelwold, which he never succeeded in completing.[36] By the same token, Ælfric excerpted the passages from Bede's *Historia Ecclesiastica* concerning Birinus and used these as the basis for the brief account of this saint embedded in his life of St. Oswald;[37] but it is nonetheless striking that Ælfric did not devote a separate life to this important Winchester saint.

In other respects, too, Ælfric's *sanctorale* departs radically from Winchester use, as it can be recovered from surviving liturgical calendars. Hence, Ælfric includes in his *Lives of Saints* an account of the Forty Soldiers of Sebaste in Armenia (*Quadraginta milites*), specified for March 9.[38] This feast is included in a large number of Anglo-Saxon calendars from various parts of England.[39] However, it is conspicuously omitted from all four calendars of certain Winchester origin: those in London, BL Cotton Titus D. xxvii (Wormald, no. 9), Cambridge, Trinity College, R. 15. 32 (Wormald, no. 10), London, BL Arundel 60 (Wormald, no. 11), and Cotton Vitellius E. xviii (Wormald, no. 12).[40] This omission can scarcely be a matter of chance and must represent some liturgical policy decision at late tenth-century Winchester. In any event, the fact that the feast of the Forty Martyrs *was* commemorated by Ælfric indicates fairly clearly that he was not following Winchester use consistently.

There are various other eccentricities in Ælfric's *sanctorale*, especially as regards the days on which certain saints are commemorated. Three such feast days are in question: those for SS Eugenia, Basil, and Julian and Basilissa. The first is St. Eugenia, whom Ælfric commemorates on December 25, the same day as Christ's Nativity. The commemoration of St. Eugenia is not found on this day in a single surviving Anglo-Saxon calendar. Instead, she was commemorated on either March 16, a commemoration recorded by five calendars,[41] or May 16, recorded in four.[42] Three calendars have both dates, and one of these—Salisbury, Cathedral Library, 150—has yet a third commemoration for St. Eugenia, on December 23. But no Anglo-Saxon calendar has a commemoration for this saint on December 25, and no Winchester calendar has a feast for St. Eugenia on any date whatsoever. Where, then, did Ælfric derive this commemoration? The answer seems to be that he took the date of the feast, along with the text of the *Vita S. Eugeniae*, from the Cotton-Corpus legendary, which has St. Eugenia on that date,[43] rather than from a liturgical calendar.

A similar situation obtains in the case of St. Basil. Ælfric commemorates St. Basil on January 1. Now St. Basil is commemorated in a large number of Anglo-Saxon calendars—seven[44]—but always on June 14. Four of the calendars in question are from Winchester. In commemorating St. Basil on January 1, therefore, Ælfric was not following Winchester use. Once again, the explanation seems to be that Ælfric took the text along with the commemoration from the Cotton-Corpus legendary, which has Euphemius' *Vita S. Basilii* against January 1.[45]

However, Ælfric's use of the Cotton-Corpus legendary will not account for all the eccentric commemorations in Ælfric's *sanctorale*. Consider the case of SS Julian and Basilissa, whom Ælfric commemorates on January 13 (*id. Ian.*). These two saints are very rarely commemorated in Anglo-Saxon calendars, and no calendar has a commemoration on January 13. Only three calendars have commemorations of any kind: one for January 9 (Oxford, Bodleian Library, Douce 296: Wormald, no. 20), one for February 27 (Cambridge, Trinity College, R. 15. 32, a calendar of Winchester origin: Wormald, no. 10), and one on December 20 (London, BL Cotton Nero A. ii: Wormald, no. 2). In addition to these commemorations, it is interesting to note that the Cotton-Corpus legendary assigns the *Passio SS Iuliani et Basilissae* to January 9. In face of this evidence, one wonders whether Ælfric's date of *id. Ian.* (= January 13) is the result of a copyist's error for *.v. id. Ian.* (= January 9); but given the scarcity of commemorations in Anglo-Saxon calendars, and the widely varying dates attested in them, it is possible that Ælfric was here following a liturgical source unknown to us.

In creating his great corpus of devotional writings, whether for preaching or for private meditation, Ælfric had constantly in mind the overall shape of the liturgical year; and in selecting texts for inclusion in this corpus, he will have been guided in the first instance by liturgical considerations—the universality of the individual feast, its appropriateness to lay persons' devotions—rather than by questions of stylistic preference. Accordingly, it is pertinent to consider first what place a particular text, whether homily or saint's life, occupied in Ælfric's overall liturgical design, before turning to questions of source, style or lexis.

Appendix: Ælfric's (Reconstructed) Calendar

[January]	[February]	[March]
1 Circumcisio Domini et		
S. Basilii	2 Purificatio S. Mariae	
6 Epiphania Domini	5 S. Agathae	
		9 SS Quadraginta militum
13 SS Iuliani et Basilisse		12 S Gregorii pape
15 S. Mauri		
20 S. Sebastiani		20 S. Cuthberti
21 S. Agnetis		21 S. Benedicti
22 S. Vincentii	22 Cathedra S. Petri	
		25 Adnuntiatio S. Mariae

[April]	[May]	[June]
	1 SS Philippi et Iacobi	
	3 Inuentio S. Crucis et	
	SS Alexandri, Euentii	
	et Theodoli	
		22 S. Albani martyris
23 S. Georgii		23 S. Æþelþryðe uirginis
25 S. Marci euangeliste		24 Natiuitas S. Iohannis
		Baptistae
		29 SS Petri et Pauli
		30 S. Pauli apostoli

[July]	[August]	[September]
	1 SS Maccabeorum	
2 Depositio S. Swithuni		
	3 S. Oswaldi reg. et mart.	
	10 S. Laurentii	8 Natiuitas S. Mariae
	15 Assumptio S. Mariae	14 Exaltatio S. Crucis
		21 S. Matthaei
23 S. Apollinaris		22 S. Mauricii
25 S. Iacobi	25 S. Bartholomei	
27 SS .vii. dormientium		
	29 Decollatio S. Iohannis	29 S. Michaelis archang.
30 SS Abdon et Sennen	Baptistae	

[October]	[November]	[December]
	1 Omnium Sanctorum	
9 S. Dionisii et sociorum	11 S. Martini	
	20 S. Eadmundi reg. et mart.	
	22 S. Ceciliae	21 S. Thomae
	23 S. Clementis papae	
		25 Natiuitas Domini et
		S. Eugeniae
		26 S. Stephani
		27 Assumptio S. Iohannis
28 SS Simonis et Iudae		28 SS Innocentium
	29 SS Crisanthi et Darie	
	30 S. Andreae apost.	

Notes

1. Ælfric reveals this awareness in the preface to his First Series of *Catholic Homilies*: "nec tamen omnia Evangelia [*scil.* gospel pericopes] tangimus per circulum anni, sed illa tantummodo quibus speramus sufficere posse simplicibus ad animarum emendationem . . . " ("we have not treated all the gospel pericopes for the course of the entire year, but only those which we hope may be sufficient for the improvement of the souls of simple folk").

2. There is a clear exposition of the origin and nature of these two cycles in Gregory Dix, *The Shape of the Liturgy*, 2d ed. (London, 1945), pp. 333–85; see also A. A. McArthur, *The Evolution of the Christian Year* (London, 1953), and J. Pascher, *Das liturgische Jahr* (Munich, 1963).

3. That is, whether it was in the form of an exegetical homily or commentary on a gospel pericope, or in the form of a saint's *passio* or *vita*. Within each of Ælfric's three great collections are texts specified for both cycles. It cannot simply be assumed that all texts in the form of saints' lives were intended for the *sanctorale*, any more that it can be assumed that texts in the form of homilies were intended for the *temporale*. Only the rubric of a particular text makes clear its liturgical destination.

4. I leave out of consideration, therefore, all those homilies specified by Ælfric for the *temporale*, including those in the *Catholic Homilies* and *Lives of Saints*, as well as in the later collection of *Temporale* homilies edited by J. C. Pope, *Homilies of Ælfric: A Supplementary Collection*, EETS OS 259–60 (London, 1967–68).

5. I have raised some of these questions cursorily, without attempting to answer them, in "The Saintly Life in Anglo-Saxon England," in *The Cambridge Companion to Anglo-Saxon England*, ed. Malcolm Godden and Michael Lapidge (Cambridge, 1991), pp. 243–63, on 256–58.

6. The last attempt to reconstruct Ælfric's *sanctorale* was made by F. Piper, *Die Kalendarien und Martyrologien der Angelsachsen* (Berlin, 1862), pp. 71–82. P. A. M. Clemoes ("The Chronology of Ælfric's Works" in *The Anglo-Saxons: Studies in Some Aspects of Their History and Culture Presented to Bruce Dickins*, ed. Peter Clemoes [London, 1959; reprinted as *OEN Subsidia* 5 (1979)], pp. 212–47, on 216–17) lists those homiletic texts of Ælfric specified for the "Proper of the Saints" (= *sanctorale*), but does not include among them the items in the *Lives of Saints* collection bearing a specification of date.

7. Liturgical calendars from the later Anglo-Saxon period are conveniently edited by F. Wormald, *English Kalendars Before A.D. 1100*, Henry Bradshaw Society Publications 72 (London, 1934)[hereafter cited simply as Wormald]. To the collection of calendars edited by Wormald three should be added: that in *The Missal of Robert of Jumièges*, ed. H. A. Wilson, Henry Bradshaw Society Publications 11 (London, 1896), pp. 9–20, as well as two unprinted calendars in Paris, BN lat. 7299 (English [?Ramsey], s. x^{ex}), fols. 3–9, and lat. 10062 (?Canterbury, s. xi^1), fols. 162–63 [fragmentary]. For transcripts of these two unprinted calendars I am very grateful to T. A. Heslop, who is preparing an edition of them for the Henry Bradshaw Society.

8. B. Thorpe, ed., *The Homilies of the Anglo-Saxon Church*, 2 vols. (London, 1844–46), vol. 1.

9. The outer limits are fixed by the dates of the archbishopric of Sigeric (990–994), but it is not clear precisely when within these limits the First Series was issued. The date 989, which is frequently cited in secondary literature (e.g., J. Hurt, *Ælfric* [New York, 1972], p. 42, or S. B. Greenfield and D. G. Calder, *A New Critical History of Old English Literature* [New York, 1986], p. 75), is based on an ancient and erroneous dating of the first year of Sigeric's archbishopric.

10. Note that Ælfric specifies one item (CH I.xviii) for what he calls *letania maior* and that similar specifications are found for two homilies in CH II (nos. xix–xx). Now the feast of the *letaniae maiores* or Major Litanies (also called "Great Rogations") fell invariably on St. Mark's Day, April 25, and was so named from the great penitential processions that were instituted at Rome in the time of Gregory the Great. However, what Ælfric (mistakenly) calls the *Major Litanies* are in fact the "Minor Litanies" (also called "Lesser Rogations"), which fell on the three days preceding Ascension Day; and because Ascension Day (which fell on the fortieth day after Easter) was not a fixed day in the solar calendar, the Minor Litanies form part of the *temporale*, not the *sanctorale*. There is no doubt that by *letania maior* Ælfric was referring to the three days of fasting before Ascension Day, because he refers (CH I.xviii, Thorpe, *The Homilies*, p. 244) specifically to the story of Bishop Mamertus of Vienne and the origin of the litanies or processions instituted at that time (the story is told, *inter alia*, by Gregory of Tours, *Historia Francorum* II.34; see the discussion in Michael Lapidge, *Anglo-Saxon Litanies of the Saints*, Henry Bradshaw Society Publications 106 [London, 1991], pp. 8–11). In other words, although Ælfric specified his texts for the Major Litanies (*letania maior*), which falls on April 25 and does indeed belong to the *sanctorale*, it is clear that he was in fact thinking of the Minor Litanies, which falls on the three days before Ascension and pertains to the *temporale*. I have therefore omitted these texts from consideration here.

11. Tables helpfully setting out all the dates of the year in Roman reckoning are given in C. R. Cheney, *Handbook of Dates for Students of English History* (London, 1945; rev. ed. 1970), pp. 75–81.

12. M.R. Godden, ed., *Ælfric's Catholic Homilies, The Second Series: Text*, EETS SS 5 (London, 1979).

13. Godden (ibid., pp. xci–xciii) would date the issue of the Second Series to 995. This dating is based on arguments that Sigeric died in 995. But the arguments are without foundation: they rest on the witness of three charters attested by Sigeric and thought by Godden to date from 995. The charters in question are listed by P. H. Sawyer, *Anglo-Saxon Charters: An Annotated List and Bibliography* (London, 1968), nos. 882, 883, and 1379. However, two of these charters date unquestionably from 994, and in the third, the name of Sigeric has been inserted by a later scribe into a space left blank during the vacancy caused by his death. In other words, there is no evidence to contradict the argument that Sigeric died on October 28, 994: see Simon Keynes, *The Diplomas of King Æthelred the Unready, 978–1016* (Cambridge, 1980), pp. 251–53, who also points (p. 251, n. 40) to a previously unnoticed obit recording the death of Sigeric in 994. The incontestable implication is that both series of Ælfric's *Catholic Homilies* were issued before October 28, 994.

14. The number is ambiguous because one homily, no. xxvii, contains two separate specifications of date, one for July 25, the other for July 27 (see following).

15. The first part of the homily for SS Alexander, Eventius and Theodulus is in Pope, *Homilies of Ælfric*, vol. 2, pp. 734–48. The first part includes an account of St. Quirinus, a Roman soldier responsible for guarding Pope Alexander, but who was converted and then martyred under Hadrian. The date of his martyrdom was March 30. Although St. Quirinus is commemorated against this date in some Anglo-Saxon calendars (e.g., London, BL Cotton Vitellius A. xviii: Wormald, no. 8), Ælfric mentions no date in his account of Quirinus, and hence Quirinus has been omitted from Ælfric's *sanctorale*.

16. *Ælfric's Lives of Saints*, ed. W. W. Skeat, EETS OS 76, 82, 94 and 114 (London, 1881–1900; reprinted in 2 vols., 1966).

17. The *terminus ante quem* for the dating of the *Lives of Saints* is the death of Ealdorman Æthelweard (to whom the collection is dedicated). The date of his death cannot be fixed with absolute certainty; but his last attestation of a genuine charter occurs in 998 (Sawyer, *Anglo-Saxon Charters*, no. 895), and the assumption must be that he died very soon afterwards. See Keynes, *The Diplomas of King Æthelred*, p. 192 and n. 139.

18. On this point, see discussion by Joyce Hill, "The Dissemination of Ælfric's *Lives of Saints*: A Preliminary Survey," in this book, pp. 235–59 and Table 1.

19. It is not clear why the life of St. Sebastian is out of order; it should follow St. Maur, not precede it.

20. The copy in Julius E. vii gives the date wrongly as *.xiii. kl. Febr.* [= January 20]; the correct date (*.xii. kl. Febr.* = January 21) is found in another manuscript of the collection, London, BL Cotton Otho B. x.

21. Lucy is included with St. Agatha, hence (by implication) for February 5; the date of her feast is properly December 13.

22. The date in question should properly be *.x. kl. Iul.* [June 22]; note that the correct date has been supplied in a later manuscript of this life; namely, CUL, Ii. 1. 33, fol. 147r.

23. Given its position in the sequence, the date in question should presumably fall in July, but there is no known commemoration of St. Macarius in July. It is possible that the piece on Macarius was not intended for the *sanctorale* at all; see Pope, *Homilies of Ælfric*, vol. 2, pp. 786–98, who argues that the piece about Macarius was added to the Swithun life simply as a caution against trusting in false illusions created by magicians.

24. Julius E. vii gives the date wrongly as *.iiii. id. Oct.* [= October 12]; the correct date (*.vii. id. Oct.* = October 9) is given in CUL, Ii. 1. 33.

25. The date in question is *.iii. id. Nou.* = November 11.

26. Skeat, *Ælfric's Lives of Saints*, vol. 2, pp. 426–43. The life of St. Vincent is preserved solely in CUL Ii. 1. 33, fols. 128v–32v. It is not clear whether it was intended by Ælfric as part of his *Lives of Saints* collection or was an occasional piece intended for a specific destination such as Abingdon, which possessed a relic of the saint: see Susan E. Irvine, "Bones of Contention: the Context of Ælfric's Homily on St Vincent," *ASE* 19 (1990): 117–32.

27. *Angelsächsische Homilien und Heiligenleben*, ed. B. Assmann, rev. P. Clemoes (Darmstadt, Germany, 1964), pp. 24–48 (no. 3). On the date and circumstances of composition, see Clemoes, ibid., pp. xix–xx, as well as idem, "The Chronology of Ælfric's Works," p. 233, where it is suggested that the homily for the Nativity of BVM "was probably part of a re-issue of CH I"; see also Mary Clayton, "Ælfric and the Nativity of the Blessed Virgin Mary," *Anglia* 104 (1986): 286–315.

28. Note, however, that there is a homily treating Ambrose's dramatic confrontation with the Emperor Theodosius in Pope, *Homilies of Ælfric*, vol. 2, pp. 762–69; but no feast day is specified for this homily.

29. See F. E. Warren, *The Leofric Missal* (Oxford, 1883), p. 210; for the *Benedictional of St Æthelwold*, see Andrew Prescott, "The Text of the Benedictional of St Æthelwold," in *Bishop Æthelwold: His Career and Influence*, ed. Barbara Yorke (Woodbridge, England, 1988), pp. 119–47, on pp. 132–33; see also D. H. Turner, *The Claudius Pontificals*, Henry Bradshaw Society Publications 97 (London, 1971), pp. ix–x and xviii for further references to prayers for St. Vedastus in tenth-century Anglo-Saxon liturgical books.

30. See Peter Jackson and Michael Lapidge, "The Contents of the Cotton-Corpus Legendary," in this book on pp. 131–46.

31. C. E. Fell, *Edward King and Martyr* (Leeds, England, 1971), pp. xx–xxv; the Council of Enfield in 1008 decreed that King Edward's feast day was to be celebrated throughout England.

32. See Susan J. Ridyard, *The Royal Saints of Anglo-Saxon England: A Study of West Saxon and East Anglian Cults* (Cambridge, 1988), pp. 96–121.

33. See David W. Rollason, *The Mildrith Legend: A Study in Early Medieval Hagiography in England* (Leicester, 1982), pp. 53–68.

34. See the extensive list of manuscripts cited in Bertram Colgrave, *Felix's Life of Saint Guthlac* (Cambridge, 1956), pp. 26–46, as well as discussion by Jane Roberts, "An Inventory of Early Guthlac Materials," *Mediaeval Studies* 32 (1970): 193–233.

35. For example, in the preface to his Grammar, J. Zupitza, ed., *Ælfrics Grammatik und Glossar*, 2d ed. rev. Helmut Gneuss (Berlin, Zürich, and Dublin, 1966), p. 1: "sicut didicimus in scola Aðelwoldi" ("as we learned in the school of Æthelwold").

36. See Michael Lapidge and Michael Winterbottom, *Wulfstan of Winchester: The Life of St Æthelwold* (Oxford, 1991), p. cxlix.

37. Skeat, *Ælfric's Lives of Saints*, vol. 2, pp. 132–34.

38. Ibid. vol. 1, pp. 238–60.

39. Wormald, nos. 2, 3, 4, 5, 6, 7, 14, 15, 16, 17, 18, 19, and 20.

40. It is also omitted from London, BL Arundel 155 (Wormald, no. 13), a calendar from Christ Church, Canterbury.

41. Salisbury, Cathedral Library, 150 (Wormald, no. 2), London, BL Cotton Vitellius A. xviii (no. 8), CCCC 391 (no. 17), CCCC 9 (no. 18) and Vatican City, Biblioteca Apostolica Vaticana, Reg. lat. 12 (no. 19).

42. Salisbury, Cathedral Library, 150 (no. 2), Oxford, Bodleian Library, Hatton 113 (no. 16), CCCC 391 (no. 17) and Vatican City, Biblioteca Apostolica Vaticana, Reg. lat. 12 (no. 19).

43. See pp. 131–46.

44. London, BL Cotton Titus D. xxvii (Wormald, no. 9), Cambridge, Trinity College, R. 15. 32 (Wormald, no. 10), London, BL Arundel 60 (Wormald, no. 11), Cotton Vitellius E. xviii (Wormald, no. 12), CCCC 391 (Wormald, no. 17), CCCC 9 (Wormald, no. 18), and Oxford, Bodleian Library, Douce 296 (Wormald, no. 20). Note that the first four of these calendars are from Winchester.

45. See pp. 131–46.

The Contents of the Cotton-Corpus Legendary

Peter Jackson and Michael Lapidge

During the Middle Ages the saint's life was perhaps the most common and most characteristic literary genre.[1] The saint's life could take various literary forms. On one hand, it might contain a detailed description of the trial and death of a Christian martyr; such lives were especially common during the early centuries of Christianity (second to fourth centuries) and are known as *passiones*, so named from the sufferings of the martyr or martyrs in question.[2] On the other hand, once Christianity became established as the state religion, martyrdoms (and hence *passiones*) became less common. From the later fourth century onward, the characteristic subject of a saint's life was a confessor (that is, someone who had lived a blameless life in devotion to Christ, similar in quality to that of a martyr, but who had not suffered martyrdom on Christ's behalf)—a bishop, a monk, a hermit of the desert, a father of the Church—and the description of such a life is referred to as a *vita*.[3] From the late fourth century onward—from the time of the Greek life of St. Antony and the Latin lives of Sts. Paul the Hermit, Hilarion, and Malchus (these last three by Jerome)—the *vita* is the characteristic hagiographical form.[4] In the early Middle Ages (before, say, 750), the saint's *vita* seems to have circulated separately in the form of a *libellus* dedicated to a particular saint. From early Anglo-Saxon England, for example, we have the fragmentary remains of a *libellus* of St. Guthlac (now London, BL, Royal 4. A. XIV, fols. 107–8). From the eighth century onward, however, it became more and more usual to collect individual *passiones* or *vitae* together to constitute a single (even if multivolume) book. If the resulting book consists wholly or largely of *passiones*, it is referred to as a *passional*; a collection of saints' *vitae* intended for reading (whether public or private) is called a *legendary*.[5] Because the reading in question was associated with the liturgical year, the *vitae* or *passiones* were arranged according to the calendar date on which the particular saint's day fell. Manuscript passionals and legendaries survive in ever-increasing numbers from the eighth century onward, with the twelfth century being perhaps the period of greatest production.[6] The earliest surviving Anglo-Saxon passional is now Paris, BN, lat. 10861, a manuscript written at Canterbury in the earlier ninth century.[7] This passional is small in comparison with legendaries of the later Middle Ages (it consists solely of eighteen *passiones*). Only from the later eleventh century do we have English evidence of large, multivolume legendaries. The earliest such multivolume legendary from England is that known as the "Cotton-Corpus legendary."

The "Cotton-Corpus legendary" is so named because it now survives as separate manuscripts in the Cotton collection in London and in Corpus Christi College Cambridge: London, BL, Cotton Nero E. i, parts i and ii, and CCCC 9. The two individual manuscripts (that is, Cotton and Corpus) have evidently been separate since the late eleventh century, because each volume began to attract accretions from that time onward. Nero E. i, parts i and ii, were apparently one manuscript until early modern times, because there are accretions to the beginning of part i (but not its end), as well as to the end of part ii (but not its beginning).

The accretions to the beginning of part i now consist of fifty-four folios, containing a list of contents in a sixteenth-century hand (fols. 1–2), followed by Byrhtferth, *Vita S. Oswaldi* (fols. 3r–23v) and *Vita S. Ecgwini* (fols. 24r–34v), Lantfred, *Translatio et miracula S. Swithuni* (fols. 35r–52v), and the Winchester hymn "Aurea lux patrie" (fols. 52v–53r), all in a hand of the third quarter of the eleventh century; fols. 53v–54v, which were originally left blank by the eleventh-century scribe, contain the capitula and first ten chapters of the *Passio S. Andreae*, copied in a distinctive hand of the second quarter of the twelfth century.[8] The remainder of this text has been lost. The text of the Cotton-Corpus legendary itself, written in a hand of the third quarter of the eleventh century, begins with a list of contents on fol. 55r; the first text of the passional, the *Passio S. Martinae* (our no. 1: see below) begins on fol. 55v.

The end of part ii of Nero E. i attracted a very miscellaneous body of accretions. Following the end of the Cotton-Corpus legendary proper (fol. 155v), there are various saints' lives in the same distinctive Worcester hand of the second quarter of the twelfth century that made additions to part i. These lives are found on fols. 156–65, and include the *Vita S. Fritheswithae* (fols. 156r–157v), Rhigyfarch's *Vita S. Dauidis* (fols. 158r–162v) and the *Vita S. Margaretae Antiochenae* (fols. 162v–165r; 165v is blank).[9] Following these miscellaneous hagiographical contents comes part of the Cotton-Corpus legendary (now part ii, fols. 166–80) which seems to have been detached from the end of the Corpus manuscript, inasmuch as the text on fol. 166r represents the continuation of text on p. 458 of CCCC 9 (see later).[10] Then follow various random contents: a fragment of a Worcester cartulary (fols.

181–84) written in the late eleventh century,[11] a copy of the Anglo-Saxon law code known as *IV Edgar* (fols. 185–86),[12] a text of a *Vita S. Bedae* (fols. 187–88), and finally the remnant of what must once have been a vast, thirteenth-century passional (fols. 189–222).[13]

The second volume of the original Cotton-Corpus legendary, now CCCC 9, also attracted various accretions. Four quires (now pp. 1–60) of miscellaneous liturgical and hagiographical material were added to the beginning of the manuscript. The first quire (pp. 1–16) contains a liturgical calendar (pp. 3–14),[14] preceded by various *computistica* (pp. 1–2) and followed by Easter tables for the years 1032–1094 (pp. 15–16); the remaining three quires, written in various hands of late eleventh- and twelfth-century date, contain the *Vita S. Saluii* (pp. 17–26), the *Vita et miracula S. Nicholai* (pp. 26–53), the *Vita S. Rumwoldi* (pp. 53–59) and the *Passio SS. Ciryci et Iulittae* (pp. 59–60). The Cotton-Corpus legendary itself begins on p. 61 with a list of contents; the first text is Hincmar's *Vita S. Remigii* (our no. 120: see later), which begins on p. 62.

If these various accretions can (mentally) be stripped away, we are left with a two-volume passional dating from the late Anglo-Saxon period. Neil Ker first recognized the relationship between the disparate parts of the original legendary, and he was able to argue (on the basis of the resemblance of its script to other Worcester books and documents) that it must originally have been written at Worcester in the third quarter of the eleventh century.[15] The original two-volume constitution of the legendary was as follows:

1. January to September (Nero E. i, pt i, fols. 55–208; Nero E.i, pt ii, fols. 1–155)
2. October to December (CCCC 9, pp. 61–458; Nero E.i, pt ii, fols. 166–80)

The Cotton and Corpus manuscripts are but one English manuscript copy of this original legendary, albeit the earliest; as Wilhelm Levison was the first to recognize, the same legendary is preserved in various other English manuscripts of twelfth-century and later date.[16]

The Cotton-Corpus legendary consists of 165 saints' *vitae* arranged according to the calendar year, beginning on January 1. It bears no colophon or other indication of where or when it was compiled. To judge solely from its content, the compilation must have taken place in northern France or Flanders, because most of the localizable saints are from that region: Desiderius (14: Langres), Amandus (32: Saint-Amand), Medardus (61: Vermandois, Noyon, Soissons), Wandregisilus (77: Saint-Wandrille), Gaugericus (88: Trier, Cambrai), Audoenus (94: Rouen), Bertinus (102: Saint-Bertin), Audomarus (105: Saint-Omer), Lambertus (111: Maastricht, Liège), Remigius (120: Rheims), Vedastus (121–22: Saint-Vaast in Arras), Leodegarius (124: Autun),

Richarius (127: Saint-Riquier), Quintinus (130: Saint-Quentin), Hucbertus (133: Maastricht, Liège, Saint-Hubert), Winnocus (134: Saint-Bertin, Sint Winnoksberg/Bergues-Saint-Winnoc, Wormhoudt), Anianus (141: Orleans), Trudo (146: Sint Truiden/Saint-Trond), Eligius (150: Noyon), Iudocus (160: Saint-Josse-sur-Mer) and Columba (165: Sens). The cult centers of these saints define a geographical area extending no further west than Saint-Wandrille and Rouen, no further south than Langres, and no further east than Trier. The cult center where the Cotton-Corpus legendary was compiled must be sought within this area; probably, that is, in the diocese of Noyon-Tournai (in the archdiocese of Reims).[17] The remainder of the saints are either early Roman martyrs or else saints whose cults were, by the ninth century or so, universal, such as St. Brigid. There are no German saints, none from southern France, and with one exception, none from England.[18] Concerning the date of the compilation, it may be remarked that the latest securely datable *vita* in the legendary is Hincmar's *Vita et miracula S. Remigii* (no. 120), which was composed in 877 or 878.[19] The compilation, therefore, must date from some time in the very late ninth century, or from the earlier tenth.

By the late tenth century, a version of the Cotton-Corpus legendary had traveled to England, where as Patrick Zettel has shown,[20] it was laid heavily under contribution by Ælfric for the composition of his *Lives of Saints*, a sort of English legendary in its own right. Although the Cotton-Corpus legendary was almost certainly compiled on the continent, its manuscript transmission is wholly English, inasmuch as all the manuscripts that preserve it are of English origin. It provides a comprehensive index to the hagiography with which the late Anglo-Saxon reading public will have been familiar, and it is a pity that it has never been satisfactorily studied. Its contents deserve detailed examination, for it is possible that the transmissional history of the individual *vitae* might throw light on the (well-stocked) library in which it was compiled. Such an examination lies beyond the scope of the present chapter, the purpose of which is simply to provide an accurate list of the contents of the legendary,[21] so that students of hagiography can form some clear idea of what texts were known in late Anglo-Saxon England.

Note: In the list that follows, the name of each text has been given as it appears in BHL (with occasional silent emendation). The *Roman* dates are given where they appear either in the manuscript rubric, the contents list, or the text itself. Where no such date is given (e.g., nos. 71 and 139) the date found in Anglo-Saxon liturgical calendars is given in square brackets; in two instances in which the feasts are not found in extant calendars (nos. 14 and 97), the dates are taken from accompanying texts in the legendary (nos. 15 and 96, respectively). Occasional discrepancies are reported between the list of contents and the contents of the manuscripts themselves, but the record of these discrepancies is not intended to be exhaustive.

London, BL, Cotton Nero E. i, pt i

1. fols. 55v–61r: *Passio S. Martinae* [BHL 5587–88]; *Kl. Ian* [1 January].
2. fols. 61v–70r: Euphemius (trans.), *Vita S. Basilii* [BHL 1023]; *Kl. Ian.* [1 January].
3. fols. 70r–74r: *Vita S. Genouefae* [BHL 3336]; *.iii. non. Ian.* [3 January].
4. fols. 74r–75r: *Passio S. Theogenis* [BHL 8107]; *.iii. non. Ian.* [3 January].
5. fols. 75r–77v: *Passio S. Luciani* [BHL 5010]; *.vi. id. Ian.* [8 January].
6. fols. 77v–85v: *Passio SS. Iuliani et Basilissae et soc.* [BHL 4529, 4532]; *.v. id. Ian.* [9 January].
7. fols. 85v–87v: Venantius. Fortunatus, *Vita S. Hilarii* [BHL 3885; the *vita* is followed by Hilary, *Ep. ad Abram.* (PL 10, 549–52) on fols. 87v–88v]; *.Id. Ian.* [13 January].
8. fols. 88v–89v: *Passio S. Felicis* [BHL 2894; note that this first *passio* of Felix pertains properly to Felix of Trier]; *.xix. kl. Feb.* [14 January; *recte* 24 October].
9. fols. 89v–90r: *Passio S. Felicis* [BHL 2885]; *.xix. kl. Feb.* [14 January].
10. fols. 90r–92v: *Passio S. Marcelli* [BHL 5234, 5235]; *.xviii. kl. Feb.* [15 January; *recte* 16 January].
11. fols. 92v–93r: *Passio S. Marcelli* [BHL 5253; note that this second *passio* of Marcellus pertains properly to Marcellus of Tangier in Mauritania]; the date of the feast is given correctly in the text as *.iii. kl. Nou.* [30 October], but in the rubric as *eodem die* [15 January].
12. fols. 93r–97v: *Vita S. Fursei* [BHL 3209, 3210]; *.xvii. kl. Feb.* [16 January].
13. fols. 97v–98v: *Vita S. Sulpicii Pii* [BHL 7928]; *.xvi. kl. Feb.* [17 January].
14. fols. 98v–99r: Warnaharius, *Passio SS. Geminorum et Desiderii* [BHL 7829]; [17 January].
15. fols. 99r–102r: Warnaharius, *Passio SS. Speusippi, Eleusippi et Meleusippi* [BHL 7829]; *.xvi. kl. Feb.* [17 January].
16. fols. 102r–14r: *Passio S. Sebastiani* [BHL 7543]; *.xiii. kl. Feb.* [20 January].
17. fols. 114r–16v: *Passio S. Agnetis* [BHL 156]; *.xii. kl. Feb.* [21 January].
18. fols. 116v–17v: *Passio S. Fructuosi* [BHL 3200, 3196]; *.xii. kl. Feb.* [21 January].
19. fols. 117v–19r: *Passio S. Patrocli* [BHL 6520]; *.xii. kl. Feb.* [21 January].
20. fols. 119r–21v: *Passio S. Vincentii* [BHL 8628, 8630, 8631, 8634 (*Additamentum*)]; *.xi. kl. Feb.* [22 January].
21. fols. 121v–24v: *Passio S. Potiti* [BHL 6908]; *.xi. kl. Feb.* [22 January; *recte* 13 January].

22. fols. 124v–25r: *Passio S. Asclae* [BHL 722]; *.x. kl. Feb.* [23 January].
23. fols. 125r–27v: *Passio S. Babylae* [BHL 891]; *.ix. kl. Feb.* [24 January].
24. fols. 127v–30r: *Passio S. Polycarpi* [BHL 6870]; *.vii. kl. Feb.* [26 January].
25. fols. 130r–36v: *Passio SS. Thyrsi, Leuci, Callinici et soc.* [BHL 8280]; *.v. kl. Feb.* [28 January].
26. fols. 136v–42r: Cogitosus, *Vita S. Brigidae* [BHL 1457]; *Kl. Feb.* [1 February].
27. [See following item.]
28. [See following item.]
29. fols. 142r–44r: three homilies on the Purification of the Virgin (2 February). The first homily (Augustine, *Sermo* ccclxx.2–4) is ptd *PL* 39, 1657–79; the second (Ambrose, *Comm. in Luc.* II. 58–62) is ptd *CCSL* 14, 56–57; the third is also found in the Homiliary of Saint-Père-de-Chartres, a collection of sermons intended for delivery to a lay audience and certainly known in Anglo-Saxon England; see J. E. Cross, *Cambridge Pembroke College MS. 25: A Carolingian Sermonary Used by Anglo-Saxon Preachers*, King's College London Medieval Studies 1 (London, 1987), p. 25.
30. fols. 144r–48r: *Passio S. Tryphonis* [BHL 8338]; *.iii. non. Feb.* [3 February].
31. fols. 148r–49v: *Passio S. Agathae* [BHL 133]; *.iii. non. Feb.* [3 February; *recte* 5 February. Note that the date given in the text is *.ii. kl. Feb.* = 31 January].
32. fols. 149v–53r: Baudemund, *Vita S. Amandi* [BHL 332]; *.viii. id. Feb.* [6 February].
33. fols. 153r–54v: *Vita S. Valentini* [BHL 8460]; *.xvi. kl. Mart.* [14 February].
34. fols. 154v–57r: *Passio S. Iulianae* [BHL 4523(m)]; *.xiv. kl. Mart.* [16 February].
35. fols. 157r–60r: Eutychian (?), trans. Paul the Deacon, *Historia Theophili qui Christum negauit* [BHL 8121]; *.ii. kl. Mart.* [28 February; *recte* 4 February. Note that the date is also given as February 28 in the rubric to a copy of the *Historia* in London, BL, Harley 3020; see J. P. Carley, "More Pre-Conquest Manuscripts from Glastonbury Abbey," *ASE* 23 (1994), 265–81 (at p. 278)].
36. fols. 160r–62r: Venantius Fortunatus, *Vita S. Albini* [BHL 234]; *Kl. Mart.* [1 March].
37. fols. 162r–65r: *Passio SS. Perpetuae et Felicitatis* [BHL 6633]; *Non. Mart.* [7 March].
38. fols. 165r–66v: *Passio SS. Sebasteni (Quadraginta militum)* [BHL 7537, 7538]; *.v. id. Mart.* [11 March; *recte* 10 March].
39. fols. 166v–69v: Paul the Deacon, *Vita S. Gregorii I* [BHL 3639]; the date is correctly given as *.iv. id. Mart.* [12 March] in the rubric, but as *.iv. kl. Mart.* [26 February] in the contents list.

40. fols. 169v–74v: St. Patrick, *Confessio* and *Epistola ad Coroticum* [BHL 6492, 6493]; *.xvi. kl. Apr.* [17 March]. [Note that there is an erased entry in the contents list between St. Patrick and St. Theodosia.]

41. fols. 175r–79r: *Passio S. Theodosiae* [BHL 8090]; *.iv. non. Apr.* [2 April].

42. fols. 179r–84v: Sophronius of Jerusalem (trans. Paul the Deacon of Neapolis), *Vita S. Mariae Ægyptiacae* [BHL 5415]; the date in the contents list, *.v. id. Apr.* [9 April] has been struck through, and *eodem die* [2 April] added in a coeval hand.

43. fols. 185r–96r: Felix, *Vita S. Guthlaci* [BHL 3723]; [11 April].

44. fols. 196r–202r: Paulinus, *Vita S. Ambrosii* [BHL 377]; *.ii. non. Apr.* [4 April].

45. fols. 202r–03v: *Passio SS. Eleutherii et Antiae* [BHL 2451(a)]; *.xiv. kl. Mai.* [18 April].

46. fols. 203v–05v: *Passio S. Georgii* [BHL 3372, 3374]; *.ix. kl. Mai.* [23 April].

47. fols. 205v–06v: *Passio S. Marci* [BHL 5276]; *.vii. kl. Mai.* [25 April].

48. fols. 206v–07v: *Inuentio et passio SS. [Vitalis] et Geruasii et Protasii* [BHL 3514]; *.iv. kl. Mai.* [28 April, Vitalis only].

49. fols. 207v–08r: *Passio S. Iacobi minoris* [BHL 4093]; *Kl. Mai.* [1 May].

50. fol. 208r–v: *Vita S. Philippi* [BHL 6815, 6814]; *eodem die* [1 May].

London, BL, Cotton Nero E. i, pt ii

[To judge from the contents list, three texts have been lost from the manuscript between nos. 50 and 51: *Inuentio S. Crucis, Passio SS. Alexandri, Euentii et Theoduli* and *Passio S. Quiriaci*.]

51. fol. 1r: *Passio SS. Gordiani et Epimachi* [BHL 3612; begins acephalous (only the last twelve words and rubric remain)]; *.vi. id. Mai* [10 May].

52. fol. 1r–v: *Passio S. Pancratii* [BHL 6421]; *.iv. id. Mai.* [12 May].

53. fols. 1v–6r: *Passio SS. Nerei et Achillei* [a composite text drawn from BHL 6058, 6059 and 6060, together with the *Vita SS. Petronillae et Feliculae* (BHL 6061), *Passio S. Nicomedis* (BHL 6062), *Passio SS. Nerei et Achillei* (BHL 6063), *Passio SS. Eutychetis, Victorini et Maronis* (BHL 6064), and *Passio S. Domitillae et soc.* (BHL 6066)]; *eodem die* [12 May, Nereus and Achilleus only].

54. fols. 6r–8r: *Passio S. Torpetis* [BHL 8307]; *.xvi. kl. Iun.* [17 May].

55. fol. 8r–v: *Passio S. Pudentianae* [BHL 6991]; *.xiv. kl. Iun.* [19 May].

56. fols. 8v–15v: Venantius Fortunatus, *Vita S. Germani* [BHL 3468]; *.v. kl. Iun.* [28 May].

57. fols. 15v–16r: *Passio S. Cononis* [BHL 1912]; *.iv. kl. Iun* [29 May].

58. fols. 16r–17v: *Passio SS. Marcellini, Petri et soc.* [BHL 5230, 5231]; *.iv. non. Iun.* [2 June].

59. fols. 17v–20r: *Passio S. Erasmi* [BHL 2578, 2580]; *.iii. non. Iun.* [3 June; *recte* 2 June].

60. fols. 20r–21v: *Passio S. Bonifatii* [BHL 1413]; *Non. Iun.* [June 5; for the celebration of the feast of St. Boniface of Tarsus on this day, rather than the more usual 14 May, see *Acta Sanctorum, Mai.* III, 279; there may have been some confusion with the feast of St. Boniface, apostle of the Germans, on 5 June].

61. fols. 21v–22v: *Vita S. Medardi* [BHL 5864]; *.vi. id. Iun.* [8 June].

62. fols. 22v–24v: *Passio SS. Primi et Feliciani* [BHL 6922]; *.v. id. Iun.* [9 June].

63. fols. 24v–25v: *Passio S. Getulii, Cerealis et soc.* [BHL 3524(b), 3524]; *.iv. id. Iun.* [10 June].

64. fols. 25v–26r: *Passio SS. Basilidis et soc.* [BHL 1019]; *.ii. id. Iun.* [12 June; a coeval hand has written above the entry in the contents list *eodem die* = 10 June].

65. fols. 26r–27r: *Passio S. Symphorosae* [BHL 7971]; *.v. kl. Iul.* [27 June; on the celebration of the feast on this day, rather than the more usual 18 July, see *Acta Sanctorum, Iul.* IV, 353].

66. fol. 27r: Gregory of Tours, *Miraculum S. Martini* [BHL 5623]; *.Kl. Iul.* [1 July; *recte* 4 July].

67. fols. 27r–29v: *Passio SS. Viti, Modesti et Crescentiae* [BHL 8712, 8712(a)]; *.xvii. kl. Iul.* [15 June].

68. [See following item.]

69. fols. 29v–30v: two homilies by Augustine on the Nativity of St. John the Baptist; the first (*Sermo* ccxciii(a).2–5) is ptd *Sancti Augustini sermones post Maurinos reperti*, ed. G. Morin, Miscellanea Agostiniana I (Rome, 1930), pp. 223–26; the second (*Sermo* ccxciii(c)) is ptd. *ibid.*, pp. 351–52; *.viii. kl. Iul.* [24 June].

70. fols. 30v–32v: *Passio SS. Gallicani, Iohannis et Pauli* [BHL 3236, 3238(b)]; *.vi. kl. Iul.* [26 June].

71. fols. 32v–36v: *Passio S. Petri* [BHL 6663, 6664]; [29 June].

72. fols. 36v–40v: *Passio S. Pauli* [BHL 6574, 6570]; *.ii. kl. Iul.* [30 June].

73. fols. 40v–41v: *Passio SS. Processi et Martiniani* [BHL 6947]; *.vi. non. Iul.* [6 July].

74. fols. 41v–42v: *Passio S. Felicitatis cum septem filiis* [BHL 2853]; *.vi. id. Iul.* [10 July].

75. fols. 42v–43v: *Passio SS. Rufinae et Secundae* [BHL 7359]; *.vi. id. Iul.* [10 July].

76. fols. 43v–44r: *Vita S. Praxedis* [BHL 6920]; *.xii. kl. Aug.* [21 July].

77. fols. 44r–48v: *Vita S. Wandregisili* [BHL 8805; ends incomplete through physical loss to the MS]; *.xi. kl. Aug.* [22 July].

[Some leaves have been lost after fol. 48]

78. fols. 49r–52r: *Passio S. Apollinaris* [BHL 623; begins acephalous]; *.x. kl. Aug.* [23 July].
79. fols. 52r–53r: *Passio S. Iacobi maioris* [BHL 4057]; *.viii. kl. Aug.* [25 July].
80. fols. 53r–56v: *Passio SS. Dormientium Septem* [BHL 2316]; *.vi. kl. Aug.* [27 July].
81. fols. 56v–60r: *Passio S. Pantaleonis* [BHL 6437]; *.v. kl. Aug.* [28 July].
82. fol. 60r–v: *Passio SS. Simplicii, Faustini et Beatricis* [BHL 7790]; *.iv. kl. Aug.* [29 July].
83. fols. 60v–61r: *Passio S. Felicis II* [BHL 2857]; *.iv. kl. Aug.* [29 July].
84. fols. 61r–64r: *Passio S. Stephani I* [BHL 7845]; *.iv. non. Aug.* [2 August].
85. fols. 64r–67r: *Vita S. Cassiani* [BHL 1632]; *Non. Aug.* [5 August].
86. fols. 67r–73r: *Passio SS. Sixti, Laurentii et Hippolyti* [a composite text drawn from the *Passio SS. Polychronii et Parmenii* (BHL 6884), the *Passio SS. Abdonis et Sennetis* (BHL 6), the *Passio S. Sixti II* (BHL 7801), the *Passio S. Laurentii* (BHL 4754, 4753), and the *Passio S. Hippolyti* (BHL 3961)]; *.viii. id. Aug.* [6 August] corrected in the rubric to *.iiii. id. Aug.* [10 August (St. Laurence only)].
87. fols. 73r–75v: *Passio SS. Donati et Hilariani* [BHL 2289, 2291]; *.vii. id. Aug.* [7 August].
88. fols. 75v–77v: *Vita S. Gaugerici* [BHL 3287]; *.iii. id. Aug.* [11 August].
89. fols. 77v–78v: *Passio S. Eupli* [BHL 2728, 2729]; *.ii. id. Aug.* [12 August].
90. fols. 78v–79r: *Passio S. Eusebii* [BHL 2740]; the date of the feast is given in the rubric as *.xviii. kl. Sept.* [15 August]; the correct date, *.xix. kl. Sept.* [14 August] is given in the contents list.
91. fols. 79r–86v: Paschasius Radbertus, *Cogitis me* (= ps.-Jerome, *Ad Paulam et Eustochium de Assumptione sanctae Dei genitricis semperque uirginis Mariae*)[BHL 5355(d); ed. A. Ripberger, Spicilegium Friburgense 9 (Fribourg, 1962)]; *.xviii. kl. Sept.* [15 August].
92. fols. 86v–88r: *Passio S. Agapeti* [BHL 125]; the date of the feast is given in the rubric as *.v. kl. Sept.* [28 August]; the correct date, *.xv. kl. Sept.* [18 August] is given in the contents list and in the text itself.
93. fols. 88r–89r: *Passio S. Symphoriani* [BHL 7967]; *.xi. kl. Sept.* [22 August].
94. fols. 89r–91v: *Vita S. Audoeni* [BHL 750]; *.ix. kl. Sept.* [24 August].
95. fols. 91v–94r: *Passio S. Bartholomaei* [BHL 1002]; *.viii. kl. Sept.* [25 August].
96. fol. 94r–v: *Passio S. Genesii* [BHL 3304]; *.viii. kl. Sept.* [25 August].

97. fols. 94v–95v: *Miracula S. Genesii* [BHL 3307]; [25 August].

98. fols. 95v–105v: Possidius, *Vita S. Augustini* [BHL 785]; *.v. kl. Sept.* [28 August].

99. fols. 105v–07v: *Vita S. Sabinae* [BHL 7408]; *.iv. kl. Sept.* [29 August. This date pertains to the feast of St. Sabina, martyred at Rome (see below, no 101), but the *Vita* is that of St. Sabina, virgin of Trecis. The closing sentence of the text supplies the date *.ix. kl. Feb.* (January 24; *recte* January 29)].

100. fols. 107v–09r: *Passio S. Seraphiae* [BHL 7586]; *.iv. kl. Sept.* [29 August].

101. fol. 109r–v: *Passio S. Sabinae* [BHL 7407]; *.iv. kl. Sept.* [29 August; *recte* 23 August (see no. 99)].

102. fols. 109v–11v: *Vita S. Bertini* [not listed separately in BHL, but cf. no. 763 and item no. 105 (*Vita S. Audomari*); ptd MGH, SS. rer. Meroving. 5, 765–69; also *Miraculum Vitae additum* (BHL 1289(b)), ptd ibid., 778–80]; *Non. Sept.* [5 September].

103. fols. 111v–16v: *Passio S. Hadriani* [BHL 3744, 3744(b)]; *.vi. id. Sept.* [8 September].

104. fols. 116v–18r: *Sermo de natiuitate S. Mariae* [an extract from the apocryphal Gospel of Matthew, ed. K. Tischendorf, *Evangelia Apocrypha*, 2d ed. (Leipzig, 1876), pp. 54–64][BHL 5341]; [8 September].

105. fols. 118r–21v: *Vita S. Audomari* [not listed separately in BHL, but cf. no. 763 and above, item no. 102 (*Vita S. Bertini*); ptd. MGH, SS. rer. Meroving. 5, 754–64 and 776–78]; *.v. id. Sept.* [9 September].

106. fols. 121v–22r: *Passio S. Hyacinthi* [BHL 4053]; *.iii. id. Sept.* [11 September; note that this is the *passio* of the Hyacinthus who was martyred *in portu Romano*, but the date given pertains to the feast of the Hyacinthus who was the companion of SS. Eugenia and Protus (cf. no. 156)].

107. fol. 122r–v: *Passio S. Cornelii papae* [BHL 1958]; *.xviii. kl. Oct.* [14 September].

108. fols. 122v–23v: *Passio S. Cypriani* [BHL 2038]; *.xviii. kl. Oct.* [14 September].

109. fols. 123v–26r: *Passio S. Euphemiae* [BHL 2708]; *.xvi. kl. Oct.* [16 September].

110. fols. 126r–29v: *Passio SS. Luciae et Geminiani* [BHL 4985]; *.xvi. kl. Oct.* [16 September].

111. fols. 129v–33v: *Vita S. Lamberti* [BHL 4677]; *.xv. kl. Oct.* [17 September].

112. fols. 133v–37r: *Passio S. Matthaei* [BHL 5690]; *.xi. kl. Oct.* [21 September; *recte* 22 September].

113. fols. 137v–39v: Eucherius, *Passio SS. Mauricii et soc.* [BHL 5741, 5743]; *.x. kl. Oct.* [22 September].

114. fols. 139v–42r: *Passio S. Firmini* [BHL 3002]; *.vii. kl. Oct.* [25 September].

115. fols. 142r–43r: *Passio S. Cypriani* [BHL 2038]; *.vi. kl. Oct.* [26 September; *recte* 14 September].

116. fols. 143r–45v: *Acta et passio SS. Cypriani, Iustinae et Theoctistae* [BHL 2047, 2050]; *.vi. kl. Oct.* [26 September].

117. fols. 145v–47r: *Passio SS. Cosmae et Damiani* [BHL 1970]; *.v. kl. Oct.* [27 September].

118. fols. 147r–48v: *Apparitio in Monte Gargano (Dedicatio ecclesiae Michaelis archangeli)* [BHL 5948]; *.iii. kl. Oct.* [29 September].

119. fols. 148v–51r: *Vita S. Hieronimi* [BHL 3869; the ending has been altered in a later hand to that of 3870]. The date is given in the rubric as *.v. kl. Oct.* [27 September]; the correct date, *.ii. kl. Oct.* [30 September] is given in the contents list.

Cambridge, Corpus Christi College 9

120. pp. 62–136: Hincmar, *Vita S. Remigii* [BHL 7152, 7153, 7154, 7155 (*Vita*), 7156 (*Translatio*), 7157, 7158, 7159]; *Kl. Oct.* [1 October; note that this is the feast of the translation of St. Remigius].

121. pp. 136–45: Alcuin, *Vita S. Vedasti* [BHL 8508]; *Kl. Oct.* [1 October].

122. pp. 145–47: Alcuin, *Homilia in die natali S. Vedasti* [BHL 8509]; *Kl. Oct.* [1 October; *recte* 6 February].

123. pp. 147–53: *Passio S. Piatonis* [BHL 6845]; *Kl. Oct.* [1 October].

124. pp. 153–76: *Vita S. Leodegarii* [BHL 4849(b)]; *.vi. non. Oct.* [2 October].

125. pp. 176–200: Hilduin, *Passio S. Dionysii* [BHL 2175]; *.vii. id. Oct.* [9 October].

126. pp. 200–10: *Passio SS. Sergii et Bacchi* [BHL 7599]; *Non. Oct.* [7 October].

127. pp. 210–17: Alcuin, *Vita S. Richarii* [BHL 7224]; [9 October, the feast of the translation; see *Acta Sanctorum, Oct.* III, 442].

128. pp. 217–21: *Passio S. Callisti papae* [BHL 1523]; *.ii. id. Oct.* [14 October].

129. pp. 221–24: *Passio SS. Crispini et Crispiniani* [BHL 1990]; *.viii. kl. Nou.* [24 October; *recte* 25 October].

130. pp. 224–30: *Passio et inuentio S. Quintini* [BHL 6999 (*passio*), 7000 (*inuentio*)]; *Prid. kl. Nou.* [31 October].

131. pp. 230–34: *Passio SS. Caesarii et Iuliani* [BHL 1511]; *Kl. Nou.* [1 November].

132. pp. 234–43: *Vita et passio S. Eustachii* [BHL 2760]; the date of the feast is given in the text as *.ii. non. Nou.* [4 November] and in the rubric as *.xii. kl. Oct.* [20 September].

133. pp. 243–58: Jonas of Orléans, *Vita S. Hucberti* [BHL 3994]; *Kl. Nou.* [1 November].
134. pp. 258–61: *Vita S. Winnoci* [BHL 8952]; *.viii. id. Nou.* [6 November].
135. pp. 261–68: Porphyrius, *Passio SS. Claudii, Nicostrati, Simproniani, Castorii et Simplicii* [BHL 1837]; *.vi. id. Nou.* [8 November].
136. pp. 268–71: *Passio S. Theodori* [BHL 8077]; *.v. id. Nou.* [9 November].
137. pp. 271–75: *Passio S. Mennae* [BHL 5921]; *.iii. id. Nou.* [11 November].
138. pp. 275–99: Sulpicius Severus, *Vita S. Martini* (Sulpicius's *vita* is accompanied by various texts, including Letters to Eusebius and to Bassula, an account of the miracles that occurred at his first translation, etc.; see also no. 140)[BHL 5610, 5611, 5613, 5622, 5619, 5620, 5621, 5623]; *iii. id. Nou.* [11 November].
139. pp. 299–301: Gregory of Tours, *Vita S. Bricii* [BHL 1452 = *Historia Francorum* II. 1]; [13 November].
140. pp. 301–19: Sulpicius Severus, *Dialogi* ii and iii [BHL 5615, 5616]; [11 November].
141. pp. 319–23: *Vita S. Aniani* [BHL 473]; *.xv. kl. Dec.* [17 November].
142. pp. 323–36: *Passio S. Caeciliae* [BHL 1495]; *.x. kl. Dec.* [22 November].
143. pp. 336–39: *Passio S. Longini* [BHL 4965]; *.x. kl. Dec.* [22 November]. It is worth noting that, uniquely among pre-1100 English calendars, the feast of St. Longinus is commemorated on 22 November in that of the *Leofric Missal* [= "Leofric B": Wormald, *English Kalendars before* A.D. *1100*, p. 54 (no. 4); see also R. J. Peebles, *The Legend of Longinus in Ecclesiastical Tradition and in English Literature and Its Connection with the Grail* (Baltimore, 1911), p. 13; cf. no. 149].
144. pp. 339–43: *Passio S. Clementis I* [BHL 1848]; *.ix. kl. Dec.* [23 November].
145. pp. 343–45: Gregory of Tours, *Miracula S. Clementis I* [BHL 1855, 1857]; [23 November].
146. pp. 345–61: Donatus the Deacon, *Vita S. Trudonis* [BHL 8321]; *eodem die* [23 November].
147. pp. 361–77: *Passio SS. Chrysogoni, Agapes, Theodotae et Anastasiae* [BHL 1795, 1795(a)(Chrysogonus), 118 (Agape), 8093 (Theodota), 401 (Anastasia)]; *.viii. kl. Dec.* [24 November].
148. pp. 377–78: *Passio SS. Saturnini et Sisinnii* [BHL 7493]; *.iii. kl. Dec.* [29 November]. [The text of no. 148 ends four lines into the left-hand column of p. 378; the remainder of the leaf has been ruled for writing but left blank.]
149. pp. 379–89: *Passio SS. Chrysanthi et Dariae* [BHL 1787]; [? 29 November. There is no date given for this feast either in the contents list, the rubric or the text itself. However, uniquely among pre-1100 English calendars, the feast is commemorated on 29 November in that of the *Leofric*

Missal [= "Leofric B," Wormald, *English Kalendars before* A.D. *1100*, p. 54 (no. 4)]; see also *Acta Sanctorum, Oct.* XI, 438, and no. 143.

150. pp. 389–93: *Vita S. Eligii* [BHL 2477]; *Kl. Dec.* [1 December].

151. pp. 393–97: *Passio S. Sabini* [BHL 7451]; *.vii. id. Dec.* [7 December].

152. pp. 397–403: *Passio S. Eulaliae* [BHL 2700]; *.iv. id. Dec.* [10 December].

153. pp. 403–06: *Passio SS. Fusciani, Victorici et Gentiani* [BHL 3226]; *.iii. id. Dec.* [11 December].

154. pp. 406–08: *Passio SS. Luceiae, Auceiae et soc.* [BHL 4980]; *Id. Dec.* [13 December]. The compiler has confused the feast of St. Luceia of Campania (no. 154), celebrated on 25 June or 6 July, with that of St. Lucia of Syracuse, celebrated on 13 December (no. 159).

155. pp. 408–10: *Passio S. Anastasiae* [BHL 401]; *.viii. kl. Ian.* [25 December].

156. pp. 410–26: *Passio SS. Eugeniae, Proti et Hyacinthi* [BHL 2667]; *.viii. kl. Ian.* [25 December].

157. pp. 426–34: *Passio S. Marini* [BHL 5538]; *.vii. kl. Ian.* [26 December].

158. pp. 434–37: *Passio SS. Maximi et soc.* [BHL 5857(d), (e)]; *.viii. kl. Nou.* [25 October]. The feast of St. Maximus and his companions was occasionally commemorated on 15 December in pre-Conquest English calendars, for example, that in "Leofric B" (ed. Wormald, *English Kalendars before* A.D. *1100*, p. 55; cf. above, no. 143).

159. pp. 437–40: *Passio S. Luciae* [BHL 4992(c)]; *Id. Dec.* [13 December].

160. pp. 440–46: *Vita S. Iudoci* [BHL 4504]; *eodem die* [13 December].

161. pp. 446–55: *Passio S. Christinae* [BHL 1756]; *.ix. kl. Aug.* [24 July]. Uniquely among pre-1100 English calendars, this feast is celebrated on December 5 in a calendar of *c.* 1061 allegedly from Sherborne [ed. Wormald, *English Kalendars before* A.D. *1100*, p. 195 (no. 14); on the place of origin, see now D. N. Dumville, *Liturgy and the Ecclesiastical History of Late Anglo-Saxon England* (Woodbridge, 1992), p. 74.]

162. pp. 455–58: *Aduentus et exceptio corporis SS. Benedicti et Scholasticae in agrum Floriacensem* [BHL 1117]; [4 December]. [The text ends abruptly at the end of p. 458; it resumes without a break in Cotton Nero E.i, pt ii, fol. 166r.]

London, BL, Cotton Nero E. i, pt ii

[fols. 166r–67r: continuation and conclusion of no. 162]

163. fols. 167r–68r: *Exaltatio sanctae crucis* [BHL 4178]; *.xviii. kl. Oct.* [14 September].

164. fols. 168r–80r: *Gesta S. Siluestri* [BHL 7725, 7726, 7739]; *.ii. kl. Ian.* [31 December]. Note that the text of the *Gesta S. Siluestri* has been

extensively altered and added to by a hand of the second quarter of the twelfth century, probably that of John of Worcester (see above, p. 132; see also W. Levison, "Konstantinische Schenkung und Silvester-Legende," in *Miscellanea Francesco Ehrle*, Studi e Testi 38 [1924; rpt. Rome, 1962], 159–247, at 223).

165. fol. 180r–v: *Passio S. Columbae* [BHL 1893]; *.ii. kl. Ian.* [31 December].

Notes

1. There is no adequate treatment in English of medieval hagiography, and one is obliged to consult Réginald Grégoire, *Manuale di agiologia: Introduzione alla letteratura agiografica*, Bibliotheca Montisfani 12 (Fabriano, Italy, 1987), as well as the earlier (but still useful) study of René Aigrain, *L'hagiographie: ses sources, ses méthodes, son histoire* (Paris, 1953). A cursory introduction to Anglo-Saxon hagiography is provided by Michael Lapidge, "The Saintly Life in Anglo-Saxon England," in *The Cambridge Companion to Anglo-Saxon England*, ed. Malcolm Godden and Michael Lapidge (Cambridge, 1991), pp. 243–63. The vast corpus of medieval Latin hagiography is controlled by means of the Bollandists' *Bibliotheca Hagiographica Latina*, 2 vols. (Brussels, 1899–1901), with *Supplementum* by Henryk Fros (1986)[hereafter BHL]. There is an extensive bibliography of the subject in *Saints and Their Cults: Studies in Religious Sociology, Folklore and History*, ed. Stephen Wilson (Cambridge, 1983), pp. 309–417.

2. Grégoire, *Manuale*, pp. 145–51, as well as Hippolyte Delehaye, *Les passions des martyrs et les genres littéraires* (Brussels, 1921).

3. Grégoire, ibid., pp. 152–59.

4. The fundamental study of medieval Latin *vitae* is now Walter Berschin, *Biographie und Epochenstil im lateinischen Mittelalter*, 3 vols. (Stuttgart, 1986–91)[in progress].

5. See Grégoire, *Manuale*, pp. 141–44, and especially Guy Philippart, *Les légendiers latins et autres manuscrits hagiographiques*, Typologie des sources du moyen âge occidental, 24–25 (Turnhout, 1977).

6. See ibid., pp. 37–48.

7. Michelle P. Brown, "Paris, Bibliothèque Nationale, lat. 10861 and the Scriptorium of Christ Church, Canterbury," *ASE* 15 (1986): 119–37.

8. This same hand is found in the principal manuscript of John of Worcester's *Chronicon*, now Oxford, Corpus Christi College 157, as the scribe who copied the annals from 1128–31 and continued the chronicle to 1140. Among the materials copied by this scribe is found, against the year 1138, the following hexameter: "corrigat ista legens offendit si qua Iohannes" ("if in any respect John has committed an error, let any reader please correct it"). This hexameter implies that John of Worcester himself copied these materials into CCCO 157. The hand is also found in the unique

copy of John's *Chronicula* (an abbreviation of the *Chronicon*, now in Dublin, Trinity College 503), as well as in Oxford, Bodleian Library, Auct. F. 1. 19 and CUL, Kk. 4. 6. The presence of John of Worcester's hand in Cotton Nero E. i implies that that manuscript was at Worcester in the second quarter of the twelfth century. We are very grateful to Patrick McGurk for this information on John of Worcester.

9. Because fol. 165v is well worn and contains various *probationes pennae*, there is some likelihood that it once formed the final leaf of another (lost?) manuscript before it was combined with part ii of Cotton Nero E. i.

10. Note that fols. 166–80 contain various corrections in the distinctive Worcester hand (John of Worcester?), as well as two folios of text (fols. 174v–176r) interpolated into the text of the *Gesta S. Siluestri* by this same hand.

11. Another part of this fragmentary cartulary is preserved as London, BL, Add. 46204; see G. R. C. Davis, *Medieval Cartularies of Great Britain: A Short Catalogue* (London, 1958), no. 1069. The original location of Add. 46204 was between fols. 182 and 183 of Nero E. i, part ii.

12. See Ker, *Catalogue*, no. 166, who dates the script of this fragment to s. x/ xi; it is thus the earliest surviving copy of this particular law code. We are grateful to Patrick Wormald for discussion of this matter.

13. On this thirteenth-century passional, see Michael Lapidge and Michael Winterbottom, *Wulfstan of Winchester: The Life of St Æthelwold* (Oxford, 1991), pp. clxxv–clxxvii.

14. Francis Wormald, ed., *English Kalendars before A.D. 1100*, Henry Bradshaw Society Publications 72 (London, 1934), pp. 225–37 (no. 18).

15. N. R. Ker, "Membra Disiecta, Second Series," *British Museum Quarterly* 14 (1939–40):82–83; on the date of the script, see also his *Catalogue*, p. 41 (no. 29), and *English Manuscripts in the Century after the Norman Conquest* (Oxford, 1960), pp. 49, 53 and pl. 26, as well as T. A. M. Bishop, *English Caroline Minuscule* (Oxford, 1971), p. 20, n. 1.

16. "Conspectus codicum hagiographicorum," MGH, Scriptores rerum Merovingicarum, 7 (1920), 529–706, on 545–46. Levison identified three separate English recensions of the original passional. His first recension (a) consists of Cotton Nero E. i + CCCC 9, as well as a two-volume passional now in Salisbury, Cathedral Library, 221 + 222 (formerly in Oxford, Bodleian Library, Fell 4 + 1); the second recension (b) consists solely of Oxford, Bodleian Library, Bodley 354 (? West Country, s. xii[2]); the third recension (c) consists of Hereford, Cathedral Library, P. 7. VI (Hereford, s. xii[med]) and Oxford, Bodleian Library, Fell 2. Note that Zettel (cited in note 20) would eliminate this last manuscript from Levison's c-recension.

17. It *may* be significant that St. Vedastus (nos. 121–22) is accorded special prominence in the legendary, being commemorated with prayers and poems as well as with a *vita*; but without a full examination of the contents, this must remain no more than an impression.

18. The exception is St. Guthlac (our no. 43). However, the *Vita S. Guthlaci* does not appear in the scribe's list of contents (Nero E. i, pt i, fol. 55r), and was therefore possibly an ad hoc scribal addition.

19. The dating was established by Heinrich Schrörs, *Hinkmar, Erzbischof von Reims* (Freiburg, 1884), pp. 446–47, who demonstrated that in c. 9 (no. 134), Hincmar recounts an incident said to have happened twenty-five years ago, in 852, where in the same chapter (no. 130) he refers to something that is mentioned in a letter by Hincmar dated 878; the composition must therefore fall in one of these two years.

20. Patrick H. Zettel, "Saints' Lives in Old English: Latin Manuscripts and Vernacular Accounts: Ælfric," *Peritia* 1 (1982): 17–37. It is well to remember, however, that Zettel claimed only that "some early form of the collection, or at least something very similar to it, must have served as Ælfric's chief quarry for hagiographic matter both in the *Homilies* and in the *Lives*" (p. 22). Martin Brett, while accepting that "something similar to at least that part of the legendary which deals with the more widely celebrated saints must have been available to Aelfric," believes that Cotton-Corpus was copied from an exemplar that had not been long in England, for three reasons: it is very long; there are no clear signs of its influence on the pre-1100 English calendars printed by Wormald; and the original form of the legendary had almost no saints specific to England (Martin Brett, "The Use of Universal Chronicle at Worcester," in *L'historiographie médiévale en Europe*, ed. Jean-Philippe Genet (Paris, 1991), 277–85 (at p. 283, n. 28)). Similar reservations are expressed by Teresa Webber (*Scribes and Scholars at Salisbury Cathedral, c. 1075–c. 1125* (Oxford, 1992), p. 70). Certain correspondences between individual festal dates in Cotton-Corpus and those in extant pre-1100 English calendars are pointed out below (see nos. 143, 149, 158 and 161), but the subject deserves closer examination. In any case, the main contention of the present chapter—that Cotton-Corpus "provides a comprehensive index to the hagiography with which the late Anglo-Saxon reading (or listening) public will have been familiar"—is not seriously affected, though the precise date at which the collection in its present form reached England admittedly remains open to investigation.

21. A list of contents was compiled by Patrick H. Zettel, "Ælfric's Hagiographic Sources and the Latin Legendary Preserved in B.L. MS Cotton Nero E. i + CCCC MS 9 and other Manuscripts," (D.Phil. dissertation, Oxford University, 1979), pp. 15–34; however, this list was unavailable for consultation at the time that work on the present list was begun in 1984. We have also consulted an unpublished list by Rosalind Love (Cambridge), to whom we are grateful for discussion of various matters. We are also indebted to James Carley, David Dumville, and Paul Hayward for advice and assistance.

Hermits and the Contemplative Life in Anglo-Saxon England

Mary Clayton

One of the more striking differences between the early and late Anglo-Saxon Church concerns the question of how sanctity is to be achieved: is it by the active life of pastoral work, caring for the poor, teaching, and attempting to cure the ills of society, or is it by cutting oneself off from all society and seeking to achieve a vision of God? This is, of course, a fundamental problem of Christianity, to which all ages have had to respond. In this chapter I should like first to trace the early Christian background to the Anglo-Saxon formulations of this problem, a background molded by the desert fathers and the influence which they exerted. I shall then look at early insular responses to this debate, a debate conducted, both explicitly and implicitly, through the models of sanctity held up for emulation. The major part of this chapter concentrates, however, on Ælfric and his treatment of the active and contemplative lives, both theoretically and in terms of the types of saints on which he focuses in the *Sermones Catholici* and in the *Lives of Saints*. This is an aspect of Ælfric's spirituality that has not been commented on, but that, I believe, sheds light on his approach to sanctity, shows once again how consistently and deeply he had absorbed the principles of the peculiarly Anglo-Saxon type of Benedictine monasticism under which he lived and which helps to explain some of the choices he made in his compilation of the *Lives of Saints*.

I

From the third century the life of the hermit captured the Christian imagination: the desert solitaries, renouncing the world and aspiring to union with God through a life of penitence and contemplation, took the place of the martyrs once the persecution of the church had ended. The Egyptian desert, in particular, became the home of hundreds of monks, and in the fourth century we find there two forms of the ascetic life, both of which were to be fundamental to the life of the church.[1] The solitary monk, wrestling with temptation and practicing a life of austerity and prayer, took his inspiration from St. Antony (c. 251–356), the enormously influential story of whose life was written by St. Athanasius.[2] These monks lived either totally alone or in colonies whose members gathered to celebrate weekly mass, spending the rest of their time in their cells. In striving to overcome all distractions, they aimed to empty themselves of selfhood, to open themselves to God, and they rejected all society except that of other contemplatives (though not always successfully, as a reputation for holiness and wisdom resulted in a stream of people seeking advice). The second type of life, the communal one of the organized monastery, seems to have originated with St. Pachomius (c. 292–346), who had been a soldier in the Roman army before becoming a Christian. He established a series of large monasteries, in which the monks lived a life of obedience and work, with the profits of the latter being distributed to the poor. Basil the Great of Caesarea (c. 330–79), having experienced both the life of the desert solitary and that of the Pachomian monastery, also advocated the cenobitic life, though in smaller monasteries than those of Pachomius, arguing that only it allowed the monk to practice Christian charity toward others and that the solitary life held too many dangers. For Basil social obligations could not be ignored: both active charity and contemplative prayer were necessary, and he believed that to leave the monastery for the hermit's cell should be considered a regression.

Eastern eremeticism and monasticism were transmitted to the West both through literature (the life of individual saints, accounts of communities of monks, collections of anecdotes and sayings, monastic rules) and by individuals traveling either from West to East or East to West. From the fourth century on, Western ascetics, like St. Jerome (c. 342–420), fled to the Eastern deserts or, like Martin of Tours (316– or 335–397), became hermits in the West. Martin was joined by other hermits and established a monastery, isolated from the world, in which the monks devoted themselves to contemplative prayer. Although he himself was elected bishop of Tours and preached, his monks were not active pastorally and did not work. The Martinian monastery was, then, unlike the Pachomian or Basilian models in that the monks were basically contemplatives who, instead of living as solitaries, as in the East, lived communally. Cassian (c. 360–435), an Eastern monk whose *Collationes* were responsible for disseminating the theory of Eastern monasticism in the West, also placed primary value upon the contemplative life (which was for him a solitary one), upon the individual opening himself entirely to God. Other monastic foundations were not, however, so resolutely isolated from the world: Lérins, founded by Honoratus (c. 350–419) had hermitages to which individuals could withdraw, but most monks lived communally and were not unaware of the outside world. Benedict of Nursia (c. 480–c. 550), whose rule was the cornerstone of Western monasticism, also seems to have considered the life of the hermit as the higher vocation, but regarded the cenobitic life as better suited to the majority, and his monks worked and spent much of their time in communal worship.

Already, then, there were different models, based on different responses to the demands of the Christian life: that of the solitary hermit, that of the community whose members devoted themselves to contemplative prayer, that of a mixture of solitaries (regarded as superior) and cenobites, that of the cenobitic monastery cut off from the outside world in which the monks devoted themselves to work and communal celebration of the Divine Office, and that of the cenobitic and socially oriented monastery. Contemplative prayer could be part of the life of any of these models but, clearly, to differing degrees, ranging as they did from lives devoted entirely to seeking participation in the vision of God to lives of work and service for others, in which concentration on the individual's inner life is subordinated to the demands of charity.

The practice of different forms of the religious life was accompanied by a theory of the different Christian lives. Early discussions distinguish two lives, the active and the contemplative: the theory of the contemplative life reflects the Eastern anchoritic model, which demanded complete renunciation of the world and devotion instead to a life of solitary penitence and asceticism; the active life demands, on the other hand, participation in works of charity, such as feeding the hungry, clothing the naked, tending to the sick, and teaching.[3] Of the two lives, the contemplative was regarded as superior, a judgment that had its basis in the Martha and Mary story in Luke 10:39–42, where Mary's passivity is preferred by Christ to Martha's activity. Cassian, for example, therefore argued that the monastery was only a place of preparation for the hermitage, in which the solitary monk could attain spiritual purity to a degree impossible in the cenobitic life: "The perfection of the hermit lies in his having freed himself from all earthly concerns and, in so far as human frailty allows, of uniting himself with Christ."[4] This life cannot be reconciled with the demands of the active life: "Who can contemplate the immeasurable blessedness of heaven at that very moment when he is ministering alms to the poor, when he is welcoming visitors with gracious hospitality, when he is concerned with caring for the needs of his brethren?"[5]

The influence of this model was profound, and it is reflected in Western theologians like Augustine and Gregory the Great, but not without alteration. Augustine departed from it in that he argued that on earth we can hope only for intermittent glimpses of God and that, while here, the claims of this world should not be abandoned but that all should strive to practice the active virtues of Christianity. Augustine's position is linked with his views on monasticism: for him "true monasticism is coenobitical, not hermitical and . . . it is apostolic, or, in modern terminology, mixed rather than purely contemplative."[6] In his exegesis of the Martha and Mary story, for example, he did not follow the common exegesis of seeing in the two sisters figures of the active and contemplative lives, but instead saw them as standing for the two churches, the terrestrial and the celestial, the present and the future.[7] Augustine, therefore, to some extent departs from the exaltation of isolation and of total concentration on the vision of God: for him, Mary's life is that of heaven and of this we can have only fleeting glimpses on earth. In arguing thus, Augustine dissociated contemplation from the hermit's life: as he describes it, contemplation is available, though only occasionally, to all, and is not the exclusive preserve of the solitary. While it should be striven for, Augustine held that the true Christian should always be ready to undertake works of charity: it is more virtuous to abandon contemplation in case of necessity than to ignore the claims of others. Augustine himself lived a cenobitic life with his clergy, balancing active charity with contemplative prayer.

Gregory the Great shows a not always easy compromise between the traditional view and that of Augustine. He did not adopt Augustine's interpretation of Martha and Mary as this life and the next, retaining instead the traditional and more common exegesis of the two sisters as the active and the contemplative lives and providing what was to become the classic definition:

> Duae etenim uitae sunt, in quibus eos omnipotens Deus per sacrum eloquium erudit, actiua uidelicet et contemplatiua. Actiua enim uita est, panem esurienti tribuere, uerbo sapientiae nescientem docere, errantem corrigere, ad humilitatis uiam superbientem proximum reuocare, infirmantis curam gerere, quae singulis quibusque expediant dispensare, et commissis nobis qualiter subsistere ualeant prouidere. Contemplatiua uero uita est caritatem quidem Dei proximi tota mente retinere, sed ab exteriore actione quiescere, soli desiderio conditoris inhaerere, ut nil iam agere libeat, sed, calcatis curis omnibus, ad uidendam faciem sui Creatoris animus inardescat . . . [8]

Although Gregory retains the traditional polarized notion of the superiority of the contemplative to the active, in practice he advocates as best of all a union of both lives, much as Augustine did. For Gregory, the best Christian life on earth seems to be what was known later as the "mixed" life, a combination of action and contemplation, exemplified for him in teachers and preachers whose pastoral duties and instructions alternate with periods of withdrawal and prayer: "Cum enim longe sit a continentibus et tacentibus excellentia praedicatorum, et ualde a coniugatis distet eminentia continentium. . . . Praedicatores uero non solum se a uitiis coercent sed etiam alios peccare prohibent, ad fidem ducunt, in studio bonae conuersationis instruunt."[9] Christ is the example of this life:

atque aliter, quia coniunctae utriusque uitae, actiuae uidelicet et
contemplatiuae, in se exempla monstrauit. Ab actiua enim uita longe
contemplatiua distat, sed incarnatus Redemptor noster ueniens, dum utramque
exhibuit, in se utramque sociauit.[10]

Hinc est quod humani generis Redemptor per diem miracula in urbibus
exhibet et ad orationis studium in monte pernoctat, ut perfectis uidelicet
praedicatoribus innuat quatenus nec actiuam uitam amore speculationis
funditus deserant, nec contemplationis gaudia penitus operationis nimietate
contemnant; sed quieti contemplantes sorbeant quod occupati erga proximos
loquentes refundant.[11]

Although, then, the life of contemplation is exalted by Gregory, it does not
seem to be advocated as in itself the best life of the Christian while in this
world: that is reserved for those who unite action and contemplation, the
preachers whom Gregory instructs in his *Cura Pastoralis*. Again, therefore,
the contemplative life no longer involves living the life of the hermit; it is
those periods that can be spared from ecclesiastical administration or teaching or works of charity, and the contemplative-active contrast becomes largely
one between different aspects of the life of a monk or cleric or, indeed,of a
lay person. His treatment of the two (now really three) lives was enormously
influential and his classic definition of the active and contemplative was
followed by, for example, Bede, who, like Gregory, regarded a combination
of teaching and contemplation as the Christian ideal.[12]

By Gregory's time, therefore, the contemplative-active distinction can
be defined in different ways: as a contrast between the life of the hermit and
that of cenobites or other religious; between the monastic life and that of
pastoral clergy, or as different states within an individual's life. Whereas the
early Eastern discussions associate the contemplative life chiefly with the
solitary, in the West the tradition rapidly became more complicated as attempts were made to reconcile social responsibilities with the wish to live a
life of prayer and devotion. The notion of the superiority of the contemplative
life, rooted as it was in Luke 10, remained a constant, but was no longer
viewed as a justification for abandoning all else: the ideal Christian balanced
both lives.

II

The different forms of the Christian life and the theological discussions
of these forms were both transmitted to the newly Christianized areas of
Europe as they were converted. In Ireland the influence of the eremitic saints
and the appeal of the desert seem to have outweighed the importance of
Augustine and Gregory, and the contemplative life appears to have been

regarded as superior to any other. Hermits' settlements still survive, such as, for example, that of Skellig Michael off the west coast of County Kerry, which display a remarkable agreement with the literary sources describing their lives.[13] For hermits in such isolated settings, pastoral responsibilities clearly did not come into question. The hermit's life was particularly linked with the idea of pilgrimage, of the *peregrinatio*, which from an early period was enthusiastically practiced in Ireland.[14] This was of two kinds: the lesser *peregrinatio* within Ireland and the *potior peregrinatio* that involved journeying overseas to live a life of asceticism in a foreign country. Charles-Edwards has demonstrated the connections between Irish social organization and *peregrinatio*, which made it "the most intelligible form of ascetic renunciation available to Irishmen."[15] The *deorad Dé*, the exile of God, was very highly regarded in Irish society: "like the bishop or the chief poet, the *deorad Dé* has a legal status equal to that of the normal Irish king"[16] and he was "the representative on earth of God and the saints."[17]

In the saints' lives there is abundant evidence of the anchoritic ways of life: Adamnán's Life of Columba, for instance, describes two kinds of hermit. Some of those mentioned in it were in fairly close connection with a community, probably still owing allegiance to an abbot.[18] Others lived as solitaries, frequently leaving Ireland altogether as *peregrini* seeking a deserted retreat: "the wanderer in the desert of the ocean, on the other hand, must frequently have been beyond all contact with the church at large, whether his *peregrinatio* was permanent or seasonal."[19] The "wanderers in the desert of the ocean" are those who totally abandoned their homeland and set out in search of solitude, often settling in the northern islands and even in Iceland. Even those Irish saints who did not permanently embrace the hermit's life usually alternated periods of withdrawal with their pastoral work.[20] At the end of the eighth century and in the ninth, the ascetic impulse, which seems to have suffered a decline in the previous century, was renewed in the Irish church with the *Celi Dé* or Culdee movement.[21]

Maelruain (d. 792), founder of Tallaght, is particularly associated with this new asceticism, whose adherents seem to have lived principally in groups and in which the former practice of leaving Ireland was no longer approved. The Culdees seem not, however, to have been a movement of hermits strictly speaking: they were the successors of the ascetic communities (monks in the full sense) who had always been only one of the different groups within the Irish monastic *ciuitas*: "The monastic revival of the late eighth century ... sought to invigorate the small religious communities within the churches or living separately as small ascetic monasteries."[22] In the early Irish church the contemplative life, therefore, was associated with withdrawal from society: either by living as a hermit or by living within that section of the monastic community which was composed of the most religious monks, who had nothing to do with the temporal and pastoral responsibilities of the monastery.

Irish Christianity was, of course, particularly influential in the north of England, and here, too, there is abundant evidence for the importance of the eremitic life, similarly viewed. Early English monasteries were centers of missionary and pastoral activity, and the contemplative life is again associated principally with the hermit. Aidan (d. 651), who led the Irish mission to Northumbria, periodically retreated to an island hermitage on Farne for prayer and meditation.[23] Cuthbert (643–687) was clearly inspired by Irish models, and he eventually left the monastery of Lindisfarne to become a recluse on Farne, before reluctantly leaving it when he was appointed bishop.[24] On realizing that death was approaching, he retired again to Farne and ended his life there, being succeeded by another hermit, Æthelwald. The Lindisfarne Gospels were provided with an ornate jeweled casing by Billfrith the anchorite in the first half of the eighth century: he probably lived close to, but not in, the Lindisfarne community.[25] When news of Bishop Wilfrid's (634–709/ 710) death spread, his biographer Stephen tells us, "omnes abbates eius de suis locis et anachoritae concito cursu pergentes die et nocte festinanter,"[26] and at the end of his life he allowed Caelin, who had been ruling the monastery of Ripon, "nunc ad pristinum statum conuersationis atque ad deserta loca reuertere et contemplatiuam uitam, sicut olim, exercere et soli Deo seruire."[27] We know that Wilgils, father of St. Willibrord (658–739), ended his life as a hermit near the mouth of the Humber, living in a cell amidst a monastic congregation,[28] as happened also in the Irish monasteries. Cynefrith, the brother of Abbot Ceolfrid (d. 716) of Wearmouth and Jarrow, had been abbot of Gilling, but retired to Ireland to study the Scriptures and serve "liberius Domino in lacrimis precibusque";[29] Ceolfrid himself, when an old man, gave up his abbacy and set out for Rome "imitatus exemplum fratris sui Cynefridi, qui . . . studio uitae contemplatiuae monasterii curam reliquit, et patriam propter Dominum spontaneo mutauit exsilio."[30] The author of his *vita* portrays him mounting his horse and departing "abiectis saecularium rerum curis, festinans ab ipsa quoque cognata sibi Anglorum gente peregrinari in terris quo liberior puriorque animo ad contemplanda angelorum consortia redderetur in celis."[31] Bede mentions several hermits: Hereberht, who lived on an island in a lake;[32] Wictbert, who preached in Frisia having lived "multos annos in Hibernia peregrinus anchoreticam in magna perfectione uitam";[33] Hæmgils, who, influenced by Dryhthelm's vision of the next world, "in Hibernia insula solitarius ultimam uitae aetatem pane cibario et frigida aqua sustentat."[34] Toward the end of the eighth century Alchfrith *anchorita* lived in the area of Lindisfarne and left behind a letter, which, drawing on sermons by Columbanus, clearly shows the influence of Irish spirituality, and three prayers, preserved in the ninth-century Book of Cerne.[35] The ninth-century

Liber vitae of Durham includes a list of "nomina anchoritarum" with twenty-eight names, all described as *presbyter.* in the manuscript they follow the "nomina regum uel ducum" and the "nomina reginarum et abbatissarum," an order of precedence that reflects their importance.[36] Anglo-Saxons did not, moreover, travel only to Ireland to live as hermits: an Anglo-Saxon called Philip lived as a hermit in the Palatinate in the time of King Pippin;[37] Sola died in 704 as a hermit in Solnhofen, west of Eichstätt;[38] and two Anglo-Saxon sisters were hermits at Oberalteich in ninth-century Bavaria.[39]

The most famous Northumbrian monument, the eighth-century Ruthwell Cross, also has a strong eremitic orientation, as was pointed out nearly fifty years ago by Schapiro and Saxl.[40] The north side of the cross has John the Baptist, "a prototype of Christian asceticism";[41] a large panel depicting Christ between two beasts, with an inscription drawing attention to the theme of Christ in the desert; and the hermits Paul and Antony breaking bread in the desert. The eucharist is the primary theme of all these of these panels, but it is consistently placed in a desert setting "epitomis[ing] the importance both of the eucharist and of the eremitic vocation."[42] Éamonn Ó Carragáin points out that the Paul and Antony scene "presented the monastic vocation as a paradigm of faith: as a call to risk the desert in order to live on bread daily given from heaven."[43]

In Mercia, too, we have evidence of hermits, in particular, of course, Guthlac (d. 714) and his successor in Crowland, Cissa. At the age of twenty-four, Guthlac renounced the life of raiding and pillaging he had led up to then and entered the monastery of Repton, leaving it two years later for the life of a solitary in the marshes of Crowland: "heremum cum curioso eximiae sollicitudinis animo petere meditabatur. Cum enim priscorum monachorum solitariam uitam legebat, tum inluminatio cordis gremio auida cupiditas heremum quaerere feruebat."[44] He retained an affiliation to Repton, which he regarded as his mother house. The *vita* of Guthlac, written c. 740 by the monk Felix, was composed under the influence of early Christian hagiography, especially that of the *vita* of Antony by Athanasius; and as Mayr-Harting points out, there is no reason why Guthlac himself should not have known and have been inspired by this life.[45] His ascetic practices and the temptations which he is described as undergoing are remarkably similar to those of Antony, and the similarity may well be of life as well as of hagiography, particularly as Felix describes Guthlac as having been inspired by the desert hermits. The *Old English Martyrology*, a Mercian compilation probably composed c. 800, points to a milieu with a developed interest in the eremitic and it includes many solitaries among its selection of saints: Paul the Hermit, Antony, Cuthbert, Guthlac, Æthelwald (Cuthbert's successor on Farne), Simeon the Stylite, Pelagia, Hilarion, and Martin of Tours.[46]

The lives of the desert hermits profoundly influenced the surviving *vitae* written in the early Anglo-Saxon period.[47] The anonymous *vita* of Cuthbert, written by a monk of Lindisfarne (699–705), borrows much from Athanasius's *Vita S. Antonii* and Sulpicius Severus's *Vita Martini*, as does the anonymous life of Gregory the Great. Jerome's *Vita S. Pauli* was drawn upon for the *vitae* of Gregory the Great, Cuthbert, and Guthlac, and Aldhelm used it for his portrait of Paul the Hermit in his prose *De virginitate*, drawing also on Athanasius for his portrait of Antony. There can be no doubt, therefore, of the importance of the model of the desert saint in early Anglo-Saxon England.

The unqualified celebration of the values of the solitary ascetic was not, however, universal. The striking exception in the early Northumbrian church was Bede, who was deeply imbued with the teaching of Gregory the Great and who shared Gregory's preoccupation with the role of teachers and preachers. Alan Thacker has shown how Bede's anxiety about the contemporary church led him to stress, in hagiography, history, and commentaries, the necessity for a reform of both Church and society, with a reformed monasticism taking the leading role in achieving this.[48] He wished to see in Britain "an intellectual and moral elite"[49] of *doctores* or *praedicatores*, who would combine and balance both action and contemplation: "on the one hand, the preacher and teacher could only fulfil his role successfully if he essayed the monastic skill of withdrawal and contemplation, on the other, the monk could only achieve the contemplative ideal after long practice in virtuous living, in *bona actio*."[50] Although Bede retained the traditional belief in the superiority of the contemplative life, he does not seem to have believed in a total retirement from the world and, indeed, clearly regarded the contemporary English church as too much in need of instruction and warning to be able to sacrifice some of its most pious members to a life of solitary prayer. Where Bede exalts the life of contemplation, it is only one part of a saint's life, as in the case of Cuthbert.

Bede's source for his lives of Cuthbert (one in verse and a second in prose) was the anonymous *vita*, which "with its account of Cuthbert's attempted anachoresis when prior and the contemplative's somewhat negative attitude towards episcopacy, belongs in the Egyptian, Martinian and Irish traditions."[51] As Thacker shows, Bede restructures this source to show how the saint's roles as active monk, contemplative, and *magister* unfold in turn, with Cuthbert's solitude on Farne "viewed as the crowning accomplishment of the monk: from the long *perfectio* of the active life Cuthbert rose to the ultimate *otium* of divine contemplation."[52] Despite this new stress on a progression from one state to the next, which seems to privilege contemplation over action, Bede alters the emphasis of his source to decrease the contemplative elements, as in, for example, the way in which his "version of the story of Cuthbert's journey into Pictland transformed a *peregrinatio* of uncertain length into a temporary expedition on specific monastic business; he discreetly omitted the Lindisfarne author's revelation that Cuthbert eventually sailed away to a secret retreat and had to be constrained to return to

monastic life, probably because he was conscious that such behaviour con-
sorted ill with the Benedictine virtue of *stabilitas*."[53] Bede stresses, moreover,
that Cuthbert's withdrawal to the hermitage was carried out with the consent
of his abbot and fellow monks and, of course, that the saint, although reluctant, did not refuse to leave his retreat when asked to become bishop. For
Bede, Cuthbert's "mixed" life as bishop is the culmination of his spiritual
advancement. Cuthbert's own life fits into an Irish pattern of eremitic asceticism alternating with, but more important than, teaching.[54] Bede's version,
however, even though he takes care to portray Cuthbert as outstanding in the
ascetic life of the contemplative, remaining in his hermitage and living
"solitariam in ieiuniis orationibus et uigiliis . . . uitam,"[55] is stylized to accord
with his own Gregorian ideals, which demanded a balance of action and
contemplation and subordinated the solitary life to the demands of the church.

In the Anglo-Saxon Church of the seventh and eighth centuries, therefore, there is a widespread interest in the eremitic life, manifesting itself in
the numbers of Anglo-Saxons who adopted the contemplative life, both in
England and abroad, and in the influence exerted by the lives of the desert
saints as hagiographic and as actual models. There can be little doubt that the
Anglo-Saxon Church was in this indebted to the Irish Church, in which the
call of the desert was for centuries a powerful force in the religious life.
Because of this model, it is clear that many in the early Anglo-Saxon Church
valued the contemplative life above any other: Bede, in promoting instead a
balance of action and contemplation in each individual, is the main exception
to this. His model was the Gregorian one, in which the interests of the church
at large are preferred to those of the individual.

III

Bede's influence is evident in Alcuin's (c. 735–804) treatment of the
two lives and in the importance he attributes to preaching.[56] From Alcuin on,
however, we have little evidence for assessing the relative importance of
active or contemplative lives in England until the end of the ninth century,
when Gregorian teaching again came into prominence in England with the
Alfredian translation of the *Pastoral Care*.[57] The *Pastoral Care* is largely
concerned with describing the qualities of the ideal preacher and with practical and spiritual advice and has little on the contemplative life, but Gregory,
followed by the Old English translation, makes the point very strongly that
those with the necessary talents have a moral obligation to use them for the
benefit of others. If they refuse to help others because they wish to devote
themselves to contemplation, then they incur the guilt of all the sins which
they have neglected to correct:

Monige men sindon, swæ swæ we ær cwædon, þe bioð geweorðod mid
miclum & mid monegum Godes gifum, & ðonne bioð onælede mid ðære
girninge ðara smeaunga Godes wisdomes anes, & fleoð ðonne þa nytwierðan
hiersumnesse ðære lare, & nyllað ðæs ðencean hu hie mægen nytwierðuste
bion hiera nihstum, ac lufiað digla stowa, & fleoð monna ansine. Gif him
ðonne God ryhtlice & streclice deman wile, & he him for his mildheortnesse
ne arað, ðonne bioð hie swæ monegum scyldum scyldige swæ hie monegra
unðeawa gestieran meahton mid hiora larum & bisnum, gif hie ongemong
monnum bion woldon. Hwæt ðenceað ða þe on swelcum weorcum scinað,
& magon hiera nihstum swæ nytte bion, hwy hie þara geearnunga hiora
digelnesse & anette bet truwian ðonne ðære hu hie oðerra monna mæst
gehelpen? Hwæt se ancenda Godes sunu of his fæder bosme wæs ferende
to urre andweardnesse ðæt he ure gehulpe.[58]

Alfred's own Preface to the *Pastoral Care* is also permeated with the importance of teaching as a means of regenerating the English people.

There is almost no evidence in this period for hermits in England, although this may be due to the shortage of evidence in general from the
second half of the ninth and the first half of the tenth centuries. Only with the
Benedictine reform from the mid-tenth century onward do sources again
become available in any abundance, and then they naturally relate primarily
to the reform movement. As this is exclusively cenobitic, we lack much
evidence for hermits in England, although there is some: the reformers concentrate mainly on relating the progress of Benedictine values and castigating
their clerical predecessors, and what hermits there were in England do not
figure largely in the sources.[59] The reform movement in general does not
seem to have objected to the ideal of the eremitic life: Thacker's recent
discussion of Æthelwold's devotion to the monastic past of Anglo-Saxon
England draws attention to the way in which he appropriated "the remains of
early monastic or eremitic saints."[60] The remains of Cissa, Guthlac's successor at Crowland, for example, went to Thorney, to which monastery were
translated, too, the remains of Saints Tancred, Torhtred, and Tova, "in local
tradition three siblings who lived as hermits near the site of the abbey."[61]
References to contemporary hermits, however, are rare: only once does Ælfric,
for example, refer to a contemporary anchorite, but the context of this single
reference is intriguing. In the introduction to his letter to Sigefyrð on chastity,
Ælfric explains why he is writing:

Ælfric abbod gret   Sigefyrð freondlice!
Me is gesæd,   þæt þu sædest be me,
þæt ic oðer tæhte   on Engliscum gewritum,
oðer eower ancor   æt ham mid eow tæhð,
forþan þe he swutelice sægð,   þæt hit sy alyfed,

þæt mæssepreostas   wel moton wifian,
and mine gewritu   wiðcweðað þysum.
Nu secge ic þe, leof man,   þæt me is lað to tælenne
agenne godes freond,   gyf he godes riht drifð,
ac we sceolon secgan   and forswugian ne durron
þa halgan lare,   þe se hælend tæhte:
Seo lare mæg eaðe   unc emlice seman.[62]

The allusion here to the anchorite is notable for its casual nature: "eower
ancor æt ham." It suggests a background in which anchorites were accepted,
even taken for granted, with the possessive adjective implying that Sigefyrð
maintained this anchorite on his estate. This was common in the later Middle
Ages and the practice would seem to date, therefore, from the late Anglo-
Saxon period. In the eleventh century, there are several references to recluses:
three Evesham monks lived as hermits in the neighborhood of the abbey in
the time of the prior Æfic, who was a friend of Cnut (1015–1035);[63] and
around the middle of the eleventh century, Aldwin, an unlettered monk of
Worcester, settled as a hermit in the wilds near Malvern.[64] In a will preserved
only in a late corrupt form there is a reference to "Mantat ancer, Godes
wrǣcca" in the time of Cnut.[65] Whitelock argues that "the use of the title
ancer in connection with Thorney looks like a piece of exaggerated antiquari-
anism" but says that "there must have been at least a tradition that these
estates were given by Cnut to a hermit and that the latter left them to the
abbey in return for right of burial there."[66] The idea of an anchorite at Thorney
in the time of Cnut is not implausible, however, given the other evidence of
eleventh-century anchorites: there were not many of whom traces survive,
admittedly, but they were clearly not unknown. Ælfric's reference, in particular, indicates that they may have been much more common than the surviving
evidence suggests. From the twelfth century onward, anchorites are relatively
common in England.

IV

Although evidence of hermits from the Benedictine reform period is
relatively scarce, there is some discussion of the different forms of Christian
life. In his homily for the feast of the Assumption of the Virgin in *Sermones
Catholici II*, for example, Ælfric discusses the Martha and Mary story in
Luke, the locus classicus for a treatment of the active and contemplative
lives.[67] He must have been acquainted with both exegetical traditions on this
passage: that on the active and contemplative lives followed by Origen, Cassian,
Gregory the Great, Bede and Haymo (which Ælfric would have known at

least from Bede's *Commentary on Luke* and from Haymo) and that of Augustine (whom he follows in this text) on the terrestrial and celestial churches. His sources are Augustine's *Sermones* 103 and 104, which he reorganizes to give a running gloss on the pericope.[68] He discusses Christ's corporal needs and the necessity that we should not complain that he is not now present in the world, turning then to the two women as symbols of the two lives, the present and the future, the transitory and the eternal.

Martha's manifold cares are contrasted with the unity of Mary's concern for Christ's teaching and the superiority of Mary's choice is set forth in a passage contrasting the transitory nature of Martha's toils with Mary's concentrated stillness. Ælfric then continues:

> Swiðe god ðenung is and herigendlic. þæt gehwa godes ðearfum ðenige. and swiðost ðam eawfæstum godes ðeowum. ac swa ðeah mare is þæt man þa heofenlican lare secge þam ungelæredum. and heora sawla gereordige þe næfre ne ateoriað. þonne man ðone deadlican lichaman mid brosniendlicum mettum afylle; Ægðres men behofiað. ge bigleofan ge lare. ac swa ðeah hwonlice fremað þæs mannes lif. ðe bið nytene gelic. ðe hawað symle to ðære eorðan þæt is to eorðlicum ðingum. and for andgitleaste ne cann his mod awendan to ðam upplicum ðingum ne to ðam ecan life.[69]

The starting point here seems to have been Augustine's insistence on the good, albeit the inferior good, of Martha's life:

> Bona sunt ministeria circa pauperes, et maxime circa sanctos Dei seruitia debita, obsequia religiosa. Redduntur enim, non dantur, dicente Apostolo, Si nos uobis spiritualia seminauimus, magnum est si carnalia uestra metamus. Bona sunt, exhortamur ad haec, et in uerbo Domini aedificamus uos, nolite pigri esse ad suscipiendos sanctos. Aliquando nescientes, suscipiendo quos nesciebant, Angelos susceperunt. "Bona sunt haec: melius est tamen quod elegit Maria. Illud enim habet ex necessitate occupationem: istud autem ex charitate suauitatem."[70]

Ælfric's passage begins like this part of *Sermo* 103 and one would expect it to continue in a similar fashion, with a contrast between Martha's service, which was good, and Mary's being served spiritually, which was better. This is what is implied by an earlier passage in Ælfric's homily: "Martha wæs geornful hu heo mihte god fedan. maria hogode swiðor hu heo mihte þurh godes lare hire sawle gereordigan. for ðan þe ðæs modes gereordung is betere. þonne ðære wambe . . .". [71]

Instead, however, Ælfric changes the distinction from one between providing corporal nourishment, as an image of this life, and receiving spiritual, as an image of the next life, to a distinction between those who provide corporal nourishment and those who provide spiritual nourishment, in Augustine's terms both aspects of this present life. The terms in which this new distinction is presented equate feeding with Martha and teaching with Mary, as the "god" and "mare" clearly take up the earlier contrast between the sisters: "God wæs marthan ðenung ða ða heo ðam ælmihtigan þenode. ac swa ðeah maria geceas þone selran dæl."[72] Ælfric's argument becomes, therefore, one for the superiority of teachers. This new argument cannot be explained by the straightforward influence of the alternative exegetical tradition, as both feeding and teaching are aspects of the active life. Strictly speaking, therefore, teaching should not be equated with Mary according to any exposition known to Ælfric, but this passage in the Old English text certainly implies such an equation. Although this could have been made a consistent and coherent part of the exegesis by introducing a new equation of Christ with the teachers, Ælfric does not explicitly do this; instead, he seems to extend the idea of the superiority of heavenly knowledge, of which Mary is an image, to include the notion that those engaged in providing such knowledge for others are also to be numbered among those who have chosen the "optimam partem." Teaching as an activity seems to share in, indeed to appropriate, the superiority of contemplation.

Having thus departed from his source, Ælfric then returns to *Sermo* 103, with a statement of man's duties in this world and a contrast to the next life, continuing:

> For ði is marthan ðenung swiðe herigendlic. ðurh hi wæs maria geherod. þeah ðe se lareow halig beo. hraðe ascleacað his tunge to ðære godcundan bodunge. gif he næfð þone lichamlican fodan. is swa ðeah selre þæt þæt ece is . . .[73]

This sentence again seems to imply that Mary is like the teacher, Martha like those who supply him with food, whereas Augustine, at the end of *Sermo* 104, implies that he himself, in his role of preacher, is like Martha and his congregation like Mary: "Nam et modo inde aliquid agimus, remoti a negotiis, sepositis familiaribus curis, conuenistis, statis, auditis. In quantum hoc agitis, Mariae similes estis. Et facilius uos quod agit Maria, quam ego qui praerogo."[74] Ælfric himself, later in his homily, also says that the congregation in church is like Mary listening to the word of God. Here, therefore, the implied parallel between Mary and the teacher is again puzzling in terms of the relationship between Ælfric and his source: for the second time and by the same kind of sleight of hand, teaching is substituted for the role of pupil or listener, with the result that it is the teacher, who, by implication, has chosen the "optimam partem." After this interpolation, the remainder of the exegesis is taken from *Sermo* 104 and is closely translated.

What Ælfric is doing here, therefore, is elevating the role of the teacher, albeit in a somewhat covert fashion. His predecessors in this are, as will be obvious from the discussion of the active and contemplative lives, Gregory and Bede. Much of Gregory's discussion of the lives comes in his homilies on Ezechiel and in the *Moralia* on Job: there seems to be no evidence that Ælfric knew the first of these, although he does seem to have known the second. The importance of preaching also, however, features in Gregory's *Homiliae in Euangelia*, which Ælfric undoubtedly knew, in, of course, the *Cura Pastoralis* itself, and, probably even more significantly, Gregory's ideas were deeply influential on Bede. Bede's importance for the entire Benedictine reform movement has been highlighted[75] and Ælfric's knowledge of his work was extensive: from Bede, perhaps, more than anyone else, Ælfric acquired his sense of the superiority of teachers and of the urgent need for good teachers.

While following Augustine for the greater part of his exegesis, therefore, Ælfric departs from his sources to introduce a concept that has no place in them. What seems to be at the root of Ælfric's treatment of his source here is his wish to follow Augustine's exegesis, combined with a desire to follow Gregory and Bede's promotion of the life of the teacher as the highest form of the Christian life. He does not succeed in integrating these two elements in his Old English homily, probably in part because the commentaries on the pericope for the feast impose a structure of two contrasting lives, whereas the life of the teacher, as advocated by Gregory and Bede, is a combination of both. The exegetical tradition centers from the beginning on the contrast between the sisters, and even those commentators whom one would expect to expand the exegesis to take into account the role of Christ as teacher fail to do so. Ælfric, therefore, here imports into the Martha and Mary story an aspect of the active-contemplative debate that had hitherto been applied only in other contexts; hence, the awkward inconsequentiality of his treatment here. In addition, of course, there are no clear statements in either Gregory or Bede that teaching was superior even to contemplation: both adopt the traditional Christian teaching that contemplation is the highest state and, although a belief in the teacher's combination of action and contemplation as being in practice the best life is evident in the work of both, neither says so in such a way as to run the risk of denigrating the traditionally celebrated life of contemplation. Much in Ælfric's work points to his agreement with the implicit conclusions of Gregory and Bede, but he had no unequivocal statements in either and this probably contributes to the problematic nature of his treatment of the issue in his homily for the Assumption. His wish not to present the contemplative life as the most praiseworthy may also lie behind his choice of sources in this text: he knew, for example, the exegesis in terms of the active and contemplative lives in Bede's *Commentary on Luke*, but chose not to use it. Augustine's exegesis of the pericope enabled Ælfric to avoid praising the life of the contemplative. A similar avoidance can be seen in his *Sermones Catholici I* text for the feast of the Purification of the Virgin: here Ælfric is following Bede and Haymo for most of his exegesis, but he does not adopt their interpretation of the pigeons and turtledoves as the active and contemplative lives, preferring to expound them in terms of innocence and purity.[76]

                                   V

If this is the reason for Ælfric's alterations to his sources here, then it can be seen to fit in with other features of his work. In the first place, there is a clear avoidance of eremitic saints in Ælfric: he seems to have deliberately refrained from presenting the life of the contemplative hermit as an ideal. We find in his work no Antony, Paul the Hermit, Mary of Egypt, Hilary, Paphnutius, Guthlac, to name only a few of those of whom he undoubtedly knew. Apostles, martyrs, and confessors are the groups of saints to which he devotes his energies: teachers and those who gave up their lives for the faith are, therefore, the saints whom he considered important. Malcolm Godden has shown that the *Lives of Saints* "were to be read, in part at least, as providing important political and ethical lessons for the present"[77] and that Ælfric saw "both Old Testament history and the quasi-history embedded in saints' legends as providing parallels and precedents for the lay nobility and the clergy in the face of the troubles of his own time."[78] These lessons and precedents clearly did not include those offered by the *vitae* of the anchoritic saints: hermits are notable by their absence. The selection of saints, as Zettel has shown, is guided mainly by the importance of their feasts in the calendar of the Anglo-Saxon church and by the sources available to him.[79] The eremitic saints are not accorded great prominence in the English calendars, but even in Zettel's count we should expect Guthlac to figure in the *Lives of Saints*. There is no *vita* of Guthlac in the Cotton-Corpus legendary, Ælfric's principal hagiographic source collection, but the work was certainly available in late Anglo-Saxon England, and vernacular versions of it circulated as well as the Latin text: while we cannot be sure whether or not Ælfric knew the *vita*, he had plainly read more than was available in the Cotton-Corpus collection and his knowledge of the Guthlac text seems reasonably probable. The life of Mary of Egypt, though available in the Cotton-Corpus legendary, was ignored by Ælfric, but it was considered of sufficient importance to be translated into Anglo-Saxon and incorporated in the principal surviving manuscript of the *Lives of Saints*. There is no doubt that Ælfric could have included solitaries, had he so desired, but he obviously did not wish to provide models of the hermit's life. It is probably no accident that Ælfric's sole reference to a contemporary hermit is a critical one: the hermit taught that priests were allowed to marry, a concept anathema to Ælfric, and it is to contradict this that Ælfric composed his letter to Sigefyrð.

One of the few saints in Ælfric's work in whose life the eremitic, contemplative element featured prominently is Cuthbert, whose *vita* is related in *Sermones Catholici II*, drawing on Bede's prose and metrical *vitae* of the saint.[80] Bede stresses the pastoral and preaching aspects of Cuthbert's career to a much greater extent than his source, the anonymous life, and his depiction of the saint "omits Cuthbert's *anachoresis* and all negative phraseology about pastoral care and episcopacy, emphasizing instead Cuthbert's obedience to his abbot, that the solitary life was not necessarily superior to the cenobitic, and that Cuthbert, even as an enclosed contemplative, never ceased teaching other people."[81] Ælfric's portrait of Cuthbert takes this change of direction even further and stresses the pastoral element to an greater degree again. He cuts down considerably the sections on Cuthbert as solitary ascetic, and in describing his life on Farne, for example, he does not mention the saint's increasing wish for isolation or his cutting himself off in his cell so that he could not even be seen. Cuthbert's death scenes are also drastically abbreviated, again in the direction of minimizing the desert elements, the temptations he endured in his last days. Ælfric retains throughout the references to Cuthbert as teacher:

> Witodlice cuþbertus ferde swa swa his gewuna wæs. ymbe geleaffulre bodunge. þæt he ðam ungelæredum folce. lifes weig tæhte . . . [82]

> cuþbertus ðam folce fægere bodade. þæt hi wære wæron wið deofles syrwum. ðy læs ðe he mid leasunge heora geleafan awyrde . . . [83]

> he wolde gelome. leodum bodian. on fyrlenum lande. unforhtigende; Hwæt ða him geuðe. se ælmihtiga god. fægre getingnysse. ðam folce to lare . . . [84]

> þa wunode se halga wer manega gear. on ðam ancerlife swiðlice stiðe. and hine geneosodon gelome eawfæste menn. and be his lare heora lif gerihtlæhton . . . [85]

> Hwæt ða siððan se halge cuðbertus lindisfarnensiscere gelaðunge leodbiscop. mid ealre gecneordnysse. his folces gymde to geefenlæcunge. ðæra eadigra apostola. and hi mid singalum gebedum gescylde wið deofl. and mid halwendum myngungum. to heofonan tihte . . . [86]

For Ælfric, then, Cuthbert is above all the teacher and preacher par excellence, and he does not follow Bede in his shaping of Cuthbert's life to show a steady progress toward contemplation, before he becomes bishop.

Ælfric's attitude to the *Vitae Patrum*, one of the primary texts dealing with the lives and teaching of the desert fathers, is also instructive.[87] He clearly had access to a copy and used it throughout his career, referring to it on those rare occasions when he praises the anchoritic life:

> þysum fyligð ancersetlena drohtnung, and synderlic ingehyd. þa on westenum wunigende, woruldlice estas and gælsan mid strecum mode and stiðum life fortrædon ... Seo boc þe is gehaten *Uitae Patrum* sprecð menigfealdlice embe þyssera ancersetlena, and eac gemænelicra muneca drohtnunge, and cwyð, þæt heora wæs fela ðusenda gehwær on westenum and on mynstrum wundorlice drohtnigende, ac swa-þeah swyðost on Egypta-lande.[88]

> On westenum wunedon þa wisan fæderas
> Antonius and Paulus, Hilarion and Macharius,
> Iohannes and Arsenius, Pafnutius and Apollonius,
> and fela þusenda, swa swa *Vita Patrum* segð,
> muneca and mynecena, on mycelre drohtnunge
> Criste þeowigende on modes clænnysse.[89]

His praise, however, is always brief and when he uses the work directly, it is always only to extract from it exempla which he uses in support of dogmatic points: there is no extended treatment of the *Verba Seniorum*, the book that appears to have been known to Ælfric under the title *Vitae Patrum*. Moreover, in the Preface to the *Lives of Saints*, he voiced doubts about using the work, saying that it contains many subtle points which were not fitting for the laity: "Nec tamen plura promitto me scripturum hac lingua, quia nec conuenit huic sermocinationi plura inseri; ne forte despectui habeantur margarite christi. Ideoque reticemus de libro uitae patrum, in quo multa subtilia habentur quae non conueniunt aperiri laicis, nec nos ipsi ea quimus implere."[90] Given Ælfric's use of the work, this is surprising, particularly as the *Vitae Patrum* was a hallowed and popular text. His avoidance throughout his career of the *Vitae Patrum*'s central theme of the ascetic, contemplative life may furnish the explanation for his refusal to use it in the *Lives of Saints*. Ælfric's use of the *Vitae Patrum* is restricted to exempla that do not explicitly treat of the contemplative life: he employs it for exempla on prayer, on the prohibition of castration, on visions of departing souls, and on the Eucharist. He may well have shunned the *Vitae Patrum*'s main theme because he himself was not totally comfortable with the idea of the eremitic life as the highest ideal, though criticism of such a revered model would probably have seemed inconceivable.

Ælfric's avoidance of the eremitic and contemplative as an ideal is clearly connected with his urgent emphasis on the necessity for good teachers, as his treatment of the Martha and Mary story suggests. The theme of the importance of teachers is found throughout his work: this, he says, is the last age of the world, when men are in greater need than ever of good teachers.[91] Beginning with the Preface to *Sermones Catholici I*, he laments the lack of such men: "is nu to lyt ðe wile wel tæcan and wel bysnian"[92] and at the end of his life, he was still preoccupied with the lack of good *lareowas*. In an independently composed passage in the *Sermo de Die Iudicii*, which Pope dates to after the year 1000, Ælfric again deplores the shortage of preachers who carry out the duties of their office:

Is swaþeah to lyt þæra lareowa nu
þe þus don wille, and is manncynn forþi
miclum geyrmed, for þam þe þæra is
feawa folces lareowa þe geornlice hogie
hu man yfel alecge and unrihtwisnysse,
and riht arære, swa swa we rædað on bocum:
Canes muti non possunt latrare:
Hi synd þa dumban hundas, and hy ne magon beorcan.
þis cwæð se witega be Godes lareowum,
þe noldon bodian and gebigan manncynn
to Godes willan þa on þam timan þe hi wæron.
Nu is gyt wyrse on urum timan,
þæt þæt we ealle suwiað, and unriht gæð forð
openlice and digollice, and we embe ne hogiað.
Witodlice þa lareowas þe us lar of com,
hi bododon þam hæðenum and þam hetelum ehterum,
and heora lif sealdon for Godes geleafan;
ac we ne durron nu to þam gedyrstlæcan,
þæt we Cristenum cyninge oððe Cristenum folce
Godes beboda and Godes willan secgan.[93]

Ælfric here appeals to the example of the martyrs, who gave their lives because of their preaching, to castigate contemporary *lareowas*, including, it would seem, himself, because they do not dare openly to condemn the rampant wrongdoing which is evident everywhere. His works constantly come back to what makes a good *lareow*: he should teach and live well,[94] but those priests who cannot teach should at least set a good example by living well,[95] and if their teachers do not live virtuously, then the people should strive to follow their teaching and ignore their example.[96] Teachers should be well educated ("Lange sceal leornian. se ðe læran sceal");[97] they should not cease from teaching no matter how obstinate their listeners;[98] and those preachers who accept the offerings of the people and do not preach feed on the sins of the people.[99] The people should always pray for good teachers.[100] Because of the difficulties of their office, *lareowas* will be rewarded more than the laity in the next life: "þa lareowas swincað swiðor þonne þa læwedan, ge on heora þeowdome, þe hi gode þeowiað, ge on heora gehealdsumnysse, þe hi healdan sceolon, ge on þære boclican lare þe hi bodian sceolon, and bið for ði mare heora med mid gode."[101]

Whereas in contemporary continental discussions this teaching role was assigned to the secular clergy and monks were expected to be enclosed and removed from such concerns, in England the Benedictine Reform cathedral-monasteries meant that monks were much more involved with the laity.[102] Wormald has emphasized how "very odd an arrangement it was"[103] compared with continental Europe, where one of the motives of the enormously influential Benedict of Aniane "for drawing so careful a line between the respective spheres of monk and canon was to isolate the former from the cares of the Church in the world . . . ; the last thing he had in mind was the mingling of Martha's life with Mary."[104] What seems to have given rise to the peculiar Anglo-Saxon situation was the influence of Bede on Æthelwold, in particular: because for Bede "almost everyone who was anyone in the first century of the English Church was what he rightly or wrongly called a monk,"[105] the tenth-century reformers aimed at making all English religious communities monastic. The monks portrayed in Bede are very much engaged in pastoral work and preaching and this must also have been the case in the reform period, at least for those monks in cathedral monasteries. So although Ælfric, for example, keeps his source's praise of Martin's monks who do nothing except pray and copy books[106] and explicitly states that bishops and "sacerdas" (secular priests) should preach but that monks should live their lives "on stilnysse,"[107] nevertheless this cannot have corresponded to the reality of contemporary Anglo-Saxon monasticism. Those monks who served cathedrals cannot have lived lives of cloistered contemplation and prayer, and we know, too, that Anglo-Saxon abbots and monk-bishops were heavily involved in government as well as ecclesiastical administration. Ælfric even felt it necessary, as indeed it was, to preach against monks taking part in battles.[108] The ideal of enclosed asceticism, therefore, was far from being fact. The contemporary situation and the clash between it and the theory of the monastic life help, I believe, explain Ælfric's stance on the problem of the contemplative life: educated to believe in the superiority of monasticism to all other ways of life, but of a uniquely English type of pastoral monasticism, he was somewhat at a loss when confronting statements on the superiority of contemplation. His training cannot have been conducive to viewing withdrawal and total "stilnysse" as the monastic ideal, especially in an England rife with apostasy and where education outside the monasteries was poor. So, although some lip service is paid to the ideal of monasticism as dissociated from the world (an ideal that also, of course, allowed him to defend the freedom of monks from those aspects of worldly involvement of which he disapproved), Ælfric in practice seems to have been far more concerned to exalt the ideal of teachers and preachers.

For Ælfric, then, the concept of the solitary anchoritic life seems to have held little appeal. As a member of a reformed church that stressed the corporate element very strongly and was devoted to the ideal of Benedictine monasticism, redefined in English terms, he appears to have viewed the lone hermit's life with some suspicion, although the traditional eulogies of such a life would have prevented him from directly voicing these doubts. Although the reform movement in general, so far as the scanty evidence allows us to judge, did not object to the anchoritic life, Ælfric's sense of the urgent need for pastoral preaching would have predisposed him against an ideal that encouraged a concentration on the individual's spiritual life to the detriment of social concerns. In an age when apostasy was widespread and the country in a state of crisis, such an ideal had obvious shortcomings. Because he obviously could not preach against the eremitic life, Ælfric seems to have chosen to ignore it as far as possible and exalt instead the ideal of the preacher and teacher, who sets a good example and spreads the word of God.

VI

The ideal of the contemplative life, then, has an interesting history in Anglo-Saxon England. In the early period, and under the influence of the Irish Church in particular, it exercised a strong appeal on some of the most devout members of the Church: they renounced the world, and sometimes even abandoned their native countries, and devoted themselves to prayer and ascetic practices. From the later Anglo-Saxon period, however, we have less evidence of hermits or, indeed, the type of asceticism associated with this life, and the individualism that allowed the anchoritic ideal to coexist with the cenobitic in the early period seems to have been less common. The outstanding saints of the later period are all cenobitic, propagating the ideal of Benedictinism and a sense of community, although not adverse to looking back with approval at the eremitic saints of early Anglo-Saxon England. Ælfric, however, the most prolific exponent of Benedictine values, appears not to have entirely shared this sense of approval and the evidence of his selection of sources and hagiographic models points to an alternative ideal of pastoral involvement.[109]

Notes

1. For general introductions to the early hermits and early monasticism see Derwas J. Chitty, *The Desert a City* (Oxford, 1966); Clifford H. Lawrence, *Medieval Monasticism* (London, 1984), pp. 1–16; Kathleen Hughes, *The Church in Early Irish Society*

(London, 1966), pp. 10–24; and John Ryan, *Irish Monasticism, Its Origins and Early Development* (London, 1931).

2. Athanasius, *Life of St. Antony*, trans. R. T. Meyer (London, 1950).

3. On the active and contemplative lives, see Cuthbert Butler, *Western Mysticism* (London, 1922).

4. Cited by Henrietta Leyser, *Hermits and the New Monasticism* (London, 1984), p. 11.

5. Cited by Hughes, *The Church*, p. 18.

6. Gerhart B. Ladner, *The Idea of Reform* (Cambridge, Mass., 1959), p. 340.

7. *Sermones* 103 and 104, *PL* 38, 613–18.

8. *Homiliae in Hiezechihelem Prophetam*, ed. Marcus Adriaen, CCSL 142 (Turnhout, Belgium, 1971), II. ii. 178–79 and 186–96: "There are two lives in which Almighty God by this holy word instructs us—the active and the contemplative. . . . The active life is: to give bread to the hungry, to teach the ignorant the word of wisdom, to correct the erring, to recall to the path of humility our neighbour when he waxes proud, to tend the sick, to dispense to all what they need, and to provide those entrusted to us with the means of subsistence. But the contemplative life is: to retain indeed with all one's mind the love of God and neighbour, but to rest from exterior action, and cleave only to the desire of the Maker, that the mind may take no pleasure in doing anything, but having spurned all cares, may be aglow to see the face of its Creator . . . " (trans. Butler, pp. 171–72).

9. Ibid., II. vi. 186–98: "The excellence of preachers is far above that of the continent and silent, and the eminence of the continent outdistances greatly that of married people. . . . But preachers not only withhold themselves from vices, but restrain others from sinning, lead them to the faith and instruct them in the pursuit of holy living" (p. 184).

10. *Moralia in Iob Libri XXIII–XXXV*, ed. Marcus Adriaen, CCSL 143B (Turnhout, Belgium 1985), XXVIII. xiii. 33: "Christ set forth in Himself patterns of both lives, that is the active and the contemplative, united together. For the contemplative life differs very much from the active. But our Redeemer, by becoming incarnate, while He gave a pattern of both, united both in Himself" (trans. Butler, p. 176).

11. *Moralia in Iob, Libri I–X*, ed. M. Adriaen, CCSL 143 (Turnhout, Belgium, 1979), VI. xxxvii. 56: "It is hence that the Redeemer of mankind in the daytime exhibits His miracles in cities, and spends the night in devotion to prayer upon the mountain, namely, that He may teach all perfect preachers, that they should neither entirely leave the active life from love of the speculative, nor wholly slight the joys of contemplation from excess in working; but in quiet imbibe in contemplation what in employment they may pour back to their neighbours by word of mouth" (trans. Butler, p. 177).

12. On action and contemplation in Bede, see Alan Thacker, "Bede's Ideal of Reform" in *Ideal and Reality in Frankish and Anglo-Saxon Society*, ed. Patrick Wormald (Oxford, 1982), pp. 130–53, particularly p. 132 and pp. 138–43.

13. See Michael Herity, "Early Irish Hermitages in the Light of the Lives of Cuthbert" in *St. Cuthbert, His Cult and His Community to A.D. 1200*, ed. Gerald Bonner, David Rollason, and Clare Stancliffe (Woodbridge, England, 1989), pp. 45–63.

14. Thomas Charles-Edwards, "The Social Background to Irish Peregrinatio," *Celtica* 2 (1976): 43–59; Patrick L. Henry, *The Early English and Celtic Lyric* (London, 1966), pp. 29–39.

15. Charles-Edwards, ibid., p. 56.

16. Ibid., p. 53.

17. Ibid.

18. A. D. S. MacDonald, "Aspects of the Monastery and Monastic Life in Adomnan's Life of Columba," *Peritia* 3 (1984): 299.

19. Ibid., p. 299.

20. Clare Stancliffe, "Cuthbert and the Polarity Between Pastor and Solitary," in *St Cuthbert, His Cult*, pp. 21–44.

21. See, e.g., Hughes, *The Church*, pp. 173–84.

22. Richard Sharpe, "Some Problems Concerning the Organization of the Church in Early Medieval Ireland," *Peritia* 3 (1984): 267.

23. *Historia Ecclesiastica*, III.16, in *Venerabilis Baedae Opera Historica*, ed. Charles Plummer (Oxford, 1896), p. 159.

24. For Cuthbert's life, see *Two Lives of St. Cuthbert*, ed. Bertram Colgrave (Cambridge, 1940).

25. Thomas D. Kendrick et al., *Codex Lindisfarnesis*, vol. 2 (London, 1960), p. 5.

26. *The Life of Bishop Wilfrid by Eddius Stephanus*, ed. Bertram Colgrave (Cambridge, 1927), p. 134: "all his abbots and hermits came hastening from their homes by day and by night" (trans. Colgrave, p. 135).

27. Ibid., p. 138: "to return to his former manner of life, to go back to the desert places and to live a life of contemplation, as he once did, serving God alone" (p. 139).

28. Wilhelm Levison, *England and the Continent in the Eighth Century* (Oxford, 1946), pp. 54–55.

29. *Historia abbatum auctore anonymo* in Plummer, *Venerabilis Baedae Opera Historica*, ed. Plummer, p. 388, para. 2: "more freely in tears and prayers."

30. Ibid., p. 395: "imitating the example of his brother Cynefrith who . . . gave up the charge of the monastery in his zeal for the contemplative life, and exchanged his own land for voluntary exile for the sake of the Lord" (trans. Dorothy Whitelock, *English Historical Documents, c. 500–1042* [London, 1955], p. 702).

31. Plummer, ibid., p. 398: "his secular cares laid aside, hastening also from the English people, his kindred, to be a stranger in foreign lands, that he might with greater freedom and purity of mind devote himself to the contemplation of the companies of angels in heaven" (trans. Whitelock, ibid., p. 704).

32. Plummer, *Historia Ecclesiastica*, IV. 27, p. 274.

33. Ibid., V. 9, p. 298: "lived the life of a hermit in great perfection for many years in Ireland" (trans. L. Sherley-Price, *Bede: A History of the English Church and People* [Harmondsworth, England, 1955], p. 284).

34. Ibid., V.12, p. 309: "went to be a hermit in Ireland, supporting his latter years on a diet of bread and cold water" (trans. Sherley-Price, ibid., p. 293).

35. See Levison, *England and the Continent*, pp. 296–302; and Kathleen Hughes, "Some Aspects of Irish Influence on Early English Private Prayer," *Studia Celtica* 5 (1970): 48–61.

36. *Liber Vitae Ecclesiae Dunelmensis*, ed. J. Stevenson, Surtees Society 13 (London, 1841), p. 6.

37. Levison, *England and the Continent*, p. 168.

38. Ibid., p. 168.

39. Louis Gougaud, *Ermites et reclus*, Moines et monastères 3 (Vienne, France, 1928), p. 81.

40. Meyer Schapiro, "The Religious Meaning of the Ruthwell Cross," *Art Bulletin* 26 (1944): 232–45; Fritz Saxl, "The Ruthwell Cross," *Journal of the Warburg and Courtauld Institutes* 6 (1943): 1–19.

41. Schapiro, ibid., p. 236.

42. Éamonn Ó Carragáin, "The Meeting of Saint Paul and Saint Anthony: Visual and Literary Uses of a Eucharistic Motif" in *Keimelia: Studies in Medieval Archaeology and History in Memory of Tom Delaney*, ed. Gearóid Mac Niocaill and P. F. Wallace (Galway, Ireland, 1988), p. 44.

43. Ibid., p. 44.

44. *Felix's Life of St Guthlac*, ed. and trans. Bertram Colgrave (Cambridge, 1956), p. 87: "he planned to seek the desert with the greatest diligence and the utmost earnestness of mind. For when he read about the solitary life of monks of former days, then his heart was enlightened and burned with an eager desire to make his way to the desert."

45. Henry Mayr-Harting, *The Coming of Christianity to Anglo-Saxon England* (London, 1972), p. 239.

46. *An Old English Martyrology*, ed. George Herzfeld, EETS OS 116 (London, 1900) and Gunter Kotzor, *Das altenglische Martyrologium*, Bayerische Akademie der Wissenschaften, Phil.-hist. Klasse no. 88 (Munich, 1981).

47. See Bertram Colgrave, "The Earliest Saints' Lives Written in England," *Proceedings of the British Academy* 44 (1958): 35–60, passim.

48. Thacker, "Bede's Ideal of Reform," p. 149.

49. Ibid., p. 131.

50. Ibid., p. 132.

51. Stancliffe, "Cuthbert and the Polarity," p. 40.

52. Thacker, "Bede's Ideal of Reform," p. 141.

53. Ibid., p. 140.

54. Stancliffe, "Cuthbert and the Polarity," p. 41.

55. Colgrave, *Two Lives of Cuthbert*, p. 220: "a solitary life of fasting, prayer and vigils."

56. Thacker, "Bede's Ideal of Reform," pp. 151–53.

57. *King Alfred's West-Saxon Version of Gregory's Pastoral Care*, ed. Henry Sweet, EETS OS 45 (Oxford, 1871).

58. Ibid., pp. 44 and 46: "There are many men, as we have remarked above, who are honoured with great and many gifts of God, and then are inflamed with the desire of the contemplation of God's wisdom alone, and so avoid the profitable obedience of teaching, and will not consider how they can be most useful to their neighbours, but love solitude and shun the faces of men. But if God determines to judge them righteously and severely, and does not of his mercy spare them, they are guilty of as many sins as they could have corrected faults with their instruction and example, if they had been willing to associate with men. What reason have those, who shine with such words and can be so useful to their neighbours, for trusting rather to the merits of retirement and solitude then aiding other men as much as possible? Did not the only born Son of God come from his Father's bosom to be with us and help us?" (trans. Sweet, pp. 45–46).

59. Allusions in later saints' lives to Anglo-Saxons of the tenth and eleventh centuries living as hermits must be viewed with caution. The *vita* of St. Ælfheah, written c. 1080 by Osbern, for example, says that he lived as a hermit near Bath, attracting followers and eventually founding a monastery. As Brooks points out, however, this is more likely to reflect "Osbern's desire to satisfy late eleventh-century Norman ideals of sanctity" than any authentic tradition (Nicholas Brooks, *The Early History of the Church of Canterbury* [Leicester, England, 1984], p. 279.) Similarly, in his *vita* of St. Dunstan, Osbern describes Dunstan as living in a tiny cell, like an anchorite, but this is missing from the earlier *vitae* and it is, again, most probably a late addition (see *Memorials of St Dunstan*, ed. William Stubbs, Rolls Series 63 [London, 1874], pp. 83–84, for the description of Dunstan's cell).

60. Alan Thacker, "Æthelwold and Abingdon," in *Bishop Æthelwold: His Career and Influence*, ed. Barbara Yorke (Woodbridge, Conn., 1988), p. 62.

61. Ibid., p. 61.

62. *Angelsächsische Homilien und Heiligenleben*, ed. Bruno Assman, reprinted with a supplementary introduction by Peter Clemoes (Darmstadt, Germany, 1964), p. 13, ll. 1–12: "Abbot Ælfric greets Sigefyrð in a friendly fashion! It has been said to me that you said about me that I taught in English writings otherwise than your anchorite at home with you teaches, because he clearly says that masspriests are allowed to marry, and my writings deny this. Now I say to you, dear man, that it is unpleasant for me to speak evil against a friend of God, if he practises God's law, but we must declare, and dare not pass over in silence, the holy teaching which the Saviour taught: that teaching can easily satisfy us both equally."

63. David Knowles, *The Monastic Order in England* (Cambridge, 1941), p. 75.

64. Ibid., p. 78.

65. Dorothy Whitelock, *Anglo-Saxon Wills* (Cambridge, 1930), p. 66.

66. Ibid., p. 177.

67. *Ælfric's Catholic Homilies: The Second Series*, ed. Malcolm Godden, EETS SS 5 (1979), pp. 255–59. This edition is hereafter cited as *CH II*.

68. *PL* 38, 613–18. For a detailed discussion of Ælfric's treatment of his sources, see my "The Cult of the Virgin Mary in Anglo-Saxon England, with Special Reference to the Vernacular Texts" (dissertation, Oxford University, 1983), pp. 355–67).

69. *CH II*, p. 257, ll. 70–80: "It is very good and praiseworthy ministering, that every one minister to God's poor, and above all to the pious servants of God; but yet it is greater to declare the heavenly lore to the ignorant, and refect their souls, which never perish, than to fill the mortal body with corruptible meats. Man stands in need of both, of sustenance and of lore; but yet little profits that man's life who is like unto a beast that ever looks to the earth, that is, to earthly things, and for lack of understanding cannot turn his mind to things on high, nor to the everlasting life" (trans. B. Thorpe, *The Homilies of the Anglo-Saxon Church II* [London, 1846], pp. 441–43).

70. *PL* 38, 615: "Good are ministrations done to the poor, and especially the due services and the religious offices done to the saints of God. For they are a payment, not a gift, as the Apostle says, 'If we have sown unto you spiritual things, is it a great thing if we shall reap your carnal things?'. Good are they, we exhort you to them, yea by the word of the Lord we build you up, 'be not slow to entertain' the saints. Sometimes, they who were not aware of it, by entertaining those whom they knew not, have entertained angels. These things are good; yet better is that thing which Mary hath chosen. For the one thing hath manifold trouble from necessity; the other hath sweetness from charity" (trans. Philip Schaff, *A Select Library of the Nicene and Post-Nicene Fathers of the Christian Church*, vol. 6 [reprinted Grand Rapids, Mich., 1956], p. 428).

71. *CH II*, p. 257, ll. 54–58: "Martha was anxious how she might feed God; Mary was more solicitous how she might, through God's lore, refect her soul; for the refection of the mind is better than of the belly" (trans. Thorpe, vol. 2, p. 441).

72. Ibid., p. 257, ll. 60–62: "Good was Martha's ministering, when she ministered to the Almighty, but, nevertheless, Mary chose the better part" (p. 441).

73. Ibid., p. 258, ll. 92–96: "therefore is the service of Martha very praiseworthy, through it was Mary praised. Though the teacher be holy, his tongue will quickly slacken from divine preaching, if he have not bodily food; nevertheless, that is better which is eternal" (p. 443).

74. *PL* 38, 618: "For in some measure we are employed in it now, and ye too when removed from business, and laying aside domestic cares, ye meet together, stand, listen. In so far as ye do this, ye are like Mary. And with greater facility do ye that which Mary doeth, than I who have to distribute" (trans. Schaff, *A Select Library*, p. 430).

75. See Patrick Wormald, "Æthelwold and his Continental Counterparts: Contact Comparison, Contrast" in Yorke, *Bishop Æthelwold*, pp. 13–42.

76. See my discussion in "The Cult of the Virgin Mary," pp. 319–20.

77. Malcolm Godden, "Ælfric's Saints' Lives and the Problem of Miracles," *Leeds Studies in English*, n.s. 16 (1985): 94.

78. Ibid., p. 97.

79. Patrick Zettel, "Ælfric's Hagiographic Sources and the Latin Legendary Preserved in BL MS Cotton Nero E.i + CCCC MS 9 and Other Manuscripts" (dissertation, Oxford University, 1979).

80. *CH II*, pp. 81–91.

81. Stancliffe, "Cuthbert and the Polarity," p. 40.

82. *CH II*, p. 84, ll. 97–99: "But Cuthbert, as was his wont, went preaching the faith, that he might teach the ignorant people the way of life" (trans. Thorpe, vol. 2, p. 139).

83. Ibid., p. 84, ll. 113–15: "Cuthbert beautifully preached to the people, that they should be guarded against the wiles of the devil, lest with the leasing he should corrupt their faith" (p. 141).

84. Ibid., p. 85, ll. 131–33: "He would oftentimes fearlessly preach to the people in distant lands. Verily the Almighty had given him a sweet eloquence for people's instruction" (p. 141).

85. Ibid., p. 87, ll. 210–12: "There the saint dwelt many years, living very rigidly an anchoret's life, and pious men frequently visited him, and by his instruction rectified their lives" (p. 147).

86. Ibid., p. 88, ll. 259–63: "The holy Cuthbert then, suffragan bishop of the church of Lindisfarne, with all diligence took care of his people, in imitation of the blessed apostles, and with continual prayers shielded them against the devil, and with salutary admonitions excited them to heaven" (p. 149).

87. I am grateful to Peter Jackson for making available to me the results of his research on the Anglo-Saxon use of the *Vitae Patrum*.

88. *The Homilies of the Anglo-Saxon Church I*, ed. Benjamin Thorpe (London, 1844), pp. 544–46: "This is followed by the life and extraordinary knowledge of anchorites. These dwelling in the waste, trampled with stern mind and rigid life on worldly delicacies and luxuries. . . . The book which is called *Vitæ Patrum* speaks manifoldly concerning the lives of these anchorites, and also of common monks, and says that there were many thousands of them living wonderfully everywhere in the deserts and in monasteries, but yet especially in Egypt" (trans. Thorpe, pp. 545–47). This edition will hereafter be cited as *CH I*.

89. Assmann, *Angelsächsische Homilien und Heiligenleben*, p. 23, ll. 215–20 (my translation): "The wise fathers, Antony and Paul, Hilarion and Macarius, John and Arsenius, Paphnutius, and Apollonius, and many thousands of monks and nuns lived in the deserts, as the *Vitae Patrum* says, in a great way of life, serving Christ in purity of spirit."

90. *Ælfric's Lives of Saints I*, ed. Walter W. Skeat, EETS 76 and 82 (London, 1881), p. 2: "I do not promise, however, to write very many in this tongue, because it is not fitting that many should be translated into our language, lest peradventure the pearls of Christ be had in disrespect. And therefore I hold my peace as to the book called *Vitæ Patrum*, wherein are contained many subtle points which ought not to be laid open to the laity, nor indeed are we ourselves quite able to fathom them" (trans. Skeat, p. 3).

91. *CH II*, p. 212, ll. 191–96.

92. *CH I*, p. 6: "there are too few who will well teach and well exemplify" (trans. Thorpe, p. 7).

93. *Homilies of Ælfric: A Supplementary Collection*, vol. 2, ed. John Pope, EETS OS 260 (London, 1968), pp. 597–98 (my translation): "Nevertheless there are now too few teachers willing to do this, and therefore mankind is greatly afflicted, because there are few teachers of the people who earnestly consider how evil and unrighteousness may be suppressed and what is right may be established, as we read in books: *Canes muti non possunt latrare*: They are dumb dogs and they cannot bark. The prophet said this about God's teachers, who were not willing to preach and convert mankind to God's will at the time when they lived. Now it is even worse in our times in that we are all silent, and unrighteousness continues openly and secretly, and we do not think about it. Assuredly the teachers from whom doctrine came to us preached to the heathen and to hostile persecutors and gave their lives for their faith in God; but we do not dare now to presume to declare God's commands and God's will to a Christian king or a Christian people."

94. *CH II*, pp. 183–84, ll. 100–27.

95. *CH II*, p. 306, ll. 66–68.

96. *CH I*, p. 243; and *CH II*, p. 26, ll. 235–38.

97. *CH II*, p. 183, ll. 111–112: "Long shall he learn who is to teach" (trans. Thorpe, p. 321).

98. *CH II*, p. 132, ll. 145–49.

99. *CH II*, p. 308, ll. 120–130.

100. *CH II*, p. 305, ll. 37–40.

101. Assmann, *Angelsächsische Homilien und Heiligenleben*, p. 57, ll. 163–67 (my translation): "Teachers work more than lay people, both in their service, by which they serve God, and in the moral practices, which they must observe, and in the scriptural teaching, which they must preach, and therefore their reward will be greater with God."

102. On this see my "Homiliaries and Preaching in Anglo-Saxon England," *Peritia* 4 (1985): 232–37.

103. Wormald, *Ideal and Reality*, p. 37.

104. Ibid., p. 38.

105. Ibid., p. 40.

106. *CH II*, p. 291, ll. 120–27.

107. *CH II*, p. 195, ll. 186–88.

108. Skeat, *Ælfric's Lives of Saints*, p. 123, ll. 827–32.

109. I am grateful to Malcolm Godden and Colin Ireland for discussing this paper with me.

Saint Cuthbert: The Post-Conquest Appropriation of an Anglo-Saxon Cult*

Barbara Abou-El-Haj

The cult of St. Cuthbert, like so many early medieval cults, can be traced over centuries from its Anglo-Saxon origins to its post-Conquest appropriation. Nonetheless, this apparent continuity conceals significant interruptions, discontinuities which suggest that the cult of saints was no unbroken phenomenon, but rather was configured and reconfigured at critical historical junctures. Gaps, sometimes half a millenium, separate early biographies from characteristic additions in the eleventh and twelfth centuries across Europe when cults were spectacularly elaborated, textually, spatially, and visually, frequently to take advantage of pilgrimage and assert property and patrimony rights.[1] Nowhere is this more dramatic than in the strategic reception and appropriation of Anglo-Saxon cults by the Normans in the post-Conquest Anglo-Norman kingdom. Premier among them was the cult of St. Cuthbert.[2]

Development of Cuthbert's Cult

Thirty-four years after Cuthbert died in 687, Bede wrote his *Life and Miracles* (c. 721) of the hermit, abbot, and bishop of Lindisfarne based on an anonymous life written between 698 and 705. Nothing enters the surviving record for more than 200 years.[3] In the mid-tenth century or perhaps as late as the eleventh century, the *Historia de Sancto Cuthberto* was composed, largely devoted to royal donations to Cuthbert as its subtitle suggests: *Historia de Sancto Cuthberto et de commemoratione locorum regionumque eius priscae possessionis a primordio usque nunc temporis [A History of St. Cuthbert and a Record of the Places and Regions of his Ancient Possessions from the Beginning Until the Present Time].*[4]

The *Historia* records the cult's possessions from its inception at Lindisfarne—evacuated during the Danish attacks on Northumbria—to its long sojourn at Chester-le-Street from 883 until 995, when the community moved to Durham. Cuthbert himself designated Durham, after a brief shelter at Ripon, by refusing to allow his body to be moved further, a *topos*.[5] The text ends in one MS with King Edmund's visit to the shrine around 945, but continues in another copy with gifts up to the time of King Cnut (1020–1035).

Only after the Norman Conquest, almost forty years later (between 1072 and 1083), does the record begin to expand at an increasing pace. A new *Chronicle* was composed by the community, also comprising royal donations.[6] By this time the texts formed only a portion of the activities centered around the cult, advanced by William of St. Calais, Norman bishop of Durham, who inaugurated an ambitious program to reorganize Durham spiritually and expand it economically. He began by expelling Cuthbert's congregation of secular clerks and installing Benedictine monks between 1081 and 1083.[7] William's centerpiece was to be an extravagant new cathedral, begun in 1093. The high point of the enterprise was accomplished in 1104, when Cuthbert's body was discovered incorrupt and translated into the partly finished cathedral. Just before (perhaps around 1100), the Durham monks had copied and illustrated a little book of Bede's life and miracles of Cuthbert, together with seven recently compiled miracles.[8]

Soon after another ten miracles were added to the record, and just following the translation, Symeon wrote his *History of the Church of Durham* [*Historia Dunelmensis Ecclesiae*] using the *Historia de Sancto Cuthberto*, which he described as a cartulary of the generosities given by kings and clergy.[9] Sometime around 1123 three more miracles and an anonymous account of the 1104 translation were written.[10] By this time the church was dedicated to Saint Cuthbert alone (in the clerk's chronicle it was also dedicated to the Virgin). The pace of cult activities increased again in the latter twelfth century, when Reginald of Durham composed a different version of the translation (between 1165 and 1172) and substantially increased the record of miracles in his *Libellus de Admirandis Beati Cuthberti Virtutibus*,[11] and about twenty-five years later, around 1200, Cuthbert's miracles were copied and painted in an even smaller, but luxurious book of quite a different character from the Oxford MS.[12]

The foregoing account is typical of the constellation of cult activities that may begin in the early Middle Ages, but expand dramatically from the late eleventh century, which at Durham marked the appropriation of the secular community by the Benedictines and their incorporation into the Anglo-Norman kingdom of William the Conqueror and his successors. But they are not a simple progression or expansion. They reveal shifts in emphasis arising from the post-Conquest consolidation, which was particularly violent in Northumbria and at Durham.

Norman Pressures on Durham

Just three years after the Conquest William's newly appointed Earl of Northumbria, Robert de Comines, whose men were accused of slaughtering and plundering in the town, was assassinated in Durham as he escaped from a burning house. William brought his troops north in a ferocious raid leaving not one inhabited village between York and Durham, in the words of the *Historia Regum*. Durham's last Anglo-Saxon bishop, Aethelwine (1057–1071), who had fled with Cuthbert's body and his clerks to their Anglo-Saxon monastery at Lindisfarne for three months, died in prison following the rebels' defeat at Ely in 1071. The conqueror's appointee Walcher (Bishop of Durham and in 1076 Earl of Northumbria), also accused of allowing his men to plunder and failing to resist one of the recurrent Scottish attacks (1079), was massacred with his retinue at Gateshead (1080) in an ensuing feud.[13]

Two accounts of a visit by William the Conqueror to Durham during the height of this violence highlight how the cult was defensively activated between the time of the clerks and that of the monks who replaced them in 1083. According to the clerk's account, William came to the shrine, listened to an account of royal donations read from the *Historia*, and offered gifts to Cuthbert as his predecessors were said to have done. By the time Symeon wrote his version (1104–1107),[14] the encounter had changed dramatically. William is said to have publicly doubted whether Cuthbert's body was indeed in the coffin-reliquary, demanded it be opened, and threatened to kill all the prelates assembled if his suspicions were confirmed. Instead he was struck with intolerable heat and galloped away without stopping until he reached the River Tees.[15]

William's threats have been linked to a scheme to levy a tax on the men of St. Cuthbert. This was naturally viewed as a violation of the privileges and immunities listed in the *Historia de Sancto Cuthberto* and the *Chronicle*, enjoyed not by Durham, but rather, conventionally by its sainted proprietor Cuthbert. The clergy responded in stereotypical fashion with a report that Cuthbert himself appeared to the tax agent and "belabored him" with his pastoral staff. The man is said not to have recovered until he left the diocese entirely.[16] Both stories, written after 1104 by Symeon in his *Historia Dunelmensis*, together with the account of the 1104 translation, suggest how skepticism about the saint's body, real and contrived, could have been dramatically and publicly satisfied when Cuthbert's body was indeed discovered in his coffin not only present but incorrupt, just as the 1104 translation was about to be celebrated (see later).

Between the writing of the clerk's *Chronicle* and Symeon's *History* Durham was incorporated into the Norman ecclesiastical hierarchy and the clerks lost their shrine to the Benedictines in more or less violent circumstances. After Bishop Walcher was murdered, the king appointed William of St. Calais, who energized the cult as the focus for a sweeping reorganization of the see.

William of St. Calais (1080–1096)

In 1081–1083 William delivered his ultimatum to the clerks. Only one chose to join the Benedictine monks. Ten years later (after a three-year exile), William initiated plans for a new cathedral.[17] Beginning in 1093, foundations were set for a Norman church of contemporary design and extravagant proportions.[18] In a parallel endeavor, beginning in 1091–1092, the monks began to assemble systematically segments of the ancient patrimony lost by the clerks they had displaced. The last acquisition is recorded in 1101, shortly after King William Rufus, who had kept the see vacant for three years and collected the bishop's income, appointed as bishop of Durham his notorious tax collector, Ranulf Flambard (1099), a throroughly scurrilous plunderer in the estimations of Symeon and William of Malmesbury. With Henry's accession and Anselm's return in 1101, Flambard was imprisoned and escaped to Normandy; he was restored in 1102.[19]

Ranulf Flambard (1099/1102–1128)

According to Symeon, Ranulf "demanded 'many an immoderate sum of money' from the inhabitants of the bishopric of Durham in order to buy back the king's favor." William of Malmesbury called him "a plunderer of the rich, 'an exterminator of the poor,' a confiscator of other men's inheritance." The monks are said to have quarreled with him over an endowment promised by William of St. Calais and may have been suspicious of his archdeacon, whom Ranulf appointed to rival their own prior.[20] Under the new bishop, the monks and their prior continued the building program, advancing the cult both independent of and in response to the vicissitudes of Anglo-Norman political and ecclesiastical politics. They had to maneuver between their bishop and his archdeacon and an audience they seem to have animated in stages, as they secured their claims to Cuthbert's ancient properties from the community of clerks they had displaced. Despite their apparent success, the monks nevertheless felt impelled to denounce the clerks for more than forty years.

The Cult from 1100–1104

In the years between 1100 and 1104, then, the monks completed their most elaborate additions to the cult: they acquired the last segment of Cuthbert's lost property (1101); they had an illustrated copy of Cuthbert's life and miracles drawn up; and they translated Cuthbert's body into the partly finished cathedral. In 1104 they had reached the midpoint in consolidating their possession of Durham between the expulsion of the clerks and the final confirmation of their possession of the cathedral by Calixtus II in 1123, the year the translation account may have been written.[21] The events surrounding the translation put to rest real and contrived challenges to the cult over the presence of the saint's body by the conqueror in 1072 (in Symeon's account) and again in 1104, if we are to believe the translation account. As activated twenty years later, not only was the body confirmed in the reliquary-coffin in 1104, it was also discovered incorrupt in a series of spectacles in which the monks staged their possession of Cuthbert's body. They seem to have proceeded by creating and heightening a controversy over the saint's body, and then publicly resolving it on the day of translation when the audience, first excluded, then invited, reached a calculated intensity so familiar in medieval narratives. The illustrations in the little book seem to have prepared the way for these events, while striking omissions helped displace the cult from Anglo-Saxon Lindisfarne to Anglo-Norman Durham.

Picturing the Cult: Oxford, Bodleian Library, University College MS 165

Of the thirty-six extant copies of Bede's prose life, the Oxford and London MSS (BL, Yates Thompson MS 26) are the only two illustrated, both apparently at Durham;[22] thus, although they are really tiny (slightly larger than 5 × 7 and 3 × 5 in.), their illustrations (originally fifty-five each) amount to an extravagant undertaking. In both manuscripts the illustrations are comprehensive and intimately linked with the text, introducing each chapter. Yet the painted MS of c. 1200 is quite distinct from the version of around 1100, where key pictures seem to articulate and confirm contemporary cult activities.

Lindisfarne and Durham in MS 165

Malcolm Baker concluded that the illustrations of Cuthbert instructing his monks aimed to link closely post-Conquest Durham with Anglo-Saxon

Lindisfarne, where Cuthbert had introduced Benedictine practices to the reluctant brothers just as his eleventh-century successors had reintroduced Benedictine practices at Durham. Without pressing this argument too far, even the simplified version of Anglo-Saxon colored outline drawing and the lively narrative style of MS 165, so different from the stately MS paintings of the next generation, may have furthered this association.[23] But Lindisfarne was evoked at Durham in a very circumspect fashion. Unlike the London MS of a hundred years later, where Baker observed how Cuthbert appears emphatically episcopal, MS 165 is distinguished by its unconventional omission of a scene of episcopal elevation, in striking contrast to the thirty or so hagiographies illustrated in the eleventh and twelfth centuries in Europe, where consecration, investiture or acclamation are standard scenes (Figure 1)[24] and in contrast to the pattern of text and illustration in the Oxford manuscript.

There, Cuthbert's life as a hermit and abbot and his ministry as Bishop of Lindisfarne are given chapter by chapter illustration, except for Bede's account of his consecration as a bishop, Chapter 24:

> congregata sinodo . . . sub praesentia . . . regis Egfridi, . . . Theodorus archiepiscopus praesidebat unanimo omnium consensu ad episcopatum ecclesiae Lindisfarnensis electus est. . . . ad se praemissis nequaquam suo loco posset erui . . . rex ipse . . . cum . . . Trumwine . . . adiurant . . . , lacrimas fundunt . . . , atque ad sinodum pertrahunt. . . . quamvis multum renitens unanima . . . ad suscipiendum episcopatus officium collum summittere compellitur. Nec tamen statim ordinatio, sed peracta hieme quae imminebat expleta est.[25]

> [when no small synod had gathered together, in the presence of . . . King Ecgfrith, over which Archbishop Theodore . . . presided, he was elected to the bishopric of the church at Lindisfarne with the unanimous consent of all. And when he could by no means be dragged from his place . . . , this same king himself, together with . . . Bishop Trumwine . . . adjured him . . . with tears and prayers, until at last they drew him, also shedding many tears . . . and led him to the synod. . . . He was overcome by the unanimous will of them all and compelled to submit his neck to the yoke of the bishopric. His consecration, however, was not carried out until after the end of that winter, which was then beginning.]

Though the ceremony was postponed, omitting this scene is striking because the saint's modest refusal is a *topos* in hagiographical literature, always followed by his acclamation or investiture by popular outcry, and conventionally illustrated. Scenes of acclamation and investiture illustrate texts in which the controversy over royal investiture was entirely

Figure 1. Amand is consecrated. He saves a boy from a foul spirit, Saint-Amand d'Elnone, 1160–1180, Valenciennes, Bibl. Mun. MS 500, fol. 65v.

unproblematic. Many follow the old texts; a few seem to represent the contemporary papal position. Because royal investiture was also under dispute between Henry I, Anselm, and Paschal II in these very years (1101 ff.), accompanied by a "flood of polemical literature," one might have expected a scene of Cuthbert's episcopal elevation in the Oxford manuscript as well.[26]

Figure 2. Cuthbert predicts his death to Hereberht, Durham, 1100–1104, Oxford, Bodl. Lib. Univ. Coll. MS 165, fol. 84. (Photo: Courtesy of the Master and Fellows of University College, Oxford.)

One hundred years later the Durham painter of the London MS seems to have "corrected" this anomaly by painting a conventional scene, now torn out of the MS.[27] In the earlier MS the monks seem to have achieved a balance between evoking Lindisfarne while de-emphasizing Cuthbert's episcopal office there, now that the cult was promoted at Durham (scarcely two decades after Benedictine monks had replaced Cuthbert's clerks and repossessed their properties). A different set of issues was addressed 100 years later.[28]

Death and Burial

Even more singular and conspicuous is the absence of death and burial scenes, particularly because the text and scenes prefatory to the saint's death are in fact expansive (Figures 2, 3, and 4). In three scenes Cuthbert predicts his death, gives elaborate instructions for his burial, and reluctantly agrees to be transferred from his hermitage on Farne to be buried at his monastery at Lindisfarne. On his deathbed he commanded his monks to take his body with them if ever Lindisfarne were evacuated, which indeed happened in the course of the Danish invasions. In this way, following his own instructions, confirmed

Figure 3. Cuthbert, sick, gives instructions for his burial, Durham, 1100–1104, Oxford, Bodl.Lib. Univ. Coll. MS 165, fol. 102. (Photo: Courtesy of the Master and Fellows of University College, Oxford.)

Figure 4. Cuthbert's last commands before his death, Durham, 1100–1104, Oxford, Bodl. Lib. Univ. coll. MS 165, fol. 110. (Photo: Courtesy of the Master and Fellows of University College, Oxford.)

Figure 5. Amand dies and his soul is taken to heaven, Saint-Amand d'Elnone, between 1066 and 1107, Valenciennes, Bibl. Mun. MS 502, fol. 30.

by the miracle of 995 when the saint would not allow his body to move further, Cuthbert came to rest at Durham.[29]

According to Colgrave, Bede's long and vivid account of Cuthbert's death is his chief addition to the anonymous life written shortly before.[30] In fact a very traditional description of Cuthbert's soul carried to heaven by ministering angels is already given in the course of the saint's predictions about his death. Not only is Bede's text a *topos*, the designer of the Oxford miniatures knew very well the pictorial formulas for saints' deaths, because

Figure 6. Cuthbert as a shepherd sees St. Aidan's soul carried to heaven, Oxford, Durham, 1100–1104, Oxford, Bodl. Lib. Univ. Coll. MS 165, fol. 18. (Photo: Courtesy of the Master and Fellows of University College, Oxford.)

he used one for Cuthbert's vision of Aidan's soul carried to heaven (Figures 5 and 6). Here he used a standard format to depict the crucial and stereotyped image in illustrated saints' lives that displays the central claim for a successful shrine; viz., that the saint's body venerated on earth is the conduit to his soul, residing in heaven where he or she will intervene on behalf of his or her community and pilgrims.[31] One hundred years later, in the London MS, Cuthbert's death was depicted according to Bede's description. In the earlier MS his last instructions never to abandon his body substitute for a death scene (Figure 4).

Cuthbert's burial was also omitted, even more unusual because it is even more stereotypical and standard for the genre. As with the death, there is a similar discrepancy between the painter's otherwise comprehensive illustration of the life and Bede's lengthy description of Cuthbert's preparations for burial. The designer knew and used conventional burial formulae twice, not for the saint's burial, but for two posthumous events that followed Cuthbert's translation to Lindisfarne:[32] (1) Cuthbert's body was discovered incorrupt on

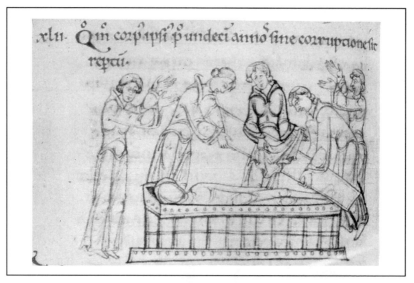

Figure 7. Cuthbert's body discovered incorrupt, Durham, 1100–1104, Oxford, Bodl. Lib. Univ. Coll. MS 165, fol. 118. (Photo: Courtesy of the Master and Fellows of University College, Oxford.)

the eleventh anniversary of his death (March 20, 698), when the monks were instructed by Bishop Eadberht to transfer his body to a wood chest already prepared, and (2) two months later (May 6) Bishop Eadberht was laid in Cuthbert's sarcophagus (Figures 7 and 8).[33] Eadberht's entombment displays the standard burial formula with one interesting variation that touches upon events that preceded the 1104 translation of Cuthbert, shortly after the MS was painted. Unlike most figures lowered into coffins (Christ and saints are normally stiff as boards) Eadberht's body sags (Figure 8).

1104 Discovery of Cuthbert's Body Incorrupt and His Translation[34]

In 1104, just after the miniatures were painted, Cuthbert's body was again discovered incorrupt. The monks staged the events of 1104 in a way that self-consciously reenacted Bede's text and matched its new illustrations. On August 24, five days before Cuthbert's body was to be translated into the partly finished cathedral, the prior and nine monks "ante venerabilem sepulcrum prosternuntur, effusisque lacrimis et precibus, manus non sine timore ac tremore apponunt, ut illud aperiant"[35] ['prostrated themselves before the venerable coffin, and amid tears and prayers they laid hands upon it, not without fear and trembling, to open it . . . '] to discover Cuthbert's body fragrant and incorrupt, just as it had

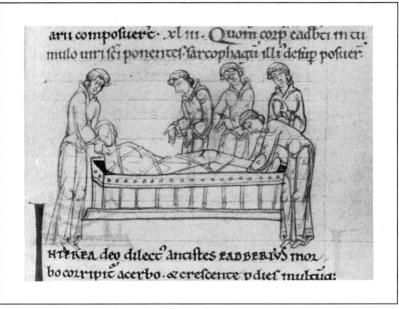

Figure 8. Eadberht, placed in Cuthbert's tomb, Durham, 1100–1104, Oxford, Bodl. Lib. Univ. Coll. MS 165, fol. 121. (Photo: Courtesy of the Master and Fellows of University College, Oxford.)

Figure 9. Maur dies and is buried, St. Maur-des-Fossés, first quarter of the twelfth century, Troyes, Bibl. mun. MS 2273, fol. 73v. (Photo: Otto-Karl Werckmeister).

been 400 years earlier in Bede's biography, having "memores dictorum Bedae, qui corpus beati Cuthberti a fratribus quondam Lindisfarnensis ecclesiae post xi sepulturae annos incorruptum inventum . . ."[36] ['called to mind the words of Bede, which record that the body of St. Cuthbert had been found by the brethren of Lindisfarne in a state of incorruption, eleven years after its burial . . . '].

According to Bede, in 698 the monks planned to deposit the saint's decomposed bones in a wood chest already prepared, but

> Et aperientes sepulchrum invenerunt corpus totum quasi adhuc viveret integrum, et flexibilibus artuum compagibus multo dormienti quam mortuo similius. . . . Quod ubi viderunt, nimio mox timore sunt et tremore perculsi. . . . Extremam autem indumentorum eius partem pro ostendendo incorruptionis signo tollentes. . . . "Nova," inquit, "indumenta corpori . . . et sic reponite in thecam quam parastis."[37]

> [Opening the sepulchre, they found the body intact and whole, as if it were still alive, and the joints of the limbs flexible, and much more like a sleeping than a dead man. . . . When they saw this, they were struck with great fear and trembling. . . . They took away outer garments to show the miracle of his incorruption. . . . <The bishop instructed them>: "Put fresh garments around the body . . . and then replace it in the chest which you have prepared."]

In 1104 the monks found Cuthbert's shrouded body packed with relics: "Et, ecce! beati patris venerabile corpus, scilicet fructum desiderii sui, reperiunt, quod, in dextro latere jacens, tota sui integritate artuumque flexibilitate dormientem magis repraesentabat quam mortuum."[38] ['And behold, they discovered the body of the venerable father, naturally the reward for their longing, which, lying on its right side in a perfect state and from the flexibility if its joints, represented more a sleeping person than a dead one.'] He is depicted thus in the picture of the 698 discovery painted just a few years earlier.

As in 698 the monks, highly excited, decided to revest the body and replace Cuthbert on his back in a more suitable (gravestone) posture, as he was depicted 100 years later in the London MS, thus following Bede's script: "Prostrati toto tandem corpore, lacrimis ubertim fluentibus, septem Poenitentialibus Psalmis supplicant Dominum . . . "[39] ['After a short interval, they all fell flat on the ground, and amid a deluge of tears, beseeching the lord with the seven penitential psalms'], and "Cum ergo duo quibus jussum fuerat, unus a capite, alter a pedibus venerabile corpus de loco suae dormitionis elevarent, coepit illud quasi adhuc vivens per medium inflecti, carneque solidum et ossibus pondere naturali ad ima demergi."[40] ['When therefore the two, whom he had ordered, raised the venerable body from its place of rest, one by the head, the other by the feet, it began to bend in the middle just as a living man and sink downwards by the natural weight of solid flesh and bones.'] This is the posture depicted in the Oxford MS for one of the scenes that the designers substituted for the more standard saint's entombment: Bishop Eadberht lowered into Cuthbert's tomb. The posture is distinguished from the standard formula for depositions, for the burial of Christ, and for the burials of saints, only in the way the body sinks downward. The monks chose to depict Cuthbert's discovery with gestures of acclamation. The dead saint's suppleness seems to have been suggested in the only scene in which a body is handled, Eadberht lowered into the coffin. Flexibility was not automatically linked to incorrup-tion, thus the bishop's posture seems to allude to Cuthbert's most unusual characteristic.[41]

In Bede's time the miracle prompted Cuthbert's elevation; for the post-Conquest cult, the miracle authenticated the saint's translation into the new Norman cathedral. But not everyone participated so readily in the monks' project. The monks had conducted the discovery clandestinely, in the middle of the night; then they promptly publicized it when the morning came in a full assembly of the brethren, whereupon they were disputed by their own bishop: "At episcopus, non facile his accommodans fidem, omnino judicabat incredibile, corpus, quamlibet sanctum, tamen humanum, per tantum temporis, id est per quadringentos, decem et octo annos, ab omni corruptionis labe intactum perdurare."[42] ['But the bishop, did not easily credit their report and judged it altogether beyond belief that the body, however holy, but nevertheless human, remain free from all taint of corruption for so much time, that is, for 418 years.']

So the following night the brothers again examined the body: "ergo nervis solidum et ex integro incorruptum corpus visu et manibus tractando, levando, ac deponendo certo percepissent. . . . "[43] ["they discovered the body firm in its sinews and free from corruption by looking at it and by exercising, raising, and lowering it . . ."]. To this point the witnesses are largely internal. The monks, however, had a wider audience in mind to witness their undisputed possession of Cuthbert's cult and properties. Having "discovered" the body five days before the translation, a great crowd assembled: "Interea promulgato longe lateque venturae Translationis die, ingens fit undecumque Dunelmum usque populorum concursus; sicut diversae dignitatis et aetatis, ita et professionis, saecularis videlicet vitae et spiritualis, personae perplures, qui agnito incorrupti tam longo tempore corporis miraculo, plurimum in Domino laetantur . . ."[44] ['Meanwhile, the approaching Translation <August 29> being made known far and wide, there was a great flocking to Durham from every side. Many people of all ranks, ages, and professions, the secular and the spiritual, who, having heard of the miracle of the body incorrupt for so long a time, greatly took joy in the Lord, <hastened to be present>.']

The monks were now in a position to raise the level of spectacle, which is exactly what they did.

To their "dismay" the discovery was again disputed by an abbot who had come for the translation. Complaining that he and others had been excluded from "their secret proceedings," he accused them: "non tam verum de suo Sancto dicere, quam fingere.... Haec in auribus illorum qui cum eo venerant saepius replicans, animos quorumdam in suum inclinavit assensum."[45] ['of telling not what was true, but rather of fantasizing.... These remarks he took care to repeat frequently in the hearing of those who had assembled, converting others to his view.'] Here we have a moment, at least as activated in the report, which might have gone for or against the monks' theater.

Strenuously protesting, until the contention was at its highest pitch, and no end seemed likely to be put to it, the monks were at length persuaded by the abbot of Séez: "His ita contendentibus, cum contentioni nullus potuisset finis imponi ... aliis qui digni viderentur, ad novam miraculi inspectionem admittantur ... "[46] ["these things having been contested, when no end to the contention could be imposed ... those who seemed worthy were admitted to a new inspection of the miracle"]—including the doubting abbot, the abbot of St. Albans (with whom Durham had an outstanding property dispute), the Archbishop of Canterbury, and monks and clerks. Excluded was the public waiting for the translation. The bishop absented himself to dedicate an altar in the new cathedral.

So on the Day of Translation, before fifty to sixty men inside, and a crowd attracted by the controversy outside, the abbot of Séez explored Cuthbert's body in a brutally tactile demonstration of particularly the saint's flexibility;

> involuta explicans vestimenta circa venerandum caput, utraque illud manu cunctis aspicientibus paululum erexit, et in diversas reflectando partes integra omnibus juncturis colli compage reliquo id corpori cohaerere invenit. Deinde, manu admota, firmius aurem trahens et retrahens, et post hoc alias quoque corporis partes manu perscrutante explorans, solidum nervis et ossibus, cum carnis mollitie repperit corpus. Id etiam per caput tenendo concutiens, adeo in sublime erexit, ut in habitaculo suae quietis pene sedere visum fuerit ... [47]

[unfolding the vestments around the venerable head, he raised [the head] a little in both hands for all who were looking on, and by bending it in different directions found it to be connected with all joints of the neck to the rest of the skeleton of the body. Then, probing, more firmly pulling and tugging the ear, and examining other parts of the body with his probing hand, he found the body solid in sinews and bones with the softness of flesh. Also shaking it by holding the head, he raised it up so that it was seen almost to sit in its abode of quiet ...]

to everyone's horror—and satisfaction. Immediately the monks brought Cuthbert out: "populus, in lacrimas prae gaudio resolutus, totus obviam ruit, ut portitores sancti corporis vix in tanta constipatione procedere potuissent . . . "[48] ["the whole crowd, unrestrained in tears beyond joy, rushed forward so that the bearers of the holy body could scarcely proceed in so dense a throng"]. Within this melee Bishop Ranulf maneuvered to dampen enthusiasm:[49]

> Jam dies in altum processerat et episcopus, multa quae praesentis negotii non postulaverat causa interserens, longioris multos sermonis fecerat taedere. Sed cum tanta esset caeli serenitas ut nullum venturae pluviae signum in aere appareret, tanta coeperunt inundatione subito imbres ruere, ut confestim interrupto sermone loculum sancti corporis fratres corriperent, et ecclesiae concite inferre festinarent. Quo illato, pluvia continuo cessavit . . . [50]

> [Now the day had far advanced and the bishop, touching on many points not at all appropriate to the business at hand, had made many weary by his lengthy talk. But when the brightness of the day had been such that no sign of rain to come had appeared, suddenly such torrents of rain had begun to fall, the talk being interrupted, that the brethren snatched the coffin and hurried it into the church. When this was done, the rain ceased.]

Of the two public events in 1104 at Durham that reenacted the inauguration of Cuthbert's cult at Lindisfarne, his discovery once again incorrupt and his reentombment in the new shrine, the discovery far outplayed the translation and ceremonial deposition. Normally the chief event in inaugurating and renewing cults, the deposition is reported in an indifferent sentence at the end of the translation account. At the same time, its prototype, Cuthbert's entombment at Lindisfarne 400 years earlier, is extraordinarily absent from the illustrated MS just completed.

The monks had a stake in underplaying the installation of Cuthbert's body at Lindisfarne now that he was entombed at Durham, but they also needed historical continuity. Continuity was worked out not only in selective illustration within an apparently comprehensive set of manuscript pictures, but also in their building activities, where they reached a balance between their historical connection with, and their displacement of, Lindisfarne. In the same years that the Norman cathedral was under construction to house the cult at Durham, the monks installed a secondary cult center by building a church of similar design at Lindisfarne. On the site of Cuthbert's original tomb, they erected a cenotaph, an empty grave,[51] so that the cult was marked precisely by the absence of the body, while at the same time the body was rediscovered present and incorrupt for its audiences now at Durham. Publicly staged dramatic ceremonies were the arenas for these activities. The monks and their bishop maneuvered before the crowd generated by their spectacle. Although the little book and its pictures were destined for private use, it nonetheless displays how the events of Cuthbert's life were configured for his newly expanded Norman setting. Together, the illustrated MS, the events of 1104 recorded in c.1123, and the description in Durham's earliest relic list: "Corpus Sancti Patris Cuthberti cum carne et ossibus totum integrum quasi adhuc vivus." ['the body of the holy father Cuthbert whole with flesh and bones, as if he were yet alive'],[52] all responded to the same agenda.

At Durham, then, public ceremony, or its retrospective narration, was one stage in the monks' continuing project: to confirm possession of Cuthbert and his patrimony by responding publicly to real and contrived skepticism about the body before the bishop and his archdeacon. At the time of the translation, twenty years had passed since the Benedictine monks had displaced Cuthbert's clerks, but only three since the last segment of the ancient patrimony had been handed over to Durham. The monks continued to argue their case aggressively and defensively for at least another twenty years, beginning with Symeon, who repeatedly accuses the clerks of corruption, while he argues Durham's rightful claim to Cuthbert's property. In Meehan's words, they "stridently denounce[d] the 'depraved and incorrigible behavior of the clerks' formerly in residence"[53] to Calixtus II , the pope who confirmed their possession of the cathedral in 1123. In the same year the Translation Account was likely written; it must have been part of the same effort.

Cuthbert's property is the subject of a series of illustrations that close the Oxford MS.

The Post-Bede Miracles in Univ. MS 165

Cuthbert's posthumous miracles illustrated in the Oxford MS also display how the little book helped set the stage for the monks' project to confirm their possession of the saint's patrimony, particularly in the miracles compiled by the monks just before the MS was copied. Altogether the recent miracles doubled Bede's posthumous stories from seven to fourteen. Four derive from the *Historia de Sancto Cuthberto* and three were added between 1083 and 1100 because, according to the author, "in recent times, too, miracles have been happening."[54] Whereas Bede's posthumous miracles are uniformly benevolent (Figure 10), among the post-Bede miracles only two are benevolent; one is a protection miracle with no victim; four are terrorizing interventions. Three, including a benevolent miracle, have Cuthbert's property as their subject.

In the first, Cuthbert appears as a pilgrim to the fugitive King Alfred and prophesies his victory (Figure 11). In return, Alfred entrusts his son Edward

Figure 10. A sick man is cured at Cuthbert's tomb, Durham, 1100–1104, Oxford, Bodl. Lib. Univ. Coll. MS 165, fol. 122. (Photo: Courtesy of the Master and Fellows of University College, Oxford.)

Figure 11. Cuthbert appears as a pilgrim to King Alfred, Durham, 1100–1104, Oxford, Bodl. Lib. Univ. Coll. MS 165, fol. 135. (Photo: Courtesy of the Master and Fellows of University College, Oxford.)

Figure 12. Onlafbald, who mocked Cuthbert, is struck down, Durham, 1100–1104, Oxford, Bodl. Lib. Univ. Coll. MS 165, fol. 149. (Photo: Courtesy of the Master and Fellows of University College, Oxford.)

with gifts for Cuthbert, setting the model for all later royal donations to Cuthbert's shrine recorded in the *Historia de Sancto Cuthberto* and in the *Chronicle*. Each of these accounts typically enhanced its predecessor. In the *Historia* Alfred's are the second donations recorded. The clerks' *Chronicle* (between 1072 and 1083, used by Symeon for his *History*) makes Alfred together with Guthred joint founder of Cuthbert's laws and customs and gives a fuller account of privileges. From the beginning of the eleventh century, grants are described as *cum saca et socne*, (as now including rights of justice and jurisdiction). The *Chronicle* expands Guthred's immunities in the royal gifts listed from the tenth century and enlarges threats against usurpers: "Cum saca et socne et plena libertate et quietudine donavit . . . omnes, qui hec infringere vel auferre vel minuere presumerent, excommunicavit et excommunicando in die iudicii maledictis in ignem eternum discessuris associavit."[55] ['With 'sac' and 'socn' and full freedom and peace he gave . . . all, those who presume to infringe upon, carry off, or diminish these things he excommunicated and by excommunicating he put them on the day of judgment with the accursed who are separated into the eternal fire'.] This posthumous vision displays the sort of spiritual exchange on which the pilgrimage industry was modeled. The punitive miracles in the Oxford MS vividly

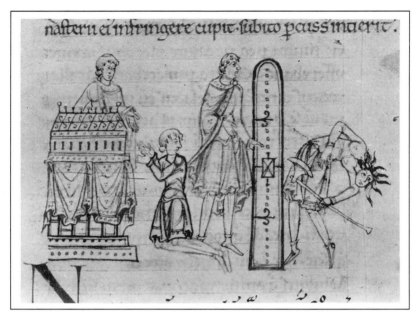

Figure 13. Barcwith, who invaded Cuthbert's sanctuary, is struck down, Durham, 1100–1104, Oxford, Bodl. Lib. Univ. Coll. MS 165, fol. 157. (Photo: Courtesy of the Master and Fellows of University College, Oxford.)

display the threats incorporated into this exchange. Those who usurp or violate Cuthbert's property are punished, immediately. In the pictures no one has to wait for judgment day, as the monks recorded in their *Chronicle*.

When Onlafblad was given Cuthbert's lands by the Norwegian king Regnald in 918, he entered the cathedral (then at Chester-le-Street) swearing enmity by his gods to the bishop (Cutheard) and congregation, whereupon he was struck mad and soon died. "After this, Cuthbert recovered his land" (Figure 12). Here is the standard conjunction of property, sacrilege and retribution to be found in punitive miracles illustrated in saints' lives.[56]

The last three miracles illustrated in the Oxford MS occurred between 1055–1065 and 1080. So they are the last of the clerks' stories, written up and illustrated between 1083 and 1100 by their successors, the monks, between the time the monks appropriated Cuthbert's cult and were preparing to install his body in their new cathedral. They comprise a protection story and two vengeance miracles, one before and one after the Conquest. The knight Barcwith fell down in a fit and died after three days' torture for having violated Cuthbert's sanctuary, which had been established by King Alfred (Figure 13). This was a heavy price, since the penalty for violating sanctuary,

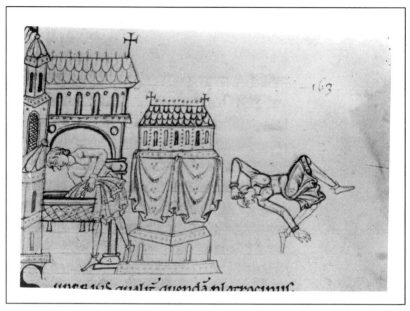

Figure 14. A Norman thief who stole from Cuthbert's shrine is struck dead, Durham, 1100–1104, Oxford, Bodl. Lib. Univ. Coll. MS 165, fol. 163. (Photo: Courtesy of the Master and Fellows of University College, Oxford.)

and only if the fugitive were killed, was a fine (96 pounds).[57] According to the story Barcwith's master, the Earl of Northumbria from whom the robber had fled to sanctuary, and all who had participated in the incident gave a cross and Gospel book adorned with gold and precious stones to the church. Not the donation but the retribution was pictured. Durham was a notorious haven for felons and murderers in the decades after the Conquest, perhaps seeking to make use of the ancient custom of sanctuary. In the late eleventh century, sanctuary boundaries came to be identified with the ecclesiastical *banleuca*, a taxable jurisdiction claimed by Durham for the entire county. Thus, violation of sanctuary infringed upon the entirety of Durham's territorial jurisdiction. David Hall compares Symeon's fine with the steeply graduated fines recorded by Richard of Hexham, which dramatically increased for the sort of violation of the church choir pictured in Cuthbert's posthumous miracle. However, death was reserved only for homicide either at the bishop's throne or at the shrine behind the altar. So Cuthbert's retribution goes far beyond current law. Current practice is more difficult to ascertain.[58] Finally, in a miracle dated 1080, a Norman soldier who stole Cuthbert's relics was attacked with a burning fever and died in torment, confessing his crimes (Figure 14). In these two miniatures retribution is more instantaneous than the text specifies. These stories may be associated with the aggressive assembly of Cuthbert's patrimony during these same years.

In 1083, three years after this last story, the clerks were expelled. Between then and 1101–1104, when the later miracles were compiled and illustrated, the monks embarked on a campaign to restore to Durham segments of Cuthbert's patrimony held by local ecclesiastical and lay lords. Each was returned to Durham's proprietor, St. Cuthbert: 1091–1092—Earl Robert Mowbray of Northumbria "relinquished all rights over the land and men of Saint Cuthbert," establishing the Durham bishop's extraordinary palatinate;[59] 1092—Carlisle (lost during Ranulf's exile) was temporarily returned by King William Rufus and the Archbishop of York; 1094—Tynningham (using a charter of doubtful authenticity, according to Craster); 1100—Coldinghamshire; 1101—the Durham bishop's house and land in York. The monks, then, established their continuity with the tradition they had usurped not only spiritually, by reintroducing Benedictine practices Cuthbert had taught at Lindisfarne, but also materially.[60]

In the MS, composed and illustrated before 1104, the effort to recover Cuthbert's patrimony is given a fantastic pictorial equivalent: the punishment meted out by the saint to those who violate his church and relics. By contrast, neither before nor after the period of intense acquisition (in the clerks' chronicle of the 1070s or in the miracles recorded after 1104), are miracles punitive in an equivalent way; and though the same miracles were copied into the British Library MS 100 years later, only the benevolent miracles were illustrated.[61]

Thus, augmenting Cuthbert's hagiography was a principal ideological line in the monks' agenda during the post-Conquest years when the cathedral shrine, the pictures, the texts, and especially ceremonies reconfigured the cult. The conjunction between property and hagiography initiated in the *Historia de Sancto Cuthberto* became a central feature in the post-Conquest cult, which saw the Norman bishop William of St. Calais reform the church and rebuild the cathedral and his new Benedictines consolidate their claim on their church and its properties through an expanding variety of activities: among them illustrations of MS 165 selective omissions of key events in Cuthbert's history at Lindisfarne and scenes of fantastic punishments of adversaries; architectural projects that underplayed Anglo-Saxon Lindisfarne in favor of Anglo-Norman Durham; and public spectacle forged around the 1104 discovery of Cuthbert's incorrupt body and his translation into the new cathedral. The monks' appeals to the cult were backed by their pragmatic pursuit of properties belonging to Cuthbert's patrimony, which had been lost over time, and by the confirmation of their possessions granted by Calixtus II. Their program can be epitomized by the book they fastened with an iron chain to the high altar before Cuthbert's shrine, the *Liber Summi Altaris*. Now lost, it contained a chronicle of the see to the time of William the Conqueror,

including the original endowments of the church of Durham. It was opened
with a key only on solemn occasions.[62]

Notes

*I am indebted to Paul E. Szarmach and David Rollason for close critical read-
ings of this chapter. I would also like to thank David Rollason for sending me type-
scripts of his chapter in this volume and his article "Symeon of Durham and the
Community of Durham in the Eleventh Century," delivered at the Seventh Harlaxton
Symposium, forthcoming in the Harlaxton volume on the eleventh century.

1. For a discussion, see Abou-El-Haj, *The Medieval Cult of Saints: Formations
and Transformations* (Cambridge, 1994).

2. See especially Susan Ridyard, "Condigna Veneratio, 'Post-Conquest Atti-
tudes to the Saints' of the Anglo-Saxons," *Anglo-Norman Studies* 9 (1986): 179–206,
especially pp. 198–200, 204–6; and *The Royal Saints of Anglo-Saxon England: A
Study of West Saxon and East Anglian Cults* (Cambridge, 1988). See also David
Rollason, *Saints and Relics in Anglo-Saxon England* (Oxford, 1989) and "Symeon of
Durham."

3. For an account of the early cult as opulent and unusually public, promoted
by the early *vitae* and the *Historia Ecclesiastica* at a time of ecclesiastical tension in
Northumbria, see Alan Thacker, "Lindisfarne and the Origins of the Cult of St.
Cuthbert," in Gerald Bonner, David Rollason, and Clare Stancliffe, eds., *St. Cuthbert,
His Cult and His Community to AD 1200* (Woodbridge, England, 1989), pp. 103–22,
especially pp. 104–10, 120–22. I am excluding the nonlocal references discussed by
David Rollason, "Why Was St Cuthbert so Popular?" in *Cuthbert Saint and Patron*,
ed. D. W. Rollason (Durham, 1987), pp. 9–22. For his comments on Lindisfarne's
power and its early cult, pp. 17–21.

4. Characterized as a pre-Conquest narrative cartulary by H. H. E. Craster,
"The Red Book of Durham," *English Historical Review* 40 (1925): 504–32, p. 518.
See Luisella Simpson, "The King Alfred/St Cuthbert Episode in the Historia de sancto
Cuthbert: Its Significance for mid-tenth-century English History," in Bonner et al.,
eds., *St. Cuthbert*, pp. 397–411, especially pp. 397–98; H. H. E. Craster, "The Patri-
mony of St. Cuthbert," *English Historical Review* 271 (1954): 177–99, especially
177–78; and Bertram Colgrave, "The Post-Bedan Miracles and Translations of St.
Cuthbert," in Sir C. Fox and B. Dickins, eds., *The Early Cultures of North West
Europe*, H. M. Chadwick Memorial Studies (Cambridge, 1950), pp. 307–32 (written
in 1920), especially pp. 307–8. For the later dating, see Ted Johnson-South, "Changing Images of Sainthood: St. Cuthbert in the Historia de Sancto Cuthberto," in Sandro
Sticca, ed., *Studies in Medieval Hagiography* (in press, Binghamton, N.Y.). Luisella
Simpson argues that the *Historia*'s emphasis on patrons of the West Saxon dynasty
places it, including the Alfred story, mainly in the mid-tenth century with some mid-
eleventh-century additions; "The King Alfred/St Cuthbert Episode," pp. 397–411.

5. See C. F. Battiscomb, ed., *The Relics of St Cuthbert* (Oxford, 1956), p. 36, a story related by Durham's historian, Symeon, *Historia Dunelmensis Ecclesiae*, ed. T. Arnold, *Symeonis Monachi Opera Omnia*, 2 vols., Rolls Series (London, 1882–85); see also *Symeonis Dunelmensis Opera et Collectanea*, ed. I. Hodgson-Hinde, Surtees Society (London, 1868), and *The Church Historians of England*, vol. 3, part 2, *Symeon's Historical Works*, trans. J. Stevenson (London, 1855). Aubin, James, Mary Magdalen, and other saints either refused to be moved or became so heavy they could not be moved beyond the locations of their choice.

6. Craster identifies this as belonging to one of two books chained to Durham's high altar, and a main source for Symeon's history, "Red Book of Durham," pp. 519–22, 529–31. See also H. H. E. Craster "A Contemporary Record of the Pontificate of Ranulf Flambard," *Archaeologia Aeliana*, 4th ser. 7 (1930): 33–56, especially p. 34, where he notes additions were made at least to 1085.

7. Cuthbert's community was originally comprised of a bishop and secular clergy and an abbot and monks. Over the centuries, it came to be composed entirely of seculars. See Craster, "Patrimony," pp. 197–98; Battiscomb, *Relics*, pp. 51–53 with lit.; B. Meehan, "Outsiders, Insiders and Property in Durham Around 1100," *Studies in Church History*, 12 (1975): 45–58; and A. J. Piper, "The First Generations of Durham Monks and the Cult of St Cuthbert," in G. Bonner et al., *St. Cuthbert*, pp. 437–46.

8. The translation is not mentioned in the MS. See Malcolm Baker, "Medieval Illustrations of Bede's Life of St Cuthbert," *Journal of the Warburg and Courtauld Institutes* 41 (1978): 16–49, especially on pp. 19–20, and Appendix D by D. H. Farmer, pp. 46–49. The years 1100–1120 are proposed for the MS by Jonathan J. G. Alexander and Elżbieta Temple, *Illustrated Manuscripts in Oxford Libraries, the University Archives and the Taylor Institution* (Oxford, 1985), pp. 4–5, cat. 17. See also C. M. Kauffmann, *Romanesque Manuscripts, 1066–1190, A Survey of Manuscripts Illuminated in the British Isles*, vol. 3 (London, 1975), cat. no. 26. The later miracles record events between 877–878 and 1080. According to Colgrave, they were written between 1083 and 1104, but nearer the earlier date, "Post-Bedan Miracles," p. 327. Four were taken from the *Historia*. These are discussed later.

9. "Ecclesiae cartula, quae antiquam regum et quorumque religiosorum munificentiam erga ipsam sanctum continet." See Colgrave, "Post-Bedan Miracles," p. 308, and Craster, "Patrimony," p. 177.

10. Colgrave dates the second set of ten or eleven miracles, nos. 8–17 and possibly 21 in his categories, to 1100–1115, and likely closer to the beginning of the century because the translation is not mentioned, "Post-Bedan Miracles," pp. 327–28. For the three miracles, nos. 18–20, and the translation story, written around 1123, see pp. 329–31.

11. Identified as the *Little Book About the Wonderful Miracles of Blessed Cuthbert Which Were Performed in Recent Times* by Victoria Tudor, "The Cult of St Cuthbert in the Twelfth Century: The Evidence of Reginald of Durham," in Bonner et al., *St. Cuthbert*, pp. 447–67, especially p. 448.

12. For comparisons between the Oxford and British Library MSS, see Baker, "Medieval Illustrations," and M. E. Stringer, "The Twelfth Century Illustrations of the Life of Saint Cuthbert," dissertation, Harvard University (1973). For reproductions, description, and literature, see Nigel J. Morgan, *Early Gothic Manuscripts I, 1190–1250, A Survey of Manuscripts Illuminated in the British Isles*, IV, vol. 1 (London, 1982), cat. no. XX.

13. The *Historia Regum* is attributed to Symeon. Some identify the house where Walcher died as the bishop's residence. On William's raid and Aethelwine, see Battiscomb, *Relics* pp. 48–49, and W. E. Kapelle, *The Norman Conquest of the North. The Region and Its Transformation 1000–1135* (Chapel Hill, N.C., 1979), pp. 112–13, 126, 138.

14. I use David Rollason's dating, "Symeon of Durham."

15. See Meehan, "Outsiders, Insiders," pp. 48–49. For the clerk's version in their *Chronicle*, see Craster, "Red Book of Durham," p. 528: "multa rex audiens, . . . preciosum pallium super sepulcrum incorrupti corporis sancti patris Cuthberti, ut erat largi cordis, offerens 'omnia,' inquit, 'que me antecessores huic ecclesie sancte Dei genitricis et sancti Cuthberti confessoris . . .' " For Symeon's version, see Battiscomb, *Relics*, p. 49.

16. See Battiscomb, ibid., pp. 49–50 (citing Symeon, *Historia Dunelmensis Ecclesiae*, book iii, cap. xix). See also Meehan, "Outsiders, Insiders," p. 49. In a similar story Edmund transfixes King Sweyn with his spear when he tried to impose the Danegeld on Bury, with however a crucial difference that explains why the story was circulated and pictured at Bury, whereas Durham treated the conqueror more discreetly. Sweyn was a dead and reviled conqueror; William's line was established. See my "Bury St Edmunds Abbey Between 1070 and 1124: A History of Property, Privilege, and Monastic Art Production," *Art History* 6 (1983): 1–29, especially pp. 12–13.

17. On the clerks expelled, see Battiscomb, ibid., pp. 51–53; Meehan, "Outsiders, Insiders," pp. 45 ff.; and Piper, "Durham Monks," pp. 437, 441. On the transformation of Cuthbert's community from monks to seculars, see Craster, "Patrimony," pp. 196–98. William was restored in 1092 after an exile imposed on him for siding with the barons in their revolt against William Rufus.

18. This was part of the wholesale destruction of Anglo-Saxon churches, replaced by Norman churches, that together with castles marked the new political order. See R. Morris, *Cathedrals and Abbeys of England and Wales. The Building Church, 600–1540* (New York, 1979), especially pp. 181–94, 250; and Colin Platt, *The Architecture of Medieval Britain* (New Haven, Conn., 1990), pp. 1–27.

19. On contemporary descriptions of Flambard, see Battiscomb, *Relics*, p. 55; Craster, "Pontificate of Ranulf Flambard," p. 49, for charters that obliquely mention misdeeds at the time of his restoration and an order to a sheriff and barons in Northumberland and Yorkshire not to receive any of the men fleeing from his land nor their money "because of the money which the bishop gives me," p. 52.

20. The monks had been unsuccessful in extracting from Flambard usurped properties Bishop William had promised for an endowment; see Piper, "Durham Monks," p. 442, citing for this and for Flambard's archdeacon, H. S. Offler, ed., *Durham Episcopal Charters 1071–1152* (Gateshead, England, 1968), nos. 14–18, 20–21. According to R. E. Southern, Flambard repented on his deathbed for wrongful exactions, which he argues were very much overstated by monastic historians and largely used for cathedral building; see his *Medieval Humanism and Other Studies* (Oxford, 1970), pp. 183–205, especially p. 202.

21. *Historia Translationum Sancti Cuthberti Auctore Anonymo*, in Hodgson-Hinde, *Symeonis Dunelmensis*, pp. 188-97, translated in Battiscomb, *Relics*, Appendix I, pp. 99–107, followed by Reginald of Durham's late-twelfth-century version (chs. xl–xliii of his book on Cuthbert), pp. 107–12, and a twelfth-century list of relics, pp. 112–14. See Battiscomb's discussion of the two accounts, pp. 55 ff. For the papal confirmation, see Meehan, "Outsiders, Insiders," p. 47.

22. Baker, "Medieval Illustrations," projects an earlier MS, not extant. See note 12. See Colgrave's survey of the surviving texts of Bede's life, *Two Lives of Saint Cuthbert* (Cambridge, 1940; paperback reprint 1985), pp. 20–42.

23. See Temple, *Anglo-Saxon Manuscripts*. In a comparable instance, Turner and Dodwell have argued that Saint Augustine's linear MS painting was self-consciously anti-Norman in a house where there was a "full-scale riot," forcing Abbot Wido, a Norman appointed by Lanfranc in 1087, to flee after Lanfranc's death in 1089. See D. H. Turner's entry on BL MS Arundel 91 in *The Golden Age of Anglo-Saxon Art* (London, 1984), cat. no. 264, p. 198 and C. R. Dodwell, *Canterbury School of Illumination 1066–1200* (Cambridge, 1954), p. 26. Leslie Dale Ross argues that rivalry at Saint Augustine and Canterbury was local and internal rather than "national" and political, "Anglo-Norman Hagiographic Illustration at Canterbury in the Early Romanesque Period," dissertation, University of California at Santa Barbara (1987), pp. 207–8, and that the struggle over primacy between York and Canterbury was much more significant, p. 215.

24. According to Baker, the emphasis on Cuthbert as bishop in liturgical postures and vestments in the London MS celebrates the monks' successful struggle against their bishops over their right to elect freely their prior ("Medieval Illustrations," pp. 39–40). Around the same years a mural painted at Durham displays Cuthbert in formal episcopal portrait, his feet kissed by prostrated monks. See Battiscomb, *Relics*, plate 1.

25. For an account of the core scenes of pictorial hagiography, see my *Medieval Cult of Saints*, Chapter Two. Colgrave, *Two Lives*, pp. 238–39 [Latin and English *en face*].

26. In Norman F. Cantor's words, *Church, Kingship and Lay Investiture in England 1089–1135* (Princeton, N.J., 1958), especially pp. 168–74. Most scenes of consecration, acclamation, and investiture are depicted in continental hagiographies according to conventional formulas described in early medieval *vitae*. In three instances, old texts were visually revised to adapt and support papal reforms. See my discussion in *Medieval Cult of Saints*, pp. 37–40.

27. It has been reconstructed using the Carlisle Cathedral choir stalls modeled on the cycle in 1485, which displayed a traditional hierarchical consecration. See Stringer, "Twelfth-century Illustrations," p. 171, and Bertram Colgrave, "The Saint Cuthbert Paintings on the Carlisle Cathedral Stalls," *Burlington Magazine* 73 (1938): 16–21, especially 21, who cautions, however, that little is left of this panel.

28. See note 24.

29. Colgrave, *Two Lives*, pp. 270–81, 282–85. For the miracle of the body not moving beyond Durham, see note 5.

30. Ibid., p. 14.

31. Cuthbert's predictions are made to Hereberht in Chapter 28, ten chapters before his death, see Colgrave, ibid., pp. 250–51. For a discussion and reproductions of death and burial scenes, see my *Medieval Cult of Saints*, pp. 49–55.

32. Against Cuthbert's wishes, the monks wanted to bury him with "fitting honor" inside Lindisfarne church, and Cuthbert reluctantly agreed; see Colgrave, ibid., pp. 278–80, 279–81. Lindisfarne was notified of his death and his body was transferred by boat from Farne and prepared for burial in linen drapes, pp. 286–88, 287–89.

33. Ibid., pp. 292–94, 293–95 for the discovery; and the very short chapter, pp. 296–97, for Eadberht.

34. I have also discussed this in my article, "The Audiences for the Medieval Cult of Saints," *Gesta* 30 (1991): 3–15, especially pp. 4–7.

35. *Symeonis Dunelmensis*, p. 189; Battiscomb, *Relics*, p. 100.

36. *Symeonis Dunelmensis*, p. 189; Battiscomb, ibid., p. 100. In 1104 those who affirmed the body was present in its tomb and still incorrupt had become anxious by skepticism; cf. Battiscomb, ibid., p. 99.

37. Colgrave, *Two Lives*, pp. 292, 294 and 293, 295.

38. *Symeonis Dunelmensis*, p. 191; Battiscomb, *Relics*, p. 101.

39. *Symeonis Dunelmensis*, p. 191; Battiscomb, ibid., p. 102.

40. *Symeonis Dunelmensis*, p. 192; Battiscomb, ibid., p. 102.

41. Cuthbert was apparently mummified. See Battiscomb, ibid., on the examinations of 1827 and 1899, pp. 8–9, and the examination of the skeleton, pp. 92–98, which should be read together with R. Bailey, who has examined the partisan ecclesiastical maneuvers in which the excavations were undertaken and discusses "alternative" accounts, "St Cuthbert's Relics: Some Neglected Evidence," Bonner et al., *St. Cuthbert*, pp. 231–46.

42. *Symeonis Dunelmensis*, p. 192; Battiscomb, ibid., pp. 102–3.

43. *Symeonis Dunelmensis*, p. 193; Battiscomb, ibid., p. 103. They vested it and returned it behind the altar as in 698. For Bede's description, see Colgrave, *Two Lives*, p. 295.

44. *Symeonis Dunelmensis*, p. 193; Battiscomb, ibid., p. 103.

45. *Symeonis Dunelmensis*, p. 194; Battiscomb, ibid., p. 104. We can wonder whether this abbot participated with the monks in raising the level of their drama, just as Symeon of Durham developed his account of skepticism on the part of the Conqueror, who, shortly after the Translation, publicly doubted whether Cuthbert's body was indeed in the coffin-reliquary and threatened to kill all the prelates assembled if his suspicions were confirmed. See note 16 above.

46. The account of disbelief is particularly lengthy; efforts to persuade the monks to accede to another inspection dramatically satisfied all skepticism. See *Symeonis Dunelmensis*, pp. 194–95; Battiscomb, ibid., pp. 103–5.

47. *Symeonis Dunelmensis*, p. 196. Battiscomb, ibid., pp. 105–6. Reginald's version of the translation, later in the century, does not include this miracle, so it seems to pertain especially to events in the first few years as recalled twenty years later; see Battiscomb, ibid., pp. 107–12.

48. *Symeonis Dunelmensis*, p. 196; Battiscomb, ibid., p. 106.

49. Though, as he began his sermon, "there stood by his side men to inform the assembled multitudes of . . . the miracle of incorruption," Battiscomb, ibid., 106. The account of the translation, written twenty years after the event, represents the bishop, who had a number of outstanding quarrels with the monks, first as a skeptic and finally as an obstacle.

50. *Symeonis Dunelmensis*, p. 197 who continues, "and the inference from this is plain, that it was not pleasing to God that the sacred body of his servant should be any longer detained in holy ground"; Battiscomb, ibid., p. 106

51. See Piper, "Durham Monks," pp. 444–45 and J. P. McAleer, "The Upper Nave Elevation and High Vaults of Lindisfarne Priory," *Durham Archaeological Journal* 2 (1986): 43–53. Colgrave, "Post-Bedan Miracles," p. 325, noted that when Symeon incorporated the 1069 miracle in which Cuthbert's body was carried to Lindisfarne island in high tide without anyone's feet getting wet, as the community fled from William the Conqueror's raid, he omitted descriptions describing the "geography and peculiar situation of Lindisfarne and its connection with the saint."

52. Part of a list drawn up after 1104 but no later than the middle of the twelfth century, found in three MSS of Bede's prose life, the earliest from Durham priory under the episcopate of William of St. Barbara (1143–1152); see Battiscomb, *Relics*, p. 113.

53. Quoted by Meehan, "Outsiders, Insiders," p. 47. See Piper, "Durham Monks," pp. 442–43, on a series of actions by Bishop Flambard that undermined the monks' and the prior's interests.

54. See Colgrave "Post-Bedan Miracles," pp. 312, 326. The miracle stories that follow are taken from Colgrave's article. Of the four miracles transcribed from the *Historia*, two are thought to be late additions and so may also belong to the post-Conquest shaping of Cuthbert's cult.

55. For the addition of Alfred, see Simpson, "The King Alfred/St Cuthbert Episode," pp. 408–9. See also Craster, "Patrimony," p. 189, and for the references to *sac* and *soc*, pp. 192–93, 198. For the threat incorporated in Cnut's gifts, see Craster, "Red Book," p. 528.

56. See my article, "Bury St Edmunds Abbey," especially pp. 8–13, and my book, pp. 45–46, 55–60, 98–106.

57. See David Hall, "The Sanctuary of St Cuthbert," in Bonner et al., *St. Cuthbert*, pp. 425–36, especially pp. 426–27.

58. On the increase in brigands and robbers, especially after William's 1069 raid, see Kapelle, *Norman Conquest*, pp. 131–33. For the conjunction of sanctuary and jurisdiction at Durham, see Hall, ibid., p. 435, and for sanctuary and homicide, see note 57.

59. Craster, "Patrimony," p. 199.

60. Some of their acquisitions may have funded the new cathedral, whose expense so strained revenues that Bishop Ranulf repented on his deathbed for wrongful exactions, attributed to the building enterprise (see note 20). The extravagant setting for the cult enhanced and endangered the monks' strategies, encapsulated in the 1104 discovery and translation.

61. Meehan noted the clerks were "noticeably less strident . . . than the monks towards their property," "Outsiders, Insiders," pp. 48–49. Colgrave observed that in the miracles written later and not inscribed in MS 165 violators are restored to health after they are punished, "Post-Bedan Miracles," p. 328. Reginald's 129 miracles date between 875 and the 1170s, but most took place between 1135 and 1154. One fifth are miracles of retribution, but none concerns Durham's security and after 1170 cures dramatically increase, especially at the cathedral; see Tudor, "Reginald of Durham," pp. 454–55.

62. From an early-eighteenth-century description based upon an early-fifteenth-century history by Prior Wessington of Durham. See Craster, "Red Book of Durham," pp. 520–22.

Part Two

Old English Prose

The Corpus of Anonymous Lives
and Their Manuscript Context

D. G. Scragg

Saints' lives written in Old English that are not attributable to Ælfric are relatively thin on the ground, and the few that survive often do so in only a single copy. The following survey examines all the anonymous saints' lives in their manuscript context to try to determine more about the pre-Ælfrician tradition and to discover if there is any evidence that the poverty of that tradition is the result of accident of transmission rather than failure of the genre in the tenth century.

The category "saint's life" is here used in the widest sense, incorporating *vita* and *passio* and including items for all the Marian festivals and the cross. No more than half of the items discussed offer anything like a full *vita*.

The Manuscripts

A¹ (Vercelli, Biblioteca Capitolare, CXVII, The Vercelli Book. Ker 394. s. x²)

A is a tenth-century collection of homilies and saints' lives in prose and verse.[2] Of the twenty-nine items in random order, six are in verse, including three hagiographical pieces, *Andreas, The Fates of the Apostles* and *Elene* (the last two signed by Cynewulf). Three of the prose pieces, all of which are anonymous, are saints' lives. One scribe wrote all 135 original folios, but he drew his material from different exemplars, hence item 29, for example, is unlikely to have shared the transmission history of items 19 and 20.

Ker 19, *Purification of the Virgin,* B3.3.19 (f.d. February 2). Unique. This is a homily closely tied to the pericope, Luke 2:22–32, with relatively little attention being given to Mary.[3] The copy in A seems to have been taken by the Vercelli scribe from the same source as his homilies XV, XVI, and

XVIII (Martin); all four thus appear to have formed part of an early homiliary that was either composed or copied in a center using a Mercian writing system.[4]

Ker 20, *Martin*, B3.3.17 (f.d. November 11). This Old English life is based on extracts from Sulpicius Severus and associated material but it was probably composed first in Latin and what we have here is a literal rendering of that Latin.[5] It is found in the three manuscripts that give the best evidence of the early homiletic tradition in English, A, B, and C. The version preserved in A is fuller, although it has many copying errors and two leaves, from different points in the text, are lost.

Ker 29, *Guthlac*, B3.3.10 (f.d. April 11). Almost all of Chapters 28–32 of Felix's *Vita Sancti Guthlaci* in an Old English translation is here presented in crude homiletic dress. The translation of the whole life is preserved in Z, where, however, it has been subjected to large-scale linguistic modernization. Consequently, the copy in A is important in the evidence it gives of the early and non-West Saxon form of the original translation.

B *(Princeton University Library, W. H. Scheide Collection 71, The Blickling Homilies. Ker 382. s. x/xi)*

B is an ordered homiliary consisting entirely of pre-Ælfrician items arranged for Sundays and feast days up to Pentecost followed by five items of a *sanctorale*. It is an original collection, assembled by its two scribes from a variety of exemplars.[6] Items 13, 14, and 15 may be drawn from a different exemplar from items 16, 17, and 18 because the opening of item 16 was written by a different scribe on a fresh quire. The manuscript is incomplete, having lost quires at the beginning as well as the outer leaves of what survives as the final quire, so that it is not now possible to see how complete the set was, but the limited range of saints included is clear enough.

Ker 1, *Annunciation*, B3.4.18 (f.d. March 25). Unique. A close translation, with omissions and occasional expansion, of pseudo-Augustine *Sermo cxx* (PL 39, XX-XXX), which is set for Christmas. One of the expansions makes it clear that the piece in English is set for the Annunciation.[7] The opening is lost but the Latin source indicates that little is missing. Since the first surviving quire of B is complete, it follows that this item began part way through a quire, perhaps then having been copied continuously from the same source as the previous item(s).

Ker 13, *Assumption of the Virgin*, B3.3.20 (f.d. August 15). The piece is out of chronological order, at the beginning of the sanctorale.[8] One leaf is missing from the copy in B near the beginning, but a complete version survives in F. B and F appear to draw on a common exemplar at no great distance. As a translation of Latin apocrypha, the piece suggests grave limitation in the Latinity of the translator.[9]

Ker 14, *Nativity of John the Baptist*, B3.3.12 (f.d. June 24). Unique. A translation of pseudo-Augustine *Sermo cxcix* (PL 39, XX–XXX) in a version somewhat longer than that printed by Migne.

Ker 15, *Peter and Paul*, B3.3.32 (f.d. June 29). Unique. A translation of a known *passio*, BHL 6657.

Ker 16, *Michael*, B3.3.25 (f.d. September 29). Unique. Most of the piece is a translation of *De Apparitione Sancti Michaelis in Monte Gargano* but a short extract from a *Visio Pauli* is used for the final paragraph.

Ker 17, *Martin*, B3.3.17 (f.d. November 11). Also in A and C, although the B version is textually closer to C than to A.

Ker 18, *Andrew*, B3.3.1 (f.d. November 30). Incomplete, but a full version survives in F. B and F are textually very close.[10] Again the piece is based closely on a Latin original, *Acta Andreae et Matthiae*.

C (Oxford, Bodleian Library, Junius 85 and 86. Ker 336. s. xi med.)

C was perhaps once an ordered homiliary, but it is now very fragmentary. It was considerably adapted during the eleventh century and divided into two books in modern times. It contains, in whole or in part, six anonymous items, one of which is relevant here.[11]

Ker 8, *Martin*, B3.3.17 (f.d. November 11). This also appears in A and B. B and C are textually close, except where a copyist has modernized the language of C.

D (Cambridge, Corpus Christi College 41. Ker 32. s. xi¹ or xi med.)

D contains a late copy of the Old English Bede, with additional entries made by a single hand perhaps a generation after the Bede had been copied. The additional items are in blank spaces and in the margins and include six anonymous homiletic pieces. Four of these, Ker's items 9, 11, 12, and 13, are copied on consecutive leaves. The last two, items 17 and 18, are each copied separately from the rest. There is no indication that the two items relevant here were drawn by the scribe from the same archetype, but both pieces have items of vocabulary (e.g., *nimðe*), which suggest tenth-century composition.

Ker 11, *Assumption of the Virgin*, B3.3.21 (f.d. August 15). An independent translation of one of the Latin sources used for the Assumption piece in B.[12]

Ker 17, *Michael*, B3.3.24 (f.d. September 29). Unique. This anaphoric list of the virtues of St. Michael, with no known source, has some idiosyncratic spellings that mark it off from the rest of the manuscript.[13]

E *(Oxford, Bodleian Library, Bodley 340 and 342. Ker 309. s. xi. in. – xi med.)*

E is a two-volume copy of a homiliary that originated in Canterbury, containing homilies from the First and Second Series of Ælfric's *Catholic Homilies* rearranged into a single annual cycle and supplemented by eleven early anonymous pieces. None of the anonymous items is a saint's life. The Ælfric items in the Canterbury homiliary appear to be drawn from the original sets sent by Ælfric to Archbishop Sigeric. A number of other surviving manuscripts drew on the same homiliary (see later, MSS G, H, I, and especially F).

It is likely that E was made in Canterbury circa 1000 and moved to Rochester early in the eleventh century, where two Ælfric items on St. Andrew, the patron saint of Rochester, were added in xi[1].[14] About the middle of the century the whole homiliary was worked over by a scribe who altered passages in pencil and then inked most of them over. Apparently the intention was to delete words and phrases not acceptable linguistically and substitute those that were.[15] He also added a brief *Life of Paulinus* in a space at the end of the original volume 2 (Bodley 342). This item refers to Rochester (where Paulinus is buried) as *þes stede*, "this place."

Ker 75, *Paulinus*, B3.3.31 (f.d. October 10). Unique. The item gives every appearance of having been created to fit the manuscript context in which it is now found. Although the last lines of text have been cut off by a binder, the sense indicates that restoration of them would have completed the Life. All the information, except the local reference to Paulinus' burial, is drawn from Bede. Nothing in the language conflicts with eleventh-century composition (there are frequent late spellings, e.g., *cyng, wærð, liues, Æþelbrihtes*, and inflections, e.g., *on Euerwic, Norðhembram* (acc. pl.), and there is no sign of early or non-West Saxon vocabulary). The item is out of chronological order, having been added where there was space.

F *(Cambridge, Corpus Christi College 198. Ker 48. s. xi[1], xi[2])*

F is an incomplete copy of the Canterbury homiliary represented by E, with extensive additions made during the eleventh century.[16] The only items relevant to this study are two of the late additions, and both are versions of pieces also in B, with the copies in B and F being derived from a common exemplar at no great distance.

Ker 54, *Assumption of the Virgin*, B3.3.20 (f.d. August 15).

Ker 64, *Andrew*, B3.3.1 (f.d. November 30).

G (Cambridge, Corpus Christi College 162. Ker 38. s. xi in.)

G is a collection that draws thirty-one items (occasionally slightly adapted) from the Canterbury homiliary represented by E and incorporates further items, some by Ælfric and some anonymous, from other sources. Like E, G was at Rochester during the eleventh century and may have been written there, but there are also signs of a Canterbury origin. The book has features of script and decoration similar to those in E, some of which are very like those found in BL, Royal 6.C.i, a later eleventh-century manuscript from St. Augustine's, Canterbury,[17] and a further link with that center is perhaps suggested by an early addition, the following, that is relevant here.

Ker 55, *Deposition of Augustine of Canterbury*, B3.3.2 (f.d. May 26). Only the beginning of this unique item was entered on a blank page at the end of the manuscript in a hand contemporary with that of the principal scribe. The fragment stops at the end of the page, leaving the verso blank. Our understanding that the piece relates to Augustine comes from the Latin heading, *In Die Depositionis Beati Augustini Anglorum Doctoris*, because the text does not mention him.

H (Cambridge, Corpus Christi College 303. Ker 57. s. xii¹)

H is a large, late collection of homilies and saints' lives drawn from southeastern sources. Most of the items are by Ælfric, but eleven are anonymous, five of them unique. The manuscript is in two parts, a change of hand coinciding with a new quire and a new item at page 203. Part I consists of two blocks of items, the first (made fragmentary by the loss of 44 leaves at the beginning, as a medieval pagination makes clear) consisting of homilies for Sundays and holy days other than saints' days in chronological sequence to Easter, the second for saints' days from May 3 (Invention of the Cross) to December 6 (Nicholas) followed by five pieces for the common of saints. (A short item, Ker 40, added on a blank space at the end clearly did not form part of the original plan.) Part II completes the *temporale* sequence, beginning with a general homily and continuing with pieces assigned chronologically to the period from Rogationtide to the Twenty-First Sunday after Pentecost, again excluding saints' days, and ends with a miscellaneous collection of items, all but one by Ælfric, including the items found at the end of the *Lives of Saints* set in MS W. Two scribes shared the copying of the book, with a third hand perhaps intervening occasionally toward the end. Hand 1 wrote what are now the opening quires, hand 2 took over partway through Quire 4 and wrote to the end of Quire 13. The four items of interest here all occur in the second block in Part I and are copied by hand 2. There is some evidence, considered briefly in the Appendix to this chapter, that items 23, 26, and 34, although now separated by the chronological arrangement of H, were drawn by the scribe from a single exemplar.

Ker 18, *Invention of the Cross*, B3.3.6 (f.d. May 3). Also in U. Substantive differences between the two copies are minor and probably due to the intervention of the latest scribe in H who shows a tendency to modernize vocabulary throughout his stint.[18]

Ker 23, *Margaret*, B3.3.15 (f.d. July 20). Unique. There are significant differences of both vocabulary and content between this and the life of the same saint in M. See also the Appendix to this chapter.

Ker 26, *Giles*, B3.3.9 (f.d. September 1). Unique. See also the Appendix to this chapter.

Ker 34, *Nicholas*, B3.3.29 (f.d. December 6). Unique. See also the Appendix to this chapter.

I (Oxford, Bodleian Library, Bodley 343. Ker 310. s. xii²)

I is another large, late collection assembled by a single scribe from a variety of sources, including part of a copy of the Canterbury homiliary textually similar to the version used for F and G. The language of all texts is heavily modernized throughout. The two items listed here are found in different sections of the manuscript and were clearly drawn from different sources.

Ker 12, *Legendary History of the Cross*, B3.3.5 (*Invention* f.d. May 3). Also in part in f[b]. Napier dated the translation early eleventh century[19] but without any firm evidence. The vocabulary is mixed,[20] and the piece may be earlier or composed at some distance from Winchester. It is worth observing that other items in the block to which item 12 belongs in I are certainly drawn from a southeastern source.[21] Further investigation of the origin of this piece might begin with the possibility that it stems from Canterbury.

Ker 16, *Nativity of the Virgin Mary*, B3.3.18 (f.d. September 8). Also appears in O and f[a]. The version in I has considerable linguistic modernization and some abbreviation. I and O are printed in parallel columns as Assmann X.[22] The source is the first twelve chapters of the apocryphal pseudo-Matthew Gospel. Chapters 13–25 of the same work are a source for Vercelli homily VI but the two Old English items appear quite independent. Despite the lateness of all three extant copies of this item, there is reason to suspect that it derives from an early, perhaps pre-Ælfrician, translation.[23] There is room for a full linguistic analysis of this piece. Again it is possible that it stems from Canterbury.

M *(BL, Cotton Tiberius A.iii, fols. 2–173. Ker 186. s. xi med.)*

M is a composite manuscript, much of it in Latin, belonging to Christ Church, Canterbury.[24] The margins of the manuscript suffered so badly in the Cotton fire that leaves are now mounted separately, but it is possible to distinguish a distinct group of four quires (probably eights although the last now lacks a leaf) occupying fols. 65–95, which contain, among other items, the only piece relevant to the present study, Ker's item 15. The first of these quires, pricked for twenty-nine lines, was presumably prepared by the scribe (Ker hand 2) who ended the previous quire with Ælfric's colloquy in Latin, since he used the first leaf of the new quire to copy four sets of prognostics in Latin. The rest of this quire was used by a new scribe (Ker hand 3), who added Old English material and continued it on the three subsequent quires that have thirty-five lines (a lineation otherwise unknown in this manuscript). This same scribe is also responsible for the Old English gloss to the colloquy, and further overlap between his work and that of hand 2 may be seen in the fact that his first item, Ælfric's version of Bede's *De Temporibus,* may have been derived from the same source as hand 2's copy of the Latin prognostics.[25] Scribe 3 was evidently assembling a commonplace collection. Having begun with the Ælfric *De Temporibus,* he continued with a series of notes on the size of religious buildings and objects, then item 15, which follows, and finally a long series of homiletic pieces (interrupted toward the end by a Latin *ordo*).

Almost all of the work of Scribe 3 occurs again in other manuscripts, and it is interesting to note that in almost every case the version in M has been significantly altered. An Ælfric homily (Ker 16) is supplemented with quotations from an earlier anonymous piece,[26] a Sunday letter (Ker 17) is expanded with bits of anonymous homilies, an incident that forms part of Vercelli homily IX is reconstructed as an independent story (Ker 18),[27] and bits of various Wulfstan homilies are assembled in a scissors-and-paste fashion (Ker 19). Even the *De Temporibus* is in an inferior version.[28] It is hardly surprising that the saint's life is in a form otherwise unknown in English and Latin. It is not clear if the idiosyncracies of this section of M are the result of the use of inferior copies or if the copying scribe is in some way responsible, but the language and content of this group of four quires need to be looked at in some depth.

Ker 15, *Margaret,* B3.3.16 (f.d. July 20). Unique. The piece shows extensive modification of the supposed source (BHL 5303), and it is unlike the life of the same saint that survives in H. (That in f^g survives as an incipit only.)

O *(Oxford, Bodleian Library, Junius 121 and Hatton 113 and 114. Ker 338 and 331. s. xi third quarter)*

O is a set of three volumes made by a single scribe of Worcester, with some later additions. The Hatton volumes taken together constitute a large homiliary that begins with general items and continues with two ordered sets, the first containing items for Sundays and feast days from Christmas to November 1. Among the latter, only one item, the Nativity of the Virgin, is not by Ælfric. This is included in O presumably to supply a need created by Ælfric's stated reluctance to provide a homily for the feast.[29]

Ker 72 (Hatton 114), *Nativity of the Virgin Mary*, B3.3.18 (f.d. September 8). Also in I and f[a]. On the date of the piece, see the discussion under I.

T *(Oxford, Bodleian Library, Hatton 116. Ker 333. s. xii[1])*

T is a manuscript from the Worcester region that begins with an orderly collection of saints' lives (items 1–16), followed by a disorderly collection of homiletic pieces. All but item 1 of the orderly collection are by Ælfric, and Pope has shown that they were drawn from a single exemplar. The disordered items are all by Ælfric except the last. Vleeskruyer's analysis of the language of the manuscript, published in conjunction with his edition of item 1,[30] suggests that the scribe was faithful to the language of his exemplars, drawing on three separate sources for items 1, 2–16, and 17–26, respectively.

Ker 1, *Chad*, B3.3.3 (f.d. March 2). Unique. Vleeskruyer's thesis of this as a late copy of a ninth-century Mercian original has not been universally accepted, and one critic has even suggested a date for its composition close to that of the manuscript itself.[31] The truth probably lies between these extremes: the piece is certainly pre-Conquest and probably pre-Ælfric, but nothing in the language proves that it was composed before the tenth century.

U *(Oxford, Bodleian Library, Auct.F.4.32, fols. 10–18. Ker 297. s. xi[2])*

U is a single quire added to an unrelated larger manuscript in medieval times. It contains only one item.

Ker a, *Invention of the Cross*, B3.3.6 (f.d. May 3). Also in H, in a late copy. The piece includes some short quotations from Ælfric, "interpolated into an already existing account,"[32] although this says little about the date of the original composition. The language has some late features.[33]

W (BL, Cotton Julius E.vii. Ker 162. s. xi in.)

W is now the principal manuscript for Ælfric's *Lives of Saints* set, but it is not arranged in the order issued by Ælfric. Clemoes has suggested that item 21, the *Memory of Saints*, was intended to open the *Lives* set,[34] and there are now four non-Ælfrician items intervening at three points. A single scribe copied almost all of the surviving forty-nine items (the manuscript is fragmentary at the end), but the copying may have extended over a long period of time because differences appear in the character of the hand as the writing proceeds.[35] The scribe copied in two blocks of quires, now 2–14 and 19–31. Quire 19 begins a new item on a new page, something that does not happen elsewhere in the book, even though Quire 14, apparently the last written by the main scribe before he began on 19, was left with two and a half sides blank at the end. Having completed the whole book in regular quires of eight, the scribe added a bifolium at the beginning in which he copied Ælfric's Latin Preface and his letter to Æthelweard, together with a list of the contents of the book. By this time, another scribe had utilized the break in the manuscript before the present Quire 19 to insert part of an additional item, the anonymous piece on the Seven Sleepers, the copying of which was taken over partway through by a third scribe. This third scribe was thought by Ker to be possibly the main scribe "but the writing is more compressed than elsewhere"; however, Clemoes thinks the hand different.[36] In either case, the hand continued to write after the main scribe had added his list of contents at the beginning, because, although the Seven Sleepers is listed in its present place in the manuscript, the scribe who wrote the latter part of it continued with another anonymous item, Mary of Egypt, which is not in the list of contents. That the Seven Sleepers is in the table of contents and Mary of Egypt is not suggests some dislocation between them. It would appear that the copying of the Seven Sleepers was broken off abruptly. Comparison with the burnt MS f[g] suggests that about a tenth of the piece is missing at the end of the copy in W. A later scribe noticed the oddity of the ending and added a doxology similar to that added to the dislocated *Memory of Saints* earlier in the manuscript.[37]

A study by Roland Torkar[38] of the spelling of possessives *minre, minra, þinre, þinra* sometimes with and sometimes without *n* in this manuscript suggests that three of the anonymous items, 30, 41, and 44, had a transmission history in common that they did not share with either the fourth anonymous item, 31, or with any of the Ælfric items. Item 44, which is set for February 11, is out of place chronologically, appearing between items for November 20 and November 22, respectively. A possible explanation for this is that a legend of a virgin saint, Euphrosyne, is therefore placed immediately before the only Ælfric account of a virgin saint, Cecilia, to appear in the second half of the book. I assume that at some point in the compiling of W, it was decided to incorporate three items from a source independent of that used for the Ælfric items. The decision was made after the scribe had completed the quires containing Ælfric's February pieces and possibly after he had begun the second half of the book with Quire 19. Another scribe, perhaps the main scribe's master, fitted item 30 on the blank end of Quire 14 and added an additional quire (15), before handing over either to a third scribe or perhaps back to the main scribe after the latter had finished the whole of his book. Meanwhile, the main scribe had been able to fit item 41 (from the same archetype as item 30) into its proper place chronologically and had put the third item from that source, item 44, into what seemed an appropriate place late in the volume. Whoever completed the writing of item 30 finally added item 31, but this was drawn from a new source (because Torkar has shown that it does not display the distinctive spellings of the other anonymous items), and it was added after the main scribe had appended his list of contents of the manuscript at the beginning. It is also out of chronological order.

My view of the chronology of writing is thus:

1. Hand 1 wrote items 2–29 in sequence, broke off, and began a new set of quires with item 32, adding items 41 and 44 to the original collection in the course of copying.

2. Hand 2 began item 30.

3. Item 30 was continued by hand 3 (possibly identical with hand 1) but was left incomplete.

4. Hand 1 added the table of contents and item 1.

5. Hand 3 (= 1?) added item 31.

6. Another hand added the doxology to item 30.

Ker 30, *Seven Sleepers*, B3.3.34 (f.d. July 27). Also in f^g. In W it breaks off abruptly, the scribe leaving a blank line before beginning another item (a feature not found elsewhere in W).

Ker 31, *Mary of Egypt*, B3.3.23 (f.d. April 2). Also in f^d, in a copy with frequent minor differences that very occasionally suggest access to a better reading, and in f^g, where the differences are mainly of spelling. The readable text in f^d and f^g does not overlap. W lacks a long passage at Skeat line 246, with no indication that the scribe was aware of the loss. Presumably the copy text lacked a leaf or leaves. It would seem that all three versions are drawn independently from the archetype, with W and f^g being closer to each other than either is to f^d.

Ker 41, *Eustace and his Companions*, B3.3.8 (f.d. November 2). Also in f^k, where the readable passages show spelling differences only.

Ker 44, *Euphrosyne*, B3.3.7 (f.d. February 11). Also in f^g, where the readable passages suggest that its scribe had access to a better copy.

Z *(BL, Cotton Vespasian D.xxi, fols. 18–40. Ker 344. s. xi²)*

Z was separated into two parts probably by Cotton.[39] The larger portion, now Oxford, Bodleian Library, Laud Misc. 509, is mainly by Ælfric. The Cotton part contains only one item.

Ker 5, *Guthlac*, B3.3.10 (f.d. April 11). This is the only surviving complete copy of the translation of Felix's *Vita Sancti Guthlaci*, part of which is excerpted as item 29 in A.

Xʰ *(BL, Cotton Vespasian D.xiv, fols. 4–169. Ker 209. s.xii med.)*

Xʰ is a large collection of mainly homiletic pieces, some originating in the twelfth century as their Latin sources show, but others abstracted from earlier writings, especially those of Ælfric. There is significant intervention of a copying scribe or scribes in all the items, in both content and language, so that it is hard to be precise about the date of composition of the anonymous ones. Cameron includes item 44, *In Festis Sancte Marie*, in his list of Old English texts (B3.3.22), but this is patently of twelfth-century origin. Items 11 and 43, listed here, are more difficult to date. The manuscript is made up of blocks of quires originally separate,[40] and these may reflect the sources drawn upon by the scribe. The first block includes Ker's items 3–19. It begins with the Distichs of Cato, but all other items are either saints' lives or associated material, and all but item 11 are by Ælfric. The fourth block, items 35–48, includes twelfth-century pieces, but there are also some by Ælfric. It is doubtful if the manuscript association of the two items that follow can tell us anything of their date of origin.

Ker 11, *James the Greater*, B3.3.11 (f.d. July 25). Unique. It is one of the longer pieces in a manuscript, which consists mainly of short extracts. A close comparison with the Latin source, copies of which are known from Anglo-Saxon England, might reveal something of the manuscript tradition to which the translation is indebted.

Ker 43, *Neot*, B3.3.28 (f.d. July 31). Unique. The Latin source was composed before the Norman Conquest according to its latest editors,[41] but there is no clear evidence that the English version was made in the eleventh century[42] and some linguistic pointers to twelfth-century composition (e.g., the indefinite pronoun *me*).

fᵃ *(Cambridge, Corpus Christi College 367, Part II, fols. 3–6 and 11–29. Ker 63. s. xii)*

A collection of fragments, evidently once part of a large manuscript. Eight of the ten items are by Ælfric, the other two being Vercelli homily IV and the item described here.

Ker 6, *Nativity of the Virgin Mary*, B3.3.18 (f.d. September 8). Almost all of Assmann X (lacking probably only one leaf at the end), in a copy independent of those in I and O.

f^b (Cambridge, Corpus Christi College 557, and Lawrence, Kansas, Kenneth Spencer Research Library, University of Kansas, C2, item 1. Ker 73(S). s. xi med.)

Three fragments of a single item, the latest discovery in Kansas proving that the piece is a copy of a known Invention homily.

Ker 1, *Legendary History of the Cross*, B3.3.5 (*Invention* f.d. May 3). The complete text is found in I.

f^d (Gloucester, Cathedral Library 35. Ker 117. s. xi)

Fragments from bindings. Ker recognizes three hands of different dates, the second, of s. xi med., writing only the item of interest here.

Ker 2, *Mary of Egypt*, B3.3.23 (f.d. April 2). This is also in W and f^g.

f^e (BL, Cotton Caligula A.xiv, fols. 93–130. Ker 138. s. xi med.)

Five quires remain of what was once a much larger manuscript. Of the three surviving items, two are saints' lives by Ælfric and the third is the item described here.

Ker 3, *Mildred*, B3.3.26 (f.d. July 13). The Latin rubric identifies this item as a Life of Mildred, but all that remains of the text is concerned with historical background, principally of the foundation of Minster-in-Thanet. The opening paragraph[43] is verbally close to the text known as the Kentish Royal Legend, which is itself related, somewhat tangentially, to lists of the resting places of the saints.[44] It would appear that earlier material has here been adapted to serve as suitable reading for a saint's day. A further extract (or more likely two extracts) from almost certainly the same item (although there is no textual overlap) occurs in f^1. The details of the founding of Minster-in-Thanet might suggest that the item was written there before Mildred's relics were moved to St. Augustine's, Canterbury, in 1035,[45] although this cannot be confirmed without the full text. Linguistically there is no doubt that the item is pre-Conquest, written in good West Saxon with occasional Kentish spellings.

f^f (BL, Cotton Otho A.viii, fols. 7–34, and Cotton Otho B.x, fol. 66. Ker 168. s. xi in.)

Most of our knowledge of f[f] is derived from seventeenth-century catalogues of the Cotton Library,[46] which list a variety of Latin pieces (two
glossed in Old English) and one vernacular item, which follows here.

Ker 1: *Machutus*, B3.3.13 (f.d. May 14 or November 15). The language
of this unique piece is late West Saxon, and it probably originated in Winchester at the end of the tenth or early in the eleventh century.[47]

f[g] (BL, Cotton Otho B.x, fols. 1–28, 31–50, 52–54, 56–57, 59–60, 65, and
67, and Oxford, Bodleian Library, Rawlinson Q.e.20. Ker 177. s.xi[1])

Fragment f[g] was badly burnt in the Cotton fire and we are now largely
dependent upon Wanley for a description of its contents. Ker defines three
sections, A, B, and C, which may have been originally in separate manuscripts.

Section A is a disorderly collection of twenty-four items, principally
saints' lives and therefore comparable with W. Seventeen items are by Ælfric,
one probably by Wulfstan (item 17 = Bethurum XIII). Four, occurring as a
group, are anonymous saints' lives, all of which are probably pre-Ælfrician
since other copies of c.1000 survive.

Ker 10, *Euphrosyne*, B3.3.7 (f.d. February 11). Also in W. Some legible
parts are collated in Skeat and reveal frequent minor differences, with f[g]
usually having the better readings.

Ker 11, *Christopher*, B3.3.4 (f.d. July 25). The explicit, quoted by Wanley
and now partly legible,[48] is identical with that in f[j]. Wanley's transcription of
the incipit from f[g] is the sole witness to the opening of this life.

Ker 12, *Mary of Egypt*, B3.3.23 (f.d. April 2). Also in W and f[d].

Ker 13, *Seven Sleepers*, B3.3.34 (f.d. July 27). Also in W, where it lacks
the conclusion, as Wanley's explicit from f[g] shows.

All that remains of Section C is the incipit and explicit of the single item
as printed by Wanley.

Margaret, B3.3.15 (f.d. July 20). There is no indication in Wanley's two
sentences how early this life might have been translated, but it is evident that
it is independent of the lives in H and M.

f[i] (BL, Cotton Vitellius A.xv, fols. 4–93. Ker 215. s.xii med.)

Fragment f[i] is the principal authority for Alfred's adaptation of
Augustine's *Soliloquies*, and it also has a translation of the *Gospel of
Nicodemus* and the prose *Solomon and Saturn*, together with the item that

follows. Seventeenth-century records show in addition a "fragmentum Saxonicum quod forte continet aliquam partem historiae sive legendae Thomae Apostoli."[49] Ker gives details of palaeographic features that point to the use of an early copy for at least the first item.

Ker 4, *Quintin*, B3.3.33 (f.d. October 31). Only the opening few lines of this unique piece remain. The language suggests that, like the other pieces in the manuscript, it derives from an early copy, perhaps even one that is pre-Conquest.

f^j (BL, Cotton Vitellius A.xv, fols. 94–209. Ker 216. s. x/xi)

The *Beowulf* manuscript opens with three prose pieces, the first fragmentary because of the loss of quire(s) before the present opening.

Ker 1, *Christopher*, B3.3.4 (f.d. July 25). Also in f^g, where little remains. Sisam has a full discussion of the development of the saint's cult in tenth-century England.[50]

f^k (BL, Cotton Vitellius D.xvii, fols. 4–92. Ker 222. s. xi med.)

Fragment f^k was badly burnt in the Cotton fire, 123 of its 211 leaves being totally lost, but much of what remains is at least partly legible (Skeat comments: "Such readings as can be made out are sometimes serviceable," vol. 2, p. 445). Fifty-one saints' lives, all but two by Ælfric, in no discernible order, plus two Ælfric pieces for a confessor, Ælfric's dedication of a church, and a copy of the resting places of the saints, are in Wanley's account.

Ker 14, *Pantaleon*, B3.3.30 (f.d. July 27). All but one of the leaves remain. No satisfactory printed edition of this unique copy exists. The incipit ("Gehera∂ nu men þa leofestan hwæt her seg∂ on þysum b[ocum] be þam halgan Pantaleone þam cnihte") is like that found in tenth-century pieces (cf. especially Blickling XIII, *Assumption of the Virgin,* but similarly in Blickling II and IV, Assmann 11, and elsewhere), and tenth-century origin is further suggested by the language.[51]

Ker 29, *Eustace and His Companions*, B3.3.8 (f.d. September 20). Also in W. Only one leaf is now legible in f^k (collated by Skeat, lines 121–69), but this is enough to show that the two versions differ only in very minor details of spelling.

f^l (London, Lambeth Palace Library, 427, fols. 210–11. Ker 281. s. xi²)

Two non-adjacent leaves which were preserved in a medieval binding. Ker links the script with Exeter, but there is no western feature in the language, which is good late West Saxon, the only distinctive feature being the word *woruldprydum,* which marks the text as of the eleventh-century. Cameron listed the manuscript as a (fragmentary) Life of St. Mildred, B3.3.27, independent of the fragment in MS f^e, which is listed as B3.3.26. The *Dictionary of Old English* has modified this by splitting B3.3.27 into B.3.3.27.1 (Mildred) and B.3.3.27.2 (Seaxburg), but if the two Mildred pieces, B3.3.26 and B3.3.27.1, are part of the same, although in different recensions—as seems likely—this numbering remains confusing. It would be better to see the fragment in f^e and the two fragments here as separate parts of a single item (though this needs now to be tested by a thorough linguistic analysis) and to abandon this as an Old English Life of Seaxburg.[52]

Leaf 210. *Mildred,* B3.3.27.1 (f.d. July 13). This brief fragment is probably a continuation of the item begun in MS f^e.

Leaf 211. This continues the history of Minster-in-Thanet and is probably part of the same item. Although a few sentences are here given to Seaxburg, their content suggests considerable confusion and probably represents a Kentish writer's attempt to conflate conflicting information from a variety of sources.[53] As with the excerpt in MS f^e, this fragment has verbal overlap with the Kentish Royal Saints.

f^n (BL, Cotton Otho C.i, vol. 2. Ker 182. s. xi med.)

The fire-damaged f^n is fully described by Kenneth Sisam.[54] It contains the first two books of Wærferth's translation of Gregory's *Dialogues* copied early in the eleventh century, books III and IV being added some decades later by a scribe who then went on to write Ker's items 2a and 2b, which are translated from *Vitas Patrum.* Other scribes subsequently added further items, loosely related. The first of these, Ker 2c, also draws on *Vitas Patrum,* and this has led to considerable confusion in the modern period. Assmann's edition[55] printed 2a, 2b, and 2c as *Drei Leben aus: De Vitis Patrum,* Ker listed the three as parts of one item, and Cameron gave them a single entry. But Sisam's analysis makes it clear that 2c is quite distinct palaeographically and linguistically.

Ker 2a and 2b. These are two brief lives of anonymous Egyptian anchorites translated from *Vitas Patrum,* B3.3.35a and B3.3.35b. The language is good late West Saxon, with some eleventh-century spellings.[56]

Ker 2c, *Malchus,* B3.3.35c. To judge by the language, this piece is of tenth-century origin.

Conclusions

This volume of studies on the vernacular saints' lives is exploratory, and
conclusions drawn in any chapter must be partial and to some extent prema-
ture. The range of hagiographical material available in the vernacular in the
tenth century includes the Old English Martyrology and the Alfredian translations of Bede and of Gregory, and account must be taken too of the verse
saints' lives. But if we confine our attention to the prose lives within the
definition offered at the opening of this survey, it is clear from the previous
discussion that the manuscript evidence suggests that many of the pieces
described existed in English before the year 1000; for, although only A is
dated tenth century on palaeographic grounds, two other major sources of our
knowledge, B and W, were written very early in the eleventh century, and
both drew their material from yet earlier copies. Other manuscripts (notably
D, G, I, T, f^g, and f^k), themselves copied much later, were probably drawing
on similarly early copy texts, even if for indication of this we have to rely
on the more suspect linguistic evidence—more suspect because we have
relatively little provably tenth-century material for comparison. The items in
H and X^h are probably of post-Conquest origin. This leaves very few items
that seem to have originated in the eleventh century, perhaps the most interesting conclusion of this survey.

It is impossible on present evidence to date the pre-1000 material any
more closely. The items in A, B, D, and T look archaic linguistically, but this
might simply be because they are not written in the Winchester language that
characterizes the majority of surviving late Old English texts. What we can
say, however, is that when Ælfric was preparing his *Lives of Saints* set, there
probably existed, in English, homilies or *vitae* for the following saints: Andrew,
Chad, Christopher, Euphrosyne, Eustace, Guthlac, Malchus, Martin, Mary of
Egypt, Peter and Paul, the Seven Sleepers, and perhaps Margaret and Pantaleon,
and also pieces for the Marian festivals of the Annunciation, the Purification,
and the Assumption (and perhaps the Nativity also), and for the Nativity of
John the Baptist. Once Ælfric's *Lives* set became available, an English reader
had a very wide choice of hagiographical material, and the evidence for the
addition of further pieces is slight. In Winchester, interest in Breton saints
(which began in the tenth century) produced a vernacular life of Machutus,
and in Kent, local associations gave rise to the creation of hagiographical
material linked to the names Augustine (of Canterbury) and Mildred. Though
the traditions drawn upon for these compositions are undoubtedly pre-Ælfrician,
the manuscript evidence (fragmentary as it is) points toward the surviving
pieces being of eleventh century origin. Norman veneration perhaps added a
few further saints to the list, although it must be noted that Norman influence
should not here be seen as beginning only in 1066. But I should stress finally

that it has not been my intention in this survey to examine the evidence for the veneration of saints in England but to look primarily at the manuscript context of such vernacular lives as survive.

The range of lives available before Ælfric is about what we should expect, given the relative paucity of vernacular material in the tenth century. What is noticeable is the number of items that survive in a single manuscript copy, often a mutilated one at that. This is in contrast with the homiletic tradition, where we find larger numbers of tenth-century items surviving (usually, of course, in eleventh-century copies), and those often in multiple copies.[57] The difference must lie in the nature of the material. Whereas homiletic prose might be selectively reused in a scissors and paste manner, items or parts of items being reordered and revised for use in different contexts, saints' lives had a definable and limited application. Thus, then, although it must be admitted that Ælfric appears to have done for the vernacular saint's life what he had already done for the vernacular sermon, in providing a more comprehensive set than was available when he began, he in no sense filled a total vacuum. However he may be shown to have transmuted it, the genre was already well established in English.

Table 1—List of Lives Included in This Survey and Their Manuscript Distribution

MSS	A	B	C	D	E	F	G	H	I	M	O	T	U	W	Z	X^h	f^a	f^b	f^c	f^d	f^e	f^f	f^g	f^h	f^i	f^j	f^k	f^l	f^m
Andrew	18																												
Augustine						64																							
Chad							55																						
Christopher																							11		1				
Legendary History of the Cross								18	12							1													
Invention of the Cross													1										10						
Euphrosyne														44															
Eustace														41													29		
Giles								26																					
Guthlac	29																												
James the Greater															5														
Nativity of John the Baptist		14														11													
Machutus																						1							
Margaret A								23																					
Margaret B																							C						
Margaret C											15																		
Martin	20	17	8																										
Annunciation		1																											
Nativity of the Virgin Mary									16		72						6												
Purification of the Virgin Mary	19	13																											
Assumption of the Virgin Mary						54																							
Assumption of the Virgin Mary				11																									
Malchus																													2c
Mary of Egypt														31						2			12						
Michael A		16																											
Michael B				17																									
Mildred A																					3								
Mildred B																										1			
Neot								34								43													
Nicholas																													
Pantaleon																											14		
Paulinus					75																								
Peter and Paul		15																											
Quintin																						4							
Seven Sleepers														30									13						
Vitas Patrum																													2

Notes

1. The sigla used are those of my analysis of the anonymous homiletic corpus, "The Corpus of Vernacular Homilies and Prose Saints' Lives Before Ælfric," *ASE* 8 (1979): 223–77. The present review excludes physical description of the manuscripts and detailed discussion of their contents beyond what is necessary in a consideration of items relevant to this chapter, because both are dealt with fully by N. R. Ker, *Catalogue of Manuscripts Containing Anglo-Saxon* (Oxford, 1957; cited as Ker, *Catalogue*), whose dating is universally adopted here. His "A Supplement to *Catalogue of Manuscripts Containing Anglo-Saxon*," *ASE* 5 (1976): 121–31, is cited as (S).

2. For a full discussion, see my "The Compilation of the Vercelli Book," *ASE* 2 (1973): 189–207, and my edition *The Vercelli Homilies and Related Texts*, EETS 300 (London, 1992), together with *The Vercelli Book*, ed. Celia Sisam, EEMF 19 (Copenhagen, 1976).

3. See the discussion in Mary Clayton, *The Cult of the Virgin Mary in Anglo-Saxon England* (Cambridge, 1990), pp. 218 ff.

4. See my "Compilation," pp. 202–3.

5. Latin quotations are recorded in two copies of the Old English life, and these are then translated. In one case, the Latin does not correspond to anything in Sulpicius, cf. *The Blickling Homilies*, ed. Richard Morris, EETS 58, 63, 73 (London, 1874–80), p. 219, line 33, and my *The Vercelli Homilies*, p. 290.

6. For details, see my "The Homilies of the Blickling Manuscript," *Learning and Literature in Anglo-Saxon England*, ed. Michael Lapidge and Helmut Gneuss (Cambridge, 1985), pp. 299–316.

7. See Clayton, *Cult of the Virgin Mary*, p. 223.

8. Rudolph Willard, in *The Blickling Homilies*, EEMF 10 (Copenhagen, 1960), p. 38n, suggests that this is deliberate, but see the answer in Milton McC. Gatch, "Eschatology in the Anonymous Old English Homilies," *Traditio* 21 (1965): 117–65 on p. 118, n. 7.

9. On the textual transmission, see my "Homilies of the Blickling Manuscript," pp. 313–14. On the relationship with sources, see Clayton, *Cult of the Virgin Mary*, pp. 232–24.

10. See my "Homilies of the Blickling Manuscript," p. 314.

11. For a fuller analysis of the manuscript and its contents, see J. N. Chadbon, "Oxford, Bodleian Library, MSS Junius 85 and 86: an Edition of a Witness to the Old English Homiletic Tradition," D. Phil. dissertation, University of Leeds (1994).

12. See Mary Clayton, "The Assumption Homily in CCCC 41," *Notes and Queries* 234 (1989): 293–95. The text is edited by Raymond J. S. Grant in *Three Homilies from Cambridge, Corpus Christi College 41* (Ottawa, 1982).

13. The piece is edited in *Vier Altenglische Predigten aus der Heterodoxen Tradition*, ed. H. L. C. Tristram (Freiburg im Breisgau, Germany, 1970), cited as Tristram, and by Grant (see previous note).

14. See Kenneth Sisam, *Studies in the History of Old English Literature* (Oxford, 1953), pp. 148–98.

15. Details are in N. R. Ker, "A Study of the Additions and Alterations in MSS Bodley 340 and 342," DPhil. dissertation, Oxford University (1933).

16. See Sisam, *Studies*, p. 155; my "Homilies of the Blickling Manuscript" has a full discussion of the compilation of F.

17. See Ker, *Catalogue*, p. 56.

18. *The Old English Finding of the True Cross*, ed. and trans. Mary Catherine Bodden (Cambridge, 1987), pp. 20–21, lists differences of vocabulary between the two copies but her commentary on them is unreliable.

19. *History of the Holy Rood-Tree*, ed. A. S. Napier, EETS 103 (London, 1894), pp. lvii–lix.

20. See Walter Hofstetter, *Winchester und der Spätaltenglische Sprachgebrauch* (Munich, 1987), pp. 223–24.

21. See *Ælfric's Catholic Homilies: The Second Series*, ed. M. R. Godden, EETS SS 5 (London, 1979), pp. xxxvii–xxxix.

22. *Angelsächsische Homilien und Heiligenleben*, ed. Bruno Assmann, Bibliothek der Angelsäschsichen Prosa 3 (Kassel, Germany, 1889), referred to as Assmann.

23. Mary Clayton has expressed the view that the text is of eleventh-century composition (*Cult of the Virgin Mary*, pp. 245–53), and few would quarrel with her ability to judge on grounds of content. But the evidence here is far from clearcut, and some linguistic features point to earlier composition (cf. Hofstetter, *Winchester und der Spätaltenglische Sprachgebrauch*, p. 237).

24. For details see F. Wormald, *English Drawings of the Tenth and Eleventh Centuries* (London, 1952), no. 31.

25. The prognostics and the Ælfric are together also in another manuscript, BL, Cotton Titus D.xxvi–xxvii; see *Ælfric's De Temporibus Anni*, ed. Heinrich Henel, EETS 213 (London, 1942), pp. x–xxxix, for details of errors common to Titus and Tiberius A.iii.

26. Printed in Godden, *Ælfric's Catholic Homilies*, Appendix.

27. See my "'The Devil's Account of the Next World' Revisited," *AN&Q* 24 (1986): 107–10.

28. See Henel's *Ælfric's De Temporibus Anni*, pp. x ff.

29. See Clayton, *Cult of the Virgin Mary*, p. 244.

30. *The Life of St Chad*, ed. R. Vleeskruyer (Amsterdam, 1953).

31. *Middle English Religious Prose*, ed. N. F. Blake (London, 1972), p. 2.

32. Godden, *Ælfric's Catholic Homilies*, p. 362.

33. Bodden, *Finding of the True Cross*, pp. 12–23, lists some, although I cannot agree with all of her commentary.

34. P. A. M. Clemoes, "The Chronology of Ælfric's Works," in *The Anglo-Saxons: Studies presented to Bruce Dickins*, ed. Peter Clemoes (London, 1959), pp. 212–47, on p. 222. The article is available now as a reprint in *Old English Newsletter, Subsidia* 5 (1980).

35. See Ker, *Catalogue*, p. 210.

36. Ker, ibid.; Clemoes, "Chronology," p. 219, n. 2.

37. Noted by Ker, ibid., p. 208.

38. "Zu den Vorlagen der ae. Handschrift Cotton Julius E.vii," *Neuphilologische Mitteilungen* 72 (1971): 711–15. A wider linguistic analysis is available in Hugh Magennis, "Contrasting Features in the Non-Ælfrician Lives in the Old English *Lives of Saints*," *Anglia* 104 (1986): 316–48.

39. See Ker, *Catalogue*, p. 424.

40. See ibid., p. 271, and Peter Clemoes, "Supplementary Introduction," added to the reissue of Bruno Assmann, *Angelsächsische Homilien und Heiligenleben* (Darmstadt, Germany, 1964), p. xvi.

41. *The Anglo-Saxon Chronicle: A Collaborative Edition*, ed. David Dumville and Simon Keynes, vol. 17. *The Annals of St. Neots with Vita Prima Sancti Neoti*, ed. David Dumville and Michael Lapidge (Cambridge, 1984), p. lxxxii.

42. Ibid., p. cxvi.

43. The text is in *Leechdoms, Wortcunning, and Starcraft of Early England*, ed. T. O. Cockayne (London, 1864–66), vol. 3, pp. 422–28; the parallel section runs from the beginning to p. 424, line 2. See also M. J. Swanton, "A Fragmentary Life of St. Mildred and Other Kentish Royal Saints," *Archaeologia Cantiana* 91 (1975): 15–27.

44. See Ker, p. 173, and D. W. Rollason, "Lists of Saints' Resting Places in Anglo-Saxon England," *ASE* 7 (1978): 61–93 on pp. 73–75.

45. See D. W. Rollason, *The Mildrith Legend* (Leicester, England, 1982).

46. See *The Old English Life of Machutus*, ed. David Yerkes (Toronto, 1984), pp. xxvii ff.

47. Ibid., pp. xxxvi–ix.

48. Details in Ker, *Catalogue*, p. 226.

49. Ibid., p. 280.

50. K. Sisam, *Studies*, pp. 68–72.

51. See Hofstetter, *Winchester und der Spätaltenglische Sprachgebrauch*, p. 246, to which may be added the spelling *þeossum*.

52. There is a twelfth-century Latin life of Seaxburg in Cambridge, Trinity College 0.2.1, with a reference to a vernacular life earlier, but there is no evidence that the fragment here is the latter, although it may have drawn on it. For a different view, see Rollason, *Mildrith Legend*.

53. Seaxburg, queen of the Kentish king Eorcenbriht (640–664), became the second abbess of Ely. This text has her ruling Kent as a widow for thirty years before handing over the kingdom to her son Hloðhere. But this ignores Hloðhere's elder brother Egbert, who ruled Kent until 673, and Hloðhere himself died in 685. See F. M. Stenton, *Anglo-Saxon England*, 3d ed. (Oxford, 1971), p. 61, and D. P. Kirby, *The Earliest English Kings* (London, 1991), p. 44.

54. K. Sisam, *Studies*, pp. 199–224.

55. *Angelsächsische Homilien und Heiligenleben*, no. 18.

56. See Hofstetter, *Winchester und der Spätaltenglische Sprachgebrauch*, p. 247, and the references there.

57. See my "Corpus."

Appendix: The Three Anonymous Lives in Cambridge, Corpus Christi College 303

D. G. Scragg and Elaine Treharne

Considered individually or as a group, the lives of Margaret, Giles, and Nicholas in MS H have attracted little scholarly interest.[1] Yet within what has been written there are some broad claims concerning their origin; for example, that the pieces are of mid or late eleventh-century composition,[2] and that at least two of them are by the same author.[3] This appendix briefly reviews the evidence.

The unique copies of the three lives are found in Part I of MS H among *sanctorale* items incorporated into the second half of the annual cycle.[4] All three were copied by the second principal scribe of the manuscript. That they are copied in H and not composed there is clear from scribal errors such as dittography and homeoteleuton; for example, in Giles a sequence of three lines was copied twice (p. 126, lines 3–6). All three share the leveling and confusion of inflections in nouns, adjectives (especially noticeably in the determiner), and verbs characteristic of the twelfth-century language of the copyist and found throughout his stint. However, these morphological and syntactical features are noticeably more frequent in the three unique saints' lives; for example, the prepositional phrase *to ures sceppendes gode ælmihtigne* (Margaret, p. 100, lines 9–10) suggests considerable confusion of the Old English inflectional system (the scribe or a later reader excised final *s* from the first two words, but left *ælmihtigne*). Gender confusion is widely apparent in determiners, such as *uppan þære sastrande* (OE *strand* is neuter).[5] Verbs consistently have vowel leveling, such as *ge sculon finden* (Margaret, p. 100, line 11) and *heo wolden healdon* (Nicholas, p. 177, line 12). But such confusion in the grammar of the pieces, widespread though it is, may be the work of a copyist. For an indication of the date of their translation into English we need to examine other evidence.

On the basis of church dedications and entries in monastic calendars, William Schipper came to the conclusion that "the cults of St. Giles and St.

Nicholas entered England at about the same time as the Norman conquerors did," and he adds: "a tentative date between 1067 and 1090 for the introduction of these cults into England . . . provides a convenient historical context for the translations into English of the lives of these saints."[6] Schipper's evidence and conclusions now need modification in respect of Nicholas, who appears in at least one pre-Conquest calendar entry, in BL Cotton Nero A.ii.[7] Furthermore, the earliest manuscript copy of the Latin life of Nicholas known to have been written in England, BL Cotton Nero E.i, was made by a Worcester scribe in the third quarter of the eleventh century, probably around 1060,[8] which means that the Latin life was circulating in England before the Conquest, possibly well before. The existence of a Margaret cult in England long before the Conquest is, of course, well attested. There is, then, no firm evidence that the translation into English of the three unique lives in H can be seen as part of a peculiarly Norman veneration of those saints.

There is no space here for a full linguistic analysis of the three pieces,[9] but a number of points of both similarity and dissimilarity between them can easily be demonstrated. First, the especially frequent instances of confusion of inflections referred to earlier, which might indicate that the three lives, although not consecutive pieces in H, were drawn from a single exemplar, should be seen alongside two lexical items that link them: the word *sæint-/seint-/seagnt-*, which appears only in post-Conquest texts, principally in charters and in late pieces in BL Cotton Vespasian D.xiv (see X[h]), occurs once in the Life of Nicholas and once in that of Margaret; and the lexeme *me*, which is first recorded in the Peterborough Chronicle s.v. 1110,[10] and again, perhaps significantly, in Vespasian D.xiv, occurs frequently in the Lives of Margaret and Nicholas as the indefinite pronoun. But this is evidence of no more than association of the two lives during their transmission, for there is a clear indication that the two were not translated together in the word used in each of them to represent "prison": *carcern* in Margaret (a term frequently used in early West Saxon and non-West Saxon texts but avoided in late West Saxon) and *cw(e)artern* in Nicholas (the term favored by Ælfric). Many linguistic features suggest a close association between the lives of Nicholas and Giles. J. E. Cross[11] has given a list of rare or unique lexical items in the two pieces, and others might be added; for example, in Giles we find *for hire anre sace*, which is perhaps the earliest recorded use of "sake" in its modern sense. Rare forms that the two have in common are *þærrihtes* with a late adverbial final *s* (six examples in Nicholas and sixteen in Giles, only very rarely elsewhere), the Latin borrowing *mægster* (one example in each) and the phrase *Godes deorling* (five examples in Nicholas and fifteen in Giles). These certainly point to Nicholas and Giles having a common origin.

However, in the last analysis it has to be admitted that tracing the history of these three pieces is made difficult by the proven linguistic intervention of the latest scribe, or at the very least of a twelfth-century predecessor. Throughout H there is ample evidence to suggest that a twelfth-century copyist imposed his own forms on the material, not necessarily in any regular or consistent way, but sufficiently frequently for us to doubt that the surviving texts are close to the form in which they were originally written. Two simple examples of scribal adulteration of the text are the frequent occurrence of the curious word *þonum* (= *þonne*), which may be a sign of the misunderstanding by late scribes of an Anglo-Saxon abbreviation, and the representation of the past plural 'saw' as *geseagon*, which is found throughout H, even in material (such as homilies by Ælfric) where the form is clearly not authorial. The substitution here is more than spelling: *geseagon* for *gesawon* is more analogous to word replacement. Scribal intervention, then, probably explains the occurrence of *sæint* and *me* in Margaret and Nicholas and might also (although less certainly) explain the common features of Nicholas and Giles. Thus, although the evidence of the cult of Giles, which is post-Conquest, points to the Giles piece having been translated into English no earlier than the second half of the eleventh century, the linguistic links between the Giles and Nicholas lives are not sufficiently strong for it to be certain that Nicholas is post-Conquest too, although the probability must be that it is. And there is no unambiguous linguistic evidence that associates the translation of the Margaret life with the same period.

Notes

1. See for example G. H. Gerould, "A New Text of the *Passio S. Margaretæ* with Some Account of the Latin and English Relations," *Publications of the Modern Language Assocation* 39 (1924): 525–56; C. W. Jones, *Saint Nicholas of Myra, Bari and Manhattan* (Chicago, 1978); and A. M. Luiselli Fadda, "La Versione anglosassone della *Vita sancti Ægidi abbatis*," *Romanobarbarica* 7 (1982–83): 273–352. Other works are cited in the following.

2. D. E. Ahern, "An Edition of Two Old English Saints' Lives: 'The Life of St. Giles' and 'The Life of St. Nicholas'," dissertation, University of Arizona (1975); B. Picard, *Das altenglische Aegidiusleben in MS CCCC 303*, Hochschulsammlung Philosophie, Literaturwissenschaft Bd. 7 (Freiburg, 1980); William Schipper, "The Normans and the Old English Lives of S. Giles and S. Nicholas," *International Christian University Language Research Bulletin* 1 (1985): 97–108.

3. Schipper, ibid.; Walter Hofstetter, *Winchester und der Spätaltenglische Sprachgebrauch* (Munich, 1987), p. 245.

4. See MS H, pp. 213–14.

5. *The Life of Margaret* is edited by Bruno Assmann as his no. 15 in *Angelsächsische Homilien und Heiligenleben*. There is no widely available edition of

the others. No reference is given in this chapter to examples that can be found easily in the Toronto Microfiche Concordance.

6. Schipper, "The Normans," p. 102.

7. See *A Pre-Conquest English Prayer-Book*, ed. Bernard James Muir, Henry Bradshaw Society 103 (London, 1988), p. 14.

8. See *Two Anglo-Saxon Pontificals*, ed. H. M. J. Banting, Henry Bradshaw Society 104 (London, 1989), p. 1.

9. For such an analysis, see Elaine Margaret Treharne, "Corpus Christi College, Cambridge 303 and the Lives of Saints Margaret, Giles and Nicholas," dissertation, University of Manchester (1992).

10. See *The Peterborough Chronicle 1070–1154*, ed. Cecily Clark, 2d ed. (Oxford, 1970), p. 35, line 26.

11. "Lexicographical Notes on the Old English 'Life of St. Giles' and the 'Life of St. Nicholas'," *Notes and Queries* 216 (1971): 369–72.

The Dissemination of Ælfric's *Lives of Saints*: A Preliminary Survey

Joyce Hill

When Ælfric issued his *Lives of Saints* collection, he concluded his English preface with the directive to subsequent users that copies should be accurately made and that no material should be added: "Ic bidde nu on godes naman gif hwa þas boc awritan wille . þæt he hi wel gerihte be þære bysne . and þær namare betwux ne sette þonne we awendon."[1] He had issued a similar but more strongly worded directive at the end of the *Catholic Homilies:* "Gif hwa ma awendan wille. ðonne bidde ic hine for godes lufon þæt he gesette his boc onsundron. fram ðam twam bocum ðe we awend habbað we truwiað þurh godes diht."[2] In neither case, however, was Ælfric's directive followed. Even during his lifetime, as exemplified by Oxford, Bodleian Library, Bodley 340, the *Catholic Homilies* were being anthologized with anonymous ones, and three of them were even used to provide for the last three days of Holy Week, contrary to Ælfric's unambiguous, repeated statements that no homilies should be preached on these days.[3] Likewise, the *Lives of Saints* collection, in the form of London, British Library, Cotton Julius E. vii, as early as the beginning of the eleventh century already incorporated non-Ælfric items.[4] For the *Catholic Homilies* we are fortunate in having manuscripts that take us very close indeed to Ælfric's original series before they were modified by others, and there are also manuscripts that give some insight into how Ælfric himself developed the collection. By contrast, for the *Lives of Saints* only Julius E. vii survives undamaged as a witness to the *sanctorale* in year order, beginning with the Nativity on 25 December and concluding with Thomas on the subsequent December 21. It has the advantage of being an early manuscript, and it is evidently not far removed from the original, since it includes Ælfric's Latin and Old English prefaces.[5] Yet, as already noted, it incorporates non-Ælfric items in defiance of Ælfric's prefatory directive. A further complication is that it includes items by Ælfric that are non-hagiographical, and we have no certain knowledge whether these were all part of Ælfric's original conception.[6]

The preeminent position that Julius E. vii must necessarily have in a study of the dissemination and use of Ælfric's *Lives of Saints* is therefore simply a result of accident of survival. It does not represent the collection as issued by Ælfric, and it is not the manuscript from which all other copies of Julius E. vii items ultimately derive; consequently it is important to establish the nature and presentation of the somewhat mixed contents of Julius E. vii before proceeding with a survey of the items represented in it. Additionally, attention will need to be paid to the presentation of this manuscript in Skeat's edition of the *Lives of Saints,* because this inevitably conditions our conception of the collection and influences the terms in which it is usually discussed. Only then will it be possible to present a tabulated survey of the occurrence in all other manuscripts of Julius E. vii texts. The three final items, which do not fall within the December to December cycle, will be excluded,[7] as will Ælfric's prefaces, which are unique to Julius E. vii; all other items will be represented, including the non-Ælfrician saints' lives and Ælfric's non-hagiographical pieces. The survey attempts to be comprehensive and therefore includes whole, damaged, and lost texts (insofar as these can be positively identified), texts accidentally incomplete, and extracts, whether free-standing or combined with other material. In this survey I depend principally on Ker's *Catalogue*;[8] if there are corrections or additions to be made, I should be glad to receive notice of them.

Julius E. vii and Skeat's Edition

Ælfric's Old English preface indicates that the *Lives of Saints* collection was worked on over a period of time; composition and completion is datable to the decade 992–1002.[9] Julius E. vii, the best extant witness, is dated by Ker as s. xi in.[10] It is mainly in one hand, although it has been modified since first being put together. The non-Ælfrician Mary of Egypt (122v–36r, Skeat XXIIIB), apparently copied from a faulty exemplar,[11] was added after the main scribe drew up the table of contents on fol. 4v, because it is not listed. Additionally, there is evidence of insertion at the point where the text occurs. The writing of Mary of Egypt, as well as part of the non-Ælfrician preceding item, the Seven Sleepers (107v–22v, Skeat XXIII), is more compressed than elsewhere, and Mary of Egypt ends part way down 136r, with the rest of the recto and all of the verso blank, the blank space completing a four-leaved quire before the next item begins on 137r. The Seven Sleepers is probably also an addition,[12] although it is included in the scribe's contents list, as are the two other non-Ælfrician lives, Eustace (163v–69v, Skeat XXIX) and

Eufrasia or Euphrosyne (207r–13v, Skeat XXXIII). The text of the Seven
Sleepers ends abruptly and has been provided by another scribe with a brief
formal doxology by way of conclusion (Skeat XXIII, 838–40). The copy in
London, British Library, Cotton Otho B. x does not have the Julius doxology
but it formerly continued beyond the point where the abrupt end occurs in the
Julius copy, and in Otho B. x this further material must have amounted to
about 100 lines.[13] There are no peculiarities of this sort in connection with
Eustace and Euphrosyne, although one wonders why Euphrosyne (feast day
February 11) is written out between Edmund (November 20) and Cecilia
(November 22) in what is otherwise a well-ordered collection.[14]

The non-hagiographical items by Ælfric are all in the contents list and
evidently integral to the manuscript. These are: the Nativity (Skeat I), Ash
Wednesday (Skeat XII: recognized in the manuscript as suitable for preaching in anticipation on the previous Sunday), the Prayer of Moses (Skeat XIII:
so named, but also rubricated for Mid-Lent Sunday), the Memory of the
Saints (Skeat XVI), On Auguries (Skeat XVII: listed by the scribe as "De
Auguriis" and thus titled in other manuscripts, but rubricated on fol. 82r
simply as "Sermo in laetania maiore"), From the Book of Kings (Skeat XVIII),
and Maccabees (Skeat XXV). My classification of them as non-hagiographical,
in the sense of not being saints' lives or passions, follows Zettel,[15] although
it is possible that the Memory of the Saints, positioned midway through
Julius E. vii, was originally written by Ælfric as an introduction to the *Lives
of Saints* collection.[16]

We know, of course, that the collection did not originally include Mary
of Egypt, the Seven Sleepers, Eustace, and Euphrosyne, but we do not know
if it was ever issued without Ælfric's non-hagiographical items. It is possible
that it was,[17] but it is also probable that it was Ælfric himself who issued a
collection mixing some non-hagiographical items with saints' lives. The chief
evidence for this is that the non-hagiographical items, along with a good
number of saints' lives, are found in Cambridge, University Library Ii. 1. 33,
a twelfth century manuscript that is textually in a distinct line of transmission
from Julius E. vii.[18] The Julius manuscript is also mixed in including the
Interrogationes Sigewulfi, *De Falsis Deis*, and *De Duodecim Abusivis*, but
again the juxtapositioning may be traceable to Ælfric, because these too are
found in CUL Ii. 1. 33.[19] They are variously positioned in CUL Ii. 1. 33,
which is not an ordered collection, but in Julius E. vii they stand outside the
sanctorale sequence, following Thomas. Nevertheless, they are integral to the
manuscript and are included in the table of contents, although loss of leaves
at the end means that part of the Julius *De Falsis Deis* and the whole of its
De Duodecim Abusivis are lacking.

Thus, for all the non-hagiographical items by Ælfric, as also for the non-
Ælfric saints' lives, the scribe's table of contents has important evidential

value. Yet it is, at the same time, something of a hindrance to our understanding of the nature of the material within the *sanctorale* and consequently to any attempt to trace how this material was exploited elsewhere. The reason for this is that the scribe's listing does not acknowledge all the divisions in the manuscript; instead, he assigns one item number to each day and, with one exception, lists only one item per day (although he does not bring forward into his list the dates given in the rubrics). For most days there is only one item in the manuscript and the scribe's method consequently causes no difficulties, but there are certain days when a saint's life (duly listed and numbered in the scribal list) is followed in the body of the manuscript by another item or items, which may be significantly different; and in these cases the scribe's omission of the additional pieces is misleading, because it may disguise a marked change of subject. The omissions, however, are a logical consequence of the presentation of texts within the manuscript. What the scribe chooses to list are items that have a specific title; usually their rubrics also incorporate a date. What he ignores are companion pieces, which include no date in their rubric (because this is provided in the previous item) and which, whatever their subject, have the non-specific title of "alia sententia," "item," or "item alia." That this pattern of response governed the drawing up of the table of contents and the assigning of numbers is confirmed by the treatment of the companion narratives for Agatha and Lucy (Skeat VIII and IX). It is obvious from the opening of the Lucy narrative that Ælfric wrote these two lives as a consecutive pair, even though they do not have consecutive feast days, Agatha's being February 5 and Lucy's being December 13; that they were issued as a pair, despite the difference of date, is further confirmed by their consecutive appearance in London, British Library, Cotton Vitellius D. xvii, which is not an ordered collection. In the Julius manuscript, where they stand together as written, they are clearly intended for February 5, because Agatha comes first, in the correct calendar position, and has a rubric specifying the date; Lucy follows without a date, as is normal for a companion piece in this manuscript, but the narrative is, nevertheless, provided with a title, "De sancta lucia uirgo", which, uncharacteristically for a companion piece, identifies the new subject. At first the scribe followed his usual practice and listed Agatha only, which he numbered VIII. But he evidently noticed the distinctive title for Lucy and responded to it by carefully adding "Et sancta lucia" on the same line as Agatha, reducing the size of the lettering to squeeze it in. By its position and the use of *Et* it is clearly shown to be a companion piece to Agatha and thus correctly shares the Agatha number. The scribe's numbering is supplied thereafter without a break, except that he omits Mary of Egypt altogether (perhaps because it was not in the manuscript when the list was made),[20] and he accidentally jumps from XVII to XIX in numbering the consecutive items "De libro regum" and "De sancto Albano."

Skeat, in his edition, dealt with Mary of Egypt by numbering it XXIIIB and to Lucy he gave the number IX, with the result that for the next nine items his numbering differs from the scribe's by one; they come together again at Alban, where the scribe jumped a number. Skeat was prepared to intervene editorially to "correct" the scribe's treatment of Lucy, when in fact the scribe had been perfectly consistent in his numbering method, and yet Skeat was not otherwise prepared to institute an editorial numbering system for the manuscript's contents; instead, apart from the Lucy "correction" and its consequences and the conservative method of numbering Mary of Egypt, which has no intrinsic connection with scribal item XXIII, he imposes the scribe's system on the body of the manuscript, where no numbers are used and where there is clear marking of more divisions than the scribe's and Skeat's numbers acknowledge. The difficulty is that if, as often, Skeat's numbers are used in modern scholarly discussion as a convenient way of identifying texts, they may confuse the picture by not signaling differences of subject. Skeat XIX provides a good example of the problem. If one begins investigating this by consulting the index to Ker's *Catalogue* (p. 530), where it is listed as "Alban. Skeat, no. XIX," it seems that Alban is a relatively popular subject, because there are references to six manuscripts. But this is misleading because "Alban" is in fact two items: a self-contained account of Alban's martyrdom (Skeat XIX, 1–154) drawn from Bede's *Historia Ecclesiastica*, and an "item alia" (Skeat XIX, 155–258), which is an equally self-contained piece using the Old Testament story of Absalom and Ahitophel (2 Samuel 15–16) as an exemplum in a homily on thieves and traitors. "Alban" as such occurs only in three manuscripts (see Table 2 below); it is "Absalom and Ahitophel" which occurs in six, three times with Alban, twice independently, and once in a composite text, no doubt because, as a moral tale with practical application, it was more open to general use than the principal item for June 22. Indeed, if we may trust Wanley,[21] the title given it in Vitellius D. xvii shows a response to it as a moral piece, rather than a narrative one, since it is called "De iniustis," even though it here still has what was presumably its original position relative to Alban. In presenting the Absalom and Ahitophel story from the Julius manuscript, Skeat naturally lists the manuscript's "item alia" title in his modern table of contents, and he gives it its own heading at the point where the text begins (p. 424), supplementing the manuscript's non-specific title with an editorial adaptation of the more informative title in Cambridge, Corpus Christi College 303, p. 340, where it occurs as a separate piece. Even so, it has the Alban number and is printed under the continuing editorial running title of "Passio Sancti Albani."

The independent use of the Absalom and Ahitophel text in CCCC 303 with an explicit title "Quomodo Acitofel 7 multi alii laqueo se suspenderunt" is symptomatic—as is the presentation of the same text in Vitellius D. xvii—of the fact that distinctions were fully recognized by medieval users, even though they were disguised by the method of presentation in the principal extant manuscript, which served as Skeat's exemplar. In order to carry out an analysis of the dissemination and use of the material in the *Lives of Saints* collection as we have it in Julius E. vii, it is thus necessary to observe all the distinctions of subject, because there may well be a difference, as in the case of Skeat XIX, between the popularity of the first and second subjects bearing a given number, which may in turn be related to a difference in their suitability for use in other contexts. To clarify this, Table 1 shows the scribe's contents list from Julius E. vii, his numbering sequence and that of Skeat, and the additional divisions that need to be observed.[22]

In every case the omission of the additional divisions from the contents list is consistent with the scribe's system. However, the divisions are all clearly signaled in the body of the manuscript by Latin headings, and this points to their potential for separate treatment in other contexts. Their subjects, briefly, are as follows:

Skeat VII, 296–429: *Alia sententia quam scripsit terrentianus.*
Additional hagiographical material concerning Constance and Gallicanus, Terrentianus and John and Paul. The preceding narrative for the day (January 21) describes how Agnes cures Constance of leprosy; Agnes and the *alia sententia* were clearly written as a pair.

Skeat XV, 104–226: *Item alia.*
Information about the Four Evangelists.

Skeat XIX, 155–258: *Item alia.*
The Old Testament narrative of Absalom and Ahitophel used as an exemplum in a homily against thieves and traitors (see p. 239).

Skeat XXI, 464–95: *Item alia.*
Macarius cures a maiden apparently transformed by sorcerers into a mare. Skeat's lines 496–98 are a formal homiletic conclusion. In the manuscript these come at the end of the Swithun narrative, but an eleventh-century corrector marked them for transposition to the end of the Macarius narrative and in this, as also in other instances, Skeat follows the corrector.[23] Here, however, I follow the actual arrangement in Julius E. vii.

Skeat XXIV, 81–191: *Item alia.*
The letter of Christ to Abgarus.

Skeat XXV, 205–811: *Item.*
A continuation of Maccabees, as the manuscript indicates by using *item* (uniquely), rather than *item alia*. Ælfric provided for a break here in the way that he wrote the narrative, presumably because it was so long. In all other copies surviving to the present day, but not in Julius E.vii, there are numbered sections in the longer second part, so that a reader could easily subdivide further.[24]

Table 1

Scribal Number	Skeat Number	Scribal Title: Contents List	Additional Divisions
I	I	DE NATIUITATE *CHRISTI*	
II	II	De Sancta Eugenia	
III	III	De Sancto Basilio	
IIII	IV	DE Sancto Iuliano *et* basilissa	
V	V	DE Sancto Sebastiano	
VI	VI	DE Sancto Mauro	
VII	VII	DE Sancta Agnete	(Agnes, Skeat VII, 1–295) Alia sententia quam scripsit terrentianus, Skeat VII, 296–429
VIII	VIII	DE Sancta Agatha	
	IX	Et sancta lucia	
VIIII	X	DE Cathedra sancti petri	
X	XI	DE xl. militibus	
XI	XII	DE capite Ieiunii	
XII	XIII	DE Oratione moysi	
XIII	XIV	DE Sancto Georgio	
XIIII	XV	DE Sancto Marco euangelista	(Mark, Skeat XV, 1–103) Item alia, Skeat XV, 104–226
XV	XVI	De Memoria sanctorum	
XVI	XVII	DE Auguriis	
XVII	XVIII	De libro regum	
XIX	XIX	De sancto Albano	(Alban, Skeat XIX, 1–154) Item alia, Skeat XIX, 155–258
XX	XX	DE Sancto æðeldryða	
XXI	XXI	DE Sancto swyðuno	(Swithun, Skeat XXI, 1–463, 496–98) Item alia, Skeat XXI, 464–95
XXII	XXII	DE Sancto Appollonare	
XXIII	XXIII [XXIIIB	DE VII.tem Dormientium Mary of Egypt]	
XXIIII	XXIV	DE Abone *et* senne	(Abdon and Sennes, Skeat XXIV, 1–80) Item alia, Skeat XXIV, 81–191
XXV	XXV	DE Machabeis	(Maccabbes, Skeat XXV, 1–204) Item, Skeat XXV, 205–811 Item alia, Skeat XXV, 812–62
XXVI	XXVI	DE Sancto Oswoldo	
XXVII	XXVII	DE Sancta cruce	
XXVIII	XXVIII	DE Legione thebeorum	
XXVIIII	XXIX	DE Sancto Dionisio	
XXX	XXX	DE Sancto Eustachio	
XXXI	XXXI	DE Sancto Martino	
XXXII	XXXII	DE Sancto Eadmundo	
XXXIII	XXXIII	DE Sancta eufrosia	
XXXIIII	XXXIV	De Sancta cæcilia	
XXXV	XXXV	DE Crisanto et daria	
XXXVI	XXXVI	DE Sancto THoma Apostolo	
XXXVII	XXXVII	DE Interrogationibus sigewulfi presbyter[i]	
XXXVIII	XXXVIII	DE Falsis diis	
XXXVIIII	XXXIX	De xii. Abusiuis	

Skeat XXV, 812–62: *Item alia.*

A statement, directed mainly at monks, about the three orders of society. Skeat's Latin title, supplementing the manuscript's *item alia,* is taken, with editorial emendation, from CCCC 303, p. 355, where the piece stands as a separate item headed "Qui sint Oratores. Laboratores. Bellatores."

Using the criteria already applied, I follow Zettel[25] in classifying four of these as non-hagiographical: Skeat XV, 104–226; XIX, 155–258; XXV, 205–811; XXV, 812–62. They are therefore additional to the non-hagiographical items listed on p. 237. Skeat XXI, 464–95, is a borderline case. Zettel does not comment on it in relation to its appearance in Julius E. vii, but he excludes it from the hagiographic canon in its "extended" form, by which he means those manuscripts where the entire Macarius story is combined with "De Auguriis" and further material about Saul and the Witch of Endor.[26]

Notwithstanding the mixture of items that we have in Julius E. vii, there is no mistaking Ælfric's fundamental intention, since he carefully explains in the Old English preface that, having included in the *Catholic Homilies* "þæra halgena þrowunga and lif . þe angel-cynn mid freols-dagum wurþað," the present book is to be "be þære halgena ðrowungum and life . . . þe mynster-menn mid heora þenungum betwux him wurðiað."[27] His principal source, as Zettel has shown, was a legendary that appears to have been compiled some-where in northern France not before c. 863.[28] No recensions earlier than or contemporary with Ælfric have been identified, but four out of the five later copies of English origin identified by Zettel provide evidence of the collec-tion as Ælfric knew it; Zettel calls this collection the Cotton-Corpus legend-ary. When Ælfric made his vernacular collection, using this legendary, he naturally supplemented it with English saints (Alban, Æthelthryth, Swithun, Oswald, Edmund), and for these he had to draw upon other sources, but for almost all of the rest he used the legendary. The exceptions are all the non-hagiographical items.[29]

By contrast with some of Ælfric's own items, the four items not by Ælfric harmonize with the collection's hagiographic intent particularly well, in being outright saints' lives. Furthermore, even though the surviving recen-sions of the Cotton-Corpus legendary do not suggest that their authors used this legendary's narratives as their immediate sources,[30] recensions of the sources of the Seven Sleepers, Mary of Egypt, and Eustace are in the collec-tion as we know it and could well have been in the collection as Ælfric knew it also. Thus, although their presence in Julius E. vii flies in the face of Ælfric's desire to have only his own work included, one can argue that, in terms of subject matter and for three of them in terms of hagiographic con-text, they do not in fact disturb the fundamental nature of the collection as much as some of Ælfric's texts do.

The Dissemination of Texts

Tables showing the dissemination of texts necessarily simplify, because they cannot take account of detailed differences between copies of the same text nor can they fully represent the complex and highly variable situation regarding free-standing extracts or the incorporation of parts of texts into a new textual context, whether by the original author or in non-authorial composites. They are, nevertheless, very useful reference points for further work, as we see from Ker's tables of Ælfric's *Catholic Homilies*,[31] Pope's of Ælfric's Supplementary Homilies,[32] and Scragg's of the vernacular homilies and prose saints' lives before Ælfric.[33] For the *Lives of Saints* collection there is a table of sorts in Skeat's edition,[34] but this is not comprehensive or detailed enough for modern scholars. In providing a new one here, albeit only as a preliminary survey, I take account of the full range of textual divisions outlined in Table 1 and use item and article numbers from Ker's *Catalogue* as a means of identification.

The following list identifies the relevant manuscripts and shows how they are positioned in Table 2. Within each group the manuscripts are arranged by date as given in Ker's *Catalogue*, and by Ker's item number where the dates cannot be distinguished. It should be noted that the classification of some of the fragments is highly conjectural.

Group A. Collections that are or appear to have been wholly or predominantly hagiographic

162.   London, British Library, Cotton Julius E.vii. s. xi in.

81.   Cambridge, Queens' College (Horne) 75 [and Bloomington, Lilly Library, Poole 10].[35] s. xi in. Binding fragments.

260.   London, British Library, Royal 8 c.vii, fols. 1 and 2. s. xi in. Binding fragments.

177.   London, British Library, Cotton Otho B. x, fols. 1–28, 31–50, 52, 53, 54(?), 56, 57, 59, 60, 65, 67 + Oxford, Bodleian Library, Rawlinson Q. e. 20. s. xi[1]. Badly damaged in the Cotton fire of 1731. In classifying the manuscript here, I take account only of Part A. Parts B and C may or may not have been originally part of the same manuscript. Even if they were, they do not affect the identity of Part A.

222.   London, British Library, Cotton Vitellius D. xvii, fols. 4–92. s.xi med. Seriously damaged in the Cotton fire of 1731.

138.   London, British Library, Cotton Caligula A. xiv, fols. 93–130. s.xi med. Thirty-eight leaves, a fragment of a larger manuscript. Fols. 125–130 are misbound at the end; they should precede fol. 93.

18.   Cambridge, University Library Ii. 1. 33. s.xii[2].

Group B. Collections of homilies with some saints' lives

48. Cambridge, Corpus Christi College 198. s. xi¹, xi². The items in Table 2 are among the additions made in hands nearly contemporary with the s. xi¹ original.
117. Gloucester Cathedral Library 35. s. xi¹–xi². Binding fragments.³⁶ Of the items in Table 2, Swithun is in a hand of s. xi¹ and Mary of Egypt in a hand of s. xi med.
63. Cambridge, Corpus Christi College 367, pt. II, fols. 3–6, 11–29. s. xii. Fragments of six quires muddled together.
310. Oxford, Bodleian Library, Bodley 340. s. xii².

Group C. Manuscripts that, in using material represented in the sanctorale part of Julius E. vii, draw upon the non-hagiographical items only

15. Cambridge, University Library Gg. 3. 28. s. x/xi.
38. Cambridge, Corpus Christi College 162, pp. 1–138, 161–564. s. xi in.
41. Cambridge, Corpus Christi College, 178 + 162, pp. 139–60. s. xi¹. There are two books of homilies here, one for general occasions and one for important festivals. The items in Table 2 are from the first of these and are all in CCCC 178.
68. Cambridge, Corpus Christi College 419 + 421, pp.1, 2. s. xi¹.
182. London, British Library, Cotton Otho C. i, vol. 2. s. xi in., xi med. This was damaged in the Cotton fire of 1731, but with little loss, except in item 5.
21. Cambridge, University Library Ii. 4. 6. s. xi med.
283. London, Lambeth Palace Library 489. s. xi 3rd quarter.³⁷
331. Oxford, Bodleian Library, Hatton 113, 114 (= Skeat's Junius 22)³⁸ s. xi 3rd quarter. The item in Table 2 is in Hatton 114.
338. Oxford, Bodleian Library, Junius 121. s. xi 3rd quarter.
332. Oxford, Bodleian Library, Hatton 115 (= Skeat's Junius 23). s. xi², xii med. The items in Table 2 are in the main body of the manuscript, not in the two quires of s. xii.
56. Cambridge, Corpus Christi College 302. s. xi/xii.
57. Cambridge, Corpus Christi College 303. s. xii¹.
153. London, British Library, Cotton Faustina A. ix. s. xii¹.
333. Oxford, Bodleian Library, Hatton 116 (= Skeat's Junius 24). s. xii¹.
209. London, British Library, Cotton Vespasian D. xiv, fols. 4-169. s. xii. med.

The details given in Table 2 under Ker 81 bring together information from Ker's *Catalogue* and "Supplement,"³⁹ and a study of the strips by Collins and Clemoes.[40] The fragments come from the *Catholic Homilies* and from the *Lives of Saints*, but it seems likely that the homilies and saints' lives were written out in two ordered sets and were kept separate, and that the surviving strips showing lives of saints were once part of a very early, whole set. I have therefore grouped this manuscript with those collections that are wholly or predominantly hagiographic because, even if the *Lives of Saints* were juxtaposed with the *Catholic Homilies*, the identity of the hagiographic collection was preserved, and it would have been far more closely allied to the nature of the collection in Julius E. vii than to collections in which individual saint's lives and homilies are intermingled. For convenience in tabulating, and also in conformity with Ker's "Supplement," the column for Ker 81 is used for all the strips, although those from the *Lives of Saints* have two locations:

Strip 4 (Ker, "Supplement"; strip 1 in the *Catalogue*): Cambridge, Queens' College (Horne 75). Part of Appollinaris, corresponding, with gaps, to Skeat XXII, 97–213.

Strips 5 and 6 (Ker, "Supplement"; not reported in the *Catalogue*): Bloomington, Lilly Library, Poole 10. These two strips were sewn together in their original relation and correspond, with gaps, to the end of Apollinaris (Skeat XXII, from 213), Abdon and Sennes (Skeat XXIV, without the non-Ælfrician Seven Sleepers and Mary of Egypt, which intervene in Julius E. vii) and the opening line of Christ's Letter to Abgarus (the *item alia* to Abdon and Sennes, Skeat XXIV, 81).

Strip 7 (Ker "Supplement"; strip 2 in the *Catalogue*): Cambridge, Queens' College (Horne 75). Part of Christ's Letter to Abgarus, corresponding, with gaps, to Skeat XXIV, 83–190, and the beginning of Maccabees (Skeat XXV, 1–8).

Skeat's numbers are given in the left column of Table 2, with those of the Julius scribe in brackets where they differ. The names of the four non-Ælfric items are italicized but the texts are otherwise treated normally. The following symbols are used:

( )   lost or imperfect owing to external circumstances, but where Ker was nevertheless able to assign article numbers;

*   unequivocal evidence for existence but no article number, owing to loss of most of the manuscript;

-       extract, either free-standing or because apparently copied from an incomplete exemplar;

+   whole text combined with other material;

-+   extract combined with other material.

Table 2

	Group A							Group B				Group C													
	162	81	260	177	222	138	18	48	117	63	310	15	38	41	68	182	21	283	331	338	332	56	57	153	333	209
I Nativity	4										77-+					(5)-+										
II Eugenia	5			(9)																						
III Basil	6			(3)																						
IV Julian and Basilissa	7			(5)	(43)																					
V Sebastian	8			(6)	(13)			60																		
VI Maur	9			(4)																						
VII Agnes (1–295)	10		*	(7)	(47)																					
Alia Sententia (296–429)	11			(8)	(48)																					
VIII Agatha	12		*		(49)																					
IX [ ] Lucy	13				(50)																					
X [VIII] Chair of St Peter	14				(51)		6				22															
XI [X] 40 Soldiers	15																									
XII [XI] Ash Wednesday	16												14-+									17	67			
XIII [XIII] Prayer of Moses (Mid-Lent)	17																7 28-+									
XIV [XIII] George	18			(22)	(30)		26					(97)-+	6	7-+				6-+	47	26-+			68	18	19-+	7-
XV [XIIII] Mark (1–103)	19				8		19	59																		8-
Item alia (104–226)	20				9		20	59																		
XVI [XV] Memory of the Saints	21													7-+									62			
XVII [XVI] On Auguries	22													8-+	12						5	4	47		20-+	
XVIII [XVII] Kings	23																				33					
XIX Alban (1–154)	24				(52)		27																			
Item alia (155–258)	25				(53)		28											6-+			20		70			

Table 2 (*continued*)

	Group A							Group B				Group C														
	162	81	260	177	222	138	18	48	117	63	310	15	38	41	68	182	21	283	331	338	332	56	57	153	333	209
XX Æthelthryth	26			(23)	(54)		4																			
XXI Swithun (1–463, 496–98)	27			(20)					(1)																	
Item alia (464–95)	28																									
XXII Apollinaris	29-	*			(26)									8+											20+	
XXIII Seven Sleepers	30-			(13)																						
XXIIIB Mary of Egypt	31-			(12)					(2)																	
XXIV Abdon and Sennes (1–80)	32	*		(27)			} 37																			
Item alia (81–191)	33	*		(28)																						
XXV Maccabees (1–204)	34	*		(45)				} 52															} 71			
Item (205–811)	35			(46)			(35)							14									72			
Item alia (812–62)	36						36														11					
XXVI Oswold	37				(31)		31																			
XXVII Holy Cross	38				(37)		39																			
XXVIII Theban Legion (Maurice)	39				(33)					(7)																
XXIX Dionysius	40				(34)		32																			
XXX Eustace	41				(29)																					
XXXI Martin	42				(1)	(1)																				
XXXII Edmund	43			(21)	(42)		29-				18-31															
XXXIII Euphrosyne	44			(10)																						
XXXIV Cecilia	45				(25)																					
XXXV Chrysanthus and Daria	46			(32)	2																					
XXXVI Thomas	47						18-																			

Even in this preliminary survey, certain obvious patterns of dissemination and use are apparent. Saints' lives in themselves, being narratives, are
not readily open to selective re-use in composite homilies, and those produced by Ælfric as a fundamentally monastic collection generally appear in
a relatively small number of manuscripts, by contrast with the non-hagiographic
material, which is more widely scattered and in general more liable to adaptation.[41] As one might expect, the non-Ælfric saints' lives conform to this
rather restricted pattern. Furthermore, the hagiographical items mostly occur
either in *sanctorale* collections or in collections where saints' lives predomi-
nate (Group A in Table 2), a feature suggestive of a monastic milieu, where
there is need of a wider range of saints' lives than in the secular church.[42] By
contrast, from among the non-hagiographical items Ash Wednesday (Skeat
XII), the Prayer of Moses (Skeat XIII), Kings (Skeat XVIII), and the *item
alia* to Swithun (i.e., Macarius, Skeat XXI, 464–95) appear in conjunction
with the *Lives of Saints* hagiographies only in Julius E. vii, although they are
copied, and in some cases adapted, in other contexts. Given the loss of
manuscripts, it is unwise to put too much weight on this negative evidence,
but the fact that it is only non-hagiographical items that show this pattern of
non-association coupled with use elsewhere may support the view that they
were not all originally part of the *Lives of Saints* collection. The only other
items that do not appear in the first two groups of manuscripts are the Forty
Soldiers, and Chrysanthus and Daria, but these occur nowhere at all, beyond
Julius E. vii. Their dissemination (or lack of it) is therefore not comparable
to the non-hagiographic items and we must attribute their non-appearance
either to relative unpopularity or, more probably, to accident of survival.

If, in the present context, we may define hagiographies as those items that
are straightforward saints' lives or passions, or items that derive from the
Cotton-Corpus legendary, or both, it is noteworthy that only eight have an
existence outside the predominantly *sanctorale* collections represented by the
first block in the table and that they occur only once each. These are Sebastian
(Skeat V), Chair of St. Peter (Skeat X), Mark (Skeat XV), Swithun (Skeat
XXI), Mary of Egypt (Skeat XXIIIB), Holy Cross (Skeat XXVII), Martin
(Skeat XXXI), and Edmund (Skeat XXXII). Furthermore, they are confined to
four manuscripts that (if we admit Ker 117) provide a mixture of homilies and
saints' lives as preaching materials (the second block in the table, Ker 48–310).
What we may be seeing here, as homily collections were rearranged, is limited
transfer of hagiographic material from the monastic milieu of Ælfric's *Lives of
Saints* as originally conceived to a more secular milieu, such as Ælfric himself
had provided for in the *Catholic Homilies,* where, of course, certain major
saints were included, as they would always need to be in a secular collection.
Nevertheless, the exploitation of hagiographies once in the *Lives of Saints* set
is on a modest scale in the surviving compilations of this sort.

The Chair of St. Peter and Holy Cross may be considered together. Although each has its source in the Cotton-Corpus legendary,[43] neither of them is a saint's life as such. Each is used in a twelfth century manuscript, the Chair of St. Peter in Bodley 343 (Ker 310) and Holy Cross in CCCC 367 (Ker 63). Bodley 343 is a collection suitable for public preaching, because it brings together mainly *temporale* homilies and some major saints' life material, akin to Ælfric's mixed collection of *Catholic Homilies* for secular use, upon which it is heavily dependent; CCCC 367 although now fragmentary and muddled, was probably a similar kind of collection. The Chair of St. Peter and Holy Cross fit well into this context and their inclusion in such collections in the twelfth century perhaps reflects shifts in ecclesiastical fashion as certain feasts are more widely celebrated.

Also in Bodley 343, along with the Chair of St. Peter, are Martin and Edmund. Ælfric thought it suitable to include a life of Martin in his *Catholic Homilies* as a major saint honored by the English nation,[44] but he included him again in his "monastic" set, where he was given a much longer narrative. In Bodley 343 the longer life is exploited, but it is drastically abbreviated to a manageable preaching length, consistent with the other items in the manuscript.[45] Thus adapted, it performs the function of Ælfric's "secular" Martin narrative. It is therefore a special case in the present discussion, as it is also a special case in being the only true saint's life, as far as one can tell, to be intentionally modified.[46] Edmund must be presumed to have a place in the same collection because, as an English saint and a royal one at that, his narrative was of particular interest in a period that valued English cults.[47] In any case, even Ælfric had been prepared to expand the saints' life material in the First Series of *Catholic Homilies*,[48] so that, although in Bodley 343 we are not looking at "transfer" on any significant scale, there was good precedent for the augmentation of the hagiographical element in a secular collection.

Augmentation, although of a rather more piecemeal kind, is also what accounts for the presence of Sebastian and Mark (with the *item alia* following continuously) in CCCC 198 (Ker 48). The collection as initially written out was an ordered series of items, including some saints' lives drawn mainly from the *Catholic Homilies*, but there were then some near-contemporary additions, in which more attention was given to saints, drawing chiefly on the *Catholic Homilies* again and, to a lesser extent, on the *Lives of Saints*. Sebastian and Mark are in the third group of additions (291r–321v, 386r–94v; quires 37–41, 50), which was made by the scribe who completed the last of the homilies in the basic collection before it was augmented.

For Swithun and Mary of Egypt there is only the evidence of the binding strips in Gloucester Cathedral Library 35 (Ker 117) and these are insufficient for the original context or contexts to be determined. Three of the five items testified to by the fragments are by Ælfric (Swithun, the Passion of the Apostles

Peter and Paul from the First Series of *Catholic Homilies,* and the Feast of St. Peter from the Second Series); thus, with Mary of Egypt, four of the five items are hagiographical. The imperfect extract from the Benedictine rule (Ker 117, item 3) was probably added later. It is an open question whether this group of fragments testifies to a single manuscript consisting mainly of saints' lives. If it does, it should be classified in the first group of manuscripts in the table, rather than in the second group, where I have more cautiously placed it.

The dissemination of Maccabees (Skeat XXV), although not of the *item alia* on the three orders of society,[49] follows the same pattern as the hagiographical items just discussed in being preserved in the mixed collections of the table's second group of manuscripts, as well as in the more firmly hagiographic first group. Yet, in common with other non-hagiographic items, it also occurs separately from *Lives of Saints* material. Its characteristic title of *Passio Sanctorum Machabeorum* suggests that it could be read as if it were a hagiographic narrative, and as usual with hagiographies, it is copied entire. Yet it is something of an oddity: it is an Old Testament paraphrase, there is no source for it in the Cotton-Corpus legendary, and it is long—far too long to be adopted as a preaching text as it stands and too long perhaps even for reading at one time, as Ælfric seems to have acknowledged in writing in the opportunity for a break at Skeat XXV, 204/205. The possibility for further division, signaled by numbered sections in manuscripts other than Julius E. vii has already been noted.[50] Yet the divisions did not prompt scribes to copy part of the text. On the contrary, while the more hagiographic manuscripts at least observe Ælfric's stylistically signaled break at lines 204/205, there are no separate headings in CCCC 198 (Ker 48) and CCCC 303 (Ker 57). A further point of contrast between the occurrences of Maccabees in these two manuscripts and the more firmly hagiographic ones is that in each it stands somewhat outside the main body of material. In CCCC 198 it is in one of the blocks of near-contemporary additions, although not the same block as Swithun and Mark. Clearly it is part of the hagiographic augmentation of this collection; we might go so far as to conjecture that the additional block that includes Maccabees (328r–366v, 378r–385v; quires 42–46, 49) was taken from an ordered *sanctorale,* because it consists of homilies for saints' days in August, September, and November. Even so, Maccabees is the only one in the block taken from the *Lives of Saints* collection as we know it. It is likewise an addition to CCCC 303, where it is in a curious Old Testament group consisting of Absalom and Ahitophel (Skeat XIX, 155–258), all of Maccabees, the *item alia* to Maccabees (i.e., the three orders of society, Skeat XXV, 812–62), and Ælfric's homily on the Book of Judith (ending lost).[51] Maccabees proper is given its standard rubric *Kal. Augusti Passio Sanctorum Machabeorum.* The monastic-oriented statement on the three orders of society follows, as it does in Julius E. vii, CUL Ii. 1. 33, and CCCC 198, but it is separately titled in CCCC 303 as a distinct piece.[52] The preservation of what seems to have been the original arrangement,[53] as well as the form of the rubric to Maccabees proper, suggests that here too the exemplar might well have been a hagiographic collection not dissimilar to those represented by the first group of manuscripts in Table 2. Even so, its position in the manuscript and its immediate context do not point to any quasi-hagiographic interest or to copying for use in preaching, but to a desire by the scribe to make a collection of Old Testament narratives.

The Book of Kings is the only other Old Testament paraphrase in Julius E. vii. There is no source for it in the Cotton-Corpus legendary and, like Maccabees, it seems somewhat out of place in the Julius collection. In some respects it is even more of an anomaly because it is not attributed to a day, as Maccabees is and as hagiographical items generally are, nor, by contrast with Maccabees, does its heading *Sermo excerptus de libro regum* indicate that it has any claims to a place in a *sanctorale*. It also seems to be less popular than Maccabees, surviving only in one other manuscript, Hatton 115 (Ker 332). This anthology contains a number of homilies, but it is a varied collection of vernacular ecclesiastical materials, and its rationale, if any, is difficult to grasp. The epitome of Kings, for that is really what it is, comes very near the end of the manuscript, where its immediate context is not hagiographic, but Old Testament, since three of the four preceding items are concerned with Exodus and Numbers (a homily by Ælfric), Judges (translation), and Genesis (*Interrogationes Sigewulfi*).[54]

With Maccabees and Kings, we have moved finally into the third group of manuscripts in the table, where only items that we have identified in Julius E. vii as non-hagiographic are represented. We can see at a glance that these texts are used differently from the saints' lives. On the other hand, comparison with Ker's analysis of the *Catholic Homilies*[55] and Scragg's of the anonymous homilies[56] shows that the nature and extent of their exploitation is similar to that of the *temporale* and moral homilies by Ælfric and the anonymous homilists, since these, like the non-hagiographical items recorded in Julius E. vii, are employed in various contexts and are often adapted and re-used, sometimes by the author himself in the case of Ælfric's texts, and sometimes by others.[57] They are amenable to adaptation in not having a narrative base, while their moral concerns make them useful in a wide range of ecclesiastical contexts. Thus the Prayer of Moses (Skeat XIII) was useful enough to be copied entire on several occasions, either for mid-Lent, as rubricated in Julius E. vii, or as a general homily "quando uolueris,"[58] but additionally the statement on the need to avoid indecorous behavior and drunkenness in church (68–86) was selected for use in other contexts, as was the warning against excessive fasting (98–101).[59] Similarly the Ash Wednesday homily (Skeat XII), also presented as a *temporale* homily in the Julius collection, was copied entire and adapted, in the case of CCCC 162 (Ker 38) not radically so, but in order to give greater prominence to the address to the lay congregation by expanding Skeat XXII, 289–92 and then placing this explanation at the beginning of the homily rather than at the end.[60] The Nativity homily (Skeat I) is another *temporale* item. So also is *De Auguriis* (Skeat XVII), which, although listed thus in the scribe's table of contents, is rubricated *Sermo in laetania maiore* at the point where it occurs (82r). It also has a *temporale* rubric when used in other manuscripts[61] and, as a homily on omens, is combined with the Macarius story in CCCC 178 (Ker 41) and Hatton 166 (Ker 333) to produce a distinctly non-hagiographical text.[62] The Memory of the Saints (Skeat XVI) was a useful item in any homiletic collection, secular or monastic, but when it was drawn upon selectively, what proved to be valuable was the definition of the vices and virtues, rather than the historical narrative with which it begins.[63] Likewise the practical morality of the *item alia* to Alban (Skeat XIX, 464–95) ensured its re-use as a separate item,[64] and the general applicability to society as a whole must have accounted for the independent copying of the *item alia* to Maccabees (Skeat XXV, 812–62), described in CCCC 178 (Ker 41) as *De tribus ordinibus saeculi* and in Hatton 115 (Ker 332) as *Qui sint Oratores. Laboratores. Bellatores.*

The *Lives of Saints* collection has an unfortunate history of loss and damage, and when the surviving evidence is so incomplete, it is dangerous to rely too much upon apparent patterns of dissemination and use. Nevertheless, when one tabulates what is known or known about, there is a measure of consistency, enough at least for us to see that, with regard to the collection as we have it in Julius E. vii, there is a broad contrast between the use of hagiographic and non-hagiographic material or, to put it another way, between what is derived from the Cotton-Corpus legendary (always admitting the supplementation by English saints) and what is not. On the other hand, as one might have expected, there is no distinction between Ælfrician and non-Ælfrician saints' lives, although it would be useful to extend the comparison beyond the four included here. Whether there is a distinction between the dissemination and use of Ælfric's "monastic" hagiographies and his "secular" ones remains to be seen. Beyond that, with a collaborative edition of the *Lives of Saints* being planned, we may look forward to work being done on the textual transmission of the material tabulated here, so that the relationships of the various recensions and adaptations may be more thoroughly understood.

Notes

1. *Ælfric's Lives of Saints*, ed. Walter W. Skeat, 2 vols. in 4 parts, EETS OS 76, 82, 94, 114 (London, 1881–1900); reprinted as 2 vols. (London, 1966) vol. 1, p. 6. References to the Skeat edition throughout are to the two-volume reprint.

2. *Ælfric's Catholic Homilies: The Second Series. Text*, ed. Malcolm Godden, EETS SS 5 (London, 1979), p. 345.

3. For an account of this early eleventh century manuscript, see *Ælfric's Catholic Homilies*, ed. Godden, pp. xxv–xxviii; for detailed discussion of Ælfric's refusal, in both series, to provide homilies for Maundy Thursday, Good Friday, and Holy Saturday and the overriding of his pronouncements by using anonymous homilies, see Joyce Hill, "Ælfric's 'Silent Days'," *Leeds Studies in English*, n.s. 16 (1985): 118-31. For further information on the tradition of silence on the last three days of Holy Week, see Roberta Frank, "A Note on Old English *Swigdagas* 'Silent Days'," *Studies in Honour of René Derolez*, ed. A. M. Simon-Vandenbergen (Ghent, 1987), pp. 180–89.

4. Seven Sleepers (Skeat XXIII), Mary of Egypt (Skeat XXIIIB), Eustace (Skeat XXX), Eufrasia or Euphrosyne (Skeat XXXIII). Hugh Magennis, "Contrasting Features in the Non-Ælfrician Lives in the Old English Lives of Saints," *Anglia* 104 (1986): 316–48, reviews the scholarship that established the recognition that these pieces are not by Ælfric; his own study leads to the further conclusion that each is by a different author. On the Seven Sleepers in particular, see Hugh Magennis, "Style and Method in the Old English Version of the Legend of the Seven Sleepers," *English Studies* 66 (1985): 285–95. See also the articles by Magennis listed in note 30, and *The Anonymous Legend of the Seven Sleepers*, ed. Hugh Magennis (Durham, 1994).

5. It is the only manuscript to do so. The manuscripts of the *Catholic Homilies* show that prefatory material of this sort is dropped at a fairly early stage in the transmission process.

6. See pp. 248–52. Ælfric's Life of St. Vincent is printed by Skeat in an Appendix as XXXVII, but since it did not form part of Ælfric's *Lives of Saints* collection and is not in Julius E. vii, it will not be discussed in this article. On its composition and use, see Susan E. Irvine, "Bones of contention: the context of Ælfric's homily on St. Vincent," *ASE* 19 (1990): 117–32, and Alex Nicholls, "Ælfric's 'Life of St. Vincent': the Question of Form and Function," *Notes and Queries* 241 (1991): 445–50.

7. For these, see p. 237.

8. N. R. Ker, *Catalogue of Manuscripts Containing Anglo-Saxon* (Oxford, 1957). For further comment on many of the manuscripts referred to in the course of this survey, see P. A. M. Clemoes, "The Chronology of Ælfric's Works," *The Anglo-Saxons: Studies in Some Aspects of their History and Culture, Presented to Bruce Dickins*, ed. P. A. M. Clemoes (London, 1959), pp. 212–47 (now reprinted as *Old English Newsletter, Subdidia* 5 [1980]); *The Homilies of Ælfric: A Supplementary Collection*, ed. John C. Pope, EETS OS 259, 260 (London, 1967–68); Godden, *Ælfric's Catholic Homilies*; D. G. Scragg, "The Corpus of Vernacular Homilies and Prose Saints' Lives Before Ælfric," *ASE* 8 (1979): 223–77.

9. Clemoes, "Chronology," p. 244. Ælfric explains to Æðelweard that he has proceeded with the collection only as he has had leisure to do so (Skeat, p. 4).

10. Ker, *Catalogue*, item 162. Reference to Ker is by item number throughout, with the addition of article numbers as necessary. There is a thirteenth-century inscription on fol. 3 which shows that the manuscript belonged to Bury St. Edmunds.

Pope, *The Homilies of Ælfric*, vol. 1, p. 85, note 1, reports Clemoes as observing that, if Ker is correct in his estimate of s.xi.in as the date of the manuscript, it was probably written before 1020, when the Benedictine Abbey was founded. However, the status of Bury before this date and the reliability of the 1020 annal have recently been reassessed by David Dumville, *English Caroline Script and Monastic History: Studies in Benedictinism*. A. D. 950–1030 (Woodbridge, 1993), pp. 30–48. In the context of this reassessment, Dumville concludes that Bury had significant scriptorial activity "up to half a century earlier than has previously been allowed" (p. 48). If Dumville is correct, it is now necessary to reconsider the origin and date of Anglo-Saxon manuscripts with a Bury provenance (listed by Dumville on pp. 78–9).

11. On fol. 127r the Julius text jumps from "eorþan" (Skeat XXIIIB, 246) to "þa ðincg" (Skeat XXIIIB, 318), but what is missing can, in the main, be supplied from Gloucester Cathedral Library 35 (Ker 117).

12. Ker 162. Clemoes, "Chronology," pp. 219–20, takes a different view of the evidence, but agrees that Mary of Egypt and the Seven Sleepers are both additions. On the basis of two binding fragments, Cambridge, Queens' College (Horne 75), Clemoes was able to deduce that there was at least one manuscript of the *Lives of Saints* without these two items (pp. 220, 237). This has since been confirmed by the discovery of two further fragments: see pp. 244–45.

13. See Ker 162, item 30, and 177, item 13. We do not know, of course, that the scribe who copied the Seven Sleepers into Julius E. vii had access to the text as it must have been in Otho B. x before it was burnt.

14. The only other saint out of calendar order is Lucy, but that is a different case; see p. 238. For a further description of this manuscript, with particular reference to the non-Ælfric items, see D. G. Scragg's study of "The Corpus of Anonymous Lives and Their Manuscript Context" immediately preceding in this volume. Ker, *Catalogue*, no. 177, notes that fols. 52 and 54 of Cotton Otho B.x cannot be identified, but they have recently been shown to contain parts of the lives of Eugenia and Euphrosyne (fol. 52r and fol. 52v, respectively) and Sebastian (fol. 54r and 54v), lives already known to have been in this manuscript. See S. D. Lee, "Two Fragments from Cotton MS. Otho B.X," *British Library Journal* 17 (1991): 83–87.

15. Patrick H. Zettel, "Ælfric's Hagiographic Sources and the Latin Legendary Preserved in B. L. MS Cotton Nero E.i. + CCCC MS 9 and Other Manuscripts," D. Phil. Diss., Oxford University, (1979), p. 42.

16. Clemoes, "Chronology," p. 222.

17. Ælfric's prefaces imply a "purer" version than we have in Julius E. vii, as noted by Milton McCormick Gatch, *Preaching and Theology in Anglo-Saxon England: Ælfric and Wulfstan* (Toronto and Buffalo, N.Y., 1977), p.189, n. 49. See also pp. 240, 242.

18. Clemoes, "Chronology," p. 220.

19. Ibid., p. 220. The three items form an "appendix" to Julius E. vii, and Clemoes believes that their order "may reflect their order of composition like that of

the items at the end of Gg. 3. 28" (p. 224, n. 1). If we work on the analogy of Gg. 3. 28, the assumption would be that Ælfric had copies of these pieces written out for safekeeping (i.e., as "file copies") at the end of a manuscript of the *Lives of Saints* and that the Julius copy, even with its non-Ælfrician expansion of the *sanctorale*, was sufficiently close to this copy to preserve the "appendix." For Gg. 3. 28 and Ælfric's practice in having new short pieces copied into the end of a suitable codex, see Kenneth Sisam, *Studies in the History of Old English Literature* (Oxford, 1953), pp. 165–68.

20. See p. 236.

21. Because the manuscript was very badly damaged in the Cotton fire, we are obliged for most items, including this one, to depend on the account in Humphrey Wanley's *Librorum Veterum Septentrionalium*, in vol. 2 of George Hickes, *Linguarum Veterum Septentrionalium Thesaurus* (Oxford, 1705).

22. In the manuscript the scribe's list is laid out in a double column; the left column ends with Alban and the right begins with Æðelþryð. No entry runs on to a second line. For the *D* of "De" the scribe consistently uses a square capital in the left column, and an uncial in the right. Eight of the numerals have superscript corrections: VIIII corrected to VIIII; XIII corrected to XIIII; XVI corrected to XVII; XXI corrected to XXIII; XXIII corrected to XXIIII; XXVI corrected to XXVII; XXXI corrected to XXXIII; and XXXVIII corrected to XXXVIIII. The scribal numbering given in Table 1 shows the numbers as corrected in the manuscript. There is no number XVIII and the manuscript shows no attempt to remedy this. For the Seven Sleepers "item" is written above VII, thus clarifying that this numeral is part of the title and not part of the numbering sequence. In the edited text given here, *w* is substituted for the letter-form *wynn*.

23. Geoffrey Needham, "Additions and Alterations in Cotton MS. Julius E VII," *Review of English Studies*, n.s. 9 (1958): 160–64. For the Swithun-Macarius doxology in particular, see p. 162, n. 3. Skeat's editorial responses to the Julius copy are further discussed by Robert J. Alexander, "W. W. Skeat and Ælfric," *Annuale Medievale* 22 (1982): 36–53.

24. See Table 2 below: CUL Ii. 1. 33 (Ker 18), CCCC 198 (Ker 48), CCCC 303 (Ker 57).

25. See note 15.

26. For copies of the "extended" Macarius narrative, see Table 2 below: CCCC 178 (Ker 41) and Hatton 116 (Ker 333). The combination of Macarius with other material is discussed in Pope, *The Homilies of Ælfric*, vol. 2, pp. 786–89; and in Audrey L. Meaney, "Ælfric's Use of His Sources in His Homily on Auguries," *English Studies* 66 (1985): 477–95.

27. Skeat, *Ælfric's Lives of Saints*, p. 4. Bernadette Moloney, "Be Godes Halgum: Ælfric's Hagiography and the Cult of Saints in England in the Tenth Century," *Literature and Learning in Medieval and Renaissance England: Essays Presented to Fitzroy Pyle*, ed. John Scattergood (Dublin, 1984), pp. 25–40, on 34,

notes that Ælfric's claim to have provided lives of saints mainly celebrated by monks is quite well authenticated. As both the Latin and Old English prefaces acknowledge, the immediate users in this case were to be two laymen, Æðelwerd and Æðelmær, but they had evidently asked for a vernacular version of the monastic legendary. In origin, then, the *Lives of Saints* differed from the *Catholic Homilies* in not being intended for public use as a body of preaching materials within the secular church, although Ælfric recognized that others might wish to copy the collection once it was in the vernacular. Therefore when we consider the initial impetus for producing the *Lives of Saints* as well as its declared content, the non-hagiographical items, and the *temporale* homilies in particular, do seem to be anomalous. It is revealing that it is these which are most exploited in general homiletic collections (see pp. 251–52). For the use of legendaries in private devotion (as presumably intended by Æðelweard and Æðelmær), see Guy Philippart, *Les Légendiers latins et autres manuscrits hagiographiques*, Typologie des Sources du Moyen Âge Occidental, Fasc. 24–25 (Turnhout, Belgium, 1977).

28. Patrick H. Zettel, "Saints' Lives in Old English: Latin Manuscripts and Vernacular Accounts: Ælfric," *Peritia* 1 (1982): 17–37, on p. 18. Details of the contents of this legendary are provided by Peter Jackson and Michael Lapidge, "The Contents of the Cotton-Corpus Legendary," on pp. 131–46 of the present volume. As noted immediately below, Ælfric supplemented this collection with English saints. Paris BN lat. 5362 is a later copy (*c.* 1100) of a hagiographical commonplace book which seems to have been compiled by Ælfric himself, and this preserves extracted and abbreviated Latin material on Ælfric's English saints, which he probably compiled in preparation for his vernacular narratives. For an account of this manuscript's contents, see *Wulfstan of Winchester: the Life of St. Æthelwold*, ed. Michael Lapidge and Michael Winterbottom (Oxford, 1991), pp. cxlvii–cxlix.

29. Listed on p. 237.

30. Hugh Magennis, "On the Sources of Non-Ælfrician Lives in the Old English Lives of Saints, with reference to the Cotton-Corpus Legendary," *Notes and Queries*, 230 (1985): 292–99 and "The Anonymous Old English *Legend of the Seven Sleepers* and its Latin Source," *Leeds Studies in English*, n.s. 22 (1991): 43–56.

31. Ker, *Catalogue*, pp. 511–15.

32. Pope, *The Homilies of Ælfric*, vol. 1, pp. 92–93.

33. Scragg, "The Corpus," pp. 270–77. For further analysis of the manuscript distribution of the anonymous saints' lives, see also D. G. Scragg's contribution to the present volume, "The Corpus of Anonymous Lives and Their Manuscript Context," immediately preceding.

34. Skeat, *Ælfric's Lives of Saints*, vol. 2, p. lxii. In addition to the incomplete coverage, the shelf marks are not in all cases the ones in modern use, and the article numbers differ from those that we have since become accustomed to in Ker's *Catalogue*.

35. See pp. 244–45.

36. See pp. 249–50 on the difficulty of classifying the material bearing this shelf mark.

37. Ker's *Catalogue* reads "s. xi quarter," but because this makes no sense and *quarter* is used only in association with *3rd*, it must be an error for "s. xi 3rd quarter."

38. When Skeat uses old shelf marks in his account of the manuscripts (*Ælfric's Lives of Saints*, vol. 2, pp. vii–xxii), he usually also provides the shelf marks by which the manuscripts are identified today. The exceptions are Skeat's Junius 22, 23, and 24, which are now Hatton 113 + 114, 115, and 116, respectively.

39. Ker, *Catalogue*, pp. 127–28 and N. R. Ker, "A Supplement to *Catalogue of Manuscripts Containing Anglo-Saxon*," *ASE* 5 (1976): 121–31, on p. 123.

40. Rowland L. Collins and Peter Clemoes, "The Common Origin of Ælfric Fragments at New Haven, Oxford, Cambridge, and Bloomington," *Old English Studies in Honour of John C. Pope*, ed. Robert B. Burlin and Edward B. Irving, Jr. (Toronto, 1974), pp. 285–326.

41. In his contribution to this volume, Scragg reaches the same conclusions in discussing the distribution and use of the anonymous texts. See pp. 209–30.

42. For usages of legendaries, see Philippart, *Les Légendiers latins*.

43. Zettel, "Ælfric's Hagiographic Sources," pp. 217–18 (Chair of St Peter) and 228–34 (Exaltation of the Holy Cross). By contrast with lives and passions, however, where the Cotton-Corpus legendary provided Ælfric with all, or almost all, of his material, these two homilies draw upon a number of sources, as Zettel shows in his analyses. Most of the source identifications excluding those relating to the Cotton-Corpus legendary were made by: Max Förster, *Über die Quellen von Ælfrics Homiliae Catholicae. Vol. 1. Legenden* (Berlin, 1892), p. 20, and J. H. Ott, *Über die Quellen der Heiligenleben in Ælfrics Lives of Saints*, Vol. 1 (Halle, 1892), pp. 34–36, for the Chair of St Peter; Grant Loomis, "Further Sources of Ælfric's Saints' Lives," *Harvard Studies and Notes in Philology and Literature* 13 (1931): 1–8, on pp. 3–4, for Holy Cross.

44. Godden, *Ælfric's Catholic Homilies*, pp. 288–97. As Zettel has shown, "Ælfric's Hagiographic Sources," pp. 74–82, Ælfric chose to include in the *Catholic Homilies* those saints who were the highest ranking or most significant in the Anglo-Saxon Church, and Martin comes into this group. The saints in the *Lives of Saints* collection are from farther down the rank order and include some that have special significance for monks. Presumably for this latter reason Martin was included here also, in a more detailed form than in the *Catholic Homilies*.

45. In Julius E. vii Martin takes up fols. 179v–203r; the abbreviated version in Bodley 343 is on fols. 35r–39v, and there is no great difference between the amount of text per page in the two manuscripts. The Julius version is longer than most of the other *sanctorale* items in that manuscript. By contrast, the version in Bodley 343 is comparable, for example, to its three immediately preceding items, which are on fols. 26v–30r, 30r–33v, 33v–35r.

46. The only other true saints' lives that are shown in Table 2 to be abbreviated are not comparable: for Mary of Egypt and the Seven Sleepers, see pp. 236–37; in the case of Edmund and Thomas, both in CUL Ii. 1. 33 (Ker 18), it is simply that in this late copy (s. xii²) Ælfric's Prefaces are omitted (Old English for Edmund, corresponding to Skeat XXXII, 1–12, and Latin for Thomas, corresponding to Skeat XXXVI, 1–12).

47. On this general topic, see Susan J. Ridyard, "Condigna Veneratio: Post-Conquest Attitudes to the Saints of the Anglo-Saxons," *Anglo-Norman Studies 9: Proceedings of the Battle Conference 1986*, ed. R. Allen Brown (Woodbridge, 1987), pp. 179–206; and David Rollason, *Saints and Relics in Anglo-Saxon England* (Oxford, 1989), esp. ch. 9. Ridyard, pp. 187–88, has some particular comments on the cult of Edmund.

48. Clemoes, "Chronology," pp. 233–35.

49. For the item on the three orders of society, see p. 242 and p. 252.

50. See p. 240.

51. ˙The Judith homily is edited by Bruno Assmann, *Angelsächsische Homilien und Heiligenleben*, Bibliothek der angelsächsischen Prosa 3 (Kassel, 1889; rpt. with a Supplementary Introduction by Peter Clemoes, Darmstadt, 1964), pp. 102–16. The group of Old Testament items at the end of CCCC 303 is very obviously distinct from the main homiletic contents because it is separated from them by two pages of Latin and Old English forms of excommunication.

52. See p. 242.

53. Manuscripts that include both Maccabees and the passage on the three orders of society copy them consecutively, as in Julius E. vii, even though in other respects the manuscripts differ markedly from Julius and from each other.

54. For published texts, see respectively Pope, *The Homilies of Ælfric*, pp. 638–66 (Homily XX); *The Old English Version of the Heptateuch*, ed. S. J. Crawford, EETS OS 160 (London, 1922), pp. 402–17 (edited from Oxford, Bodleian Library, Laud Misc. 482 and collated with Hatton 115); and George Edwin MacLean, "Ælfric's Version of *Alcuini Interrogationes Sigeuulfi in Genesin*," *Anglia* 7 (1884): 1–59 (edited from CCCC 162).

55. See p. 242 and note 31.

56. See p. 243 and note 33.

57. In the context of this preliminary survey, I do not distinguish between adaptations and re-use of Ælfric's own work by Ælfric himself and adaptations and re-use by others. It will obviously be useful on another occasion to develop the survey by analyzing this distinction with respect to the adapted and reused texts in Table 2.

58. In CCCC 162 (Ker 38) it is rubricated *De oratione moysi in medio .xl. uel quando uolueris;* in CUL Ii. 4. 6 (Ker 21) it is simply *De oratione moysi,* but it is positioned for mid-Lent; in Hatton 114 (Ker 331), CCCC 303 (Ker 57), and Cotton Faustina A. ix (Ker 153) it is *De oratione moysi in media quadragesima.*

59. The adaptation shown in Table 2 for CUL Gg. 3. 28 (Ker 15) is the same as that in Junius 121 (Ker 338) and it is by Ælfric, in his pastoral letter for Wulfsige of Sherborne, in which he uses Skeat XIII, 68–86, corresponding to *Die Hirtenbriefe Ælfrics*, ed. Bernhard Fehr, Bibliothek der angelsächsischen Prosa 9 (Hamburg, 1914; reprinted with a Supplementary Introduction by Peter Clemoes, Darmstadt, 1964), pp. 24–25, para. 105–10. The copy in CUL Gg. 3. 28 breaks off partway through para. 108, owing to loss of leaves. This passage from the Prayer of Moses homily is presumably a modification to the letter made by Ælfric after he had already sent the first version to Wulfsige; see my "Monastic Reform and the Secular Church: Ælfric's Pastoral Letters in Context," *England in the Eleventh Century: Proceedings of the 1990 Harlaxton Symposium*, ed. Carola Hickes (Stamford, England, 1992), pp. 103–17. Ker notes the use of the homily in commenting on the Junius copy of the letter for Wulfsige (Ker 338, art. 26) but he fails to note it in commenting on the copy in CUL Gg. 3. 28 (Ker 15, art. 97), even though his index (p. 528) lists "15 art. 97 (extr.)" as an occurrence for Skeat XIII (Fourth Sunday in Lent). The adaptation in CCCC 178 (Ker 41) is the same as that in Hatton 116 (Ker 333), using Skeat XIII, 98–101, as well as a passage from the Memory of the Saints (Skeat XVI, 267–381). The homily to which the passages contribute, *De octo uitiis et de duodecim abusiuis*, is printed (from CCCC 178) in *Old English Homilies and Homiletic Treatises of the Twelfth and Thirteenth Centuries*, ed. Richard Morris, EETS OS 29 and 34 (London, 1867–68), pp. 296–304. The adaptation in Lambeth 489 (Ker 283), which uses Skeat XIII, 75–86, as well as Skeat XIX, 248–54, is a homily for the dedication of a church.

60. The homily is headed *Alia narratio doctrina populi*, but the previous homily, to which it is an alternate, is rubricated *Dominica in quinguagesima*. It was noted previously, p. 237, that in Julius E. vii the possibility of preaching the homily in anticipation of Ash Wednesday was allowed for in the rubric. It is also allowed for in lines 289–92 of the Julius version of the text, which acknowledges, as does the expanded opening to the copy in CCCC 162, that the mid-week congregation will be smaller.

61. It is *De auguriis* in CCCC 162 (Ker 41), Hatton 115 (Ker 332), and Hatton 116 (Ker 333), and *Epistola pauli* in CUL Ii. 1. 33, but it is *Sermo in letania maiore de epistola pauli et de auguriis* in CCCC 303 (Ker 57), *Sermo in letanie maiore uel quando uolueris* in CCCC 419 (Ker 68), and *Dominica .IIIa. Uel quando uolueris* in CCCC 302 (Ker 56), where the rubrics of the two preceding homilies are explicit in naming the season as Advent.

62. See p. 242.

63. For the adaptations in CCCC 178 (Ker 41) and Hatton 116 (Ker 333), see note 59. It is the same adaptation in Vespasian D. xiv (Ker 209) but here the material that forms one substantial homily in CCCC 178 is divided up into shorter pieces with separate Latin headings.

64. See p. 239.

Experiments in Genre:
The Saints' Lives in Ælfric's *Catholic Homilies*

M. R. Godden

Medieval hagiography was a highly varied genre, serving several different functions and drawing on a variety of traditions. As Rosemary Woolf puts it, describing the literary saint's life, "in origins it is part panegyric, part epic, part romance, part sermon, and historical fact dissolves within the conventions of these forms."[1] Thomas Hill's chapter in this volume has already shown the complexity of the genre, its variety of functions, and its relation to other genres. Such complexities were probably as evident to medieval writers as they are to us, and one of the major interests in examining Ælfric's writing of hagiography is the opportunity to watch a writer responding to the questions of genre and mode.

In considering his treatment of hagiography it would seem natural to concentrate on the collection traditionally known as Ælfric's *Lives of Saints*.[2] The title is editorial and in various ways misrepresents the contents of the collection—it includes several pieces on doctrinal issues, ranging from the nature of the soul to folklore and superstition, and some narrative pieces drawn from the Old Testament, such as the stories of the Maccabees—but in his preface Ælfric defines the contents simply as the *passiones vel vitas sanctorum* and the *halgena prowunga*,[3] and the twenty-seven saints' lives by him that are included do form the bulk of the volume. Ælfric identifies these saints as those whose feasts were celebrated by the monks rather than the laity, but the lives seem not to have been designed for use in the liturgy: they do not refer to the feast day as the occasion for reading them, they are often very long, and they frequently include attached pieces on other issues. They are, as Clemoes defines them when listing the canon, "narrative pieces intended not for reading as part of the liturgy, but for pious reading at any time."[4] Though they may have been read by monks in the refectory they seem actually to have been commissioned or prompted by Ælfric's two lay patrons,

Æthelweard and Æthelmær, and, like the rest of the collection, reflect their
interests as much as those of the monastic order.[5]

These lives were not, however, Ælfric's first attempts at the genre: he
had already written a large number of hagiographic texts for inclusion in his
two series of *Catholic Homilies*,[6] and these differ in many ways from the
texts included in the *Lives of Saints* collection. The precise nature and function of the two sets of forty "homilies" that make up the *Catholic Homilies*
is very difficult to define, and it is still unclear how far they were intended
for verbatim preaching, how far for private reading, and how far as models
for others' preaching.[7] Ælfric calls them *sermones* and in terms of their register, their mode of discourse, they present themselves, at least initially, as
addresses to a listening audience in a liturgical context, with occasional references to "the Gospel passage that you have just heard read" and to the saint
who died "on this day." About twenty-six pieces in the two volumes might
be designated hagiography, though boundaries are hard to draw. Some are
clearly "passions" in the strict sense; that is, narratives of the sufferings and
deaths of martyrs:[8] there are five in the First Series, covering Laurence,
Bartholomew, Clement, Peter and Paul, and Andrew; and five more in the
Second, covering James the Greater, Alexander, James the Less, Simon and
Jude, and Matthew. Also some may clearly be defined as *vitae* or "lives"; that
is, narratives of the actions and biographies of saints: such are the accounts
of John the Evangelist in the First Series and Gregory, Cuthbert, Benedict,
and Martin in the Second. But many suggest the fluidity of generic boundaries and the difficulties of definition. Ælfric's first piece on Stephen is an
account of the saint's martyrdom, and perhaps therefore a passion, but it is
simultaneously a close exposition of a biblical text, in this case the passage
from Acts that formed the epistle for the day, and its sources are homiletic
rather than hagiographic. Similar cases are the homilies on the nativity of
John the Baptist, using the gospel account as basis for a partial narrative of
the saint's life, and on the decollation of John, using the Gospel text as basis
for an account of his martyrdom. A different problem is presented by the
Second Series homily for Tuesday in Rogationtide, which gives an account
of the otherworld experiences of Fursey: the source is a conventional saint's
life, but what Ælfric actually gives us is really eschatology rather than
hagiography. Nor can this piece easily be separated from the following one,
on Drihthelm's journey to the otherworld, although Drihthelm seems not to
have been considered a saint and the source here is history (Bede's *Historia
Ecclesiastica*) rather than hagiography. With the Invention of the Cross (*CH*
II xviii) we have an occasion that was liturgically treated like saints' days and
a story that seems in content very like a saint's life, but has no saint as
protagonist and uses history as source. Beyond that, we can point to cases
where conventional hagiographical texts provided material for entirely non-

hagiographic homilies.[9] Even within these groups there are substantial variations in approach: the accounts of Gregory and Cuthbert, placed next to each other in *Catholic Homilies* II and both fitting the category of lives of confessors, could not be more different in their content, style, and structure.

In the preface to the First Series Ælfric notes that he has included two kinds of writing in the volume: "nec solum Evangeliorum tractatus in isto libello exposuimus, verum etiam Sanctorum passiones vel vitas" [*CH* I p. 1; "we have presented in this volume not only the expositions of the Gospels but also the passions or lives of saints"]. He makes a similar distinction, in English, in the preface to his Second Series: "hi ne sind na ealle of godspellum genumene . ac sind forwel fela of godes halgena life oððe þrowunge gegaderode" [*CH* II p.2; "they are not all taken from the Gospels, but very many are collected from the life or passion of God's saints"]. In doing so, he draws attention to the fact that he was combining into a single preaching collection two distinct kinds of text, drawn from two very different models. On the one hand, there were homilies on the Gospels, drawn from the great homiliary of Paul the Deacon, which was the major source for the *Catholic Homilies*, and from the homiliaries of Haymo and Smaragdus: these source collections were designed for use in the monastic night office, and for private reading, and insofar as they provided for saints' days generally used Gospel commentary rather than narratives.[10] On the other hand, there were lives and passions of saints, drawn particularly from the massive Cotton-Corpus legendary identified by Patrick Zettel:[11] such legendaries were mainly designed for monastic reading.

Ælfric was not the first to combine homilies on the gospels and narratives of saints into a single preaching collection. That had already been done in some Latin collections designed for preaching to the laity, such as the homiliary found in Pembroke College Cambridge MS 25 (formerly known as the homiliary of St. Père de Chartres),[12] and the second homiliary of Hrabanus Maurus. Probably such collections provided the model for the Blickling Homilies,[13] which similarly combine exegetical homilies and saints' legends within the same volume. But, though it seems possible that Ælfric knew such collections and was influenced by them,[14] these were not his sources, as we have seen, and the Latin homiliaries at least were of little help as models, using only very brief and cursory narratives of saints. In adapting hagiographic material for a preaching collection, Ælfric had to experiment for himself in developing a kind of hagiography appropriate to the collections and functions that he had conceived and in finding ways of combining the often spectacular narratives of miracles with the more sober and discursive discourse of exegesis and preaching.

Several major issues presented themselves to Ælfric. First there was the problem of the truth content and authority of hagiography, and its relationship to history. In his preface to the First Series Ælfric testifies that the *gedwyld* (a word that covers both folly and heresy) widely current in contemporary thought and teaching prompted him to write his own homilies. It is clear that such *gedwyld* was at least in part associated with hagiography. He repudiates the apocryphal account of the Assumption of the Virgin and the story of Paul's vision of heaven and hell known as the *Visio Pauli*, and questions whether an episode in the life of Thomas the apostle is credible.[15] But the question of truth in hagiography was a hard problem to tackle. In his preface Ælfric proclaims the great authorities on whom he has based his own writings—Augustine, Jerome, Bede, Gregory, Smaragdus, and sometimes Haymo. In a wonderfully simple but persuasive picture he contrasts the true faith to be found in their writings, which he claims merely to have translated, with the opposite extreme of *gedwyld*, folly or heresy, which is to be found in other kinds of books. But one of the striking absences from Ælfric's initial citation of authority is hagiographical sources. His named authorities are relevant primarily to the exegetical homilies: they cover none of the hagiographic pieces in the First Series, only five of those in the Second. The legends of saints that he had to use were a nightmare area of conflicting versions, uncertain attributions and alarming accusations and counteraccusations of heresy and falsehood. Ælfric knew the Gelasian decree condemning a variety of hagiographic and apocryphal texts, but could not tell for certain which were the right texts and which the wrong ones.[16] This was a mad world in which notions of patristic authority were of little help.

One of the ways of avoiding such problems was to use historical or biblical sources for the lives of saints rather than anonymous or pseudonymous legends, and this is a route Ælfric took more than once. But in terms of genre and structure it involved its own kinds of problems in shaping the narrative to the conventions and expectations associated with hagiography. One such case is the homily on the Invention of the Cross [*CH* II xviii]. The Cotton-Corpus legendary had a version of the *Acta Cyriaci* (BHL 4169), the narrative of the discovery of the cross that Cynewulf used in *Elene*, but Ælfric knew a different and contradictory account of the discovery, in the *Historia Ecclesiastica* of Eusebius as translated by Rufinus. He evidently preferred this as an apparently more authoritative account, but had then to select and shape the material to create an appropriate hagiographic narrative. In shaping his account he seems to have partially imitated, consciously or not, the structure of the legend he had rejected; hence he begins in the same fashion with Constantine's vision of the cross and his battle the next day, and his representation of the forces of Maximus as invaders and aggressors recalls the presentation of the barbarian invaders in the legend.

Second, there was the question of how individual saints were to be conceived as persons: allegorical figures, representative believers, historical characters, or spiritual heroes? The exegetical tradition tended to emphasize their symbolic and representative role. If one examines the provision for saints' days in the homiliaries one is immediately struck by how little the Gospel passage for the occasion engages with the individual personality or history of the saint who is celebrated. It is a point made by Ælfric when he remarks apropos of the Gospel passage appointed for the Assumption of the Virgin Mary: "Ne sprecð þis godspel nan ðing sinderlice be cristes meder . ac man hit ræt swa ðeah gewunelice æt hire mæssan . for ðære cyrclican gesetnysse" (*CH* II xxix 18–20).[17] Many of the passages appointed for saints' days are applicable to any saint, or at least to any confessor, martyr, or apostle; indeed some of them were used for the common of saints as well as for individual saints' days. Such tendencies were accentuated by the patristic tradition of biblical commentary. Even where the passage appointed did deal, briefly or substantially, with the appropriate saint, the exegetical tradition was inclined to pass over the saint's individual role or to ignore him or treat the saint as representative of all saints or more commonly all believers. To treat instead (or as well) the story of the saint's life or passion was, to a greater or lesser extent, to acknowledge the saint's individual identity. With New Testament saints, especially the apostles, there was a particular problem when exegetical and hagiographic conventions clashed; as is shown later, John the Evangelist and Peter were troubling examples of this problem. There were also, however, questions to be faced about how far hagiographic narratives should acknowledge the individual story and context of the particular saint, in the manner of historiography, and how far they should heroicize their subjects as figures of sanctity; this was to have implications for the kind of diction used for saints' lives, as we shall see.

A third and more general issue raised by the adaptation of hagiography to a preaching collection was the question of the kind of meaning that could be found in saints' lives—their *sententia*. As a primarily homiletic preaching collection, the *Catholic Homilies* give priority to doctrinal exposition and argument rather than narrative: they explicitly attempt to confront and confound *gedwyld*, to provide the *lar* that is necessary to all humanity in the face of Antichrist, and to give the understanding and guidance that individuals need. Saints' lives, however, are essentially narratives, and their engagement with doctrine, if any, is necessarily more oblique. Purely as narratives their characteristic kind of "meaning" is exemplary: at a literal or symbolic level, the saint presents a pattern of life that reflects on the lives of others. That is the kind of reading that Ælfric suggests in his later homily on the commemoration of the saints, and a passing comment in a still later homily shows him drawing parallels between the sufferings of the saints in the time of the early persecutions and the resistance of the Anglo-Saxons to Viking pressures in his own time.[18] As he comments elsewhere, the miracles that characterize the genre can be seen also as attesting to the power of the true God.[19] There were, however, other ways, closer to the homiletic mode, in which hagiography could be made to yield *sententia*. One kind of meaning involves the saint taking on the role of preacher, merging his voice with that of the speaker of the homily or saint's life and lending the authority of his life and sanctity to the sermons, dialogues, and letters through which hagiography imitates preaching. As J. E. Cross has shown, the account of his preaching which Paul gives to Nero, in the legend of his martyrdom, later became a model for Ælfric's own teaching.[20] Such uses of the saint as preacher is a recurrent feature of Ælfric's early saints' lives, but one could take his story of Matthew (*CH* II xxxii) as a relatively simple example. Here he drastically summarizes the legendary account of the apostle's conflicts with wizards and dragons, but highlights the moment when Matthew has to take a stand against the king's attempts to marry the daughter of his predecessor, who has become a nun; here Anglo-Saxon anxieties about the relations of ecclesiastical and dynastic needs find their voice in Matthew, in a dispute much developed by Ælfric himself:

> þa het se apostol þone cyning cuman to cyrcan mid his folce . and ealle ða mædenu samod ; Hi ða comon swa heora gewuna wæs . and se apostol him eallum sæde . hwæt gebyrað to sinscipe . hwæt to wydewan hade . hwæt to mægðhade . and hwæt to ælces mannes ðeawum þe on godes gelaðunge mid geleafan wunað ; And cwæð ða æt nextan þæt gif hwa þæs cyninges bryde gewemde . þæt he wyrðe wære þæt hine man on byrnendum ligum bescufe ; þu min leofe bearn Irtace . nu ðu wast þæt effigenia ðines foregengan dohtor is þæs heofenlican cyniges bryd . and mid haligrefte gehalgod . Hu miht ðu þam ælmihtigan his bryde beniman . and ðinum sinscipe geðeodan? (*CH* II xxxii 155-66)[21]

Other kinds of meaning, however, are drawn out by means of commentary or moralization; thus Ælfric attaches to his account of Bartholomew (*CH* I xxxi) a discussion of the doctrinal issues associated with medicine and healing, prompted by the healing miracles in the saint's life, and his account of Clement (*CH* I xxxvii) prompts a long discussion of the problems raised by God's apparent toleration of the sufferings of the faithful.

Such questions of generic mode and style are raised by most of Ælfric's early saints' lives, but a closer look at some representative examples will help clarify the nature of the problem and some of the attempts at solution.

John the Evangelist (*CH* I iv)

When he came to write this piece, the first genuine saint's life in the First Series, Ælfric was faced with a large range of potential sources and models, partially in conflict with each other. The original version of Paul the Deacon's homiliary had three items for this occasion: a homily by Bede on the Gospel for the day, John 21; an excerpt from Ps-Isidore *De Ortu et Obitu Patrum*, giving summary details of the apostle's origins and death; and an excerpt from the *Ecclesiastical History* of Rufinus, narrating a story of John's conversion of a young outlaw.[22] Later versions of the homiliary, which often seem to be closer to what Ælfric saw, have the Bede homily and an extract from Augustine's *Tractates on John*, expounding John 21 again.[23] Ælfric would also have seen two more Latin homilies on the Gospel passage for the day in the homiliaries of Haymo and Smaragdus. The Cotton-Corpus legendary provided him with an apocryphal legend of the apostle's life and his end, a version of BHL 4320. If Ælfric knew the Pembroke 25 homiliary, he would have found there this same legend and another as well, BHL 4316. The anonymous Old English homilies that have survived contain nothing on John, but the *Old English Martyrology* has a summary account of his life, which mentions some miracles and his mysterious end.

The major issue which Ælfric faced here was reconciling the exegetical tradition with the hagiographical. The problem starts with the Gospel for the day John 21:21–23, which suggests the possibility that John may not die: "Hunc ergo cum vidisset Petrus, dixit Iesu: Domine, hic autem quid? Dicit ei Iesus: Sic eum volo manere donec veniam, quid ad te? tu me sequere. Exiit ergo sermo iste inter fratres quia discipulus ille non moritur."[24] The author of the Gospel quickly counters this interpretation in the next verse by claiming that Christ meant the words only hypothetically: "Et non dixit ei Iesus: Non moritur, sed: Si eum volo manere donec veniam, quid ad te?"[25] The patristic and later commentators known to Ælfric faced the problem in their turn and similarly worked at repudiating the view of the brethren that John would not die. Somewhat surprisingly they seem to have ignored the evangelist's own explanation but argued instead that what Christ meant was that John would die a peaceful and natural death, in contrast to the violent death under persecution that the other apostles would face.[26] Yet the view of the brethren seems to have had its effect on traditions about John's end. A Pseudo-Jerome text on the assumption of the Virgin Mary, well known to Ælfric, reports the tradition that only manna was found in John's tomb, though the author refuses to commit himself on this tradition.[27] The *Old English Martyrology* records another tradition and differences of opinion: "æt þære byrigine bið wellmicel wundor gesewen and gehired: hwilon heo eðað swa lifiende man slape; hwilon þonne man þa byrigine sceawað, þonne ne bið þær nan lichoma gesewen, ac bið micel swetnisse stenc. Forþam nat nænig man hwæþer se Iohannes si þe cwicu þe dead."[28] When Ælfric consulted his legendary, this gave him an account of the saint matching the report of "Jerome" and the *Martyrology*, strongly implying that the apostle's body was immediately assumed into heaven, in a form of bodily resurrection.[29] The people watch in the church as John walks into his tomb, but a blinding and enduring light then prevents them seeing what follows, and when it fades and they investigate the tomb, they find it containing only manna. The story presumably developed in response to the tradition recorded in John 21: whether it is taken as implying that John did not die, like Enoch and Elijah, or only that he died and was immediately carried up, body and soul, to heaven, it reflects an acceptance of the literal meaning of Christ's words, a meaning that the exegetes were so anxious to refute.

Ælfric must have been exercised over the conflicts raised here. It was by no means simply a difference between the views of his patristic and Carolingian authorities on the Gospel passage and the testimony of anonymous legends, for the commentators themselves appeared to give credence to the legend. As we have seen, the epistle supposedly by Jerome at least acknowledged its plausibility. Haymo and Smaragdus both cite details from it as true, though implicitly disagreeing with its main point. Jerome (in another work genuinely by him) and Bede both mention episodes found in the legend approvingly, though they confused the issue by misattributing them to the *Historia Ecclesiastica* of Eusebius.[30] Perhaps for those reasons, Ælfric decided to accept the legendary account and ignore the exegetical tradition. He incorporates details of John's life from Bede's homily on the Gospel and from Haymo's, and also from Augustine's commentary on the Gospel, but his main concern is the story of John's acts and his end, as given by the apocryphal legend. Characteristically, having made up his own mind he shields his readers from doubt and controversy. He carefully records that John was "taken up" to heaven rather than saying that he died, and follows the legend in reporting that only manna was found in the tomb. He makes no mention of John 21 and the problems raised by it.

If Ælfric chose in the end to use the legend of John's acts and miracles and exclude Gospel exegesis, it was perhaps in part because the legend incorporated its own homiletic *sententia*. It was a powerful and often moving story, and in adapting it he highlighted the moments of revelation and devotion and argument. The central event is the apostle's confrontation with two young disciples of a Stoic philosopher, who convert all their wealth into gold pieces and diamonds, which they then destroy to show their repudiation of wealth; they are then taught by John the superior Christian law of giving to the poor and become his disciples, but subsequently regret becoming poor themselves when they see the finery of their former servants and are soundly rebuked by the apostle for their backsliding. The powerful speech in which he contrasts their worldly materialism with spiritual verities (99–133) is one of Ælfric's finest pieces of writing, using all his rhetorical skill to enhance the already eloquent qualities of the original:

"Nimað þis gold, and ðas gymstanas, and farað, and bicgað eow land-are; forðan þe ge forluron ða heofenlican speda. Bicgað eow pællene cyrtlas, þæt ge to lytelre hwile scinon swa swa rose, þæt ge hrædlice forweornion. Beoð blowende and welige hwilwendlice, þæt ge ecelice wædlion. . . . Þa heofenlican æhta sind us eallum gemæne. Nacode we wæron acennede, and nacode we gewitað. Þære sunnan beorhtnys, and þæs monan leoht, and ealra tungla sind gemæne þam rican and ðam heanan" (*CH* I iv, p. 64).[31] The apostle becomes Ælfric's own spokesman as preacher, directing his arguments through the two disciples to the Anglo-Saxon audience. Miracles here serve the ends of teaching: when John turns the crushed diamonds back into flawless whole ones, or later converts pebbles into gems and sticks into rods of gold, it is to create occasions for his arguments about the proper use of wealth rather than to demonstrate power. The narrative is in fact studded with powerful prayers and preaching, reaching beyond the confines of the narrative situation. The story of the saint's acts and miracles thus becomes a framework for the preaching role of the saint, substituting for Ælfric's own preaching role.

Peter and Paul (*CH* I xxvi)

Here too Ælfric was faced with a multiplicity of possibilities. First, there were general sermons for the occasion: the original version of Paul the Deacon's *Homiliary* contained six of these, five by Maximus and one by Leo; two of these survive into the later version printed in PL 95. Second, there were exegetical homilies on the Gospel passage for the day, Matthew 16:13–19; the original version had one by Bede, the later version one by Hericus, and there were two more in the homiliaries of Haymo and Smaragdus, both closely based on Bede. Third, there were hagiographic legends describing the acts and martyrdom of the apostles: there was one in the Cotton-Corpus legendary, and another in the *Blickling Homilies* for this occasion. Ælfric's decision was to combine exegesis with legend in a two-part homily, though not without raising problems. The Gospel passage records how Christ named Peter as the rock on which his church would be built and promised him the keys of the kingdom. It is thus a fitting prelude to an account of Peter's mission to Rome and his heroic martyrdom there. However, in his interpretation of the passage Ælfric chose to follow Bede[32] in seeing Peter as primarily a representative figure, exemplifying true faith and the intercessory role shared by all the apostles; both commentators are resistant to the Gospel text's tendency to present Peter as *primus inter pares*. Thus the rock on which the Church is to be built is not Peter but faith and Christ: " 'And ic timbrige mine cyrcan uppon ðisum stane': þæt is, ofer ðone geleafan ðe ðu andetst. Eal

Godes gelaðung is ofer ðam stane gebytlod, þæt is ofer Criste" (*CH* I xxvi, p. 368).[33] The exegetical tradition that Ælfric follows reads Peter in a very different way from that suggested by the following account of his heroic martyrdom.

The legendary part encompassed a much more difficult doctrinal problem. There were two quite different traditions about the martyrdom of the two apostles: one, probably the older and more historical one, recorded that Paul was martyred a year or more after Peter; the other reported that they were martyred together on the same day (probably a later deduction from the establishment of a joint feast on July 29). The latter seems to have been the Anglo-Saxon belief, reflected in calendars and the *Blickling Homilies*, and probably the *Old English Martyrology*.[34] Ælfric too takes this view, repeatedly insisting that this was the correct version and the older one erroneous. The legend he found in the Cotton-Corpus collection follows the older tradition and describes the martyrdom of Peter alone, which made it unusable for Ælfric. Wishing, even so, to mark the occasion with a narrative of the saints' passion, he looked more widely for parallel but orthodox versions. Somewhere he located an alternative, and orthodox, legend of the passion that describes the apostles' teaching and suffering together.[35] This begins very abruptly with the entry of Paul into Rome to join Peter, saying nothing of Peter's arrival at Rome or the preceding conflicts between Peter and Simon Magus; it was perhaps designed as an alternative ending to the older account of Peter's acts and martyrdom rather than as an autonomous text, but Ælfric evidently preferred to distance himself entirely from the "false" version. He dealt with this abruptness partly by writing a brief introductory account of Peter's missionary travels before he reached Rome, drawing on the first epistle of Peter and perhaps Isidore and Jerome. But he also managed to locate an alternative version of Peter's struggle with Simon Magus, in a text purporting to be a letter of Marcellus (a former disciple of the magus) and included in the Cotton-Corpus collection as part of the legend of Saints Nereus and Achilles.[36] From this he selected two representative incidents, a competition with the magus to resurrect a widow's son and a confrontation with a ferocious dog conjured into existence by Simon but turned against him by Peter. He then linked this into the account of the final events, from the arrival of Paul, and reproduced fairly fully the Latin legend.

As far as we can tell, then, Ælfric created his text on Peter and Paul out of a variety of sources and with no model:

1. Gospel exegesis drawing on homilies by Bede and Hericus which he probably found in Paul the Deacon's homiliary;

2. An account of Peter's preaching missions drawing on a variety of sources;

3. Incidents from Peter's conflict with Simon Magus drawing on the letter of Marcellus that he found in the Cotton-Corpus legendary;

4. An account of the martyrdom of the two apostles, taken from a Latin legend found in some other collection.

The preaching role of the *Catholic Homilies* is reflected in the Gospel exegesis and in Paul's account to Nero of his own preaching to all ranks of society, in which he demonstrates that his teaching has not been hostile to the concerns of the state and society. At the same time, Ælfric's work on the legend attests to a genuine interest in the narrative aspect, and particularly the miraculous and even the spectacular. Peter's miracle competitions with the magus are fully reported, and Ælfric went out of his way to find and add the story of the dog. These are stories of divine and apostolic power in competition with diabolic power, reflecting an interest in the nature of black magic and diabolic illusions that we see frequently elsewhere in Ælfric's work.[37]

Paul (*CH* I xxvii)

This homily similarly combines Gospel exegesis with hagiographic narrative. Ælfric had already used the saint's *passio* in the homily for the feast day of Peter and Paul, and so for this occasion seems to have constructed his own hagiographic *vita* of the saint out of biblical material. The narrative part is pieced together from a variety of scattered references in the Acts of the Apostles, to construct a story that runs from Paul's origins through his persecution of the faithful and conversion, to his rise to prominence among the apostles and his missionary journeys. In the process Ælfric creates an image of the saint strikingly different from that implied by the Bible and patristic exegesis. For Augustine, Paul's life had been an exemplary tale of the conversion of a notorious sinner, the great example of divine mercy and grace; in his comments he emphasizes the savagery of Paul before conversion and the immensity of his transformation.[38] Ælfric sees his story more on the model of the life of a confessor saint. He resolutely defends Paul from criticism, even before his conversion, arguing that he persecuted the Christians out of ignorance and from an honest concern to defend divine law. Augustine ingeniously argues that Paul, by holding the coats of all those who stoned Stephen, contributed more to his death than any other individual and was thus the greatest sinner of all Stephen's persecutors. Ælfric takes a strongly contrasting view, arguing that there is no record that Paul personally killed any of the faithful. He selects and shapes material to present Paul as a dominant and saintly figure, justifying him for taking flight from his enemies in terms similar to those he uses of Christ, and omits the account in Acts of the disciples' suspicion of Paul. The language too is resonant of hagiography, using characteristic epithets like *Godes cempa* and *ðam gecorenan cempan*. The delicate interplay between scriptural authority and hagiographic models brings out well Ælfric's sense of the genre and its demands.

This somewhat unexpected but heroic way of reading the life of Paul has its repercussions for the exposition of the Gospel reading for the day which forms the second half of the homily. The reading has no apparent reference to Paul, but in a linking passage at the end of the hagiographic narrative Ælfric strikingly suggests a way of relating it to the apostle, because of Paul's insistence on supporting himself by his labor: "Þa oðre apostoli, be Godes hæse, leofodon be heora lare unpleolice; ac ðeah-hwæðere Paulus ana, seðe wæs on woruld-cræfte teld-wyrhta, nolde ða alyfdan bigleofan onfon, ac mid agenre teolunge his and his geferena neode foresceawode. . . . He forlet ealle woruld-ðing, and ðam Hælende anum folgode, swa swa ðis godspel cwyð, ðe ge nu æt ðisre ðenunge gehyrdon" (*CH* I xxvii, p. 392).[39] This leads directly into the Gospel passage, which begins with Peter's words to Christ: "Efne we forleton ealle woruld-ðing, and ðe anum fyligað" ("Behold we have abandoned all worldly things and follow you alone"). The Gospel exegesis is thus used to support a heroicizing reading of Paul, seen here as apparently superior to the other disciples who depended on the rewards of preaching.

Andrew (*CH* I xxxviii)

For his homily for Andrew Ælfric's source texts and models provided a variety of suggestions and materials. The original homiliary of Paul the Deacon had Gregory's homily on the Gospel for the day, Matthew 4:18ff., to which the later version of PL 95 adds a sermon by Augustine, on martyrdom and the vicissitudes of the world, and a homily by Hericus on the Gospel text assigned to the Octave of Andrew.[40] Haymo and Smaragdus too provided further homilies on the Gospel, and the Cotton-Corpus legendary provided a *passio* (BHL 428) describing the persecution and martyrdom of the saint in Achaia at the hands of Egeas.[41] For comparison one might note that the Pembroke homiliary has a narrative piece based mainly on the same *passio*, although prefacing it with biographical material from the Gospels and Isidore, and the *Old English Martyrology* gives a brief account of the saint's martyrdom probably based on BHL 428 again.[42] A quite different story of Andrew, his experiences among the cannibals, is told in the Old English poem *Andreas* and in the Blickling homily on the saint. Whether Ælfric knew this story is hard to say. Neither in his remarks on Andrew nor in his discussion of

Matthew does he ever refer to the Mermedonian experiences, but he may well have considered it fallacious and deliberately remained silent about it.

In its earliest form his homily was devoted entirely to exegesis of the Gospel text, reflecting the influence of the exegetical homiliaries of Paul the Deacon, Haymo, and Smaragdus. But a note surviving in the Royal manuscript shows that at a very early stage he was already thinking that it would be appropriate to include a narrative of the passion as well: "Hit wære gelimplic, gif þises dæges scortnys us geþafian wolde, þæt we eow þæs halgan apostoles Andrees þrowunge gerehton. Ac we wyllað on oðrum sæle, gif we gesundfulle beoð, eow gelæstan, gif we hwæt lytles hwonlicor gefyldon."[43] The narrative in fact appears in the Royal manuscript and in all later copies and must have been added by Ælfric at a very early stage. The Gospel passage tells how Andrew and Simon abandoned their fishing to follow Christ, and in his exposition Ælfric primarily follows Gregory, interpreting the disciple' action as an image of worldly renunciation. The central concern is with the disciples in their symbolic function as models for the true believer, and the interpretation threatens to ignore the literal situation of the disciples, treating poor fishermen as representatives of the rich, as Ælfric acknowledges: "Wen is þæt eower sum cweðe to him sylfum on stillum geðohtum, 'Hwæt forleton þas gebroðru, Petrus and Andreas, þe for nean nan ðing næfdon?' " (*CH* I xxxviii, p. 580)[44]

But Ælfric frames this symbolic interpretation with a different kind of reading, which engages with the individuality of the disciples and relates more closely to the subsequent account of Andrew's passion. In a powerful and rhetorical passage near the beginning he examines the significance of Christ's choice of poor fishermen to represent him rather than emperors or philosophers:

> Fisceras and ungetogene menn geceas Drihten him to leorning-cnihtum, and hi swa geteah, þæt heora lar oferstah ealne woruld-wisdom, and hi mid heora bodunge caseras and cyningas to soðum geleafan gebigdon. Gif se Hælend gecure æt fruman getinge lareowas, and woruldlice uðwitan, and ðyllice to bodigenne sende, þonne wære geðuht swilce se soða geleafa ne asprunge ðurh Godes mihte, ac of woruldlicere getingnysse. He geceas fisceras ærðan ðe he cure caseras, forðan ðe betere is þæt se casere, þonne he to Romebyrig becymð, þæt he wurpe his cynehelm, and gecneowige æt ðæs fisceres gemynde, þonne se fiscere cneowige æt þæs caseres gemynde. Caseras he geceas, ac ðeah he geendebyrde þone unspedigan fiscere ætforan ðam rican casere. Eft siððan he geceas ða welegan; ac him wære geðuht swilce hi gecorene wæron for heora æhtum, gif he ær ne gecure þearfan. He geceas siððan woruldlice uðwitan, ac hi modegodon, gif he ær ne gecure þa ungetogenan fisceras. (*CH* I xxxviii, pp. 576, 578)[45]

He concludes his exposition of the Gospel by returning to the story of the calling of the disciples and discussing the significance of their names; the interpretation of Andrew suggests a way of reading him which relates appropriately to the ensuing legend: "Eornostlice Simon is gereht 'gehyrsum' and . . . Andreas 'ðegenlic'. . . . Gif he ðegenlice, for Godes naman, earfoðnysse forberð, and werlice deofles costnungum wiðstent, ðonne gefylð he on his ðeawum Andrees getacnunge, þe is gereht 'ðegenlic' " (*CH* I xxxviii, p. 586)[46] Ælfric is probably drawing in part here on Hericus (PL 95, 1460) who interprets the name as *virilis*, but his use of the term *ðegenlic* seems to relate to the subsequent legend's presentation of Andrew as the heroic follower of Christ.

The account of the saint's martyrdom that follows draws on a version of the Latin *passio* found in the Cotton-Corpus legendary; the Latin text is itself fairly brief and Ælfric follows it very closely. Its concern is as much with doctrine and ideas, expressed through the theological debate between Andrew and Egeas and the saint's willingness to face death, as with the narrative of event. There are no prolonged tortures and the only miracle is that which prevents the soldiers freeing Andrew from the cross when Egeas changes his mind under pressure from the people. The miracle has its own doctrinal point, demonstrating that the martyrdom is not, as Egeas thinks, an act initiated and controlled by him but one ultimately willed by God and willingly accepted by the saint; it thus neatly symbolizes the earlier argument of Andrew in his debate with Egeas that Christ willingly undertook death on the cross despite the apparent responsibility of the Jews and Romans. The central theme is that willingness to face death: it is explored in the dialogue between Andrew and Egeas, developed further in the saint's dissuasion of the people from intervening against the persecutor, and culminates in Andrew's ecstatic salute to the Cross as he is about to embrace it in death:

> Hal sy ðu, rod, þe on Cristes lichaman gehalgod wære, and mid his limum gefrætwod, swa swa mid meregrotum. Þu hæfdest eorðlicne ege, ærðande ure Drihten þe astige; nu ðu hæfst heofonlice lufe, and byst astigen for behate. Orsorh and blissigende ic cume to ðe, swa þæt ðu me blissigende underfo, ðæs leorning-cniht ðe on ðe hangode, forðan ðe ic þe symle lufode, and ic gewilnode ðe to ymbclyppenne. Eala ðu gode rod, þe wlite and fægernysse of Drihtnes lymum underfenge, ðu wære gefyrn gewilnod and carfullice gelufod, butan to-forlætennysse gesoht, and nu æt nextan minum wilnigendum mode gegearcod. Onfoh me fram mannum, and agif me minum Lareowe, þæt he ðurh ðe me underfo, seðe þurh ðe me alysde. (*CH* I xxxviii, p. 596)[47]

(Both the personalization of the cross and the loving tenderness with which Andrew addresses it remind us that this legend is a probable source for *The Dream of the Rood*.) In contrast to the agonies the apostle suffers in the legend used in *Andreas*, here he departs mysteriously and peacefully amid a blinding light, his soul journeying immediately up to heaven with the departing light. Narrative and debate work harmoniously together in developing an emotional counterargument to the story of persecution and oppression, as Andrew gains power over his persecutor. If the Gospel exposition has been adapted in part to harmonize with the legend, the legend in turn relates back to the exposition. The dialogues and speeches within the narrative harmonize well with the preaching role of the homilies; Andrew's willingness to renounce life appropriately parallels the earlier willingness to renounce his nets and the material world.

Gregory (*CH* II ix)

In this, the first of the genuine saints' lives in the Second Series, the question of an exegetical approach was probably not seriously considered. The Latin homiliaries did not provide for this occasion, and although Ælfric could have offered an exposition of the text for the occasion, Matthew 25:14–23, this is really a reading for the common of a confessor and obviously had no specific relevance to this saint. In considering an account of his life, Ælfric was perhaps baffled by the possibilities. He remarks at the outset that many books tell of the saint's life, specifying Bede's *Historia Ecclesiastica* in particular because it was available in English. The earliest known life was that composed by an anonymous monk of Whitby around 700, making extensive use of miracle stories that, as the author acknowledges, may have been linked to other saints rather than Gregory. Paul the Deacon's life, composed around 800, draws on both Bede and Gregory of Tours's *Historia Francorum*, whereas the later life by John the Deacon draws on Paul and the Whitby Life. The *Old English Martyrology* just records two miracles associated with Gregory, derived ultimately from the Whitby life. The tradition thus ranges from the historical to the frankly hagiographic and miraculous.

It was Paul the Deacon's life that Ælfric found in the Cotton-Corpus legendary and he used this as his main source and model.[48] Paul's life is a sober account that eschews miracle stories and concentrates especially on Gregory's writings and the issues raised in them that relate to his life; a particular concern is the problem of reconciling monastic ideals with the needs of pastoral work and ecclesiastical administration. Ælfric adopts the framework of this life but excludes most of the material on Gregory's writings and plays down the conflict between monastic ideals and pastoral activity. Thus he records Gregory's attempt to escape election to the papacy, but relates this to his fears about the corrupting tendencies of worldly glory rather than attributing it to the higher ideals of monasticism. What he emphasizes instead is Gregory's speech to the populace amid the ravages of plague, which takes up forty-five lines in Ælfric's version. In its powerful call to repentance under the threat of imminent death, with the promise of mercy and warnings against despair, it recalls Ælfric's own words in his preface to the *Catholic Homilies*; Ælfric speaks here through Gregory, inviting a parallel between the Roman plague and the contemporary troubles of the world's end.

The other major feature of Ælfric's account of Gregory is the story of the conversion of England. Paul told the story of the slaveboys in the mar-ketplace, as did all accounts of the saint, but gave only the most cursory account of the mission itself. Ælfric highlights it, making it the central act of Gregory's life and devoting to it over a third of his homily. His source is Bede's *Historia Ecclesiastica*, but history is here adapted to fit the conven-tions of hagiography and homiletics. He suppresses the fact that Augustine took fright before reaching England and turned back before being forced to go on by Gregory and the fact that the first mission almost failed and had to be reinforced from Rome (just as he minimizes Gregory's own reluctance to take on the duties of the church and pastoral work). Ælfric is seeking to generalize and heroicize the events of the past. At the same time, he contin-ues to use his saint as a preaching voice: central features of the mission account are Gregory's exhortatory letters to Augustine (175–87 and 239–46).

If the framework of his account owes its main features to Paul, the emphasis and content are distinct. Where Paul the Deacon had seen Gregory as a representative example of the problems of the active and contemplative lives, Ælfric turns the life into the story of an evangelist, modeled on the accounts of the apostles converting the heathen; Gregory is introduced as the apostle of the English, and his engagement with their conversion is the domi-nant concern of his life and the text.

Cuthbert (*CH* II x)

What marks the homily on Gregory is the way in which hagiography, history, and preaching are combined. Yet it is immediately followed in the Second Series by an experiment in a radically different kind of hagiographic writing, one that was to set the pattern for all of Ælfric's subsequent writing in this genre. He had before him three distinct ways of handling the same essential legend of Cuthbert: Bede's verse life, his subsequent prose expan-sion of it, and his *Historia Ecclesiastica*.[49] The verse life is essentially an account of the miracles that punctuated Cuthbert's life, described in a roughly chronological series but kept rigorously free of any attempt to connect them meaningfully or contextualize them: the life asserts the heroic glory of the saint and the divine power and calling with which he was marked out. The prose life invests the miracles with much circumstantial detail and shapes them into a biographical account of the saint, showing how the miracles prompted the course of his life or reflected on its sanctity. The *Historia Ecclesiastica* takes this historicizing and contextualizing process further, setting Cuthbert's life within the context of contemporary history and politics.

Ælfric takes details evenhandedly from the verse life and the prose life, both of which he mentions in his opening lines, and evidently knew the *Historia* well, because he mentions it elsewhere and draws on it for other texts, such as the homily on Gregory. But he chooses the verse life as his structural model. His version is striking in its starkness. The context of history is pared away to be almost invisible. There is no indication of the period of history at the beginning, and not until line 213 do we have a reference to historical context at all, and then only what is necessary to explain an inspired act of prophecy: "Ða com him to sum abbudysse seo wæs Ælflæd gehaten . ðæs cyninges sweoster Ecgfrides" (*CH* II x 212–14).[50] Even the biographical shape of Cuthbert's life is attenuated. Thus in Bede's prose life Cuthbert sees Aidan's soul being transported to heaven and is inspired by the vision to become a monk himself; on his way to the monastery he is miraculously fed while taking shelter; he reaches the monastery and becomes a monk; he is appointed to take charge of hospitality to visitors and is visited by an angel in disguise. The miracles accompany, and attest to, the idea of a divine calling to monasticism. Ælfric tells the three miracles in turn but makes no connection between them or with the decision to become a monk; they are simply three miracles linked only chronologically and introduced by *Eft, Hwilon eac, æfter ðisum* and *þa æt sumon sæle.* The biographically crucial moment when Cuthbert becomes a monk is buried within the same sentence as his appointment to take charge of hospitality: "Se eadiga cuþberhtus æfter ðisum ealle woruldðing eallunge forlet. and mid halgum ðeawum hine sylfne to munuclife geðeodde. and he hrædlice siððan he munuc wæs wearð geset cumena ðen. þæt he cumena huses gymde. and mynsterlicum cumum geðensum wære" (*CH* II x 59–63)[51] The whole story becomes a series of miracles loosely linked by *then, Next, after this.* Doctrinal discussion and explicit *sententia* are entirely absent.

The opportunity of making a close comparison of three very different presentations of the same narrative material by the same author must surely have affected the way Ælfric thought about hagiography, and the technique of the Cuthbert piece evidently owes much to Bede's verse life. This radically different mode of writing is no isolated case, however, for similar techniques of structure and style are evident in the next piece, on Benedict (*CH* II xi). Ælfric's source here was not a strictly hagiographical work but the *Dialogues* of Gregory the Great, a work that tells numerous stories of Italian saints and holy figures within the framework of a dialogue between Gregory and his deacon Peter, which comments on the doctrinal and moral implications of the stories.[52] The story of Benedict, told in Book 2, is thus presented in the context of moral and doctrinal debate, and the account also sets his life within the story of relations between church and secular rulers in a troubled period of Italian history. Ælfric's version excludes all but one of the doctrinal and metaphysical discussions of the significance of the miracles, and pares away the circumstantial details and historical references. Events are presented in series without even the temporal connectives seen in Cuthbert: "Twa mynecena . . . "; "Sum munuccild . . . "; "Sum oðer munuc . . . "; "Benedictus eac . . . "; "Sum hafenleas mann . . . "; Sumum men . . . "; "An subdiacon . . . " (CH II xi 334, 362, 376, 393, 396, 408, 413). The technique seems to be entirely deliberate: thus the last of these miracles just cited, the appearance of an ever-flowing barrel of oil when the last drop has apparently been given away, is introduced in the source with the phrase eo quoque tempore and an explanation of the relevant circumstances, linking the story to the preceding episodes; Ælfric begins immediately with the event. The story becomes a list of miracles. The same techniques can be seen in the homily on Martin (CH II xxxiv), where the historical context and biographical structure supplied by Sulpicius Severus are largely left out by Ælfric. His interest in creating a hagiographic rather than biographical structure for Martin is evident in the way he recasts the detail of earlier church customs: whereas the source carefully distinguishes successive stages of conversion, first as catechumen and then as fully baptized Christian, Ælfric imposes the pattern of his own time, having Martin move directly from heathendom to baptism. The difference between these lives and the coherently linear and individualized lives of Gregory or Clement could not be more marked.

This change of technique is accompanied by a radical experiment in prose style, for all three texts are written in a distinct kind of prose using regular rhythm and alliteration.[53] Sporadic examples of this prose occur in passages in the First Series but in the Second Series it is used in a much more sustained fashion in several narrative homilies, and it was soon to become Ælfric's standard mode of writing. Surely Bede's verse life prompted this extensive use of the alliterative style. The Cuthbert life is the first text within the sequence of the Second Series to use this style, and it is the earliest work by Ælfric known to have a verse text as a substantial source. The basic resemblance of this style to Old English verse is well established: sentences divide up into units with two stresses that are linked in pairs by alliteration:

> ða dyde cuþberhtus swa his gewuna wæs.
> sang his gebedu on sælicere yðe.
> standende oð þone swyran.
> and syððan his cneowa on ðam ceosle gebigde.
> astrehtum handbredum to heofenlicum rodore;

Efne ða comon twegen seolas of sælicum grunde.
and hi mid heora flyse his fet drygdon.
and mid heora blæde his leoma beðedon.
and siððan mid gebeacne his bletsunge bædon.
licgende æt his foton on fealwun ceosle; (*CH* II x 78–85)

The similarity to verse is more marked in Cuthbert than later examples. In his later work the rhythms are much looser than in verse and the units generally longer, with more unstressed syllables, but in the earliest texts that use the style the phrases or half lines are often short and the rhythms tight. Again, later examples are marked by their avoidance of the specialized diction of poetry, but in the early uses we find poetic words like *metod, heolstor, brim*;[54] thus Cuthbert stands *on ðam sealtan brymme* (75), where both phrasing and vocabulary are poetic. The alliterative style is accompanied in Cuthbert by occasional attempts at a colorful dramatic language of a kind not seen again or indeed earlier. There is the yellow sand of the scene with the seals or the snow-white horse of Cuthbert's angelic visitor. There are also occasional examples of rhyme (such as at 72–73). Though Ælfric had clearly been experimenting with the alliterative style earlier for brief passages, it seems likely that the example of Latin verse hagiography, with its implications of a different mode of discourse, prompted him to experiment with using the style as a sustained form of writing rather than just for occasional passages and to enrich it so fully with poetic diction.

Associated with these changes in structure and style is the deployment of a specialized hagiographic diction. What particularly characterizes the specialized diction is the use of generalizing epithets to mark the saint and the tyrant. There are traces in early lives, such as *se reða cwellere* for Egeas the persecutor of Andrew. It is marked in Ælfric's recasting of the narrative in Acts of the Apostles for his account of Stephen: Stephen is *se eadiga Stephanus, þæs eadigan martyres, ðam eadigan cyðere, se halga wer, se halga Stephanus, ðone eadigan Stephanum, se halga cyðere*. It is a language that universalizes, persistently asserting the archetypal nature of Stephen's role. Persecutors are similarly characterized with adjectives like *reðe* and *wælhreow*. Domitian in the homily on John is *sum wælhreow casere, se wælreowa, se wælhreowa Domicianus*. In the homily on Laurence epithets like *se wælhreowa casere, se reða casere, se reða cwellere* are matched with phrases such as *se eadiga martyr, ðone halgan diacon*. That it is not an inevitable way of writing such narratives is suggested by the homily on Peter and Paul, which is singularly devoid of expressions of this kind, as is the account of Gregory. But they are particularly dense in the later lives. Cuthbert is *se halga biscop, se eadiga Cuðberhtus, ðone halgan* and so on, even before he has expressed in his life the sanctity that had been foretold for him. Benedict is *ðam halgan benedicte, se halga wer*, whereas his occasional persecutors are *sum reðe cyning, se wælhreowa ehtere* (450–51). Martin is *se halga* and his persecutor is *se wælhreowa* (50).

Such language is essentially formulaic, a prose hagiographic equivalent of the heroic epithets that are similarly used in poetry for a range of different characters: *folces hyrde, folces weard, har hilderinc*. In both poetry and prose formulaic epithets assert the essential likeness of individual characters to a traditional type. But, for all the similarities to verse, there is a curious absence of the florid and emotional. In Ælfric's later hagiographical pieces, from Cuthbert on, the style becomes associated with a succinct, rather understated narrative technique. The repetitive diction and the regular balance of sentences insists on pattern and order rather than passion. Its very consistency of tone and rhythm works to universalize rather than individualize its subjects.

These later lives within the *Catholic Homilies* set the pattern for Ælfric's subsequent hagiographic and narrative writing in the *Lives of Saints* collection. They too concentrate on narrative rather than preaching and debate, they use the universalizing hagiographic diction and employ the balanced, succinct, rhythmical style that had first appeared extensively in Cuthbert. Their concentration on narrative, but at the same time a narrative which resists biographical structuring or historical contextualizing, has been noted by Dorothy Bethurum: "He was interested in narrative in the *Lives of Saints* and very little in homiletic material, and omitted all that did not contribute to effective storytelling. . . . Ælfric omits doctrinal matter, historical detail, and names that would be unfamiliar to his hearers. . . . One event follows another in the English story in a fashion that often seems purely fortuitous, though in the Latin original there are skilful connectives indicating cause and effect."[55] Neither in the use of poetic features nor in the exclusion of narrative sequentiality and biographical structure were the later writings to be as extreme or experimental as the lives of Cuthbert, Benedict, and Martin, but the basic similarities are clear. The technique is evidently deliberate, worked out through a series of experiments while writing the *Catholic Homilies*. Though the later type of saint's life may seem curiously stark to a modern critical mind, it is evidently a considered mode of writing by someone who could and did write saints' lives of a very different kind, using all the features that are absent from those in the *Lives of Saints* collection. There was clearly a change of heart about the genre.

One of the factors in this changed technique is the separation of direct *sententia*, or doctrinal material, from narrative. To explain this as reflecting a lack of interest in doctrinal issues on the part of Ælfric and his readers, as Bethurum suggests, is not wholly convincing. Æthelweard and Æthelmær, who asked for these lives, had also asked for homilies from the earlier collections, and even within the *Lives of Saints* collection there are still homi-letic pieces and doctrinal discussions, though no longer embedded within the hagiographic narrative. This perhaps has partly something to do with a change of view about the relationship of hagiography and preaching texts. The *Lives of Saints* items are, as we have seen, reading pieces rather than preaching texts. That is perhaps also true about the latest of the saints' lives in the *Catholic Homilies*. The earlier, nonalliterative saints' lives often begin with some kind of homiletic address from preacher to audience, but the lives of Cuthbert, Benedict, and Martin launch straight into narrative without a hint of the audience's presence. They are also very much longer than most of the homilies. The sense or pretense of a preaching text is clearly fading; Ælfric seems to have largely abandoned the attempt to adapt hagiography to a preaching genre even before he had completed the *Catholic Homilies* and begun to treat the saint's life as a distinct kind of discourse.

The change of technique and style seems also to be associated, however, with a change of emphasis on the kind of *sententia* to be found in saints' lives. What we see in these later lives, beginning with Cuthbert, is not just a concentration on the narrative of events but a particular kind of narrative, one that resists historical and biographical contextualization. Both style and narrative technique insist upon the universality of the life of the saint. Though the individuality of Cuthbert and Benedict, Oswald and Edmund, remains clear, events tend always to detach themselves from individual backgrounds and causes to reveal basic patterns of action common to all periods and regions. Bethurum comments that "the story of Oswald told by Bede against the background of the stirring events in Northumbria in the seventh century . . . becomes in Ælfric's account merely the *Acta Sancti Oswaldi*."[56] That is true, but one should add that in doing so the story acquires a curious and surely not accidental resemblance to the legend of Constantine, the archetype of Christian emperors. The movement from moral discourse to narrative of event is accompanied by an interest in making event symbolic rather than individual.

One final point is the possibility that the change in mode was related to an anxiety about the distinction between hagiography and history. Ælfric's concern about the status of saints' legends is evident in his comments on the legend of Thomas and on the Assumption of the Virgin and is implicit in his treatment of the legend of Peter and Paul. His hesitations about miracles have been described elsewhere. The movement away from a form of narrative that uses plain prose and sets the saint's life in a historical context and toward a form that employs a style modeled on verse and repeatedly signals its difference from historical narration may have been one of the factors by which Ælfric reconciled himself to the troubling qualities of hagiography. In clearly identifying it as a special form of writing, a genre with its own mode of discourse, he was implicitly inviting his public to read it in a particular and appropriate way, which could be different from the way they read history or homily.

Notes

1. Rosemary Woolf, "Saint's Lives," in *Continuations and Beginnings*, ed. E. G. Stanley (London, 1966), p. 40.

2. *Ælfric's Lives of Saints*, ed. and trans. W. W. Skeat, EETS OS 76, 82, 94, 114 (London, 1881–1900; reprinted as two volumes, 1966), cited by number and line.

3. Ibid., pp. 2, 4.

4. P[eter] A. M. Clemoes, "The Chronology of Ælfric's Works," *The Anglo-Saxons: Studies in Some Aspects of Their History and Culture presented to Bruce Dickins*, ed. Peter Clemoes (London, 1959), p. 221. [Reprinted as *Old English Newsletter, Subsidia* 5 (1980).]

5. See Malcolm R. Godden, "Ælfric's Saints' Lives and the Problem of Miracles," *Leeds Studies in English* 16 (1985): 83–100, especially pp. 94–97.

6. *The Homilies of the Anglo-Saxon Church: The First Part, Containing the Sermones Catholici or Homilies of Ælfric*, ed. and trans. Benjamin Thorpe, 2 vols. (London, 1844–46), vol. 1, for the First Series, identified as *CH* I followed by homily number and pages in Thorpe's edition; and *Ælfric's Catholic Homilies: The Second Series, Text*, ed. Malcolm R. Godden, EETS SS 5 (London, 1979), for the Second Series, identified as *CH* II followed by homily number and line number. Unless otherwise noted, translations from Ælfric are mine.

7. See Milton McC. Gatch, *Preaching and Theology in Anglo-Saxon England* (Toronto, 1977), and Mary Clayton, "Homiliaries and Preaching in Anglo-Saxon England," *Peritia* 4 (1985): 207–42.

8. On the distinction between *passiones* and *vitae*, see especially Michael Lapidge, "The Saintly Life," *The Cambridge Companion to Old English Literature*, ed. Malcolm R. Godden and Michael Lapidge (Cambridge, 1991), pp. 252–53.

9. For instance, some of the Old Testament prophecies of Christ used in *CH* II i are taken from the Latin legend of James, which Ælfric used as source for *CH* II xxvii.

10. Clayton, "Homiliaries," pp. 208-11.

11. Patrick Zettel, "Ælfric's Hagiographic Sources and the Latin Legendary Preserved in BL MS Cotton Nero E i + CCCC MS 9 and other manuscripts," D.Ph. dissertation, Oxford University (1979), and "Saint's Lives in Old English: Latin Manuscripts and Vernacular Accounts: Ælfric," *Peritia*, 1 (1982): 17–37.

12. See Clayton, "Homilaries," pp. 212–16, and for the Pembroke collection J. E. Cross, *Cambridge Pembroke College MS 25: A Carolingian Sermonary Used by Anglo-Saxon Preachers*, King's College London Medieval Studies 1 (London, 1987).

13. *The Blickling Homilies* ed. Richard Morris, EETS OS 58, 63, 73 (London, 1874, 1876, 1880; reprinted in two volumes, 1966).

14. See Malcolm R. Godden, "Ælfric and the Vernacular Prose Tradition," *The Old English Homily and Its Backgrounds*, ed. Paul E. Szarmach and Bernard F. Huppé (Albany, N.Y., 1978), pp. 99–118.

15. *CH* I 436–38; *CH* II xx 14–16; *CH* II p. 298. See further Godden, "Ælfric's Saints' Lives."

16. Ibid., p. 90.

17. "This Gospel does not say anything specifically about Christ's mother, but it is nevertheless customarily read at her mass, because of the ecclesiastical ordinance."

18. Skeat, *Lives of Saints*, xvi 9–12; *Homilies of Ælfric: A Supplementary Collection*, ed. John C. Pope, EETS OS 259 and 260 (London, 1967–8), vol. 2, Homily xiv, 128–46.

19. Skeat, *Lives of Saints*, xxxii 267–68.

20. J. E. Cross, "The Literate Anglo-Saxon—on Sources and Disseminations," *Proceedings of the British Academy* 58 (1972), and separately, especially pp. 26–28 and 33–36.

21. "Then the apostle ordered the king to come to the church with his people, and all the virgins too. They then came as their custom was, and the apostle told them all what belongs to marriage, what to widowhood, what to virginity, and what to the morality of everyone who lives with faith within God's church. And then at last he said that if anyone seduced the king's bride he would deserve to be thrust into burning fire. 'My beloved son Irtacus, now that you know that Effigenia your predecessor's daughter is the heavenly king's bride, and sanctified with the holy veil, how can you deprive the almighty of his bride and join her in marriage to you?' "

22. For the contents of the original version of Paul the Deacon's homiliary, see Cyril L. Smetana, "Ælfric and the Early Medieval Homiliary," *Traditio* 15 (1959): 163–204.

23. See the later and fuller version of Paul the Deacon's homiliary printed in PL 95.

24. "When Peter caught sight of him [John] he asked, 'Lord, what will happen to him?' Jesus said, 'If it should be my will that he wait until I come, what is it to you? Follow me.' That saying of Jesus became current in the brotherhood, and was taken to mean that that disciple would not die."

25. "But in fact Jesus did not say that he would not die; he only said, 'If it should be my will that he wait until I come, what is it to you?' "

26. See, for instance, Smaragdus, PL 102, 44–47, and Haymo, PL 118, 70–75, and Bede, *Homilia* I 9

27. *Der Pseudo-Hieronymus-Brief IX "Cogitis me": Ein erster marianischer Traktat des Mittelalters von Paschasius Radbert*, ed. A. Ripberger, Spicilegium Friburgense 9 (Fribourg, Switzerland, 1962).

28. *Das altenglische Martyrologium*, ed. Günter Kotzor, 2 vols. (Munich, 1981), vol. 2, p. 7. "At the grave a great miracle is seen and heard: sometimes it breathes as if a living person were sleeping, sometimes when one looks at the grave there is no body to be seen but there is a great odour of sweetness. Therefore no-one knows whether John is alive or dead."

29. The account is essentially the one listed as BHL 4320 and printed by Fabricius, *Codex Apocryphus Novi Testamenti* (Hamburg, 1719), vol. 2, 604, but Zettel ("Saint's Lives," pp. 32–34) demonstrates that the Hereford MS of the legendary contains a version much closer to Ælfric.

30. Cf. Smaragdus, PL 102, 47 and Haymo, PL 118, 74–75, and also Godden, "The Problem of Miracles," pp. 91–92.

31. "Take this gold and these jewels, and go and buy yourselves land, for you have lost the heavenly treasures. Buy yourselves purple tunics, so that you may glitter for a little while like a rose, and quickly perish. Be prosperous and rich for a while, so that you may eternally be poor. . . . The heavenly treasures are common to us all. Naked were we born, and naked we shall depart. The sun's brightness, and the light of the moon and all the stars, are common to rich and poor."

32. *Bedae Opera Homiletica*, ed. David Hurst, CCSL 122 (Turnhout, Belgium, 1955), Homilia 20.

33. " 'And I will build my church upon this rock': that is, upon the faith which you confess. All God's church is built on that rock, that is on Christ."

34. See Zettel, "Ælfric's Hagiographic Sources," pp. 94–97 and 177–78 for an excellent discussion of this issue.

35. *Acta Apostolorum Apocrypha*, ed. R. A. Lipsius and M. Bonnet, 2 parts (Leipzig, 1891–1903), vol. 1, pp. 119–77. The source was identified by Max Förster, *Über die Quellen von Ælfric's Homiliae Catholicae. Vol. 1. Legenden* (Berlin, 1892), §10.

36. Printed in *Acta Sanctorum*, ed. I. Bollandus, G. Henschenius, et al., 67 vols (Antwerp, 1643–1770, Brussels 1780–), Maii III, pp. 9–10; the source was identified by Förster, *Legenden*, §10, and its inclusion in the legendary shown by Zettel, "Ælfric's Hagiographic Sources," pp. 94–97.

37. See especially Skeat, *Lives of Saints*, xxi 464–98, and Pope, *Homilies of Ælfric*, homily xxix. One further problem about this text and its sources remains. At

the beginning of his account Ælfric remarks: "We wyllað æfter ðisum godspelle eow gereccan ðæra apostola drohtnunga and geendunge, mid scortre race; forðan ðe heora ðrowung is gehwær on Engliscum gereorde fullice geendebyrd" (CH I xxvi, p. 370) ['I will describe for you the sufferings and ending of the apostles with a short narrative because their passion is everywhere fully narrated in the English language']. He may have been referring to the Blickling version, which also uses the Latin legend beginning with the arrival of Paul. Yet the comment is puzzling. The Blickling version does reproduce this account a little more fully than Ælfric, including for instance the substance of Pilate's letter to Rome reporting his experience of Christ, but it has nothing on the earlier conflict between Peter and Simon Magus, and it is difficult to see how he could describe it therefore as a full account in comparison with his own short one. Yet if he was referring to some other lost English version it was presumably one that gave the "correct" version of the apostles' martyrdom and either a detailed account of Peter's conflict with the magus or an expanded version of the final events. There is in fact no evidence of even a Latin text that would have answered that description. Possibly he was referring to a version of a long Latin legend that has not survived or been traced; possibly it was a vague gesture toward the Blickling version as a justification for giving a short account when other motives made him reluctant to write anything fuller.

38. Augustine, *Sermo* 279, PL 38, 1276.

39. "The other apostles, following God's command, lived by their teaching without risk; but Paul alone, who was a tent-maker in his secular trade, would not take the permitted sustenance but provided for his own and his companions' needs by his own toil.... He abandoned all worldly things and followed the Saviour alone, as this Gospel says, which you heard now at this service."

40. The homily by Gregory is in PL 76, 1092–99. The homily by Hericus appears as an anonymous item in the later and fuller version of Paul the Deacon's homiliary printed in PL 95, 1457–60. The authorship was established by Henri Barré, *Les homéliaires de l'École d'Auxerre*, Studi et Testi 223 (Vatican City, Italy, 1962).

41. Haymo's homily is in PL 118, 747–55, and the one by Smaragdus is in PL 102, 510–12. The *passio* is a version of BHL 428. Zettel demonstrated ("Ælfric's Hagiographic Sources," pp. 166–71) that the version in the Hereford manuscript of the legendary is closer to Ælfric than the version found in the earlier manuscripts; the Hereford version is in fact more or less identical to the one edited in *Acta Apostolorum Apocrypha*, ed. R. A. Lipsius and M. Bonnet, vol. 2 (Leipzig, 1898), pp. 1–37.

42. Cross, *Cambridge Pembroke College MS 25*, p. 39; Kotzor, *Das altenglische Martyrologium*, vol. 2, p. 260.

43. "It would be fitting, if the shortness of the day would permit, to tell you of the holy apostle Andrew's passion. But, if we have health, we will make it good another time, if we have fallen short in any detail." The note is printed by Kenneth Sisam, *Studies in the History of Old English Literature* (Oxford, 1953), p. 174.

44. "No doubt one of you is saying in his silent thoughts, 'What did these brothers, Peter and Andrew, who scarcely owned anything, give up?'."

45. "The Lord chose fishermen and uneducated people as his disciples, and so educated them that their learning excelled all worldly wisdom, and with their preaching they turned emperors and kings to true belief. If the Saviour had chosen in the beginning eloquent teachers and worldly philosophers and sent such people out to preach, then it might have seemed as if the true faith had not sprung up through God's power but through worldly eloquence. He chose fishermen before he chose emperors, because it is better that the emperor, when he comes to Rome, should cast aside his crown and kneel at the fisherman's memorial than that the fisherman should kneel at the emperor's memorial. He chose emperors, but he placed the indigent fisherman before the rich emperor. Afterwards he chose the wealthy; but it would have seemed as if they had been chosen because of their possessions if he had not chosen the poor previously. He subsequently chose worldly philosophers, but they would have become proud if he had not chosen the uneducated fishermen before."

46. "Truly Simon is interpreted 'obedient' and . . . Andrew 'thegn-like'. . . . If someone endures hardship like a thegn, for God's sake, and bravely withstands the devil's assaults, then he fulfills in his character the meaning of Andrew, which is interpreted 'thegnlike.' "

47. "Hail to you, O Cross, sanctified in Christ's body, and adorned with his limbs, as with pearls. You received earthly terror before our Lord ascended you; now you have heavenly love, and are raised up as a promise. Carefree and rejoicing I come to you, so that you may receive me rejoicing, the disciple of him who hung on you, because I have always loved you and desired to embrace you. O good Cross, who received beauty and fairness from the Lord's limbs, you were of old desired and sorrowfully loved, sought without remission, and now at last prepared for my longing heart. Take me from mankind, and give me to my teacher, so that he may receive me through you, he who redeemed me through you."

48. On the sources, see Malcolm R. Godden, "The Sources for Ælfric's Homily on St. Gregory," *Anglia* 86 (1968): 79–88. Paul the Deacon's life is printed in PL 75, 41–60, though a shorter and more original version, close to the text Ælfric used, is printed by H. Grisar in *Zeitschrift für katholische Theologie* 11 (1887): 158–73; and by W. Stuhlfath in *Gregor I der Grosse* (Heidelberg, 1913).

49. The prose life is edited in Bertram Colgrave, *Two Lives of St. Cuthbert* (Cambridge, 1940), and the verse life by W. Jaager, *Bedas metrische Vita sancti Cuthberti*, Palaestra 198 (Leipzig, 1935). The sources were identified by Förster, *Legenden.*

50. "Then a certain abbess who was called Ælflæd, sister of King Ecgfrith, came to him."

51. "The blessed Cuthbert utterly abandoned all worldly things after this, and with holy virtues associated himself with the monastic life and as soon as he became

a monk he was appointed the visitors' servant, so that he should look after the guesthouse and serve the monastic visitors."

52. A. de Vogüe, ed., *Grégoire le Grand, Dialogues*, 3 vols., Sources Chrétiennes 244, 253, and 257 (Paris, 1978–80).

53. The fullest discussion of this style is in Pope, *Homilies of Ælfric*, pp. 105–36.

54. See M. R. Godden, "Ælfric's Changing Vocabulary," *English Studies* 61 (1980): 217–19.

55. Dorothy Bethurum, "The Form of Ælfric's 'Lives of Saints'," *Studies in Philology* 29 (1932): 515–33, on pp. 519–20.

56. Ibid., p. 520.

Ælfric as Historian: His Use of Alcuin's *Laudationes* and Sulpicius's *Dialogues* in His Two Lives of Martin

Frederick M. Biggs

Ælfric's insistence on orthodoxy has received much attention: he rejects the Apocrypha when confronting legends concerning the Virgin Mary and as a translator of the Bible his concern is to conserve the literal text.[1] My subject in this chapter, however, is his changing attitude toward an authority that he had no immediate reason to doubt, the work on Saint Martin by Alcuin, his well-known countryman who had become schoolmaster in the court of Charlemagne. In 1892 Max Förster identified sources for Ælfric's *Depositio Sancti Martini Episcopi* (his first life of Saint Martin, which appears in the Second Series of *Catholic Homilies*) in the works of Sulpicius Severus, primarily his *Vita Sancti Martini*, but also his *Epistulae* and his *Dialogorum Libri Tres*, the same works that largely underlie his second life of Martin in the *Lives of Saints*.[2] Until recently this view, with some qualifications, was accepted by other scholars;[3] however, in his Oxford dissertation,[4] Patrick H. Zettel substantially altered our understanding of the situation by discovering Ælfric's use of Alcuin's *Laudationes*.[5] As Zettel notes, this work, which also derives largely from Sulpicius,[6] cannot be the sole source for Ælfric's first life of Martin, because it lacks much material that the Old English writer includes. The discovery, however, reopens the question of what materials Ælfric had at his disposal in writing the two lives, and how he chose to use them. In this chapter, I would like to argue that Ælfric probably did not consult Sulpicius's *Dialogues* when he wrote the *Depositio* and that, when he used this work in writing his second Life of Martin, it led him to reject the *Laudationes* as authoritative.[7] In doing so, Ælfric shows an awareness of the relative value of historical sources, ultimately preferring Sulpicius's firsthand account to Alcuin's redaction.

Much of the manuscript evidence suggests that Ælfric would have had access to Sulpicius's *Dialogues* as well as to the *Vita* and Epistles when he wrote the *Depositio*. Many manuscripts of *Martiniana* contain most if not all of Sulpicius's writings concerning the saint, and the Irish "Book of Armagh" (Dublin, Trinity College 52) indicates that all three were known in an Insular context from the beginning of the ninth century.[8] Manuscripts known in Anglo-Saxon England that contain the *Vita, Dialogues*, and Epistles include London, BL Additional 40074;[9] Cambridge, Trinity Hall 21;[10] Vatican, Reg. Lat. 489;[11] and Hereford Cathedral Library O.6.xi.[12] Moreover all three works are included in the Cotton-Corpus legendary, which Zettel has identified as Ælfric's "chief quarry for hagiographic matter both in the *Homilies* and in the *Lives*."[13] However, the exact contents of this collection at the moment when Ælfric would have known it are still open to dispute. The earliest version— contained in London, BL Cotton Nero E.i parts 1 and 2, and Cambridge, Corpus Christi College 9—includes among other texts about the saint the two books of the *Dialogues* that concern Martin, but the manuscript was written some fifty years after Ælfric's death.[14] Two twelfth-century versions of the collection—Oxford, Bodleian Library Bodley 354 and Hereford, Cathedral Library P.7.vi[15]—include all three books of the *Dialogues* and differ in some other respects in the material that they include about Martin, one of which will be discussed later. These differences create the impression that the contents of the collection, at least as far as Martin is concerned, grew over time, and so it is at least possible that Ælfric's version of the legendary did not contain the *Dialogues*.[16] Of course, it is also possible that the *Dialogues* were available to Ælfric when he wrote the *Depositio*, but that he did not consult them carefully.

The manuscript evidence for Ælfric's knowledge of Alcuin's *Laudationes* also raises some questions about the contents of the Cotton-Corpus legendary. The presence of this text in Bodley 354 leads Zettel to propose that it may have been part of the version of the collection that Ælfric used. However, because the text does not appear in CCCC 9, nor indeed in Hereford P.7.vi, it may well be a later addition. Indeed Alcuin's redaction has been identified in only one manuscript known in Anglo-Saxon England, Cambridge, Pembroke College 25.[17] This manuscript, as Henri Barré established, is one of six witnesses of the *Homiliary of Saint-Père*, Chartres, a ninth-century Carolingian collection.[18] Recently James E. Cross has shown this collection to be the source for a number of Old English vernacular homilies, providing further evidence for its circulation in Anglo-Saxon England.[19] Moreover, the text of the *Laudationes* in the Pembroke manuscript is significant at several points for understanding Ælfric's *Depositio*, whereas the text in Bodley 354 is substantially that of Migne in the *Patrologia Latina*.[20] Hence, although it is certainly too soon to conclude that Ælfric knew the *Homiliary of Saint Père*, or even that the version of the *Laudationes* is limited to this collection,[21] Zettel's discovery of Ælfric's use of Alcuin may not simply point to his use of the Cotton-Corpus legendary.

To turn from the external evidence of surviving manuscripts to the internal evidence of the works themselves, we may begin with Zettel's discovery that Alcuin's *Laudationes* is the immediate source for the passages in Ælfric's *Depositio* (ed. Godden, lines 146–54, 219–25, and 241–66) derived ultimately from the *Dialogues*.[22] Indeed, only three details in these passages may be more closely paralleled in the *Dialogues* than in the *Laudationes*, and on closer examination, only one appears significant. This phrase occurs in the account of miraculous manifestation that takes place while Martin celebrates mass. Ælfric relates the event: "Hwilon æt his mæssan men gesawon scinan færlice æt his hnolle swilce fyren clywen. swa þæt se scinenda líg his locc up ateah."[23] Alcuin's redaction provides the immediate source for most of the material here: "Et eodem beato viro celebrante sanctum mysterium ad altare, globus igneus subito de vertice fulsit illius."[24] For Ælfric's final comment, however, one must return to the *Dialogues* 2.2, which after describing the fiery ball emanating from the saint's head, adds "ita ut in sublime contendens longum admodum crinem flamma produceret."[25] Although there is some confusion over the image here—Ælfric, or his immediate source, understands *crinem* to refer to the saint's hair, apparently unaware of the meaning "tail of a comet"[26]—when Ælfric retells this story in the *Lives of Saints* the confusion remains: "swa þæt se líg abræd þone loc up feor."[27] This detail is the strongest evidence for Ælfric's knowledge of the *Dialogues* when writing the *Depositio*, although it remains possible that the phrase appeared in the manuscript of Alcuin that Ælfric used.[28]

The other details possibly shared by the *Dialogues* and the *Depositio* offer less convincing evidence of Ælfric's use of this work. The first occurs in a passage in which Martin revives a dead person: "Hit gelamp eac swilce on oðrum timan. þæt anre wydewan sunu wearð to deaðe gebroht. and hrædlice gewát fram woruldlicum bricum. and se halga martinus for hine gebæd on ðæs folces gesihðe. and hé sona arás to ðam lænan life þe hé ær forlet; þurh ðam tacne gelyfdon of ðære leode gehwilce on ðone lifigendan god. ðe hine to life arærde."[29] In presenting the story in this way, Ælfric clearly follows Alcuin's account: "Tertium ab eodem sancto viro, in Carnoteno oppido, cujusdam muleris flentem filium sola oratione in conspectu populi resuscitavit. Quo miraculo viso, plurimi ex populo crediderunt Christo."[30] However, one detail, Ælfric's identification of the woman as a widow, has no source in Alcuin. At least a possible source for this detail is in Sulpicius's account (*Dialogues* 2.4), where the woman begs the saint to restore her son, "quia unicus mihi est,"[31] a phrase that might have been misread to imply not that the woman has no other sons but that she has no one else. Yet the ultimate source of the detail, Luke's Gospel, makes it unnecessary to posit the *Dialogues* as an intermediary; this account of Christ's raising a young man specifies that his mother is a widow (Luke 7:12). Moreover, when Ælfric retells this story in his second life of Martin following the account in the

Dialogues, he clearly identifies the woman as a "wif" and translates her argument, "forþan-ðe he is me ancenned."[32] Thus it is possible that Ælfric's source for the *Depositio* contained the word for widow and so does not correspond to any of the manuscripts that I have yet consulted;[33] but it is also possible that Ælfric himself recalled Christ's miracle when describing Martin's.

The final possible correspondence between the *Depositio* and the *Dialogues* appears in Ælfric's discussion of how Martin heals a boy bitten by a snake: "Þa wæs ðær án cnapa geættrod þurh næddran swiðe toswollen. þurh ðæs wyrmes slege. unwene his lifes. ac he wearð ahred þurh martines hrepunge fram ðam reðan attre."[34] Alcuin again provides most of these details in his version of this incident: "In eadem quoque domo puerum a serpente percussum, sanctorum tactu digitorum a periculo mortis eruit."[35] The phrase *swiðe toswollen* may go back to Sulpicius's description (*Dialogues* 2.2): "cerneres omnibus uenis inflatam cutem."[36] However, it is also possible that Ælfric added this naturalistic detail. In the *Lives of Saints* he develops the image further—describing the boy's body as "eall toblawen on anre bytte gelicnysse"[37]—following a phrase—"et ad utris instar tensa uitalia"[38]—in the *Dialogues*.

Other details, however, suggest that Ælfric did not consult the *Dialogues* when he wrote his first life of Martin. In one instance, he relates how a man is healed by sitting where Martin had sat: "Hit gelamp hwilon þæt an wód man gesæt þær ðær se eadiga wer hine ær gereste. and he wearð gewittig ðurh þæs weres geearnungum þe on ær þæt setl swa gebletsode."[39] The printed version of Alcuin's text introduces a complication by identifying the deranged person as a "puella," but many manuscripts of Alcuin simply read "persona," and it is this that Ælfric follows: "Quaedam persona daemoniaco arrepta spiritu, stramine, ubi sanctus Martinus sedebat, a potestate erepta est inimica."[40] Sulpicius's version of the story in the *Dialogues* 2.8 is substantially more complicated: "ecclesia ibi est celebris religione sanctorum nec minus gloriosa sacrarum uirginum multitudine. praeteriens ergo Martinus in secretario ecclesiae habuit mansionem. post discessum illius cunctae in secretarium illud uirgines inruerunt: adlambunt singula loca, ubi aut sederat uir beatus aut steterat, stramentum etiam, in quo iacuerat, partiuntur. una earum post dies paucos partem straminis, quam sibi pro benedictione collegerat, energumeno, quem spiritus erroris agitabat, de ceruice suspendit. nec mora, dicto citius eiecto daemone persona curata est."[41] It seems unlikely that Ælfric would have followed Alcuin's simplified account had he known the full version from Sulpicius, and when he comes to retell the story in the second life, he corrects some details: "Eac swilce of his bedstrewe man band on anne wodne þa ge-wat se deofol him of and he his ge-wit underfeng."[42] Ælfric restores the role of the straw in effecting the cure, which must have seemed to him a superfluous detail in Alcuin's account, and he reintroduces the intermediary between the saint and the cured person. It is striking, however, that Ælfric uses the impersonal construction *man band*, and thus avoids identifying the gender of the person who assists in the miracle. Although it is difficult to identify exactly what he might have objected to in the story, the impersonal construction may indicate that perhaps for personal or theological reasons he was offended by the suggestion of intimacy between the saint and a woman. The impression of some uneasiness on his part with the story is increased by his condensing it into three clauses. This issue will become more important when considering the structure of the second life; the point here is that when Ælfric finds information in the *Dialogues* that clarifies an event, he follows it even if he does not wish to provide a longer account of an incident.

A second example of Ælfric's reliance on the *Dialogues* in the *Lives of Saints* to correct an account he had previously derived from Alcuin is provided by the description of the appearance of the Virgin, Peter and Paul, and two virgins to the saint.[43] In the *Depositio* Ælfric states: "Seo halige MARIA eac swilce gecom to ðam halgan were on sumere tide mid twám apostolum. Petre. and Paule. mid twám mædenum. Tecla. and Agna. and mid hire geneosunge hine gearwurðode. and micclum gehyrte. þurh hir andwerdnesse."[44] This version clearly rests on Alcuin's: "Quodam vero die beatissimae Genitircis Dei et domini nostri Jesu Christi, et sanctorum apostolorum Petri et Pauli; nec non sanctarum virginum Theclae et Agnetis visitatione vir Dei honoratus et confortatus est."[45] The account in the *Dialogues* 2.13 is substantially different. Rather than describing a single event with all five saints present, Sulpicius (writing in the voice of Martin's disciple, Gallus) states that Martin receives repeated visits from the three women, and other visions of Peter and Paul:

Quodam die ego et iste Sulpicius pro foribus illius excubantes iam per aliquot horas cum silentio sedebamus, ingenti horrore et tremore, ac si ante angeli tabernaculum mandatas excubias duceremus, cum quidem nos, clauso cellulae suae ostio, ibi esse nesciret. interim conloquentium murmur audimus et mox horrore quodam circumfundimur ac stupore, nec ignorare potuimus nescio quid fuisse diuinum. post duas fere horas ad nos Martinus egreditur: ac tum eum iste Sulpicius, sicut apud eum nemo familiarius loquebatur, coepit orare, ut pie quaerentibus indicaret, quid illud diuini fuisset horroris, quod fatebamur nos ambo sensisse, uel cum quibus fuisset in cellula conlocatus: tenuem enim nos scilicet et uix intellectum sermocinantium sonum pro foribus audisse. tum ille diu multumque cunctatus—sed nihil erat quod ei Sulpicius non extorqueret inuito: incredibiliora forte dicturus sum, sed Christo teste non mentior, nisi quisquam est tam sacrilegus, ut Martinum aestimet fuisse mentitum—: dicam, inquit, uobis, sed uos nulli quaeso dicatis: Agnes, Thecla et Maria mecum fuerunt. referebat autem nobis uultum adque habitum singularum. nec uero illo tantum die, sed frequenter se ab eis confessus est uisitari: Petrum etiam et Paulum Apostolos uideri a se saepius non negauit.[46]

In his second version, Ælfric clearly follows the *Dialogues*:

> Ða halgan apostolas petrum and paulum he ge-seah ge-lome
> swa swa he sæde him-sylf sulpicio þam writere
> þe hine axian dorste ælces þinges þe he wolde.
> Se ylca sulpicius and sum oðer broðor
> sæton sume dæg swiðe afyrhte
> ætforan martines inne and he hi þær-ute nyste.
> Þa gehyrdon hí motian wið martine lange
> and he wæs ana ær innan þam huse belocen.
> Eft þa ða he ut-eode þa axode sulpicius
> and hine eadmodlice bæd þæt he him ge-openian sceolde
> hwa him wið-spræce. Þa wandode he lange
> him þæt to secgenne ac he sæde swa-þeah
> ic hasige eow nu þæt ge hit nanum ne secgan
> Maria cristes modor com to he hider
> mid twam oþrum mædenum tecla and agne
> and na on þisum anum dæge ac oft rædlice ær
> hi comon to me and he sæde him eac
> hwilc heora wlitu wæs and hu hi wæron ge-scrydde.[47]

In itself, Ælfric's careful use of the *Dialogues* again suggests that the Anglo-Saxon writer did not have access to this work when he composed his first Life of Martin. But the passage seems even more pointed. Ælfric takes up Sulpicius's last point—the visions of Peter and Paul—first and transforms Gallus's negative statement that Martin did not deny ("non negauit") these visions into a positive one based specifically on the *authority* of Sulpicius, "as he himself said, Sulpicius, *the writer*." Then, anticipating a detail in the following narrative, he explains the basis for this authority: Sulpicius was able to ask Martin anything that he wanted to know. Finally, he turns to the event at which Sulpicius was present, rendering Gallus's "iste Sulpicius" as "se ylca Sulpicius," driving home the direct authority for this account. Ælfric, then, rewrites the account to exploit fully the authority of his source as a witness of the event.

Indeed these remarks about Sulpicius's direct access to the saint echo the opening passage of the second life of Martin, where Ælfric clearly identifies Sulpicius as his source:

> Sulpicius hatte sum snoter writere
> ðe wolde awritan þa wundra and mihta
> þe martinus se mære mihtiglice gefremode
> of þisre worulde and he wrat þa be him
> þa ðing þe he of-axode oððe æt him sylfum

oððe æt oþrum mannum forðan þe manegum wæron
his wundra cuþe þe god worhte þurh hine
and we þæt englisc nimað of þære ylcan gesetnysse
ac we ne writað na mare butan his agene wundra.[48]

Underlying this comment may be in part Sulpicius's own reassurances to the reader that conclude his explanation of why he has written the *Vita*: "Obsecro autem eos qui lecturi sunt, ut fidem dictis adhibeant, neque me quicquam nisi conpertum et probatum scripsisse arbitrentur: alioquin tacere quam falsa dicere maluissem."[49] The passage also rests on Sulpicius's discussion near the end of the *Vita* of how he visited Martin and gathered his information "partim ab ipso, in quantum ille interrogari potuit . . . partim ab his qui interfuerant uel sciebant."[50] The final two lines, however, which recall other Ælfrician remarks on translation such as the one in the Preface to Genesis,[51] indicate his discontent with some of the material that he knows about Martin. This comment is not directed at Gregory of Tours because, as Gerould notes, he draws more heavily on Gregory's work in this later version.[52] Instead, I would argue that it refers to the *Laudationes* and shows that Ælfric became dissatisfied with Alcuin's redaction, which he had previously used, when he compared it with Sulpicius's contemporary accounts of the saint. In this context, his comment that he works from "þære ylcan gesetnysse," that is, from Sulpicius's own account, appears quite pointed.

If Ælfric had become familiar with the *Dialogues* only after writing the *Depositio*, this work would have provided him with more information not only about the individual events of Martin's life, but also about the order of these events. Establishing the chronology of the saint's life is complicated by the nature of Sulpicius's own writings. The *Vita*, which was completed before Martin's death, obviously omits details from the end of the life that later authors, including Ælfric, fill in mainly from Sulpicius's epistle to Bassula.[53] Moreover, the structure of the *Vita* is Suetonian in that it follows the chronology of the subject's life until success is attained, and then summarizes thematically further achievements; as Clare Stancliffe writes, "chapters 2–10 do contain a chronological account of Martin's career up to his election as bishop and the foundation of Marmoutier; the following fourteen devoted to his miraculous deeds as bishop are strictly arranged according to subject-matter."[54] The situation is further complicated by the *Dialogues*, purportedly a conversation between Sulpicius, Postumianus—who relates his journey to the east in *Dialogue* I—and Gallus, who in *Dialogues* II and III compares Martin with Postumianus's eastern saints. The difficulty is that Gallus's remarks are not structured on the order of events in the saint's life, but do include some chronological references. To this mixture of chronological and nonchronological information can be added the evidence of the order of the

composition of the works themselves: internal details make it clear that the
Vita was written before the *Dialogues* and the epistles concerning Martin.
This complicated situation makes it more difficult to determine Ælfric's attitude toward his sources from the way he structures his accounts of the
saint's life than from his rewriting of individual incidents; however, these
changes also indicate that he turns away from Alcuin's redaction for reasons
of historical accuracy. In general, the structure of the *Depositio*, which is
dominated at the end by the structure of Alcuin's work, contrasts sharply with
that of the *Lives of Saints*, in which Ælfric attempts his own integration of
Sulpicius's works.

Perhaps the most dramatic example of Ælfric's restructuring of material
between the *Depositio* and the *Lives of Saints* occurs because of his first use
in the earlier life of two incidents from Alcuin, the story of the healing of the
widow's son mentioned earlier, and the account of the saint healing a girl
who had been mute from birth (ed. Godden, lines 152–54). Ælfric clearly
follows Alcuin in linking these legends, even accepting his phrase "in eodem
oppido," which he renders "on ðære ylcan byrig" ("in that same city"). In fact
in Sulpicius's text these miracles do not occur in the same place: Martin heals
the dumb girl "in Carnutena . . . ciuitate,"[55] but he has resuscitated the young
man on the way to that city: "fuerat causa nescio qua Carnotum oppidum
petebamus. interea, dum uicum quendam habitatium multitudine frequentis-
simum praeterimus. . . . "[56] When Ælfric comes to these miracles in the *Lives
of Saints*, he apparently felt no need to link them and so separates them by
some seventy lines in his text. Indeed he even fails to mention where the first
miracle takes place, identifying it only as "þone feld . . . þær martinus ferde."[57]

It is not, however, simply the separating of the two incidents, but their
placement within the larger narrative that shows Ælfric's move away from
the *Laudationes* in the later version, although the argument here is complicated by some textual uncertainties. As printed by Migne, Alcuin's text summarizes several miracles that the saint performs after returning to Gaul but
before becoming a bishop: three resurrections and the healing of the girl. In
combining these events, Alcuin violates the chronology of the saint's life as
set out in the *Dialogues* because here it is stated specifically that the third
resurrection takes place after Martin had become a bishop (*Dialogues* 2.4).
Even in the *Depositio* Ælfric avoids this suggestion by including the material
from Alcuin after relating how Martin was selected Bishop of Tours, and so
if it were from a text such as Migne's that he worked, his placement of the
material could be taken to show a knowledge of the *Dialogues* even at this
time. However, the version of Alcuin's text in Pembroke 25 makes it much
less clear when Martin became a bishop, following the miracles under consideration with the comment: "et alia multa in episcopatu sanctarum insignia
uirtutum gessit miracula et multa caelestis vitae dogmata docens privatae

continentiam vitae in multitudine populi constitutus non amisit."[58] If it were a text such as this that Ælfric used, there would be no reason to assume that the miracles were not performed after Martin had become a bishop.

The more likely explanation for Ælfric's use of the material at this point in the *Depositio* indicates the high regard he has for his countryman's work at this time. Although his and Alcuin's accounts do not agree on the order of events that lead up to these two miracles, they do overlap in the incident that follows: Ælfric immediately turns to the story of the saint halting a pagan burial, which is also the next miracle recounted in the *Laudationes*.[59] It appears, then, that in comparing the *Vita* and the *Laudationes* Ælfric confronts in Alcuin material that he does not find in Sulpicius's *Vita*, and, unsure where else to include it, he places it before the next point where the two texts coincide. In the *Lives of Saints*, which he structures quite differently, 600 lines separate the story of the pagan burial and third resurrection. From this experience alone, Ælfric would have had reason to question the structure of Alcuin's ordering of events had he consulted the *Dialogues* when writing the *Depositio*, and he certainly moves away from the intermediary account when writing the *Lives of Saints*.

The extent of Ælfric's debt to Alcuin becomes clearer in the section of the *Depositio* that precedes the description of Martin's death. Here, unlike the previous instance, following the *Laudationes* does not lead him into any gross historical inaccuracy, in part because Alcuin too has followed Sulpicius's writings and in part because the chronology of this phase of Martin's life is less certain. But a historical issue is raised simply because Ælfric comes to prefer his countryman's version even to Sulpicius's *Vita*. He does so, I would argue, not only because the *Vita* and the *Laudationes* agree in many details, but also because Alcuin's version contained details that he may not have known at this time from other sources and so appeared as authoritative as Sulpicius's own writings.

The exact point in the *Depositio* where Ælfric shifts from relying primarily on Sulpicius's *Vita* to following the *Laudationes* is difficult to determine because of the overlapping of material. From line 154, the order of events follows that of Alcuin's version, and Ælfric gradually shifts from the fuller accounts in the *Vita* to the much condensed ones of the *Laudationes*. One possible place to identify the shift is in line 211 where, after describing in three sentences how Martin expels a demon,[60] Ælfric follows Alcuin in turning directly to an account of how Martin heals a leper, passing over a miracle that occurs at the beginning of Chapter 18 of the *Vita*. He then summarizes three more miracles in single sentences,[61] and in one detail he may have been misled by the wording of Alcuin's condensed version. In describing how Martin is healed by angels after a fall, Ælfric locates the place of the fall as "on ðam healicum gradum æt þam halgum weofode,"[62] understanding the

more restricted, medieval meaning of *gradus* as "the elevated part of a church
in front of the altar" in Alcuin's brief phrase *cadens per gradus*.[63] In contrast,
the *Vita* specifies that this stair descends "de cenaculo." At this point, then,
it appears that Ælfric is working primarily from Alcuin's redaction.

In any case, Ælfric like Alcuin omits Chapter 20 of the *Vita*, which
relates the saint's confrontation with Maximus, and immediately turns to
commenting on other angelic visitations (ed. Godden, lines 219–21), a detail
that, as Zettel notes, could have been drawn from the *Vita* 21.1, the *Dialogues*
2.13, or directly from Alcuin.[64] The following passage (ed. Godden, lines
221–25), as noted previously, comes ultimately from the *Dialogues*, but by
way of the *Laudationes*. Like Alcuin, Ælfric then turns to discussing the
saint's confrontations with devils, but apparently the single sentence in the
Laudationes ("nam daemonum phantasmata, et in diversis figuris horribiles
aspectus nihil metuens, nec ullis eorum fallaciis illudi potuit"[65]) recalls to his
mind the much longer discussion of Satan's appearance to Martin in the *Vita*,
a story that he recounts (ed. Godden, lines 226–38) before returning to Alcuin's
redaction. The implication again is that Ælfric is working primarily from
Alcuin, although he still consults Sulpicius's *Vita*. Indeed, Ælfric ends his
account of Martin's miracles with the last one that Alcuin includes—the
woman healed from a flow of blood by touching Martin's clothes (ed. Godden,
lines 264-66; PL 101, 661)—and does not return to the final chapters of the
Vita at all. Thus it appears that Ælfric in the *Depositio* comes to rely almost
totally on Alcuin's version, perhaps even for his summarizing comment, "ne
mage we awritan ealle his wundra on ðisum scortan cwyde,"[66] which may
echo Alcuin's: "talibus etiam et aliis innumerabilibus electus Dei sacerdos in
mundo claruit miraculis."[67] In any case, he appears to have no doubt at this
time that in following Alcuin he writes "mid cuðum gereorde."[68]

In the *Lives of Saints* Ælfric provides his own synthesis of material from
the *Vita* and the *Dialogues*, including virtually all of the miracles in both. In
many cases, he too must rely on thematic links to join the material; however,
the significant juncture between the two works again shows his awareness of
the historical potential of his sources. This juncture, I will argue, takes place
after Ælfric has used material through Chapter 20 of the *Vita*, but even if it
occurs slightly earlier, his structure makes sense in a general way. In the
Dialogues Gallus explicitly limits his subject to the later part of Martin's life
(after he has become a bishop) to avoid repeating the events covered so fully
in Sulpicius's first work (*Dialogues* 1.27). Ælfric's strategy is to follow the
Vita until he perceives a compelling reason to begin introducing material
from the *Dialogues*; he then in general uses material from the *Dialogues* in
their narrative order unless he perceives some thematic reason for linking
particular passages.

The first use of material from the *Dialogues* in the *Lives of Saints* is somewhat misleading because it is not typical of how Ælfric works. The miracle itself has already been discussed: a nun uses Martin's bed straw to cast out a demon (ed. Skeat, lines 572–73). It may simply be a thematic link that explains Ælfric's decision to place these lines where he does: Chapter 18 of the *Vita* ends with the brief comment that threads from Martin's garments often heal people, and this may have seemed a natural context to include a miracle that concerned another object endowed with special properties because it came in contact with the saint. However, as noted before, both the impersonal "man" construction and the extreme brevity of Ælfric's rendering suggest that he is embarrassed by this account. If so, the context of the miracle in the *Dialogues* would not have reassured him. In the *Dialogues* 2.6, Gallus relates how the wife of Emperor Maximus chose to serve Martin, which leads in Chapters 7 and 8 to a discussion of how other monks should behave toward women. Although Gallus claims to leave this subject to return to his recounting of miracles, the last part of Chapter 8, the miracle under consideration here, at some level continues the theme. Because the surrounding discussion does not contain miracles, Ælfric, whose emphasis is on the "wundra and mihta" (ed. Skeat, line 2) of Martin,[69] is justified in omitting it. By doing so, he implicitly follows Sulpicius's own advice near the end of the discussion when he comments in his fictional voice, "tota nobis istorum memoria relinquatur: ad Martinum potius reuertamur."[70] Ælfric does include the miracle itself, but appears to want to minimize its importance both in the way he tells it, and in the place that he puts it—before the obvious shift to material from the *Dialogues*.

The next juncture in the *Lives of Saints* between the material from the *Vita* and from the *Dialogues* is significant not only because it shows Ælfric attempting—albeit mistakenly—to construct a historically accurate narrative, but also because it challenges the thesis of this chapter that Ælfric turned away from Alcuin's work in his second life of Martin. To begin with the second point, lines 239–65 of the *Depositio* all come directly from the *Laudationes*, but include some material ultimately from the *Vita* as well as from the *Dialogues*. One place where the two sources are mixed is in a series of remarks about Martin's attitude toward secular authority: "Hé nolde olæcan ænigum rican mid geswæsum wordum. ne eac soð forsuwian; Gif him ænig heafodman hwilces ðinges forwyrnde. ðonne wende he to gode mid gewunelicum gebedum. and him sona getiðode his scyppendes arfæstnys þæs ðe se woruldrica him forwyrnde on ær."[71] The passage in the *Laudationes* reads, "Nemini adulando blandiebatur; principi nulli veritatis verba tacuit, ad nota semper orationum subsidia recurrens. Unde si quid ei potestas renuit saecularis, mox divina praestitit pietas."[72] Although these two thoughts seem closely related, Alcuin has apparently taken them from different works. As Zettel notes,[73] the first draws on Martin's dealings with Maximus (*Vita* 20): "cum ad imperatorem Maximum, ferocis ingenii uirum et bellorum ciuilium victoria elatum, plures ex diuersis orbis partibus episcopi conuenissent et foeda circa principem omnium adulatio notaretur seque degenere inconstantia regiae clientelae sacerdotalis dignitas subdidisset, in solo Martino apostolica auctoritas permanebat. Nam et si pro aliquibus regi supplicandum fuit, imperauit potius quam rogauit."[74] The second is less specific, but may come from the account of Martin's dealings with Valentinian, who tries to deny the saint access to his court but who eventually must even rise to greet him because a fire breaks out on his throne (*Dialogues* 2.5).[75] Thus it is possible that Ælfric, remembering his earlier life of Martin, or Alcuin's version, follows the story in the *Lives of Saints* drawn on the *Vita* (20) with the full account from the *Dialogues* (ed. Skeat, lines 610–81). Although this explanation would not undercut part of my thesis—that Ælfric probably did not consult the *Dialogues* when he wrote the *Depositio*—it would suggest that he continued to be influenced by Alcuin's work even after he had become familiar with Sulpicius's work.

A closer reading of the *Lives of Saints*, however, suggests that the correspondence to Alcuin's work is coincidence, and that Ælfric has more specific reasons for joining the two accounts: he attempts his own historical synthesis of the material. Chapter 20 of the *Vita* ends with Martin prophesying to Maximus how the emperor would eventually die at the hands of Valentinian, and Ælfric translates this scene:

> He sæde þa þam casere swa swa him becom siððan
> þæt gif he ferde to ge-feohte swa he gemynte
> ongean ualentinianum þe he aflymde ær
> of his cyne-dome, þæt him come sige,
> ac æfter lytlum fyrste he sceolde feallan ofslagan,
> and hit gewearð swa swa him gewitegode martinus.[76]

The following section in the *Lives of Saints* begins with Martin traveling to visit Valentinian: "Martinus ferde hwilon to ualentiniane þam casere wolde for sumere neode wið hine spræcan."[77] In point of fact, these are different people: Valentinian I ruled from 364–375, and although Valentinian II became Augustus in name in 375, in reality he did not begin exercising power until after the death of Maximus in 387. Ælfric, however, is apparently unaware that he is conflating two emperors of the same name and that he has in fact reversed the chronology.[78] Without this information, Ælfric's version makes good sense: he relates how Martin prophesies that a first emperor will be conquered by a second and then continues with a story about this second emperor. It may also be significant that this is the first developed material from the *Dialogues* that he includes: in the frame material in the *Dialogues*—which Ælfric omits here as elsewhere—Postumianus remarks that Martin's dealings with Valentinian took place "eo fere tempore, quo primum episcopus datus est."[79] It may well be that Ælfric worked this material into his narrative as soon as he found an opportunity.

If this suggestion is correct, then it is of particular interest because it shows Ælfric trying to establish a historical connection between his two sources. For the next 260 lines, he is forced to rely mainly on thematic links: he discusses Martin's dealings with angels (ed. Skeat, lines 682–705; drawn primarily from *Dialogues* 2.13) and then his dealings with devils (ed. Skeat, lines 706–844; from *Dialogues* 2.13, *Vita* 23, *Vita* 24, *Vita* 21, and *Vita* 23, and *Vita* 24). Yet he again betrays his interest in historical accuracy by his next structural decision: after having included all of the material in the *Vita* but before turning to the rest of the material from the *Dialogues,* he takes up a miracle recorded by Sulpicius in a letter to Eusebius (ed. Skeat, lines 845–900), which was written because the author had heard an incorrect account of one of the miracles that he had omitted from the *Vita.* Without internal evidence to help him locate this event in the saint's life, he accepts the external evidence of the chronology of Sulpicius's writings to place it where he does. He continues this general procedure when he next turns to the *Dialogues* 2.1 and follows the events in this source, omitting material that is more didactic than miraculous, and occasionally linking items that shares a common theme.

This analysis, however sketchy, of the structures of Ælfric's two lives of Martin suggests not only that the Anglo-Saxon writer turns away from Alcuin's *Laudationes* when he comes to write the *Lives of Saints,* but also that he does so for historical reasons. His newly gained familiarity with the *Dialogues* frees him from dependency on Alcuin's work and in fact allows him to see the liberties that his predecessor had taken with his sources. Indeed, the one structural correspondence that remains between the second life and the *Laudationes* is better explained precisely by Ælfric's interest in a chronologically accurate narrative than by assuming his continued dependence on Alcuin. Of course, he too must cope with the limitations of his sources: when he cannot establish a chronological structure, he relies on thematic links. But he also relies on the narrative structure of Sulpicius' works in their historical order to guide his own work. The weight of the evidence suggests that Ælfric turned away from the *Laudationes* when he came to write his second life of Martin because he had become aware of a more precise record of the events of the saint's life.

Indeed, apparently the only extended passage from Alcuin's work that he introduces into the *Lives of Saints* helps to confirm this explanation. After describing how Martin continued to live like a monk even after having been elected Bishop of Tours, Ælfric continues:

He wæs soðfæst on dome, and est-ful on bodunge,
arwurð-ful on þeawum, and þurhwacol on ge-bedum,
singal on rædinge, gestæððig on his lece,
arfæst on gewilnunge, and arwurðful on his þenungum.[80]

The following passage continues to praise the saint with expressions that
recall Chapters 26 and 27 of the *Vita*; but, as Zettel notes,[81] the direct source
of these four lines is in Alcuin's description: "devotus in praedicatione, verax
in judicio, venerabilis in moribus, pervigil in orationibus, assiduus in lectione,
constans in vultu, pius in affectu, honorabilis in ministerio sacerdotali . . ."[82]
Ælfric, who here does no more than transpose the first two items, had not in
fact used this passage in the *Depositio*, which follows the *Vita* closely at this
point. Of course, this general praise would have little chance of containing
any historical inaccuracy, and so Ælfric is content to use it.

The difficulty in concluding an argument such as this one is similar to
the difficulty that Ælfric faced in writing his two lives of Martin: there is
always the possibility that new source material—or the more careful reading
of the existing evidence—will lead to new insights into how authors shape
their works. To Förster and Gerould, the question of Ælfric's sources appeared relatively simple: Sulpicius and Gregory of Tours provided all the
necessary information. Zettel discovered that the situation is more complicated in that Alcuin's redaction clearly underlies much of the *Depositio*,
which for him helped to confirm the status of the Cotton-Corpus legendary
as Ælfric's primary source for hagiographic material. One purpose of this
essay has been to suggest that we may not yet have reached a full understanding of the situation, because a particular manuscript such as Pembroke College 25 may provide a Latin source even closer to Ælfric's version than the
printed edition in the *Patrologia Latina*. The main object, however, of a
source study such as this one is not solely to find the exact text that an author
used, but rather to use the available information to discover what authors
themselves thought of their sources. In the case of Ælfric's two Lives of
Martin, this larger question is particularly interesting because—if the argument of this essay is correct—Ælfric himself comes to discriminate between
his sources: he eventually favors Sulpicius's works to Alcuin's redaction, and
in doing so he shows good historical judgment even while working in a genre
as notoriously unhistorical as hagiography.

Appendix: Pembroke College, Cambridge, MS 25, fols. 133v–36v

The intention here is to present the text with a minimum of editorial
intervention: I have expanded abbreviations, introduced some punctuation,

and offered a few notes; but I have made no attempt to regularize spelling or to smooth out grammatical problems. I have included the sectional divisions, but have not followed them since they are not consistent. Because largely the introduction of material from the *Vita* separates this redaction from that printed in the PL, I have indicated these borrowings with italics and references to the chapter and section of Sulpicius's work.

{133v} LXV. Omelia in natale sancti Martini episcopi.

{134} i. Postquam Dominus noster Iesus Christus triumphator ad alta caelorum ascendit et in maiestate paterna consedit, multis saeculi partibus doctorum lumina concessit, quatinus ignorantiae tenebris effugatis, ad uerum lumen agnoscendum gentes ubique conuerteret. Et quasi stellae diuersis in caeli partibus clarescunt, ita et doctores sancti per uarias mundi partes lucescerent, ut omnibus uia patesceret salutis, et ueritatis lux claresceret cunctis. Unde et beatissimum Martinum Galliae direxit in partes, ut populos gentilitatis errore torpentes luce ueritatis inradiaret, et plurimas de antiqui hostis faucibus extraheret gentes, et sacratissimo Christi coniungeret corpori. ii. Iste igitur Martinus primum *sub rege Constantino in adolescentia* sua, *deinde sub Iuliano cesare* [*Vita* 2.2] inuitus militans, magis elegit Deo caelesti seruire, quam imperatori militare terreno, quia *cum decem annorum esset inuitis parentibus ad aecclesiam fugiens, caticuminum se fieri postulauit* [2.3]. Et post sacri baptismatis misterium quod uigesimo secundo aetatis suae anno accepit,[83] magnis in mundo claruit miraculis. Haec sunt enim prima eius insignia. Quia dum adhuc caticuminus esset, in frigore hiemali, quod multum *inhorruerat* [3.1], media clamidis suae parte, *in porta Ambientium ciuitatis* [3.1], pauperem uestiuit; qua etiam parte clamidis suae, inter angelicos exercitus, Dominum Iesum nocte sequente uidit uestitam *clara uoce dicentem: "Martinus adhuc caticuminus hac me ueste contexit"* [3.3], ut uerum intelligeret esse {134v} Martinus, quod in euangelio dixerat Dominus: "Quandiu fecistis uni ex his minimis, mihi fecistis."[84] iii. In eodem quippe habitu quem pauper acceperat dignatus est Iesus se ostendere, ut similia studeamus agere [cf. 3.4].

Deinde post haec terrenae renuntiauit militiae,[85] inquiens *ad cesaram: "actenus tibi militaui pater, ut nunc militem Deo donatium tuum pugnaturus accipiat; Christi enim sum miles, pugnare mihi non licet"* [4.3].[86] Tunc pro hac uoce indignatus est tirannus dicens, certe *non religionis gratia, sed metu futurae pugnae detractat militiae* [4.4]. At Martinus ad hanc uocem constantissime inquit, "*si ignauiae hoc michi asscribitur non fidei, crastina die* [4.4] sine armis ante exercitum stabo, et *in nomine Iesu signo crucis non clipeo protectus aut galea, hostium cuneos penetrabo securus*" [4.4] iiii. Postero autem die sancti uiri merito *hostes legatos de pace miserunt, sua omnia seque dedentes, ne inermis ad proelium mitteretur* [4.4], sed omnis absque uindicta eius meritis liberarentur.

Post haec quidem *relicta militia sanctum Hilarium* [5.1] antistitem uenerabilem *expetiuit* [5.1], quia tunc temporis, sicut lucifer in caelo caeteris clarior stellis clarescit, ita ille uir sanctus in aecclesia Christi omnibus laudabilis, magnitudine fame et uitae sanctitate, et doctrinarum ueritate sanctarum, excelsior effulgebat cunctis. Huius disciplinis sanctus Martinus uoluit se sociari, ut talis uiri intrepidus exemplis, contra omnia maligni spiritis tela muniretur et dictis.

Post haec quidem diuino *per saporem* [5.3] ammonitus est aeloquio, *ut patriam parentesque quos adhuc gentilitas detinebat religiosa sollicitudine uisitaret* [5.3], et ad sacre conuerteret fidei {135} professionem. At ille peregrinationem illam adgressus est, reuelans fratribus *multa se aduersa passurum* [5.3], et postea ita euenit. *Primum enim inter Alpes incidit in latrones. Cumque unus securi in caput eleuasset, sustinuit alter. Sed uinctis post [t]ergum manibus uni traditus est aduersantium, cui se interroganti an timeret. Respondit, numquam se fuisse tam securum, quia sciebat miseracordiam Dei maxime in temptationibus adfuturam se ille dicebat: "magis autem de te doleo, ne Christi miseracordia latrocinia exercens indignus sis." Et uerbum Dei ad eum predicauit. Statimque latro credidit, Martinumque prosperae reddidit uiae, orans ut pro se Dominum precaretur* [5.4–6].

Deinde item *progressus est, et obuiam sibi in humana specie diabolus in itinere se obtulit* [6.1], quo pergeret interrogans. *Cumque ad*[87] *a Martino responsi accepisset se quo Dominus mittebat pergeret, ait ad eum: "ubicumque ambulaueris, aduersabitur tibi zabulus.*[88] *Tunc respondit ei prophetica uoce* [6.1–2] "Dominus mihi adiutor est, non timebo minas tuas." *Statimque e conspectu eius euanuit* [6.2]. Et postea matrem quae se mundo genuit ipse regenerauit Christo, *absoluens gentilitatis errore, tamen patre in malis perseuerante* [6.3].

Sed post multas hereticorum tribulationes *plures suo saluans exemplo* [6.3], iterum ad Hilarium repedauit. Et prope ciuitatem monasterium sibi construxet, in quo ei quidam caticuminus adhesit, uolens eius instrui disciplinis, subitoque mons[89] sed absente uiro *u*[90] *febrium* [7.1] illum praerepsit, quem uir Dei *rediens post triduum* [7.2] precibus pro eo ad Deum profusis resuscitauit, uiteque redditum baptizauit, qui multis postea uixit annis. *Ab hoc quidem tempore beati istius uiri nomen enituit ut qui sanctus iam ab omnibus habebatur potens etiam et uere apostolicus haberetur* [7.7].

Alterum quoque in Lupicini {135v} cuiusdam *uiri honorati* [8.1] agro laqueo suspensum, sacris orationibus pristinae restituit vitae. uii. Tertius ab eodem sancto uiro in Carnoteno oppido, filius cuiusdam mulieris flentis, sola oratione in conspectu populi resuscitatus est, quo uiso miraculo, plurimi ex populo unanimiter crediderunt Christo. Et iterum succendente tempore, in eodem oppido mutam ab infantia puellam oleo benedicto sanauit. Et alia multa in episcopatu, sanctarum insigna uirtutum gessit miracula, et multa caelestis uitae dogmata docens, priuatae continentiam uitae in multitudine populi constitutus non amisit. Humilis enim erat in habitu, iocundus in sermone, deuotus in predicatione, uerax in iudicio, uenerabilis in moribus, peruigil in orationibus, assiduus in lectione, constans in uultu, pius in affectu, honorabilis in sacerdotali ministerio, infatigabilis uerbi Dei seminator, impiger acceptam Domini sui pecuniam multiplicare; cum gaudentibus gaudens, cum lugentibus lugens, omnibus omnia factus, ut omnes lucrificaret Christo; uirtutibus insignis, bonitate laudabilis, pietate amabilis multis in episcopatu fulgens uirtutibus.

Nam turbam paganorum ritu tumultuantem in obsequio cuiusdam corporis uerbo orationis uno ligauit in loco. Iterumque resoluens, suis permisit dominari uestigiis. Ruentem pinum super se signo crucis apposito auertit, mirantemque turbam Christo credere fecit; seipsum in tectu cuiusdam domus flammis opposuit, ne innotua lederet ignis tecta, qui fanum incendit idolatriae. Aliud quoque templum antiquo errore daemonibus dedicatum, dum manu non potuit {136} humana, angelico uultus[91] auxilio subuertit; nec non alio loco gentilium sacra subuertens, a quodam pagano gladio appetitus, ille nudum ferientis ictui collum opposuit. Sed impius retro cadens, suam intelligens impietatem ueniam postulauit a sancto. Alteroque librante iocum[92] in sanctum caput, ferrum fugit de manibus.

Treueris paraliticam puellam totisque resolutis membris, sacra benedicti olei infusione, asstante populo pristinae reddidit sanitati. Tetradii proconsularis uiri seruum manus impositione a doemonio liberauit; unde et ille Tetradus cum tota domo sua ad Christianam conuersus est religionem. Cuiusdam quoque patris familias pueri a daemone arrepti digitos in os mittens, spiritum malignum per pudenda patientis exire compulit. Leprosum in porta Parisiae ciuitatis a deformitate sui corporis solo saluauit osculo. Sed et fimbria uestimenti eius uel filis cilicii, multos sanare morbos non dubium est. Filia Arborii prefecti per impositionem aepistolae sancti Martini a grauissimis liberata est febribus. Paulini oculum penniculo superposito sanauit a dolore atque caligine.

Idem quoque sanctus Martinus cadens super gradus caenaculi, grauiter pene totis adtritus est membris; et nocte ab angelo Dei ad integram recreatus est sanitatem; sepiusque angelicis uisitationibus et familiari collocutione fruebatur. Quadam uero die beatissimae Genitricis Dei et Domini nostri Iesu Christi, et sanctorum apostolorum Petri et Pauli, nec non sanctarum uirginum Teclae et Agnetis uisitatione iste uir Dei honoratus et confortatus est. Nam doemonum fantasmata et in diuersis figuris horribiles aspectus nihil metuens, nec ullis eorum fallaciis inludi potuit.

Spiritu uero prophetarum {136v} ita claruit, ut multis multa praedixerit futura, ueluti Maximo in Italia uictoriam, et in Aquileia interitum praedixerat. Eodem beato uiro sacrum caelebrante mysterium ad altarae, globus igneus subito de uertice fulsit illius. Euantius quidam aegrotus properante ad se beato uiro prius sanitatem recepit, quam sanctus Martinus domum intraret. In eadem quoque domo puerum a serpente percussum, sanctorum tactu digitorum a periculo mortis eruit.

Nam tantae fuit uir Dei patientiae, ut conuitia non doluit obprobria non sensit. Immo et quorundam rusticorum flagella placido sustinuit animo, et eorum fixa terris animalia solo soluebat sermone. Nemini adulando blandiebatur principi, nulli ueritatis uerba tacuit, sed semper ad nota orationum subsidia recurrebat. Unde si quid ei potestas rennueret saecularis, mox diuina illi prestabat pietas Dei. Quaedam persona a daemonio uexata, stramine ubi sanctus Martinus iacebat liberata est. Et non solum homines sed etiam animalia a daemonum liberabat potestate, et mansuetos in suum redire gregem precipiebat. Etiam tante fuit miseracordiae, ut canibus insequentibus lepusculum imperauit stare, et miseram bestiolam a morte presente eripuit. Villa quedam in Senonico grandinum tempestate sepius uastata, ad preces sancti Martini multis liberata est annis. Quaedam mulier a sanguinis fluxu uestimentorum illius tactu sanata est. Talibus etiam et aliis innumerabilibus electus Dei sacerdos in mundo claruit miraculis, quae per se Dominus ostendere dignatus est, ut per eius exempla ducatum nobis preberet ad celestia regna. Prestante Domino nostro Iesu Christo quicumque eodem Patre et Spiritu sancto uiuit et regnat in saecula saeculorum. Amen.

Notes

Research on this chapter was supported during the Summer of 1989 by the American Philosophical Society and during 1990 by the American Council of Learned Societies and the National Endowment for the Humanities. The edition of Alcuin's *Laudationes* in the appendix is reproduced by kind permission of the Master and Fellows of Pembroke College, Cambridge. I have also profited from the comments and criticisms of Deeana Copeland Klepper, Malcolm Godden, and Thomas D. Hill; remaining mistakes of fact and interpretation are my own.

1. See, for example, Mary Clayton, "Delivering the Damned: A Motif in OE Homiletic Prose," *Medium Ævum* 55 (1986): 92–102; and my "Biblical Glosses in Ælfric's Translation of Genesis," *Notes and Queries*, n.s. 38 (1991): 286–92.

2. Max Förster, *Über die Quellen von Ælfric's Homiliae Catholicae. Vol. 1. Legenden* (Berlin, 1892), pp. 41–42. He also noted that Ælfric uses Gregory of Tours's *Historia Francorum*.

3. A little more than thirty years after Förster's article, Gordon Hall Gerould restated the case, clearing up some details; see "Ælfric's Lives of St. Martin of

Tours," *Journal of English and Germanic Philology* 24 (1925): 206–10. More recent critics include Paul E. Szarmach, "The Vercelli Homilies: Style and Structure" in *The Old English Homily and Its Backgrounds*, ed. P. Szarmach and Bernard F. Huppé (Albany, N.Y., 1978), p. 260; and Marcia A. Dalbey, "The Good Shepherd and the Soldier of God," *Neuphilologische Mitteilungen* 85 (1984): 422–23.

4. Patrick H. Zettel, "Ælfric's Hagiographic Sources and the Latin Legendary Preserved in BL MS Cotton Nero E i + CCCC MS 9 and Other Manuscripts," dissertation, Oxford University (1979). Zettel has reported only part of his research in "Saints' Lives in Old English: Latin Manuscripts and Vernacular Accounts: Ælfric," *Peritia* 1 (1982): 17–37. See also Lapidge and Jackson in this book.

5. Alcuin's work is identified by the Bollandists in the BHL as number 5625. It is printed in PL 101, 657–62. I came upon this source independently and would like to thank James E. Cross and Malcolm Godden for calling my attention to Zettel's dissertation.

6. I Deug-Su discusses the sources of Alcuin's work in his *L'opera agiografica di Alcuino*, Biblioteca degli Studi Medievali vol. 13 (Spoleto, Italy, 1983), pp. 167–72.

7. This focus limits the present study primarily to the miracles that Martin performed during his life and thus excludes the account of his death.

8. E. A. Lowe dates the manuscript to ca. 807; see the *Codices Latini Antiquiores. Part II. Great Britain and Ireland*, 2d ed. (Oxford, 1972), no. 270. See also the edition by John Gwynn (Dublin, 1913) and the discussion in James F. Kenny, *The Sources for the Early History of Ireland. Ecclesiastical* (1929; reprinted New York, 1966), p. 668.

9. I rely here in part on the work of Helmut Gneuss, "A Preliminary List of Manuscripts Written or Owned in England up to 1100," *ASE* 9 (1981): 1–60; and Paul E. Szarmach's entry on Sulpicius Severus in the *Sources of Anglo-Saxon Literary Culture: A Trial Version*, ed. Frederick M. Biggs, Thomas D. Hill, and Paul E. Szarmach (Binghamton, N.Y., 1990), pp. 158–60. This manuscript is Gneuss's no. 296. See also the *British Museum Catalogue of Additions to Manuscripts 1921–1925* (London, 1950), pp. 20–21.

10. Gneuss, "A Preliminary List," no. 201; see also M. R. James, *A Descriptive Catalogue of the Manuscripts in the Library of Trinity Hall* (Cambridge, 1907), pp. 37–39.

11. Gneuss, "A Preliminary List," no. 915; see also A. Wilmart, *Codices Reginenses Latini*, vol. 2 (Vatican City, Italy, 1845), pp. 684–85.

12. Gneuss, "A Preliminary List," no. 264; see also Arthur Thomas Bannister, *Hereford Cathedral Library: Descriptive Catalogue* (Hereford, England, 1927), p. 70; and H. Schenkl, "Bibliotheca patrum latinorum Britannica X," *Sitzungsberichte der kaiserlichen Akademie der Wissenschaften* 139 (1898): section 9, pp. 17–18.

13. Zettel, "Saints' Lives," p. 22.

14. Zettel asserts that this version was "written at Worcester c. 1060"; ibid., p. 19. The material on Martin occurs in the Cambridge manuscript; see Gneuss, "A Preliminary," no. 36; see also M. R. James *A Descriptive Catalogue of the Manuscripts in the Library of Corpus Christi College*, vol. 1 (Cambridge, 1912), pp. 24–30.

15. Zettel, citing Malcolm Parkes, asserts that the Bodleian manuscript "was written in England, perhaps in the west country, in the latter half of the twelfth century"; "Saints' Lives," p. 20; see also Falconer Madan, *A Summary Catalogue of Western Manuscripts in the Bodleian Library at Oxford*, vol. 2, part I (Oxford, 1922), no. 2432. On the Hereford manuscript, see Bannister, *Hereford Cathedral Library*, pp. 172–77.

16. Other evidence for the circulation in Anglo-Saxon England of Sulpicius's *Vita* and Epistles without the *Dialogues* is slight: Avranches, BM 29 contains extracts from the *Vita* and from the epistle to Bassula, but not from the *Dialogues*, and *Vercelli Homily* 18 uses only these two works. On the Avranches manuscript, see Gneuss, "A Preliminary List," no. 782, and the *Catalogue général des manuscrits des bibliothèques publiques de France. Departments*, vol. 10 (Paris, 1889); for *Vercelli* 18, see *Vercelli Homilies IX–XXIII*, ed. Paul E. Szarmach (Toronto, 1981), p. 57.

17. Gneuss, "A Preliminary List," no. 131; see also M. R. James, *A Descriptive Catalogue of the Manuscripts in the Library of Pembroke College, Cambridge* (Cambridge, 1905), pp. 25–29.

18. Henri Barré, *Les Homèliaires Carolingiens de l'Ecole d'Auxerre*, Studi e Testi 225 (Vatican City, Italy, 1962), pp. 17–25.

19. James E. Cross, *Cambridge Pembroke College MS. 25: A Carolingian Sermonary Used by Anglo-Saxon Preachers*, King's College London Medieval Studies 1 (London, 1987). There are two twelfth-century English witnesses of this collection, Cambridge, St John's College 42; and Lincoln, Cathedral Chapter Library 199. On the latter manuscript, see Cross, ibid., pp. 241 ff. BL Arundel 169, another twelfth-century manuscript, preserves Alcuin's redaction without Sulpicius's work; see J. Forshall, *Catalogue of Manuscripts in the British Museum. New Series* vol. 1 (London, 1834), pp. 46–47.

20. For the reader's convenience, I have provided a transcription of the Pembroke text in the Appendix to this chapter.

21. The text in Cambridge, St John's College 42 follows Pembroke. I have not yet checked Lincoln, Cathedral Library 199 fols. 327–29v; see R. M. Thomson, *Catalogue of the Manuscripts of the Lincoln Cathedral Chapter Library* (Cambridge, 1989).

22. Zettel, "Ælfric's Hagiographic Sources," pp. 100–10. His references to the *Depositio* are to the edition of Benjamin Thorpe, *The Homilies of the Anglo-Saxon Church. The First Part, Containing the Sermones Catholici or Homilies of Ælfric*, 2 vols. (London, 1844–46), vol. 2, pp. 498–519. I have changed these to the edition by Malcolm Godden, *Ælfric's Catholic Homilies. The Second Series. Text*. EETS SS 5 (London, 1979), the one used throughout this chapter.

23. Godden, ibid., lines 241–43: "once during Mass, men saw [something] like a fiery ball shine unexpectedly on the top of his head, so that the flashing flame drew up his hair."

24. PL 101, 661: "and while the same blessed man celebrated holy communion at the altar, a ball of fire suddenly shone from the top of his head."

25. Quotations from the *Dialogues* are from the edition of C. Halm, *Sulpicii Severi Libri qui supersunt* CSEL 1 (Vienna, 1866). I provide translations from Sulpicius's works from Alexander Roberts, *The Works of Sulpitius Severus*, A Select Library of Nicene and Post-Nicene Fathers of the Christian Church, second series, vol. 11 (reprinted Grand Rapids, Mich., 1964). Here, p. 38, "so that as it rose on high, the flame produced a hair of extraordinary length."

26. This use appears for example in Virgil (*Aeneid* 5.528) and Ovid (*Metamorphoses* 15.849). Hereford, Cathedral Library MS 0.6.vi (fols. 64–64v) also confuses the image: "globum ignis de capite illius uidimus emicare, ita ut in sublime contendens longius collum crinemque flamma produceret" ("we saw a ball of fire shine forth from his head so that, stretching on high, the flame drew further forth the neck and the hair"); see also Vatican, Pal. lat. 845, fol. 46.

27. References are to the edition of W. W. Skeat, *Ælfric's Lives of Saints*, EETS OS 76, 82, 94, and 114, 2 vols. (London, 1881–1900); the life of Martin appears in vol. 2, pp. 218–312. I have generally relied on the translations in this volume; here, line 938, "so that the flame drew the hair far up."

28. I have checked the reading in the original or microfilm of the following manuscripts: Cambridge, Pembroke College 25; Cambridge, St John's College 42; London, BL Arundel 169; Oxford, Bodleian Library, Bodley 354; Paris, BN lat. 2854, 3788, 3817, 5280, 5334, 5325, 5359, 5583, 8995; Paris, Bibliothèque de l'Arsenal 474, 995, 1030; Valenciennes, BM 518; Montpellier, Bibliothèque de l'École de Médecine 42; Saint-Omer, BM 765; Clemont-Ferrand, BM 147 (83A3); Rouen, BM 1343; Le Mans, BM 10; Vatican, Reg. Lat. 495, 529, 543, 586. The presence of additional material from the *Vita* in Pembroke 25 indicates that such a change could take place.

29. Godden, *Ælfric's Catholic Homilies,* lines 146–52: "it happened similarly another time that a widow's son died and suddenly departed from worldly joys; and this holy Martin prayed for him in the sight of the people, and he immediately arose to the transitory life that he had previously forsaken. Through that sign, all of the people believed in the living God, who had raised him to life."

30. PL 101, 660: "the third, by the same holy man in Chartres: by prayer alone he resurrected the son of a certain weeping woman in the sight of the people; by which miraculous vision, most of the people believed in Christ."

31. Halm, *Sulpicii Severi Libri,* p. 185; Roberts, *The Works,* p. 40; "who is my only one."

32. Skeat, *Ælfric's Lives,* lines 1021–25; "for he is my only son."

33. Malcolm Godden has called to my attention Ælfric's use of *wuduwe* in describing the resurrection of Drusiana in his homily on the "Assumption of Saint John the Apostle" (Thorpe, vol. 1, p. 60). The apparent source for the passage, the pseudo Mellitus *Vita* (BHL 4321), does not identify Drusiana in this way, although it does specify widows as among the crowd that entreats John to raise the woman; for a printed text, see Boninus Mombritius, *Sanctuarium seu Vitae Sanctorum* (1910; reprinted Hildesheim, Germany, 1978), vol. 2, p. 56.

34. Godden, *Ælfric's Catholic Homilies*, lines 245–48: "then there was a boy poisoned by an adder, greatly swollen through the stroke of the worm, [and] not expected to live. But he was saved by Martin's touch from that cruel adder."

35. PL 101, 661: "in the same house, by the touch of his holy fingers he plucked from the danger of death a boy bitten by a snake."

36. Halm, *Sulpicii Severi Libri*, p. 182; Roberts, *The Works*, p. 38: "one could see his skin swollen in all his veins."

37. Skeat, *Ælfric's Lives*, line 953: "all swollen up in the likeness of a bottle."

38. Halm, *Sulpicii Severi Libri*, p. 182; Roberts, *The Works*, p. 38: "and his vitals strung up like a leather bottle."

39. Godden, *Ælfric's Catholic Homilies*, lines 256–59: "it happened once that a deranged man sat where previously the holy man had rested himself; and he was made sane through the merit of the man who previously had blessed that seat."

40. PL 101, 661: "a certain person, caught by a demonic spirit, was rescued from the hostile power by straw where Saint Martin had sat." The reading "persona" is found in Pembroke 25, and St John's 42 (fol. 54v, col. 2) as well as in Bodley 354 (fol. 84v, col. 1) and thus offers no evidence as to which collection—the *Homiliary of Saint-Père*, Chartres, or the Cotton-Corpus legendary—Ælfric may have used. This reading is in fact much more common, occuring in Paris, BN Lat. 3788 (fol. 227v), 5280 (fol. 289), 5287 (fol. 101), 8995 (fol 107v); Paris, Bibliothèque de l'Arsenal 474 (fol. 117), 995 (fol 93v, col. 1); Valenciennes, BM 518 (fol. 160v); Montpellier, Bibliothèque de l'École de Médecine 42 (fol. 53); and Vatican, Reg. lat. 529 (fol 83v) and 586 (fol. 131). Indeed, the only manuscript that I have noted that supports Migne's reading is Arsenal 1030 (fol. 304v).

41. Halm, *Sulpicii Severi Libri*, p. 190; Roberts, *The Works*, p. 42: "The church there is celebrated for the piety of the saints, and is not less illustrious for the multitude of the holy virgins. Well, Martin, being in the habit of passing that way, had an apartment in the private part of the church. After he left, all the virgins used to rush into that retirement: they kiss every place where the blessed man had either sat or stood, and distribute among themselves the very straw on which he had lain. One of them, a few days afterwards, took a part of the straw which she had collected for a blessing to herself, and hung it from the neck of a possessed person, whom a spirit of error was troubling. There was no delay; but sooner than one could speak the demon was cast out, and the person was cured."

42. Skeat, *Ælfric's Lives*, lines 572–73: "in like manner one bound some of his bedstraw on a lunatic; then the devil went from him and he received his reason." Skeat translates *man band* as "men bound"; I have also changed his *when* to *then*.

43. For an analysis of the correspondences between the *Depositio* and the *Laudationes*, see Zettel, "Ælfric's Hagiographic Sources," p. 104.

44. Godden, *Ælfric's Catholic Homilies*, lines 221–25: "similarly, the blessed Mary came to the holy man on a particular occasion with two apostles, Peter and Paul, [and] with two virgins, Thecla and Agnes, and with her visit honored him, and greatly encouraged him by her presence."

45. PL 101, 661: "truly one day the holy man was honored and comforted by a visit from the most blessed Mother of God and our Lord Jesus Christ, and from the holy apostles Peter and Paul, and also from the holy virgins Thecla and Agnes."

46. Halm, *Sulpicii Severi Libri*, pp. 195–96; Roberts, *The Works*, p 45: "One day, I and Sulpitius there were watching before Martin's door, and had already sat in silence for several hours. We did so with deep reverence and awe, as if we were carrying out a watch prescribed to us before the tent of an angel; while, all the time, the door of his cell being closed, he did not know that we were there. Meanwhile, we heard the sound of people conversing, and by and by we were filled with a kind of awe and amazement, for we could not help perceiving that something divine was going on. After nearly two hours, Martin comes out to us; and then our friend Sulpitius (for no one was accustomed to speak to him more familiarly) began to entreat him to make known to us, piously enquiring on the subject, what meant that sort of divine awe which we confessed we had both felt, and with whom he had been conversing in his cell. We added that, as we stood before the door, we had undoubtedly heard a feeble sound of people talking, but had scarcely understood it. Then he after a long delay (but there was really nothing which Sulpitius could not extort from him even against his will: I am about to relate things somewhat difficult to belief, but, as Christ is my witness, I lie not, unless any one is so impious as to think that Martin himself lied) said: 'I will tell you, but I beg you will not speak to it to any one else. Agnes, Thecla, and Mary were there with me.' He proceeded to describe to us the face and general aspect of each. And he acknowledged that, not merely on that day, but frequently, he received visits from them. Nor did he deny that Peter also and Paul, the Apostles, were pretty frequently seen by him." On the possible debt of this passage to Ambrose's *De virginibus*, see Clare Stancliffe, *St. Martin and His Hagiographer. History and Miracle in Sulpicius Severus* (Oxford, 1983), p. 66.

47. Skeat, *Ælfric's Lives*, lines 688–705: "The holy apostles Peter and Paul he saw frequently, even as he said himself to Sulpicius the writer, who dared ask him anything that he would. The same Sulpicius and another brother sat one day, greatly afraid, before Martin's room, and he knew not that they were outside; then they heard some one conferring with Martin a long while, and he had previously been locked in alone in the house. Afterwards, as he came out, Sulpicius asked and humbly besought him that he would reveal to him who had been speaking with him; and he hesitated

long to tell it to him, but he said nevertheless, 'I adjure you now that you tell it to no one; Mary, Christ's mother, came to me here with two other virgins, Thecla and Agnes, not on this one day but often readily before have they come to me.' And he told them also what their appearance had been and how they were clothed."

48. Skeat, *Ælfric's Lives*, lines 1–9: "There was a certain wise writer, called Sulpicius, who desired to write the miracles and mighty deeds which the great Martin mightily performed in this world, and he therefore wrote concerning him the things which he had learned, either from himself or from other men, because the miracles, which God wrought by him, were known to many; and we take the English from the same account; but we will write no more but his own miracles."

49. Quotations are from the edition of Jacques Fontaine, *Sulpice Sévère. Vie de Saint Martin*, 3 vols., Sources Chrétiennes 133–35 (Paris, 1967–69); the text is in volume 1. This passage appears on pp. 252–54; Roberts, *The Works*, p. 4: "but I implore those who are to read what follows to give full faith to the things narrated, and to believe that I have written nothing of which I had not certain knowledge and evidence. I should, in fact, have preferred to be silent rather than to narrate things which are false."

50. Fontaine, *Sulpice Sévère*, p. 310; Roberts, *The Works*, p. 16: "partly from himself, in so far as I could venture to question him, and partly from those who had lived with him, or well knew the facts of the case."

51. "Nu is seo foresæde boc on manegum stowum swyðe nearolice gesett, 7 ðeah swyðe deoplice on ðam gastlican andgyte; 7 heo is swa geendebyrd, swa swa God sylf hi gedihte ðam writere Moyse, 7 we ne durron na mare awritan on Englisc þonne ðt Leden hæfð, ne ða endebyrdnysse awendan, buton ðam anum, ðæt ðæt Leden 7 ðæt Englisc nabbað ne ane wisan on ðære spræce fandunge;" S. J. Crawford, *The Old English Version of the Heptateuch, Ælfric's Treatise on the Old and New Testament and His Preface to Genesis* EETS OS 160 (London, 1922), p. 79. The following translation adopts several suggestions (including the reading "fadunge") in the fourth edition of *A Guide to Old English*, Bruce Mitchell and Fred C. Robinson (Oxford, 1986), p. 186: "Now the aforementioned book in many places is set down very densely and yet very profoundly in spiritual meaning; and it is so arranged as God himself dictated it to the writer Moses, and we dare not write any more in English than the Latin has, nor change the sequence, except for the one reason [namely that] the Latin and the English do not have one manner in the disposition of language."

52. Gerould, "Ælfric's Lives," p. 209; see, however, Zettel, "Saints' Lives," who argues that Ælfric used extracts of Gregory's work.

53. For a discussion of the historical context of Sulpicius's writings, see Stancliffe, *St. Martin*, especially pp. 71–85.

54. Ibid., p. 90.

55. Ed. Halm, *Sulpicii Severi Libri*, p. 199; Roberts, *The Works*, p. 46: "in the city of the Carnutes."

56. Halm, ibid., p. 185; Roberts, ibid., p. 40: "For some reason, I know not what, we were on our way to the town of the Carnutes. In the meantime, as we pass by a certain village most populous in inhabitants. . . . "

57. Skeat, *Ælfric's Catholic Homilies*, line 1013: "the field through which Martin was passing."

58. Fol. 135: "and performed many other signs of holy virtue—miracles—and teaching much dogma concerning the heavenly life, he did not forsake the self-restraint of his life, [although] placed in a multitude of people."

59. Like the printed version, Pembroke 25 continues to discuss Martin's virtue before returning to his miracles.

60. This miracle occupies six sentences in the *Vita*, whereas Alcuin reduces it to a single sentence.

61. He omits any reference to Martin curing Paulinus's vision, included in both the *Vita* and *Laudationes*.

62. Godden, *Ælfric's Catholic Homilies*, lines 216–17: "on the high steps, at the holy altar."

63. PL 101, 661: "falling on the steps." On the meaning of *gradus*, see *Mediae Latinitatis Lexicon Minus*, J. F. Niermeyer (Leiden, 1976), s.v. In the *Lives of Saints*, Ælfric returns to the *Vita*, rendering *cenaculum* as *upflor*. See also the discussion in Fontaine's "Commentaire," vol. 2, pp. 888–89. Pembroke 25, however, reads "super gradus caenaculi." If this was the reading from which Ælfric worked, he may have associated *cenaculum* with *cena*, the eucharistic meal; see Albert Blaise, *Le Vocabulaire Latin des principaux thèmes liturgique* (Turnhout, Belgium, 1966), s.v. *cena*. In this case, it may have been the adjective *confragosus* in the *Vita* that led him to reevaluate the passage.

64. Zettel, "Ælfric's Hagiographic Sources," p. 101.

65. PL 101, 661: "For fearing not at all the illusions of demons and their appearence in diverse and terrible forms, he was not able to be tricked by any of their deceits."

66. Godden, *Ælfric's Catholic Homilies*, lines 266–67: "we may not write all his miracles in this short homily."

67. Pembroke 25, fol. 136v: "with such miracles and innumerable others the chosen priest of God shone in this world."

68. Godden, *Ælfric's Catholic Homilies*, line 267: "with known speech." Malcolm Godden has pointed out to me that the phrase may be used primarily for the alliteration and that the precise meaning of *cuð* in this context is difficult to determine. It seems, however, at least to indicate Ælfric's favorable attitude toward his summary derived from Alcuin.

69. He attributes this emphasis to Sulpicius, but there are other points where he omits nonmiraculous material; for example, *Dialogues* 2.10, which concerns Martin's teachings.

70. Halm, *Sulpicii Severi Libri*, p. 190; Roberts, *The Works*, p. 42: "Let us entirely blot out these things from our memory, and let us return to Martin."

71. Godden, *Ælfric's Catholic Homilies*, lines 251–56: "he would not flatter any ruler with sweet speech, nor suppress the truth; if any leader denied him anything, he would go to God with his usual prayers, and at once the mercy of his Creator would grant him what the earthly ruler had denied him earlier."

72. PL 100, 661: "he would flatter no one by fawning; he would silence true speech for no ruler, returning always to the familiar place of prayer. If a secular power denied him something, divine mercy would at once fulfill it."

73. Zettel, "Ælfric's Hagiographic Sources," p. 102.

74. Fontaine, *Sulpice Sévère*, pp. 295–96; Roberts, *The Works*, p. 13: "when a number of bishops from various parts had assembled to the Emperor Maximus, a man of fierce character, and at that time elated with the victory he had won in the civil wars, and when disgraceful flattery of all around the emperor was generally remarked, while the priestly dignity had, with degenerate submissiveness, taken a second place to the royal retinue, in Martin alone, apostolic authority continued to assert itself. For even if he had to make suit to the sovereign for some things, he commanded rather than etreated him."

75. See Zettel, "Ælfric's Hagiographic Sources," p. 102.

76. Skeat, *Ælfric's Lives*, lines 639–44: "then he told the emperor, even as it happened to him afterwards, that if he went into battle, as he intended, against Valentinian whom he had before banished from his kingdom, that victory would come to him, but after a little space he would fall slain; and it befell him even as Martin had prophesied to him."

77. Skeat, ibid., lines 650–51: "once Martin was journeying to Valentinian the emperor, wishing to speak with him for some needful cause."

78. Ælfric might have been alerted to the problem by the "wicked consort" of Valentinian, who followed the Arian heresy. The reference is apparently to Justina, wife of Valentinian I and mother of Valentinian II; however, she is referred to in the *Dialogues* as *Arriana* (Halm, *Sulpicii Severi Libri*, p. 191).

79. Halm, ibid., p. 190; Roberts, *The Works*, p. 40: "just about that time when he first became a bishop." In contrast *Dialogues* 2.6, which includes further details about Maximus, begins without any clear indication of where it fits into the chronology of Martin's life: "Et quia palatium semel ingressi sumus, licet diversis in palatio temporibus gesta conectam" (Halm, ibid., p. 191); Roberts, ibid., p. 41: "and as we have, once for all, entered the palace, I shall string together events which there took place, although they happened at different times."

80. Skeat, *Ælfric's Lives*, lines 294–97: "he was just in judgement, and devout in preaching, venerable in manners, and vigilant in prayers, constant in reading, steadfast in his look, virtuous in desire, and reverent in his duties."

81. Zettel, "Ælfric's Hagiographic Sources," p. 124.

82. PL 101.660: "devout in preaching, true in judgment, honorable in his habits, ever watchful in prayer, untiring in reading, constant in countenance, pious in manner, and honorable in his priestly duties."

83. According to Sulpicius [*Vita* 2.6], Martin was baptized three years after joining the army at fifteen.

84. Unlike the text in the PL, here the biblical passage applies specifically to Martin.

85. This entire paragraph is drawn from the *Vita* 4; only close verbal parallels are noted.

86. The *Vita* reads: "hactenus, inquit ad Caesarem, militaui tibi; patere ut nunc militem Deo. Donatiuum tuum pugnaturus accipiat . . . "; the pointing, however, may suggest that the scribe understood *pater* to be the subject of the first sentence (i.e., *militauit*). Further corruption is indicated by the lack of punctuation between *Deo* and *donatiuum*.

87. Read "id."

88. The *Vita* reads "diabolus."

89. The obvious reading of *mors* for the MS *mons* suggests the syntax of the *Vita* [7.2]: "ita subita mors fuerat . . . "

90. Read "ui."

91. The PL text reads "fultus."

92. The *Vita* [5.4] reads "ictum."

Ælfric and the Legend of the Seven Sleepers

Hugh Magennis

The version of the legend of the Seven Sleepers of Ephesus that appears in the Second Series of Ælfric's *Catholic Homilies* under the title *Sanctorum Septem Dormientium* is extremely brief even by Ælfric's standards. This version amounts to not much more than a page in Godden's edition[1] and could be described as a summary rather than a developed narrative. The very fact that the text is so short, however, and that its abbreviation of source is so pronounced makes it a particularly revealing illustration of Ælfric's approach to hagiography and of the kinds of interests he extracts from his hagiographical sources. In his treatment of the Seven Sleepers Ælfric focuses on what he sees as the essential significance of the legend and disregards everything else. As explained here, some of these essential interests are reflected again in a later passage on the Seven Sleepers written by Ælfric, in an addition he made to a homily in the First Series of *Catholic Homilies*. In considering Ælfric's response to the legend it is also fortuitous that we have, probably closely contemporary with Ælfric's own writings, a second Old English version of it, which can be compared to that of Ælfric. This second version, the anonymous *Legend of the Seven Sleepers*,[2] appears in the manuscript of Ælfric's *Lives of Saints*, but it presents an approach to its material that is diametrically opposed to that of Ælfric himself.

After a discussion of the question of the source of the *Sanctorum Septem Dormientium*, the present chapter will consider Ælfric's careful tailoring of his inherited material to his underlying doctrinal and hagiographical ends. Because the doctrinal concerns of the *Sanctorum Septem Dormientium* are also reflected in Ælfric's other passage on the Seven Sleepers (in the First Series of *Catholic Homilies*), the text of this other passage, which is not yet accessible in a printed edition, will be set out here. Our examination of the *Sanctorum Septem Dormientium* will show Ælfric transforming a legend rich in incident and human interest into a serene revelation of Christian mystery.

Patrick Zettel has identified the source of Ælfric's version of the legend as the anonymous Latin *Passio Septem Dormientium* (BHL 2316),[3] a text of which was also the source of the other Old English version.[4] Ælfric's dependence on this *passio* is revealed by a whole series of correspondences, from the very order in which the names of the saints are given,[5] to the number of years (372) they are supposed to have slept, to the prayer of the Sleepers that God will protect the realm of the Christian emperor Theodosius against the temptations of the devil ("wið deofles costnungum," 224–25): this reading follows the Latin "custodiat imperium tuum in nomine suo a tentationibus et laqueis satanae" ["may he preserve your imperial authority in his name against the temptations and snares of Satan," p. 76, 4–5]. Zettel goes on to propose that the particular variant of BHL 2316 that served as Ælfric's source is that preserved in the Cotton-Corpus legendary, a collection of Latin saints' lives that Zettel shows to have been Ælfric's main quarry for his hagiographical material. With regard to *Sanctorum Septem Dormientium*, Zettel admits that the sheer brevity of the piece makes it difficult to tell whether the Old English is following a particular variant or not, but if Ælfric uses the Cotton-Corpus collection for many of his other saints' lives, then it would seem not unreasonable to suggest that this legendary also contains the source of his version of the legend of the Seven Sleepers.

Two notable readings in Ælfric's version, however, contrast with the corresponding readings in the text of the surviving copies of the Cotton-Corpus legendary, and these suggest that Ælfric must have been following a different manuscript tradition of the *passio*, or that, if he did base his Old English on the Cotton-Corpus text, the version of it he used cannot have been identical to that in either of the surviving copies. First, the Cotton-Corpus text in the course of the narrative gives the number of years of the sleep of the seven saints as 370, instead of the 372 years found in the other manuscripts and in Ælfric (see 204–05).[6] Near the end of the *passio* the length of the sleep is referred to again, and this time the Cotton-Corpus copies have the regular figure of 372 years.[7] Ælfric's Latin text may have had the anomalous *370* in the former passage, but if so he was evidently able to recognize this as an error and transfer the correct figure to the earlier part of his narrative.

Ælfric's second departure from the Cotton-Corpus text comes when he relates that the seven saints secretly distributed money to the poor—"þearfum digellice dældon" (197). The corresponding reading in most manuscripts of the Latin, including those of the Cotton-Corpus legendary, is "dabant mendicis occulte et aperte" ["they gave to the poor secretly and openly"].[8] The omission of an equivalent in Ælfric to "aperte" might easily be explained as due to a local scribal slip in the particular manuscript of the Cotton-Corpus legendary that Ælfric was following. It is notable, however, that certain non-Cotton-Corpus textual traditions of BHL 2316 distinctively lack the reading "et aperte,"[9] and it is possible that overall Ælfric might be following one of these, instead of the Cotton-Corpus variant. On purely internal grounds, we cannot be sure which strand of the *passio* provided Ælfric with his immediate source. He may have worked from a form of the Cotton-Corpus text that did not exhibit the discrepancies noted here. The evidence for his use of this legendary is entirely circumstantial, however, as no decisive Cotton-Corpus readings are preserved in his brief narrative.[10]

Further examination of Ælfric's *Sanctorum Septem Dormientium* reveals the presence in it of details which do not occur in BHL 2316 at all, but are paralleled only in a work not otherwise known to have been read in Anglo-Saxon England, Gregory of Tours' *Passio Septem Dormientium apud Ephesum* (BHL 2312).[11] Ælfric characteristically adds emotive details in his saints' lives, of course, and it might be argued that the apparent correspondences with Gregory could really be the result of independent additions by Ælfric, which happen to resemble features in Gregory. Examples of emotive additions in Ælfric's account of the Seven Sleepers are the references to the persecuting emperor Decius as "ðam hæðenan cwellere" (190) and as "gehathyrt" (201)—in the latter case Gregory, in contrast, speaks of Decius being troubled—"commotus" (p. 764, 13)—and the anonymous *passio* (p. 52, 12) says that he did not wish to harm the seven young men. The correspondences seem too precise to be coincidental, however, and they point to Ælfric's knowledge of details from Gregory's version.

The first such correspondence comes with Ælfric's description, in the opening lines of his version, of the saints as "Ðas seofon geleaffullan godes cempan" (187–88): with the emotive addition of *geleaffullan* ["believing"] this corresponds closely to Gregory's "hii septem adletae Christi" ["these seven champions of Christ"] at the beginning of his version (p. 762, 7). There is no such description in the anonymous *passio*. A second correspondence can be seen in the threat of Decius in Ælfric's version to torture the saints with various kinds of torments—"mid mislicum tintregum gecwylmede" (194). This again has no parallel in the anonymous *passio*, but it closely follows Gregory's "experietis diversa genera tormentorum" (p. 763, 2–3), with the direct speech, typically for Ælfric, being recast as indirect. At the corresponding part of the *passio* (see pp. 46–47) Decius is relatively sympathetic toward the seven. Again, Ælfric's statement that the saints sold their possessions to obtain money to give to the poor has no equivalent in the anonymous *passio*, which does not mention their possessions at all (see p. 47). Gregory does not actually speak of them selling their possessions, but he does say that they took their possessions, specifically clothes and furniture, and gave them to the poor—"abstulerunt aurum argentumque et vestimenta cunctaque [*sic*] suppellectilem. Quae distributa pauperibus . . . " (p. 763, 17–18). ["they took silver and gold and clothing and all their household furniture. Having distributed these to the poor . . . ," p. 769, 6], although here the *memoriam magnam* of BHL 2316 (see p. 78) could also be the source of Ælfric's phrase.[12] Another parallel with Gregory comes at the end of Ælfric's text, where the Old English *mære cyrcan* (230) recalls Gregory's *basilica magna*.

Although suggestions about source must remain fairly tentative, given the extreme brevity and concentration of his treatment, we may conclude that Ælfric primarily followed the anonymous *passio* but that he seems also to have been able to use details derived from Gregory of Tours. What is very clear, however, is that he has stripped his inherited material back to what he considers its bare essentials. The resulting organization of material and the particular emphases that can be seen in the Old English are entirely Ælfric's own, and they produce a version quite unlike any other.

In examining Ælfric's approach to his material, two aspects of the legend, as he inherited it, are of particular note. One is its preoccupation with the theological doctrine of the resurrection of the body. This element is centrally present in all the main versions of the legend and gives the miracle of the long sleep its whole purpose and meaning. Gregory of Tours has Malchus declare, on discovering that he has really been asleep for many years, that God has awakened him and his companions so that every age may know that the resurrection of the dead will come to pass: "Et nunc suscitavit me Dominus cum fratribus meis, ut cognoscat omnis saeculus, quia fiet resurrectio mortuorum" (p. 767, 13–14) ["And now the Lord has raised me up with my brothers so that every age may understand that there will be a sresurrection of the dead"]. Similarly, at the end of the anonymous Latin *passio*, Maximianus, the leader of the seven, addresses the Christian emperor Theodosius and tells him that it was so that he might believe in the resurrection of the dead that God caused the miracle to take place: "propter te suscitavit nos Deus a terra ante diem magnum resurrectionis, ut credas sine dubitatione, quoniam est resurrectio mortuorum" (p. 76, 6–8). ["Because of you God raised us from the earth before the great day of the Resurrection so that you may believe without doubt that there is a resurrection of the dead"]. The latter passage is taken over directly by Ælfric: "for ðe arærde se ælmihtiga god us of eorðan ær ðam micclum dæge. þæt ðu buton twyn gelyfe. þæt deadra manna ærist bið" (220–22) ["For you almighty God raised us from the earth before the great day that you may believe without doubt that there will be a resurrection of the dead"].

Early medieval saints' lives characteristically focus on the inspiring acts of the saints whom they celebrate. They aim to show these saints as the exemplary heroes of the church.[13] In the legend of the Seven Sleepers, however, the doctrine of the resurrection, rather than the actions of the saints, is at the center of the edification the narrative offers. The saints are faithful in the face of persecution, but their role throughout is essentially passive, not active. They are not in control of their own destinies: to all intents and purposes they are martyred without knowing it, for God causes them to fall into a miraculous sleep before they are walled up in the cave. They become instruments in a larger divine plan whose object is to offer to Theodosius, and to Christians generally, proof that the body will rise again: it is God's wish, we read in the *passio*, to reveal through the Sleepers the hope of life in the resurrection of the dead at the time of Theodosius: "revelare spem vitae in resurrectione mortuorum in illo tempore" ["to reveal the hope of life in the resurrection of the dead at that time," p. 57, 8–9]. The miracle of the Seven Sleepers presents itself primarily as a triumphant vindication of this doctrine of the resurrection of the body. It has been suggested indeed that the legend was composed in the first place, in fifth-century Ephesus, and soon after the supposed occurrence of the miracle itself, to combat a revival of Origenistic beliefs denying the resurrection of the body.[14] This historical context of theological controversy can be seen as giving the treatment of the theme of the resurrection the urgency and insistence that it receives in the story of the Sleepers, even in versions composed long after such controversy was settled.

The second aspect to be noted is the legend's concern with what might be called the *human* dimension of the story. This aspect grows out of the doctrinal basis of the legend. Because the events that happen in it are essentially beyond the control of the saints themselves there is scope to develop in the legend an interest in their fears, insecurities, and ignorance about what is happening to them. The interest in the human dimension of the story is centered above all on the episode of Malchus's expedition to Ephesus after the long sleep, when Malchus thinks that he has been asleep for only one night. The youth's astonishment and bewilderment at the changes that have come upon Ephesus are vividly described in Gregory and even more so in the *passio*—in both of these versions Malchus wonders if he is dreaming (Gregory, p. 766, 17–18; *passio*, p. 62, 15–16)—but they are emphasized above all in the anonymous Old English version, in which Malchus's distracted progress is followed with particular fascination and sympathy. Malchus and his companions emerge from these and other versions of the legend as essentially human and vulnerable, in some ways more like ordinary people than like the larger-than-life heroes of conventional hagiography.

Ælfric is drawn to the doctrinal significance of the legend, but he ignores entirely its human dimension. His interest in this doctrinal significance of the Seven Sleepers story is vividly illustrated by the second reference to it in his writings, in a passage, mentioned earlier, that he added to his homily for the first Sunday after Easter when he was revising the First Series of *Catholic Homilies*. As noted by Gatch, this addition appears in six of the eleven surviving manuscripts of the collection, although it is not given in Thorpe's edition.[15] The addition consists of seventy-eight lines of rhythmical prose, which elaborate on the theme with which the original homily was dealing at this point. The theme is that of the resurrection of the body, and the addition provides a series of exempla intended to give proof of this doctrine. Ælfric evidently felt that his original composition required further discussion of this difficult element of Christian teaching. His demonstrations in the added passage represent, as Gatch puts it, "an honest attempt by reference to natural science and hagiography to elucidate one of the most puzzling mysteries of the faith so as to make it more easily understandable to a lay congregation."[16]

Since the part of the addition dealing with the Seven Sleepers has yet to appear in print in a published form, it is relevant to present it here in full:

Us secgað eac bec swa swa hit full soð is.
þæt ða seofan slæperas þa slepon on ðam timan
fram decies dagum ðæs deofollican caseres.
oð theodosies timan ðe on crist gelyfde.
þreo hund geara fæc 7 twa 7 hundseofantig geara.   5
þæt hi ða upp arison of þære eorðan acucode.
for ðan ðe crist wolde þam casere geswutelian
þæt we ealle sceolon of deaðe arisan
on þam endenextan dæge urum drihtne togeanes.
7 underfon edlean eallra ure dæda   10
be þam ðe we ær gewrohton on þissere worulde;
Wylle we. nelle we we wuniað æfre cuce
æfter urum æriste be urum gewyrhtum
oððe wel. oððe yfele. be þam ðe we geworhton ær;[17]

[Books tell us, just as it is quite true, that the Seven Sleepers then slept at that time from the days of the devilish emperor Decius to the time of Theodosius, who believed in Christ, for a period of 372 years; that they then rose up from the earth alive because Christ wished to reveal to the emperor that we shall all arise from death on the last day to meet our Lord and to receive the reward for all our deeds, according as we have acted beforehand in this world. Willingly or unwillingly, we shall remain forever alive after our resurrection according to our deserts, for good or for ill, according as we have acted beforehand.]

The context of this passage in the homily for the First Sunday after Easter is a purely doctrinal one, a context concerned with the explication of Christian teaching, not with the glorification of the saints. The Sleepers arose, says Ælfric (7–8), because Christ wished to reveal to Theodosius the truth of the resurrection of the body, and he goes on to bring out the full relevance of this teaching for his audience by moving from the indirect statement of the þæt clause of lines 8–11 to direct address of his audience in the final three lines of the passage: "Wylle we. nelle we we wuniað æfre cuce . . . " ["willingly or unwillingly we shall remain forever alive"]. The Seven Sleepers serve Ælfric as an exemplum of the doctrine of the resurrection of the body. Indeed an interest in the saints for their own sakes in this passage would divert attention away from the essential point which Ælfric is making.

Ælfric's *Sanctorum Septem Dormientium* in the Second Series of the *Catholic Homilies* forms a self-contained unit rather than, like the reference in the First Series, contributing to a larger discussion. In the *Sanctorum Septem Dormientium* Ælfric—albeit "sceortlice"["briefly"] (184)—focuses in on the seven saints themselves, giving their names (186–87), telling of their noble birth (189), of their persecution by Decius (190–91), and of how he has them walled up in a cave "mid ormætum weorcstanum" (202). In this hagiographical narrative Ælfric sets the good servants of God—"godes þegnas" (196)—against the raging Decius, and he shows the merciful God—"se mildheorta god" (202–03)—watching over them. He describes their miraculous awakening (206–11) and, in greater detail, their joyful meeting with Theodosius (211–26), before they finally send forth their souls (226–31).

The theme of the resurrection is mentioned only in this closing part of the narrative and in Ælfric's statement that when the stone was moved from the mouth of the cave the Creator gave the saints life and resurrection—"lif and ærist" (210). In the closing part, however, when the miracle is revealed to Theodosius, the centrality of this theme of the resurrection becomes fully apparent. Theodosius himself, as in Gregory and in the anonymous *passio*, compares the resurrection of the seven to that of Lazarus (218–19), and Maximianus informs Theodosius, in a passage echoed in the reference in the First Series of *Catholic Homilies* (see 7–8 of text quoted previously), that it was to give him proof of the resurrection that they arose: "þæt ðu buton twyn gelyfe. þæt deadra manna ærist bið" ["that you may believe without doubt that there will be a resurrection of the dead," 221–22]. The orthodoxy of the doctrine of the resurrection is highlighted in Maximianus's prayer that the empire of Theodosius should stand "on soðum geleafan" ["in true faith"] (224): the adjective *soðum* introduces a different emphasis from that of "permaneat . . . in fortitudine fidei tuae" ["may remain in the fortitude of your faith"] in the *passio* (p. 76, 3–4). The rejoicing and glory with which the passage ends are those of the recognition of this "true belief," brought out all the more by the antithesis of the temptations of the devil—"wið deofles costnungum" ["against the temptations of the devil," 224–25].

In his treatment of the doctrinal theme, however, as in other aspects of his handling of the legend, Ælfric deliberately excises much of the specific detail found in the sources and analogues. Numbers, biblical quotations, names, and even characters that appear in the other versions are left out where Ælfric feels them to be less than necessary to the celebration of the miracle. Even the pivotal figure of the venerable bishop Marinus, who in other versions realizes the truth of the miracle, makes no appearance in Ælfric.

The emphasis on the historical setting of the legend is reduced in Ælfric's version to the point that it virtually disappears. Ælfric assumes that his audience will know enough about the Decian persecutions of the Christians without his dwelling on them, and he simplifies the relationship between Decius and the seven saints in terms of the conventional confrontation of raging emperor and Christian heroes. In the anonymous Latin *passio* and in the other Old English version the attitude of Decius to the saints is complicated by the fact that they are members of his household and he does not wish to harm them, whereas Ælfric (here agreeing with Gregory) emphasizes the ferocity of the emperor and the idea that he wishes to inflict tortures upon them.

In the second part of the story Ælfric leaves out all reference to a heresy at the time of Theodosius denying the orthodox teaching of the resurrection of the dead. This omission has the effect of depriving the miracle of its context of theological turmoil and controversy and necessarily weakens the impact of the vindication of doctrinal truth in the legend, although it also allows Ælfric to present Theodosius more positively than he appears in other versions. Maximianus tells Theodosius that the miracle occurred so that he would believe "buton twyn" that there will be a resurrection of the dead, but stripped of its supporting context of doctrinal controversy this assertion loses its full force and immediacy, as we have no reason to believe that Theodosius should doubt the resurrection. Because of Ælfric's drastic pruning of his sources and his excision of the theme of heresy, the most immediate reason for Theodosius's sublime joy at the end of the narrative is not elucidated, and the legend becomes a general glorification of doctrinal truth, rather than having part of its significance in belonging to a particular historical moment.

This playing-down of the individual and the specific is an aspect of Ælfric's highly iconographic and stylized approach to his material. He omits the personal concern, so apparent in the other Old English version of the legend, with the worries and fears of the seven saints as they face persecution from Decius. He reduces their understandably mixed human emotions to an exemplary perseverence in the face of torture. When we first see the saints in the anonymous Old English version, they are lamenting and weeping and fading away in their sorrow at the sufferings of their fellow Christians and in their fear of being brought before the emperor (Skeat, 125–27). They are much more impassive in Ælfric's presentation. There is no mention of their sorrow or fear: they are simply "godes cempan." Indeed, the whole of the graphic account of the persecution of the Christians found in other versions of the legend is left out by Ælfric, and with it the emphasis on the terror and flight of Christians before Decius. The other Old English version has the affective comparison of these Christians to little grasshoppers being swept away before them by Decius's men: "hi hi ut drifon. and him beforan feredon swilce lytle gærstapan" ["they drove them out and carried them before them like little grasshoppers," Skeat, 56–57]. The other Christians do not appear at all in Ælfric's version.

Most strikingly of all in his adaptation of his inherited material, Ælfric disregards entirely the feature that the other Old English writer finds most compelling and that gives this other version much of its interest and attractiveness, its concern about the perplexed Malchus, the youth chosen by the other Sleepers to leave their cave and go into Ephesus to buy bread for them. After the sleep Malchus finds Ephesus incredibly changed, apparently after only one night, and its inhabitants have suddenly all become Christian. He is faced with suspicion and hostility and can make no sense of what he sees. The account of Malchus's expedition to Ephesus takes up about a third of the whole text in the anonymous Old English version. In Ælfric's version, however, it is not even mentioned. We are simply told that when, after a period of 372 years, the stone was rolled away from the mouth of the cave, the saints awoke and they were revealed to the citizens of Ephesus: "hi wurdon ða ameldode þam burhwarum" (211).

The treatment of the emperor Theodosius is also modified in Ælfric's version, to the extent that he, not the Sleepers themselves, becomes the character to whom most attention is given. In the anonymous Old English legend, as in the Latin versions, Theodosius is shown at the time of the heresy as uncertain and longing for spiritual enlightenment. He is a figure of humility who does not know what to believe: "he nyste hwæs he gelyfan sceolde" ["he did not know what he should believe," Skeat, 396–97]. In Ælfric, however, there is no sense that he is anything but a confident figure of benevolent authority. He proceeds on his journey to Ephesus not with anxiety but with the sense of assurance that characterizes his actions throughout.

It is noticeable that the tableaulike scene between Theodosius and the seven saints is the only one that Ælfric attempts to realize with any fullness of detail. He even gives us the direct words of Theodosius and Maximianus (217–25), the first time direct speech has been used in the narrative. He also retains the biblical allusion to the raising of Lazarus (218–19) found in the other versions of the legend, this being his only scriptural reference. At the center of the scene is the gesturally significant picture of Theodosius falling in veneration before the saints and kissing and embracing them (216–18).

The attention to dramatic and symbolic detail in this stylized scene highlights its position as the climax of the whole story. God's miracle is revealed and God's guiding oversight of the faith of his people is symbolized in the embrace of Theodosius, a figure of Christian kingship, and the saints. The special role of Theodosius in the story of the Seven Sleepers is exemplified by the fact that when the saints go out of the cave to meet him their faces shine like the sun: "heora nebwlitu scean swa swa sunne" (215–16). So important for Ælfric is this scene between Theodosius and the Sleepers that he allows it to overshadow the rest of the narrative. It takes up a third of his text, whereas in the Latin *passio* (we are unable to compare the anonymous Old English version at this point, as part of the scene between Theodosius and the Sleepers is missing in the manuscript) it represents only about one-twentieth of the total. Ælfric combines in his relatively extended treatment of this scene—and therefore in his *Sanctorum Septem Dormientium* as a whole—a concern about confirming orthodox teaching with an interest in the theme of spiritual authority and Christian kingship, as illustrated by the emperor Theodosius. What remains evident as well is that in his account he is not so interested in the details of what happened to the Seven Sleepers themselves, nor in their state of mind.

These saints are not shown as people with whom the audience can identify or sympathize. They exist on a rarified and emotionless level, on which there is no concern with worldly needs or with fears. In their transfigured state at the end of the narrative their faces may shine like the sun, but the saints are also in a sense transfigured from ordinary life in the rest of the narrative as well, being presented as changeless icons rather than as striving human beings at a time of trial. Ælfric's source would have concerned itself with such human considerations but they are not of interest to Ælfric in his presentation of the story as a revelation of spiritual truth.

The *Sanctorum Septem Dormientium* provides an unusually extreme example of Ælfric's approach to hagiographical writing, and one in which doctrine receives more explicit attention than usual. In key respects, however, this text is typical of the way in which Ælfric treats his hagiographical material elsewhere.[18] Emphasizing the exemplary and iconographic aspects of the legend and deemphasizing the saints' individual humanity and vulnerability and the specific details of the historical setting of the story are, of course, particularly appropriate in the strongly doctrinal context of the *Catholic Homilies*. The whole of the *Catholic Homilies* is underlain by the principle of imparting good teaching: as Ælfric puts it in the Old English Preface to the First Series, "menn behofiað godre lare" ["people have need of good teaching," p. 2]. Ælfric's emphasis in the *Sanctorum Septem Dormientium* is also, however, in accordance with his usual hagiographical practice. In one of the first detailed examinations of Ælfric's approach to hagiography, Dorothy Bethurum spoke of his habitual "exchange of concrete detail [as found in his sources] for a summarizing phrase" and of the consequent "loss of vividness" in his saints' lives.[19] And the study of Ælfric's saints' lives has led Raymon S. Farrar to describe the heroes of hagiography as "at times slightly depersonalized representations of various aspects of Christian life."[20] Ælfric presents his saints as elevated and exemplary figures, in whom, as he declares in the Old English Preface to *Lives of Saints*, the wonders of God are seen:

> god is wundor-lic
> on his halgum swa swa we ær sædon . and his halgena wundra
> wurðiað hine . forþan þe he worhte þa wundra þurh hi.
>
> (Skeat, 56–58)

[God is wonderful in his saints, as we have said before, and the wonders of his saints honor him because he has performed the wonders through them.]

The lives of the saints are written so that they may be remembered and so that the faith of future generations may be confirmed:

> halige lareowas
> hit awriton on leden-spræce . to langum gemynde .
> and to trymmincge þam towerdum mannum.
>
> (Skeat, 50–52)

[Holy teachers wrote it in the Latin language as a lasting memorial and to confirm the faith of future generations.]

In his Latin Preface to *Lives of Saints* Ælfric speaks of his aim of refreshing his audience by the exhortations—"hortationibus" (16)—contained in his saints' lives, because, as he puts it, the passions of the martyrs greatly revive a failing faith—"quia martyrum passiones nimium fidem erigant languentem" (16–17).

Ælfric's approach, in his version of the legend of the Seven Sleepers as in his other saints' lives, reflects definitive characteristics of early medieval hagiography as a whole, as these have been discerned by modern scholars. Hagiography, of course, encompasses a range of styles, approaches, and attitudes on the part of its authors, and individual works will not all uniformly reflect its typical elements. Nonetheless, such features as the idealizing and symbolic qualities of this literature are widely recognized.[21] Its heroes are larger than life, abstracted from everyday reality, and presented in highly conventional terms. They are, typically, secure and indestructible in their faith in the protection of God and beyond criticism in their behavior. They are idealized and exemplary: "The very basis of hagiography," writes Régis Boyer, "is the exemplum, these texts have been, first of all, born of a pedogogical, edifying intention."[22] The remarks of C. W. Jones on Bede's approach in his prose *Life of St. Cuthbert*, a work written in Latin for a monastic audience, apply too to that of Ælfric, who wrote in the vernacular for a wider audience: "His primary aim was to generalize and to idealize the picture and to point it more clearly to its proper end. So we find him eliminating facts and detail . . . and making clear the moral rightness of the acts."[23]

The legend of the Seven Sleepers, however (as it appears in most versions), with its use of dramatic irony at the expense of the saints and with its interest in the feelings of ordinary people in an extraordinary situation, could be seen as conflicting with some of the principles of hagiographical writing, certainly as practiced by Ælfric. The legend is also extravagant in its plot and allows only a passive role for the saints themselves.

Furthermore, in including the legend in the Second Series of *Catholic Homilies* at all Ælfric might be said to be contradicting his declared intentions for the collection. He announces in the Old English Preface that the book is intended to include not monastic saints but only those saints whom the English nation honors with feast days: "þæra anra þe angelcynn mid freolsdagum wurðað" (p. 2, line 40). The Seven Sleepers do not come into this category, as Ælfric himself implies at the beginning of his account of them, when he informs his audience that the feast of the Seven Sleepers is kept two days after that of St. James: "We willað eow eac gereccan sceortlice þæt nu æfter twam dagum is ðæra seofon slapera gemynd" (184–85). This sentence suggests that the congregation being addressed in the homily would not be present when the feast was being celebrated.

The legend of the Seven Sleepers fits in with the overall principles of the *Catholic Homilies*, however, in that it has a strongly doctrinal theme. This theme draws Ælfric to the Seven Sleepers in the first place, and when he does turn to this celebrated tale it is in such a way as singlemindedly to give prominence to its edifying purposes, doctrinal and exemplary, and to reduce, or omit, everything else. Ælfric gets rid of those aspects that could be thought of as distracting from pure edification, and he presents his story with his customary evenness of narrative progression and serenity of tone. Further detail is not needed in his treatment and might even be counterproductive. What remains, although somewhat severe and lacking the discursive richness of the longer Old English version of the legend of the Seven Sleepers, provides a refined and abstracted example of what Ælfric would have regarded as sound hagiographical writing. In this text we see Ælfric assimilating the legend of the Seven Sleepers more fully to the conventions and principles of early medieval hagiography, as he practiced them. His practice is "purer" and more uncompromising than that of some of his contemporaries. In reflecting this practice the *Sanctorum Septem Dormientium* is characteristically Ælfrician.[24]

Notes

1. *Ælfric's Catholic Homilies: The Second Series: Text*, ed. Malcolm Godden, EETS SS 5 (Oxford, 1979), "Sanctorum Septem Dormientium," pp. 247–48. References to this text are by line number.

2. Walter W. Skeat, ed. *Ælfric's Lives of Saints*, EETS OS 76, 82, 94, and 114 (London, 1881–1900; reprinted as two vols., 1966), vol. 1, pp. 488–541; I have also edited this *vita* separately, *The Anonymous Old English Legend of the Seven Sleepers*, Durham Medieval Texts 7 (Durham, England, 1994). References in the present chapter are to Skeat's edition, by line number.

3. See Patrick H. Zettel, "Ælfric's Hagiographic Sources and the Latin Legendary Preserved in BL MS Cotton Nero E i and CCCC MS 9 and Other Manuscripts," dissertation, Oxford University (1979), pp. 192–91. The text of the *passio* is edited by P. Michael Huber, in his "Beitrag zur Visionsliteratur und Siebenschlaferlegende des Mittelalters, I Teil: Text," *Beilage zum Jahresbericht des humanistischen Gymnasiums Metten* (1902–3): 39–78. References to this edition are by page and line number.

4. See my article, "The Anonymous Old English Legend of the Seven Sleepers and its Latin Source," *Leeds Studies in English*, n.s. 22 (1991): 43–56.

5. In the Gregory of Tours version referred to in note 11, Constantinus appears not at the end of the list but after Martinianus (p. 762, 2).

6. See London, BL Cotton Nero E. i, Part II, fol. 55r, i, 41; compare Huber's edition of the *passio*, p. 61, 7. The British Library MS referred to here and in subsequent notes (by folio, column, and line number) is the earlier of the two MSS containing the Cotton-Corpus text of the *passio*. It was written at Worcester c. 1060 (text of Seven Sleepers, fols. 53r–56r). The other copy appears in the later eleventh-century MS, Salisbury, Cathedral Library 222 (formerly Oxford, Bodleian Library, Fell 1), fols. 35v–41v.

7. See Cotton Nero, fol. 56r, i, 15–16; Huber, "Beitrag zur Visionsliteratur," p. 69, 12.

8. See Cotton Nero, fol. 53v, ii, 24; Huber, ibid., p. 47, 8.

9. Note especially the MSS Namur 53 and Brussels 9290. The article referred to in note 4 shows that these MSS throw significant light on the source of the anonymous Old English version of the legend.

10. The Cotton-Corpus reading "memoriam maximam," which Zettel (p. 193) identifies as the source of Ælfric's "mære cyrcan" (230) and which he contrasts with the "memoriam Maximiani" of Huber's "Beitrag zur Visionsliteratur," (p. 78, 5), is not significant, because Huber's collations show that most MSS of the *passio* have *maximam* instead of *Maximiani*.

11. Edited by B. Krusch, in *Passiones Vitaeque Sanctorum Aevi Merovingici*, ed. B. Krusch and W. Levison, MGH, Scriptores Rerum Merovingicarum, VII, ii, (Hannover and Leipzig, 1919–20), Appendix, vol. 1, pp. 757–69. References to this edition are by page and line number.

12. See further note 10. For *memoria* as meaning "shrine," see J. F. Niermeyer, *Mediae Latinitatis Lexicon Minoris* (Leiden, 1976), and A. Souter, *A Glossary of Later Latin to 600 A.D.* (Oxford, 1949), s.v.

13. Note Ælfric's own statement on this in his "Passion of Chrysanthus and his Wife Daria":

> We wurþiað godes halgan . ac wite ge swa-þeah
> þæt þam halgum nis nan neod ure herunge on þam life .
> ac us sylfum fremað þæt þæt we secgað be him .
> ærest to gebysnunge . þæt we þe beteran beon .
> and eft to þing-rædene þonne us þearf bið .
> (lines 341–45, Skeat, *Ælfric's Lives*, vol. 2, p. 396)

14. See Ernst Honigmann, "Stephen of Ephesus (April 15, 448–Oct. 29, 451) and the Legend of the Seven Sleepers," *Studi e Testi* 173 (1953): 125–68.

15. See M. McC. Gatch, *Preaching and Theology in Anglo-Saxon England: Ælfric and Wulfstan* (Toronto and Buffalo, N.Y., 1977), pp. 86–88. For Thorpe's edition of this homily, see *The Homilies of the Anglo-Saxon Church. The First Part, Containing the Sermones Catholici, or Homilies of Ælfric*, ed. Benjamin Thorpe, 2 vols. (London, 1844 and 1846), vol. 1, pp. 230–39 (the addition to this homily occurs at the point corresponding to Thorpe's p. 236, between lines 22 and 23). Subsequent references to the First Series of the *Catholic Homilies*, other than to the unpublished addition, are to Thorpe's edition, by page number.

16. Gatch, *Preaching and Theology*, pp. 87–88.

17. The text is that of CCCC 188, p. 172. I also examined the texts of the passage in CCCC 178 (p. 242); London, BL Cotton Faustina A. ix (fol. 149v); and Cotton Vitellius C. v (fol. 95v). The other MSS that contain the addition are Oxford, Bodleian Library, Hatton 114 (fol. 96r ff.); and Cambridge, Trinity College B.15.34 (p.40 ff.). I am particularly grateful to P. A. M. Clemoes for allowing me to see his collation of the passage, which he carried out in preparing his dissertation, "Ælfric's 'Catholic Homilies,' First Series: The Text and Manuscript Tradition," 2 vols., dissertation, Cambridge University (1956).

18. On Ælfric's approach to hagiography see further my article, "Contrasting Features in the Non-Ælfrician Lives in the Old English Lives of Saints," *Anglia* 104 (1986): 319–27.

19. Dorothy Bethurum, "The Form of Ælfric's Lives of Saints," *Studies in Philology* 29 (1932): 522.

20. Raymon S. Farrar, "Structure and Function in Representative Old English Saints' Lives," *Neophilologus* 57 (1973): 88.

21. See especially Hippolyte Delehaye, *Les Légendes Hagiographiques*, 4th ed., Subsidia Hagiographica, 18a (Brussels, 1955), ch. 2 (Delehaye sees the stylization and simplicity of saints' legends as being due to the limited intellectual capacity of their popular audiences); and R. Aigrain, *L'Hagiographie: Ses Sources, Ses Methodes, Son Histoire* (Paris, 1953), especially pp. 195–290.

22. Regis Boyer, "An Attempt to Define the Typology of Medieval Hagiography," in *Hagiography and Medieval Literature: A Symposium*, ed. H. Bekker-Nielson, P. Foote, J. Højgaard Jørgensen, and P. Nyberg (Odense, Denmark, 1981), p. 28. See also S. C. Aston, "The Saint in Medieval Literature," *Modern Language Review* 65 (1970): xxxiv. Note too the Ælfric quotation given in note 13.

23. Charles W. Jones, *Saints' Lives and Chronicles in Early England* (Ithaca, N.Y., 1947), p. 74.

24. I wish to thank Mary Clayton for her helpful comments on an earlier draft of this essay.

Discourse and Hypersignification in Two of Ælfric's Saints' Lives

Ruth Waterhouse

When Ælfric in the late tenth century was writing his *Lives of Saints* for his lay audience, he had in mind not a single homogeneous audience (for one thing he specifically addressed both readers and hearers[1]) but a multiple audience with differing backgrounds and experiences, and varying sensitivities to language that would have enabled some to perceive merely the more obvious and others also the more subtle aspects of his hortatory message. He would hardly have had in mind an audience located in a period a thousand years later. The present-day reader-audience of his texts is distanced from him in so many ways (for instance, from his language and from his religious message and the socio-cultural assumptions informing it) that any twentieth-century reading needs to work from a theoretical model that can point to aspects of his texts which are relevant to both periods.

One result of the burgeoning of critical theories about literary texts in recent decades has been that readers are now much more sensitive to the part that *they* play in reconstructing a text, and because no readers in any period remain unaffected by their socio-cultural context, their reading may well reveal as much about their own period and its dominant ideologies as about the text and the socio-cultural context in which *it* was written.[2] Yet they also remain individuals. Therefore, in any consideration of the three-way transaction between writer or encoder, text, and reader-audience or decoder, any theoretical standpoint now chosen by a reader will necessarily entail a whole complex of selectively differing emphases on how the transaction functions and on its impact.

In this post-modern period, when theories devised initially with reference to Renaissance and later English literature are now being applied to earlier literature, the simplistic binary oppositions of structuralism are more and more being replaced by models that bring in a broader field of contexts that get away from such too-convenient symmetry, and the model used in

333

what follows assumes that triads can be more helpful in emphasizing the close interaction of multiple aspects of the discourse.

More general and more specific influences can be detected in any text: macro-influences upon the encoder are those of the period's society and culture and its concomitant ideology, the genre with all its conventions, as they affect features such as the *topoi* and the form, and the pre-texts and intertexts that for Old English writers have particular authority. Micro-influences are the constraints of the particular language available, especially in any form of "translation": the paradigm (the word choices), the syntagm (the chaining together of the choices), and the signifier-signified relationship (including the relative weighting of denotation as against connotative associations).

For the decoder, too, the period in all its aspects is inevitably an influence, as are his or her knowledge and expectations of the genre and the intertexts (which naturally vary from period to period and from individual to individual). But other than having to work within the framework of the micro-influence of the basic structure of the language, the decoder is more concerned with another triad: that of the discourse (the language of the text itself), the "story" of the events befalling the protagonists that each reader will deduce from it, and the hypersignification (the thematic elements over and above what is overtly stated) which can be drawn from discourse and story combined. Figure 1 shows in schematized form the relationship of these various aspects.

In my work on Ælfric's *Lives of Saints*,[3] I have tended to concentrate upon the encoder's microtriad, Ælfric's choice and use of language, as they relate to the intertexts (the Latin sources) and the broad generic influences (both of hagiography and of his own version of the alliterative line) within which he situates his discourse. But I have been less concerned until now to situate these aspects in the broader context (relevant for both encoder and decoder) of their interrelationship with the period, especially the difference between a tenth and a twentieth century reader's perception of the hypersignification of Ælfric's discourse and what that perception (necessarily hypothetical as regards a tenth century reader and generalized as regards a twentieth century reader) suggests about either period's cultural assumptions. Although the following discussion is not attempting exotic new readings, the application of this model can provide some suggestive insights.

A brief look at a couple of passages from Ælfric's *Life of Oswald* shows how the model functions. It illustrates, for instance, how the change of socio-cultural and ideological background from the tenth and twentieth centuries (and indeed between the eighth and the tenth centuries) can affect the hypersignification quite markedly. It is well-known that this particular life shows how Ælfric, as decoder of the Latin and reencoder into the vernacular

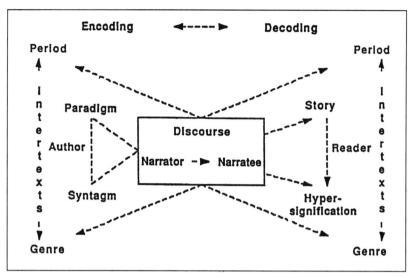

Figure 1. Writer-Text-Reader Relationships

of some half dozen chapters of Bede's *Historia Ecclesiastica*,[4] conflates and rearranges Bede's nonchronological information into a continuous chronologically ordered narrative. But he also makes additions to Bede, as in the first line of his introduction, which places Oswald's life into a spatio-temporal relationship not only to England generally (before the later particularization that Oswald is king of Northumbria), but also to the coming of Augustine:

> Æfter ðan ðe Augustinus to Engla lande becom .
> wæs sum æðele cyning Oswold gehaten
> on norðhymbra lande gelyfed swyþe on god .
> se ferde on his iugoðe fram freondum and magum.
> to scot-lande on sæ . and þær sona wearð gefullod
> and his geferan samod þe mid him siþedon .
>
> (1–6)

[After Augustine came to England there was a certain noble king called Oswald in Northumbria, believing strongly in God, who in his youth went from friends and relations to Ireland by sea, and there was at once baptized together with his companions who journeyed with him.]

Ælfric seems to assume that dating Oswald's life by his own initial added reference to Augustine's coming to England will function to give his lay (as well as any religious) audience a well-known and easily recognizable date, and even that may remind them of Augustine's mission, which was to introduce Roman Christianity to the heathen Anglo-Saxons of Kent. But, following that, Ælfric goes on to stress that the great belief in God which by implication makes Oswald "noble" is formalized as that of the Irish Celtic (not Roman) Christianity into which Oswald and his companions were baptized. Ælfric's first sentence, then, juxtaposes the two branches of Christianity, the conflict between which had to be resolved during the reign of Oswald's brother and successor, Oswiu, who in 664 convened the Synod of Whitby, which declared the Roman Church and its practices (those of Ælfric himself) to be preeminent.

Later, Ælfric recounts how, after Oswald had secured his kingdom by defeating Cadwalla, he wished to "gebigan / his leoda to geleafan . and to þam lifigendan gode ." ["convert his people to belief and to the living God" (46–47)], and says that Oswald sent to Ireland "þær se geleafa wæs ða" ["where the faith was then," (48)], and Aidan was sent by the Celtic Church of Ireland to help convert the Northumbrians.

In re-encoding the early chapters of Book III of Bede's *History*, Ælfric's choice and rearrangement of his source material alters its hypersignification. Bede's later chapters in Book III include a detailed narration of the wrangle between the Roman and the Celtic Church representatives at the Synod of Whitby. The speeches attributed to Wilfrid and to Colman[5] suggest that the issue was for Bede a live and important one, not only for the history of the English Church, but also for him personally and for the religious audience for whom he is writing. So when Bede in III.3 introduces Aidan, he speaks of his zeal for God "quamuis non plene secundum scientiam" ["although not entirely in accordance with knowledge," (p. 218)]. And he goes on to spell out how Aidan and the Celts celebrated Easter at the wrong time, adding: "Quod an uerum sit, peritus quisque facillime cognoscit" ["As to what is true or not, an instructed person can very easily judge," (p. 218)]. Such a rhetorical appeal to judge the Irish Church's dating of Easter as being wrong tends to undercut his preceding praise of Aidan and virtually functions as an instruction to his audience to perceive the relative inferiority of Celtic to Roman Christianity.

For the Latin-educated and Roman-biased eighth-century audience of Bede's religious readers (who, he seems to assume, have some prior knowledge of the still live issue of the differences—in both senses—between the Celtic and the Roman Churches), Bede's encoding presupposes the superiority of the Roman Church. Ælfric removes this emphasis in reencoding the information for his lay audience, both in his introduction to the life that situates Oswald relative to Augustine *and* to the Celtic Church, and especially in his parenthetic comment in 48b about Ireland being the place where "the faith was then." For Ælfric, as a second-generation monk intimately involved in the Benedictine revival of the tenth century,[6] monasticism (a mode of religious life closely associated with the Celtic Church, even though the reformed Benedictine rule derived from the Roman Church) naturally provides an ideal, but for the lay folk belief in God is far more important than are details of differing religious practice. Indeed, his discourse makes the concept of belief a key motif throughout the life: in just the introductory section, verbal or noun terms alluding to belief occur in lines 3, 8, 15, 27; and they recur thereafter throughout the life, suggesting at the level of hypersignification that belief connects rather than divides different Churches within Anglo-Saxon Christianity.

Judging from the way that Ælfric encodes these unelaborated references to the coming of Augustine and to belief and baptism, they were for his tenth century lay (not initially religious) Christian audience allusions to well-known foundations of their fundamental ideology. Those twentieth-century readers (lay or religious) who pass over these introductory allusions as of little significance may merely be indicating their lack of knowledge of the history of the times, but may also reflect a society most of whose ideologies are basically non-Christian.

A twentieth century reader, accustomed to modern canons of pertinency, may also have difficulty perceiving the relevance to the Life of Oswald of the later section about Birinus (119–39), who comes from Rome to convert Cynegils, king of Wessex, and his people, and who becomes Bishop of Dorchester under the auspices of both Cynegils and Oswald. Although the *Anglo-Saxon Chronicle*[7] in the annal for 827 lists Oswald as the sixth Bretwalda, and so by implication overlord of Wessex, the undue attention Ælfric pays to the seemingly peripheral episode of Birinus (as contrasted with the passages dealing with Aidan who plays a much more central role in Oswald's story) can appear an intrusive disruption to the narrative progression of the "story." In Bede, the whole of III.7, in which the information about Birinus is originally encoded, deals with the kingdom of Wessex, and because Bede's practice is to separate out information about the various kingdoms, there is no such problem for an audience (either eighth or twentieth) when the chapter break marks a transition to another strand of the English Church's history.

However, for a tenth-century reader-hearer who had any awareness of the tension which seems to have been building up between the Celtic and Roman Churches at about the time when Oswald was king of Northumbria, prior to the Synod of Whitby, the welcome extended by the Celtic Christian king Oswald to the Roman Christian bishop Birinus, and Oswald's presence at the baptism of Cynegils, and his association with Cynegils in giving Birinus his bishopric, is encoded to become a further significant reminder by Ælfric that "geleafa" (a term also chosen for inclusion in 127, 130, 131, 138) in God overrides factional boundaries, and Oswald's saintliness derives from belief, not from any particular practice of it.

The hypersignification of the episode is enhanced by the ordering whereby Oswald's treatment of Birinus and of Cynegils sets up a contrast between the conversion of the king of Wessex and the following report of the obstinate refusal by Penda (the Mercian king who finally kills Oswald) to accept Christianity. Ælfric records that

> se penda ne cuðe be criste nan þincg .
> and eall myrcena folc wæs unfullod þa git .
> (153–54)[8]

[This Penda did not know anything about Christ, and all the Mercian people was as yet unbaptized.]

The final temporal pointer "yet" foreshadows the conclusion to the life, where Ælfric narrates what happens to Oswald's bones (in contradistinction to his right arm, the incorruption of which fulfills Aidan's prophecy made during Oswald's life):[9]

> þæs halgan oswoldes ban wurdon eft gebroht
> æfter manegum gearum to myrcena lande
> into gleawceastre . and god þær geswutelode
> oft feala wundra þurh þone halgan wer .
> (283–86)

[The holy Oswald's bones were afterwards brought after many years to the land of the Mercians into Gloucester, and God there often showed many miracles through the holy man.]

Ælfric does not spell out that Mercia has become Christian since Penda's death, but he implies it, hinting that the miracles performed by and through the saintly Oswald are part of the conversion process.

The Oswald story, then, provides instances of how broader influences upon the encoder such as historical aspects of the period as well as its ideological presuppositions affect the discourse, and how changes in both in later periods also affect its decoding, especially perceptions of hypersignification, which may reveal as much about a decoder's period and assumptions (as for instance the prevailing loss of Christian belief in the twentieth century, which cannot help but influence readings of Ælfric's stress on "belief in God") as those of the encoder.

Period differences as they affect more material socio-cultural conditions can also have an impact upon the encoding, and naturally these aspects of the discourse are more immediately accessible to a tenth than to a twentieth century audience, as can be seen in Ælfric's reencoding of Bede's narration of the life of Æthelthryth. I have already treated this life in some detail in earlier work,[10] but I want to take up a few points here, though from a different perspective that is relevant to the model just proposed.

First, and most obviously, the text focuses upon a real (not a fictional) woman, and to a lesser extent on male-female relationships. Socio-cultural attitudes toward these subjects, which fluctuate markedly from period to period (as do those of individuals), cannot but influence a text, especially when so many periods are involved in encoding and decoding this particular text: the seventh century, when Æthelthryth actually lived, the eighth, when Bede wrote the Latin pre-text on which Ælfric draws in the tenth, and the twentieth that has seen the latest upsurge in feminism and the recent prominence of feminist readings of discourses dealing with women.[11]

A feminist decoding of the Life of Æthelthryth could begin by concentrating upon the power struggle between Æthelthryth and her husband, which centers upon their sexual relationship. Withholding her sexual favors finally gives Æthelthryth the upper hand in this struggle, and she achieves her desire to become a nun; however, because her refusal to allow her husband into her bed is apparently her only weapon against King Ecgfrith, Ælfric reflects the patriarchal hegemony of a culture that seems to rate a woman very largely in terms of her sexuality. Indeed, Ælfric's repeated stress upon Æthelthryth's virginity (as on that of the other female saints he includes in his collection) as being the reason for her saintliness could in itself be taken by a feminist decoder as a patronizing male writer's differentiation between the male and the female saints, because basically this one aspect of sexual restraint becomes the major criterion of female saintliness,[12] as contrasted with the more diverse criteria accorded the male saints.

This particular type of twentieth century reading could be supported by the coda to the Life of Æthelthryth, which seems to be added to show that men can emulate women in sexual abstinence, but because both man and wife live "on clænnysse" ["in chastity" (124)], after they have their three sons and it is the *man*'s soul that the angels bear to heaven "mid sange" ["with song" (130)], with no reference to the wife's soul, the continuing bias against women could easily be decoded even here.

Associated with what some twentieth century female readers might perceive as antifeminist presuppositions is Ælfric's overt ideological and hortatory (even propagandist) message about the ideal of virginity and chastity within a Christian culture and society. For decoders living within a sexually permissive twentieth century society, this message may seem to be impossibly old-fashioned. Ælfric both proclaims that Æthelthryth is a saint (and as such set apart from the general run of her society) because of her virginity, and yet in the concluding appeal to his audience in his coda about the man and wife he indicates that others within his society may also live in "clænnesse." If they do not quite emulate her virginity, they are still conforming to Christian teaching.

Thus major differences are immediately apparent between what Ælfric's contemporary audience and what a twentieth century audience might decode from his discourse, because of the very different socio-cultural context from which each derives presuppositions about male-female relationships. The different impact of the broad context upon a reader is increased because of different assumptions about the type of genre in which the narrative discourse is cast, hagiography, which would presumably be perceived as a type of historical fact in the tenth century and as a type of fiction in the twentieth. I shall return to this point later. Furthermore, given the constantly changing nature of English, the semantic field of chosen signifiers differs between the two periods, with consequent differences in the hypersignification that can be drawn from the text.

A less contentious but still revealing small instance of period differences occurs at the end of the section that generalizes the circumstances of Æthelthryth's life as abbess at Ely. I have in a previous piece[13] summarized the broad differences between the chronological disruptions of Bede's imme- diate pre-text and Ælfric's chronologically continuous narrative. In this one small section about the features of her religious life, there is again a differ- ence in the syntagmatic ordering of the discourse. Bede says (in this order) that she would wear only woolen garments; that she would seldom bathe (and then last, after the others); that she rarely ate more than once a day; and that she remained at prayer from matins until dawn (IV.19, p. 392). Ælfric in- cludes all four actions, but changes the order and also what he foregrounds, by devoting a line each first to her eating only one meal, and then to her love of prayers; and then he mentions her wearing of woolens in a half line, and to round off and climax the section he gives four and a half lines to her bathing:

> and wyllen weorode . and wolde seldhwænne
> hire lice baðian butan to heahtidum .
> and ðonne heo wolde ærest ealle ða baðian
> þe on ðam mynstre wæron . and wolde him ðenian
> mid hire þinenum . and þonne hi sylfe baðian .
>
> (44–48)

[and wore woolen garments, and would seldom bathe her body except at feast times, and then she would first bathe all those who were in the con- vent, and would serve them with her servants, and then bathe herself.]

The attitude here, especially with the foregrounded threefold repetition of "baðian,"[14] is one that implies that Æthelthryth's wearing of wool and her abstinence from bathing are Christian virtues and reflects a culture alien to most twentieth century readers to whom bathing is a commonplace. Indeed, such (non)action may only too easily be perceived as a comic (not to say totally irrelevant) criterion for the saintliness of Æthelthryth's life. There has been a change in material culture that makes woolen clothing (at least in winter) desirable rather than penitential or a symbol of poverty, and bathing something that not only can be achieved easily but also is reminiscent of the now humorously regarded attitude summed up in the phrase "Cleanliness is next to godliness." Such material changes cannot help but influence any period's decoding of a text that evokes them.

However, other features of the passage are relevant for a decoder approaching the text with an awareness of both its macro- and micro-influences, because of their impact not only on the story but also upon its hypersignification. This section, as I have pointed out, concludes the general overview of Æthelthryth's life as abbess of Ely, and Ælfric follows it immediately with the more particularized and closely focalized description of her last sickness and death, which Bede leaves until much later in his discourse, when Cynefrith, the leech, upon the opening of Æthelthryth's wooden coffin, retrospectively relates the details that Ælfric includes in their chronological position.

A close focus upon the structuring of the text cannot but note the heavy emphasis upon bathing (following upon the reference to what Æthelthryth wears) that Ælfric builds into his discourse, and it can easily bring to mind for a decoder the associated concept of water and its cleansing capacity, because bathing presupposes water. This signified concept then anticipates the actions after the opening of her coffin (97–98), including the washing of Æthelthryth's healed and uncorrupt body and the rewinding of it in new clothes. The "gewæda" ["clothes"] in which the corpse was originally wound are found to be "swa ansunde . swylce hi eall niwe wæron" ["as sound as if they were all new," (95)], but Æthelthryth is reclothed (and presumably not in wool) after being washed (the order of the events is encoded similarly in both Bede and Ælfric), so that she who had served others by bathing them is herself washed and reclothed as climactic actions before she is translated to the church and laid in the miraculous coffin found by Sexburh's monks.

This reversal in the relative ordering of the early information about the woolen clothing and the bathing and the later information about the uncorrupt body and the new winding bands, the washing of the uncorrupted body, and of the relationship between the one who served and those served points to a thematic level of hypersignification whereby her actions in life are mirrored by others performed after her death and for her uncorrupt body as part of the confirmation of her saintly status.

Intertextuality extends that hypersignification further, for the lines about the bathing of others includes a double reference to her serving those she bathes (47), and both the verbal and the noun forms (*ðenian* and *þinenum*) occur within two lines. The signified concept here can also be decoded by those who know the intertext as carrying connotations that allude to Christ washing the disciples' feet, as recorded in John 13. Furthermore, the Benedictine rule lays down that this is one of the duties of the brother serving for that particular week,[15] and as the abbess herself undertakes the duty, this type of conceptual parallel foregrounds Æthelthryth's Christlike qualities, and the generalized comment made earlier and that she "hi [the nuns] modorlice heold / mid godum gebysnungum to þam gastlican life" ["kept them in motherly fashion though good examples in the spiritual life," (39–40)] is exemplified by the specific example. (This attention to the micro-context of the discourse thus helps to balance and qualify a narrowly feminist reading that might see Æthelthryth as merely being pejorated by the presuppositions encoded in the text.)

There is a further instance of how significant for the hypersignification is the placement of the bathing episode: in the only direct speech in the life, that accorded by Ælfric to Æthelthryth (where Bede embeds her speech within that of the leech Cynefrith at the end), which follows on from the generalized section about her life as an abbess, she comments upon the tumor that afflicts her neck as punishment for the adornments she wore in her youth, and says: "and me is nu geþuht / þæt godes arfæstnyss þone gylt *aclænsige*" (57–58) ["and it now seems to me that God's justice cleanses the guilt"]. The metaphor Ælfric chooses here is his own unconstrained paradigmatic choice, as it is not the alliterating term in the line and as Bede in the pre-text has the verb *absoluar* [IV.19, p. 396], whereas the earlier translation, *The Old English Bede*,[16] has "wæron onlesed" [322.22] and can, because of the triple reference to bathing some ten lines earlier, carry for a decoder connotations of God's symbolic cleansing of her (as she has physically cleansed others) by means of the tumor. When her coffin is opened sixteen years later, the wound where the leech attempted to remove the tumor is healed, which is the evidence that the cleansing has indeed taken place.

The verb carrying the metaphor is also carrying a wider penumbra of associations because of its link with the result of bathing (cleanness) and the noun signifier *clænnyss* is a key term used several times throughout the life. The references are (after the first use) clustered near the end, where Ælfric is spelling out his hortatory (if pragmatic, for the man and his wife had three sons) message; at a time when the monastic revival's campaign against married priests must have been fresh in mind,[17] he is emphasizing for the lay folk also the Christian virtue of chastity.

The micro- and the macro-contexts are thus interacting to suggest that what for a twentieth century decoder can easily seem so comically peculiar in the increased focus in Ælfric's (as against the pre-text's) discourse on

Æthelthryth's bathing those at the convent has a hypersignification over and above its immediate contextual function, and so reflects back upon how twentieth century preoccupations can affect decoding.

I have already suggested how a narrow twentieth-century feminist perspective on the life could precondition the type of decoding carried out on the early part of the life, which concerns Æthelthryth's two marriages, first to the ealdorman whom Ælfric does not name (though Bede [IV.19, p. 390] gives his name as Tondberht), and then to King Ecgfrith. Given the double triad of contexts that I have suggested, a broader analysis reveals more about both the encoding and the challenge to participate in the decoding that Ælfric sets up in his thirty-line introductory section.

The first four lines summarize the whole of the following life, and their patterning and structure foreshadow how Ælfric manipulates his encoding:

> We wyllað nv awritan þeah ðe hit wundorlic sy
> be ðære halgan sancte æðeldryðe þam engliscan mædene
> þe wæs mid twam werum and swaðeah wunode mæden
> swa swa þa wundra geswuteliað þe heo wyrcð gelome .
>
> (1–4)

[We will now write (though it be wonderful / miraculous) about the holy saint Æthelthryth, the English maiden who lived with two men and nevertheless remained a virgin, as the miracles show that she often works.]

The very conventional and flat first half line has three words beginning with *w* that alliterate with the key word of the *b* half line, *wundorlic* . The narratorial viewpoint carried both by the paradigmatic choice of that term and by its syntagmatic context of the embedded concessive clause stresses that what is to follow will be not only wonderful or miraculous, but also surprising, and so both emotive attitudes are evoked *before* the audience knows whom they concern. Even within the next line, the present status of the protagonist as a holy saint precedes her identification by her name, followed by her past status in life as an English maid. The next line provides the information that makes the choice of the term *mæden* either problematic[18] or miraculous, that she had two husbands. But immediately juxtaposed is the emphatic reassertion of her virginity, with the word *mæden* repeated, while the fourth line provides evidence for her double status, as virgin and as saint, with the subject, *þa wundra* repeating the root of *wundorlice,* to alert a decoder to what is to follow. Ælfric's choice of the present tense verb in that fourth line, associated with *gelome*, challenges his audience to perceive her activities as continuing to the present (for the twentieth century by contrast a pointed reminder that they no longer occur).

Ælfric immediately recognizes the incredulity with which decoders may well greet the statement that Æthelthryth has had two husbands and remains a virgin. Indeed, he spends about a quarter of the lines in the life (the first 30 out of 135 lines) in stressing the sheer unlikeliness and also the proofs that Æthelthryth remains a virgin. This proportioning of his discourse is itself significant, for his treatment is necessarily selective, and only half the discourse treats her life, the other half dealing with the miracles that follow her death. In accordance with the contemporary monastic pressure for the religious to remain celibate,[19] the exemplary function of the practice of virginity by one in the secular (and monarchic) realm is for Ælfric very important for the propagandist message he is putting forward in his discourse.

The variation within and between the attitudes engendered by the socio-cultural conditions and the ideologies of the tenth and the twentieth centuries will influence the relative weight given to these proofs by individual readers. In particular, twentieth century readers are likely to be familiar with many later literary treatments of marriage, from those in the romance genre[20] in medieval literature, and in other genres such as drama and poetry, to the novel's long tradition of seeing consummated marriage as the culmination of sexual desire and wooing. Such intertexts cannot but influence a reader who in the sexually permissive late twentieth century sets out to decode this early discourse, just because he or she has experience of fictional intertexts and social attitudes toward sex and marriage other than those evoked in Ælfric's discourse; indeed, Æthelthryth's virginity may seem more miraculous to a twentieth than to a tenth century reader.

No matter one's cultural presuppositions, any reader has also to begin decoding the treatment of Æthelthryth's marriages within the micro-context of the discourse and especially with the placement of certain selected details and terms, such as the explicit paradigmatic choice, *un(ge)wemme(d)* (unstained), which recurs several times throughout the life.[21] Ælfric's initial general proof of Æthelthryth's virginity is given in 4; namely, the miracles that she performs after death. This presupposes the underlying ideological stance to be expected from a Christian monk, that takes for granted a link between virginity and the postmortem ability to perform miracles.

His second proof spells out more overtly the Christian argument, that God did not wish her virginity to be despoiled by the ealdorman, with a pun on "ælmihtig god" (11) and "his mihte" (12):

> ac hit nolde se ælmihtig god þæt hire mægðhad wurde
> mid hæmede adylegod . ac heold hi on clænnysse
> forðan þe he is ælmihtig god and mæg don eall þæt he wile .
> and on manegum widum his mihte geswutelað .
>
> (9–12)

[But Almighty God did not wish that her virginity should be destroyed with sexual intercourse, but kept her in cleanness, because he is Almighty God and may do all that he wills, and in many ways shows his might.]

The overt ideological argument is underlined when the past tense narration of the first two lines stresses that God's action rather than Æthelthryth's is paramount. The following explanatory causal clauses in the present tense retrospectively validate (for the Christian audience) the preceding statement with the generalization about God's power to achieve anything.

That Æthelthryth remains a virgin within her second royal marriage is treated in more detail in what follows, first with the repetition of *wundra* (16), but then with an entirely different and far more secular proof added: that Ecgfrith tried to bribe Wilfrid to persuade her to consummate the marriage:

> and he [Wilfrid] sæde bedan
> þæt se cyning ecfrid him oft behete mycel
> on lande and on feo . gif he læran mihte
> æðeldryðe his gebeddan . þæt heo bruce his synscipes.
> (20–24)

[and he told Bede that King Ecgfrith often promised him much in land and money if he would persuade Æthelthryth his bed-fellow to accept his sexual advances.]

What is very revealing here is that Ælfric adduces the chain of human reportage that has allowed this piece of evidence to be passed on, with Wilfrid telling Bede, and Bede providing the pre-text for Ælfric, who promptly goes on to cite at length Bede's comment (attributing it overtly to Bede) that God can cause such a happening now, "on urum dagum" (26), as "on ealdum dagum" (28). The link and contrast between the two periods, "in olden days" and "in our days," pointed to in Bede's discourse, and continued in Ælfric's, implicitly encodes the same challenge to audiences of any period, as they decode a text from the past.

Ælfric makes it perfectly clear that he realizes that his contemporary audience (no less than Bede's) will find it hard to accept that Æthelthryth remains a virgin. His narrative strategy is twofold: first, there is his repetition of the signified concept of virginity, using differing signifiers, *clænnyss* (10) and *un(ge)wemme(d)* (15, 18, 27), and his choice of positive attitudinal terms such as *wundorlic* (1) and *wundra* (4, 16), *halgan* (2, 24), and *halgum* (30), set against *hæmede adylegod* (10), all of which paradigmatic selections evaluate the concepts and the protagonists in a particular way that reveals *his* ideological point of view as being one that accords much more weight to the religious proof of God's action, though he also brings in the secular proof of the king's attempted bribery of Wilfrid for those whose ideological stance discounts the religious proof.

The most problematic influence of the macro-context is that of genre. At a time when the very concept of genre is being problematized, it is still apparent that the conventions associated with any "genre" influence the macro-context, though its impact upon an individual reader naturally varies. Generic expectations cannot help but play a considerable part in the macro-context of every reader's decoding of a text, especially as conventions are gradually built up within a "genre." I have already mentioned the retrospective impact for the twentieth century of the romance genre, and how it influences expectations about a "story" culminating in marriage. Equally important for the Æthelthryth text are the generic expectations evoked by hagiography, on the one hand, and the novel, on the other:[22] the latter is overtly fictional; the status of the former in relation to the twentieth century's fact-fiction dichotomy (and the attempt of later twentieth century writers to break down and blur that dichotomy) is far less clear-cut. On the one hand, the sheer repetition of conventional *topoi* in saints' lives (such as the virginity *topos* and the postmortem miracles *topos*) suggests that an element of fictionality pervades them and that their exemplary nature rather than their factuality is significant, and yet, on the other, part of their hortatory message depends upon their contemporary audience's acceptance of them as "reality," as they deal with behavior achievable for them too.

Most twentieth century readers are familiar with narrative fiction, but many are unfamiliar with the more specialized form of hagiography, and conventions that have become associated with the novel (as it in its turn draws upon the romance) tend to influence their decoding of other aspects of Ælfric's discourse. One that has been shown to be particularly important in recent narrative theory[23] is that of focalization, which has a large part to play in evoking the "realism" of the setting; it also reveals a great deal about the focalizer, whether narrator or protagonist within the discourse. The importance of focalization can be shown from the differential impact of two small sections of Ælfric's discourse that depend heavily upon it.

The first occurs at the point where, sixteen years after Æthelthryth's death, her abbess sister Sexburh wishes to translate her bones into the church and sends brothers to seek for stone (in an area where stone is rare) for a coffin to replace the wooden one in which Æthelthryth was initially placed. At this point in the "story," the narrator in TV fashion pans in on the miracle that foreshadows the greatest miracle, that it is not bones, but Æthelthryth's uncorrupted body, they find in the wooden coffin.

> Hi hreowan þa to grantanceastre . and god hi sona gehradode.
> swa þæt hi þær gemetton ane mære þruh

wið þone weall standende . geworht of marmstane
eall hwites bleos bufan þære eorðan .
and þæt hlyd ðærto gelimplice gefeged .
eac of hwitum marmstane . swa swa hit macode god.

(78–83)

[They rowed then to Grantchester, and God at once prospered them in that they there found a glorious coffin standing against the wall, made of marble, all of white hue, above the earth, and the lid of it exactly fitted, also of white marble, as God made it.]

The focalization is that of the brothers, as the narration gives the location of the sarcophagus, standing against the wall (a detail deduced from, but not overtly stated in, the pre-text), and then the material of which it is constructed, and the color. The lid is specifically described, and the color term (neither instance of *hwit* alliterating in its line) repeated. Then in the final half line the narrative switches from detailed focalization to the explanation (not taken from the pre-text), which gives to the foregrounding of the color of the coffin a symbolic association of purity, as God's making of the coffin foreshadows the proof of Æthelthryth's virginity in her noncorruption.

The hagiographical assumption that God made the coffin, rather than the historical one that it was likely to have been a Roman sarcophagus, might well seem comically jarring to a seemingly more objective twentieth century reader, who may also reveal his or her acculturation in reacting with amusement to the later passage (102–6) that stresses that the exact measurement of the coffin to Æthelthryth's proportions is "wundorlic," the term repeated from the first line of the life to generalize about Æthelthryth's saintliness. Such a response tends to prevent a twentieth century reader from accepting the "realism" of the focalization, whereas for the tenth century audience, the details could well help to make for a noncomic realism that supports both the factual and the symbolic nature of the incident.

But this nonmatching of responses across a long period of time is not always the case, as another instance of focalization illustrates. In the only direct speech attributed to Æthelthryth, she compares and contrasts the tumor on her neck (the lancing of which indirectly kills her) with the neckrings which she wore in her youth, first in general and then in much more specific terms. The temporal contrast is marked by the difference between "on iugoðe" ["in youth"] (56) and "nu" (57) and also by the sensory and emotive double vision of the visually perceived "geswel" (51, 59)[24] taking the place of the "gold" (59), with the tactile "hata bryne" ["hot burning"] (60) in place of "healicum gymstanum" ["excellent gemstones"] (60). Like the double vision in the lyric poem *The Dream of the Rood*, with its blood-stained and bejeweled cross, the neckring-tumor here has a complex function for an audience-reader. Focalized by the speaker for unidentified addressees, the signifiers for the respective adornments would seem to place the value of the gold and gemstones above the swelling and the hot burning, but because the syntagmatic context makes of the "geswel" and the "hata bryne" the purgatorial cleansing of Æthelthryth's guilt through "godes arfæstnyss" ["God's justice," (58)] *before* they are specifically focalized, the attitude toward them by speaker and invited of addressees is to reverse the normal response (in all periods) to gold and jewels, on the one hand, and to a tumor, on the other. The discourse moves from the sensory immediacy of focalization to the attitude being encoded through the syntagmatic ordering.

The focalization in this small passage adds to the hypersignification being built up throughout the life, whereby conventional responses to sociocultural norms as evidenced in artifacts and marital behavior are being turned upside down and reformulated to accord with the particular Christian ideology which Ælfric is advancing. His syntagmatic ordering of Æthelthryth's speech invites a reversal of expected responses in both a twentieth and a tenth century decoder.

For one last instance of the complex functioning of the narrative transaction between writer and reader in Ælfric's *Lives of Saints,* I want to return to a small section of the Life of Oswald that, although providing factual information about how Oswald, on Aidan's arrival from Ireland, translated for him because Aidan did not initially know Northumbrian well enough, also has a broader function:

> Hit gelamp þa swa þæt se geleaffulla cyning
> gerehte his witan on heora agenum gereorde
> þæs bisceopes bodunge mid bliþum mode .
> and wæs his wealhstod forþan þe he wel cuþe scyttysc .
> and se bisceop aidan ne mihte gebigan his spræce
> to norðhymbriscum gereorde swa hraþe þa git .
>
> (66–69)

[It happened then that the believing king explained to his *witan* in their own language the bishop's preaching with glad mind, and was his translator, because he knew Irish well, and Bishop Aidan could not as yet turn his speech into Northumbrian language so quickly.]

These lines provide a *myse en abyme*[25] illustration of the problem faced by encoder and decoder of a discourse derived from a different language, and it hints at the further problem of the hypersignification of a discourse whose original and later audiences are separated by a large temporal-spatial-ideological gap. "Translator" is the normal gloss for *wealhstod* (67), and Ælfric is "translating" or reencoding his Latin pre-text, the discourse of Bede, into the vernacular for his contemporary tenth century audience, "on heora agenum gereorde" (66), and the reason is that he well knows Latin, as Oswald well knows Irish, though the status of Aidan and of Bede does not correspond in quite the same way. For twentieth century readers, however, Ælfric is much more in the position of Aidan, and the development in the English language, quite apart from the very radical changes in the whole socio-cultural-ideological context of twentieth century readers, is such that another "wealhstod" is now needed to convey "þæs . . . bodunge mid bliþum mode" (66). The model that a present-day "wealhstod" uses for decoding and reencoding for others needs now to take account of the whole complex context in which the transaction between writer, text, and reader takes place.[26]

Notes

1. The text used here is *Ælfric's Lives of Saints*, ed. Walter W. Skeat, EETS OS 76, 82, 94, 114 (London, 1881–1900). Passages cited from the Lives of Æthelthryth (Skeat's XX) and Oswald (Skeat's XXVI) are identified by the line numbers of Skeat's edition. Ælfric's reference to his readers and hearers occurs on p. 2: "siue legendo, seu Audiendo."

2. This concept is a central thesis informing Lee Patterson's *Negotiating the Past: The Historical Understanding of Medieval Literature* (Madison, Wisc., 1987). See also Ch. 1 of John Stephens and Ruth Waterhouse, *Literature, Language and Change: From Chaucer to the Present* (London and New York, 1990).

3. Particularly my "Ælfric's Use of Discourse in Some Saints' Lives," *ASE* 5 (1976): 83–103; and "Ælfric's 'Usitatus' Use of Language in *Lives of Saints*," *Parergon*, n.s. 7 (1989): 1–45.

4. The text of the *Historia Ecclesiastica* (hereafter *HE*) is that edited by Bertram Colgrave and R. A. B. Mynors (Oxford, 1969) with the page numbers of that edition.

5. *HE*, III.25, pp. 298–306. See Margaret Deanesly's account of the Synod of Whitby and its aftermath in *The Pre-Conquest Church in England* (London, 1961).

6. In another Saint's life, his Life of Swithun, Ælfric recalls being associated with the monks at Winchester under Bishop Æthelwold, when he switches from the third to the first person (plural) pronoun at line 262:

> Hi hit heoldon þa syððan symle on gewunon .
> swa swa we gesawon sylfe for oft .
> and þone sang we sungon unseldon mid heom .

[Then afterwards they always kept it up as a custom, as we ourselves have seen very often, and we have sung the song with them frequently.]

James Hurt, *Ælfric,* (New York, 1972), p. 79, cites the example.

7. *The Anglo-Saxon Chronicle,* ed. J. Earle and C. Plummer, 2 vols. (Oxford, 1892–99).

8. Bede records the episode of Birinus in *HE* III.7, and it is not until III.9, p. 242 that the information about Mercia and Penda being heathen is recorded.

9. See P. Clemoes's brief but pertinent analysis of the setting of Aidan's prophecy in "Late Old English Literature," in *Tenth Century Studies,* ed. David Parsons (London and Chichester, England, 1975), pp. 103–14, on p. 112. Oswald's bones were translated to Gloucester in 909, a piece of information that Ælfric obviously did not derive from Bede (*HE* III.13, p. 252, n.1).

10. See note 2; also my *Triangular Clause Relationship in Ælfric's Lives of Saints and in Other Works* (New York, Frankfort, Berne, 1983). Susan Ridyard, in *The Royal Saints of Anglo-Saxon England: A Study of West Saxon and East Anglian Cults* (Cambridge, 1988), p. 54, remarks that "Ælfric adds nothing to Bede's narrative, although the sequence of events is slightly modified." In view of my recent work, this seems an instance of litotes.

11. The collection of essays by Helen Damico and Alexandra Hennessy Olsen, *New Readings on Women in Old English Literature* (Bloomington, Ind., 1990), is an indication of the growing interest in feminist approaches to OE literature. For the medieval period in general there have been many recent books dealing with women. Of special interest in the present context are Pauline Stafford, *Queens, Concubines, and Dowagers: The King's Wife in the Early Middle Ages* (Athens, Ga., 1983), and Stephanie Hollis, *Anglo-Saxon Women and the Church* (Woodbridge, England, 1992); the latter includes a detailed analysis of Bede's treatment of Æthelthryth, in the context of Theodore's *Penitential.* She makes only a brief comment on Ælfric's changes to Bede.

12. All the female saints that Ælfric treats in his *Lives of Saints* are accorded saintly status because they maintain their virginity against formidable odds, usually to the point of martyrdom; Æthelthryth is an exception in that she does not suffer martyrdom (the tumor that indirectly kills her is perhaps her symbolic martyrdom). See Peter R. Brown, *The Body and Society: Men, Women and Sexual Renunciation in Early Christianity* (New York, 1988), especially the Epilogue, pp. 428–47, dealing with the early Middle Ages.

13. See especially "Ælfric's 'Usitatus' Use of Language," pp. 40–43.

14. The examples of the verb *baþian* recorded by A. diPaolo Healey and R. L. Venezky, *A Microfiche Concordance to Old English* (Toronto 1980), have a literal reference, but the semantic field of the related noun forms for *bath* is wider ranging, with Bede extending it to allude to "baptism"; Ælfric himself in other saints' lives

(Lives of the Forty Soldiers and Life of Cecilia) contextually activates connotations for the term, of purgatorial cleansing leading to heavenly blessing for the saints, and of hellfire for the backslider. The associated terms *þinen* and *þenian* are used by Ælfric of the Virgin Mary, of female saints, and of those who serve God or minister to the poor.

15. In *The Rule of S. Benet. Latin and Anglo-Saxon Interlinear Version*, ed. H. Logeman, EETS OS 90 (London, 1888), p. 66, the interlinear gloss for Ch. 35 and 53 use the term *þwean* for the Latin *laveo;* in Ch. 36, where there is an instruction that the sick be given baths as often as expedient, the gloss has "þaða brice þa untruman swa oft swa hit fremeð sigeþoden." Chapter 55 deals with clothing, with woollen clothes laid down for the winter, but with the general proviso that cheapness is the main criterion. The OE version is that edited by A. Schröer, in *Die Angelsächsischen Prosabearbeitungen der Benediktinrregel*, Bibliothek der Angelsächsischen Prosa 2, 2d ed. with supplement by H. Gneuss (Darmstadt, Germany, 1964).

16. *The Old English Version of Bede's Ecclesiastical History of the English People*, ed. Thomas Miller, EETS OS 95, 96, 110, 111 (London, 1890–98).

17. Ælfric's Latin *Life of Æthelwold*, which appears in *Three Lives of English Saints*, ed. Michael Winterbottom (Toronto, 1972), relates how Æthelwold expelled the evil-living clerics from the Old Minster at Winchester, which suggests also Ælfric's concern for chastity and celibacy as being key aspects of the monastic life. In his vernacular Life of Swithhun, Ælfric puts into Swithhun's mouth a further reference to the events, when Swithhun addresses a priest, Eadsige: "þe wæs of ealdan mynster mid ðam oðrum preostum adræfed for heora unþeawum þurh aðelwold bisceop" (27-28) ["who was driven from the Old Minster with other priests for their misconduct by Bishop Æthelwold"]. MS A of *The Anglo-Saxon Chronicle* in its 964 annal also records that Edgar drove the priests from the Old and New Minsters and from Chertsey and Milton Abbas and replaced them with monks.

18. In lines 10, 124, and 133 its choice is not constrained by the need for alliteration; in 121 and 134 it is alliterating. The concordance listing of the term suggests that its semantic field drifts its basic signification to include not only virginity, but also physical chastity, celibacy, and the broad general sense of avoiding mortal sin, of both men and women; so although not gender specific, it seems to be more commonly associated with men, whereas *mægðhad* is more frequently used for women.

According to the Concordance, Ælfric in his *Grammar* translates both *puella* and *virgo* as "mæden," but of the six uses in Æthelthryth, four are qualified (one by *halig*, three by *ungewemmed*) to limit the meaning to the "virgo" sense. The term *mægðhad* occurs in 9 and 17, reinforcing *mæden*.

19. *The Benedictine Rule* in Ch. 4 lays down in its Rules of Conduct that monks must not fulfill the desires of the flesh and must love chastity; in the interlinear gloss these become "gewilnunga lichaman [non] gefremman" and "clænnesse lufian"; the first degree of humility (in Ch. 7) spells out in some detail the need to avoid the

desires of the flesh ("gewilnunga lichaman"). Ælfric himself stresses in his pastoral letters to Wulfsige and Wulfstan how Christ established "clænysse" and taught it. See *Die Hirtenbriefe Ælfrics*, ed. B. Fehr, reprinted with Supplement to the Introduction by Peter Clemoes (Darmstadt, Germany, 1966), pp. 2, 5, 74, 122. The section quoted on p. 74 stresses that monks, nuns, and mass priests should serve Christ "on clænnysse"; although, as n. 14 points out, the semantic field shows drifting of the term's signification.

20. Rosemary Woolf, in "Saints' Lives," in *Continuations and Beginnings*, ed. E. G. Stanley (London, 1966), pp. 37–66, sees the saint's life as part romance in origin (p. 40). See also p. 43.

21. In lines 18 and 107, it is nonalliterating; in 15 and 27 it alliterates. The concordance listing of the terms *un(ge)wemme(d)* suggests that the semantic field covers both literal and figurative uses. Apart from Æthelthryth, the only other saints in *Lives of Saints* who are *ungewemmed* are Martin and Cecilia (used once each), whereas it is used four times of Æthelthryth to stress that her "cleanness" is virginity, rather than chastity.

22. Rosemary Woolf, in "Saints' Lives," touches on the differential attitudes between contemporary and modern audiences toward hagiography; see especially p. 65.

23. The concept of focalization is summarized in Shlomith Rimmon-Kenan, *Narrative Fiction: Contemporary Poetics* (London and New York, 1983), Ch. 6; and in Michael Toolan, *Narrative: A Critical Linguistic Introduction* (London and New York, 1988), Ch. 3.

24. The concordance listing of the term shows that apart from Ælfric, it occurs in medical contexts only. Ælfric uses the term figuratively as well as literally. And here, although literal in reference, it is also symbolic. The term *swura* occurs four times near *geswel*, in 51, 53, 55, 56, and as part of a compound in 57; Ælfric seems sometimes to make a distinction between *swura* and *hnecca*, whereby the former can carry the association of submission to God (as here), where the latter is sometimes associated with the devil.

25. See the discussion of the concept in Ann Jefferson, "*Mise en abyme* and the Prophetic in Narrative," *Style* 17 (1983): 196–208.

26. Thanks are expressed to my research assistants Gwen Griffiths and Alison James for their help in this work. See Gwen Griffiths, "Reading Ælfric's Saint Æthelthryth as a Woman," *Parergon*, n.s. 10 (1992): 35–49.

St. Euphrosyne: Holy Transvestite

Paul E. Szarmach

Once considered to have been written by Ælfric and now relegated to the anonymous tradition, the Life of St. Euphrosyne would appear to be a likely candidate for literary obscurity.[1] Yet most recent interest in women in Anglo-Saxon culture (and literature), as well as the growing study of Old English prose for its own sake, may make it possible to retrieve this work for the future canon of prose works that are to be actively read both for cultural meaning and literary style.[2] Within this dual movement toward new topics and new works this chapter offers an analytical reading of this anonymous life. The specific focus must nevertheless be on sexuality, both explicit and implicit, and Euphrosyne's holy transvestitism that enables her to live as a man in a monastery for some thirty-eight years and convert her father to the good and moral life. Because Ælfric is the measure for achievement in prose, how the anonymous writer treats themes found similarly in Ælfric will likewise be a consideration. All such saints' lives have been called *sensational novelettes,* containing episodes "unelevated even when the underlying doctrine is remembered,"[3] but the final point here will be that the renewed interest in human sexuality, fostered in part by issues highlighted by women's studies, has a liberating effect in the study of Old English prose. Before looking closely at the Old English anonymous Life of Euphrosyne, however, it might be useful to set the context for "holy transvestites" in the early medieval period.

In his *The Legends of the Saints* the Bollandist Hippolyte Delehaye presents a discussion of transvestite saints as part of a larger consideration of pagan legend and myth in hagiographic form.[4] Delehaye considers several saints who, disguising themselves as men, might ultimately in their actions represent a Christianized form of homage to Aphrodite and, by extension, the goddess Amathus in Cyprus, who was Aphrodite-Aphroditos, or simply a hermaphrodite. It is not surprising that Delehaye would be hostile to this

latter point of origin for transvestite saints—he calls this cult a "most mon-
strous" development—but his list of transvestite saints is long.[5] There is one
group containing Pelagia-Margarito of Antioch (a former dancing girl), a
second Pelagia of Antioch, a Pelagia of Tarsus, a Marina of Antioch, and a
Margaret of Antioch, all of whom have similar biographies. There is another
group—Margaret (Reparata), Eugenia, Apollinaria, Maria-Marina, Theodora,
and Euphrosyne—whose *vitae* contain enough similarities to make them a
group apart from the first. These women who dressed as men can be considered different from bearded women saints or from a later phenomenon such
as Joan of Arc.[6] In short, Christian literature of the earlier period provides
ample precedent for women who dressed as men for various reasons (usually
to protect virginity or chastity) and yet attained sainthood.

The doctrinal basis for such Christian, saintly behavior needs comment
as well. It is evident that in early Christianity questions regarding the human
body admitted many possible answers as thinkers and theologians began the
long process of refinement that led to the comparative doctrinal rigor generally associated with the High Middle Ages. St. Paul's many pronouncements
on sexual ethics and behavior, trailing Neoplatonic biases as they do, were
central to the development of Christian sexuality. In 1 Corinthians 11, e.g.,
Paul gives rules for headdresses at prayer, which require men and women to
dress differently as is appropriate to nature: "Nec ipsa natura docet vos, quod
vir quidem si comam nutriat, ignomina est illi; mulier vero si comam nutriat,
gloris est illi; quoniam capilli pro velamine ei data sunt" (vv. 14–15).[7] Yet in
Galatians 3:28 Paul, describing the state of those baptized into Christ, those
who have "put on Christ" therefore, says: "Non est Iudaeus, neque Graecus;
non est servus, neque liber; non est masculus, neque femina. Omnes enim vos
unum estis in Christo Iesu."[8] This state of sexlessness, or at least the blurring
of sexual differences, is part of the complicated system of beliefs and rituals
now described as "gnostic bisexual cosmogonies and the androgynous visions
of the Montanist priestesses," as John Anson has put it, where "male attire
represented communion with Christ."[9] These beliefs and customs in turn gave
shape and rationale to Egyptian scribes as they recorded the lives of female
monks (i.e., transvestite virgins) who can be dated from the middle of the
fifth century, which stories include Lives of Eugenia and Euphrosyne. But
even commentators now perceived as more orthodox endorsed the notion that
women should be more like men. Thus, Jerome says: "Sin autem Christo
magis voluerit servire quam saeculo, mulier esse cessabit, et dicetur vir, quia
omnes in perfectum virum cupimus occurrere."[10] Ambrose likewise lends his
authority to this issue: "Quae non credit, mulier est, et adhuc corporei sexus
appellatione signatur; nam quae credit, occurrit in virum perfectum, in
mensuram aetatis plenitudinis Christi, carens jam nomine saeculi, corporis
sexu, lubrico juventutis, multiloquio senectutis."[11] There is no similar warrant

or endorsement of male transvestitism. Vern Bullough puts the matter succinctly in his important historical-sociological study: "the female who wore
male clothes and adopted the role of the male would be trying to imitate the
superior sex, to become more rational, while the man who wore women's
clothes, who tried to take on the gender attributes of the female, would be
losing status, becoming less rational."[12] Having sketched the narrative and
doctrinal traditions that form the general background to the Life of Euphrosyne,
I would now like to look closely at the Old English text.

As is often the case in holy biography, the anonymous author begins
with the saint's "pre-history"; that is, her parents. The initial emphasis is on
Paphnutius, Euphrosyne's father who kept *Godes beboda geornlice* ["God's
commandments zeaously"], and her unnamed mother, who, likewise virtuous,
was nevertheless barren. The mother, particularly moved by her husband's
gedrefed mod ["troubled mind"] over their childlessness, daily gave her wealth
(*hire speda*) to the poor and prayed to God for a child. There is no dramatic
presentation of Paphnutius's distress, but the OE author does specify the
father's concern that there would be no one *æfter his forðsiðe to his æhtum
fenge* ["after his death inherit his possessions"]. This comment seems inno-
cent and quiet enough, but the emphasis here on *his* wealth (as opposed to
her wealth) anticipates some future developments in the story.

Indeed, father and mother have a different attitude toward wealth, a
difference that is not morally culpable at this point in the story but that will
have moral and narrative importance later. Father and mother do appear to
have nearly parallel quests for an heir, however. The mother *cyrcan sohte*
["visited church(es)"]; the father traveled *gif he weninga hwilcne godes man
findan mihte þæt his gewilnunga gefultumian mihte* ["if he could perhaps find
any man of God who was able to give him his wish"]. The father's travel is
less focused and more ambiguous in its motivation to fulfill his *gewilnunga*,
but it is at least successful for he visits a minster with a compassionate and
efficacious abbot. The two of them pray to God: *þa gehyrde god heora begra
bene and forgeaf him ane dohtor* ["who heard the prayers of both of them and
gave him/them a daughter"]. The text is quite specific that the prayers of
father and abbot are successful (the mother is not mentioned at all here) and
felicitously ambiguous as to whose daughter it might be. The vagaries of OE
pronoun reference allow the reading that Euphrosyne is daughter to father
and abbot, a biological impossibility of course but (eventually) a thematic
reality for these "father figures."

Indeed, in a few short lines Euphrosyne is born, is baptized at seven, and
left motherless at twelve. The rapid treatment of this part of Euphrosyne's life
carries further the notion that this life is, at its root, a story about father(s) and
daughter. From a strictly narrative point of view it becomes evident that
Euphrosyne's mother is not necessary to the action. From a thematic point of

view the values that the mother personified are now transferred to Euphrosyne, in part, and to the abbot. The pairing is complicated: Euphrosyne is her mother's daughter, so to speak, and she has her mother's values, most notably toward wealth, but it is the abbot who is the external teacher, who sets out the moral ideas for her that she chooses. The father is not without his positive qualities, but as before Euphrosyne's birth, he is not totally blameless. The moral tension of this story is to maintain the moral rectitude of the father but not to present his moral superiority: he must be good enough to be the saint's real father but flawed enough to inspire the narrative complications.

This intricate family triangle plays itself out to the point that Euphrosyne enters the monastery in male disguise, the narrative complexities developing in this way: Paphnutius raises an attractive daughter through adolescence, teaching her holy writings, divine readings, and worldly wisdom. Paphnutius declines proposals of marriage until a thegn *weligra and wurþra þonne ealle þa oþre* ["more wealthy and more worthy than all the others"] makes a winning offer. At this key juncture in her life (Euphrosyne is eighteen), Paphnutius and Euphrosyne visit the abbot. Paphnutius declares: "Ic hæbbe broht hider þone wæstm þinra gebeda, mine dohtor, þæt þu hire sylle þine bletsunge forþam ic wille hi were syllan."[13] The abbot-father teaches Euphrosyne the ways of the monastery and monastic virtues so that she observes, beatitudelike: "Eadige synd þas weras þe on þisse worulde syndon englum gelice and þurh þæt ece lif."[14] Euphrosyne's comment about "men like unto angels" is a foreshadowing of her transformation. Her spiritual father has shown her that the path to eternal salvation lies in this kind of transformation.

But how can Euphrosyne enter the minster? The resolution of this narrative problem has aspects of classical and dramatic comedy: disguise, strategem and subterfuge, willing servants and intermediaries.[15] All these elements help lovers thwart unwanted marriages or unwanted lovers and overbearing parents—except in this application of the motifs Christ is the bridegroom and the celibate life the aim.[16] In its use for these Christian purposes the comic pattern appears ironic. Like many an active heroine, Euphrosyne takes charge of her own situation, helped by secondary characters.

When a brother of the minster comes to invite her father to the abbot's ordination day, Euphrosyne confirms that the monastery life is for her by crossexamining him. She concludes: "Ic wolde gecyrran to þyllicre drohtnunga, ac ic onsitte þæt ic beo minum fæder ungehyrsum, se for his idlum welum me wile to were geþeodan."[17] For Euphrosyne the moral dilemma is that she wishes to honor her father. This unnamed brother urges a higher morality, "Eala swustor ne geþafa ðu þæt ænig man þinne lichaman besmite, ne ne syle þu þinne wlite to ænigum hospe, ac bewedde þe sylfe Criste, se þe mæg for þisum gewitenlicum þingum syllan þæt heofonlice rice," and outlines a plan of deception; "far nu to mynstre digellice and alege þine woruldlican gegyrlan and gegyre þe mid munucreafe."[18] When Paphnutius is away, Euphrosyne follows the plan by summoning a second unnamed brother. To him she explains her dilemma again, indicating her father's attachment to worldly riches and her qualms about filial obedience, and he responds with the classic Gospel text spoken by Christ: "Swa hwa swa ne wiþsæcð fæder and meder and eallum his magum and þærtoeacan his agenre sawle, ne mæg he beon min leorningman."[19]

This second brother invests Euphrosyne *mid munucreafe* ["with a monk's habit"] and blesses her. Euphrosyne had asked him to cut her hair as well, but it is not absolutely clear from the text that this ritual ceremony took place. But Euphrosyne's unwomaning does explicitly continue, however, as she reasons herself into taking on man's clothing. Euphrosyne believes that her father would take her from a woman's convent, should he find her there, but that he would not think to look for her in a monastery. Dressed as a monk and taking fifty mancuses, she escapes from her home to the monastery that her father had visited and the one that contributes the "spirit of place" to the life.

Euphrosyne's reception at the minster and her acceptance into the community there mark the third and final step in her sexual and moral transformation. The porter introduces her to the abbot as a eunuch from the king's household and Euphrosyne herself makes this speech to the abbot: "ic wæs on cinges herede and ic eom eunuchus and ic symle wilnode to munuclifum gecyrran, ac þyllic lif nis gewunelic on ure ceastre. Nu geaxode ic eowre mæran drohtnunge and min willa is þæt ic mid eow eardian mote, gif eower willa þæt bið. Ic hæbbe mænigfealde æhta and gif me her god reste forgifen wile, ic gedo þæt hi cumað hider."[20]

Euphrosyne is now "neither man nor woman" by her own self-description and through her own will and action. The themes of sexuality and wealth, which have accompanied Paphnutius's marriage plans for his daughter, take on an inverted possibility here as Euphrosyne offers a dowry of sorts in choosing to be a bride of Christ. The OE narrator changes his narration at this point in telling how the abbot asks for Euphrosyne's name: "þa axode he [= se abbod] *hine* hwæt *his* nama wære. þa cwæð *he*: 'Smaragdus ic eom geciged' "[21] (emphasis mine). The change to the masculine pronoun to refer to Euphrosyne signals her change of sex status in the author's view. In this name-poor work the choice of a name is significant. *Smaragdus* means "emerald," signifying in the biblical commentaries those whose faith is solid and whose doctrine is worthy.[22] The abbot assigns Smaragdus-Euphrosyne to the care of the elder brother Agapitus, saying to the latter that the new monk will be his *sunu* ["son"].

It might be a narrative expectation that in avoiding the snares of sexuality in the world Smaragdus-Euphrosyne would face a temptation in the monastery. This theme, however, takes a twist. There is no fiendish apparition or falling monk or sex-thirsty pagan; rather, Smaragdus-Euphrosyne nearly becomes the occasion of sin in others. He-she is *wlitig on ansyne* ["good-looking"] with the result that "swa oft swa ða broðra comon to cyrcan, þonne besende se awyregda gast mænigfelade geþohtas on heora mod and wurdon þearle gecostnode þurh his fægernysse."[23] The tempted monks appeal to the abbot, who orders Smaragdus-Euphrosyne to live in a solitary cell. Are these temptations homosexual—one wonders, the temptation is *þurh HIS fægernysse*—or heterosexual? Or is the OE author simply toying—metaphysically, so to speak—with the sexual theme? The consignment to solitary does advance the narrative, however. Smaragdus-Euphrosyne excels in deprivations, serving as moral exemplar, and his/her isolation adds a realistic dimension to his/her distance from Paphnutius.

The narrative focus in this father-daughter narrative returns to the father again to relate his anguish and grief over the disappearance of his daughter. Just as Euphrosyne's flight from her father takes three stages, Paphnutius's reunion with his daughter takes three narrative stages. The discovery of her disappearance and the great lamentation over her apparent death, which constitute the first stage, have some powerful, even poetic, moments. Paphnutius has a lament that echoes biblical rhythms in a series of parallel metaphors describing loss:

> Hwa bereafode me minra speda
> > oððe tostencte mine æhta?
> Hwa forcearf minne wingeard
> > oððe hwa adwæscte min leohtfæt?
> Hwa bescirede me mines hihtes
> > oððe hwa gewemde þone wlite mire dohtor?[24]

The imagery of wealth, given the recurrence of this theme in the whole Life, would seem to mark a stage in Paphnutius's moral development. It is indeed the first time that wealth is metaphorical for Paphnutius. At least on one level he sees Euphrosyne as a nonmaterial treasure—his own "pearl of great price." Finding no relief from his sorrow, Paphnutius seeks consolation from the abbot and the monastery. The brethren fast and pray, but no revelation comes. The abbot consoles Paphnutius, concluding that Euphrosyne *sumne godne ræd hire geceas* ["chose for herself a certain good counsel"] and saying, "ac ic getrywe on God þæt he gyt on þissum life hi geswutelie."[25] This second stage is inconclusive because of its delay of reunion and recognition. The overall effect of this delay is to heighten the suffering of Paphnutius and to inject a form of suspense as to how father and daughter will be reunited. The abbot, though ignorant of Euphrosyne's fate, is correct in his inference that all is (somehow) well, which is a reaffirmation of the theme of God's controlling Providence.

Paphnutius actually achieves a kind of double reunion with Euphrosyne. In a state of depression he returns to the abbot for more counsel and guidance. The abbot suggests that Paphnutius meet with brother Smaragdus, a reunion that is not really a reunion, for it is a dramatic irony at everyone's expense except Euphrosyne's. Euphrosyne cries at the sight of her father, but Paphnutius does not recognize his daughter because austerities have transformed her and she furthermore covers her head with her cowl. At this juncture the narrator resumes the use of *heo* as the pronoun of reference for Euphrosyne. Euphrosyne gives her father various counsels of hope and teaches him various doctrines, most notably that *man ne sceolde fæder and modor and oþre woruldlice þing lufian toforan Gode* ["a person should not love father and mother and other worldly things before God"]. (The Skeat translation translates *man* by "a man," which is surely an incorrect rendering for the true impersonal here.) Paphnutius is relieved from his depression, observing with an irony lost on him: "Min mod is gestrangod þurh þisne broþor and ic eom swa bliðe swilce ic mine dohtor funden hæbbe."[26]

Thirty-eight years later (!), Euphrosyne-Smaragdus is on her/his deathbed, and Paphnutius comes to her with recriminations that she/he has not kept her promises that he would see his daughter. Having asked Paphnuntis to wait three more days and now certain that she is to die, Euphrosyne makes her deathbed declaration: "Nelle þu leng beon hohful be þinre dehter Eufrosinan. Soðlice ic earme eom sio sio sylfe, and þu eart Pafnuntius min fæder. Efne nu þu me hæfst gesewen and þin gewilnung is gefylled . . . Eac swilce ic cyðde þam abbode þæt ic hæfde miccle æhta, and ic him behet þæt ic hider ingesyllan [wolde] gif ic her þurhwunode. Nu gelæst ðu þæt ic behet, forþam þeos stowe is arwyrðe. . . ."[27] This recognition speech quickly unravels the major narrative complication, which involves the disguise, and reasserts the continuing major theme of wealth. The reference to *þin gewilnung* recalls the very beginning of the Life where Paphnutius is pursuing his "will" in seeking an heir. The distress that Paphnutius feels now is more of a release, to be sure, but there is a note of humanity mixed with a right morality that is easy to find in his outburst: "Wa me, min sweteste bearn, forhwam noldest þu ðe sylfe me gecyðan þæt ic mihte mid þe sylfwilles drohtian! Wa me þæt þu swa lange þe sylfe dyrndest!"[28] Taken at face value, these words suggest that Paphnutius would have allowed Euphrosyne to live as a bride of Christ and that he would have joined her in the monastery. Presumably, the total action portrays Euphrosyne's singleminded devotion to Christ at the expense of all other considerations, most notably her father, and Paphnutius's declaration of good will at this point continues that moral tension in his character: a good but flawed man. A slightly different reading of the total action, however, could suggest that Euphrosyne is indeed a strong, self-willed woman who acts independently within the framework of her own society. Fortunately, her strong will is focused on Christ.

Euphrosyne's moral success, both for herself and for her father, ends with public recognition. The abbot and the brethren celebrate her triumphs, and a one-eyed man, having kissed and touched the corpse of Euphrosyne, receives his eye back. But the moral conversion of the father is the true success. Paphnutius takes the great part of his posessions, lives in his daughter's cell for ten years, dies, and is buried beside her.

What then does a close reading of the Life of Euphrosyne, which attempts to consider the narrative on its own terms, reveal about its nature and shape? At its narrative root this Life is a father-daughter story, a subcategory of the vast romance genre, adapted to illustrate doctrines of Christian sexuality. Romance motifs and themes such as identity, disguise, and recognition serve the development of Christian ideas such as chastity and celibacy. In this Life the idea of sexual identity becomes particularly complex, for Euphrosyne is daughter, transvestite, eunuch, monk, saint, and bride of Christ on earth and in heaven. Euphrosyne "unwomans" herself in her transformation to sainthood in taking on a monk's appearance. Such a metamorphosis is not sensational: it is thematic, for she/he is becoming one with Christ and is achieving the heavenly state where there is neither male nor female. Her singleminded purpose overturns and inverts earthly expectations, and although her father bears an earthly burden, he too achieves the blissful state through her example.

In the presentation of these challenging ideas the anonymous OE writer has sought to shape and render the story he has received so as to sharpen and clarify the major narrative and thematic elements. The acknowledged Latin source for this work, an anonymous *Vita Sanctae Euphrosynae,* provides the basis for comparison.[29] The Old English writer makes no major structural change in the narrative: he follows the ordering of elements as they are presented there. He retains many of the features of the Latin, such as, the suppression of personal names (which makes the story more exemplary), the moments of dialogue, and the biblical allusions that underlie points of action. The changes that he effects help sharpen some of the themes, here most notably the theme of wealth. As I have suggested already, the central tension of the narrative is that Paphnutius must be flawed enough to make Euphrosyne's disobedience acceptable and her transvestitism rational to the narrative scheme, but Paphnutius must be good enough to be the saint's father. In the Latin section of the "prehistory," Paphnutius is more pious and observant, thus making Euphrosyne's disobedience even less morally acceptable. The structure of Old English further requires the vernacular author to make decisions about pronoun reference, forcing him, if you like, to interpret when Euphrosyne is Euphrosyne or Smaragdus. The Old English does seem to make thematic choices, observing the dramatic irony of disguise consistently. There are several differences that might be authorial in the Old English—or might be the result of manuscript problems. Only more manuscript research on my part might answer why in the Latin it is clear that Euphrosyne is shorn before entering the monastery, whereas in the Old English there is a muddle. It could be manuscript, doctrine-observance—a recollection of biblical injunctions of crossdressing—or perhaps a move toward narrative economy. Likewise not all the Old English speeches are as long as the Latin.

These relations to the Latin help define the Old English writer's craft vis-à-vis Ælfric, especially in his treatment of Eugenia, which Delehaye classes with the Life of Euphrosyne in a subgenre of sorts.[30] There are many points of similarity between the two lives: an intelligent and beautiful woman chooses to join a monastery, where there is a test of her sexuality, and where there is a public recognition scene. The Eugenia story is, however, more complex in its structure and in its complexities of characters. Ælfric "offers an erotic story with no erotic content."[31] The comparison between Ælfric and the anonymous writer—which is necessary to establish some sense of relative place in the Old English prose canon—cannot be direct. Suffice it to say, Ælfric has more to do and he does it well in his cool, restrained, abbreviated style, whereas the anonymous writer keeps the father's cry as part of the message of renunciation that teaches salvation at any cost. It is that distinction of attitude wherein lies the beginning of a detailed comparison. Both authors depict the lives of holy women who sought to control their bodies through the resources that their milieu gave them: monastic refuge and concealed identity. In the process they do not so much repudiate woman's sexuality as to elevate it to the blissful state of sexlessness described in Galatians 3:28. Historians of ideas still have to establish the place of these early vernacular Lives in the developing scheme of Christianity, but Old English prose writers reacted to them with the resources their language and their own skills so specially provided them, making these Lives part of the achievement of Old English prose.

Notes

1. The Life appears in the standard edition of Ælfric's *Lives*: W. W. Skeat, ed. and trans., *Ælfric's Lives of Saints*, EETS OS 76, 82, 94, 114 (reprinted in two vols., 1966), vol. 1, pp. 334–55. For comments on the non-Ælfrician contents of this edition and the main manuscript, BL Cotton Julius E.vii, see Joyce Hill, in this volume, pp. 235–59 passim; see also Hugh Magennis, "Contrasting Features in the Non-Ælfrician Lives in the Old English *Lives of the Saints*," *Anglia* 104 (1986): 316–48. Magennis offers a succinct introduction—with due cautions—to the Life in his entry "*Euphrosyne*

vita," for the main entry *Acta Sanctorum*, in *Sources of Anglo-Saxon Literary Culture: A Trial Version*, ed. Frederick M. Biggs, Thomas D. Hill, and Paul E. Szarmach, with the assistance of Karen Hammond, Medieval and Renaissance Texts and Studies 74 (Binghamton, N.Y., 1990), p. 6. Magennis also considers the sources of the non-Ælfrician pieces in "On the Sources of Non-Ælfrician Lives in the Old English *Lives of Saints*, with Reference to the Cotton-Corpus Legendary," *Notes and Queries*, n.s. 32 (1985): 292–99.

No one seems to be much bothered by the manuscript heading in Cotton Julius E. vii, fol. 207, which refers to Euphrasia, who is different from Euphrosyne. See *Bibliotheca Hagiographica Latina* s.n.

This study is conceived as a twin to my "Ælfric's Women Saints: Eugenia," in *New Readings on Women in Old English Literature*, ed. Helen Damico and Alexandra Hennessey Olsen (Bloomington, Ind. 1990), pp. 146–57, and it necessarily covers similar ground. For reaction to my study of Eugenia, see Theodore Leinbaugh's review article "Prose," in "The Year's Work in Old English Studies," *Old English Newsletter*, 25, no. 2 (1992): 56; Leinbaugh does not see "abnormal desires" in Eugenia and thus does not see her as a "transvestite." See also Gopa Roy, "A Virgin Acts Manfully: Ælfric's *Life of St. Eugenia* and the Latin Versions," *Leeds Studies in English*, n.s. 23 (1992): 2–27. Roy is right to point out the importance of Patrick Zettel's Oxford dissertation, which was not easily available to me and was, I understood, not available to scholars for their use. One notes that it appeared then that Zettel was about to begin publishing out of his dissertation (as I suggest on p. 152), but now such publication is not likely, unfortunately, and Zettel has graciously indicated to me that his work is available for fair use.

An earlier version of this chapter was read at the annual meeting of the Rocky Mountain Medieval and Renaissance Association, held at the Grand Canyon, April 22, 1989. I want to thank Dana-Linn Whiteside for reading the final version of it and Helene Scheck and Virginia Blanton-Whetsell for their comments on an earlier version.

2. For a brief overview of the status of prose, see my "Old English Prose," *ANQ*, n.s. 3, no. 2 (1990): 56–59.

3. Rosemary Woolf, "Saints Lives," in *Continuations and Beginnings*, ed. E. G. Stanley (London, 1966), p. 61.

4. Hippolyte Delehaye, *The Legends of the Saints*, trans. Donald Attwater (New York, 1962), pp. 119–69.

5. Ibid., p. 155.

6. Ibid. p. 156; for an overview of transvestite saints, see also Marie Delcourt, *Hermaphrodite* (London, 1961), pp. 84–102, "Appendix: Female Saints in Masculine Clothing"; Szarmach, "Ælfric's Women Saints," p. 156 n. 4; Valerie Hotchkiss, "Clothes Make the Man: Female Transvestism in the Middle Ages," dissertation, Yale University (1990) [presumably soon to be a book]; Evelyne Patlagean, "L'Histoire de la Femme Déguisé en Moine et l'Evolution de la Sainteté Féminine à Byzance," *Studi Medievali*, 3d ser. no. 17, 2 (1976): 597–623. There are no male transvestite saints. Indeed, when St. Jerome was tricked by his enemies into putting on a woman's dress, he lost his chance to become pope; see Millard Meiss and Elizabeth H. Beatson, *The*

Belles Heures of Jean Duc De Berry (New York, 1974), fol. 184v [facsimile]. David Lorenzo Boyd and Ruth Mazo Karras will publish a paper in *Gay and Lesbian Quarterly* on "*Ut cum muliere*: A Male Transvestite Prostitute in Fourteenth-Century London," having discovered a document regarding one John Rykener, who was arrested, in women's clothing, for having sex with another man. Thomas Middleton and Thomas Dekker offer *The Roaring Girl* (ed. Andor Gomme [London,1976]), whose Moll [= Mary Frith, b. 1589?] was an active cutpurse in London, among other things, and who wore men's clothes. For the references to Patlagean, St. Jerome, and *The Roaring Girl* I wish to thank respectively Gordon Whatley, Robin Oggins, and Albert Tricomi; Dr. Karras kindly gave me a copy of "*Ut cum muliere . . .*" For a clinical view see Leslie Martin Lothstein, *Female-to-Male Transsexualism* (Boston and London, 1983), who offers a very brief historical overview, pp. 19–21.

7. Bible, Douay-Rheims trans.: "For does not nature itself teach you, that if a man has long hair, it is a shame to him: but truly if a woman has long hair, it is a glory to her; because her hair is given to her as a covering."

8. Ibid. "There is not Jew, nor Greek; there is not slave, nor free; there is not male, nor female. For ye are all one in Christ Jesus." For an analysis of Galatians 3:28, see Ben Witherington III, *Women in the Earliest Churches* (Cambridge, 1988), pp. 76–78, and his earlier study, "Rite and Rights for Women—Galatians 3:28," *New Testament Studies* 27, no. 5 (1981): 593–604, which offers useful analysis of the verse and helpful bibliography for the controversies.

9. John Anson, "The Female Transvestite in Early Monasticism: The Origin and Development of a Motif," *Viator* 5 (1974): 10, 11. Anson offers an appreciative reading of Euphrosyne on pp. 15–17.

10. Jerome, *Commentariorum in Epistolam ad Ephesios Libri Tres*, PL 26, 567: "If moreover [a woman] would wish to serve Christ more than the world, she will cease to be a woman and will be called a man because we all wish to attain the perfect man."

11. Ambrose, *Expositionis in Evangelium secundum Lucam Libri X*, PL 15 (1938): "Who does not believe is a woman, and is designated thus by the name of the sex of her body; for who believes attains the perfect man, to the degree of the fullness of the age of Christ, now being empty of name of the world, the sex of her body, the slippery slope of youth, the chattiness of old age."

12. Vern Bullough, "Transvestites in the Middle Ages," *American Journal of Sociology* 79 (1974): 1383.

13. Skeat, *Ælfric's Lives*, p. 337: " 'I have brought hither the fruit of thy prayers, my daughter, that thou mayest give her blessing, because I wish to give her a husband.' "

14. Ibid., p. 339: " 'Blessed are these men who in the world are like unto angels, and by such means shall obtain everlasting life.' "

15. The Life of Eugenia similarly has comic potential. See my "Ælfric's Women Saints," pp. 149–51.

16. For the motif of Christ as Bridegroom, see Stephen Morrison, "The Figure of *Christus Sponsus* in Old English Prose," in *Liebe-Ehe-Ehebruck in der Literatur des Mittelalters*, ed. Xenja von Ertzdorff and Marianne Wynn, *Beiträge zur Deutschen Philologie* 58 (1984): 5–15.

17. Skeat, *Ælfric's Lives*, p. 339: " 'I would turn to such a life, but I fear to be disobedient to my father, who, for his vain (and transitory) riches desireth to join me to a husband.' "

18. Ibid., pp. 339, 341: " 'O sister! suffer thou not that any man defile thy body, neither give thou thy beauty to any shame; but wed thyself to Christ, who for these transitory things can give thee the heavenly kingdom. . . . go now to a minster secretly, and lay aside thy worldly garments and clothe thyself with the monastic habit.' "

19. Ibid., p. 343: " 'Whoever will not forsake father and mother and all his kindred, and moreover his own soul, he cannot be my disciple.' "

20. Ibid., p. 345: " 'I was in the king's household and I am a eunuch; and I ever desired to turn to the monastic life, but such a life is not customary in our city; now I have heard of your illustrious conduct, and my will is that I may dwell with you if that be your will. I have manifold possessions; and if God will grant me rest here, I will cause them to come hither.' "

21. Ibid., p. 345: "Then he asked him what his name was. Then said *he*, 'I am called Smaragdus.' "

22. See Jean Leclercq's observation on the name in connection with his study of the Carolingian Smaragdus in *An Introduction to the Medieval Mystics of Europe*, ed. Paul E. Szarmach (Albany, N.Y., 1984), p. 37: "a name that has symbolic import: the emerald (*smaragdus* in Latin) is one of the precious stones mentioned in the Book of the Apocalypse, and has been interpreted as applying to men whose faith is solid and whose doctrine is worthy of note."

23. Skeat, *Ælfric's Lives*, p. 345: "as often as the brothers came to church, the accursed spirit sent manifold thoughts into their minds, and they were exceedingly tempted by his fairness." Female saint-heroes are good-looking; cf. Judith and Juliana. See Paul Beekman Taylor, "The Old English Poetic Vocabulary of Beauty," in *New Readings on Women in Old English Literature*, ed. Helen Damico and Alexandra Hennessey Olsen (Bloomington, Ind., 1990), pp. 211–21.

24. Skeat, ibid., p. 347: " 'Who hath bereaved me of my treasures or scattered my goods? Who hath cut away my vineyard, or who hath quenched my lamp? Who hath deprived me of my hope, or who hath polluted the beauty of my daughter?' "

25. Ibid., p. 349: " 'but I trust in God that He will yet in this life reveal her.' "

26. Ibid., p. 351: " 'My mind is strengthened by help of this brother and I am as blithe as if I had found my daughter.' "

27. Ibid., p. 353: "Be no longer careful about thy daughter Euphrosyne. Verily, I miserable one, am she herself; and thou art Paphnutius my father, Lo! now thou hast

seen me, and thy desire is fulfilled. . . . Moreover, I told the abbot that I had great possessions, and I promised him that I [would] bring them in hither if I continued here; now perform thou that which I promised, for this place is worthy."

28. Ibid., pp. 353, 354: " 'Woe is me, my sweetest child! wherefore wouldest thou not make thyself known to me, that I might of my own will have lived here with thee? Woe is me! that thou hast so long concealed thyself!' "

29. Magennis, "Contrasting Features," pp. 342–48, offers a fairly detailed comparison of the Life of Euphrosyne in the context of Latin sources and Ælfric's style, giving a balanced assessment of the anonymous writer's work. My focus on sexuality and gender requires me to value certain passages more than Magennis' more "philological" interests require; hence, I have found significance in Paphnutius's speech where Magennis (p. 344) sees the author erring in taking the focus away from Euphrosyne and putting it on her father. Yet Magennis and I have much in common, e.g., in considering Ælfric to be cooler in his emotional effects.

Latin versions of Euphrosyne are found in PL 73, 645–52 (Rosweyde's edition) and in *Acta Sanctorum*, (February 11), pp. 537–41. Magennis, "On the Sources," p. 299 compares the Old English with Cotton Vespasian E.iv, fols. 100v–03v, a twelfth century Latin version. Agnes Smith Lewis offers a translation of a Syriac version of the legend, which she apparently discovered in 1892 at St. Catherine's, Sinai; now reprinted in *Vox Benedictina* 1, no. 3 (1984): 140–56, the translation first appeared in *Select Narratives of Holy Women from the Syro-Antiochene or Sinai Palimpsest . . .* , Studia Sinaitica 9.

30. Delehaye, *The Legends*, pp. 150–55.

31. Szarmach, "Ælfric's Women Saints," p. 155.

Index of Manuscripts

Index of Saints

[See also Subject Index]

Subject Index

[See also Index of Saints]